Capital Markets
Institutions and Instruments
Second Edition

Frank J. Fabozzi
School of Management
Yale University

Franco Modigliani
Sloan School of Management
Massachusetts Institute of Technology

Prentice Hall
Upper Saddle River, New Jersey 07458

Fabozzi, Frank J.
    Capital markets: institutions and instruments / Frank J. Fabozzi,
Franco Modigliani. --2nd ed.
        p.   cm.
    Includes bibliographical references and index.
    ISBN 0-13-300187-3
    1. Capital market.   I. Modigliani, Franco.   II. Title.
HG4523.F33   1995
332'.0414--dc20   95-42745
                                              CIP

To our wives, Donna Marie Fabozzi and Serena Modigliani

Acquisitions Editor: Paul Donnelly
Associate Editor: Teresa Cohan
Production and Interior Design: Benchmark Productions, Inc.
Marketing Manager: Susan McLaughlin
Cover Design: Lorraine Castellano
Design Director: Patrica H. Wosczyk
Prepress and Manufacturing Buyer: Marie McNamara
Editorial Assistant: MaryBeth Sanok
Cover Art: David Bishop/Phototake

© 1992, 1996 by Prentice Hall, Inc.
A Simon & Schuster Company
Upper Saddle River, New Jersey 07458

Printed in the United States of America

10 9 8 7 6 5 4 3 2

ISBN 0-13-300187-3

Prentice-Hall International (UK) Limited, *London*
Prentice-Hall of Australia Pty. Limited, *Sydney*
Prentice-Hall Canada Inc., *Toronto*
Prentice-Hall Hispanoamericana, S. A., *Mexico*
Prentice-Hall of India Private Limited, *New Delhi*
Prentice-Hall of Japan, Inc., *Tokyo*
Simon & Schuster Asia Pte. Ltd., *Singapore*
Editora Prentice-Hall do Brasil, Ltda., *Rio de Janeiro*

Contents

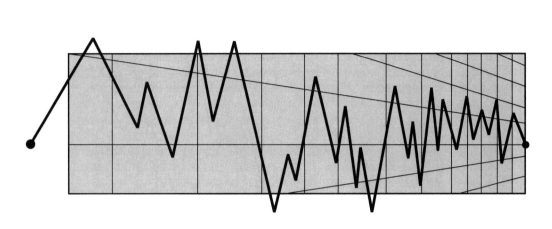

Section III: Risk and Return Theories

Section IV: Derivatives Markets

Preface

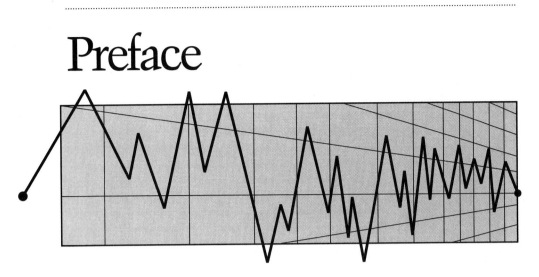

The revolution that has taken place in the world financial markets was aptly described by a noted economist, Henry Kaufman, in the 1985 Annual Report of Phibro-Salomon:

> If a modern-day Rip Van Winkle had fallen asleep twenty years ago, or for that matter even ten years back, on awakening today, he would be astonished as to what has happened in the financial markets. Instead of a world of isolated national capital markets and a preponderance of fixed-rate financing, he would discover a world of highly integrated capital markets, an extensive array of financing instruments, and new methods of addressing market risk.

The purpose of this book is to describe the wide range of instruments for financing, investing, and controlling risk that are available in today's financial markets. New financial instruments are not created simply because someone on Wall Street believes that it would be "fun" to introduce an instrument with more "bells and whistles" than existing instruments. The demand for new instruments is driven by the needs of borrowers and investors based on their asset/liability management situation, regulatory constraints (if any), financial accounting considerations, and tax considerations. For these reasons, to comprehend the financial innovations that have occurred and are expected to occur in the future, a general understanding of the asset/liability management problem of major institutional investors is required. Therefore, in addition to coverage of the markets for all financial instruments, we provide an overview of the asset/liability management problem faced by major institutional investors and the strategies they employ.

We believe that the coverage provided in this book on the institutional investors and financial instruments is as up-to-date as possible in a market facing rapid changes in the characteristics of the players and those making the rules as to how the game can be played. New financial instruments are introduced on a regular basis; however, armed with an understanding of the needs of borrowers and institutional investors and the attributes of existing financial instruments, the reader will be able to recognize the contribution made by a new financial instrument.

This book deviates in several ways from the traditional capital markets textbook. One important way is in our coverage of derivative markets (futures, options, swaps, etc.). These markets are an integral part of the global capital market. They are not—as often categorized by the popular press and some of our less informed congressional representatives and regulators—"exotic" markets. These instruments permit a mechanism by which market participants can control risk—borrowers can control borrowing costs and investors can control the market risk of their portfolio. It is safe to say that without the derivative markets, there would not be an efficient global capital market.

In addition, it is important to appreciate the basic principles of option theory not only as a stand-alone instrument, but because many financial instruments have embedded options. Also, the liabilities of many financial institutions have embedded options. Thus, it is difficult to appreciate the complex nature of assets and liabilities without understanding the fundamentals of option theory.

While we recognize that many colleges offer a specialized course in derivative markets, our purpose here is not to delve deeply into the various trading strategies and the nuances of pricing models that characterize such a course. Instead, we provide the fundamentals of the role of these instruments in financial markets, the principles of pricing them, and a general description of how they are used by market participants to control risk.

A special feature of this book is the extensive coverage of the mortgage market and the securitization of assets. Asset securitization refers to the creation of securities whose collateral is the cash flow from the underlying pool of assets. The process of asset securitization is radically different from the traditional system for financing the acquisition of assets. By far the largest part of the securitized asset market is the mortgage-backed securities market, where the assets collateralizing the securities are mortgage loans. Securitized assets backed by non-real estate mortgage loans are a small but growing part of the market.

Another key feature of this book is an emphasis on the role played by foreign investors in the U.S. market. Although the bulk of this book covers the U.S. financial markets, we discuss other major financial markets throughout.

In deciding the topics to cover in this book we discriminated between what belongs in a course on capital markets and what is the province of investment management. Oftentimes, because the needs of institutional investors dictate the need for financial instruments with certain investment characteristics or for a particular strategy employing a capital market instrument, we had to cross the line. The approach taken in this book makes it adaptable for a course in investment banking and as a supplement for a derivative markets course.

DIFFERENCES BETWEEN SECOND AND FIRST EDITIONS

The second edition greatly expands on the topics in the first edition. The number of chapters has been increased from 22 to 31. The differences between the two editions are summarized below:

- Chapter 1 in the first edition was fairly lengthy. In the second edition, the coverage has been split between Chapters 1 and 2. The reasons for the globalization of financial markets and the classification of global markets have been shifted from the last chapter in the first edition to Chapter 1 of the second edition.

- There are chapters devoted exclusively to the primary market (Chapter 6) and secondary market (Chapter 7). In the first edition, coverage of the primary and secondary markets was spread out in several chapters.

- The coverage of risk and return theories has been expanded to two chapters (Chapters 8 and 9) from one in the first edition.

- A new chapter (Chapter 12) introducing the swaps market has been included early in the book. The new chapter demonstrates how a swap can be used to create a security. More detailed information about specific types of swaps is then covered in later chapters. Chapter 15 includes a discussion of equity swaps, a topic not covered in the previous edition.

- The coverage of interest rate determination has been expanded from two chapters in the first edition to three chapters (Chapters 16, 17, and 18).

- Coverage of the debt obligations of corporations has been augmented from one chapter to two chapters (Chapters 21 and 22). There is greater coverage of the medium-term note market and the loan market. A discussion of the bankruptcy process is also included.

- The coverage of mortgage-backed securities has been expanded to two chapters: mortgage pass-through securities (Chapter 25) and collateralized mortgage obligations (Chapter 26). The presentation of collateralized mortgage obligations begins with a pool of mortgage pass-through securities and shows how the cash flows for the pool can be carved up to create various types of bonds. By presenting collateralized mortgage obligations in this manner, the student can see the structuring process that is now being used in other sectors of the financial market.

- There is a new chapter (Chapter 27) devoted to asset-backed securities.

- The two chapters on interest rate risk control tools in the first edition have been reorganized and expanded. Chapter 28 covers exchange-traded interest rate options and futures markets while Chapter 29 covers over-the-counter interest rate derivative markets.

- The chapter on foreign exchange markets in the first edition has been split into two chapters (Chapters 30 and 31).

- Coverage of the global financial markets was in the last chapter of the first edition. In the second edition, the material has been integrated into the other chapters.

- We have added at least 50% more questions to each chapter.

ACKNOWLEDGMENTS

We are indebted to many individuals for providing us with various forms of assistance. Michael Ferri (George Mason University) provided significant assistance for several of the chapters. Steve Boxer and Arun Muralidhar provided us with helpful comments on most of the chapters in the first edition. Laurence Siegel (Ford Foundation) reviewed many of the chapters and provided insightful comments, as well as encouragement. Chapter 3 benefitted significantly from the comments of Elizabeth Mays (Office of Thrift Supervision).

Others who have read portions of the manuscript and provided feedback include: Joseph Bencivenga (Salomon Brothers), Anand Bhattacharya (Prudential Securities), Mark Castelino (Rutgers University), Daniel T. Coggin (Consultant), Bruce Collins (Western Connecticut State University), Jack Clark Francis (Baruch College, CUNY), Gary L. Gastineau (Consultant), Robert L. Gilligan II (Brokers & Reinsurance Markets Association), Ramzi Gedeou, K.C. Ma (Consultant), Scott Richard (Miller, Anderson & Sherrerd), and Uzi Yaari (Rutgers University).

Portions of the manuscript were used in our courses at MIT and in Fabozzi's courses at Yale University. We received helpful comments from many of our students. In particular, we wish to thank Barbara Addo, Alan Gerstein, and Stefano Roscini.

We also benefitted from discussions with the following individuals on various topics: Robert Arnott (First Quadrant), Paul Asquith (MIT), Douglas Bendt (Mortgage Risk Assessment Corp.) Peter L. Bernstein (Peter L. Bernstein Inc.), David Canuel (Aeltus Investment Management), John H. Carlson (Fidelity Investments), Peter Carrill (Lehman Brothers), Andrew S. Carron (First Boston), Peter E. Christensen (PaineWebber), Ravi Dattatreya (Sumitomo Bank Capital Markets), Sylvan Feldstein (Merrill Lynch), Henry Gabbay (BlackRock Financial Management), Sean Gallop (Nomura Securities), Hal Hinkle (Goldman Sachs), Jane Howe (Pacific Investment Management Company), David P. Jacob (Nomura Securities),Joseph Guagliardo, Jr. (Gifford Fong Associates), Frank J. Jones (Guardian Life Insurance Company), Andrew Kalotay (Andrew Kalotay Associates), Martin Leibowitz (CREF), Ed Murphy (Merchants Mutual Insurance Company), Scott Pinkus (Goldman Sachs), Mark Pitts (White Oak Capital Management), Chuck Ramsey (First Southwest and Mortgage Risk Assement Corp.), Sharmin Mossavar-Rahmani (Goldman Sachs Asset Management), Frank Ramirez (First Southwest), Michael Rosenberg (Merrill Lynch), Dexter Senft (Lehman Brothers), and Richard Wilson (Fitch Investors Service).

In our end-of-chapter questions, we used excerpts from *Institutional Investor* and several weekly publications of Institutional Investor Inc., *Wall Street Letter, Bank Letter, BondWeek, Corporate Financing Week, Derivatives Week, Money Management Letter,* and *Portfolio Letter.* We are grateful to Tom Lamont, editor of the weekly publications, for permission to use the material. The source for the largest U.S. and global banks reported in Chapter 3 is EURABANK^R database of Sleigh Corporation (Franklin Lakes, New Jersey). Jan D. Slee and Elaine Kallenbach furnished the information.

In addition, the authors would like to thank the following reviewers: John S. Strong (College of William and Mary), Jim Kolari (Texas A & M University), William

A. Kracaw (Purdue University), Peter Williamson (Dartmouth College), Don M. Chance (Virginia Polytechnic Institute & State University), Peggy Fletcher (Northeastern University), Robert E. Lamy (Wake Forest University), Colleen Pantalone (Northeastern University), and Andrea Heuson (University of Miami).

Frank J. Fabozzi
Franco Modigliani

Biographical Sketches

Frank J. Fabozzi is Adjunct Professor of Finance at the School of Management at Yale University and editor of the *Journal of Portfolio Management*. From 1986 to 1992, he was a full-time member of the Finance faculty at the Sloan School of Management at MIT. Dr. Fabozzi has authored and edited several widely acclaimed books in finance. He is on the board of directors of the BlackRock complex of closed-end funds and the Guardian Park Avenue Portfolio family of open-end funds, and on the board of supervisory directors of two offshore funds. He earned a doctorate in Economics in 1972 from The Graduate Center of the City University of New York and is a Chartered Financial Analyst. In 1994 he was awarded an honorary doctorate of Humane Letters from NOVA Southeastern University.

Franco Modigliani is Institute Professor and Professor of Finance and Economics at MIT. He is an Honorary President of the International Economic Association and a former President of the American Economic Association, the American Finance Association, and the Econometric Society. He is a member of several academies, including the National Academy of Science. Professor Modigliani has authored numerous books and articles in economics and finance. In October 1985, he was awarded the Alfred Nobel Memorial Prize in Economic Sciences. He has served as a consultant to the Federal Reserve System, the U.S. Treasury Department, and a number of European banks, as well as to many businesses, and is on several Boards of Directors. Professor Modigliani received a Doctor of Jurisprudence in 1939 from the University of Rome and a Doctor of Social Science in 1944 from the New School for Social Research, as well as several honorary degrees.

Introduction

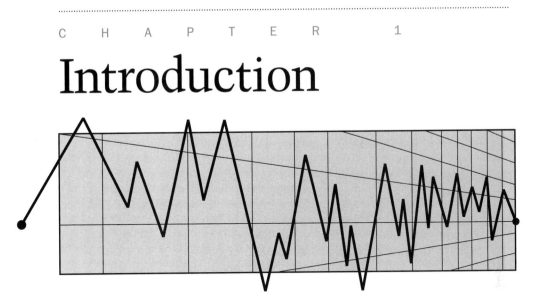

LEARNING OBJECTIVES

After reading this chapter you will understand:

- what a financial asset is.

- the distinction between a debt instrument and an equity instrument.

- the general principles for determining the price of a financial asset.

- ten properties of financial assets: moneyness, divisibility and denomination, reversibility, term to maturity, liquidity, convertibility, currency, cash flow and return predictability, complexity, and tax status.

- the principal economic functions of financial assets.

- what a financial market is and the principal economic functions it performs.

- the different ways to classify financial markets.

- what is meant by a derivative instrument.

- the reasons for the globalization of financial markets.

- the classification of global financial markets.

In a market economy, the allocation of economic resources is driven by the outcome of many private decisions. Prices are the signals that direct economic resources to their best use. The types of markets in an economy can be divided into: (1) the market for products (manufactured goods and services), or the *product market*; and (2) the market for the factors of production (labor and capital), or the *factor market*. Our purpose in this book is to focus on one part of the factor market, the market for financial assets, or, more simply, the *financial market*. It is in this market that the cost of capital is determined. In this chapter we will look at the basic characteristics and functions of financial assets and financial markets.

FINANCIAL ASSETS

We begin with a few basic definitions. An **asset** is any possession that has value in an exchange. Assets can be classified as tangible or intangible. A **tangible asset** is one whose value depends on particular physical properties— examples are buildings, land, or machinery. Tangible assets may be classified further into reproducible assets such as machinery, or non-reproducible assets such as land, a mine, or a work of art.

Intangible assets, by contrast, represent legal claims to some future benefit. Their value bears no relation to the form, physical or otherwise, in which the claims are recorded. **Financial assets**, financial instruments, or securities are intangible assets. For these instruments, the typical future benefit is a claim to future cash. This book deals with the various types of financial assets, the markets where they are traded (i.e., bought and sold), and the principles for valuing them.

The entity that has agreed to make future cash payments is called the issuer of the financial asset; the owner of the financial asset is referred to as the **investor**. The following are a few examples of financial assets:

a bond issued by the U.S. Department of the Treasury

a bond issued by General Electric Corporation

a bond issued by the state of California

a bond issued by the government of France

an automobile loan

a home mortgage loan

common stock issued by Digital Equipment Corporation

common stock issued by Honda Motor Company

In the case of the bond issued by the U.S. Department of the Treasury, the U.S. government (the issuer) agrees to pay the investor interest until the bond matures, then at the maturity date repay the amount borrowed. For the bonds issued by General Electric Corporation, and the state of California, just as with the bond issued by the U.S. Department of the Treasury, the issuer agrees to pay the investor interest until the bond matures, then at the maturity date repay the amount borrowed.

In the case of the French government bond, the cash payments are known if the French government does not default. However, the cash payments may be denominated not in U.S. dollars but in the currency of France, the French franc. Thus, while the cash payments are known in terms of the number of French francs that will be received, from the perspective of a U.S. investor, the number of U.S. dollars is unknown. The number of U.S. dollars will depend on the exchange rate between the French franc and the U.S. dollar at the time the cash payments are received and converted into U.S. dollars.

For the automobile loan and the home mortgage loan, the issuer is the individual who borrowed the funds. The investor is the entity, such as a bank, that lent the funds to the individual. The loan agreement will include a schedule specifying how the borrower will repay the loan and how the interest will be paid.

The common stock of Digital Equipment Corporation entitles the investor to receive dividends distributed by the company. The investor in this case also has a claim to a pro rata share of the net asset value of the company in case of liquidation.

The same is true for the cash payments of the common stock of Honda Motor Company, a Japanese corporation. In addition, from the perspective of a U.S. investor, since Honda will make dividend payments in Japanese yen, there is the uncertainty about the cash payments in terms of U.S. dollars. The cash payments in U.S. dollars will depend on the exchange rate at the time of conversion between U.S. dollars and the Japanese yen.

Debt *versus* Equity Claims

The claim that the holder of a financial asset has may be either a fixed dollar amount or a varying, or residual, amount. In the former case, the financial asset is referred to as a **debt instrument**. The bond issued by the U.S. Department of the Treasury, General Electric Corporation, and the state of California cited above are examples of debt instruments requiring fixed dollar payments to borrow the funds. The two loans are also debt instruments.

An equity claim (also called a **residual claim**) obligates the issuer of the financial asset to pay the holder an amount based on earnings, if any, after holders of debt instruments have been paid. Common stock is an example of an equity claim. A partnership share in a business is another example.

Some financial assets fall into both categories. Preferred stock, for example, is an equity claim that entitles the investor to receive a fixed dollar amount. This payment is contingent, however, due only after payments to debt instrument holders are made. Another instrument is convertible bonds, which allow the investor to convert debt into equity under certain circumstances. Both debt and preferred stock that pays a fixed dollar amount are called **fixed-income instruments**.

The Value of a Financial Asset

Valuation is the process of determining the fair value or price of a financial asset. The fundamental principle of valuation is that the value of any financial asset is the present value of the cash flow expected. This principle applies regardless of the financial asset. Consequently, it applies equally to common stock, a bond, a loan, and real estate.

The principle is simple: just determine the cash flow and then calculate the present value. However, accomplishing the task is not that simple.

Estimating the cash flow—The first problem encountered in valuing a financial asset is interpreting what is meant by "cash flow." Accountants have a set answer: it is the net income after taxes plus noncash outlays such as depreciation. This is a nice definition, but useless for our purposes. **Cash flow** is simply the cash that is expected to be received each period from investing in a particular financial asset.

The type of financial asset, whether debt instrument or equity instrument, and the characteristics of the issuer determine the degree of certainty of the cash flow expected. For example, assuming that the U.S. government never defaults on the debt instruments it issues, the cash flow of securities issued by the U.S. Department of the Treasury is known with certainty.

The cash flow of other debt instruments is not known with certainty. There are three reasons for this. First, the issuer might default. Second, there are provisions that are included in most debt instruments that grant the issuer and/or the investor the right to change how the borrowed funds are repaid (these features are discussed in Section VI.) Finally, as also explained in Section VI, there are some debt instruments where the interest rate the issuer pays can change over the time that the borrowed funds are outstanding.

The holder of common stock of a corporation is uncertain as to the amount and the timing of dividend payments. Dividend payments will be related to corporate profits. Moreover, unlike debt instruments in which the borrowed funds are to be repaid, an investor in common stock typically must sell the stock in order to try to recover the amount invested. Whether the amount received when the stock is sold is more or less than the amount initially invested depends on the stock's price at the time of sale, which is uncertain.

Regardless of whether we are talking about the cash flow of a debt or equity instrument, the above discussion of cash flow pertains to the nominal dollar amount, not the amount adjusted for the purchasing power of those dollars. Because of inflation, the purchasing power of the cash flow is uncertain even if the nominal dollar amount of the cash flow is certain.

The appropriate interest rate for discounting the cash flow—Once the cash flow for a financial asset is estimated, the next step is to determine the appropriate interest rate that should be used to calculate the present value (or discounted value). To determine the appropriate rate, the investor must address the following two questions:

1. What is the minimum interest rate the investor should require?

2. How much more than the minimum interest rate should the investor require?

Figure 1-1
Summary of the Process for Valuing a Financial Asset

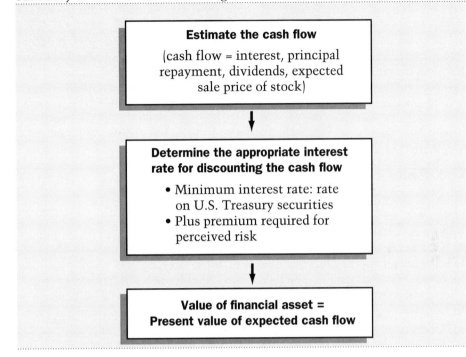

The minimum interest rate that an investor should require is the interest rate available in the financial market on a default-free cash flow. In the U.S., this is the interest rate on securities issued by the U.S. Department of the Treasury. This is the reason why the market for U.S. Treasury securities plays an extremely important role.

The premium over the interest rate on a U.S. Treasury security that the investor should require should reflect the risks associated with realizing the cash flow expected. The greater the perceived risk, the larger the premium investors will require. The valuation process is summarized in Figure 1-1.

While there are various types of risks that we will discuss in this chapter and those to follow, we can see three of them in our examples. The first is the risk that the issuer or borrower will default on the obligation. This is called **credit risk**, or **default risk**. The second is the risk attached to the potential purchasing power of the cash flow expected. This is called **purchasing power risk**, or **inflation risk**. Finally, for financial assets whose cash flow is not denominated in U.S. dollars, there is the risk that the exchange rate will change adversely resulting in less U.S. dollars. This risk is referred to as **foreign-exchange risk**.

Financial Assets *versus* Tangible Assets

A tangible asset, such as a plant or equipment purchased by a business entity, shares at least one characteristic with a financial asset: both are expected to generate future cash flow for their owner. For example, suppose a U.S. airline purchases a fleet of aircraft for $350 million. By purchasing the aircraft, the airline expects to realize cash flow from passenger travel.

Financial assets and tangible assets are linked. Ownership of tangible assets is financed by the issuance of some type of financial asset—either debt instruments or equity instruments. For example, in the case of the airline, suppose that a debt instrument was issued to raise the $350 million to purchase the fleet of aircraft. The cash flow from the passenger travel will be used to service the obligation of the debt instrument. Ultimately, therefore, the cash flow for a financial asset is generated by some tangible asset.

The Role of Financial Assets

Financial assets have two principal economic functions. The first is to transfer funds from those who have surplus funds to invest to those who need funds to invest in tangible assets. The second function is transferring funds in such a way as to redistribute the unavoidable risk associated with the cash flow generated by tangible assets among those seeking and those providing the funds. However, the claims held by the final wealth holders are generally different from the liabilities issued by the final demanders of funds because of the activity of entities operating in financial markets, called **financial intermediaries**, who seek to transform the final liabilities into different financial assets which the public prefers. Financial intermediaries are discussed in the next chapter.

To illustrate these two economic functions, consider three situations.

1. Joe Grasso has obtained a license to manufacture Teenage Mutant Ninja Turtles wristwatches. Joe estimates that he will need $1 million to purchase the plant and equipment to manufacture the watches. Unfortunately, he has only $200,000 to invest, and that is his life savings, which he does not want to invest even though he has confidence that there will be a receptive market for the watches.

2. Susan Carlson has recently inherited $730,000. She plans to spend $30,000 on some jewelry, furniture, and a few cruises, and to invest the balance of $700,000.

3. Larry Stein, an up-and-coming attorney with a major New York law firm, has received a bonus check that after taxes has netted him $270,000. He plans to spend $70,000 on a BMW and invest the balance, $200,000.

Suppose that, quite by accident, Joe, Susan, and Larry meet in New York City. Sometime during their conversation, they discuss their financial plans. By the end of the evening, they agree to a deal. Joe agrees to invest $100,000 of his savings in the business and sell a 50% interest to Susan for $700,000. Larry agrees to lend Joe $200,000 for four years at an interest rate of 18% per year. Joe will be responsible for operating the business without the assistance of Susan or Larry. Joe now has his $1 million to manufacture the watches.

Two financial claims came out of this agreement. The first is an equity instrument issued by Joe and purchased by Susan for $700,000. The other is a debt instrument issued by Joe and purchased by Larry for $200,000. Thus, the two financial assets allowed funds to be transferred from Susan and Larry, who had surplus funds to invest, to Joe, who needed funds to invest in tangible assets in order to manufacture the watches. This transfer of funds is the first economic function of financial assets.

The fact that Joe is not willing to invest his life savings of $200,000 means that he wanted to transfer part of that risk. He does so by selling Susan a financial asset that gives her a financial claim equal to one-half the cash flow from the business after paying the interest expense. He further secures an additional amount of capital from Larry, who is not willing to share in the risk of the business (except for the credit risk), in the form of an obligation requiring payment of a fixed cash flow, regardless of the outcome of the venture. This shifting of risk is the second economic function of financial assets.

Properties of Financial Assets

Financial assets have certain properties that determine or influence their attractiveness to different classes of investors. The ten properties of financial assets are (1) moneyness, (2) divisibility and denomination, (3) reversibility, (4) term to maturity, (5) liquidity, (6) convertibility, (7) currency, (8) cash flow and return predictability, (9) complexity, and (10) tax status.[1] Each property will be described below.

Moneyness—Some financial assets are used as a medium of exchange or in settlement of transactions. These assets are called **money.** In the United States they consist of currency and all forms of deposits that permit check writing. Other financial assets, although not money, are very close to money in that they can be transformed into money at little cost, delay, or risk. They are referred to as **near money.** In the United States, these include time and savings deposits and a security issued by the U.S. government with a maturity of three months called a three-month Treasury bill.[2] Moneyness is clearly a desirable property for investors.

Divisibility and denomination—**Divisibility** relates to the minimum size at which a financial asset can be liquidated and exchanged for money. The smaller the size, the more the financial asset is divisible. A financial asset such as a deposit at a bank is typically infinitely divisible (down to the penny), but other financial assets have varying degrees of divisibility depending on their denomination, which is the dollar value of the amount that each unit of the asset will pay at maturity. Thus many bonds come in $1,000 denominations while some debt instruments come in $1 million denominations. In general, divisibility is desirable for investors.

Reversibility—**Reversibility** refers to the cost of investing in a financial asset and then getting out of it and back into cash again. Consequently, reversibility is also referred to as **round-trip cost**.

---

[1] Some of these properties are taken from James Tobin, "Properties of Assets," undated manuscript, New Haven, Yale.

[2] U.S. Treasury bills are discussed in Chapter 19.

A financial asset such as a deposit at a bank is obviously highly reversible because usually there is no charge for adding to or withdrawing from it. Other transaction costs may be unavoidable, but these are small. For financial assets traded in organized markets or with "market makers" (discussed in Chapter 7), the most relevant component of round-trip cost is the so-called bid-ask spread, to which might be added commissions and the time and cost, if any, of delivering the asset. The **bid-ask spread** is the difference between the price that a market maker is willing to sell a financial asset for (i.e., the price it is asking) and the price that a market maker is willing to buy the financial asset for (i.e., the price it is bidding). For example, if a market maker is willing to sell some financial asset for $70.50 (the ask price) and buy it for $70.00 (the bid price), the bid-ask spread is $0.50. The bid-ask spread is also referred to as the bid-offer spread.

The spread charged by a market maker varies sharply from one financial asset to another, reflecting primarily the amount of risk the market maker is assuming by "making" a market. This market-making risk can be related to two main forces. One is the variability of the price as measured, say, by some measure of dispersion of the relative price over time. The greater the variability, the greater the probability of the market maker incurring a loss in excess of a stated bound between the time of buying and reselling the financial asset. The variability of prices differs widely across financial assets. Three-month Treasury bills, for example, have a very stable price (as explained in Chapter 17), while a common stock generally tends to exhibit much larger short-run variations.

The second determining factor of the bid-ask spread charged by a market maker is what is commonly referred to as the **thickness of the market** which is essentially the prevailing rate at which buying and selling orders reach the market maker (i.e., the frequency of transactions). A "thin market" is one which has few trades on a regular or continuing basis. Clearly, the greater the frequency of orders coming into the market for the financial asset (referred to as the "order flow"), the shorter the time that the financial asset will have to be held in the market maker's inventory, and hence the smaller the probability of an unfavorable price movement while held.

Thickness also varies from market to market. A three-month U.S. Treasury bill is easily the thickest market in the world. In contrast, trading in stock of small companies is said to be thin. Because Treasury bills dominate other instruments both in price stability and thickness, the bid-ask spread tends to be the smallest in the market. A low round-trip cost is clearly a desirable property of a financial asset, and as a result thickness itself is a valuable property. This explains the potential advantage of large over smaller markets (economies of scale), and a market's endeavor to standardize the instruments offered to the public.

Term to maturity—The **term to maturity** is the length of the interval until the date when the instrument is scheduled to make its final payment, or the owner is entitled to demand liquidation. Often, term to maturity is simply referred to as maturity, and this is the practice that we will follow in this book.

Instruments for which the creditor can ask for repayment at any time, such as checking accounts and many savings accounts, are called **demand instruments**. Maturity is an important characteristic of financial assets such as debt instruments, and in the United States can range from one day to 100 years. For example, there are U.S. Treasury bills that mature in one day. At the other extreme, in 1993, The Walt Disney Company issued a debt instrument that matures in 100 years, dubbed by Wall Street as "Mickey Mouse" bonds. Many other instruments, including equities, have no maturity and are thus a form of perpetual instrument.[3]

It should be understood that even a financial asset with a stated maturity may terminate before its stated maturity. This may occur for several reasons, including bankruptcy or reorganization, or because of provisions entitling the debtor to repay in advance, or the investor may have the privilege of asking for early repayment.[4]

Liquidity—**Liquidity** is an important and widely used notion, although there is at present no uniformly accepted definition of liquidity. A useful way to think of liquidity and illiquidity, proposed by Professor James Tobin,[5] is in terms of how much sellers stand to lose if they wish to sell immediately as against engaging in a costly and time-consuming search.

An example of a quite illiquid financial asset is the stock of a small corporation or the bond issued by a small school district, for which the market is extremely thin, and one must search for one of a very few suitable buyers. Less suitable buyers, including speculators and market makers, may be located more promptly, but will have to be enticed to invest in the illiquid financial asset by an appropriate discount in price.

For many other financial assets, liquidity is determined by contractual arrangements. Ordinary deposits at a bank, for example, are perfectly liquid because the bank has a contractual obligation to convert them at par on demand. In contrast, financial contracts representing a claim on a private pension fund may be regarded as totally illiquid, because these can be cashed only at retirement.

Liquidity may depend not only on the financial asset but also on the quantity one wishes to sell (or buy). While a small quantity may be quite liquid, a large lot may run into illiquidity problems. Note that liquidity is again closely related to whether a market is thick or thin. Thinness always has the effect of increasing the round-trip cost, even of a liquid financial asset. But beyond some point it becomes an obstacle to the formation of a market, and has a direct effect on the illiquidity of the financial asset.

Convertibility—An important property of some financial assets is that they are convertible into other financial assets. In some cases, the conversion takes place within one class of financial assets, as when a bond is converted into another bond. In other situations, the conversion spans classes. For example, a corporate convertible bond is a bond that the bondholder can change into equity shares. There is preferred stock that may be convertible into common stock. The timing, costs, and conditions for conversion are clearly

---

[3] In the United Kingdom, there is one well-known type of bond that promises to pay a fixed amount per year indefinitely and not to repay the principal at any time: such an instrument is called a *perpetual*, or a *consul*.

[4] Some assets have maturities that may be increased or extended at the discretion of the issuer or the investor. For example, the French government issues a six-year *obligation renouvelable du Tresor* which allows the investor, after the end of the third year, to switch into a new six-year debt.

[5] Tobin, "Properties of Assets."

spelled out in the legal descriptions of the convertible security at the time it is issued.

Currency—Most financial assets are denominated in one currency, such as U.S. dollars or yen or deutsche marks, and investors must choose them with that feature in mind. Some issuers, responding to investors' wishes to reduce foreign-exchange risk, have issued dual-currency securities. For example, some pay interest in one currency but principal or redemption value in a second. Further, some bonds carry a currency option which allows the investor to specify that payments of either interest or principal be made in either one of two major currencies.

Cash flow and return predictability—As explained earlier, the return that an investor will realize by holding a financial asset depends on the cash flow that is expected to be received. This includes dividend payments on stock and interest payments on debt instruments, as well as the repayment of principal for a debt instrument and the expected sale price of a stock. Therefore, the predictability of the expected return depends on the predictability of the cash flow. Return predictability is a basic property of financial assets, in that it is a major determinant of their value. Assuming investors are risk averse, as we will see in later chapters, the riskiness of an asset can be equated with the uncertainty or unpredictability of its return.

In a world of non-negligible inflation, it is further important to distinguish between nominal expected return and the real expected return. The **nominal expected return** considers the dollars that are expected to be received but does not adjust those dollars to take into consideration changes in their purchasing power. The **real expected return** is the nominal expected return but after adjustment for the loss of purchasing power of the financial asset as a result of inflation.

For example, if the nominal expected return for a one-year investment of $1,000 is 6%, then at the end of one year the investor expects to realize $1,060, consisting of interest of $60 and the repayment of the $1,000 investment. However, if the inflation rate over the same period of time is expected to be 4%, then the purchasing power of $1,060 is only $1,019.23 ($1,060 divided by 1.04). Thus the return in terms of purchasing power, or real expected return, is 1.9%. In general, the real expected return can be approximated by subtracting from the nominal expected return the expected inflation rate. In our example, it is approximately 2% (6% minus 4%).

Complexity—Some financial assets are complex in the sense that they are actually combinations of two or more simpler assets. To find the true value of such an asset, one must "decompose" it into its component parts and price each component separately. We will encounter numerous complex financial assets throughout this book. Indeed, there have been many innovations involving debt instruments since the early 1980s that have resulted in complex financial assets.

Most complex financial assets involve a choice or option granted to the issuer or investor to do something to alter the cash flow. Because the value of such financial assets depends on the value of the choices or options granted to the issuer or investor, it becomes essential to understand how to determine the value of an option.

Tax status—An important feature of any financial asset is its tax status. Governmental codes for taxing the income from the ownership or sale of financial assets vary widely if not wildly. Tax rates differ from year to year, country to country, and even among municipal units within a country (as with state and local taxes in the United States). Moreover, tax rates may differ from financial asset to financial asset, depending on the type of issuer, the length of time the asset is held, the nature of the owner, and so on.

FINANCIAL MARKETS

A **financial market** is a market where financial assets are exchanged (i.e., traded). Although the existence of a financial market is not a necessary condition for the creation and exchange of a financial asset, in most economies financial assets are created and subsequently traded in some type of organized financial market structure.

The Role of Financial Markets

The two primary economic functions of financial assets were discussed above. Financial markets provide three additional economic functions. First, the interactions of buyers and sellers in a financial market determine the price of the traded asset; or, equivalently, the required return on a financial asset is determined. The inducement for firms to acquire funds depends on the required return that investors demand, and it is this feature of financial markets that signals how the funds in the economy should be allocated among financial assets. This is called the **price discovery process**. Whether these signals are correct or not is an issue that we discuss in Chapter 7 when we examine the question of the efficiency of financial markets.

Second, financial markets provide a mechanism for an investor to sell a financial asset. Because of this feature, it is said that a financial market offers liquidity, an attractive feature when circumstances either force or motivate an investor to sell. In the absence of liquidity, the owner will be forced to hold a debt instrument until it matures and an equity instrument until the company is either voluntarily or involuntarily liquidated. While all financial markets provide some form of liquidity, the degree of liquidity is one of the factors that characterize different markets.

The third economic function of a financial market is that it reduces the search and information costs of transacting. **Search costs** represent explicit costs, such as the money spent to advertise the desire to sell or purchase a financial asset, and implicit costs, such as the value of time spent in locating a counterparty. The presence of some form of organized financial market reduces search costs. **Information costs** are those entailed with assessing the investment merits of a financial asset; that is, the amount and the likelihood of the cash flow expected to be generated. In an efficient market, prices reflect the aggregate information collected by all market participants.

Classification of Financial Markets

There are many ways to classify financial markets. One way is by the type of financial claim. The claims traded in a financial market may be either for a fixed dollar amount or a residual amount. As explained earlier, the former financial assets are referred to as debt instruments, and the financial market in which such instruments are traded is referred to as the **debt market**. The latter financial assets are called equity instruments and the financial market where such instruments are traded is referred to as the **equity market**. Alternatively, this market is referred to as the **stock market**. Preferred stock is an equity claim that entitles the investor to receive a fixed dollar amount. Consequently, preferred stock shares characteristics of instruments classified as part of the debt market and the equity market. Generally, debt instruments and preferred stock are classified as part of the **fixed-income market**. The sector of the stock market that does not include preferred stock is called the **common stock market**. These classifications are summarized in Figure 1-2.

Another way to classify financial markets is by the maturity of the claims. For example, there is a financial market for short-term financial assets, called the **money market**, and one for longer maturity financial assets, called the **capital market**. The traditional cut-off between short term and long term is one year. That is, a financial asset with a maturity of one year or less is considered short term and therefore part of the money market. A financial asset with a maturity of more than one year is part of the capital market. Thus, the debt market can be divided into those debt instruments which are part of the money market and part of the capital market depending on the number of years to maturity. Since equity instruments are generally perpetual, they are classified as part of the capital market. This is depicted in Figure 1-3.

Figure 1-2
Classification of Financial Markets by Type of Claim

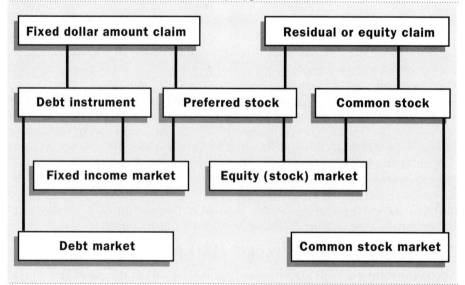

Figure 1-3

Classification of Financial Markets by Maturity of Claim

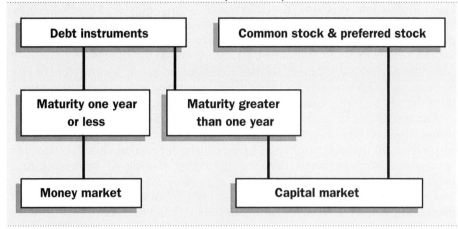

A third way to classify financial markets is by whether the financial claims are newly issued or not. When an issuer sells a new financial asset to the public, it is said to "issue" the financial asset. The market for newly-issued financial assets is called the **primary market**. After a certain period of time, the financial asset is bought and sold (i.e., exchanged or traded) amongst investors. The market where this activity takes place is referred to as the **secondary market**.

Finally, a market can be classified by its organizational structure. These organizational structures can be classified as auction markets, over-the-counter markets, and intermediate markets. We describe each type in later chapters.

Globalization of Financial Markets

Globalization means the integration of financial markets throughout the world into an international financial market. Because of the globalization of financial markets, entities in any country seeking to raise funds need not be limited to their domestic financial market. Nor are investors in a country limited to the financial assets issued in their domestic market.

The factors that have led to the integration of financial markets are (1) deregulation or liberalization of markets and the activities of market participants in key financial centers of the world; (2) technological advances for monitoring world markets, executing orders, and analyzing financial opportunities; and (3) increased institutionalization of financial markets. These factors are not mutually exclusive.

Global competition has forced governments to deregulate or liberalize various aspects of their financial markets so that their financial enterprises can compete effectively around the world. Technological advances have increased the integration and efficiency of the global financial market. Advances in telecommunication systems link market participants throughout the world with the result that orders can be executed within seconds. Advances in computer technology, coupled with advanced telecommunication systems, allow the transmission of real-time information on security prices and other key information to many participants in many places. Therefore, many investors can monitor global markets and simultaneously assess how this information will impact the risk/reward profile of their portfolios. Significantly improved computing power allows the instant manipulation of real-time market information so that attractive investment opportunities can be identified. Once these opportunities are identified, telecommunication systems permit the rapid execution of orders to capture them.

The shifting of the roles of the two types of investors, retail and institutional investors, in financial markets is the third factor that has led to the integration of financial markets. The U.S. financial markets have shifted from being dominated by retail investors to being dominated by institutional investors. Retail investors are individuals, while institutional investors are financial institutions such as pension funds, insurance companies, investment companies, commercial banks, and savings and loan associations. These financial institutions are described in Section I.

The shifting of the financial markets in the U.S. and other major industrialized countries from dominance by retail investors to institutional investors is referred to as the **institutionalization of financial markets**. Unlike retail investors, institutional investors have been more willing to transfer funds across national borders to improve the risk/reward opportunities of a portfolio that includes financial assets of foreign issuers. The potential portfolio benefits associated with global investing have been documented in numerous studies, which have heightened the awareness of investors about the virtues of global investing. Moreover, investors have not limited their participation in foreign markets to those of developed economies. There has been increased participation in the financial markets of developing economies, popularly referred to as **emerging markets**.

Classification of Global Financial Markets

While there is no uniform system for classifying the global financial markets, Figure 1-4 provides a schematic presentation of an appropriate classification system. From the perspective of a given country, financial markets can be

Figure 1-4
Classification of Global Financial Markets

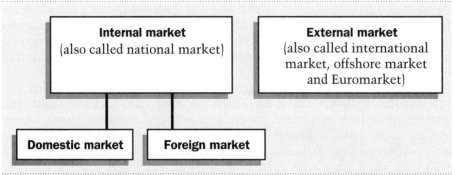

classified as either internal or external. The **internal market**, also called the **national market**, it can be decomposed into two parts: the **domestic market** and the **foreign market**. The domestic market is where issuers domiciled in the country issue securities and where those securities are subsequently traded.

The foreign market of a country is where the securities of issuers not domiciled in the country are sold and traded. The rules governing the issuance of foreign securities are those imposed by regulatory authorities where the security is issued. For example, securities issued by non-U.S. corporations in the United States must comply with the regulations set forth in U.S. securities law. A non-Japanese corporation that seeks to offer securities in Japan must comply with Japanese securities law and regulations imposed by the Japanese Ministry of Finance. Nicknames have been used to describe the various foreign markets. For example, the foreign market in the U.S. is called the "Yankee market." The foreign market in Japan is nicknamed the "Samurai market," in the United Kingdom the "Bulldog market," in the Netherlands the "Rembrandt market," and in Spain the "Matador market."

The **external market**, also called the **international market**, includes securities with the following distinguishing features: at issuance they are offered simultaneously to investors in a number of countries; and they are issued outside the jurisdiction of any single country. The external market is commonly referred to as the **offshore market**, or more popularly, the **Euromarket** (even though this market is not limited to Europe, it began there).[6]

DERIVATIVE MARKETS

Some contracts give the contract holder either the obligation or the choice to buy or sell a financial asset. Such contracts derive their value from the price of the underlying financial asset. Consequently, these contracts are called **derivative instruments**. The array of derivative instruments include options contracts, futures contracts, forward contracts, swap agreements, cap and floor agreements. Each of these derivative instruments and the role that they play in financial markets will be discussed throughout this book.

The existence of derivative instruments is the key reason why investors can more effectively implement investment decisions to achieve their financial goals and issuers can more effectively raise funds on more satisfactory terms. Several of the financial innovations and strategies discussed throughout this book rely on the market for derivative instruments.

As with any financial asset, derivative instruments can be used for speculative purposes as well as for accomplishing a specific financial or investment objective. Unfortunately, there have been several financial fiascos that have involved the use of derivative instruments. As a result, some regulators and lawmakers have been concerned with derivative instruments, viewing them as the "product of the devil." The problem with the derivative instruments is not with the instruments per se but the lack of understanding of their risk/return characteristics by some users. Hopefully, the discussion in this book will help dispel the misconceptions associated with derivative instruments.

---

[6] The classification we use is by no means universally accepted. Some market observers and compilers of statistical data on market activity refer to the external market as consisting of the foreign market and the Euromarket.

SUMMARY

In this chapter we explained the characteristics of financial assets and the markets where they are traded. A financial asset (financial instrument or security) entitles the owner to future cash flows to be paid by the issuer. The claim can be either an equity or debt claim.

The value of any financial asset is equal to the present value of the cash flow expected. The cash flow is the cash payments (dividends, interest, repayment of borrowed funds for a debt instrument, and the expected sale price of an equity instrument). For most financial assets, the cash flow is not known with certainty. The first step to value a financial asset is to estimate the cash flow. The minimum interest rate that should be used to discount the cash flow is the interest rate on U.S. Treasury securities. To that rate a premium must be added to reflect the risks associated with realizing the cash flow.

Financial assets have certain properties that determine or influence their attractiveness to different classes of investors. There are ten properties of financial assets: moneyness, divisibility and denomination, reversibility, term to maturity, liquidity, convertibility, currency, cash flow and return predictability, complexity, and tax status.

The two principal economic functions of a financial asset are (1) transferring funds from those who have surplus funds to invest to those who need funds to invest in tangible assets, and (2) transferring funds in such a way that redistributes the unavoidable risk associated with the cash flow generated by tangible assets among those seeking and those providing the funds.

Financial markets provide the following three additional functions beyond that of financial assets themselves: (1) they provide a mechanism for determining the price (or, equivalently, the required return) of financial assets, (2) they make assets more liquid, and (3) they reduce the costs of exchanging assets. The costs associated with transacting are search costs and information costs.

There are many ways to classify financial markets: by types of financial claim (debt instrument versus equity claim), by the maturity of claims (money market versus capital market), by whether the security is newly-issued or seasoned (primary market versus secondary market), or by the type of organizational structure.

Derivative instruments derive their value from an underlying financial asset. These instruments allow market players to more efficiently accomplish their financial goals.

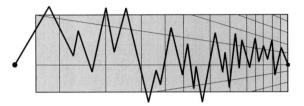

QUESTIONS

1. What is the difference between a financial asset and a tangible asset?

2. What is the difference between the claim of a debt holder of Ford Motor Corporation and a common stockholder of Ford Motor Corporation?

3. What is the basic principle in determining the value of a financial asset?

4. Why is it difficult to determine the cash flow of a financial asset?

5. What factors affect the interest rate that should be used to discount the cash flow expected from a financial asset?

6. A U.S. investor who purchases the bonds issued by the Japanese government made the following comment: "Assuming that the Japanese government does not default, I know what the cash flow of the bond will be." Explain why you agree or disagree with this statement.

7. A U.S. investor who purchases the bonds issued by the U.S. government made the following statement: "By buying this debt instrument I am not exposed to default risk or purchasing power risk." Explain why you agree or disagree with this statement.

8. You just inherited 30,000 shares of a company you have never heard of, ABC Corporation. You call your broker to find out if you have finally struck it rich. After several minutes she comes back on the telephone and says: "I don't have a clue about these shares. It's too bad they are not traded in a financial market. That would make life a lot easier for you." What does she mean by this?

9. Explain why liquidity may depend not only on the type of financial asset but also on the quantity one wishes to sell or buy.

10. What are the two basic roles of financial assets?

11. Give three reasons for the greater integration of financial markets throughout the world.

12. In January 1992, the U.S.-based Atlantic Richfield Corporation issued $250 million of bonds with a maturity of 30 years in the United States. From the perspective of the U.S. financial market, indicate whether this issue is classified as being issued in the

domestic market, the foreign market, or the offshore market.

13. In January 1992, the Korea Development Bank issued $500 million of bonds with a maturity of ten years in the United States. From the perspective of the U.S. financial market, indicate whether this issue is classified as being issued in the domestic market, the foreign market, or the offshore market.

14. In September 1990, a study by the U.S. Congress Office of Technology Assessment, entitled "Electronic Bulls & Bears: U.S. Securities Markets and Information Technology," included this statement:

    Securities markets have five basic functions in a capitalistic economy:

    1. they make it possible for corporations and governmental units to raise capital;

    2. they help to allocate capital toward productive uses;

    3. they provide an opportunity for people to increase their savings by investing in them;

    4. they reveal investors' judgments about the potential earning capacity of corporations, thus giving guidance to corporate managers; and

    5. they generate employment and income.

    For each of the functions cited above, explain how financial markets (or securities markets, in the parlance of this Congressional study) perform each function.

15. Indicate whether each of the following instruments trades in the money market or the capital market:

    a. General Motors Acceptance Corporation issues a financial instrument with 4 months to maturity.

    b. The U.S. Treasury issues a security with 30 years to maturity.

    c. IBM Corporation issues common stock.

16. Give three examples of derivative instruments and explain why they are called derivative instruments.

Overview of Market Participants and Financial Innovation

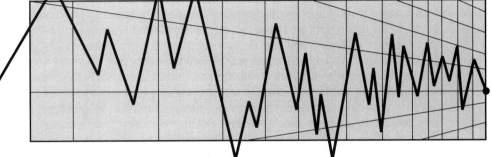

LEARNING OBJECTIVES

After reading this chapter you will understand:

- the participants in financial markets: central governments, agencies of central governments, municipal governments, supranationals, nonfinancial businesses, financial businesses, and households.

- the business of financial institutions.

- what a financial intermediary is.

- how financial intermediaries provide at least one of four economic functions: maturity intermediation, risk reduction via diversification, reducing the costs of contracting and information processing, and a payments mechanism.

- the nature of the management of assets and liabilities by financial intermediaries.

- how different financial institutions have differing degrees of knowledge and certainty about the amount and timing of the cash outlay of their liabilities.

- the typical justification for governmental regulation of markets.

- how the government regulates financial markets through disclosure regulation, financial activity regulation, regulation of financial institutions, and regulation of foreign participants.

• the primary reasons for financial innovation.

• different ways to understand the emergence and success of financial innovations.

With an understanding of what financial assets are and the role of financial assets and financial markets, we can now identify who the players are in the financial markets. By this we mean, who are the entities that issue financial assets and who are the entities that invest in financial assets. We will focus on one particular group of market players, called financial intermediaries, because of the key economic functions that they perform in financial markets. In addition to reviewing their economic function, we will set forth the basic asset/liability problem faced by managers of financial intermediaries.

Other key players in financial markets are regulators. Because financial markets play a prominent role in any economy, governments have deemed it necessary to regulate certain aspects of these markets. In the United States, regulation occurs at the federal or state level, and in some cases both. While we introduce specific regulatory bodies and legislation in the chapters to follow, our objective in this chapter is to provide an overview of the various types of regulation.

We live in a time marked by an unusually rapid pace of financial innovation. This innovation reflects and responds to the needs of issuers and investors in attempting to accomplish their financial goals. At the end of the chapter we provide a brief overview of some of the reasons for and benefits of financial innovation.

ISSUERS AND INVESTORS

There are entities that issue financial assets, both debt instruments and equity instruments. There are investors who purchase these financial assets. This does not mean that these two groups are mutually exclusive—it is common for an entity to both issue a financial asset and at the same time invest in a different financial asset. Thus, it makes little sense to discuss issuers and investors separately. Instead, we shall refer to both issuers and investors as entities that participate in the financial market.

Classification of Entities

A simple classification of these entities is as follows: (1) central governments, (2) agencies of central governments, (3) municipal governments, (4) supranationals, (5) nonfinancial businesses, (6) financial enterprises, and (7) households. Central governments borrow funds for a wide variety of reasons. Debt obligations issued by central governments carry the full faith and credit of the borrowing government. In the United States, the role of raising funds rests with the Department of the Treasury. Funds are raised by the issuance of debt obligations called **Treasury securities**. In Japan, the Ministry of Finance is responsible for raising funds via the sale of securities.

Many central governments establish agencies to raise funds to perform specific functions. In the United States, for example, federal agencies were created by Congress to reduce the cost of raising funds for certain borrowing sectors of the economy deemed to be important enough to warrant assistance. The entities in these privileged sectors include farmers, homeowners, and students. There are two types of government agencies in the United States: **federally-related institutions** and **government-sponsored enterprises**. The former are arms of the federal government, such as the Farmers Housing Administration. Government-sponsored enterprises, also called federally-sponsored agencies, are privately owned, publicly chartered entities. An example is the Federal Home Loan Mortgage Corporation, popularly referred to as Fannie Mae. In Germany, two federal agencies that issue securities are the Federal Railway (Bundesbahn) and the Post Office (Bundespost). Agency obligations may or may not be guaranteed by the full faith and credit of the central government that created the agency.

Most countries have municipalities that raise funds in the capital market. For example, in the United States municipal governments include states, counties, and cities. These entities also create "authorities" and special districts to raise funds for a specific purpose, an example being the Port Authority of New York and New Jersey.

A supranational institution is an organization that is formed by two or more central governments through international treaties. The purpose for creating a supranational institution is to promote economic development for the member countries. Two examples of supranational institutions are the International Bank for Reconstruction and Development, popularly referred to as the World Bank, and the Inter-American Development Bank. The general objective of the former is to improve the efficiency of the international financial and trading markets. The objective of the latter is to promote economic growth in the developing countries of the Americas.

Businesses are classified into nonfinancial and financial businesses. These entities borrow funds in the debt market and raise funds in the equity market. Nonfinancial businesses are divided into three categories: corporations, farms, and nonfarm/noncorporate businesses. The first category includes corporations that manufacture products (e.g., cars, steel, computers) and/or provide nonfinancial services (e.g., transportation, utilities, computer programming). In the last category are businesses that produce the same products or provide the same services but are not incorporated.

Financial businesses, more popularly referred to as **financial institutions**, provide services related to one or more of the following:

1. transforming financial assets acquired through the market and constituting them into a different, and more widely preferable, type of asset—which becomes their liability. This is the function performed by **financial intermediaries**, the most important type of financial institution.
2. exchanging financial assets on behalf of customers.
3. exchanging financial assets for their own account.
4. assisting in the creation of financial assets for their customers and then selling those financial assets to other market participants.
5. providing investment advice to other market participants.
6. managing the portfolios of other market participants.

Financial intermediaries include depository institutions (commercial banks, savings and loan associations, savings banks, and credit unions), who acquire the bulk of their funds by offering their liabilities to the public mostly in the form of deposits; insurance companies (life and property and casualty companies); pension funds; and finance companies. Deposit accepting, or depository institutions, are discussed in Chapter 3. Other financial intermediaries are covered in Chapter 4.

The second and third services in the list above are the broker and dealer functions discussed in Chapters 5 and 7. The fourth service is referred to as underwriting. As will be explained in Chapters 5 and 6, typically a financial institution that provides an underwriting service also provides a brokerage and/or dealer service.

Some nonfinancial businesses have subsidiaries that provide financial services. For example, many large manufacturing firms have subsidiaries that provide financing for the parent company's customer. These financial institutions are called **captive finance companies**. Examples include General Motors Acceptance Corporation (a subsidiary of General Motors) and General Electric Credit Corporation (a subsidiary of General Electric).

Snapshot of the Entities in the U.S. Credit Market

Table 2-1 shows the participation of the entities above in the U.S. debt (or credit) market as reported by the Federal Reserve Board for the third quarter of 1994. The total debt outstanding was $16.7 trillion. Notice how the Federal Reserve Board divides the debt market into three major sectors: domestic non-financial sector, domestic financial sector, and foreign sector. The domestic financial sector includes not only financial businesses but also government agencies that raise funds in the U.S. debt market (government-sponsored entities and certain federally-related agencies).

ROLE OF FINANCIAL INTERMEDIARIES

Financial intermediaries obtain funds by issuing financial claims against themselves to market participants, then investing those funds. The investments made by financial intermediaries—their assets—can be in loans and/or securities. These investments are referred to as **direct investments**. Two examples will illustrate this. Most readers of this book are familiar with what a commercial bank does. Commercial banks accept deposits and may use the proceeds to lend funds to consumers and businesses. The deposits represent the IOU of the commercial bank and a financial asset owned by the depositor. The loan represents an IOU of the borrowing entity and a financial asset of the commercial bank. The commercial bank has made a direct investment in the borrowing entity; the depositor effectively has made an indirect investment in that borrowing entity.

As a second example, consider an investment company that pools the funds of investors and uses those funds to buy a portfolio of securities such as stocks and bonds. Investors providing funds to the investment company receive an equity claim that entitles the investor to a pro rata share of the outcome of the portfolio. The equity claim is issued by the investment company. The portfolio of financial assets acquired by the investment company represents a direct investment that it has made. By owning an equity claim against the investment company, those who invest in the investment company have made an indirect investment.

We have stressed that financial intermediaries play the basic role of transforming financial assets that are less desirable for a large part of the public into other financial assets—their own liabilities—which are more widely preferred by the public. This transformation involves at least one of four economic functions: (1) providing maturity intermediation, (2) risk reduction via

Table 2-1
Summary of Credit Market Debt Outstanding as of the Third Quarter of 1994

Domestic Nonfinancial Sector		$ 2,765.5
U.S. government	$ 202.6	
Household	1,826.8	
Nonfinancial business		
Nonfarm/noncorporate	37.9	
Corporate	249.6	
State and local government	448.6	
Domestic Financial Sector		$ 12,675.1
Government-sponsored enterprises	631.9	
Federally-related mortgage pools	1,437.6	
Monetary authority	356.8	
Funding corporations	111.0	
Private financial sector		
Commercial banks	3,203.1	
Thrift institutions	1,157.9	
Life insurance companies	1,417.8	
Other insurance companies	438.8	
Private pension funds	735.1	
Finance companies	524.2	
Mortgage companies	25.0	
Mutual funds	718.2	
Closed-end funds	81.3	
Money market funds	425.1	
Real estate investment trusts (REITs)	9.1	
Brokers and dealers	95.6	
Asset-backed securities issuers	484.2	
Bank personal trusts	245.3	
State and local pension funds	577.0	
Foreign Sector		$ 1,250.4
Total credit market assets		$ 16,691.0

Source: Federal Reserve Bulletin

diversification, (3) reducing the costs of contracting and information processing, and (4) providing a payments mechanism.

Maturity Intermediation

In our example of the commercial bank, two things should be noted. First, the maturity of at least a portion of the deposits accepted is typically short term. For example, certain types of deposit are payable upon demand; others have a specific maturity date, but most are less than two years. Second, the maturity of the loans made by a commercial bank may be considerably longer than two years. In the absence of a commercial bank, the borrower would have to borrow for a shorter term or find an entity that is willing to invest for the length of the loan sought, and/or investors who make deposits in the bank would have to commit funds for a longer length of time than they want. By issuing its own financial claims the commercial bank in essence transforms a longer term asset into a shorter term one by giving the borrower a loan for the length of time sought and the investor/depositor a financial asset for the desired investment horizon. This function of a financial intermediary is called **maturity intermediation**.

Maturity intermediation has two implications for financial markets. First, investors have more choices concerning maturity for their investments; borrowers have more choices for the length of their debt obligations. Second, because investors are reluctant to commit funds for a long period of time, they will require that long-term borrowers pay a higher interest rate than on short-term borrowing. In contrast, a financial intermediary will be willing to make longer term loans, and at a lower cost to the borrower than an individual investor would, by counting on successive deposits providing the funds until maturity (although at some risk as discussed below). Thus, the second implication is that the cost of longer-term borrowing is likely to be reduced.

Risk Reduction via Diversification

Consider the example of the investor who places funds in an investment company. Suppose that the investment company invests the funds received in the stock of a large number of companies. By doing so, the investment company has diversified and reduced its risk. Investors who have a small sum to invest would find it difficult to achieve the same degree of diversification because they would not have sufficient funds to buy shares of a large number of companies. Yet by investing in the investment company for the same sum of money investors can accomplish this diversification, thereby reducing risk.

This economic function of financial intermediaries—transforming more risky assets into less risky ones—is called **diversification**. While individual investors can do it on their own, they may not be able to do it as cost effectively as a financial intermediary, depending on the amount of funds they have to invest. Attaining cost effective diversification in order to reduce risk by purchasing the financial assets of a financial intermediary is an important economic benefit for financial markets.

Reducing the Costs of
Contracting and Information Processing

Investors purchasing financial assets should develop skills necessary to understand how to evaluate an investment. Once those skills are developed, investors should apply them to the analysis of specific financial assets that are candidates for purchase (or subsequent sale). Investors who want to make a loan to a consumer or business will need to write the loan contract (or hire an attorney to do so). While there are some people who enjoy devoting leisure time to this task, most of us find that leisure time is in short supply, so to sacrifice it, we have to be compensated. The form of compensation could be a higher return obtained from an investment.

In addition to the opportunity cost of the time to process the information about the financial asset and its issuer, there is the cost of acquiring that information. All these costs are called **information processing costs**. The costs of writing loan contracts are referred to as **contracting costs**. Another dimension to contracting costs is the cost of enforcing the terms of the loan agreement.

With this in mind, consider our two examples of financial intermediaries—the commercial bank and the investment company. Their staffs include investment professionals who are trained to analyze financial assets and manage them. In the case of loan agreements, either standardized contracts can be prepared, or legal counsel can be part of the professional staff to write contracts involving more complex transactions. The investment professionals can monitor compliance with the terms of the loan agreement and take any necessary action to protect the interests of the financial intermediary. The employment of such professionals is cost-effective for financial intermediaries because investing funds is their normal business.

In other words, there are economies of scale in contracting and processing information about financial assets, because of the amount of funds managed by financial intermediaries. The lower costs accrue to the benefit of the investor who purchases a financial claim of the financial intermediary and to the issuers of financial assets, who benefit from a lower borrowing cost.

Providing a Payments Mechanism

While the previous three economic functions may not have been immediately obvious, this last function should be. Most transactions made today are not done with cash. Instead, payments are made using checks, credit cards, debit cards, and electronic transfers of funds. These methods for making payments are provided by certain financial intermediaries.

At one time, noncash payments were restricted to checks written against noninterest-bearing accounts at commercial banks. Similar check writing privileges were provided later by savings and loan associations and savings banks, and by certain types of investment companies. Payment by credit card was also at one time the exclusive domain of commercial banks, but now other depository institutions offer this service. Debit cards are offered by various financial intermediaries. A debit card differs from a credit card in that a bill is sent to the credit cardholder periodically (usually once a month) requesting payment for transactions that have been made in the past. With a debit card, funds are immediately withdrawn (debited) from the purchaser's account at the time the transaction takes place.

The ability to make payments without the use of cash is critical for the functioning of a financial market. In short, depository institutions transform assets that cannot be used to make payments into other assets that offer that property.

OVERVIEW OF ASSET/LIABILITY MANAGEMENT FOR FINANCIAL INSTITUTIONS

In Chapters 3 and 4, we will discuss the major financial institutions. To understand why managers of financial institutions invest in particular types of financial assets and the types of investment strategies employed, it is necessary to have a general understanding of the asset/liability problem faced.

The nature of the liabilities dictates the investment strategy a financial institution will pursue. For example, depository institutions seek to generate income by the difference between the return that they earn on assets and the cost of their funds. This difference is referred to as a **spread**. That is, they buy money and sell money seeking to realize a profit. They buy money by borrowing from depositors or through other sources of funds. They sell money when they make loans and buy securities. Their objective is to sell money for more than it costs to buy money. The cost of the funds and the return on the funds sold is expressed in terms of an interest rate per unit of time. Consequently, the objective of a depository institution is to earn a positive spread between the assets it invests in (what it has sold the money for) and the cost of its funds (what is has purchased the money for). As we shall see in Chapter 4, life insurance companies are in the spread business.

Pension funds are not in the spread business in that they do not raise funds themselves in the market. They seek to cover the cost of pension obligations at a minimum cost that is borne by the sponsor of the pension plan. Investment companies face no explicit costs for the funds they acquire and must satisfy no specific liability obligations, except in the case of one type of investment company that agrees to repurchase shares at any time.

Nature of Liabilities

By the liabilities of a financial institution we mean the amount and timing of the cash outlays that must be made to satisfy the contractual terms of the obligations issued. The liabilities of any financial institution can be categorized according to four types, as shown in Table 2-2. The categorization in the table assumes that the entity that must be paid the obligation will not cancel the financial institution's obligation prior to any actual or projected payout date.

The descriptions of cash outlays as either known or uncertain are undoubtedly broad. When we refer to a cash outlay as being uncertain, we do not mean that it cannot be predicted. There are some liabilities where the "law of large numbers" makes it easier to predict the timing and/or amount of cash outlays. This is the work typically done by actuaries, but even actuaries have difficulty predicting natural catastrophes such as floods and earthquakes.

These risk categories will be further discussed in later chapters. Here we will give a brief illustration of each one.

Type I liabilities—With Type I liabilities both the amount and timing of the liabilities are known with certainty, such as when a financial institution knows that it must pay $50,000 in six months time. For example, depository institutions know the amount that they are committed to pay (principal plus interest) on the maturity date of a fixed-rate deposit, assuming that the depositor does not withdraw funds prior to the maturity date.

Type I liabilities, however, are not limited to depository institutions. A major product sold by life insurance companies is a **guaranteed investment contract**, popularly referred to as a GIC. The obligation of the life insurance company under this contract is that, for a sum of money (called a premium), it will guarantee an interest rate up to some specified maturity date.[1] For example, suppose a life insurance company, for a premium of $10 million, issues a five year GIC agreeing to pay 10% compounded annually. The life insurance company knows that it must pay $16.11 million to the GIC policyholder in five years.[2]

---

[1] A GIC does not seem like a product we would associate with a life insurance company, because the policyholder does not have to die in order for someone to be paid. Yet, as discussed in Chapter 4, a major group of insurance company financial products are in the pension benefit area—GIC is one such product.

[2] This amount is determined as follows: $10,000,000 (1.10)^5$.

Table 2-2
Nature of Liabilities of Financial Institutions

Liability Type	Amount of Cash Outlay	Timing of Cash Outlay
Type I	known	known
Type II	known	uncertain
Type III	uncertain	known
Type IV	uncertain	uncertain

Type II liabilities—With Type II liabilities the amount of the cash outlay is known, but the timing of the cash outlay is uncertain. The most obvious example of a Type II liability is a life insurance policy. Although there are many types of life insurance policy, the most basic type is that, for an annual premium, a life insurance company agrees to make a specified dollar payment to policy beneficiaries upon the death of the insured.

Type III liabilities—With this type of liability, the timing of the cash outlay is known but the amount is uncertain, such as when a financial institution has issued an obligation in which the interest rate adjusts periodically based on some interest rate benchmark. Depository institutions, for example, issue liabilities called certificates of deposit which have a stated maturity. The interest rate paid need not be fixed over the life of the deposit but may fluctuate. If a depository institution issues a three-year floating-rate certificate of deposit that adjusts every three months and the interest rate paid is the three-month Treasury bill rate plus one percentage point, the depository institution knows it has a liability that must be paid off in three years but the dollar amount of the liability is not known. It will depend on three-month Treasury bill rates over the three years.

Type IV liabilities—There are numerous insurance products and pension obligations where there is uncertainty as to both the amount and the timing of the cash outlay. Probably the most obvious examples are automobile and home insurance policies issued by property and casualty insurance companies. When, and if, a payment will have to be made to the policyholder is uncertain. Whenever damage is done to an insured asset, the amount of the payment that must be made is uncertain.

As we discuss in Chapter 4, sponsors of pension plans can agree to various types of pension obligations to the beneficiaries of the plan. There are plans where retirement benefits depend on the participant's income for a specified number of years before retirement and the total number of years the participant worked. This will affect the amount of the cash outlay. The timing of the cash outlay depends on when the employee elects to retire, and whether the employee remains with the sponsoring plan until retirement. Moreover, both the amount and the timing will depend on how the employee elects to have payments made—over only the employee's life or those of the employee and spouse.

Liquidity Needs

Because of uncertainty about the timing and/or the amount of the cash outlays, a financial institution must be prepared to have sufficient cash to satisfy its obligations. Also keep in mind that our discussion of liabilities assumes that the entity that holds the obligation against the financial institution may have the right to change the nature of the obligation, perhaps incurring some penalty. For example, in the case of a certificate of deposit, the depositor may request the withdrawal of funds prior to the maturity date. Typically, the deposit-accepting institution will grant this request, but assess an early withdrawal penalty. In the case of certain types of investment companies, shareholders have the right to redeem their shares at any time.

Some life insurance products have a cash-surrender value. This means that, at specified dates, the policyholder can exchange the policy for a lump sum payment. Typically, the lump sum payment will penalize the policyholder for turning in the policy. There are some life insurance products that have a loan value, which means that the policyholder has the right to borrow against the cash value of the policy.

In addition to uncertainty about the timing and amount of the cash outlays, and the potential for the depositor or policyholder to withdraw cash early or borrow against a policy, a financial institution has to be concerned with possible reduction in cash inflows. In the case of a depository institution, this means the inability to obtain deposits. For insurance companies, it means reduced premiums because of the cancellation of policies. For certain types of investment companies, it means not being able to find new buyers for shares.

REGULATION OF FINANCIAL MARKETS

Financial markets play a prominent role in many economies, and governments around the world have long deemed it necessary to regulate certain aspects of these markets. In their regulatory capacities, governments have greatly influenced the development and evolution of financial markets and institutions. It is important to realize that governments, issuers, and investors tend to behave interactively and to affect one another's actions in certain ways. Thus, it is not surprising to find that a market's reactions to regulations often prompt a new response by the government, which can cause the institutions of the market to change their behavior further, and so on. A sense of how the government can affect a market and its participants is important to an understanding of the numerous markets and securities that will be described in the chapters to come.

In this section, we will discuss regulation in the United States. Our purpose is not to provide a detailed account of the U.S. regulatory structures and rules. Rather, we provide a broad view of the goals and types of regulations currently in place in the United States.

Justification for Regulation

The standard explanation or justification for governmental regulation of a market is that the market, left to itself, will not produce its particular goods or services in an efficient manner and at the lowest possible cost. Efficiency and low-cost production are hallmarks of a perfectly competitive market. Thus, a market unable to produce efficiently must be one that is not competitive at the time and that will not gain that status by itself in the foreseeable future. Of course, it is also possible that governments may regulate markets that are viewed as competitive currently but unable to sustain competition, and thus low-cost production, over the long run. A version of this justification for regulation is that the government controls a feature of the economy that the market mechanisms of competition and pricing could not manage without help. A short-hand expression used by economists to describe the reasons for regulation is "market failure." A market is said to fail if it cannot, by itself, maintain all the requirements for a competitive situation.

The regulatory structure in the United States is largely the result of financial crises that have occurred at various times. Most regulatory mechanisms are the products of the stock market crash of 1929 and the Great Depression in the 1930s. Some of the regulations may make little economic sense in the current financial market, but they can be traced back to some abuse that legislators encountered, or thought they encountered, at one time. Further, with the exception of financial institution regulation, the three other forms of regulation discussed below are most often a function of the federal government, with state governments playing a secondary role. For that reason, the present discussion of regulation concentrates on the federal government and its agencies. We will examine the role of state governments in Chapters 3 and 4.

Forms of Federal Government Regulation of Financial Markets

Government regulation of financial markets takes one of four forms: (1) disclosure regulation, (2) financial activity regulation, (3) regulation of financial institutions, and (4) regulation of foreign participants. Each is described below along with a discussion of this form of regulation in the United States.

Disclosure regulation—Disclosure regulation requires issuers of securities to make public a large amount of financial information to actual and potential investors. The standard justification for disclosure rules is that the managers of the issuing firm have more information about the financial health and future of the firm than investors who own or are considering the purchase of the firm's securities. The cause of market failure here, if indeed it occurs, is commonly described as "asymmetric information," which means investors and managers have uneven access to or uneven possession of information. Also, the problem is said to be one of "agency," in the sense that the firm's managers, who act as agents for investors, may act in their own interests to the disadvantage of those investors. The advocates of disclosure rules say that, in the absence of the rules, the investors' comparatively limited knowledge about the firm would allow the agents to engage in such practices.

The United States is firmly committed to disclosure regulation. The Securities Act of 1933 and the Securities Exchange Act of 1934 led to the creation of the Securities and Exchange Commission (SEC), which is responsible for gathering and publicizing relevant information and for punishing those issuers who supply fraudulent or misleading data. None of the SEC's requirements or actions constitutes a guarantee, a certification, or an approval of the securities being issued. Moreover, the government's rules do not represent an attempt to prevent the issuance of risky assets. Rather, the government's (and the SEC's) sole motivation in this regard is to supply diligent and intelligent investors with the information needed for a fair evaluation of the securities.

It is interesting to note that several prominent economists deny the need and justification for disclosure rules. Led by George Benston, they argue that the securities market would, without governmental assistance, get all the information necessary for a fair pricing of new as well as existing securities. In this view, the rules supposedly extracting key data from agent-managers are redundant.[3] One way to look at this argument is to ask what investors would do if a firm trying to sell new shares did not provide all the data investors would want. In that case, investors either would refuse to buy that firm's securities, giving them a zero value, or would discount or underprice the securities. Thus, a firm concealing important information would pay a penalty in the form of reduced proceeds from the sale of the new securities. The prospect of this penalty is potentially as much incentive to disclose as the rules of a governmental agency.

Financial activity regulation—Financial activity regulation consists of rules about traders of securities and trading on financial markets. A prime example of this form of regulation is the set of rules against trading by insiders who are corporate officers and others in positions to know more about a firm's prospects than the general investing public. Insider trading is another problem posed by asymmetric information. A second example of this type of regulation would be rules regarding the structure and operations of exchanges where securities are traded. The argument supporting these rules rests on the possibility that members of exchanges may be able, under certain circumstances, to collude and defraud the general investing public.

Like disclosure, financial activity regulation is also widely implemented in the United States. The SEC has the duty of carefully monitoring the trades that corporate officers, directors, or major stockholders ("insiders") make in the securities of their firms. The SEC and another federal government entity, The Commodity Futures Trading Commission (CFTC), share responsibility for the federal regulation of trading in derivative instruments.

Regulation of financial institutions—Regulation of financial institutions is that form of governmental monitoring that restricts these institutions' activities in the vital areas of lending, borrowing, and funding. The justification for this form of government regulation is that these financial firms have a special role to play in a modern economy. Financial institutions help households and firms to save; as depository institutions, they also facilitate the complex payments among many elements of the economy; and they serve as conduits for the government's monetary policy. Thus, it is often argued that the failure of these financial institutions would disturb the economy in a severe way.

The U.S. government has imposed an extensive array of regulations on financial institutions. Most of these regulations restrict what financial institutions do in the markets and how those institutions manage their liabilities and assets. A recent development has been the imposition of risk-based capital requirements that certain financial institutions must maintain in order to

---

[3] George J. Benston, "Required Disclosure and the Stock Market: An Evaluation of the Securities Exchange Act of 1934," *American Economic Review* 63 (March 1973), pp. 132–55.

operate. While capital requirements for certain financial institutions are not new, what is new is relating capital requirements to various risk dimensions. We will discuss risk-based capital requirements when we focus on specific financial institutions.

Regulation of foreign participants—Regulation of foreign participants is that form of governmental activity that limits the roles foreign firms can have in domestic markets and their ownership or control of finanical institutions.

Many countries regulate participation by foreign firms in domestic financial securities markets. As have most countries, the United States has been extensively reviewing and changing it policies regarding foreign firms' activities in the U.S. financial markets.

FINANCIAL INNOVATION

Competition among financial institutions has brought forth and fostered the development of new products and markets. Regulations that impede the free flow of capital and competition among financial institutions (particularly interest rate ceilings) have fostered the development of financial products and trading strategies to get around these restrictions. Finally, the global pattern of financial wealth has transformed financial markets from local markets into globally internationalized financial markets. Through technological advances and the reduction in trade and capital barriers, surplus funds in one country can be shifted more easily to those who need funds in another country. As a result, there has arisen a need for financial products and trading strategies to protect more efficiently against the adverse movements of foreign currencies.

Categorizations of Financial Innovation

Since the 1960s, there has been a surge in significant financial innovations. Observers of financial markets have categorized these innovations in different ways. Here are just three ways suggested to classify these innovations.

The Economic Council of Canada classifies financial innovations into the following three broad categories:[4]

- *market-broadening instruments*, which increase the liquidity of markets and the availability of funds by attracting new investors and offering new opportunities for borrowers;

- *risk-management instruments*, which reallocate financial risks to those who are less averse to them or who have offsetting exposure, and who are presumably better able to shoulder them; and

- *arbitraging instruments and processes*, which enable investors and borrowers to take advantage of differences in costs and returns between markets, and which reflect differences in the perception of risks, as well as in information, taxation, and regulations.

Another classification system of financial innovations based on more specific functions has been suggested by the Bank for International Settlements: *price-risk-transferring innovations*, *credit-risk-transferring instruments*,

---

[4] *Globalization and Canada's Financial Markets* (Ottawa, Canada: Supply and Services Canada, 1989), p. 32.

liquidity-generating innovations, credit-generating instruments, and *equity-generating instruments.*[5] Price-risk-transferring innovations are those that provide market participants with more efficient means for dealing with price or exchange-rate risk. Reallocating the risk of default is the function of credit-risk-transferring instruments. Liquidity-generating innovations do three things: (1) they increase the liquidity of the market, (2) they allow borrowers to draw upon new sources of funds, and (3) they allow market participants to circumvent capital constraints imposed by regulations. Instruments to increase the amount of debt funds available to borrowers and to increase the capital base of financial and nonfinancial institutions are the functions of credit-generating and equity-generating innovations, respectively.

Finally, Professor Stephen Ross suggests two classes of financial innovation: (1) new financial products (financial assets and derivative instruments) better suited to the circumstances of the time (e.g., to inflation) and to the markets in which they trade; and (2) strategies that primarily use these financial products.[6]

One of the purposes of this book is to explain these financial innovations. First, we will discuss why financial innovation takes place.

Motivation for Financial Innovation

There are two extreme views of financial innovation.[7] At one extreme are those who believe that the major impetus for innovation has been the endeavor to circumvent (or "arbitrage") regulations and find loopholes in tax rules.[8] At the other extreme are those who hold that the essence of innovation is the introduction of financial instruments that are more efficient for redistributing risks among market participants.

Many of the innovations that have passed the test of time have provided more efficient mechanisms for redistributing risk. Other innovations may just represent a more efficient way of doing things. If we consider the ultimate causes of financial innovation,[9] the following emerge as the most important:

1. increased volatility of interest rates, inflation, equity prices, and exchange rates.

2. advances in computer and telecommunication technologies.

3. greater sophistication and educational training among professional market participants.

4. financial intermediary competition.

5. incentives to get around existing regulation and tax laws.

6. changing global patterns of financial wealth.

---

[5] Bank for International Settlements, *Recent Innovations in International Banking* (Basle: BIS, April 1986).

[6] Stephen A. Ross, "Institutional Markets, Financial Marketing, and Financial Innovation," *Journal of Finance* (July 1989), p. 541.

[7] Ian Cooper, "Financial Innovations: New Market Instruments," *Oxford Review of Economic Policy* (November 1986).

[8] Merton H. Miller, "Financial Innovation: The Last Twenty Years and the Next," *Journal of Financial and Quantitative Analysis* (December 1986), pp. 459–71.

[9] Cooper "Financial Innovations," Table 9. We add inflation to the first category described.

With increased volatility comes the need for certain market participants to protect themselves against unfavorable consequences. This means new or more efficient ways of risk sharing in the financial market are needed. Many of the financial products require the use of computers to create and continually monitor them. To implement trading strategies using these financial products also requires computers, as well as telecommunication networks. Without advances in computer and telecommunication technologies, some innovations would not have been possible. Although financial products and trading strategies created by some market participants may be too complex for other market participants to use, the level of market sophistication, particularly in terms of mathematical understanding, has risen, permitting the acceptance of some complex products and trading strategies.

As you read the chapters on the various sectors of the financial markets that we review in this book, it is important to understand the factors behind any innovations in that market.

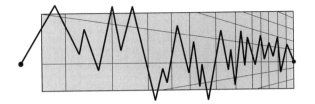

SUMMARY

Entities in the financial market can both raise funds (debt or equity) by issuing financial obligations, and invest in financial assets. These entities can be classified into one of the following categories: (1) central governments, (2) agencies of central governments, (3) municipal governments, (4) supranationals, (5) nonfinancial businesses, (6) financial enterprises, and (7) households.

Financial institutions provide various types of financial services: broker and dealer functions and underwriting functions. A special group of financial institutions are called financial intermediaries. These entities obtain funds by issuing claims to market participants and use these funds to purchase financial assets. Intermediaries transform assets they acquire into assets (their liabilities) that are more attractive to the public in four ways, by: (1) providing maturity intermediation, (2) providing risk reduction via diversification at lower cost, (3) reducing the cost of contracting and information processing, and (4) providing a payments mechanism.

The nature of their liabilities, as well as regulatory and tax considerations, determines the investment strategy pursued by all financial institutions. The liabilities of all financial institutions will generally fall into one of the four types shown in Table 2-2.

Regulation of the financial system and its various component sectors occurs in almost all countries. A useful way to organize the many instances of regulation is through four general forms: (1) disclosure regulation, (2) financial activity regulation, (3) regulation of financial institutions, and (4) regulation of foreign participants.

Financial innovation has increased dramatically since the 1960s, particularly in the late 1970s. While financial innovation can be the result of arbitrary regulations and tax rules, innovations that persist after regulations or tax rules have been changed to prevent exploitation are frequently those that have provided a more efficient means for redistributing risk.

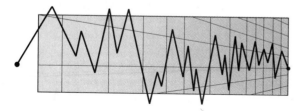

QUESTIONS

1. Explain how the household sector participates as both a borrower and lender of funds in the financial market.

2. What entities are included in the nonfinancial business sector of the financial market?

3. Explain why some subsidiaries of a nonfinancial business may be classified as financial businesses.

4. Why were government agencies created in the United States?

5. The European Investment Bank was established by the European Economic Community and charged with the role of promoting balanced regional development, serving the common interest of member states, and furthering industrial modernization. The member states include certain European countries. Would the European Investment Bank be classified as a municipal government or a financial business entity? If neither, how would it be classified?

6. a. Explain why an individual's account at a financial intermediary may be called an indirect investment in a firm that has borrowed money from the intermediary.

   b. Explain why the intermediary's loan to the firm is a direct investment.

7. Referring to Table 2-2, match the types of liabilities to these four assets that an individual might have:

   a. car insurance policy;

   b. variable rate certificate of deposit;

   c. fixed rate certificate of deposit; and

   d. a life insurance policy that allows the holder's beneficiary to receive $100,000 when the holder dies; however, if the death is accidental, the beneficiary will receive $150,000.

8. A bank issues an obligation to depositors in which it agrees to pay 8% guaranteed for one year. With the funds it obtains, the bank can invest in a wide range of financial assets. What is the risk if the bank uses the funds to invest in common stock?

9. Explain how financial intermediaries provide maturity intermediation?

10. How do financial intermediaries reduce the cost of contracting?

11. a. What is the economic rationale for the widespread use of "disclosure regulation"?

    b. Why do some economists believe that disclosure regulation is unnecessary?

12. What is meant by financial activity regulation?

13. In a 1989 study entitled "Globalization and Canada's Financial Markets," a research report prepared for the Economic Council of Canada, the following was reported:

    An important feature of the increasing significance of some aspects of financial activity is the greater use of financial markets and instruments that intermediate funds directly—a process called "market intermediation," which involves the issuance of, and trading in, securities such as bonds or stocks—as opposed to "financial intermediation," in which the financial institution raises funds by issuing a claim on itself and provides funds in the form of loans.

    a. Commercial banks are financial institutions that raise funds by issuing claims against themselves and then use the funds to provide loans. What do you think are the implications of the shift from financial intermediation to market intermediation for commercial banks?

    b. What do you think some of the obstacles are in market intermediation?

Depository Institutions

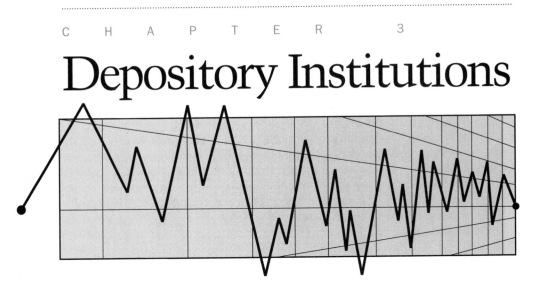

LEARNING OBJECTIVES

After reading this chapter you will understand:

• what a depository institution is.

• how a depository institution generates income.

• differences between commercial banks, savings and loan associations, savings banks, and credit unions.

• the asset/liability problem all depository institutions face.

• what is meant by funding risk.

• who regulates commercial banks and thrifts and the types of regulations imposed.

• the funding sources available to commercial banks and thrifts.

• reserve requirements imposed on banks.

• the risk-based capital requirements imposed on commercial banks and savings and loan associations.

Depository institutions include commercial banks (or simply banks), savings and loan associations (S&Ls), savings banks, and credit unions. All are financial intermediaries that accept deposits. These deposits represent the liabilities (debt) of the deposit-accepting institution. With the funds raised through deposits and other funding sources, depository institutions make direct loans to various entities and also invest in securities. Their income is derived from two sources: the income generated from the loans they make and the securities they purchase, and fee income.

It is common to refer to S&Ls, savings banks, and credit unions as "thrifts," which are specialized types of depository institutions. Traditionally, thrifts have not been permitted to accept deposits transferable by check (negotiable) through checking accounts. Instead, they have obtained funds primarily by tapping the savings of households. Since the early 1980s, however, thrifts have been allowed to offer negotiable deposits entirely equivalent to checking accounts, although they bear a different name (NOW accounts, share drafts).

Depository institutions are highly regulated because of the important role that they play in the financial system. Demand deposit accounts are the principal means that individuals and business entities use for making payments, and government monetary policy is implemented through the banking system. Because of their important role, depository institutions are afforded special privileges such as access to federal deposit insurance and access to a government entity that provides funds for liquidity or emergency needs. For example, the deposits of most depository institutions are currently insured up to $100,000 per account.

In this chapter we will look at depository institutions—the nature of their liabilities, where they invest their funds, and how they are regulated. Before we examine the specific institutions, we begin with an overview of the asset/liability problem faced by the manager of a depository institution.

ASSET/LIABILITY PROBLEM OF DEPOSITORY INSTITUTIONS

The asset/liability problem that depository institutions face is quite simple to explain—although not necessarily easy to solve. A depository institution seeks to earn a positive spread between the assets it invests in (loans and securities) and the cost of its funds (deposits and other sources). The spread is referred to as **spread income** or **margin**. The spread income should allow the institution to meet operating expenses and earn a fair profit on its capital.

In generating spread income a depository institution faces several risks. These include **credit risk, regulatory risk**, and **funding** (or interest rate) **risk**. Credit risk, also called default risk, refers to the risk that a borrower will default on a loan obligation to the depository institution or that the issuer of a security that the depository institution holds will default on its obligation. Regulatory risk is the risk that regulators will change the rules so as to impact the earnings of the institution unfavorably.

Funding Risk

Funding risk can be explained best by an illustration. Suppose that a depository institution raises $100 million by issuing a deposit account that has a maturity of one year and by agreeing to pay an interest rate of 7%. Ignoring for the time being the fact that the depository institution cannot invest the entire $100 million because of reserve requirements, which we discuss later in this chapter, suppose that $100 million is invested in a U.S. government security that matures in 15 years, paying an interest rate of 9%. Because the funds are invested in a U.S. government security, there is no credit risk in this case.

It seems at first that the depository institution has locked in a spread of 2% (9% minus 7%). This spread can be counted on only for the first year, though, because the spread in future years will depend on the interest rate this depository institution will have to pay depositors in order to raise $100 million after the one-year time deposit matures. If interest rates decline, the spread will increase because the depository institution has locked in the 9% rate. If interest rates rise, however, spread income will decline. In fact, if this depository institution must pay more than 9% to depositors at any time during for the next 14 years, the spread will be negative. That is, it will cost the depository institution more to finance the government securities than it will earn on the funds invested in those securities.

In our example, the depository institution has borrowed short (borrowed for one year) and lent long (invested for 15 years). This policy will benefit from a decline in interest rates but be disadvantaged if interest rates rise. Suppose the institution could have borrowed funds for 15 years at 7% and invested in a U.S. government security maturing in one year earning 9%—that is, borrowed long (15 years) and lent short (one year). A rise in interest rates will benefit the depository institution because it can then reinvest the proceeds from the maturing one-year government security in a new one-year government security offering a higher interest rate. In this case a decline in interest rates will reduce the spread. If interest rates fall below 7%, there will be a negative spread.

All depository institutions face this funding problem. Managers of a depository institution who have particular expectations about the future direction of interest rates will seek to benefit from these expectations. Those who expect interest rates to rise may pursue a policy to borrow funds for a long time horizon (borrow long) and lend funds for a short time horizon (lend short). If interest rates are expected to drop, managers may elect to borrow short and lend long.

The problem of pursuing a strategy of positioning a depository institution based on expectations is that considerable adverse financial consequences will result if those expectations are not realized. The evidence on interest rate forecasting suggests that it is a risky business. It is doubtful that there are managers of depository institutions who have the ability to forecast interest rate moves so consistently that the institution can benefit in the long run. The goal of management is to lock in a spread as best as possible, not to wager on interest rate movements.

Inherent in any balance sheet of a depository institution is funding risk exposure. Managers must be willing to accept some exposure, but they can take various measures to address the interest rate sensitivity of the institution's liabilities and its assets. A depository institution has (or should have) an asset/liability committee that is responsible for monitoring the interest rate risk exposure. There are several financial instruments (described in later chapters) that have been developed to help managers of depository institutions more effectively deal with their asset/liability problem.

Liquidity Concerns

Besides facing credit risk and interest rate risk, a depository institution must be prepared to satisfy withdrawals of funds by depositors and to provide loans to customers. There are several ways that a depository institution can accommodate withdrawal and loan demand: (1) attract additional deposits, (2) use existing securities as collateral for borrowing from a federal agency or other financial institution, (3) sell securities that it owns, or (4) raise short-term funds in the money market.

The first alternative is self-explanatory. The second has to do with the privilege allowed to banks to borrow at the discount window of the Federal Reserve Banks. The fourth alternative primarily includes using marketable securities owned as collateral for raising funds in the repurchase agreement market (see Chapter 19).

The third alternative, selling securities that it owns, requires that the depository institution invest a portion of its funds in securities that are both liquid and have little price risk. By price risk we refer to the prospect that the selling price of the security will be less than its purchase price, resulting in a loss. For example, as we explain in Chapter 18, while a 30-year U.S. government security is a highly liquid security, its price would change dramatically as interest rates rise. A price decline of, say, 25% would not be uncommon in a volatile interest rate environment. A 30-year government bond is therefore highly liquid, but exposes the depository institution to substantial price risk.

In general, as we explain in Chapter 17, short-term securities entail little price risk. It is therefore short-term, or money market, debt obligations in which a depository institution will invest in order to satisfy withdrawals and customer loan demand. It does this chiefly by lending federal funds, an investment vehicle that we will discuss later in this chapter. The term to maturity of the securities it holds affects the amount that depository institutions can borrow from some federal agency because only short-term securities are acceptable collateral.

Securities held for the purpose of satisfying net withdrawals and customer loan demands are sometimes referred to as "secondary reserves."[1] A disadvantage of holding secondary reserves is that securities with short maturities offer a lower yield than securities with a longer maturity in most interest rate environments. The percentage of a depository institution's assets held as secondary reserves will depend both on the institution's ability to raise funds from the other sources cited above and on its management's risk preference for liquidity (safety) versus yield.

Depository institutions hold liquid assets not only for operational purposes, but also because of the regulatory requirements that we discuss below.

COMMERCIAL BANKS

In 1992, there were about 11,500 commercial banks in the United States. A commercial bank can be chartered either by the state (state-chartered banks) or by the federal government (national banks). Of the 11,500 banks, more than half were state-chartered. All national banks must be members of the Federal Reserve System and must be insured by the Bank Insurance Fund (BIF), which is administered by the Federal Deposit Insurance Corporation (FDIC). While federal depository insurance has existed since the 1930s, and the insurance program is administered by the FDIC, BIF was created early in 1989 by the Financial

---

[1] Roland I. Robinson, *The Management of Bank Funds* (New York: McGraw-Hill, 1962), p. 15. The term "secondary reserves" is used because primary reserves are the reserves required by the Federal Reserve Board. The balance sheet of a depository institution will not use the term "secondary reserves" because a depository institution invests in short-term or money market instruments for reasons other than liquidity and does not report the purpose for which it acquires securities.

Institutions Reform, Recovery, and Enforcement Act of 1989 (FIRREA). Coverage is currently $100,000 per account. However, there have been several proposals to restructure deposit insurance coverage.

State-chartered banks may elect to join the Federal Reserve System. Their deposits must be insured by BIF. In spite of the large number of banks that elect not to be members of the Federal Reserve System, banks that are members hold more than 70% of all deposits in the United States. Moreover, with the passage of the Depository Institutions Deregulation and Monetary Control Act of 1980 (DIDMCA), the reserve requirements that apply to members of the Federal Reserve System apply also to state-chartered banks.

The size of banks varies greatly, as can be seen from Table 3-1 which shows the distribution for FDIC banks as of December 1992. Shown in the same table are total assets for each asset size. While less than 6% of the banks have total assets in excess of $500 million, these banks hold about three-quarters of the total assets.

The 50 largest U.S. commercial banks, based on total assets as of mid-1994, are listed in Table 3-2. The 20 largest bank holding companies are listed in Table 3-3. A bank holding company is a corporation that owns stock in one or more banks.

Table 3-4 shows, as of mid-1994, the 50 largest banks in the world measured in U.S. dollars and ranked in terms of total assets. The top ten banks are Japanese. The only two U.S. commercial banks in the top 50 are Citibank (34th) and Bank of America (46th). The listing in Table 3-4, however, is misleading because regulations differ across countries. Specifically, U.S. regulations prevent greater degrees of leverage for large banks; Japanese regulations do not apply this brake.

Table 3-1
Distribution of FDIC Insured Commercial Banks by Size as of December 1992

Asset Size (in millions)	Number of banks	% of banks	Assets (in billions)	% of assets
Less than $24.9	2,256	22.3	$ 41.1	1.2
$ 25.0 to $49.9	2,949	25.7	107.4	3.1
$ 50.0 to $99.9	2,785	24.3	197.4	5.6
$100.0 to $499.9	2,539	22.2	502.9	14.3
$500.0 to $999.9	252	2.2	177.4	5.1
$1 to $2.9 billion	202	1.8	350.4	10.0
$3.0 billion or more	178	1.6	2,129.4	60.7
Total	11,561	100.0	$3,506.0	100.0

Source: The data for this table come from Table No. 776, "Selected Financial Institutions — Number of Assets, by Asset Size: 1992," Statistical Abstract of the United States: 1994 (Department of Commerce, Bureau of the Census).

Table 3-2
The 50 Largest U.S. Commercial Banks
Ranked by Total Assets as of Mid-1994

Rank	Bank name	State	Total assets (in millions of U.S. dollars)
1	Citibank, N.A.	New York	$175,712
2	Bank of America NT&USA	California	136,693
3	Chemical Bank	New York	115,510
4	Morgan Guaranty Trust Co.	New York	101,902
5	Chase Manhattan Bank, N.A.	New York	84,189
6	Bankers Trust Company	New York	68,134
7	Wells Fargo Bank, N.A.	California	50,925
8	Home Savings of America, FSB	California	50,511
9	PNC Bank, N.A.	Pennsylvania	40,614
10	NationsBank of Texas, N.A.	Texas	37,109
11	Bank of New York	New York	36,088
12	Great Western Bank, FSB	California	35,869
13	First National Bank of Chicago	Illinois	34,491
14	Republic National Bank of New York	New York	29,697
15	First National Bank of Boston	Massachusetts	29,552
16	Mellon Bank, N.A.	Pennsyvania	29,294
17	World Savings & LA, FS&LA	California	28,100
18	First Union National Bank of Florida	Florida	27,765
19	NBD Bank, N.A.	Michigan	25,355
20	NationsBank of North Carolina	North Carolina	25,014
21	Comerica Bank-Detroit	Michigan	24,935
22	Continental Bank, N.A.	Illinois	22,331
23	First Union Nat Bk of North Carolina, N.A.	North Carolina	21,956
24	Society National Bank	Ohio	21,808
25	NationsBank of Florida, N.A.	Florida	21,391
26	Texas Commerce Bank, N.A.	Texas	21,387
27	First Interstate Bank of California	California	20,515
28	Wachovia Bank of North Carolina, N.A.	North Carolina	20,287
29	First Fidelity Bank, N.A.	New Jersey	20,065
30	State Street Bank and Trust Co.	Massachusetts	18,784
31	Bank One Texas, N.A.	Texas	18,173
32	CoreStates Bank, N.A.	Pennsylvania	17,829
33	Marine Midland Bank, N.A.	New York	17,485
34	American Savings Bank, FA	California	17,297
35	Glendale Federal Bank, FSB	California	16,977
36	National Westminster Bank (USA)	New York	16,675
37	Union Bank	California	16,526
38	First Bank, N.A.	Minnesota	15,803
39	First Nationwide Bank, FSB	California	15,496
40	NationsBank of Georgia, N.A.	Georgia	15,308
41	California Federal Bank, FSB	California	15,300

Table 3-2 *Continued from previous page*

Rank	Bank name	State	Total Assets (in millions of U.S. dollars)
42	Norwest Bank Minnesota, N.A.	Minnesota	15,295
43	Seafirst Bank	Washington	15,084
44	Shawmut Bank Connecticut	Connecticut	14,508
45	National Bank for Cooperatives	Colorado	14,408
46	American Express Bank Ltd.	New York	13,679
47	Key Bank of New York, N.A.	New York	13,608
48	Northern Trust Company	Illinois	13,538
49	Shawmut Bank, N.A.	Massachusetts	12,884
50	Meridian Bank	Pennsylvania	12,359

Source: Data as provided by Eurabank® database of Sleigh Corporation, Franklin Lakes, New Jersey.

Table 3-3

The 20 Largest U.S. Bank Holding Companies
Ranked by Total Assets as of Mid-1994

Rank	Bank holding company	State	Total assets (in millions of U.S. dollars)
1	Citicorp	New York	$216,574
2	BankAmerica Corporation	California	186,933
3	NationsBank Corporation	North Carolina	156,978
4	Chemical Banking Corp.	New York	149,888
5	J.P. Morgan & Co Inc.	New York	133,888
6	Chase Manhattan Corp.	New York	102,103
7	Bankers Trust New York Corp.	New York	91,627
8	Bank One Corporation	Ohio	79,919
9	First Union Corporation	North Carolina	70,541
10	PNC Bank Corp.	Pennsylvania	62,080
11	Wells Fargo & Co.	California	52,443
12	First Chicago Corporation	Illinois	52,043
13	First Interstate Bancorp	California	51,461
14	Norwest Corporation	Minnesota	50,782
15	Fleet Financial Group	Rhode Island	47,923
16	Bank of New York Co. Inc.	New York	45,546
17	NBD Bancorp Inc.	Michigan	40,776
18	Suntrust Banks Inc.	Georgia	40,728
19	Bank of Boston	Massachusetts	40,588
20	Republic New York Corporation	New York	39,493

Source: Data as provided by Eurabank® database of Sleigh Corporation, Franklin Lakes, New Jersey.

Table 3-4
The 50 Largest Banks in the World Ranked by Total Assets as of Mid-1994

Rank	Bank Name	Country	Total Assets (in millions of U.S. Dollars)
1	Dai-ichi Kangyo Bank	Japan	$502,669
2	Fuji Bank	Japan	501,729
3	Sumitomo Bank Ltd	Japan	493,473
4	Sakura Bank Ltd	Japan	491,952
5	Sanwa Bank	Japan	489,878
6	Mitsubishi Bank	Japan	455,895
7	Norinchukin Bank	Japan	428,240
8	Mitsubishi Trust & Banking	Japan	385,846
9	Industrial Bank of Japan	Japan	384,063
10	Mitsui Trust & Banking Company	Japan	370,003
11	Sumitomo Trust & Banking Ltd	Japan	369,073
12	Credit Lyonnais	France	338,906
13	Industrial & Comm Bank of China	China-People's Rep.	337,487
14	Deutsche Bank AG	Germany	319,252
15	Tokai Bank Ltd	Japan	308,433
16	Long-Term Credit Bank of Japan	Japan	298,946
17	Credit Agricole	France	282,915
18	Bank of China	China-People's Rep.	273,647
19	Yasuda Trust & Banking	Japan	271,078
20	Daiwa Bank	Japan	269,101
21	Societe Generale	France	259,838
22	Asahi Bank	Japan	259,702
23	ABN Amro Holding N.V.	Netherlands	252,984
24	Banque Nationale de Paris	France	250,486
25	Barclay's Bank PLC	United Kingdom	245,891
26	Bank of Tokyo	Japan	239,924
27	Toyo Trust & Banking	Japan	231,106
28	National Westminster Bank PLC	United Kingdom	226,419
29	Dresdner Bank	Germany	219,754
30	Union Bank of Switzerland	Switzerland	210,191
31	Westdeutsche Landesbank Girozen	Germany	191,399
32	People's Construction Bank of China	China-People's Rep.	183,584
33	Agricultural Bank of China	China-People's Rep.	181,968
34	Citibank, N.A.	USA	175,712
35	Banque Paribas	France	167,707
36	Bayerische Vereinsbank	Germany	165,660
37	Commerzbank AG	Germany	163,796
38	Nippon Credit Bank	Japan	163,325
39	CEP Caisses D'Epargne Et Prevoy	France	157,669
40	Shoko Chukin Bank	Japan	157,366
41	Credit Suisse	Switzerland	156,938
42	Bayerische Hypotheken Und Wechs	Germany	151,934

Table 3-4 *Continued from previous page*

Rank	Bank Name	Country	Total Assets (in millions of U.S. Dollars)
43	Bayerische Landesbank Girozenir	Germany	149,061
44	Hong Kong and Shanghi Bank Cor	Hong Kong	146,504
45	Swiss Bank Corporation	Switzerand	139,890
46	Bank of America NT&SA	USA	136,693
47	Zenshinren Bank	Japan	135,989
48	Chuo Trust & Banking	Japan	135,292
49	Rabobank Nederland	Netherlands	130,470
50	Deutsche Genossenschaftsbank	Germany	127,196

Source: Data as provided by Eurabank® database of Sleigh Corporation, Franklin Lakes, New Jersey.

Bank Services

Commercial banks provide numerous services in the U.S. financial system. The services can be broadly classified as follows: (1) individual banking, (2) institutional banking, and (3) global banking. Of course, different banks are more active in certain of these activities than others. For example, money center banks (defined later) are more active in global banking.

Individual banking encompasses consumer lending, residential mortgage lending, consumer installment loans, credit card financing, automobile and boat financing, brokerage services, student loans, and individual-oriented financial investment services such as personal trust and investment services. Interest and fee income are generated from mortgage lending and credit card financing. Mortgage lending is often referred to as "mortgage banking" (see Chapter 24). Fee income is generated from brokerage services and financial investment services.

Loans to nonfinancial corporations, financial corporations (such as life insurance companies), and government entities (state and local governments in the U.S. and foreign governments) fall into the category of institutional banking. Also included in this category are commercial real estate financing, leasing activities, and factoring.[2] In the case of leasing, a bank may be involved in leasing equipment either as lessors,[3] as lenders to lessors, or as purchasers of leases. Loans and leasing generate interest income, and other services that banks offer institutional customers generate fee income. These services include management of the assets of private and public pension funds, fiduciary and custodial services, and cash management services such as account maintenance, check clearing, and electronic transfers.

It is in the area of global banking that banks have begun to compete head-to-head with another financial institution—investment banking firms (see Chapter 5). Global banking covers a broad range of activities involving corporate financing and capital market and foreign exchange products and services. Most global banking activities generate fee income rather than interest income.

---

[2] The factoring business involves a bank's purchase of accounts receivable.

[3] This means that the bank buys the equipment and leases it to another party. The bank is the lessor and the party that uses the leased equipment is the lessee.

Corporate financing involves two components. First is the procuring of funds for a bank's customers. This can go beyond traditional bank loans to involve the underwriting of securities, though the Glass-Steagall Act limits bank activities in this area. In assisting its customers in obtaining funds, banks also provide bankers' acceptances, letters of credit, and other types of guarantees for their customers. That is, if a customer has borrowed funds backed by a letter of credit or other guarantee, its lenders can look to the customer's bank to fulfill the obligation. The second area of corporate financing involves advice on such matters as strategies for obtaining funds, corporate restructuring, divestitures, and acquisitions.

Capital market and foreign exchange products and services involve transactions where the bank may act as a dealer or broker in a service. Some banks, for example, are dealers in U.S. government or other securities. Customers who wish to transact in these securities can do so through the government desk of the bank. Similarly, some banks maintain a foreign-exchange operation, where foreign currency is bought and sold. Bank customers in need of foreign exchange can use the services of the bank.

In their role as dealers, banks can generate income in three ways: (1) the bid-ask spread, (2) capital gains on the securities or foreign currency used in transactions, and (3) in the case of securities, the spread between interest income earned by holding the security and the cost of funding the purchase of that security.

The financial products that banks have developed to manage risk also yield income. These products include interest rate swaps, interest rate agreements, currency swaps, forward contracts, and interest rate options. We will discuss each of these in later chapters. Banks can generate either commission income (that is, brokerage fees) or spread income from selling such products.

Bank Funding

In describing the nature of the banking business, we have focused so far on how a bank can generate income. We will now a look at how a bank can raise funds. There are three sources of funds for banks: (1) deposits, (2) nondeposit borrowing, and (3) common stock and retained earnings. Banks are highly leveraged financial institutions, which means that most of their funds come from borrowing—the first two sources we refer to. Included in nondeposit borrowing are borrowing from the Federal Reserve through the discount window facility, borrowing reserves in the federal funds market, and borrowing by the issuance of instruments in the money and bond markets.

Deposits—There are several types of deposit accounts. **Demand deposits** (checking accounts) pay no interest and can be withdrawn upon demand. Savings deposits pay interest (typically below market interest rates), do not have a specific maturity, and usually can be withdrawn upon demand.

Time deposits, also called **certificates of deposit**, have a fixed maturity date and pay either a fixed or floating interest rate. Some certificates of deposit can be sold in the open market prior to their maturity if the depositor needs funds (see Chapter 19). Other certificates of deposits cannot be sold. If a depositor elects to withdraw the funds from the bank prior to the maturity date, a withdrawal penalty is imposed. A **money-market demand account** is one that pays interest based on short-term interest rates. The market for short-term debt obligations is called the money market, which is how these deposits get their name. They are designed to compete with money market mutual funds, described in Chapter 4.

Reserve requirements and borrowing in the federal funds market—A bank cannot invest $1 for every $1 it obtains in deposit. All banks must maintain a specified percentage of their deposits in a non-interest-bearing account at one of the 12 Federal Reserve Banks. These specified percentages are called **reserve ratios**, and the dollar amounts based on them that are required to be kept on deposit at a Federal Reserve Bank are called **required reserves**. The reserve ratios are established by the Federal Reserve Board (the Fed). The reserve ratio differs by type of deposit. The Fed defines two types of deposits: transactions and nontransactions deposits. Demand deposits and what the Fed calls "other checkable deposits" are classified as transactions deposits. Savings and time deposits are nontransactions deposits. Reserve ratios are higher for transactions deposits relative to nontransactions deposits.

To arrive at its required reserves, a bank does not simply determine its transactions and nontransactions deposits at the close of each business day and then multiply each by the applicable reserve ratio. The determination of a bank's required reserves is more complex. Here we'll give a rough idea of how it is done. First, to compute required reserves, the Federal Reserve has established a two-week period called the **deposit computation period**. Required reserves are the average amount of each type of deposits held at the close of each business day in the computation period, multiplied by the reserve requirement for each type.

Reserve requirements in each period are to be satisfied by **actual reserves**, which are defined as the average amount of reserves held at the close of business at the Federal Reserve Bank during each day of a two-week reserve maintenance period, beginning on Thursday and ending on Wednesday two weeks later. For transactions deposits, the deposit computation period leads the reserve period by two days. For nontransactions deposits, the deposit computation period is the two-week period four weeks prior to the reserve maintenance period.

If actual reserves exceed required reserves, the difference is referred to as **excess reserves**. Because reserves are placed in non-interest-bearing accounts, there is an opportunity cost associated with excess reserves. At the same time, there are penalties imposed on banks that do not satisfy the reserve requirements. Thus, banks have an incentive to manage their reserves so as to satisfy reserve requirements as precisely as possible.

Banks temporarily short of their required reserves can borrow reserves from banks that have excess reserves. The market where banks can borrow or lend reserves is called the **federal funds market**. The interest rate charged to borrow funds in this market is called the **federal funds rate**.

Borrowing at the Fed discount window—The Federal Reserve Bank is the banker's bank—or, to put it another way, the bank of last resort. Banks temporarily short of funds can borrow from the Fed at its discount window. Collateral is necessary to borrow, but not just any collateral will do. The Fed establishes (and periodically changes) the type of collateral that is eligible. Currently it includes: (1) Treasury securities, federal agency securities, and municipal securities, all with a maturity of less than six months, and (2) commercial and industrial loans with 90 days or less to maturity.

The interest rate that the Fed charges to borrow funds at the discount window is called the **discount rate**. The Fed changes this rate periodically in order to implement monetary policy. Bank borrowing at the Fed to meet required reserves is quite limited in amount, despite the fact that the discount rate generally is set below the cost of other sources of short-term funding available to a bank. This is because the Fed views borrowing at the discount window as a privilege to be used to meet short-term liquidity needs, and not a device to increase earnings.

Continual borrowing for long periods and in large amounts is thereby viewed as a sign of a bank's financial weakness or as exploitation of the interest differential for profit. If a bank appears to be going to the Fed frequently to borrow, relative to its previous borrowing pattern, the Fed will make an "informational" call to ask for an explanation for the borrowing. If there is no subsequent improvement in the bank's borrowing pattern, the Fed then makes an "administrative counseling" call in which it tells the bank that it must stop its borrowing practice.

Other nondeposit borrowing—Most deposits have short maturities. Bank borrowing in the federal funds market and at the discount window of the Fed is short-term. Other nondeposit borrowing can be short-term in the form of issuing obligations in the money market, or intermediate to long-term in the form of issuing securities in the bond market. An example of the former is the repurchase agreement (or "repo") market, which we discuss in Chapter 19. An example of intermediate- or long-term borrowing is floating-rate notes and bonds.

Banks that raise most of their funds from the domestic and international money markets, relying less on depositors for funds, are called **money center banks**. A **regional bank**, by contrast, is one that relies primarily on deposits for funding and makes less use of the money markets to obtain funds. In recent years, larger regional banks have been merging with other regional banks to form so-called "superregional banks." NationsBank is the result of a merger between NCNB of Charlotte, North Carolina and C&S/Sovran of Norfolk, Virginia. With their greater size, these superregional banks can compete in certain domestic and international financial activities that were once the domain of money center banks.

Regulation

Because of the special role that commercial banks play in the financial system, banks are regulated and supervised by several federal and state government entities. At the federal level, supervision is undertaken by the Federal Reserve Board, the Office of the Comptroller of the Currency, and the Federal Deposit Insurance Corporation. While much of the legislation defining these activities dates back to the late 1930s, the nature of financial markets and commercial banking has changed in the past 20 years. Consequently, rethinking of regulation is taking place as this chapter is written. Moreover, bank regulation is becoming international in nature.

Here we will review some of the major regulations concerning the activities of commercial banks. The regulations historically cover four areas:

1. ceilings imposed on the interest rate that can be paid on deposit accounts.
2. geographical restrictions on branch banking.
3. permissible activities for commercial banks.
4. capital requirements for commercial banks.

Regulation of interest rates—While regulation of the interest rates that banks can pay has been eliminated for accounts other than demand deposits, we discuss it because of its historical relevance. Federal regulations prohibit the payment of interest on demand (checking) accounts. Regulation Q at one time imposed a ceiling on the maximum interest rate that could be paid by banks on deposits other than demand accounts.

Until the 1960s, market interest rates stayed below the ceiling (except those on checking deposits), so Regulation Q had virtually no impact on the ability of banks to compete with other financial institutions to obtain funds. As market interest rates rose above the ceiling and ceilings were extended to all depository institutions after 1966, these institutions found it difficult to compete with other financial institutions—such as money market funds—to attract funds. As a result, there was "disintermediation"—funds flowed out of commercial banks and thrift institutions and into the other financial institutions.

To circumvent the ceilings on time deposits and recapture the lost funds, banks developed the negotiable certificate of deposit, which in effect had a higher ceiling, and eventually no ceiling at all. They also opened branches outside the United States, where no ceilings were imposed on the interest rate they could offer. As all depository institutions found it difficult to compete in the 1970s, federal legislation in the form of the Depository Institutions Deregulation and Monetary Control Act of 1980 gave banks relief. With a few exceptions, the 1980 act phased out the ceilings on interest rates on time deposits and certificates of deposit. The Garn-St. Germain Act of 1982 permitted banks to offer money market accounts, accounts that were similar to those offered by money market funds.

Geographical restrictions—Each state has the right to set its own rules on intrastate branch banking, which was established by the McFadden Act, passed by Congress in 1926. This rather outdated legislation was intended to prevent large banks from expanding geographically and thereby forcing out or taking over smaller banking entities, possibly threatening competition. There are some states where banks cannot establish branches statewide; these are called **unit-banking states**. There are also **limit branch banking states** which permit some statewide branches, and other states that have virtually no restrictions on statewide branching.

State laws prohibit individual out-of-state banks from establishing a branch in their state. However, all but two states (Hawaii and Montana) have passed laws that allow an out-of-state bank holding company to expand banking operations into the state. Therefore, at this time, interstate bank expansion is only permissible at the holding company level, not the individual bank level. Most states will not permit an out-of-state holding company to establish a new bank in the state. Instead, the out-of-state bank holding company must acquire an existing bank operating in the state.[4]

---

[4] For a more detailed discussion of interstate banking and current regulations, see Paul S. Calem, "The Proconsumer Argument for Interstate Branching," *Business Review* (May-June 1993), pp. 15–29.

Permissible activities for commercial banks—The activities of banks and bank holding companies are regulated by the Federal Reserve Board. The Fed was charged with the responsibility of regulating the activities of bank holding companies by the Bank Holding Company Act of 1956, subsequently amended in 1966 and 1970. The act states that the permissible activities of bank holding companies are limited to those that are viewed by the Fed as "closely related to banking."

Early legislation governing bank activities developed against the following background:

1. Certain commercial bank lending was believed to have reinforced the stock market crash of 1929.

2. The stock market crash itself led to the breakdown of the banking system.

3. Transactions between commercial banks and their securities affiliates led to abuses. For example, it was discovered that banks were underwriting securities and then selling those securities to customers whose investment accounts they managed or advised.[5]

Against this background, Congress passed the Banking Act of 1933, which, among other provisions, created the Federal Deposit Insurance Corporation. Four sections of the 1933 act foreclosed commercial bankers from certain investment banking activities—Sections 16, 20, 21, and 32. These four sections are popularly referred to as the **Glass-Steagall Act**.

For banks that are members of the Federal Reserve System, Section 16 provides that:

> . . . *business of dealing in securities and stock by a national bank shall be limited to purchasing and selling such securities and stock without recourse, solely upon the order, and for the account of customers, and in no case for its own account, and the (national bank) shall not underwrite any issue of securities or stock.*

Banks can neither underwrite securities and stock, nor act as dealers in the secondary market for securities and stock, although Section 16 does provide two exceptions. Banks were permitted to underwrite and deal in U.S. government obligations and "general obligations of any state or any political subdivisions thereof." (The latter securities are municipal bonds, which we shall discuss in Chapter 23. The exemption applies to one type of municipal security, general obligation bonds, not another type, revenue bonds.) Section 16 also restricts the activities of banks in connection with corporate securities such as corporate bonds and commercial paper, and securities such as mortgage-backed and asset-backed securities.[6]

These restrictions were imposed on activities of commercial banks in the United States, not overseas. Commercial banks are not barred from underwriting or dealing in corporate bonds outside the United States, nor are they restricted from aiding in the private placement of corporate securities. More recently developed instruments are not specifically forbidden to commercial banks. A good example is swaps which we describe in Chapter 12.

---

[5] For a discussion of the underwriting of securities, see Chapters 5 and 6.

[6] All of these securities are discussed in Part VI of this book.

Commercial banks that are members of the Federal Reserve System are prohibited from maintaining a securities firm by Section 20 of the Banking Act, which states that no member bank shall be affiliated:

> . . . *with any organization, association, business trust, or other similar organization engaged principally in the issue, flotation, underwriting, public sale, or distribution at wholesale or retail or through syndicate participation of stocks, bonds, debentures, notes or other securities.*

Section 21 prohibits any "person, firm, corporation, association, business trust, or other similar organization" that receives deposits—that is, depository institutions—from engaging in the securities business as defined in Section 16. Section 32 further prevents banks from circumventing the restrictions on securities activities. It does so by prohibiting banks from placing bank employees or board members in positions with securities firms so that they can obtain indirect but effective control.

Subsequent legislation, court rulings, and regulatory decisions have whittled away at the barriers against commercial banks' engagement in investment banking activities. Here is a brief rundown of the significant events. In June 1987, the Fed granted approval to three bank holding companies—Citicorp, Bankers Trust, and J.P. Morgan Guaranty—to underwrite securities that were prohibited by the 1933 act: commercial paper, certain municipal revenue bonds, mortgage-backed securities, and asset-backed securities. The bank holding company must set up a separately capitalized subsidiary to underwrite these securities and must comply with rules established by the Fed regarding limits on market share, income, and revenue. The Comptroller of the Currency ruled subsequently that the 1933 act does permit national banks to underwrite mortgage-backed securities.

Court rulings in the 1980s granted commercial banks opportunities to act as investment advisors and furnish brokerage services. The Supreme Court ruled in 1981 that bank holding companies are allowed to serve as advisors to investment companies. Three years later, the Court ruled that, as long as a bank does not offer investment advice, it could provide discount brokerage services. A federal court of appeals, however, has ruled since that a bank subsidiary could operate a brokerage firm even though it offered investment advice.

The legal distinction between commercial banks and investment banks seems to have been weakened further by a ruling by the Fed in November 1986 that permitted a Japanese bank, Sumitomo Bank Ltd., to invest $500 million in an investment banking firm, Goldman Sachs. While the Fed did impose restrictions to assure that Sumitomo could not exert control over the management of Goldman Sachs' operations, the action set a precedent nonetheless. In Chapter 5, we will return to the issues surrounding the Glass-Steagall Act and the deregulation of commercial banking.

Capital requirements for commercial banks—The capital structure of banks, like that of all corporations, consists of equity and debt (i.e., borrowed funds). Commercial banks, like some other depository institutions and like investment banks, which we discuss in Chapter 5, are highly leveraged institutions. That is, the ratio of equity capital to total assets is low, typically less than 8% in the case of banks. This gives rise to regulatory concern about potential insolvency resulting from the low level of capital provided by the owners. An additional concern is that the amount of equity capital is even less adequate because of potential liabilities that do not appear on the bank's balance sheet. These so-called "off-balance sheet" obligations include commitments such as letters of credit and obligations on customized interest rate agreements (such as swaps, caps, and floors).

Prior to 1989, capital requirements for a bank were based solely on its total assets. No consideration was given to the types of assets. In January 1989, the Federal Reserve adopted guidelines for capital adequacy based on the credit risk of the assets held by the bank. These guidelines are referred to as **risk-based capital requirements**. The guidelines are based on a framework adopted in July 1988 by the Basle Committee on Banking Regulations and Supervisory Practices, which consists of the central banks and supervisory authorities of the G-10 countries.[7]

The two principal objectives of the guidelines are as follows. First, regulators in the United States and abroad have sought greater consistency in the evaluation of the capital adequacy of major banks throughout the world. Second, regulators have tried to establish capital adequacy standards that take into consideration the risk profile of the bank. Consider two banks, A and B, with $1 billion in assets. Suppose that both invest $400 million in identical assets, but the remaining $600 million in different assets. Bank A invests $500 million in U.S. government bonds and $100 million in business loans. Bank B invests $100 million in U.S. government bonds and $500 million in business loans. Obviously, the exposure to default losses is greater for Bank B. While the capital adequacy standards take this greater credit risk into account, they do not recognize liquidity factors or the market price sensitivity to which a bank may be exposed. Capital adequacy standards do give explicit recognition to off-balance sheet items.

The risk-based capital guidelines attempt to recognize credit risk by segmenting and weighting requirements. First, capital is defined as consisting of Tier 1 and Tier 2 capital, and minimum requirements are established for each tier. Tier 1 capital is considered **core capital**; it consists basically of common stockholders' equity, certain types of preferred stock, and minority interest in consolidated subsidiaries. Tier 2 capital is called **supplementary capital**; it includes loan-loss reserves, certain types of preferred stock, perpetual debt (debt with no maturity date), hybrid capital instruments and equity contract notes, and subordinated debt.

Second, the guidelines establish a credit risk weight for all assets. The weight depends on the credit risk associated with each asset. There are four credit risk classifications for banks in the U.S.: 0%, 20%, 50%, and 100%, arrived at on no particular scientific basis. Table 3-5 shows a few examples of assets that fall into each credit risk classification.[8]

---

[7] The G-10 countries include Belgium, Canada, France, Germany, Italy, Japan, Netherlands, Sweden, Switzerland, United Kingdom, and United States.

[8] There are special rules for determining the amount of capital required for off-balance sheet items. An off-balance sheet item is a position in an interest-sensitive contract and/or foreign-exchange-related product that is not reported on the balance sheet.

Table 3-5
Risk Weight Capital Requirement for Various Assets

Risk Weight	Examples of Assets Included
0%	U.S. Treasury securities Mortgage-backed securities issued by the Government National Mortgage Association
20%	Municipal general obligation bonds Mortgage-backed securities issued by the Federal Home Loan Mortgage Corporation or the Federal National Mortgage Association
50%	Municipal revenue bonds Residential mortgages
100%	Commercial loans and commercial mortgages LDC loans Corporate bonds Municipal IDA bonds

The way the credit risk weights work is as follows. The book value of the asset is multiplied by the credit risk weight to determine the amount of core and supplementary capital that the bank will need to support that asset. For example, suppose that the book values of the assets of a bank are as follows:

Asset	Book Value (in millions)
U.S. Treasury securities	$ 100
Municipal general obligation bonds	100
Residential mortgages	500
Commercial loans	300
Total book value	$1,000

The risk-weighted assets are calculated as follows:

Asset	Book Value (in millions)	Risk Weight	Product (in millions)
U.S. Treasury securities	$100	0%	$ 0
Municipal general obligation bonds	100	20	20
Residential mortgages	500	50	250
Commercial loans	300	100	300
Risk-weighted assets			$570

The risk-weighted assets for this bank would be $570 million.

The minimum core (Tier 1) capital requirement is 4% of the book value of assets; the minimum total capital (core plus supplementary capital) is 8% of the risk-weighted assets. To see how this works, consider the hypothetical bank we used earlier to illustrate the calculation of risk-weighted assets. For that bank the weighted risk assets are $570 million. The minimum core capital requirement is $40 million (0.04 × $1 billion); the minimum total capital requirement is $45.6 million (0.08 × $570 million).[9]

One implication of the new capital guidelines is that it will encourage banks to sell off their loans in the open market. By doing so, the bank need not maintain capital for the loans (assets) sold off. While the secondary market for individual bank loans has been growing, it has not reached the stage where a bank can efficiently sell large amounts of loans. An alternative is for a bank to pool loans and issue securities that are collateralized by the pool of loans. This process is referred to as "asset securitization," (this process is covered in Chapter 27).

The risk-based guidelines discussed above are based on credit risk only. No consideration is given to the interest rate risk associated with the assets held by a bank. A bank can hold only the safest securities from a credit risk perspective but be exposed to substantial price risk. For example, a 30-year U.S. government bond has no credit risk but substantial price risk; it is possible for the price of a 30-year Treasury security to decline in price by 20% if interest rates rise by 200 basis points.

The Federal Depository Insurance Corporation Improvement Act, which was passed by Congress in December 1991, required regulators of depository institutions to incorporate interest rate risk into the capital requirements. The approach proposed by bank regulators is based on measuring interest rate sensitivity of the assets and liabilities of the bank.

Interest rate sensitivity is measured by a concept called **duration** (see Chapter 17). Duration is a measure of the approximate change in the value of an asset or liability for a 100 basis point change in interest rates. Thus, if a bank's portfolio of assets has a duration of 3, then the portfolio's value will change by approximately 3% if interest rates change by 100 basis points.[10] Similarly, the duration of the bank's liabilities can be measured using duration. The difference between a bank's assets and liabilities is called its surplus. The bank's interest rate exposure is then measured by the change in the surplus, calculated using the asset and liability durations.

The assets, liabilities, and off-balance sheet instruments would be partitioned into seven maturity groups or "buckets": 0 to 3 months; 3 months to 1 year; 1 to 3 years; 3 to 5 years; 5 to 10 years; 10 to 20 years; and more than 20 years. For each bucket, the duration of a benchmark instrument representative of the assets and the liabilities in that bucket would be computed. Multiplying the durations by the balances in each bucket and netting the results for assets and liabilities results in an estimate of how much the surplus is expected to change as a result of a given change in interest rates.

The proposal by bank regulators is that a normal level of interest rate risk exposure is one in which the surplus changes by less than 1% of assets. If the surplus changes by more than 1% of assets, the bank must hold additional capital of an amount equal to the excess.[11]

---

[9] Other minimum standards imposed by the guidelines cover limitations on supplementary capital elements.

[10] A basis point is equal to 0.0001 or 0.01%. Therefore, 100 basis points equals 1%.

[11] For a further discussion, see Elizabeth Mays, "Interest-Rate Risk Models Used in the Banking and Thrift Industries," Chapter 32 in Frank J. Fabozzi and T. Dessa Fabozzi (eds.), *The Handbook of Fixed Income Securities* (Burr Ridge, IL: Irwin Professional Publishing, 1995).

Federal Deposit Insurance

Because of the important economic role played by banks, the U.S. government sought a way to protect them against depositors who, because of what they thought were real or perceived problems with a bank, would withdraw funds in a disruptive manner. Bank panics occurred frequently in the early 1930s, resulting in the failure of banks that might have survived economic difficulties had it not been for massive withdrawals. The mechanism the U.S. government devised in 1933 to prevent a "run on a bank" was to create federal deposit insurance. The insurance was provided through a new agency, the Federal Deposit Insurance Corporation. A year later, federal deposit insurance was extended to savings and loan associations with the creation of the Federal Savings and Loan Insurance Corporation.

In 1933, federal deposit insurance covered accounts up to $2,500. This amount has been subsequently raised to its current level of $100,000. Currently, deposit insurance premiums for banks and thrifts are the same, and depend on how much capital the institution has. The premium banks and thrifts pay for this insurance ranges from 23 basis points to 31 basis points, with poorly capitalized institutions paying at the high end of the range. In February 1995, the FDIC proposed to dramatically lower the premium banks would pay to a low of 4 to 21 basis points for banks with the highest capital ratios, while leaving the premiums for thrifts unchanged. Thrifts would continue to pay higher premiums which would be used to pay off the bonds that were issued to finance the thrift industry bailout in the late 1980s. Such a large disparity between the premiums paid by banks and thrifts calls into question thrifts' ability to compete for deposits and their long-term viability. As of this writing, the issue has yet to be decided.

While federal deposit insurance did achieve its objective of preventing a run on banks, it unfortunately created incentives that encourage managers of depository institutions to take on excessive risks. If highly risky investments work out, the benefits accrue to the stockholders and management; however, if they do not, it is the depositors who are supposed to absorb the losses. Yet, depositors will have little concern about the risks that a depository institution is assuming because their funds are insured by the federal government. From a depositor's perspective, so long as the amount deposited does not exceed the insurance coverage, one depository institution is as good as another.

SAVINGS AND LOAN ASSOCIATIONS

S&Ls represent a fairly old institution. The basic motivation behind creation of S&Ls was provision of funds for financing the purchase of a home. The collateral for the loans would be the home being financed.

S&Ls are either mutually owned or have corporate stock ownership. "Mutually owned" means there is no stock outstanding, so technically the depositors are the owners. To increase the ability of S&Ls to expand the sources of funding available to bolster their capital, legislation facilitated the conversion of mutually-owned companies into a corporate stock ownership structure.

Like banks, S&Ls may be chartered under either state or federal statutes. At the federal level, the primary regulator of S&Ls is the director of the Office of Thrift Supervision (OTS), created in 1989 by FIRREA. Prior to the creation of OTS, the primary regulator was the Federal Home Loan Bank Board (FHLBB). The FHLBB no longer exists. The Federal Home Loan Banks, which, along with the FHLBB comprised the Federal Home Loan Bank System, still exist and make advances to member institutions.

Like banks, S&Ls are now subject to reserve requirements on deposits established by the Fed. Prior to the passage of FIRREA, federal deposit insurance for S&Ls was provided by the Federal Savings and Loan Insurance Corporation (FSLIC). The Savings Association Insurance Fund (SAIF) has replaced FSLIC. SAIF is administered by the FDIC.

Table 3-6 shows the number of S&Ls as of December 1992 by asset size. There were only 2,391 savings institutions compared to 11,561 commercial banks. The assets of savings institutions were less than one-third of those of commercial banks.

Assets

Traditionally, the only assets in which S&Ls were allowed to invest have been mortgages, mortgage-backed securities, and government securities. Mortgage loans include fixed-rate mortgages and adjustable-rate mortgages (i.e., loans whose interest rate is periodically changed). While most mortgage loans are for the purchase of homes, S&Ls do make construction loans.

As the structures of S&L balance sheets and the consequent maturity mismatch (i.e., lending long and borrowing short) led to widespread disaster and insolvency, the Garn-St. Germain Act of 1982 expanded the types of assets in

Table 3-6

Distribution of Insured Savings Institutions by Size as of December 1992*

Asset size (in millions)	Number of institutions	% of inst.	Assets (in billions)	% of assets
Less than $24.9	199	8.3	$ 3.1	0.3
$ 25.0 to $49.9	382	16.0	14.4	1.4
$ 50.0 to $99.9	528	22.1	38.4	3.7
$100.0 to $499.9	940	39.3	208.8	20.2
$500.0 to $999.9	153	6.4	106.4	10.3
$1 to $2.9 billion	133	5.6	227.1	21.9
$3.0 billion or more	56	2.3	436.9	42.2
Total	2,391	100.0	$1,035.2	100.0

* Excludes institutions in Resolution Trust Corporation Conservatorship.

Source: The data for this table come from Table No. 776, "Selected Financial Institutions — Number of Assets, by Asset Size: 1992," Statistical Abstract of the United States: 1994 (Department of Commerce, Bureau of the Census).

which S&Ls could invest. The acceptable list of investments now includes consumer loans (loans for home improvement, automobiles, education, mobile homes, and credit cards), nonconsumer loans (commercial, corporate, business, or agricultural loans), and municipal securities.

While S&Ls had a comparative advantage in originating mortgage loans, they lacked the expertise to make commercial and corporate loans. Rather than make an investment in acquiring those skills, S&Ls took an alternative approach and invested in corporate bonds because these bonds were classified as corporate loans. More specifically, S&Ls became one of the major buyers of non-investment-grade corporate bonds, more popularly referred to as "junk" bonds or "high-yield" bonds. Under FIRREA, S&Ls are no longer permitted to invest new money in junk bonds and had to divest themselves of their current holdings.

S&Ls invest in short-term assets for operational (liquidity) and regulatory purposes. All S&Ls with federal deposit insurance must satisfy minimum liquidity requirements. These requirements are specified by the Office of Thrift Supervision. Acceptable assets include cash, short-term government agency and corporate securities, certificates of deposit of commercial banks,[12] other money market assets (described in Chapter 19), and federal funds. In the case of federal funds, the S&L is lending excess reserves to another depository institution that is short of funds.

Funding

Prior to 1981, the bulk of the liabilities of S&Ls consisted of passbook savings accounts and time deposits. The interest rate that could be offered on these deposits was regulated. S&Ls were given favored treatment over banks with respect to the maximum interest rate they could pay depositors—they were permitted to pay an interest rate 0.5% higher, later reduced to 0.25%. With the deregulation of interest rates discussed earlier in this chapter, banks and S&Ls now compete head-to-head for deposits.

Deregulation also expanded the types of accounts that may be offered by S&Ls. Traditionally, S&Ls were not been permitted to offer demand accounts. Since the early 1980s, however, S&Ls have been allowed to offer accounts that look very similar to demand deposits and that do pay interest called **negotiable order of withdrawal (NOW) accounts**. Unlike demand deposits, NOW accounts pay interest. S&Ls were also allowed to offer money market deposit accounts (MMDA).

Since the 1980s, S&Ls have been more active in raising funds in the money market. They can borrow in the federal funds market and they have access to the Fed's discount window. S&Ls can also borrow from the Federal Home Loan Banks. These borrowings, called **advances**, can be short-term or long-term in maturity, and the interest rate can be fixed or floating.

Regulation

Federal S&Ls are chartered under the provisions of the Home Owners Loan Act of 1933. Federally-chartered S&Ls are supervised by the OTS, while state-

---

[12] The S&L is an investor when it holds the certificate of deposit of a bank, but the certificate represents the liability of the issuing bank.

chartered S&Ls are supervised by the respective state. A further act in 1933 established the Federal Savings and Loan Insurance Corporation, which at that time insured the deposits of federally-chartered S&Ls up to $5,000 and allowed state-chartered S&Ls that could qualify to obtain the same insurance coverage. We discuss some of the important coverage. There is further discussion in Chapter 21 where we cover federal agency securities and in Chapter 25 where we discuss the development of the mortgage market.

As in bank regulation, S&Ls historically have been regulated with respect to the maximum interest rates on deposit accounts, geographical operations, permissible activities (types of accounts and types of investments), and capital adequacy requirements. In addition, there have been restrictions on the sources of nondeposit funds and liquidity requirements.

The maximum interest rate that is permitted on deposit accounts was phased out by the Depository Institutions Deregulation and Monetary Control Act of 1980 (DIDMCA). While this allowed S&Ls to compete with other financial institutions to raise funds, it also raised their funding costs. For reasons to be described later, while banks also faced higher funding costs, their balance sheets were better constituted than those of S&Ls to cope with the higher costs resulting from interest rate deregulation.

Besides phasing in the deregulation of interest rates on deposit accounts, DIDMCA was significant in several other ways. First, it expanded the Fed's control over the money supply by imposing reserve deposit requirements on S&Ls. In return, S&Ls were permitted to offer NOW accounts.

Subsequent legislation, the Garn-St. Germain Act, not only granted S&Ls the right to offer money market demand accounts so that S&Ls could compete with money market funds, but also broadened the types of assets in which S&Ls could invest. Permission to raise funds in the money market and the bond market was granted by the Federal Home Loan Bank Board in 1975. FHLBB permission to form finance subsidiaries was granted in 1984. Through these subsidiaries, S&Ls were able to broaden their funding sources by the issuance of mortgage-related securities.

There are risk-based capital requirements similar to those imposed on banks. Instead of two tiers of capital, however, there are three: Tier 1, tangible capital; Tier 2, core capital; and Tier 3, supplementary capital. In addition to the risk-based requirements based on credit risk, the OTS has adopted risk-based capital requirements based on interest rate risk. These requirements became effective July 1994. The OTS has taken a different approach to the measurement of interest rate risk than that proposed by bank regulators. Rather than using a duration measure, the OTS uses a simulation approach to assess the sensitivity of the surplus to interest rate changes.[13]

Geographical operations of S&Ls were restricted until 1981, when the FHLBB permitted thrifts to acquire thrifts in other states.

The S&L Crisis

The details of the growth of the S&L industry since the late 1960s and the ensuing S&L crisis cannot be described in one chapter, so only the basics of the downfall of this industry will be presented here. Until the early 1980s, S&Ls and all other lenders financed housing through traditional mortgages at inter-

---

[13] See Mays, "Interest-Rate Risk Models Used in Banking and Thrift Industries."

est rates fixed for the life of the loan. The period of the loan was typically long, frequently up to 30 years. Funding for these loans, by regulation, came from deposits having a maturity considerably shorter than the loans. As explained earlier, this is the funding problem of lending long and borrowing short. It is extremely risky, although regulators took a long time to understand it.

There is no problem, of course, if interest rates are stable or declining, but if interest rates rise above the interest rate on the mortgage loans, a negative spread will result, which must result eventually in insolvency. Regulators at first endeavored to shield the S&L industry from the need to pay high interest rates without losing deposits by imposing a ceiling on the interest rate that would be paid by S&Ls and by their immediate competitors, the other depository institutions. However, the approach did not and could not work.

With the high volatility of interest rates in the 1970s, followed by the historically high level of interest rates in the early 1980s, all depository institutions began to lose funds to competitors exempt from ceilings, such as the newly formed money market funds; this development forced some increase in ceilings. The ceilings in place since the middle of the 1960s did not protect the S&Ls; they began to suffer from diminished profits and increasingly from operating losses. A large fraction of S&Ls became technically insolvent as rising interest rates eroded the market value of their assets to the point where they fell short of the liabilities.

The regulators, anxious to cover up the debacle of their empire, let them continue to operate, worsening the problem by allowing them to value their mortgage assets at book value. Profitability worsened with deregulation of the maximum interest rate that S&Ls could pay on deposits. While deregulation allowed S&Ls to compete with other financial institutions for funds, it also raised funding costs. Banks were better equipped to cope with rising funding costs because bank portfolios were not dominated by old, fixed-rate mortgages as S&Ls were. A larger portion of bank portfolios consisted of shorter-term assets and other assets whose interest rates reset to market interest rates after short time periods.

The difficulty of borrowing short and lending long was only part of the problem faced by the industry. As the crisis progressed, and the situation of many S&Ls became hopeless, fraudulent management activities were revealed. Many S&Ls facing financial difficulties also pursued strategies that exposed the institution to greater risk, in the hope of recovering if these strategies worked out. What encouraged managers to pursue such high-risk strategies was that depositors were not concerned with the risks associated with the institution where they deposited funds because the U.S. government, through federal deposit insurance, guaranteed the deposits up to a predetermined amount. Troubled S&Ls could pay existing depositors through attracting new depositors by offering higher interest rates on deposits than financially stronger S&Ls. In turn, to earn a spread on the higher cost of funds, they had to pursue riskier investment policies.

The result of the S&L crisis was that hundreds of thrift institutions were liquidated or merged with other institutions, at a multibillion dollar cost to taxpayers and the surviving S&Ls. Today, the thrift industry is much smaller than it was prior to the crisis, numbering about 1,500 institutions as of early 1995. The surviving S&Ls, helped by the low-interest-rate environment of the late 1980s and early 1990s, and by more conservative investment practices, have rebuilt their capital and most are once again profitable.

SAVINGS BANKS

Savings banks are institutions similar to, although much older than, S&Ls. They can be either mutually owned (in which case they are called mutual savings banks) or stockholder owned. Most savings banks are of the mutual form. Only 16 states in the eastern United States charter savings banks. In 1978, Congress permitted the chartering of federal savings banks.

While the total deposits at savings banks are less than those of S&Ls, savings banks are typically larger institutions. Asset structures of savings banks and S&Ls are similar. The principal assets of savings banks are residential mortgages. Because states have permitted more portfolio diversification than was permitted by federal regulators of S&Ls, savings bank portfolios weathered funding risk far better than S&Ls. Included in savings bank portfolios are corporate bonds, Treasury and government agency securities, municipal securities, common stock, and consumer loans.

The principal source of funds for savings banks is deposits. Typically, the ratio of deposits to total assets is greater for savings banks than for S&Ls. Savings banks offer the same types of deposit accounts as S&Ls, and deposits can be insured by either the BIF or SAIF.

CREDIT UNIONS

Credit unions are the smallest and the newest of the depository institutions. Credit unions can obtain either a state or federal charter. Their unique aspect is the "common bond" requirement for credit union membership. According to the statutes that regulate federal credit unions, membership in a federal credit union "shall be limited to groups having a common bond of occupation or association, or to groups within a well-defined neighborhood, community, or rural district." They are either cooperatives or mutually owned. There is no corporate stock ownership. The dual purpose of credit unions is therefore to serve their members' saving and borrowing needs.

Table 3-7 shows the number of credit unions by asset size as of December 1992. While there are more credit unions than commercial banks, their total assets were only $258.4 billion, compared to $3.5 trillion for commercial banks, and $1 trillion for savings institutions.

Technically, because credit unions are owned by their members, member deposits are called **shares**. The distribution paid to members is therefore in the form of dividends, not interest. Since 1970, the shares of all federally-chartered credit unions have been insured by the National Credit Union Share Insurance Fund (NCUSIF) for up to $100,000, the same as other depository institutions. State-chartered credit unions may elect to have NCUSIF coverage; for those that do not, insurance coverage is provided by a state agency.

Federal regulations apply to federally-chartered credit unions and state-chartered credit unions that have elected to become members of NCUSIF.

Table 3-7

Distribution of Credit Unions by Size as of December 1992

Asset Size (in millions)	Number of credit unions	% of cu	Assets (in billions)	% of assets
Less than $ 5.0	7,008	55.6	$ 11.9	4.6
$ 5.0 to $ 9.9	1,809	14.4	13.0	5.0
$10.0 to $ 24.9	1,848	14.7	29.7	11.5
$ 25.0 to $49.9	898	7.1	32.0	12.4
$ 50.0 to $99.9	519	4.1	36.1	14.0
$100.0 to $499.9	467	3.7	90.4	35.0
$500.0 to $999.9	34	0.3	22.8	8.8
$1 to $2.9 billion	9	0.1	12.4	4.8
$3.0 billion or more	2	<0.1	10.1	3.9
Total	12,594	100.0	$258.4	100.0

Source: The data for this table come from Table No. 776, "Selected Financial Institutions— Number of Assets, by Asset Size: 1992," Statistical Abstract of the United States: 1994 (Department of Commerce, Bureau of the Census).

Most states, however, specify that state-chartered institutions must be subject to the same requirements as federally-chartered ones. Effectively, therefore, most credit unions are regulated at the federal level. The principal federal regulatory agency is the National Credit Union Administration (NCUA).

Credit unions obtain their funds primarily from deposits of their members. With deregulation, they can offer a variety of accounts, including share drafts, which are similar to checking accounts but which pay interest. Playing a role similar to the Fed, as the lender of last resort, is the Central Liquidity Facility (CLF) which is administered by NCUA. CLF provides short-term loans to member credit unions with liquidity needs.

Credit union assets consist primarily of small consumer loans to their members, although in recent years they have increasingly added single-family mortgages to their portfolios. They also provide credit card loans.

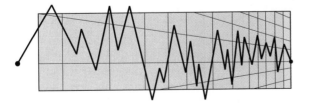

SUMMARY

Depository institutions accept various types of deposits. With the funds raised through deposits and other funding sources, they make loans to various entities and invest in securities. The deposits usually are insured by a federal agency. Income is derived from investments (loans and securities) and fee income. Thrifts (savings and loan associations, savings banks, and credit unions) are specialized types of depository institutions.

A depository institution seeks to earn a positive spread between the assets it invests in and the cost of its funds. In generating spread income, a depository institution faces credit risk and funding or interest rate risk. A depository institution must be prepared to satisfy net withdrawals of funds by depositors and provide loans to customers. It can accommodate withdrawals or loan demand by attracting additional deposits, using existing securities as collateral for borrowing from a federal agency, selling securities that it owns, or raising short-term funds in the money market.

The services provided by commercial banks can be broadly classified as individual banking, institutional banking, and global banking. There are three sources of funds for banks: deposits, nondeposit borrowing, and retained earnings and sale of equity. Banks are highly leveraged financial institutions, meaning that most of their funds are obtained from deposits and nondeposit borrowing. This includes borrowing from the Fed through the discount window facility, borrowing reserves in the federal funds market, and borrowing by the issuance of instruments in the money and bond markets.

Banks must maintain reserves at one of the 12 Federal Reserve Banks, according to reserve requirements established by the Fed. Banks temporarily short of their required reserves can borrow reserves in the federal funds market or borrow temporarily from the Fed at its discount window.

There is both federal and state regulation of banks. At the federal level, supervision of banks is the responsibility of the Federal Reserve Board, the Office of the Comptroller of the Currency, and the Federal Deposit Insurance Corporation. The major regulations involve geographical restrictions on branch banking (which are administered by the state and therefore vary widely), activities that are permissible for commercial banks, and capital requirements. Capital requirements are imposed on depository institutions. There are risk-based capital guidelines based on the credit risk associated with assets. More recently, regulators have adopted risk-based capital guidelines that incorporate interest rate risk into capital requirements.

Like banks, S&Ls may be chartered under either state or federal statutes. At the federal level, the primary regulator of S&Ls is the Director of the Office of Thrift Supervision. S&Ls are subject to reserve requirements on deposits established by the Fed. Federal deposit insurance for S&Ls is provided by the Savings Association Insurance Fund.

Much as in the case of bank regulation, S&Ls are regulated with respect to geographical operations, permissible activities, and capital adequacy requirements. S&Ls invest principally in mortgages and mortgage-related securities. Deregulation has expanded the types of investments that S&Ls are permitted to make, as well as expanding the types of deposit accounts that may be offered and the available funding sources.

The asset structures of savings banks and S&Ls are similar. As some states have permitted greater portfolio diversification than is permitted by federal regulators of S&Ls, this is reflected in savings bank portfolios. The principal source of funds for savings banks is deposits. Deposits can be federally insured by either the BIF or SAIF.

Credit unions are depository institutions that have a "common bond" requirement for membership. They are owned by their members. Although they can be state- or federally-chartered, most credit unions effectively are regulated at the federal level by the National Credit Union Administration. The assets of credit unions consist primarily of small consumer loans to their members and credit card loans.

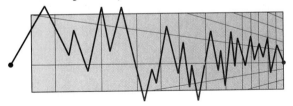

QUESTIONS

1. Explain the ways in which a commercial bank can accommodate withdrawal and loan demand.

2. Why do you think a debt instrument whose interest rate is changed periodically based on some market interest rate would be more suitable for a depository institution than a long-term debt instrument with a fixed interest rate?

3. What is meant by: a. individual banking? b. institutional banking? c. global banking?

4. Explain each of the following: a. reserve ratio; b. required reserves; c. excess reserves.

5. Explain each of the following types of deposit accounts: a. demand deposits; b. certificates of deposit; c. money market demand accounts; d. share deposits; e. negotiable order of withdrawal accounts.

6. Alan Greenspan, the Chairman of the Federal Reserve Board told the U.S. Senate on July 12, 1990:

    As you know, the Board has long supported repeal of the provisions of the Glass-Steagall Act that separated commercial and investment banking.

We still strongly advocate such repeal because we believe that technology and globalization have continued to blur the distinctions among credit markets, and have eroded the franchise value of the classic bank intermediation process. Outdated constraints will only endanger the profitability of banking organizations and their contribution to the American economy.

a. What does Mr. Greenspan mean when he says that the value of the bank intermediation process has been eroded by technology and globalization?

b. What are some of the major benefits and risks of repealing key provisions of the Glass-Steagall Act?

7. You and a friend are discussing the savings and loan crisis. She states that "the whole mess started in the early 1980s. When short-term rates skyrocketed, S&Ls got killed—their spread income went from positive to

negative. They were borrowing short and lending long."

a. What does she mean by "borrowing short and lending long"?

b. Are higher or lower interest rates beneficial to an institution that borrows short and lends long?

8. The following is the book value of the assets of a bank:

Asset	Book Value (in millions)
U.S. Treasury securities	$ 50
Municipal general obligation bonds	50
Residential mortgages	400
Commercial loans	200
Total book value	$700

a. Calculate the risk-weighted assets using the information below:

Asset	Risk Weight
U.S. Treasury securities	0%
Municipal general obligation bonds	20
Residential mortgages	50
Commercial loans	100

b. What is the minimum core capital requirement?

c. What is the minimum total capital requirement?

9. When the manager of a bank's portfolio of securities is considering alternative investments, she will also be concerned about the risk-weight assigned to the security. Why?

10. a. What is meant by the duration of an asset?

b. If the duration of an asset is 5, what does this mean?

11. a. What is the approach proposed by bank regulators for incorporating interest rate risk into capital requirements?

b. What is the proposed approach to measuring a bank's interest rate risk?

c. How is a normal level of interest rate risk exposure defined by bank regulators?

d. What happens if a bank's interest rate risk exposure is above the normal level?

12. Explain why you agree or disagree with the following statement: "Regulators of banks and S&Ls have formulated the same methodology for measuring the interest rate risk of a depository institution."

13. Consider this headline from *The New York Times* of March 26, 1933: "Bankers will fight Deposit Guarantees. . . .Bad Banking would be encouraged."

a. What do you think this headline is saying?

b. Discuss the pros and cons of whether deposits should be insured by the U.S. government.

14. The following quotation is from the October 29, 1990 issue of *Corporate Financing Week:*

Chase Manhattan Bank is preparing its first asset-backed debt issue, becoming the last major consumer bank to plan to access the growing market, Street asset-backed officials said. . . .

Asset-backed offerings enable banks to remove credit card or other loan receivables from their balance sheets, which helps them comply with capital requirements.

What capital requirements is this article referring to?

15. An article on bank funding in the October 15, 1990, issue of *Bank Letter* states:

    The steep rise in deposit insurance next year may trigger a growing preference for note issuance over wholesale deposits by top-tier banks, according to treasurers and a recent report by Keefe, Bruyette & Woods....Investor skittishness over credit quality has kept most banks out of the wholesale funding note issuance market, but when investor sentiment improves, higher quality issuers will make increased use of uninsured vehicles such as note issuance.

    Discuss this quotation. In your answer be sure to mention the three sources of bank funding.

16. Comment on this statement: "The risk-based guidelines for commercial banks gauge the interest rate risk associated with a bank's balance sheet."

17. What are the primary assets in which savings and loans associations invest?

18. Who regulates the activities of credit unions?

Nondepository Institutions

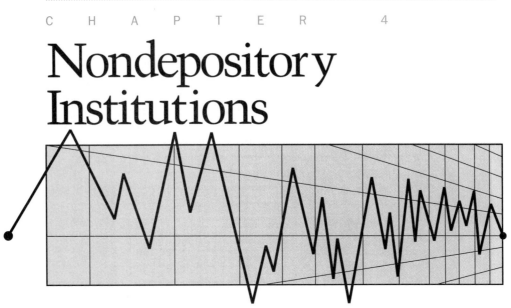

LEARNING OBJECTIVES

After reading this chapter you will understand:

- the nature of the business of insurance companies.

- the differences between the nature of the liabilities of life insurance companies and those of property and casualty insurance companies.

- how insurance companies are regulated.

- the different types of insurance policies.

- what the risk-based capital requirements are for insurance companies.

- the different types of pension plans.

- the principal provisions of the Employee Retirement Income Security Act (ERISA) of 1974.

- the different types of investment companies.

- how share prices of mutual funds and closed-end funds are determined.

- the different investment objectives of investment companies.

- how investment companies are regulated.

In this chapter we continue with our coverage of financial institutions. The four that we discuss here are life insurance companies, property and casualty companies, pension funds, and investment companies.

INSURANCE COMPANIES

Insurance companies are financial intermediaries that, for a price, will make a payment if a certain event occurs. They function as risk bearers. There are two types of insurance companies: life insurance companies ("life companies") and property and casualty insurance companies ("P&C companies"). The principal event that the former insures against is death.[1] Upon the death of a policyholder, a life company agrees to make either a lump-sum payment or a series of payments to the beneficiary of the policy. Life insurance protection is not the only financial product sold by these companies; a major portion of the business of life companies is in the area of providing retirement benefits. In contrast, P&C companies insure against a wide variety of occurrences. Two examples are automobile and home insurance.

The key distinction between life and P&C companies lies in the difficulty of projecting whether a policyholder will be paid off and, if so, how much the payment will be. While this is no simple task for either type of insurance company, from an actuarial perspective it is easier for a life company. The amount and timing of claims on P&C companies are more difficult to predict because of the randomness of natural catastrophes and the unpredictability of court awards in liability cases. This uncertainty about the timing and amount of cash outlays to satisfy claims affects the investment strategies used by the managers of the P&C companies' funds.

While we have distinguished the two types of insurance companies here by the nature of their liabilities, most large insurance companies do sell both life insurance and property and casualty insurance policies. Usually a parent company has a life company subsidiary and a P&C company subsidiary.

Fundamental Characteristics of the Insurance Industry

We begin with the fundamental characteristics of the insurance industry that are shared by life companies and P&C companies.

Insurance policy and premiums—An **insurance polic**y is a legally binding contract for which the policyholder (or owner) pays **premiums** in exchange for the insurance company's promise to pay specified sums contingent on future events. The company is said to **underwrite** the owner's risk, and acts as a buffer against the uncertainties of life. The process of underwriting can include a careful evaluation of the applicant's circumstances.

When the policy is accepted by an insurance company, it becomes an asset for the owner and a liability for the insurance company. Premiums can be paid in a single payment, or, more commonly, in a regular series of payments. If the owner fails to pay premiums, the policy is said to **lapse**, or **terminate**. Unless both parties renew the contract, the company loses the future stream of premiums, and the owner loses the protection the policy had promised.

Surplus and reserves—The surplus of an insurance company is the difference between its assets and liabilities. Since the accounting treatment of both assets and liabilities is established by state statutes covering an insurance company, surplus is commonly referred to as **statutory surplus**.

In determining the statutory surplus of an insurance company, the value of the assets and the liabilities must be determined. A complication in determining the value of liabilities arises because the insurance company has

---

[1] Life insurance companies also sell health insurance policies.

committed to make payments at some time in the future and those payments are contingent on certain events occurring. To properly reflect these contingent liabilities in its financial statement, an insurance company must establish an account called a **reserve**. A reserve is not cash that is set aside by the insurance company; it is simply an accounting entry. While there are different types of reserve accounts that must be established by an insurance company, for our purposes here it is unnecessary to discuss them.

Statutory surplus is important because regulators view this as the ultimate amount that can be drawn upon to pay policyholders. The growth of this surplus for an insurance company will determine how much future business it can underwrite. Until recently, the ability of an insurance company to take on the risks associated with underwriting policies has been measured by the ratio of the annual earned premium (discussed below) to statutory surplus. Usually, this ratio is kept at between two-to-one and three-to-one. Consequently, $2 to $3 in annual premiums can be supported for each $1 available in statutory surplus.

Determination of profits—An insurance company's revenue for a fiscal year is generated from two sources. One source is the premiums earned during the fiscal year. Not all of the premiums received are earned for that fiscal year. For example, suppose Ms. Johnson writes a check on November 1 to the All Right Insurance Company for $1,200 to cover her annual automobile insurance premium for the next 12 months. Suppose also that the insurance company's fiscal year ends on December 31. Then on December 31, the insurance company has only earned two months of the premium, or $200 (2 × $1,200/12). Thus, while Ms. Johnson paid and All Right Insurance Company received $1,200, the insurance company's earned premium is only $200. The second source of revenue is the investment income earned from invested assets.

From the revenue, costs are deducted to determine the profit. There are two general categories of costs: the first are additions to reserves; the second are the costs associated with selling insurance policies. If there is a profit, any portion of the profit not distributed to the owners as dividends is added to the statutory surplus. If there is a loss, the statutory surplus is decreased by the amount of the loss.

The overall profit or loss can be divided into two parts: investment income and underwriting income. **Investment income** is basically the revenue from the insurance company's portfolio of invested assets. **Underwriting income** is the difference between the premiums earned and the costs of settling claims.

Government guarantees—Unlike the liabilities of depository institutions, insurance policies are not guaranteed by any federal entity. However, most states have statutory "guarantee associations" that provide some protection to, at least, state residents.[2] Consequently, the premiums charged by insurance companies on policies (i.e., the pricing terms) are directly related to their financial ratings. Most market participants rely on a rating system from A.M. Best, Moody's Investors Service, or Standard & Poor's Corporation.

Regulation—Insurance companies are regulated primarily at the state level as a result of a 1945 federal statute, the McCarran-Ferguson Act. Insurance companies whose stock is publicly traded must comply with the federal regulations set forth by the Securities and Exchange Commission.

Each state establishes its own regulations to ensure the safety and soundness of insurance companies doing business in that state. One way it does so

---

[2] The New York State Guarantee Fund, for example, had $500 million available in 1993 for companies in liquidation.

is by establishing regulations with respect to (1) the types of securities that are eligible for investment, and (2) how the value of those securities must be determined for regulatory reporting purposes. As for eligible investments, a state will typically restrict the percentage of funds allocated to common stock investments to the lesser of 10% of assets (in some states 20%) or 100% of surplus. It will also restrict investments in bonds and preferred stock to those of a certain quality rating. A "basket provision" usually permits investments of about 5% of assets in any type of vehicle that is not explicitly prohibited by law.

To insure compliance with its regulations, life insurance companies licensed to do business in a state are required to file an annual statement and supporting documents with the state's insurance department. The annual statement, referred to as the **convention statement**, shows among other things the assets, liabilities, and surplus of the reporting company. As explained earlier, the surplus is closely watched by regulators and rating agencies because it is one of the determinants of the amount of business that an insurance company can underwrite.

Model laws and regulations are developed by the National Association of Insurance Commissioners (NAIC), a voluntary association of state insurance commissioners. An adoption of a model law or regulation by the NAIC is not binding on a state, but states often use these models when writing their laws and regulations.

Regulators monitor the financial well-being of insurance companies. At one time, a measure of the financial well-being related the capital of the company to its size, where size was defined as premiums earned. Capital has a well-defined meaning in the insurance industry—it is the statutory surplus plus specific statutory defined adjustments and is referred to as **adjusted regulatory capital**. The adjustments are technical in nature and need not concern us.

In 1993, the NAIC introduced a new approach to determining whether an insurance company had adequate adjusted regulatory capital. Rather than using asset size, the NAIC bases the capital needs of an insurance company on the nature of the risks to which it is exposed.[3] Based on these risks, the required amount of adjusted regulatory capital, referred to as the **risk-based capital requirement**, is determined. A formula is specified by the NAIC that involves weighting each asset and liability on the balance sheet by specified percentages (risk weights) to determine the risk-based capital requirement for an insurance company. While the risk-weightings are different, this is the same principle as the risk-based capital approach for depository institutions discussed in the previous chapter.

Of the risk factors considered in determining risk-based capital requirements, the one that has a direct bearing on decisions made by the manager of an insurance company's portfolio is the asset risk. More specifically, the risk-based capital requirements consider only credit risk associated with investing in an asset. To see how the risk-based capital requirement is determined just for asset risk, Table 4-1 shows various asset classes and the weight or capital factor for each. There are six asset categories for corporate and municipal bonds. The categories differ by the credit rating as shown in parentheses. As one moves down the table for these six asset classes, the credit risk increases—the higher the capital factor, the greater the credit risk of an asset class. Therefore, the higher the portion of the portfolio invested in asset classes with a greater credit risk, the greater the risk-based capital requirement due to asset risk.

---

[3] For a life insurance company, the risks are categorized as follows by the NAIC: asset risk, insurance risk, interest rate risk, and business risk. For a property and casualty insurance company, the risks are defined as asset risk, credit risk, loss/loss adjustment expense risk, and written premium risk.

Table 4-1

Capital Factors for Selected Asset Classes for Life
Companies for Determining Risk-Based Capital Requirements

Asset Class	Capital Factor
U.S. government securities	0.0%
Corporates, municipal, agencies, MBS, CMOs, & ABS* rated NAIC (A-AAA)	0.3%
Corporates & municipals rated:	
NAIC 2 (BBB)	1.0%
NAIC 3 (BB)	2.0%
NAIC 4 (B)	4.5%
NAIC 5 (CCC)	10.0%
NAIC 6 (Default)	30.0%
Common stocks	15.0%
Mortgage & collateral loans	5.0%
Real estate	10.0%

* MBS = mortgage- backed securities, CMO = collateralized mortgage obligations, ABS = asset-backed securities

Table 4-2 gives the asset composition for two hypothetical life companies,
A and B, and shows how the risk-based capital requirement due to asset risk
is determined for each. While the two life companies have the same asset
value, $1 billion, the risk-based capital requirements due to asset risk are $26.4
million greater for life company B than A ($68.05 million versus $41.65). This is
because of the greater proportion of funds invested in lower-rated corporate and
municipal bonds, common stock, and real estate by B compared to A.

The capital factors affect insurance companys in two ways. First, insurance
company's with low statutory surplus will have to limit their exposure to
assets with high credit risk. Second, the decision to allocate funds to particular asset classes will depend not only on the potential yield from investing in
an asset class but on the risk-based capital requirement.

Life Insurance Companies

With an understanding of the basics of the insurance industry, we can now
focus on life insurance companies. As of 1991, the total assets of U.S. life companies was $1.52 trillion.[4] The nature of the life insurance business has
changed dramatically since the 1970s, due to high and variable inflation rates
and increased domestic and global competitive pressures resulting from financial deregulation throughout the world. Moreover, consumer sophistication
has increased, forcing life companies to offer more competitive products.

Life companies compete with other life companies in providing insurance
protection. In addition, many of the products sold by life companies have an
investment feature which means that life companies compete also with other

---

[4] *Best's Insurance Reports—Life/Health*, 1992, p. vi. Assets are defined as "admitted assets," which means all assets
approved by state insurance departments as existing property in the ownership of the company.

Table 4-2

Calculation of Risk-Based Capital Requirements for
Asset Risk for Two Hypothetical Life Companies

Life Company: A
Assets in millions
Total assets: $1 billion

Asset Class	Capital factor	Dollar Allocation	Capital Factor × Dollar Allocation
U.S. government securities	0.0%	$ 200	$ 0
Corporates, municipal, agencies, MBS, CMOs, & ABS rated NAIC (A-AAA)	0.3%	300	0.90
Corporates & municipals rated:			
NAIC 2 (BBB)	1.0%	100	1.00
NAIC 3 (BB)	2.0%	50	1.00
NAIC 4 (B)	4.5%	0	0
NAIC 5 (CCC)	10.0%	0	0
NAIC 6 (Default)	30.0%	0	0
Common stocks	15.0%	150	22.50
Mortgage & collateral loans	5.0%	75	3.75
Real estate	10.0%	125	12.50
Risk-based capital requirement for asset risk			$41.65

Life Company: B
Assets in millions
Total assets: $1 billion

Asset Class	Capital factor	Dollar Allocation	Capital Factor × Dollar Allocation
U.S. government securities	0.0%	$ 80	$ 0
Corporates, municipal, agencies, MBS, CMOs, & ABS rated NAIC (A-AAA)	0.3%	100	0.30
Corporates & municipals rated:			
NAIC 2 (BBB)	1.0%	100	1.00
NAIC 3 (BB)	2.0%	150	3.00
NAIC 4 (B)	4.5%	50	2.25
NAIC 5 (CCC)	10.0%	50	0.50
NAIC 6 (Default)	30.0%	30	9.00
Common stocks	15.0%	220	33.00
Mortgage & collateral loans	5.0%	60	3.00
Real estate	10.0%	160	16.00
Risk-based capital requirement for asset risk			$68.05

financial institutions that provide investment instruments and with direct market investments in securities.

Liabilities and liability risk—The liabilities of the insurance company are the obligations set forth in insurance policies that they have underwritten. Before we describe the various types of policies, let's look at the liability risk that insurance companies face.

There are risks in the liabilities of an institution as well as in the portfolio of assets. For a life company in particular, many of the products are interest rate sensitive. The interest rate offered on an investment-type insurance policy is called the **crediting rate**. If the crediting rate of a policy is not competitive with market interest rates or rates offered by other life companies, a policyholder may allow the policy to lapse or, if permissible, may begin to borrow against the policy. In either case, this will result in an outflow of cash from the life insurance company.

Types of policies—Policies issued by life insurance companies can be classified as one of four types: (1) pure insurance protection against risk of death, (2) a package consisting of life insurance protection and an investment vehicle, (3) insurance against the risk of life, primarily designed for pension programs, and (4) pure investment-oriented vehicles.

Pure insurance protection against risk of death—**Term life insurance** provides a death benefit but no cash build-up; it has no investment component. Thus, a term life insurance policy provides pure insurance against risk of death. The premium charged by the insurance company remains constant only for a specified term of years. Most policies are automatically renewable at the end of each term, but at a higher rate. When an insurance company issues this type of contract, it knows the amount of the liability it may have to pay, but does not know the date. However, using actuarial data, the timing of the liability can be reasonably estimated for a pool of insured individuals. The premium that the insurance company charges is usually such that, no matter what happens to interest rates, the life company will have sufficient funds to meet the obligation when policyholders die.

Insurance/investment policies—**Whole life insurance** is a policy with two features: (1) it pays off a stated amount upon the death of the insured, and (2) it accumulates a cash value that the policyholder can borrow against. The first feature is an insurance protection feature—the same feature that term insurance provides. The second is an investment feature because the policy accumulates value and at every point in time has a **cash surrender value**, an amount the insurance company will pay, if the policyholder ends the policy. The policyholder has the option to borrow against the policy and the amount that can be borrowed is called the **loan value**. The interest rate at which the funds can be borrowed is specified in the policy.

The liability risk associated with the investment feature of a whole life policy is that the insurance company may not be able to earn a return on its investments greater than its policies' crediting rate. This would result in a decline in the life insurance company's surplus. Offering a lower crediting rate on a whole life policy than competitors may reduce the risk that the crediting rate will not be earned, but increases the likelihood that the owner will borrow against the policy or allow it to lapse.

Universal life is a whole life product created in response to the problem just cited for a standard whole life policy. The policyholder pays a premium for insurance protection and for a separate fee can invest in a vehicle that pays a competitive interest rate rather than the below-market crediting rates offered on a standard whole life policy. For a policyholder, the advantage of this investment alternative relative to the direct purchase of a security is that under the current tax code, the interest earned is tax deferred. The risk that the insurer faces is that the return earned is not competitive with those of other insurance companies, resulting in policy lapses.

A **variable life** policy is a whole life policy that provides a death benefit that depends on the market value of the insured's portfolio at the time of the death. Typically the company invests premiums in common stocks, and hence variable life policies are referred to as **equity-linked policies**. While the death benefits are variable, there is a guaranteed minimum death benefit that the insurer agrees to pay regardless of the market value of the portfolio. The insurer's risk is that the return earned will be less than that of its competitors, resulting in policy lapses. In addition, the insurer faces the risk that the return earned over the insured's life is less than the guaranteed minimum death benefit specified in the policy.

Insurance against the risk of life—An **annuity** is a regular periodic payment made by the insurance company to a policyholder for a specified period of time. There are two types of annuity policies: one is a life contingent policy and the other a nonlife contingent policy. To understand the first type of policy, consider a person who retires with a given amount of resources to be spread evenly over her remaining life. Clearly, she faces a problem because the length of her life is unknown. The life company, relying on the fact that the average length of life of a group can be estimated rather accurately, can offer the person a fixed annuity for the rest of her life, thus relieving her of the risk of outliving her resources. Annuities are one of the oldest types of insurance contracts.

At present most annuity policies are nonlife contingency policies and they are used primarily in connection with a pension plan. In a **single-premium deferred annuity**, the sponsor of a pension plan pays a single premium to the life insurance company; the company in turn agrees to make lifelong payments to the employee (the policyholder) when that employee retires. Most policies give the policyholder the right to take the benefits in a lump sum rather than a payout over time.

Other types of nonlife contingent annuity policies can also be purchased from a life insurance company. For example, the winner of a state lottery does not receive the winnings in a lump-sum payment—that is, a winner of a $10 million lottery does not receive $10 million today. Instead, there is a payout of a fixed amount over some specified period of time. In many states that sponsor lotteries, the state can purchase an annuity policy from a life insurance company to make payments to the lottery winner.

A second example of a nonlife contingent annuity policy is one purchased by a property and casualty insurance company to settle a legal case by making an annuity payment to someone. For example, suppose an individual is hit by an automobile and, as a result, is unable to work for the rest of his life. The individual will sue the P&C company for future lost earnings and medical care. To settle the suit, the insurance company may agree to make specified payments over time to the individual. This is called a **structured settlement**. The company will purchase a policy from a life company to make the agreed-upon payments.

Regardless of the type of annuity, the insurer faces the risk that the portfolio of assets supporting the contract will realize a return that is less than the implicit rate that the insurer has agreed to pay.

Pure investment-oriented policies—A **guaranteed investment contract** or **guaranteed income contract** (or simply GIC), is a pure investment product. In a GIC, a life company agrees, for a single premium, to pay the principal amount and a predetermined annual crediting rate over the life of the investment, all of which is paid at the maturity date. For example, a $10 million five-year GIC with a predetermined crediting rate of 10% means that, at the end of five years, the life company will pay the policyholder $16,105,100.[5] What the life company is guaranteeing is the crediting rate, not the principal. The return of the principal depends on the ability of the life company to satisfy the obligation, just as in any corporate debt obligation. The risk that the insurer faces is that the rate earned on the portfolio of supporting assets is less than the rate guaranteed.

The maturity of a GIC can vary from 1 year to 20 years. The interest rate guaranteed depends on market conditions and the rating of the life company. The interest rate will be a rate higher than the yield offered on U.S. Treasury securities of the same maturity. These policies typically are purchased by pension plan sponsors as an investment.

The popularity of GICs arises from their favorable financial accounting treatment. Specifically, the owner of a GIC, such as a pension plan sponsor, shows the value of a GIC in the portfolio at its purchase price, not at its current market value (i.e., it is not marked to market). Thus, a rise in interest rates, which would lower the value of any fixed-rate asset held by a pension fund, will not reduce the value of a GIC for financial reporting purposes. This preferential financial accounting treatment is being challenged by regulators who seek to require that they be marked to market, thereby forcing GICs to compete with other market instruments based purely on investment characteristics, not favorable financial accounting requirements.

It should be emphasized that a GIC is nothing more than the debt obligation of the life company issuing the contract. The word "guarantee" does not mean that there is a guarantor other than the life company. Effectively, a GIC is a zero coupon bond issued by a life company, and, as such, exposes the investor to the same credit risk. This credit risk has been highlighted by the default of several major issuers of GICs in recent years. The two most publicized were the prominent GIC issuers Mutual Benefit, a New Jersey-based insurer, and Executive Life, a California-based insurer, who were both seized by regulators in 1991.

Investments—The distribution of assets of U.S. life companies in 1993 is summarized in Table 4-3. In 1993 bonds plus mortgages constituted some two thirds of total life insurance assets. In fact, life companies are the largest buyers of corporate bonds.

A life company's decision to allocate most of its funds to long-term debt obligations is a result of the nature of its liabilities. As most contracts written by life companies are based on some contractually fixed interest rate that will be paid to a policyholder after an extended number of years, long-term debt obligations are a natural investment vehicle for an insurance company to use to hedge its commitments (match maturities). Or, more precisely, match the duration of their liabilities.[6]

---

[5] Determined as follows: $10,000,000 (1.10)^5 = $16,105,100.

[6] The concept of duration is discussed in Chapter 3.

Table 4-3
Distribution of Assets of U.S. Life Companies: 1993

Asset	Amount (000,000)	Percent
Government securities	$326,785	18.2
Corporate securities		
Bonds	649,860	36.1
Common stock	42,059	2.3
Preferred stock	10,127	0.6
Total corporate securities	702,046	39.0
Mortgages	220,043	12.2
Real estate	43,004	2.4
Policy loans	73,765	4.1
Cash	4,629	0.3
Short-term investments	40,660	2.2
All others	389,414	21.6
Total admitted assets	$1,800,346	100.0

Source: **1994 Best's Insurance Reports—*Life/Health, p. vi.***

As we noted earlier, the three ways that regulations affect investment decisions and strategies of insurance companies are: (1) how assets are valued for
regulatory reporting purposes, (2) guidelines for investments, and (3) risk-
based capital requirements. Publicly traded life insurance companies must
report based on GAAP accounting. However, insurance companies must also
follow regulatory accounting principles (RAP). RAP accounting requires an
insurance company that buys equity or noninvestment-grade bonds to report
any decline in their value in the periodic financial statement. That is, market
value accounting is used for these assets. An investment-grade bond, by contrast, is carried at amortized cost. By amortized cost it is meant the cost of
acquiring the asset is adjusted annually for any amortization of a premium or
accretion of a discount paid. Thus, if the market value of an investment-grade
bond declines since the time it was acquired, the reduction in value is not recognized. In other words, historical cost accounting is used for these assets.
Consequently, if $10 million is invested in a U.S. Treasury security whose
market value declines to $7 million because interest rates have increased, the
securities continue to be reported at $10 million (plus any accretion of a dis-
count paid or minus any amortization of a premium paid).

RAP accounting has an important implication. It encourages life companies to allocate only a small portion of their funds to stock and lower-quality-
rated bonds because a decline in the market value of those assets below cost
will reduce the life company's reported regulatory surplus.

Property and Casualty Insurance Companies

Property and casualty (P&C) insurance companies provide a broad range of
insurance protection against:

1. loss, damage, or destruction of property.
2. loss or impairment of income-producing ability.
3. claims for damages by third parties because of alleged negligence.
4. loss resulting from injury or death due to occupational accidents.

Property and casualty insurance products can be classified as either "personal lines" or "commercial lines." Personal lines include automobile insurance and homeowner insurance. Commercial lines include product liability insurance, commercial property insurance, and professional malpractice insurance.

State insurance commissions regulate the premiums that may be charged for insurance coverage. Competitive pressures, however, have made the need for price regulation less important. In instances where states have imposed premiums that insurers feel are uneconomic, companies have withdrawn from offering insurance.

The amount of the liability coverage is specified in the policy. The premium is invested until the insured makes a claim on all or part of the amount of the policy, and that claim is validated. For some lines of business, the P&C company will know immediately that it has incurred a liability from a policy it has underwritten; however, the amount of the claim and when it will have to be paid may not be known at that time.

To illustrate this, suppose that in 1991 an automobile policy is written that provides $1 million liability coverage for Bob Smith. The policy covers him against claims by other parties resulting from an automobile accident. Suppose that in 1993, as a result of Bob Smith's negligence, he gets into an automobile accident that results in the permanent disability of Karen Lee, a pedestrian. The P&C company recognizes that it has a liability, but how much will it have to pay Karen Lee? It may be several years before the injured party and the company settle the matter, and a trial may be necessary to determine the monetary damages that the P&C company must pay. Money managers for P&Cs need to consider the value of claims in litigation as they formulate their investment strategies.

P&Cs also have lines of business where a claim is not evident until several years after the policy period. For example, suppose that for the years 1989 through 1993 a P&C company wrote a product liability policy for a toy manufacturing company. It may not be until 1996 that it is discovered that one of the products manufactured by the toy company was defective, causing serious injury to children.

Nature of the liabilities—The liabilities of P&C companies have a shorter term than life companies and vary with the type of policy. As noted earlier, the exact timing and amount of any liability are unknown. However, the maximum amount of the liability cannot exceed the amount of the coverage specified in the policy.

Unlike many life insurance products, P&C liabilities are not interest-rate sensitive, but some are inflation sensitive. There are unique types of liability risks faced by P&C companies, the two most notable being **geographic risk** and **regulatory pricing risk. Geographic risk** arises when an insurer has policies within certain geographical areas. If a catastrophe such as a hurricane or an earthquake occurs in that geographical area, the liability exposure increases. **Regulatory pricing risk** arises when regulators restrict the premium rates that can be charged.

Investments—The distribution of the assets held by P&C companies at the end of 1991 appears in Table 4-4. Because of the nature of their liabilities, P&C companies invest more heavily in equities and less heavily in bonds than life insurance firms do.

While life companies are constrained as to eligible assets, P&C companies have greater leeway for investing. For example, a P&C company might be required to invest a minimum amount in eligible bonds and mortgages. As long as this minimum is satisfied, however, a P&C company is free to allocate its investments any way it pleases among eligible assets in the other asset classes.

PENSION FUNDS

A **pension plan** is a fund that is established for the payment of retirement benefits. The entities that establish pension plans—called the **plan sponsors**—are private business entities acting for their employees; state and local entities on behalf of their employees; unions on behalf of their members; and individuals for themselves.

The total assets of U.S. pension funds have grown rapidly since World War II. They almost tripled in the 1980s. By 1989, pension fund total assets were about $2.47 trillion. Pension funds are financed by contributions by the employer and/or the employee; in some fund plans employer contributions are matched in some measure by employees.

The great success of private pension plans is somewhat surprising because the system involves investing in an asset (i.e., the pension contract) that for the most part has been and is largely illiquid. It cannot be used—not even as collateral for borrowing—until retirement. The key factor explaining pension fund growth despite this serious limitation is that the employer's contributions

Table 4-4
Distribution of Assets of U.S. Property
and Casualty Insurance Companies: 1991

Asset	Amount ($ billions)	Percent of Total
Cash & equivalents	37.5	6.5%
Equities	106.8	18.6
U.S. Treasury securities	96.2	16.8
Federal agency securities	31.0	5.4
Municipal bonds	140.8	24.6
Corporate & foreign bonds	102.0	17.8
Mortgages	7.7	1.3
Other	51.9	9.1
Total	572.8	100.0

Note: These figures are from the group which the source calls "Other [Than Life] Insurance Companies."

Source: Board of Governors of the Federal Reserve System's **Flow of Funds Accounts, Financial Assets and Liabilities, First Quarter, 1992.**

and up to a specified amount of the employee's contributions, as well as the earnings of the fund's assets, are tax-deferred. In essence a pension is a form of employer remuneration for which the employee is not taxed until funds are withdrawn. Pension funds also have served traditionally to discourage employees from quitting, as usually the employee lost at least the accumulation resulting from the employer contribution (i.e., pension benefits have not been portable). As we will discuss later, portability of pension benefits has increased somewhat as a result of federal legislation.

Types of Pension Plans

There are two basic and widely used types of pension plans: **defined contribution plans** and **defined benefit plans**. A new idea, a hybrid often called a "designer pension," combines features of both these types.

Defined contribution plans—In a defined contribution plan, the plan sponsor is responsible only for making specified contributions into the plan on behalf of qualifying participants. The amount contributed is typically either a percentage of the employee's salary or a percentage of profits. The plan sponsor does not guarantee any certain amount at retirement. The payments that will be made to qualifying participants upon retirement will depend on the growth of the plan assets; that is, payment is determined by the investment performance of the assets in which the pension fund is invested. Therefore, in a defined contribution plan the employee bears all the investment risk.

The plan sponsor gives the participants various options as to the investment vehicles in which they may invest. Defined contribution pension plans come in several legal forms: money purchase pension plans, 401(k) plans, and employee stock ownership plans (ESOP).

By far, the fastest growing sector of the defined contribution plan is the 401(k). To the plan sponsor, this kind of plan offers fewer costs and administrative problems: the employer makes a specified contribution to a specific plan/program, and the employee chooses how it is invested.[7] To the employee, the plan offers some control over how the pension money is managed. In fact, plan sponsors frequently offer participants the opportunity to invest in one of a family of mutual funds (discussed later in this chapter). In public institutions such as state governments as well as private firms, over half of all defined contribution plans use mutual funds; and the percentage of private corporations following that path is even higher. Employees in the public and corporate sectors have responded favorably, and almost half of all assets in pensions are now invested in mutual funds, with the bulk of the money being placed in funds emphasizing equities and growth.[8]

Recent regulations from the U.S. Department of Labor require firms to offer their employees a set of distinctive choices. This development has further encouraged pension plans to opt for the mutual fund approach, because families of mutual funds can readily provide investment vehicles for different investment objectives.[9]

Defined benefit plans—In a defined benefit plan, the plan sponsor agrees to make specified dollar payments to qualifying employees at retirement (and

---

[7] "Calling it Quits," *Institutional Investor* (February 1991), p. 125.

[8] "Taking a Fancy to Mutual Funds," *Institutional Investor* (May 1992), p. 119.

[9] "The Communication Cloud over 401(k)s," *Institutional Investor* (September 1991) p. 189.

some payments to beneficiaries in case of death before retirement). The retirement payments are determined by a formula that usually takes into account the length of service of the employee and the earnings of the employee. The pension obligations are effectively the debt obligation of the plan sponsor, who assumes the risk of having insufficient funds in the plan to satisfy the contractual payments that must be made to retired employees. Thus, unlike a defined contribution plan, in a defined benefit plan, all the investment risks are borne by the plan sponsor.

A plan sponsor establishing a defined benefit plan can use the payments made into the fund to purchase an annuity policy from a life insurance company. Defined benefit plans that are guaranteed by life insurance products are called **insured plans**;[10] those that are not are called **noninsured plans**. An insured plan is not necessarily safer than an uninsured plan, as the former depends on the ability of the life insurance company to make the contractual payments.

Whether a private pension plan is insured or noninsured, a federal agency called the Pension Benefit Guaranty Corporation (PBGC), which was established in 1974 by the ERISA legislation (see below), insures the vested benefits of participants. Benefits become vested when an employee reaches a certain age and completes enough years of service so that he or she meets the minimum requirements for receiving benefits upon retirement. The payment of benefits is not contingent upon a participant's continuation with the employer or union.

Hybrid pension plans—A survey by *Institutional Investor* revealed that a new phenomenon in pension planning, hybrid plans, has attracted support.[11] These plans, which combine features of both basic types of pensions, first appeared in 1985 and have been adopted by 8% of companies and public employers in the United States. The appeal of these hybrids is that the basic types of plans have flaws: the defined contribution plan causes the employee to bear all the investment risk, while the defined benefit plan is expensive and hard to implement when few workers work for only one company over many years.

While hybrids come in many forms, a good example is the "floor-offset plan." With this plan, the employer contributes a certain amount each year to a fund, as in a defined contribution approach. The employer guarantees a certain minimum level of cash benefits, depending on an employee's years of service, as in a defined benefit plan. The employer manages the pension fund and informs the employee periodically of the value of his or her account. If the managed fund does not generate sufficient growth to achieve the pre-set level of benefits, the employee is obliged to add the amount of the deficit. In such a plan the employer and participating employees share the risk of providing retirement benefits.

Investments

The aggregate asset mix, at the end of 1994, of the 1,000 top pension plans is summarized in Table 4-5. As can be seen, for defined benefit plans, about 88% is allocated between equities and fixed-income securities. In the allocation of assets for defined contribution plans, a large proportion of assets are placed in

---

[10] Life insurance companies also manage pension funds without guaranteeing a specified payout. In this case they are acting only as money manager and the funds they manage are not insured plans.

[11] "Why Designer Pensions Are in Fashion," *Institutional Investor* (June 1992), pp. 123–31.

GICs. Qualified pension funds are exempt from federal income taxes. Thus, fund assets can accumulate tax-free. Consequently, pension funds do not invest very much in assets that have the advantage of being largely or completely tax-exempt.

There are no restrictions at the federal level on investing in non-U.S. investments. The sponsors of a fund, however, are free to restrict the allocation of the fund's assets to domestic investments. For example, the state of Oklahoma bans foreign investments for its public pension funds. It is not uncommon for union-sponsored pension funds to prohibit non-U.S. investments in their portfolios. A survey of pension fund sponsors conducted by *Institutional Investor* in 1991 found that more than half of the respondents invested in foreign securities of some type. Of those respondents that invested abroad, 96% invested in foreign stocks and 34% in foreign bonds.[12]

As can be seen from Table 4-5, the "Other" asset category is a small portion of the asset mix of pension plans. A survey by Goldman Sachs and Frank Russell Company found that from 1986 to 1992, investments other than stocks and bonds increased from $12 billion to $36 billion.[13]

Federal Regulation: ERISA

Because pension plans are so important for U.S. workers, Congress passed comprehensive legislation in 1974 to regulate corporate pension plans. The legislation, the Employee Retirement Income Security Act of 1974 (ERISA), is fairly technical in its details. For our purposes, it is necessary only to understand the major provisions of ERISA.

First, ERISA establishes minimum funding standards having to do with the minimum contributions that a plan sponsor must make to the pension plan to satisfy the actuarially projected benefit payments. Prior to enactment of ERISA, many corporate plan sponsors followed a "pay-as-you-go" funding policy. That is, when an employee retired, the corporate plan sponsor took the necessary retirement benefits out of current operations. Under ERISA, such a practice is no longer allowed.

Second, ERISA establishes fiduciary standards for pension fund trustees, managers, or advisors. Specifically, all parties responsible for the management of a pension fund are guided by the judgment of a mythical "prudent man" in seeking to determine which investments are proper.[14] Because a trustee takes care of other people's money, it is necessary to make sure that the trustee takes the role seriously. In fulfillment of responsibilities, a trustee must use the care of a reasonably prudent person to acquire and use the information that is pertinent to making an investment decision.

Third, minimum vesting standards were established by ERISA. For example, after five years of employment a plan participant is entitled to 25% of accrued pension benefits. The percentage increases to 100% after ten years. Finally, ERISA created the PBGC to insure vested benefits. The insurance program is funded from annual premiums that must be paid by pension plans.

---

[12] "Pensionforum: Over There," *Institutional Investor* (February 1991), p. 70.

[13] Thomas J. Healey and Donald J. Hardy, "Alternative Investments Grow Rapidly at Tax-Exempt Funds," *Journal of Investing* (Spring 1994), pp. 12–18.

[14] The prudent-man rule developed as part of trust law.

Table 4-5

Aggregate Asset Mix for Top 1,000 Pension Funds in 1994

Asset	Percent
Top Defined Benefit Plans	
Equity	53.9
Fixed income	33.6
Cash equivalents	3.9
Real estate equity	3.3
Mortgages	1.5
GIC/BIC	1.5
Annuities	0.2
Other	2.6
Top Defined Contribution Plans	
Company stock	23.3
Other stock	24.4
Fixed income	14.5
Cash equivalents	5.8
GIC/BIC	24.8
Annuities	1.8
Other	5.4

Source: **Pensions & Investments,** *January 23, 1995, p. 36.*

It is important to recognize that ERISA does not require that a corporation establish a pension plan. If a corporation does establish one, however, it must comply with the regulations set forth in ERISA. Responsibility for administering ERISA is delegated to the Department of Labor and the Internal Revenue Service. To ensure that a pension plan is in compliance with ERISA, periodic reporting and disclosure statements must be filed with the Department of Labor and the Internal Revenue Service.

Financial Reporting Requirements for Corporations

While the selection of assets to include in a pension fund is dictated by the actuarially projected pension obligations, another important consideration is the financial reporting requirements. Corporations report to shareholders on the basis of generally accepted accounting principles (GAAP). The reporting requirement for pension obligations is promulgated by Financial Accounting Standard Board (FASB) No. 87.

This controversial accounting standard basically requires that a corporation follow certain procedures for each pension plan it establishes. A corporation may establish more than one pension plan for different categories of workers or employees of different subsidiaries. Each year the corporation must determine the present value of the projected liabilities of the plan and compare this to the market value of the pension assets. If the market value of the assets exceeds the present value of the liabilities, there is a surplus; such a surplus is not shown on the corporation's balance sheet. However, if the present value of the liabilities exceeds the market value of the assets, there is a deficit, which must then be reported on the balance sheet as a liability. This liability must be reported even if the corporation has surpluses in all of the other plans it has established, and the surpluses exceed the deficit—that is, no offsetting is permitted.

Opponents of FASB No. 87 argue that this financial reporting requirement does not reflect the economics of the pension obligations. While full consideration of the nuances of FASB No. 87 is not appropriate here, suffice it to say that it has implications for a sponsor's decision to allocate plan assets between common stock and bonds. Specifically, FASB No. 87 encourages corporate pension plan managers to hedge the risk that the surplus will be affected adversely by a change in interest rates by holding a portfolio of bonds with certain investment characteristics.

Participants in the Noninsured Pension Fund Business

While we refer to pension funds as financial institutions, there are many types of entities in the financial services business that are involved in the pension fund business. We have already discussed the role of life insurance companies. Below, we describe other participants in the noninsured pension fund business.

A plan sponsor can do one of the following with the pension assets under its control: (1) manage all the pension assets itself—use in-house management; (2) distribute the pension assets to one or more money management firms to manage—use external money managers; or (3) combine these alternatives.

Insurance companies have been involved in the pension business through their issuance of GICs and annuities. Insurance companies also have subsidiaries that manage pension funds. Aetna Life Insurance, for example, managed $48.7 billion in pension assets as of 1991, with 36% being defined contributions for 1,000 plan sponsors.[15] The trust department of commercial banks manage funds, as do independent money management firms (i.e., firms that are not affiliated with an insurance company or bank). For example, the trust department of Norwest Bank of Minnesota manages about $8.1 billion, of which 30% is defined contributions for 1,300 plan sponsors; while the Harris Trust and Savings Bank manages $11.6 billion of assets, of which 30% is defined contributions for 245 plan sponsors.[16] Fidelity Institutional Retirement Services, an independent money management firm that is a subsidiary of Fidelity Investments, manages $27.5 billion of defined contribution funds for 2,500 pension sponsors.[17]

Managers of pension fund money obtain their income from a fee charged to manage the assets. The annual fee can range from 0.75% of assets under management to as little as 0.01% of assets under management. One study found that in 1991, the average effective fees charged by external money managers of

---

[15] "The 1992 Defined Contribution Directory," *Institutional Investor* (June 1992), p. 179.

[16] Ibid.

[17] Ibid.

public pension funds was 0.31% (31 basis points) and for corporate pension funds was 0.41% (41 basis points).[18] The fees are lower than advisory fees for investment companies (discussed later in this chapter), in which small investors tend to invest small accounts, because of the economies of scale associated with managing large amounts of money for pension funds. Some plan sponsors have been entering into management fee contracts based on performance rather than according to a fixed percentage of assets under management.

In addition to money management firms, there are advisors to plan sponsors. Advisors help the plan sponsor in several ways, through:

- developing plan investment policy and asset allocation among the major asset classes.

- actuarial advising (liability modeling and forecasting).

- designing benchmarks that the fund's money managers will be measured against.

- measuring and monitoring the performance of the fund's money managers.

- measuring trading costs and analyzing these costs.

- constructing index funds when a pension plan elects to manage indexed funds internally.

- searching for and recommending money managers to pension plans.

- providing specialized research.

INVESTMENT COMPANIES

Investment companies are financial intermediaries that sell shares to the public and invest the proceeds in a diversified portfolio of securities. Each share that they sell represents a proportionate interest in the portfolio of securities owned by the investment company. The securities purchased could be restricted to specific types of assets such as common stock, government bonds, corporate bonds, or money market instruments.

Types of Investment Companies

There are three types of investment companies: **open-end funds, closed-end funds**, and **unit trusts**.

Open-end funds—An open-end fund, more popularly referred to as a mutual fund, continually stands ready to sell new shares to the public and to redeem its outstanding shares on demand at a price equal to an appropriate share of the value of its portfolio, which is computed daily at the close of the market.

A mutual fund's share price is based on its **net asset value (NAV) per share**, which is found by subtracting from the market value of the portfolio the mutual fund's liabilities and then dividing by the number of mutual fund shares outstanding. That is:

---

[18] "Manager Fees Head South, Greenwich Says," *Money Management Letter* (March 30, 1992), p.1.

$$\text{Net asset value per share} = \frac{\text{Market value of portfolio} - \text{Liabilities}}{\text{Number of fund shares outstanding}}$$

For example, suppose that a mutual fund with 10 million shares outstanding has a portfolio with a market value of $215 million and liabilities of $15 million. The net asset value per share is $20, as shown below:

$$\frac{\$215,000,000 - 15,000,000}{10,000,000} = \$20$$

Mutual fund shares are offered directly from the mutual fund company or through a broker on its behalf. Shares are quoted on a bid-offer basis. The offer price is the price at which the mutual fund will sell the shares. It is equal to the net asset value per share plus any sales commission that the mutual fund may charge. The sales commission is referred to as a "load." A **load fund** is one that tends to impose large commissions, typically ranging from 8.5% on small amounts invested down to 1% on amounts of $500,000 or over. A mutual fund that does not impose a sales commission is called a **no-load fund**. No-load mutual funds compete directly with load funds and appeal to investors who object to paying a commission (particularly because there is no empirical evidence that suggests that load funds have outperformed no-load funds after accounting for the load charge). The relative attraction of no-load funds has forced many mutual funds to convert to no-load status. Some funds have adopted a so-called "low-load" strategy, that is, charging a relatively small load of around 3%-3.5%. For no-load funds, the offer price is the same as the net asset value per share.

The distinction between a no-load fund and a load is easy to spot in the price quotations that appear in the financial sections of newspapers. Also, the quotations indicate the size of the load, if there is one. An example of some quoted bid and offer prices, for certain funds, will illustrate these points. On one day, the following prices appeared in newspapers:

Fund	NAV	Offer Price
Vanguard Hi-Yield Corporate	7.46	NL
Safeco Equity	13.46	NL
Templeton Growth	17.63	18.71
Piper Jaffray Balance	11.79	12.28

The designation "NL" indicates that these are no-load funds. Their initial per share price to the investor equals the per share value of the fund's assets. The per share offer prices of the other two funds exceed their funds' per share NAVs. Thus, the third and fourth funds listed above are load funds. For the Templeton Growth fund, the load is ($18.71 − $17.63)/$17.63 or 6.1%. For the Piper Jaffray Balance fund, the load is 4.2%.

Even though a fund does not charge a commission for share purchases, it may still charge investors a fee to sell (redeem) shares. Such a fund, referred to as a **back-end load fund,** may charge a commission of 4% to 6%. Some back-end load funds impose a full commission if the shares are redeemed within a designated time period after purchase, such as one year, reducing the commission the longer the investor holds the shares. The formal name for the "back-end load" is the **contingent deferred sales charge** (CDSC).

There are mutual funds that do not charge an upfront or a back-end commission but instead take out up to 1.25% of average daily fund assets each year to cover the costs of selling and marketing shares. The SEC's Rule 12b-1, which was passed in 1980, allows mutual funds to use such an arrangement to cover selling and marketing costs; such funds are referred to as 12b-1 funds.

In 1986, the SEC permitted fund offerings with two types of stock with different sales structures. For example, Alliance Mortgage Securities has two shares, Class A and Class B. The former has a 3% front-end load; the latter has a back-end sales charge whose fee depends on the length of time the shares are held. Investors who may need to sell their shares in the short term might prefer the front-loaded Class A, while those intending to hold shares for a long period might prefer end-loaded Class B.

Closed-end funds—In contrast to mutual funds, closed-end funds sell shares like any other corporation and usually do not redeem their shares. Shares of closed-end funds sell on either an organized exchange, such as the New York Stock Exchange, or in the over-the-counter market. Newspapers often list quotations of the prices of these shares under the heading of "Publicly Traded Funds." Investors who wish to purchase closed-end funds must pay a brokerage commission at the time of purchase and again at the time of sale.

The price of a share in a closed-end fund is determined by supply and demand, so the price can fall below or rise above the net asset value per share. Shares selling below NAV are said to be "trading at a discount," while shares with prices above NAV are "trading at a premium." Though the divergence of price from NAV is often puzzling, in some cases the premium or discount is easy to understand. One fund's share price may be below the NAV because the fund has large tax liabilities on capital gains that have swelled the NAV, and investors are pricing the future after-tax distributions of the fund. Another fund's shares may trade at a premium to the NAV because the fund offers relatively cheap access to, and professional management of, stocks in another country where information is not readily available to small investors. In recent years, the "Spain Fund" and the "Korea Fund" have been prominent examples of this situation.[19]

An interesting feature of closed-end funds is that the initial investors bear the cost of underwriting the issuance of the funds' shares.[20] The proceeds which the managers of the fund have to work with equal the total paid by initial buyers of the shares, minus all costs of issuance. These costs, which average around 7.5% of the total amount paid for the issue, normally include selling fees or commissions paid to the retail brokerage firms which distribute them to the public. The high commissions are strong incentives for retail brokers to recommend these shares to their customers who are retail (individual) investors.

Historically, closed-end funds have been far less popular than open-end funds in the United States. One estimate is that the number of dollars in open-

---

[19] The so-called "Country Funds" were popular in the late 1980s and made up a substantial portion of the closed-end funds issued in that time.

[20] Kathleen Weiss, "The Post-Offering Price Performance of Closed-End Funds," *Financial Management* (Autumn 1989), pp. 57–67.

end funds is 12 times greater than the number in closed-end funds.[21] However, in recent years, closed-end funds have shown increasing appeal to individual investors, primarily because of their emphasis on international investment portfolios. From 1986 to 1991, the number of closed-end funds rose from 69 to 290, and their assets grew from $12 billion to $73 billion.[22]

Another reason for the popularity of closed-end funds is the introduction of a fund that has a fixed termination or maturity date. Such a fund is called a **term trust**. The first term trust, the Blackstone Target Term Trust, was a closed-end fund sold by Blackstone Financial Management (now called BlackRock Financial Management) in November 1988. Prior to this time, neither mutual funds nor closed-end funds had a fixed termination or maturity date. The fund invested in a portfolio of bonds, but specified a termination date for the fund. The objective of the fund was to return to shareholders the initial offering price, $10, plus a rate competitive with a Treasury security with the same maturity as the termination date of the trust. Effectively, term trusts are "synthetic bonds" whose performance over the term of the trust depends on the capability of the financial advisor. The implication for the management of such a fund is that there is a well-defined investment goal— to return to the shareholders the dollar amount specified at the offering date. Thus, the financial advisor manages the fund's portfolio using strategies that recognize a future liability, rather than using the strategies pursued by financial advisors of other mutual funds that need not be concerned with a future liability.

Unit trust—A **unit trust** is similar to a closed-end fund in that it issues a fixed number of ownership shares, called **unit certificates**. They are sold and redeemed only by the issuing company, like open-end funds, however. Unit trusts typically invest in bonds and differ in several ways from both mutual funds and closed-end funds that specialize in investing in bonds. First, there is no active trading of the bonds in the portfolio of the unit trust. Once the unit trust is assembled by the sponsor (usually a brokerage firm or bond underwriter) and turned over to a trustee, the trustee holds all the bonds until they are redeemed by the issuer. Usually the only time the trustee can sell an issue in the portfolio is if there is a dramatic decline in the issuer's credit quality. This means that the cost of operating the trust will be considerably less than costs incurred by either a mutual fund or a closed-end fund. Second, unit trusts have a fixed termination date, while mutual funds (with the exception of term trusts) and closed-end funds do not. Third, unlike the mutual fund and closed-end fund investor, the unit trust investor knows that the portfolio consists of a specific collection of bonds and has no concern that the trustee will alter the portfolio.

All unit trusts charge a sales commission. The initial sales charge for a unit trust is 3.5% to 5.5%. There is often a commission of 3% to sell units, but trusts sponsored by some organizations do not charge a commission when the units are sold. Since there is no active management of unit trusts, our focus on investment companies is on open-end (mutual) funds and closed-end funds. We shall refer to both as simply "funds."

The number of funds increased fourfold in the 1980s, from 250 in 1980 to more than 3,900 in 1992.[23] The amount controlled by both open-end and

---

[21] Peter Donovan, "Closed-End Funds in the United States of America," in Stefano Preda (ed.), *Funds and Portfolio Management Institutions: An International Survey* (Amsterdam: North-Holland, 1991), p. 232.

[22] Securities and Exchange Commission, *Protecting Investors: A Half-Century of Investment Company Regulation* (New York: Commerce Clearing House, Inc., 1992), p. 432.

[23] This is the number of mutual funds followed by a leading service, Lipper Analytical Services.

closed-end funds increased from $240 billion in 1982 to more than $1.5 trillion in 1992. In terms of assets under management, the funds rank behind commercial banks and nearly equal to insurance companies, but are ahead of thrifts and credit unions.[24] One reason for the growth of the assets invested in mutual funds is the use of mutual funds as an investment choice for defined contribution pension plans.

Structure and Expenses of a Fund

A fund is structured with a board of directors, a financial advisor responsible for managing the portfolio, and a distributing and selling organization. Funds enter into contracts with a financial advisor to manage the fund—typically, a company that specializes in the management of funds. The advisor can be a subsidiary of a brokerage firm, an insurance company, an investment management firm, or a bank.

The financial advisor to the fund charges a **management fee**, also called an **investment advisory fee**. This fee, which is one of the largest costs of administering a fund, is usually equal to 0.5% to 1.5% of the fund's average assets, but the fee per dollar of assets managed may be determined on a sliding scale that declines as the dollar amount of the fund increases. The management fee should reflect the difficulty of managing the particular fund.

Funds incur other costs in addition to the management fee. These include the expenses for maintaining shareholder records, providing shareholders with financial statements, and custodial and accounting services. These expenses are referred to as "other expenses" in the industry. The management fee and other expenses are referred to as annual fund operating expenses. Selling and marketing costs are also included as part of annual fund operating expenses for 12b-1 funds.

The annual fund operating expenses must be specified in the prospectus.[25] The management fee is known. How much the other expenses and the 12b-1 fees will be are not known. However, an estimate is provided in the prospectus based on the fund's historical expenses. The following are excerpts from the prospectus of two open-end funds regarding annual fund operating expenses as a percentage of average net assets:

Fidelity Magellan Fund

Management Fees	0.78%
12b-1 Fees	None
Other Expenses	0.28%
Total Fund Operating Expenses	1.06%

Dreyfus New Jersey Intermediate Municipal Bond Fund

Management Fees	0.60%
Other Expenses	0.83%
Total Fund Operating Expenses	1.43%

---

[24] *Mutual Fund Fact Book* (Washington, D.C.: Investment Company Institute, 1992), p. 25.

[25] A prospectus is a document approved by the Securities and Exchange Commission that describes the security offered.

In addition to the annual fund operating expenses that the investor in a fund incurs, there is also any sales or redemption load with buying and selling shares. The load is not an annual fee but is incurred at the time the shares are purchased and/or sold. Thus, the effective annual load depends on how long the shares are held by an investor. The longer the holding period, the lower the effective annual load.

The total fees incurred by investing in a fund are, then, the annual fund operating expenses and the load. *Money* magazine examined the prospectus of 29 large funds to determine the average annual costs of owning a share in one of these funds. In calculating the effective annual load, *Money* magazine assumed that the shares were held for three years. The study found that the average annual cost of owning a fund is 2.2%. The cost ranged from 0.4% to 3.5%. For 21 of the 29 funds, the cost ranged between 2% and 3%. For six of the funds, the cost was about 1%.

What is not included in the annual operating fund expenses are the transactions costs associated with buying and selling securities to implement the fund's portfolio strategy. To give the investor some idea of portfolio trading activity, the fund reports the portfolio turnover rate on an annualized basis. The portfolio turnover rate varies from fund to fund depending on the investment strategy pursued by the fund. Active portfolio strategies generally require frequent buying and selling of securities, and will therefore have a higher portfolio turnover rate than passive portfolio strategies.

Fund Objectives and Policies

When a fund is offered, a prospectus must be provided to the perspective investor. Every prospectus for a fund must include a statement about the investment objectives that the manager of the fund seeks to accomplish, and the policies that the manager will follow to meet the investment objectives. The investment objectives can only be changed by vote of a majority of the outstanding shares of the fund. The statement about policies indicates in broad terms the type of strategy that the fund manager will pursue and the asset classes in which the fund manager may invest.

There are funds that invest exclusively in equities, and others in bonds. Even within an asset class, there are funds with different objectives. In the case of funds that invest exclusively in equities, for example, the investment objective of one fund may be to emphasize stable income; another may emphasize capital gains, or growth; and still another a combination of income and growth. Some limit investments to specific industries so that the fund manager can presumably specialize and achieve better selection and timing. A few funds offer participation in potentially glamorous new research companies by investing in fields such as electronics, oceanography, and telecommunications. There are funds that restrict their investment to small firms and some that invest in foreign stocks. For investors who wish to achieve maximum diversification, the latest development in the mutual fund area is indexed funds that hold a portfolio mimicking the composition of a broad index such as the S&P 500.

Funds that specialize in bond investments also have a wide menu of funds. U.S. government bond funds invest only in U.S. government bonds. There are corporate bond funds which can have very different investment objectives. Some funds invest only in high-quality corporate bonds, while others invest primarily in low-quality (junk) corporate bonds. Convertible securities funds invest in convertible bonds and convertible preferred stock. Investors interested in mortgage-backed securities can turn to a fund that specializes in those securities.

There is a wide range of funds that invest exclusively in municipal bonds. Some funds specialize in municipal bond issuers within a given state so that investors can take advantage of the exemption of interest income from state and local taxes. Residents of New York and California, for example, can choose from a dozen or more mutual funds that invest in bonds of issuers within their home state; interest income is then exempt from state taxes.

Money market mutual funds invest in securities with a maturity of one year or less, called money market instruments. There are three types of money market funds. General money market funds invest in taxable money market instruments such as Treasury bills, short-term U.S. government agency issues, commercial paper, and negotiable certificates of deposit. U.S. government short-term funds invest only in Treasury bills or U.S. government agency securities. The third type of money market mutual fund is the short-term municipal fund.

A balanced fund is one that invests in both stocks and bonds. While there are often limits as to how much a fund manager may allocate to an asset class, there is room to modify the asset mix to take advantage of what the fund manager expects will be the better-performing asset class.

A **fund family**, "family of funds," "group of funds," or "complex of funds" refers to the fact that many management companies offer investors a choice of numerous funds with different investment objectives. In many cases, investors may move their assets from one fund to another within the family, at little or no cost, and with only a phone call to a toll-free number. The same policies regarding load and other costs may apply to all members of the family, but it is possible for a management company to have different fee structures for different funds under its control.

The mutual fund industry is highly concentrated, with the ten largest mutual fund groups managing close to 50% of the market share. The largest fund group is managed by Fidelity Investments, which was mentioned above. The second largest fund group manager is Merrill Lynch, an investment banking firm. The next three largest fund group managers are the Vanguard Group, Franklin Resources, and Dreyfus, all of whom are investment management firms. These five fund groups control more than 32% of mutual fund assets. [26]

Regulation

All investment companies are regulated at the federal level according to the Investment Company Act of 1940, and subsequent amendments to that legislation. The securities they issue must be registered with the SEC. Moreover, investment companies must provide periodic financial reports and disclose

---

[26] Julie Rohrer, "The Mutual Fund Battle Turns Ugly," *Institutional Investor* (September 1992), p. 41.

the investment policies that they will follow to achieve their investment objectives. The act prohibits changes in the nature of an investment company's investment objectives without the approval of shareholders. A major goal of the law was to prevent self-dealing and other examples of conflict-of-interest, such as the imposition of unreasonably high fees.

However, the most important feature of the Investment Company Act of 1940 has to do with what the law permits. The law frees any company that qualifies as a "regulated investment company" from taxation on its gains, either from income or capital appreciation. To qualify as such a company, the mutual fund must distribute to its shareholders 90% of its income each fiscal year. Further, the fund must follow certain rules about the diversification and liquidity of its investments and about short-term trading and gains.

In the past, the SEC set a limit of 8.5% on a fund's load but allowed the fund to charge certain expenses under the 12b-1 rule. Recently, the SEC has amended the rule to set, for most cases effective on July 1 of 1993, a maximum of 8.5% on the total of all fees, inclusive of front-end and back-end loads as well as expenses for advertising.

Economic Motivation for Funds

Recall from Chapter 2 that financial intermediaries obtain funds by issuing financial claims against themselves and then investing those funds. An investment company is a financial intermediary because it pools the funds of market participants and uses those funds to buy a portfolio of securities. Also recall the special role in the financial markets played by financial intermediaries. They provide at least one of the following four economic functions: (1) maturity intermediation, (2) risk reduction via diversification, (3) lower costs of contracting and information processing, and (4) a payments mechanism. We will now consider which of these economic functions a fund provides.

Consider first maturity intermediation. An investor with a short-term investment horizon wishing to invest in either stocks or debt obligations with a maturity greater than the planned investment horizon faces the risk that the securities may have to be sold at a time when their market value is less than the price paid. However, this is true even if a share of a fund is purchased, because the net asset value per share will fluctuate with market conditions. Consequently, maturity intermediation is not an economic function provided by a fund.

Next consider risk reduction through diversification. By investing in a fund, an investor can obtain broad-based ownership of a sufficient number of securities either within a sector of the financial market or across market sectors in order to reduce portfolio risk. (We'll be more specific about the type of risk that is reduced in Chapter 6.) While an individual investor may be able to acquire a broad-based portfolio of securities, the degree of diversification will be limited by the amount available to invest. By investing in the investment company, however, the investor can effectively achieve the benefits of diversification at lower cost even if the amount of money available to invest is not large.

Beyond risk reduction via diversification offered by funds, there are reduced costs of contracting and information processing because an investor purchases the services of a presumably skilled financial advisor at less cost than if the investor directly negotiated with an advisor. The advisory fee is lower because of the larger size of assets managed, as well as reduced costs of searching for an investment manager and obtaining information about the securities. Also, the costs of transacting in the securities are reduced because a fund has more clout in negotiating transactions costs, and custodial fees and bookkeeping costs are less for a fund than for an individual investor.

Finally, money market funds generally provide payment services by allowing investors to write checks drawn on the fund, although this facility is limited in various ways.

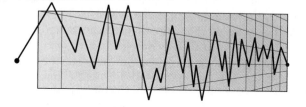

SUMMARY

Four financial institutions are discussed in this chapter: life insurance companies, property and casualty insurance companies, pension funds, and investment companies.

Life companies and P&C companies are financial intermediaries that function as risk bearers. Insurance companies are regulated at the state level. Each state establishes its own regulations with respect to the types of securities that are eligible for investment and how the value of those securities must be shown for regulatory reporting purposes.

While the principal event that life companies insure against is death, a major portion of their business has been in providing lifetime benefits in the form of retirement policies. Life insurance policies can be classified as one of four types: (1) pure insurance protection against risk of death (for example, term insurance); (2) a package consisting of insurance protection and an investment vehicle (whole life, universal life, and variable life); (3) insurance against the risk of life (annuities); and (4) an investment-oriented vehicle, primarily designed for pension programs (guaranteed investment contracts).

Property and casualty insurance companies insure against a wide variety of occurrences. They are afforded greater latitude than life companies in their investment choices. The liability of P&C companies is shorter term than for life companies and varies with the type of policy, while the exact timing and amount of any liability are unknown. P&C liabilities are not interest rate sensitive. Consequently, they tend to invest more heavily in equities and less in bonds than life insurance companies do.

A pension plan is a fund that is established by private employers, governments, or unions for the payment of retirement benefits. Qualified pension funds are exempt from federal income taxes, as are employer contributions. Pension plans have grown rapidly largely because of favorable tax treatment.

The two types of pension funds are defined contribution plans and defined benefit plans. In the former plan the sponsor is responsible only for making specified contributions into the plan on behalf of qualifying employees, but does not guarantee any specific amount at retirement. A defined benefit plan sponsor agrees to make specified payments to qualifying employees at retirement. Some hybrid plans blend features of both basic types of plans. Pension funds are managed by either the plan sponsor or by management firms hired by the sponsor. There are advisors to provide assistance to pension sponsors.

Federal regulation of pension funds, as embodied in the Employee Retirement Income Security Act of 1974, sets minimum standards for employer contributions, establishes rules of prudent management, and requires vesting in a specified period of time. Also, ERISA provides for insurance of vested benefits.

Investment companies sell shares to the public and invest the proceeds in a diversified portfolio of securities, with each share representing a proportionate interest in the underlying portfolio of securities. There are three types of investment companies: open-end or mutual funds, closed-end funds, and unit trusts. Mutual funds and closed-end funds provide two economic functions associated with financial intermediaries—risk reduction via diversification, and lower costs of contracting and information processing. Money market funds allow shareholders to write checks against their shares, thus providing a payments mechanism, another economic function of financial intermediaries.

A fund is structured with a board of directors, a financial advisor responsible for managing the portfolio, and a distributing and selling organization. Annual fund operating expenses include the management fee, other expenses, and for 12b-1 funds, the costs of distribution and marketing. There are also portfolio transactions costs associated with managing a fund.

A wide range of funds with many different investment objective and policies are available. Securities law requires that a fund clearly set forth its investment objective and policies in its prospectus. Investment companies are extensively regulated, with most of that regulation occurring at the federal level through the Investment Company Act of 1940. The key feature of the legislation in this area allows the funds to be exempt from taxation on their gains if the gains are distributed to investors within the fund's fiscal year. There are also regulations that apply to many aspects of the funds' administration, including sales fees, asset management, degree of diversification, distributions, and advertising.

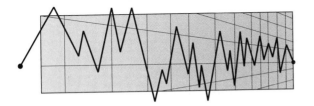

QUESTIONS

1. The quotation following is from a survey in *The Economist* on the American insurance industry:

   Life insurers, like bankers, learnt the hard way about inflation and interest rates a decade ago. Insurance was a fairly straightforward business in the old days. As late as 1979, more than 80% of new premiums were for "whole life" policies with fixed premiums, benefits and surrender values; almost all the rest was "term" insurance which pays out only on death . . . . That comfortable world had begun to change even before inflation went into double-digits in the late 1970s. Customers realized that the cash values piling up in their insurance companies did not compare favorably with returns on other instruments. Issuers had to offer policies like universal life and variable life and permutations of the two. These gave customers market-related returns, often above a guaranteed minimum, and more flexibility.

a. What is meant by whole life, universal life, and variable life insurance policies?

b. In general, what have been the consequences of life insurance companies having to offer market-related returns?

2. The following is an excerpt from *Best's Review* of June 30, 1990.

When medical waste washed up on the beaches of New Jersey and New York in several separate incidents in 1988, the public was disgusted and scared. Many ocean front resort operators and workers who depend on the allure of the beach for their livelihood were nearly ruined. But the financial losses from that lost summer of 1988 pale in comparison with the economic havoc that improperly handled medical waste can wreak on America's health care providers. . . . To date, no medical facility has been sued for injuries or damages caused by

the disposal of medical waste, but given today's consciousness of this issue and the trend in environmental legislation, such litigation is inevitable. Clearly, the eventuality represents both an emerging liability coverage issue and a thorny challenge for the commercial insurance industry.

Discuss this excerpt by addressing these issues:

a. The type of insurance company that would underwrite coverage for medical waste.

b. Some of the problems that such companies have in estimating their liabilities to policyholders.

c. The likelihood that insurance companies will be eager to start underwriting insurance for medical waste.

3. a. How is the revenue of an insurance company determined?

b. How is the profit of an insurance company determined?

4. What is the role of the National Association of Insurance Commissioners?

5. a. What is meant by a policy lapsing?

b. Why is the lapsing of a life insurance policy related to interest rates?

6. Risk-based capital requirements are based on the various risks faced by an insurance company. For life companies, one of these risks is referred to as asset risk. What does asset risk mean?

7. Calculate the risk-based capital requirements for asset risk for the Southwest Quality Life Company from the data given below (all assets are in millions of dollars):

Asset Class	Capital Factor	Dollar Allocation
U.S. government securities	0.0%	$600
Corporates, municipal, agencies, MBS, CMOs, & ABS rated NAIC (A-AAA)	0.3%	400
Corporates & municipals rated:		
NAIC 2 (BBB)	.0%	200
NAIC 3 (BB)	2.0%	300
NAIC 4 (B)	4.5%	50
NAIC 5 (CCC)	10.0%	90
NAIC 6 (Default)	30.0%	20
Common stocks	15.0%	250
Mortgage & collateral loans	5.0%	125
Real estate	10.0%	325

8. Why are the liabilities of a property and casualty insurance company more difficult to predict than those of a life company?

9. What is meant by the "crediting rate" on a life insurance policy?

10. a. What is a guaranteed investment contract?

   b. What does the "guarantee" mean? Is it a government entity that guarantees the contract?

   c. Why does the interest rate offered on a GIC depend on the rating of the life company?

11. a. Who are plan sponsors?

   b. What is the difference between a defined contribution plan and a defined benefit plan?

   c. What is a 401(k) plan?

12. What is meant by an insured pension plan?

13. What is the function of the Pension Benefit Guaranty Corporation?

14. Why are pension funds not interested in tax-advantaged investments?

15. Are U.S. pension funds free to invest in foreign securities?

16. a. What is the major legislation regulating pension funds?

   b. Does this major legislation require that a corporation establish a pension fund?

17. What types of services do advisors provide to pension sponsors?

18. Here is a quotation from the May 1, 1990, issue of *Forbes*:

   Which is a better buy, the $352 million Ameri-can Capital Harbor Fund or the closed-end $77 American Capital Convertible Securities? At first glance, it's hard to choose. They're both balanced funds. James Behrman, 45, runs both. . . . Yet Behrman has done much better with the closed-end fund. Measured by the performance of its portfolio (that is on net asset value, rather than on the trading price of the fund's shares), American Capital Convertible has returned 11.5% a year over the past five years. Harbor has returned only 8.7% a year.

   a. What are open- and closed-end funds, and what are the major differences between the two?

   b. What is meant by net asset value?

c. Can you think of a reason why a closed-end fund would out-perform an open-ended fund composed of similar securities?

19. An investment company that has 2 million shares outstanding has total assets of $40 million and total liabilities of $2 million.

    a. What is the net asset value per share?

    b. Suppose the investment company is a no-load fund, how much would an investor have to pay to purchase one share?

    c. Suppose the investment company charged a sales commission or load of 5%. What would an investor have to pay to buy a share?

20. Suppose the investment company in the previous question is a closed-end investment company. Can you determine how much an investor would have to pay to purchase one share? If so, how? If not, why not?

21. a. What is a back-end load fund?

    b. What is a 12b-1 fund?

22. "An investment company can change the investment objective at the beginning of each fiscal year." Comment on this statement.

23. In *Bogle on Mutual Funds* (Burr Ridge, IL: Irwin Professional Publishing, 1994), John C. Bogle, Chairman of the Vanguard Group of Investment Companies, in his discussion of mutual fund costs wrote: "There is one large *invisible* cost, often ignored because of its invisibility. It is the cost the fund incurs in executing portfolio transactions."

    a. Why is this cost an "invisible cost"?

    b. What figure reported by a fund gives some indication of the amount of trading activity?

24. a. What is meant by a money market fund?

    b. Explain three types of money market funds.

25. a. What types of regulatory requirements does a "regulated investment company" have to meet?

    b. What is the key advantage to a company of gaining this status?

Investment Banking Firms

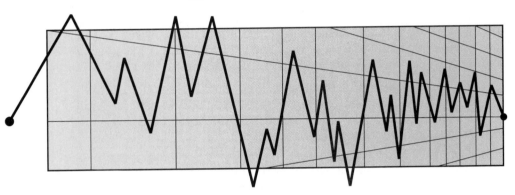

LEARNING OBJECTIVES

After reading this chapter you will understand:

• the nature of the investment banking business.

• the revenue-generating activities of investment banks.

• the activities of investment banking firms that require them to commit their own capital.

• the role investment bankers play in the underwriting of securities.

• the different types of underwriting arrangements.

• what is meant by the securitization of assets.

• the difference between riskless arbitrage and risk arbitrage.

• the various roles investment bankers play in mergers and acquisitions.

• what is meant by merchant banking.

• why investment banking firms create and trade risk control instruments.

• how investment banking firms are classified.

• the competition and challenges facing investment banking firms in the 1990s.

In this chapter, we look at investment banking firms and the key role that they play in capital markets. Investment banking firms perform two general functions. For corporations, U.S. government agencies, state and local governments, and foreign entities (sovereigns and corporations) that need funds, investment banking firms assist in obtaining those funds. For investors who wish to invest funds, investment banking firms act as brokers or dealers in the buying and selling of securities. Thus, investment banking firms perform a critical role in the primary market and the secondary market.

SCOPE OF INVESTMENT BANKING

Defining more specifically what constitutes investment banking is not a simple matter. Robert Kuhn suggests four definitions of investment banking, ranging from broadly inclusive of wide-ranging financial services to a narrow traditionalist definition (some of the terms used below will be clarified later):

1. The broadest definition includes virtually all activities of major Wall Street firms, from international corporate underwriting to retail branch marketing to a host of other financial services (e.g., real estate and insurance).

2. The next broadest definition envisions investment banking as covering all capital market activities, from underwriting and corporate finance, to mergers and acquisitions (M&A) and fairness opinions, to fund management and venture capital. Excluded, for example, are the selling of securities to retail customers, consumer real estate brokerage, mortgage banking, insurance products, and the like. Included is merchant banking, when investment bankers work and invest for their own account. Also included is the nonretail trading of blocks of securities for financial institutions.

3. Here investment banking is defined to include only some capital market activities, stressing underwriting and mergers and acquisitions. Excluded, for example, are fund management, venture capital, commodities, aspects of risk management, and the like. Depending on firm orientation, research may also be excluded if it is used primarily to support retail sales. (Note that the changing profile of investment banking would now include merchant banking in this definition.)

4. The narrowest definition takes investment banking back to its historical foundations, limiting the field strictly to underwriting and raising of capital in the primary markets, and the trading of securities (broker/dealer) in the secondary market. (It is hard to conceive of a contemporary definition of investment banking that would exclude M&A, so this one is for historians and purists.)[1]

The definition with which we basically agree is the second definition—investment banking involves all capital market activities except those involving retail-oriented sales. There are firms in the financial services business that buy or sell securities only for customers (retail or institutional) but are not

---

[1]   Robert Lawrence Kuhn, *Investment Banking: The Art and Science of High-Stakes Dealmaking* (New York: Harper & Row, 1990), pp. 5–6.

involved in the fund-raising function. These firms are called **securities** or **brokerage firms.**

According to this definition of investment banking, it would seem that many investment banking activities are similar to those performed by the larger commercial banks. This is true. As we stressed in Chapter 3, the wall between commercial banking and investment banking is being chipped away by deregulation.

NATURE OF THE BUSINESS

Investment banking firms are highly leveraged firms. Table 5-1 lists the total consolidated capital, equity capital, and long-term debt of the ten largest investment banking firms in the United States as of the end of 1993. The degree of leverage is even greater than that shown in the table because firms rely on considerable short-term borrowing as well. As we explain the activities that investment banking firms are engaged in, you will see why they have had an appetite for capital. The increasing need for capital has resulted in consolidation of firms in the industry and a change in many firms from the partnership structure to the corporate structure, the latter giving firms easier access to public funds.

In addition to needing long-term sources of capital, investment banking firms borrow on a short-term basis to finance their inventory of securities. The primary means for borrowing on a short-term basis is the repurchase agreement (see Chapter 19).

Table 5-1

Capital Structure of the Ten Largest Investment
Banking Firms Ranked by Total Consolidated Capital
(in millions, as of end of 1993)

Firm	Total Consolidated Capital	Equity Capital	Long-Term Debt
Merrill Lynch	$18,954.8	$5,485.9	$13,468.9
Salomon Inc.	17,023.0	5,331.0	11,692.0
Goldman, Sachs & Co.	15,249.0	5,008.0	10,241.0
Lehman Brothers	11,951.0	2,052.0	9,899.0
Morgan Stanley	8,208.8	3,906.2	4,302.6
Bear Stearns & Co.	4,665.3	2,040.4	2,624.9
CS First Boston	4,649.0	1,324.0	3,325.0
PaineWebber	3,131.0	1,195.0	1,936.0
Smith Barney Shearson	2,742.0	2,055.0	687.0
Prudential Securities	1,842.0	1,379.0	463.0

Source: "Ranking America's Biggest Brokers," Institutional Investor *(April 1994), p. 156. This copyrighted material is reprinted with permission from Institutional Investor, 488 Madison Avenue, New York, NY 10022.*

Investment banking firms generate revenue from commissions, fee income, spread income, and principal activities. After we describe the various activities of investment banking, we will review the revenue breakdown of the largest U.S. investment banking firms, Merrill Lynch.

According to our working definition of investment banking, the activities of firms in this business can be divided into the following specific revenue-generating activities:

- public offering (underwriting) of securities
- trading of securities
- private placement of securities
- securitization of assets
- mergers and acquisitions
- merchant banking
- trading and creation of derivative instruments
- money management

Not all investment banking firms are involved in each of these activities. In the 1980s, the philosophy in the industry was to throw people, money, and other resources at developing a market share in each of these activities—that is, to provide a full line of services. This will not be the philosophy of investment banking firms in the 1990s, as firms have reevaluated the economics of being in certain lines of business.[2]

Public Offering (Underwriting) of Securities

The traditional role associated with investment banking is the underwriting of securities. Entities that issue securities include agencies of the U.S. government, state and local governments, corporations, supranational entities, foreign governments, and foreign corporations.

The traditional process in the United States for issuing new securities involves investment bankers performing one or more of the following three functions:

1. advising the issuer on the terms and the timing of the offering.
2. buying the securities from the issuer.
3. distributing the issue to the public.

The advisor role may require investment bankers to design a security structure that is more palatable to investors than a particular traditional instrument. For example, the high interest rates in the U.S. in the late 1970s and early 80s increased the cost of borrowing for issuers of even the highest quality rating. To reduce the cost of borrowing for their clients, investment bankers designed securities with characteristics that were more attractive to investors but not onerous to issuers. They also designed security structures for low-quality bond issues, so-called high-yield or junk bond structures. We will give several examples of these financial innovations in later chapters.

---

[2] For an excellent discussion of the evolution of investment banking from its beginnings to today's global financial markets, see Samuel L. Hayes III and Philip M. Hubbard, *Investment Banking: A Tale of Three Cities* (Boston: Harvard Business School Press, 1990).

In the sale of new securities, investment bankers need not undertake the second function of buying the securities from the issuer. An investment banker may merely act as an advisor and/or distributor of the new security. The function of buying the securities from the issuer is called **underwriting**. When an investment banking firm buys the securities from the issuer and accepts the risk of selling the securities to investors at a lower price, it is referred to as an underwriter. When the investment banking firm agrees to buy the securities from the issuer at a set price, the underwriting arrangement is referred to as a **firm commitment**. The risk that the investment banking firm accepts in a firm commitment underwriting arrangement is that the price it pays to purchase the securities from the issuer will be less than the price it receives when it reoffers the securities to the public. In contrast, in a **best-efforts underwriting** arrangement, the investment banking firm agrees only to use its expertise to sell the securities, it does not buy the entire issue from the issuer.

The fee earned from underwriting a security is the difference between the price paid to the issuer and the price at which the investment bank reoffers the security to the public. This difference is called the **gross spread**, or the **underwriter discount**. There are numerous factors that affect the size of the gross spread.[3] Typical gross spreads for common stock offerings, **initial public offerings** (IPOs), and fixed-income offerings are shown in Table 5-2. IPOs are typically common stock offerings issued by companies that had not previously issued common stock to the public. Because of the risk associated with pricing and then placing IPOs, the gross spread is higher.

The typical underwritten transaction involves so much risk of capital loss that for a single investment banking firm to undertake it alone would expose it to the danger of losing a significant portion of its capital. To share this risk, an investment banking firm puts together a group of firms to underwrite the issue. This group of firms is called an **underwriting syndicate**. The gross spread is then divided among the lead underwriter(s) and the other firms in the underwriting syndicate. The lead underwriter manages the deal ("runs the books" for the deal). In many cases there may be more than one lead underwriter, in which case the lead underwriters are said to "co-lead" or "co-manage" the deal. In a bond transaction, the lead underwriters customarily receive 20% of the gross spread as compensation for managing the deal.[4]

To realize the gross spread, the entire securities issue must be sold to the public at the planned reoffering price. This usually requires a great deal of marketing muscle. Investment banking firms have an investor client base (retail and institutional) to which they attempt to sell the securities. To increase the potential investor base, the lead underwriter will put together a **selling group**. This group includes the underwriting syndicate plus other firms that are not in the syndicate. Members of the selling group can buy the security at a **concession price** (i.e., a price less than the reoffering price). The gross spread is thereby divided among the lead underwriter, members of the underwriting syndicate, and members of the selling group.

The underwriting of securities is not limited to offerings in the United States. An issuer can select among many foreign securities markets to

---

[3] For a discussion of these factors, see G. Clyde Buck, "Spreads and Fees in Investment Banking," Chapter 5 in Robert Lawrence Kuhn (ed.), *The Library of Investment Banking, Volume II* (Homewood, IL: Dow Jones-Irwin, 1990), pp.146-147.

[4] Ernest Block, *Inside Investment Banking* (Homewood, IL: Dow Jones-Irwin, 1989), p. 323.

Table 5-2
Typical Gross Spreads by Offering Size

Common Stock Offering*		Initial Public Offering	
Size (in Millions)	Gross Spread	Size (in Millions)	Gross Spread
$ 10	6.0-8.0%	$ 5	8.0-10.0%
15	5.0-7.5	10	7.5- 9.0
20	5.0-7.0	15	7.0-8.0
30	3.5-5.0	20	6.5-7.0
50	2.0-5.0	30	5.5-7.0
100	2.0-4.5	50	5.0-7.0
150	2.0-4.0	200	2.0-4.0

Fixed-Income Offering**	
Size (in millions)	Gross Spread
$ 20	1.3%
25	1.2
30	1.0
50	0.7
100	0.7
150	0.7
200	0.7

*For industrial companies, not utilities.

**Typical offering of A-rated corporate debt with 10 years to maturity.

Source: Adapted from Figures 1, 2, and 3 of G. Clyde Buck, "Spreads and Fees in Investment Banking," Chapter 5 in Robert Lawrence Kuhn (ed.), The Library of Investment Banking, Volume II (Homewood, IL: Dow Jones-Irwin, 1990).

identify the one in which to offer securities so as to reduce its cost of funds. Indeed, some securities have been offered simultaneously in several markets throughout the world.

Investment bankers have assisted in offering the securities of government-owned companies to private investors. This process is referred to as **privatization**. An example is the initial public offering of the U.S. government-owned railroad company Conrail in March of 1987. More than 58 million shares were sold, raising a total of $1.65 billion. This is the largest IPO in the history of this country. Prior to the Conrail IPO, AT&T had raised $1.5 billion in 1983. Non-U.S. examples include the U.K.'s British Telecom, Chile's Pacifica, and France's Paribas. In the case of British Telecom (the government-owned telephone company of the United Kingdom), the amount raised was $4.7 billion. This offering was a global offering; that is, it was offered simultaneously in several countries.

In the 1990s, the role of investment bankers in placing the securities of government-owned companies into the hands of private investors will increase. Eastern Europe, for example, is following a major program of privatization. It has been estimated that the combined capitalization of now-government-owned firms there will be around $200 billion.[5] In Chapter 6, we will describe the process of underwriting securities and the risks associated with this activity.

Trading of Securities

A successful underwriting of a security requires a strong sales force. The sales force provides feedback on advance interest in the deal, and the traders (or market makers) provide input in pricing the deal as well.

It would be a mistake to think that once the securities are all sold the investment banking firm's ties with the deal are ended. In the case of bonds, those who bought the securities will look to the investment banking firm to make a market in the issue. This means that the investment banking firm must be willing to take a principal position in secondary market transactions. Revenue from this activity is generated through (1) the difference between the price at which the investment banking firm sells the security and the price paid for the securities (called the bid-ask spread); and (2) appreciation of the price of the securities held in inventory. Obviously, if the securities depreciate in price, there will be a reduction in revenue.

To protect against a loss, investment banks engage in hedging strategies. There are various strategies that are employed by traders to generate revenue from positions in one or more securities: **riskless arbitrage**, **risk arbitrage**, and **speculation**.

Riskless arbitrage—Of the two types of arbitrage transactions (riskless arbitrage and risk arbitrage), riskless arbitrage calls for a trader to find a security or package of securities trading at different prices. For example, there are common stocks of companies that trade in more than one location within the United States. Also, common stock of some multinational companies trades in both the U.S. and on an exchange in one or more foreign countries (see Chapter 13 for a discussion of common stock). If there are price discrepancies in the various markets, it may be possible to lock in a profit after transactions costs by selling the security in the market where it is priced higher and buying it in the market where it is priced lower. In the case of a security priced in a foreign currency, the price must be converted based on the exchange rate.

Traders do not expect such situations to occur because they are rare. While they do exist periodically in financial markets, riskless arbitrage opportunities of the type described are short-lived. There are, however, situations where packages of securities and derivative contracts, combined with borrowing, can produce a payoff identical to another security, yet the two are priced differently. The key point is that a riskless arbitrage transaction does not expose the investor to any adverse movement in the market price of the securities in the transaction.

We will give examples of this in later chapters because the concept of riskless arbitrage provides the underlying process by which assets are priced. For now, a simple example should suffice. Consider three securities A, B, and C that can be purchased today, and for which one year from now there are only two possible outcomes (State #1 and State #2):

---

5 David Fairlamb, "The Privatizing of Eastern Europe," *Institutional Investor* (April 1, 1990), p. 172.

Security	Price	Payoff in State #1	Payoff in State #2
A	$70	$50	$100
B	60	30	120
C	80	38	112

Let W_A and W_B be the quantity of security A and B, respectively, in the portfolio. Then the payoff (i.e., the terminal value of the portfolio) under the two states can be expressed mathematically as follows:

if State #1 occurs: $\$ 50\ W_A + \$ 30\ W_B$

if State #2 occurs: $\$100\ W_A + \$120\ W_B$

Can we create a portfolio consisting of A and B that will reproduce the payoff of C regardless of the state that occurs one year from now? That is, we want to select W_A and W_B such that:

if State #1 occurs: $\$ 50\ W_A + \$ 30\ W_B = \$ 38$

if State #2 occurs: $\$100\ W_A + \$120\ W_B = \$112$

The dollar payoff on the right-hand side of the two equations is the payoff of C in each state.

We can solve these two equations algebraically, obtaining a value of 0.4 for W_A and 0.6 for W_B. Thus, a portfolio consisting of 0.4 of security A and 0.6 of security B will have the same payoff as security C. How much will it cost us to construct this portfolio? As the prices of A and B are $70 and $60, respectively, the cost is:

0.40 ($70) + 0.60 ($60) = $64

Note that the price of C is $80. Thus, for only $64 an investor can obtain the same payoff as C. This is a riskless arbitrage opportunity that can be exploited by buying A and B in the proportions given above and shorting (selling) C. (Short selling is discussed in Chapter 7.) This allows the investor to lock in a profit of $16 today regardless of what happens one year from now. By selling C, the investor must pay $38 if State #1 occurs and $112 if State #2 occurs. The investor will obtain the dollars necessary to make either payment from the payoff of A and B.

Risk arbitrage—Another type of arbitrage is called *risk arbitrage.* There are two types of risk arbitrage. The first arises in the case of exchange offers for securities of corporations coming out of a bankruptcy proceeding. For example, suppose that company A is being reorganized, and one of its bonds is now selling in the market for $200. If the trader believes that the outcome of the bankruptcy proceedings will be the exchange of three securities with an estimated value of $280 for the existing bond worth $200, then the trader will buy the existing bond. The trader will realize a profit of $80 if in fact the final exchange offer is as anticipated, and the value of the package is worth $280.

The spread between the $280 potential package and the $200 price for the bond reflects two risks: the risk that the exchange will not take place on the terms that the trader believes, and the risk that the value of the package of three securities that will be received will be less than $200. The "risk" in this risk arbitrage transaction reflects these two risks.

The other type of risk arbitrage occurs when a merger or acquisition is announced. The merger or acquisition can involve only a cash exchange, an exchange of securities, or a combination of both. First consider a cash exchange: suppose that company X announces that it plans to make an offer to buy company Y's common stock for $100 per share at a time when company Y's common stock is selling for $70. One would expect that the market price of company Y's common stock would rise to around $100. There is, however, a chance that company X will, for whatever reason, withdraw its planned purchase of the stock. The price of company Y's common stock consequently may rise to, say, $90 rather than $100. The $10 difference is the market's assessment of the likelihood of the planned purchase not being completed. An investor who buys the common stock of Y can lock in a profit of $10 if the purchase occurs at $100. The risk is that it will not occur and that the price will decline below $90.

The various takeover attempts of UAL Corp. (the parent company of United Airlines) provide a classic example of the risk associated with this type of risk arbitrage. In September 1989 there was a $300 per share bid for UAL's stock made by a group consisting of pilots and management. While the board of UAL approved the offer, the bidders could not obtain the necessary financing to complete the transaction. During this time, the stock had reached a peak of $296 per share. In mid-October, when it was determined that the transaction would not take place, the stock fell in a matter of a few days by almost 50%. In January 1990, there was once again a bid for UAL Corp. for $201 per share, the bidder this time being the union. Once again, the financing for the takeover could not be obtained, resulting in a plunge in the market price. It has been estimated that these failed takeover attempts resulted in losses to risk arbitrageurs of over $1 billion.

When the transaction involves the exchange of securities rather than cash, the announced terms of the exchange will not be reflected immediately in the price of the securities involved. For example, suppose that company B announces that it plans to acquire company T. Company B is called the bidding or acquiring firm and company T the target firm. Company B announces that it intends to offer one share of its stock in exchange for one share of company T stock. At the time of the announcement, suppose that the prices of the stock of B and T are $50 and $42, respectively. If the acquisition does take place as announced, a trader who acquires one share of company T for $42 can exchange it for stock worth $50, a spread of $8. This spread reflects three risks: (1) the acquisition may not be consummated for one reason or another and then T's stock may have to be sold, possibly at a loss; (2) there is a time delay, which means that there will be a cost to financing the position in T's stock; and (3) the price of B's stock can decline in value so that when T's stock is exchanged for B's, less of a spread is realized.

The way to protect against this last risk is for the trader to buy shares of T and sell short an equal number of shares of B (recall the transaction is a one-for-one share exchange), in order to lock in a spread of $8 if the transaction is consummated. Let's look at what happens now if the price of B's stock changes at the time the transaction is consummated. At that time, the price of the stock of both B and T will be the same. Suppose the price of B's stock falls from $50 to $45. Then, when the trader exchanges one share of stock T for stock B, there will be a profit of $3 at the purchase price of $42 for stock T. The short sale of one share of stock B for $50 can now be covered by buying it back for $45, realizing a profit of $5. The trader's overall profit will be $8, the spread that the trader wanted to lock in.

Suppose instead that at the time the exchange is consummated one share of stock B is worth $60 per share. By exchanging stock T, which was purchased at $42, for one share of stock B, which is now worth $60, a profit of $18 is realized on this leg of the transaction. However, because stock B was sold short for $50 and must now be purchased for $60 to cover the short position, a loss of $10 is realized on the second leg of the transaction. Overall, a profit of $8 still is realized.

Thus, risk arbitrage to lock in a spread, *if the exchange is consummated on the announced terms,* involves buying the shares of the target company and shorting the shares of the acquiring or bidding company. The number of shares depends on the exchange terms. Our example assumes a one-for-one exchange, so one share of B was shorted for every share of T purchased. Had the exchange been one share of B for every two shares of T, then one share of B would be shorted for every two shares of T purchased.

There remains the first risk: the risk that the deal will not be consummated. To reduce this risk, the trader or research department must carefully examine the likelihood of a successful takeover or merger.[6]

Speculation—Speculative trading is one in which the trader positions the capital of the investment banking firm to take advantage of a specific anticipated movement of prices or a spread between two prices. The benefits of being right, particularly with a highly leveraged position, are rewarding. We read in the popular press that some investment banking firms have reaped millions of dollars from a certain speculative position; remember, however, that just as often we read about large trading losses from speculative strategies.

Execution of trades for clients—Commissions are generated by executing trades for investors, both retail and institutional investors. Two common institutional trades that investment bankers are called upon to execute are block trades and program (or basket) trades. These trades are discussed in Chapter 13.

Research and trading—To encourage clients to use a firm to execute transactions so that commissions or the bid-ask spread income can be generated, investment banks provide research for clients. Typically, the research is provided free for clients that generate a certain amount of trades. For those that do not, the research is sold.

There is some research that a firm will restrict to its own traders. The purpose is to provide strategies or information that the firm's trader may be able to use to improve performance.

Private Placement of Securities

In addition to underwriting securities for distribution to the public, investment banking firms place securities with a limited number of institutional investors such as insurance companies, investment companies, and pension funds. Private placement is distinguished from the "public" offering of securities that we have described so far and will be discussed further in the next chapter.

---

[6] Of course, there is always the Dennis Levine/Ivan Boesky risk-reduction approach to risk arbitrage: through illegal means acquire material nonpublic information (called "inside information") about merger and acquisition transactions. This is, of course, not an approach we recommend.

Investment banking firms assist in the private placement of securities in several ways. They work with the issuer and potential investors on the design and pricing of the security. Often it has been in the private placement market that investment bankers first design new security structures. Field testing of many of the innovative securities that we describe in this book occurred in the private placement market.[7]

The investment bankers may be involved with lining up investors as well as designing the issue. Or, if the issuer has already identified the investors, the investment banker may serve only in an advisory capacity. Work as an advisor generates fee income, as does arranging the placement with investors. An investment banker can also participate in the transaction on a best efforts underwriting arrangement.

The fees for arranging a private placement vary depending on the issuance amount and the complexity of the transaction. Fees for the placement of an issue of senior debt might be as shown in Table 5-3. For risky subordinated debt, the fee would be higher.

In the case of fund raising for risky emerging companies, the average fee might be 5% to 6%, higher for small transactions.[8] Moreover, in raising venture capital for clients, investment bankers are frequently offered the opportunity to share in the prosperity of the company. This opportunity typically comes in the form of an option to buy a specified number of shares at a price that is set at a time the funds are raised. An arrangement that allows the investment banking firm to benefit from the company's success is referred to as an "equity kicker."

Securitization of Assets

Securitization of assets refers to the issuance of securities that have a pool of assets as collateral. The securitization of home mortgage loans to create mortgage-backed securities (which we discuss in Chapter 25) was the first example of this process. The bulk of these securities are backed by the U.S. government or an agency of the U.S. government. More recently, investment banking firms and other private entities have created mortgage-backed securities that are not guaranteed by the U.S. government or a government agency.

Table 5-3
Typical Private Placement Fees for Senior Debt

Size of Placement (in millions)	Fee
$5-10	1.5-4.0%
10-25	1.0-3.0
25-50	0.7-2.0
>50	0.5-1.5

*Source: Adapted from G. Clyde Buck, "Spreads and Fees in Investment Banking," Chapter 5 in Robert Lawrence Kuhn (ed.), **The Library of Investment Banking**, Volume II (Homewood, IL: Dow Jones-Irwin, 1990), p. 149.*

[7] For example, zero coupon corporate bonds were first publicly issued by corporations in April 1981. (The first issue was by J.C. Penney.) Prior to that there was a private offering by PepsiCo.

[8] Buck, "Spreads and Fees in Investment Banking," p. 150.

Since 1985, other assets have been securitized. The securities thus created are called **asset-backed securities**. The three most common type of asset-backed securities are those collateralized by automobile loans, credit card receivables, and home equity loans, although there are securities backed by boat loans, recreational vehicle loans, computer leases, and accounts receivable. Asset-backed securities, as well as the implications of asset securitization for financial markets, are discussed fully in Chapter 27.

Asset securitization generates revenue in one of two ways. First, when an investment banking firm securitizes assets on behalf of a client, and then underwrites the issue, it receives the gross spread, just as in any other underwriting. Second, if the investment banking firm buys the underlying assets, creates the securities, and then sells the securities, it realizes a profit on the difference between what it sells the entire issue for and the price it paid for the assets.

Mergers and Acquisitions

Investment banking firms are active in mergers and acquisitions (M&A). Under M&A activity are also included leveraged buyouts (LBOs), restructuring and recapitalization of companies, and reorganization of bankrupt and troubled companies. There has been significant activity in the M&A business in the United States in the 1980s, and it is expected that merger, LBO, and restructuring activities will be substantial in Europe in the 1990s.

Investment bankers may participate in M&A activity in one of several ways: (1) finding M&A candidates, (2) advising acquiring companies or target companies with respect to price and nonprice terms of an exchange, or helping target companies fend off an unfriendly takeover attempt, and (3) assisting acquiring companies in obtaining the necessary funds to finance a purchase.

Fees charged by investment bankers in M&A work depend on the extent of their participation and the complexity of the activities they are asked to perform. An investment banker may simply receive an advisory fee or retainer. More likely, an investment banker will receive a fee based on a percentage of the selling price. The fee structure in this case can be of one of three types: (1) the percentage can decline, the higher the selling price; (2) the percentage can be the same regardless of the selling price; or (3) the percentage can be fixed with addition of an incentive fee if the price is better than a specified amount. An example of the first fee structure is what is called the 5-4-3-2-1 "Lehman formula." In this fee structure that some firms have adopted, the fee would be 5% of the first $1 million, 4% of the second $1 million, 3% of the third $1 million, 2% of the fourth $1 million, and 1% for any excess amount. A typical flat percentage is 2% to 3% of the selling price.

Participating in an LBO can generate several fees. LBOs call for a firm to be acquired using mostly debt funds and taken private. The debt raised is from one of two sources—senior bank debt, and unsecured junior debt (called subordinated debt, or mezzanine financing). An investment banking firm can earn fees from (1) proposing the acquisition, (2) arranging the financing, (3) arranging bridge financing (that is, temporary funds loaned until permanent debt financing is completed), and (4) other advisory fees.

Under "other advisory fees" we would find fees charged by investment banking firms for providing a valuation of a firm that is the subject of a takeover or a merger, and for rendering a "fairness opinion." The question of fairness arises in such a transaction because there is an issue as to whether the purchasers of the company may have access to information that allows them to acquire the firm at a price less than its true market value. This situation is of increasing concern in LBOs, particularly management-led LBOs—that is, where the current management of the firm makes an offer to purchase the company. An investment banking firm is typically engaged by the board of directors of the company that is the subject of the takeover to render an independent and expert opinion as to the fairness of the price being offered for the shares. Fees for a fairness opinion range from $50,000 for a transaction involving a few million dollars to $1 million or more for large transactions.[9]

An investment banking firm may provide its own capital for bridge financing. This is one type of merchant banking, the activity that we turn to next.

Merchant Banking

When an investment banking firm commits its own funds by either taking an equity interest or creditor position in companies, this activity is referred to as **merchant banking**. If an equity interest is taken, there is usually substantial upside potential. The interest rate charged on debt funding provided to a client, particularly for bridge financing, is high, reflecting the high risk associated with such lending activities.

First Boston Corporation's bridge loan of $450 million to Ohio Mattress Co. to finance an LBO illustrates the risk of bridge financing for an investment banking firm. After the LBO was completed and Ohio Mattress sought to acquire permanent debt financing to refinance the bridge loan, First Boston could not sell the securities. As a result, First Boston was stuck with the loan.[10]

Bridge financing is seen as important not only for its potential source of interest income, but also as a financing vehicle that can be used to attract clients who are considering an LBO.

Trading and Creation of Derivative Instruments

Futures, options, swaps, caps, and floors are examples of instruments that can be used to control the risk of an investor's portfolio, or, in the case of an issuer, the risk associated with the issuance of a security. These instruments are referred to as derivative instruments and they allow an investment banking firm to realize revenue in several ways. Customers generate commissions from the exchange-traded instruments they buy and sell. This is no different from the commissions generated by the brokerage service performed for customers when stocks are bought and sold.

Second, there are certain derivative instruments that an investment banking firm creates for its clients where it acts as a counterparty to the agreement. These are called **over-the-counter** or **dealer-created derivative instruments**. An example is a swap, which we will describe in Chapter 12. There is the risk of loss of capital whenever an investment banking firm is a counterparty, because the investment banker becomes a principal to the transaction. To protect against capital loss, an investment banking firm will

---

[9] Buck,"Spreads and Fees in Investment Banking," p. 153.

[10] Eventually the parent company of First Boston, Credit Suisse First Boston, provided assistance by buying the bridge loan from First Boston.

seek another party to take the other side of the transaction. When this occurs, spread income is generated.

Derivative instruments are also used to protect an investment bank's own position in transactions. Here are just two examples. Suppose an investment banking firm underwrites a bond issue. The risk that the firm is exposed to is a decline in the price of the bonds purchased from the issuer, which are to be reoffered to the public. (As we explain in Chapter 17, this tends to occur if interest rates rise.) Using either interest rate futures or options (the subject of Chapter 28), the investment banking firm can protect itself. As a second example, an investment banking firm has many trading desks with either long or short positions in a security. Derivative instruments can be used by the trading desks to protect the firm against an adverse price movement.

Money Management

Investment banking firms have created subsidiaries that manage funds for either individual investors or institutional investors such as pension funds. Examples include Goldman Sachs Asset Management, a subsidiary of the investment banking firm of Goldman Sachs & Co.; Bear Stearns Asset Management, a subsidiary of Bear Stearns, an investment banking firm; and Nomura Investment Management Company, a subsidiary of Nomura Securities, a Japanese investment banking firm. Money management activities generate fee income based on a percentage of the assets under management.

Fees

Now that we have reviewed the activities of investment banking firms,we will look at the fees generated by an actual investment banking firm. In Table 5-4 we present the revenue in 1993 of Merrill Lynch, the largest investment banking firm and one that is involved in all the activities we discussed above. (The entry "Investment Banking" in the table means underwriting.)

INDUSTRY STRUCTURE

As we noted earlier, not all investment banking firms are involved in every activity described above. One way to classify firms in the investment banking

Table 5-4
Sources of Revenue in 1993 for Merrill Lynch

Source	Revenue (in thousands)	Percent of total revenue
Commissions	$ 2,894,228	17.5%
Interest and Dividends	7,099,155	42.8
Principal Transactions	2,920,439	17.6
Investment Banking	1,831,253	11.0
Asset Management and Professional Service Fees	1,557,778	9.4
Other	285,324	1.7
Total revenues	$16,588,177	100.0%

Source: 1993 Annual Report.

business is by the types of activities that they are involved in, or, more appropriately, the types of activities that they emphasize.

Relative Ranking Measures

Within an activity area, firms that specialize in the area can be ranked by some measure of market share. Depending on the activity area, there are several potential measures. As an example, consider underwriting activity. Market share can be measured by one of the following: the number of deals done in a year, or the total dollar volume of all deals done in a year. However, it is not that simple. Recall that in an underwriting an investment banking firm may be the lead manager, co-manager, or just a member of the underwriting syndicate. Consequently, ranking by number of deals or total dollar volume of deals can be made by giving full credit only to the lead manager or some proportional credit to each manager.

Table 5-5 shows the 1994 underwriting rankings as compiled by Securities Data Co. The firms shown in the table are ranked on the basis of the dollar amount of underwriting. Table 5-5 is comprised of three tables. The top table shows the global ranking of underwriters giving full credit to the lead manager. The top underwriter was Merrill Lynch. The top Japanese underwriter was Nomura Securities. The second and third tables show the ranking for just U.S. underwriters. The second table bases the ranking on full credit to the lead manager while the third table bases the ranking on full credit to each manager.

Table 5-5
Global and Domestic (U.S.) Rankings of Underwriting Firms

Global Rankings

Full Credit to Lead Manager

Manager	01/01/94–12/31/94			01/01/93–12/31/93	
	$Amount	%	Issues	$Amount	Rank
Merrill Lynch	137,761.7	12.6	862	192,826.2	1
CS First Boston/Credit Suisse	96,945.6	8.9	648	113,418.7	5
Lehman Brothers	89,432.4	8.2	653	129,726.1	4
Goldman, Sachs	86,458.1	7.9	512	151,344.4	2
Morgan Stanley	74,785.4	6.8	557	89,482.0	7
Salomon Brothers	65,447.5	6.0	542	104,180.0	6
PaineWebber	61,743.7	5.6	344	131,993.4	3
J.P. Morgan	41,242.9	3.8	271	36,795.6	10
Bear, Stearns	34,934.0	3.2	209	56,904.2	8
Nomura Securities	23,666.6	2.2	151	37,012.3	9
Donaldson, Lufkin & Jenrette	23,611.4	2.2	227	36,678.6	11
UBS	21,970.4	2.0	163	19,836.9	14
Swiss Bank	17,066.5	1.6	113	12,956.4	21
Prudential Securities	16,476.9	1.5	141	28,135.0	12
Citicorp	15,398.4	1.4	234	17,943.2	15
Top 15 Totals	806,941.6	73.8	5,627	1,159,269.0	—
Industry Totals	1,093,627.8	100.0	9,009	1,500,877.6	—

Table 5-5 *Continued from previous page*

Domestic Rankings
Full Credit to Lead Manager

Manager	01/01/94–12/31/94			01/01/93/–12/31/93	
	$Amount	%	Issues	$Amount	Rank
Merrill Lynch	116,964.2	16.5	691	173,399.1	1
Lehman Brothers	78,743.8	11.1	573	115,241.0	4
CS First Boston	73,542.1	10.4	526	89,335.0	6
Goldman, Sachs	64,420.0	9.1	396	126,799.7	2
Morgan Stanley	58,686.0	8.3	435	67,382.2	7
PaineWebber	58,199.5	8.2	309	123,689.6	3
Salomon Brothers	57,238.0	8.1	482	90,585.5	5
Bear, Stearns	34,028.8	4.8	197	55,624.6	8
J.P. Morgan	26,524.5	3.7	181	23,577.0	11
Donaldson, Lufkin & Jenrette	23,309.4	3.3	221	36,240.5	9
Prudential Securities	16,350.2	2.3	136	28,031.4	10
Smith Barney	13,922.0	2.0	172	14,965.6	12
Citicorp	11,589.8	1.6	128	14,302.3	13
First Tennessee Bank,N.A.	8,127.3	1.1	110	5,108.5	18
UBS	6,251.9	0.9	86	5,177.4	17
Top 15 Totals	647,897.7	91.3	4,643	969,459.3	—
Industry Totals	709,991.3	100.0	6,258	1,058,489.6	—

Domestic Rankings
Full Credit to Each Manager

Manager	01/01/94–12/31/94			01/01/93/–12/31/93	
	$Amount	%	Issues	$Amount	Rank
Merrill Lynch	187,799.3	26.5	947	311,091.0	1
CS First Boston	140,656.7	19.8	745	185,998.0	6
Goldman, Sachs	137,112.5	19.3	675	223,405.8	2
Lehman Brothers	135,441.4	19.1	793	209,098.8	3
Morgan Stanley	113,904.3	16.0	629	158,504.9	7
Salomon Brothers	113,422.1	16.0	698	192,075.6	4
PaineWebber	96,296.9	13.6	539	187,894.6	5
J.P. Morgan	84,997.3	12.0	358	113,739.6	8
Bear, Stearns	64,606.4	9.1	331	112,417.0	9
Smith Barney	54,265.5	7.6	415	56,073.8	12
Donaldson, Lufkin & Jenrette	47,363.7	6.7	371	87,649.3	10
Prudential Securities	34,647.1	4.9	253	61,220.1	11
Citicorp	28,140.8	4.0	193	32,472.5	14
UBS	24,098.0	3.4	124	22,425.7	16
Dean Witter Reynolds	19,963.3	2.8	165	34,331.9	13
Industry Totals	709,991.3	100.0	6,258	1,058,489.6	—

Source: Securities Data Co.

Table 5-6
Rankings of Underwriting Firms by Type of Security

Investment-Grade Debt
Full Credit to Lead Manager

Manager	$Amount	%	Issues	$Amount	Rank
	01/01/94–12/31/94			*01/01/93–12/31/93*	
Merrill Lynch	61,912.6	18.5	410	81,154.7	1
Lehman Brothers	45,095.7	13.5	391	54,699.5	3
CS First Boston	40,357.3	12.0	324	28,494.8	6
Morgan Stanley	38,028.5	11.4	315	36,133.8	5
Goldman, Sachs	34,379.4	10.3	246	65,511.9	2
Salomon Brothers	30,855.3	9.2	350	39,864.8	4
J.P. Morgan	17,941.2	5.4	138	13,435.8	7
Bear, Stearns	8,195.3	2.4	103	8,265.2	9
First Tennessee Bank,N.A.	8,119.3	2.4	109	5,105.6	11
PaineWebber	6,406.2	1.9	108	12,535.0	8
Smith Barney	5,498.5	1.6	81	2,269.6	13
UBS	5,235.4	1.6	82	1,144.4	19
Citicorp	4,547.7	1.4	98	3,531.3	12
Donaldson, Lufkin & Jenrette	3,572.6	1.1	92	1,964.6	15
Dean Witter Reynolds	2,925.1	0.9	60	5,630.3	10
Top 15 Totals	313,070.1	93.5	2.907	359,741.2	—
Industry Totals	334,970.2	100.0	3.245	377,931.0	—

Full Credit to Each Manager

Manager	$Amount	%	Issues	$Amount	Rank
	01/01/94–12/31/94			*01/01/93–12/31/93*	
Merrill Lynch	94,598.2	28.2	526	157,174.1	1
Lehman Brothers	74,285.6	22.2	482	96,281.8	4
Goldman, Sachs	70,816.4	21.1	372	129,356.7	2
Morgan Stanley	68,963.6	20.6	414	90,204.2	5
CS First Boston	67,865.7	20.3	415	87,055.0	6
Salomon Brothers	55,787.2	16.7	452	98,678.5	3
J.P. Morgan	42,502.3	12.7	216	59,454.0	7
Bear, Stearns	20,738.5	6.2	161	31,431.5	9
PaineWebber	18,536.5	5.5	174	39,202.0	8
Donaldson, Lufkin & Jenrette	16,856.4	5.0	166	27,581.2	10
Smith Barney	15,695.0	4.7	128	12,651.9	14
UBS	13,329.5	4.0	98	11,196.7	15
Citicorp	12,275.7	3.7	132	14,260.7	12
First Tennessee Bank, N.A.	10,869.3	3.2	113	6,455.6	25
Nomura Securities	9,829.2	2.9	40	15,884.6	11
Industry Totals	334,970.2	100.0	3,245	377,931.0	—

Table 5-6 *Continued from previous page*

Noninvestment-Grade Debt

Full Credit to Lead Manager

Manager	$Amount	%	Issues	$Amount	Rank
	01/01/94–12/31/94			01/01/93–12/31/93	
Merrill Lynch	4,636.0	16.8	21	8,040.3	2
Donaldson, Lufkin & Jenrette	4,213.8	15.3	26	8,176.6	1
Salomon Brothers	3,788.5	13.7	16	3,009.0	5
Goldman, Sachs	2,918.4	10.6	18	3,755.6	4
Morgan Stanley	2,605.1	9.5	17	6,281.6	3
CS First Boston	1,802.3	6.5	11	2,068.6	7
Bankers Trust	1,561.4	5.7	11	1,884.6	8
Lehman Brothers	1,288.6	4.7	8	1,349.9	11
Bear Stearns	1,178.5	4.3	6	2,498.6	6
Smith Barney	885.0	3.2	7	360.0	15
Citicorp	400.0	1.5	3	1,827.5	9
Dillon, Reed	361.5	1.3	3	1,265.0	12
Chemical Banking	360.0	1.3	3	—	—
PaineWebber	337.5	1.2	2	1,731.1	10
Alex. Brown & Sons	300.1	1.1	3	350.0	16
Top 15 Totals	26,636.6	96.6	155	42,598.4	—
Industry Totals	27,565.1	100.0	166	44,877.6	—

Full Credit to Each Manager

Manager	$Amount	%	Issues	$Amount	Rank
	01/01/94–12/31/94			01/01/93–12/31/93	
Merrill Lynch	7,282.5	26.4	32	12,761.0	1
Salomon Brothers	6,382.2	23.2	28	7,343.9	4
Donaldson, Lufkin & Jenrette	6,230.8	22.6	35	11,348.3	2
Bankers Trust	5,658.4	20.5	27	6,439.2	5
Morgan Stanley	5,612.1	20.4	29	7,815.7	3
Bear, Stearns	4,726.7	17.1	20	5,452.4	8
Goldman, Sachs	4,597.6	16.7	26	5,713.1	7
PaineWebber	3,516.3	12.8	13	3,703.1	10
Smith Barney	2,838.9	10.3	18	1,593.8	16
CS First Boston	2,834.4	10.3	18	5,888.5	6
Citicorp	2,655.8	9.6	17	3,192.9	11
Chemical Banking	2,488.3	9.0	12	1,249.6	18
J.P. Morgan	2,152.9	7.8	9	4,483.7	9
Lehman Brothers	1,762.9	6.4	11	2,783.9	13
Schoders	1,306.5	4.7	6	1,033.4	19
Industry Totals	27,565.1	100.0	166	44,877.6	—

Table 5-6 *Continued from previous page*

Asset-Backed Debt
Full Credit to Lead Manager

Manager	01/01/94–12/31/94			01/01/93–12/31/93	
	$Amount	%	Issues	$Amount	Rank
Merrill Lynch	30,839.5	27.7	72	10,602.8	2
CS First Boston	12,903.2	17.2	54	17,760.8	1
Lehman Brothers	7,162.0	9.5	37	4,355.1	4
Prudential Securities	5,788.4	7.7	47	2,396.2	8
Bear, Stearns	5,597.5	7.4	16	3,604.8	5
Salomon Brothers	5,447.0	7.2	14	6,304.2	3
J.P. Morgan	4,564.4	6.1	15	2,819.2	7
Goldman, Sachs	4,533.0	6.0	12	1,799.0	9
Dean Witter Reynolds	1,946.5	2.6	6	3,167.5	6
Citicorp	1,456.5	3.9	4	870.5	13
First Chicago	998.7	1.3	2	300.0	16
PaineWebber	877.4	1.2	4	258.0	17
Donalson, Lufkin & Jenrette	841.2	1.1	4	775.9	14
Chemical Banking	771.8	1.0	7	334.8	15
Smith Barney	605.5	0.8	7	119.5	18
Top 15 Totals	74,322.5	98.9	301	55,668.2	—
Industry Totals	75,169.2	100.0	308	59,377.7	—

Full Credit to Each Manager

Manager	01/01/94–12/31/94			01/01/93–12/31/93	
	$Amount	%	Issues	$Amount	Rank
Merrill Lynch	39,820.9	53.0	122	38,373.5	2
CS First Boston	39,175.4	52.1	117	39,317.4	1
J.P. Morgan	31,816.6	42.3	77	32,105.0	3
Salomon Brothers	23,351.9	31.1	49	23,847.5	4
Goldman, Sachs	22,963.1	30.5	50	12,776.3	8
Lehman Brothers	22,139.5	29.5	77	20,616.6	5
Bear, Stearns	13,720.1	18.3	29	17,502.1	6
UBS	8,733.0	11.6	17	6,486.9	9
Morgan Stanley	8,317.1	11.1	20	15,487.1	7
Citicorp	7,751.3	10.3	19	3,112.2	12
Prudential Securities	6,460.2	8.6	51	4,013.7	10
Smith Barney	5,185.6	6.9	24	265.7	22
NationsBank	4,166.8	5.5	14	1,324.6	17
PaineWebber	3,262.3	4.3	12	357.9	21
Dean Witter Reynolds	3,251.0	4.3	10	3,167.5	11
Industry Total	75,169.2	100.0	308	59,377.7	—

Table 5-5 *Continued from previous page*

Common Stock

Full Credit to Lead Manager

Manager	$Amount	%	Issues	$Amount	Rank
	01/01/94–12/31/94			01/01/93–12/31/93	
Merrill Lynch	9,800.4	15.9	86	18,943.3	1
Goldman, Sachs	7,722.1	12.5	44	12,903.6	2
Morgan Stanley	6,331.1	10.3	47	5,504.7	6
CS First Boston	3,561.4	5.8	36	6,087.9	5
Smith Barney	3,467.9	5.6	42	4,868.2	7
PaineWebber	3,224.2	5.2	34	6,123.8	4
Lehman Brothers	3,190.4	5.2	40	7,826.0	3
Salomon Brothers	2,488.8	4.0	23	4,865.2	8
Donaldson, Lufkin & Jenrette	2,050.5	3.3	23	4,156.1	9
Montgomery Securities	2,004.3	3.3	39	2,547.1	12
Alex. Brown & Sons	1,639.1	2.7	36	2,560.9	11
Bear, Stearns	1,224.5	2.0	26	2,513.7	13
Oppenheimer	1,049.0	1.7	14	2,218.1	14
Morgan Keegan	950.7	1.5	14	82.2	53
Robertson Stephens	887.7	1.4	19	899.7	18
Top 15 Totals	49,592.2	80.6	523	82,100.5	—
Industry Totals	61,564.7	100.0	1,049	102,412.6	—

Full Credit to Each Manager

Manager	$Amount	%	Issues	$Amount	Rank
	01/01/94–12/31/94			01/01/93–12/31/93	
Merrill Lynch	18,283.9	29.7	128	36,255.8	1
Smith Barney	15,278.0	24.8	142	20,924.0	5
Goldman, Sachs	13,716.7	22.3	83	22,743.2	4
PaineWebber	12,114.0	19.7	112	23,535.8	3
Morgan Stanley	11,693.3	19.0	77	19,598.7	7
Lehman Brothers	8,386.2	13.6	80	27,045.8	2
Donaldson, Lufkin & Jenrette	7,633.4	12.4	67	17,408.5	8
Salomon Brothers	7,245.7	11.8	62	20,202.7	6
CS First Boston	6,986.7	11.3	61	15,258.9	9
Dean Witter Reynolds	6,034.6	9.8	47	12,828.7	10
Alex. Brown & Sons	5,365.1	8.7	76	11,513.4	11
A.G. Edwards & Sons	5,012.1	8.1	37	8,814.5	14
Prudential Securities	4,853.8	7.9	44	9,309.0	13
Montgomery Securities	4,480.6	7.3	74	5,564.1	18
Bear, Stearns	3,081.5	5.0	42	10,008.8	12
Industry Totals	61,564.7	100.0	1,049	102,412.6	—

Source: Securities Data Co.

Moreover, adding to the complication, even within an activity area, such as underwriting, a firm may not be active within all segments of a given market. For example, a firm may have a major presence in the underwriting of investment-grade (high-quality) debt, but it may not be involved in the underwriting of commercial paper, noninvestment-grade (high-yield or junk) debt, or municipal securities. Table 5-6 gives some examples of rankings by the type of security (investment-grade debt, noninvestment-grade debt (i.e., high-yield bonds, asset-backed securities, and common stock). In each case, the rankings are shown two ways: full credit to lead manager, and full credit to each manager.

Some industry observers believe that measures such as the number of deals and the total dollar volume of deals are not completely adequate. One reason is that it is necessary to know how a transaction translates into profits. To draw an analogy to manufacturing, having the largest market share for a product does not necessarily mean the largest profit, particularly if the product is underpriced and/or the cost structure reflects operating inefficiencies. Returning to investment banking firms, the assembly of high-priced human capital coupled with a desire to buy market share by accepting lower gross spreads in the underwriting of some types of securities may have caused some firms to be ranked number one in that area using the measures we have described. This underwriting revenue may not necessarily flow through to the bottom line, however. As an example, Salomon Brothers Inc. was frequently ranked at the top in the underwriting of municipal securities, yet it dropped out of this business.

Investment bankers point to "reputation" as a nonquantifiable measure of the relative importance of an investment banking firm within a business activity. While ranking by the measures we have discussed may be a proxy for reputation, there are observers who feel that in some activities there is not necessarily a high correlation.

In the fall of 1992, *Institutional Investor* surveyed chief financial officers regarding underwriting firms. The survey solicited responses about reputation and bidding practices of underwriters. The results are reported in Figure 5-1.

Classification of Investment Banking Firms

A popular classification of U.S. firms is as follows: bulge-bracket firms, major bracket firms, submajor bracket firms, regional firms, specialized firms, research firms, and merchant banks.[11]

Bulge-bracket firms are those that are viewed as the premier investment banking firms because of their size, reputation, presence in key markets, and customer base. Included in this exclusive group are First Boston Corporation; Goldman Sachs; Merrill Lynch; Morgan Stanley, Salomon Brothers Inc.; and Lehman Brothers. Large investment banking firms that do not have the same status as the bulge-bracket firms but nevertheless provide full-line services are called **major bracket firms**. Included in this group are Bear Stearns & Co.; Smith Barney Shearson; PaineWebber; Donaldson, Lukfin & Jenrette; Dean Witter; and Prudential Securities.

Submajor bracket firms are frequently New York-based firms that cater to special investor groups and smaller issuing companies. Firms located outside New York and that serve regional issuers (corporate and local governments) are classified as regional firms. One example is Alex. Brown & Sons,

---

[11] Kuhn, p. 20

Figure 5-1

Who's the Top Underwriter: An *Institutional* Investor Survey

What is the size of your company (revenues)?		Morgan Stanley	13.8
		First Boston	7.3
less than $499 million	7.5%	Lehman Brothers	2.8
$500 million to $999 million	18.0	J.P. Morgan	2.8
$1 billion to $2.9 billion	36.1	Other	3.6
$3 billion to $4.9 billion	18.0		
$5 billion or more	20.3		

What is the size of your company (revenues)?

less than $499 million	7.5%
$500 million to $999 million	18.0
$1 billion to $2.9 billion	36.1
$3 billion to $4.9 billion	18.0
$5 billion or more	20.3

Is the preponderance of your company's business

Industrial?	55.7%
Financial?	15.3
Service?	29.0

Do you have a traditional investment banking relationship for underwritten debt issues?

Yes	63.8%
No	36.2

How often have you issued taxable, underwritten debt in the past twelve months?

Once	17.4%
Twice	5.3
Three times	4.5
Four times	4.5
More than four times	11.4
Not at all	56.8

Which investment banking firm has the best reputation for managing and distributing underwritten debt issues?

Goldman Sachs	41.3%
Merrill Lynch	18.3
Morgan Stanley	11.0
Salomon Brothers	10.1
First Boston	9.2
Other	10.1

Do you have a traditional investment banking relationship for underwriting your company's equity securities?

Yes	45.3%
No	54.7

How often have you issued equity during the past twelve months?

Once	10.2%
Twice	2.3
Three times	0.8
Four times	0.0
More than four times	1.6
Not at all	85.2

Which firm has the best reputation for managing the underwriting of equity securities?

Goldman Sachs	36.7%
Merrill Lynch	33.0
Morgan Stanley	13.8
First Boston	7.3
Lehman Brothers	2.8
J.P. Morgan	2.8
Other	3.6

Which firm is the most aggressive in bidding competitively for debt issues, 415 shell registrations and otherwise?

Lehman Brothers	20.7%
Merrill Lynch	20.7
Goldman Sachs	17.1
First Boston	13.4
Salomon Brothers	8.5
Other	19.5

Is there any firm that is overly aggressive in bidding for debt issues?

First Boston	17.1%
Merrill Lynch	17.1
Lehman Brothers	14.3
J.P. Morgan	11.4
Bear Stearns	5.7
Dean Witter	5.7
Donaldson, Lufkin & Jenrette	5.7
Salomon Brothers	5.7
Other	17.3

Do you have a traditional relationship with an investment bank that acts as an agent in private placements?

Yes	25.4%
No	74.6

How often has your company placed securities privately during the past twelve months?

Once	11.9%
Twice	4.8
Three times	2.4
Four times	0.8
More than four times	1.6
Not at all	78.6

Which firm has the best reputation in private placements?

Goldman Sachs	36.2%
First Boston	15.9
Morgan Stanley	10.1
Merrill Lynch	7.2
J.P. Morgan	7.2
Salomon Brothers	7.2
Other	16.2

Have you recently changed any of your investment banking relationships

For public debt?	73.3%
For equity?	26.7
For private placements?	0.0

Source: "Who's the Top Underwriter," Institutional Investor (January 1993), p. 152.

This copyrighted material is reprinted with permission from Institutional Investor, 488 Madison Avenue, New York, NY 10022.

headquartered in Baltimore, Maryland, which is the oldest investment banking firm in the United States.

There are also firms that specialize in one major activity. These firms are referred to as "boutiques." **Research firms**, as the name suggests, specialize in various research products used by investors or issuers of securities. A firm that is classified as a "specialized" firm is one that concentrates on the issuance of securities in certain industries, high technology, say.

Merchant banks are investment banking firms that focus on M&A and fund-raising activities. Examples include the Blackstone Group and Wasserstein, Perella & Co. Japanese investment banking firms have entered into joint ventures with the better-known merchant banking firms. There is a joint venture, for example, between the Blackstone Group and Nikko Securities and between Wasserstein, Perella & Co. and Nomura Securities.

COMPETITION AND CHALLENGES FOR INVESTMENT BANKING FIRMS

Investment banking firms face competition from several directions, and will have to rethink the types of activities they wish to dedicate resources to in the future.

Competition

In Chapter 3, we reviewed the Glass-Steagall Act and the separation between commercial banking and investment banking. As we emphasized, the barriers between the two are being eroded. U.S. investment banking firms face not only actual and potential competition from commercial banks (both domestic and foreign), but also competition from foreign investment banking firms. This competition will put pressure on fees and spreads from all activities.

Competition is also coming in other forms. Trading technology that may allow institutional investors to trade among themselves without the use of brokers or a need for dealers threatens the sales and trading revenue of investment banking firms. Examples of automated transaction systems are Instinet, the Cross Network, and POSIT. Trading technologies will be discussed in Chapter 13.

Underwriting revenues could be diminished if corporate issuers can succeed in placing newly issued debt obligations directly with institutional investors. One noninvestment banking firm, CapitaLink Securities, has directly linked new corporate bond issuers and institutional investors via a computerized auction. In February 1988, Great Northern Nekoosa was able to place $75 million in publicly registered bonds directly with Metropolitan Life Insurance Company. This was not a private placement; the bonds were registered.

In June 1989, Metropolitan Life actually attempted to go head-to-head with investment banking firms to bid on a $100 million bond offering of Carolina Power & Light Co. Although Metropolitan Life did not actually get to bid on the issue because it insisted on a provision that would protect it against certain risks, the event was a clear indication that the Great Northern Nekoosa transaction was not a one-time transaction but part of a longer-term plan by Metropolitan Life to deal directly with issuers for publicly registered debt securities, thereby bypassing investment banking firms. It has been estimated that in 1989 Metropolitan Life directly bought several dozen publicly registered debt obligations with an estimated par value of $1 billion.[12]

Investment bankers' response to the practice of direct purchase of publicly registered securities is that as intermediaries they add value by searching their institutional client base, which increases the likelihood that the issuer will incur the lowest cost, after adjusting for the underwriting fees. By dealing with just a few institutional investors, investment bankers argue, issuers cannot be assured of obtaining funds at the lowest cost. In addition, investment bankers often provide another important role: they make a secondary market in the securities they issue. This improves the perceived liquidity of the issue and, as a result, reduces the cost to issuers.

The question of whether investment bankers can obtain lower cost funding (after accounting for underwriting fees) for issuers compared to a direct offering is an interesting empirical question. In July 1989, Corning Corporation asked its investment bankers (Goldman Sachs & Co. and Lazard Frères & Co.) to bid on a traditional public offering of $100 million in bonds, and invited Metropolitan Life and another institutional investor to bid on a private placement of $100 million in bonds.[13] Although the traditional public offering was selected, this does not indicate that Corning chose the cheapest offering mechanism, because one was a public offering and the other a proposed private placement—investors typically want a higher yield in a private placement due to the lack of liquidity.

This example may suggest the future road that some corporate issuers will take in soliciting bids for an offering. Moreover, as a result of SEC Rule 144A (which we discuss in the next chapter), there is greater liquidity in the private placement market, driving down the yields demanded by institutional investors. In fact, insurance companies such as Prudential Securities and Cigna have units that will bid on private placements and distribute the obligations to other institutional investors.

Investment bankers also face competition from the more sophisticated corporations that are establishing in-house groups to perform some of the activities traditionally done by investment banking firms. Here are a few examples. British Petroleum established an in-house investment bank, BP Finance. The activities this group has performed for its parent company are: (1) advising on multibillion dollar divestiture transactions, (2) directly issuing British Petroleum commercial paper, and (3) handling all foreign exchange trading.[14] DuPont has set up an M&A unit that does an average of 20 deals a year, ranging from $5 million to $500 million.[15] For all but a few acquisition deals, LDDS Communications has eliminated the services of investment bankers and uses its in-house expertise. According to the firm's chief financial officer, Charles Cannada, "We've done enough of these deals to know what we're doing."[16]

---

[12] Beth Selby, "End-Running the Street," *Institutional Investor* (September 1989).

[13] Ibid., 182.

[14] David Zigas, Gary Weiss, Ted Holden and Richard A. Melcher, "Corporate America's End Run," *Business Week* (November 5, 1990), pp. 124–130.

[15] Ibid.

[16] "Top Global CFOs," *Institutional Investor* (June 1993), p. 79.

Reassessing the Business

The biggest problem the managers of investment banks face, however, is determining which lines of business are the most beneficial to pursue. While investment bankers receive high marks in the creation of new financial products and strategies, many would receive failing marks in managerial economics/managerial accounting. We refer to topics such as product pricing and cost allocation, subjects that investment bankers apparently felt they did not need in the glory days of the 1980s.

Investment banks typically have done little study to determine how costs could be controlled. Fixed-overhead costs were often incurred with no concern for long-run implications for profits. In turn, overhead costs typically were arbitrarily allocated among activities, thereby masking the true costs of creating products or providing services. This caused misallocation of resources to products or services that were either unprofitable or did not generate an adequate return relative to the resources committed.

Subsidizing unprofitable or less-profitable activities with profits from other activities has caused dissension among investment bankers. In fact, several of the boutique firms were started when key investment bankers at a firm became disenchanted with the distribution of profits to the various business units. The merchant banking boutique Wasserstein, Perella & Co., for one, was created by two former M&A investment bankers at First Boston who were dissatisfied when the large M&A fees generated were used to subsidize other firm activities, particularly unprofitable trading activities. The goal of a "financial supermarket" may be one that investment bankers will find it uneconomic to pursue.

Investment banking firms must take several steps to remain profitable. Costs have to reflect the true cost of delivering products or services, which requires examining existing products and services to determine what costs are and how they can be reduced. Investment banking firms are taking that step.

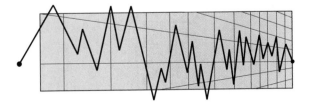

SUMMARY

Investment bankers provide two general functions: raising funds for clients and assisting clients in the sale or purchase of securities. In this chapter we have explained the various activities of investment banking and how these activities generate revenue. The activities include public offering of securities, public trading of securities, private placement of securities, securitization of assets, mergers and acquisitions, merchant banking, trading and creation of derivative instruments, and money management.

Not all firms are active participants in each activity. The premier firms, because of their size, reputation, presence in key markets, and customer base are called bulge-bracket firms. Major bracket firms do not have the same high status as the bulge-bracket firms but nevertheless provide full-line services. Submajor bracket firms, typically located in New York, focus on special investor groups and smaller issuing companies. Regional firms are located outside New York and serve regional issuers. Research firms, specialized firms, and merchant banks specialize in one activity and are referred to as boutiques.

Investment banking firms are facing increased competition that has forced them to reconsider their long-term business strategies. Competition comes not only from commercial banks, but also from new trading technologies, which are allowing institutional investors to execute trades without using investment banking firms as intermediaries, and the direct purchase by institutional investors of publicly registered securities from issuers.

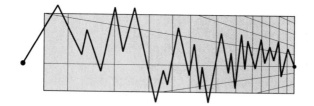

QUESTIONS

1. What are the four ways in which investment banking firms generate revenue?

2. What are the three ways in which an investment banking firm may be involved in the issuance of a new security?

3. What is meant by the underwriting function?

4. What is the difference between a firm-commitment underwriting arrangement and a best-efforts arrangement?

5. Explain at least three circumstances when investment banking firms must commit their own capital.

6. In a typical underwriting, why is it necessary to form an underwriting syndicate and a selling syndicate?

7 a. What is meant by the underwriting spread?

   b. How is the underwriting spread distributed between the lead manager, the members of the underwriting syndicate, and members of the selling syndicate?

8. What is meant by riskless arbitrage?

9. Suppose that one year from now there are the following two possible outcomes for securities X, Y, and Z:

Security	Price	Payoff in State #1	Payoff in State #2
X	$35	$25	$40
Y	30	15	60
Z	40	19	66

The prices of X, Y, and Z, are respectively $35, $30, and $40. Indicate whether a riskless arbitrage opportunity is possible?

10. Explain why an attempt to profit from a merger is not a riskless arbitrage.

11. What is meant by merchant banking?

12. What is meant by the securitization of assets?

13. How do dealers generate revenue with derivative instruments?

14. What is meant by a bulge-bracket firm?

15. a. What two measures can be used to determine the market share of an investment banking firm?

  b. What are the drawbacks of these measures?

16. The *Economist* of September 22, 1990, provided this description of recent activities of investment bankers:

    Ever since the Berlin Wall came down, the airlines, hotels and taxi ranks of Eastern Europe have been filled with business-suited Westerners hoping to make money in the wake of its collapse. In the first few months, many came, saw and left shaking their heads in disbelief at the mess. But fast on their heels came the professional advisers—accountants, management consultants, investment bankers—for whom the mess itself is money. Or may one day be.

  a. What types of functions can investment banks provide in restructuring the economies of Eastern Europe?

  b. What kinds of investment banking skills will be required?

  c. Can you think of potential problems that investment banks will face?

17. The three quotations below come from an *Institutional Investor*

article entitled "The Reeducation of Wall Street" in the January 1990 issue. Following each one there is a question to answer.

a. "In finance, size has no advantage. The most important thing is what you do not do." (Michel David-Weill, senior managing partner at the investment banking firm of Lazard Frères & Co.)

Discuss this assertion and indicate whether you agree or disagree.

b. "Market share is a proxy for how active we are in the market, and unless we're in the top group in our principal business we won't be credible enough with our customers." (Stephen Friedman, then vice chairman and chief executive officer of Goldman Sachs & Co.)

How is market share measured, and do you agree with the statement?

c. "For all their protestations that they are getting costs under control, so far most Wall Street executives are still ignoring basic above-the-line questions. As a body, the industry has attacked expenses and overcapacity only through layoffs. What it needs to do is analyze the real costs of a transaction or deal—or even a business line—by parsing it and coming up with a price for each of the component parts that go into servicing a client, from clearing to research to overhead to management."

Why is it necessary for investment banks to go through this process?

18. How do you think the trends enumerated below will impact the investment banking industry? As a senior manager at a bulge-bracket investment bank, how would you respond to these trends?

    a. Major multinational corporations increasingly set up their own in-house investment banks. These companies have in-house expertise on all major investment banking activities.

    b. Technological innovations such as CapitaLink that allow institutional investors to deal directly, in the absence of intermediaries, become increasingly common.

    c. Deregulation of financial markets eliminates the distinctions imposed by the Glass-Steagall Act between investment and commercial banking activities. J.P. Morgan, Bankers Trust, and other major banks are permitted to become major underwriters of corporate debt and equities.

19. Table 5-4 gives a breakdown of revenue of Merrill Lynch as reported in its 1993 Annual Report. Under the listing of revenues the following appears:

Investment Banking

Underwriting	$1,646,960
Strategic services	184,293
Total	$1,831,253

What do you think "Strategic services" means?

The Primary Markets

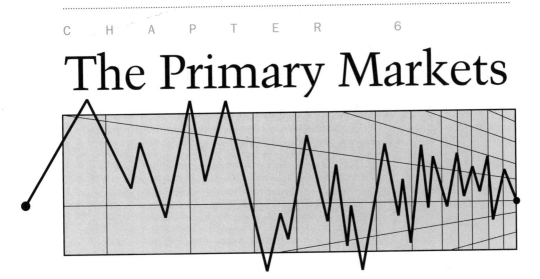

LEARNING OBJECTIVES

After reading this chapter you will understand:

• how the SEC regulates the distribution of newly issued securities.

• what a registration statement is.

• what SEC Rule 415 ("shelf registration") is.

• what a traditional private placement offering is.

• what Rule 144A is and its potential impact on the private placement market.

• what is a bought deal underwriting for a bond issue and why it is used.

• what a competitive bidding underwriting is and the different methods for determining the price of winning bidders.

• what a preemptive rights offering is and why a standby underwriting arrangement may be needed.

• what is meant by an integrated and segmented world capital market and the implications for fund raising.

• the motivation for firms to raise funds outside of their local capital market.

As we explained in Chapter 1, financial markets can be categorized as those dealing with financial claims that are newly issued, called the **primary market**; and those for exchanging financial claims previously issued, called the **secondary market**, or the market for seasoned securities. In this chapter we will focus on the primary market for securities. In the previous chapter we explained the role of investment bankers in the primary market. The next chapter will cover the secondary market.

REGULATION OF THE ISSUANCE OF SECURITIES

Underwriting activities are regulated by the Securities and Exchange Commission. The Securities Act of 1933 governs the issuance of securities. The act requires that a **registration statement** be filed with the SEC by the issuer of a security. The type of information contained in the registration statement is the nature of the business of the issuer, key provisions or features about the security, the nature of the investment risks associated with the security, and the background of management.[1] Financial statements must be included in the registration statement and they must be certified by an independent public accountant.[2]

The registration is actually divided into two parts. Part I is the **prospectus**. This part is typically distributed to the public as an offering of the securities. Part II contains supplemental information, which is not distributed to the public as part of the offering but is available from the SEC upon request.

The act provides for penalties in the form of fines and/or imprisonment if the information provided is inaccurate or material information is omitted. Moreover, investors who purchased the security are entitled to sue the issuer to recover damages if they incurred a loss as a result of misleading information. The underwriter may also be sued if it can be demonstrated that the underwriter did not conduct a reasonable investigation of the information reported by the issuer.

One of the most important duties of an underwriter is to perform **due diligence**. The following quote is taken from a court decision that explains the obligation of an underwriter to perform due diligence:

> An underwriter by participating in an offering constructively represents that statements made in the registration materials are complete and accurate. The investing public properly relies upon the underwriter to check the accuracy of the statements and the soundness of the offer; when the underwriter does not speak out, the investor reasonably assumes that there are no undisclosed material deficiencies. The representations in the registration statement are those of the underwriter as much as they are those of the issuer.[3]

The filing of a registration statement with the SEC does not mean that the security can be offered to the public. The registration statement must be reviewed and approved by the SEC's Division of Corporate Finance before the security can be offered to the public. Typically, the staff of this division will find a problem with the registration statement. The staff then sends a "letter of comments" or "deficiency letter" to the issuer explaining the problem it

---

[1] SEC Regulation S-K and the Industry Guidelines (SEC Securities Act Release No. 6384, March 3, 1982) specify the information that must be included in the registration statement.

[2] SEC Regulation S-X specifies the financial statements that must be disclosed.

[3] Chris-Craft Industries, Inc. *v*. Piper Aircraft Corp., 1973.

has encountered. The issuer must then remedy any problem by filing an amendment to the registration statement. If the SEC staff is then satisfied, they will issue an order declaring that the registration statement is "effective" and the underwriter can solicit sales. The approval of the SEC, however, does not mean that the securities have investment merit or are properly priced or that the information is accurate. It merely means that the appropriate information appears to have been disclosed.

The time interval between the initial filing of the registration statement and the time the registration statement becomes effective is referred to as the **waiting period**. During the waiting period, the SEC does allow the underwriters to distribute a preliminary prospectus. Because the prospectus is not effective, the cover page of the prospectus states this in red ink and as a result, the preliminary prospectus is commonly referred to as a **red herring**. During the waiting period, the underwriter cannot sell the security nor may it accept written offers from investors to buy the security.

Rule 415: Shelf Registration Rule

In 1982 the SEC approved Rule 415, which permits certain issuers to file a single registration document indicating that it intends to sell a certain amount of a certain class of securities at one or more times within the next two years.[4] Rule 415 is popularly referred to as the **shelf registration rule** because the securities can be viewed as sitting on a "shelf" and can be taken off that shelf and sold to the public without obtaining additional SEC approval.

In essence, the filing of a single registration document allows the issuer to come to market quickly because the sale of the security has been preapproved by the SEC. Prior to establishment of Rule 415, there was a lengthy period required before a security could be sold to the public. As a result, in a fast-moving market, issuers could not come to market quickly with an offering to take advantage of what it perceived to be attractive financing opportunities. For example, if a corporation felt that interest rates were attractive and wanted to issue a bond, it had to file a registration statement and could not issue the bond until the registration statement became effective. The corporation then takes the chance that during the waiting period interest rates will rise, making the bond offering more costly.

Continued Reporting Requirement

Any company that publicly offers a security in the United States becomes a **reporting company** and, as such, is subject to the Securities Exchange Act of 1934. This act specifies that a reporting company file with the SEC annual and periodic financial reports. The financial reports must be prepared according to generally accepted accounting principles (GAAP).

The cost of complying with the disclosure requirements can be quite costly for small companies. The disclosure requirements hold for non-U.S. companies as well who have publicly offered a security in the United States. Thus, non-U.S. companies must file financial statements not based on their home country's GAAP, but reconciled to U.S. GAAP. These disclosure requirements

---

[4] The issuer qualifies for Rule 415 registration if the securities are investment-grade securities and/or are the securities of companies that have historically filed a registration statement and whose securities comply with minimum flotation requirements.

have made the raising of funds in the United States by non-U.S. companies less attractive. However, as discussed later, the SEC has made access to the U.S. capital market easier for small companies and non-U.S. companies by amending the U.S. securities law.

Subject to certain exceptions, the reporting requirements also hold for companies whose securities are traded in the secondary market in the United States, despite the fact that the securities were not initially publicly offered in the United States. The significance of this (as we explain in Chapter 13) is that non-U.S. companies have been listing their common stock on United States stock exchanges. As such, companies that follow this practice would become a reporting company. Once again, the SEC has amended the U.S. securities law so that if certain requirements are satisfied, a non-U.S. company need not comply with the full disclosure requirements.

Private Placement of Securities

Public and private offerings of securities differ in terms of the regulatory requirements that must be satisfied by the issuer. The Securities Act of 1933 and the Securities Exchange Act of 1934 require that all securities offered to the general public must be registered with the SEC, unless there is a specific exemption. The Securities Acts allow three exemptions from federal registration. First, intrastate offerings—that is, securities sold only within a state—are exempt. Second, there is a small-offering exemption (Regulation A). Specifically, if the offering is for $1 million or less, the securities need not be registered. Finally, Section 4(2) of the 1933 Act exempts from registration "transactions by an issuer not involving any public offering." At the same time, the 1933 Act does not provide specific guidelines to identify what is a private offering or placement.

In 1982, the SEC adopted Regulation D, which sets forth the specific guidelines that must be satisfied to qualify for exemption from registration under Section 4(2). The guidelines require that, in general, the securities cannot be offered through any form of general advertising or general solicitation that would prevail for public offerings. Most importantly, the guidelines restrict the sale of securities to "sophisticated" investors. Such "accredited" investors are defined as those who (1) have the capability to evaluate (or who can afford to employ an advisor to evaluate) the risk and return characteristics of the securities, and (2) have the resources to bear the economic risks.[5]

The exemption of an offering does not mean that the issuer need not disclose information to potential investors. The issuer must still furnish the same information deemed material by the SEC. This is provided in a private placement memorandum, as opposed to a prospectus for a public offering. The distinction between the private placement memorandum and the prospectus is that the former does not include information deemed by the SEC as "non-material," whereas such information is required in a prospectus. Moreover, unlike a prospectus, the private placement memorandum is not subject to SEC review.

Rule 144A

In the United States, one restriction imposed on buyers of privately placed securities is that they may not be resold for two years after acquisition. Thus,

---

[5] Under the current law, an accredited investor is one who satisfies either a net worth test (at least $1 million excluding automobiles, home, and home furnishings) or an annual income test (at least $200,000 for a single individual, $300,000 for a couple for the last two years, with expectations of such income to continue for the current year).

there is no liquidity in the market for that time period. Buyers of privately placed securities must be compensated for the lack of liquidity which raises the cost to the issuer of the securities.

In April 1990, however, SEC Rule 144A became effective. This rule eliminates the two-year holding period by permitting large institutions to trade securities acquired in a private placement among themselves without having to register these securities with the SEC. Under Rule 144A, a large institution is defined as one holding at least $100 million of the security.

Private placements are now classified as Rule 144A offerings or non-Rule 144A offerings. The latter are more commonly referred to as traditional private placements. Rule 144A offerings are underwritten by investment bankers.

Rule 144A will encourage non-U.S. corporations to issue securities in the U.S. private placement market for two reasons. First, it will attract new large institutional investors into the market who were unwilling previously to buy private placements because of the requirement to hold the securities for two years. Such an increase in the number of institutional investors may encourage non-U.S. entities to issue securities. Second, foreign entities have been unwilling to raise funds in the United States prior to establishment of Rule 144A because they had to register their securities and furnish the necessary disclosure set forth by U.S. securities laws. Private placement requires less disclosure. Rule 144A also improves liquidity, reducing the cost of raising funds.

Figure 6-1 shows the results of an *Institutional Investor* survey of chief financial officers regarding private placements as a financing alternative. The majority of respondents indicated that they had a positive experience with Rule 144A and that most believed the rule increased liquidity in the private placement market. Almost half indicated that price was the most important factor in deciding to do a private placement. More than half responded that the cost of a private placement that they recently completed was less than it would have cost for a public issue.

VARIATIONS IN THE UNDERWRITING OF SECURITIES

In our discussion of the role of investment bankers in Chapter 5, we described the traditional syndication process; however, not all deals are underwritten using the traditional syndicate process. Variations include the "bought deal" for the underwriting of bonds, the auction process for both stocks and bonds, and a rights offering for common stock.

Bought Deal

The bought deal was introduced in the Eurobond market in 1981 when Credit Suisse First Boston purchased from General Motors Acceptance Corporation a $100 million issue without lining up an underwriting syndicate prior to the purchase. Thus, Credit Suisse First Boston did not use the traditional syndication process to diversify the capital risk exposure associated with an underwriting that we described in Chapter 5.

The mechanics of a bought deal—which has been used solely for debt securities—are as follows. The lead manager, or a group of managers, offers a

Figure 6-1

Institutional Investor CFO Survey on
Private Placement as a Financing Alternative

How important are private placements as a financing option for your company?

Extremely important	8.5%
Very important	14.6
Fairly important	17.1
Not very important	39.0
Unimportant	20.7

Have you completed a private placement within the past 12 months?

Yes	24.4%
No	75.6

Was this done under Securities and Exchange Commission Rule 144A?

Yes	28.4%
No	71.6

Do you anticipate doing a Rule 144A private placement within the next 12 months

Yes	12.5%
No	87.5

If you are considering a private placement of any kind, why?

Rates are favorable	36.2%
Strong investor interest	8.5
Persuasive proposal from bankers	6.4
Public market is less attractive	23.4
Other	25.5

If you did a Rule 144A placement, how would you characterize your experience?

Positive	67.6%
Negative	2.9
Neutral	29.4

Do you think Rule 144A has had the effect of increasing liquidity in the private-placement market?

Yes	90.4%
No	9.6

If you anticipate doing a private placement, what type will it be?

Debt	85.1%
Equity	1.1
Preferred stock	3.4
Combination	8.0

Other	2.3

If you have done a private placement in the last 12 months, how much did you raise?

Less than $10 million	2.6%
$10 million to $49 million	28.2
$50 million to $99 million	23.1
$100 million to $199 million	23.1
$200 million to $299 million	15.4
More than $300 million	7.7

How much do you anticipate placing in the next 12 months?

Less than $10 million	43.5%
$10 million to $49 million	24.2
$50 million to $99 million	21.0
$100 million to $199 million	6.5
$200 million to $299 million	4.8
More than $300 million	0.0

If you have done a private placement lately, how did its cost compare with what a public issue would have cost?

It was cheaper	54.2%
It was more expensive	27.1
It cost about the same	18.8

If you have done a Rule 144A private placement lately, did you make use of standardized offering documents?

Yes	43.3%
No	56.7

If so, would you make use of them again?

Yes	90.9%
No	9.1

What is the most important factor to your company in deciding to do private placement?

Price	48.2%
Placing power of the agent	7.0
Company's relationship with agent	4.4
Agressive, well-thought-out proposal	28.9
Other	11.4

Because of rounding some responses do not total 100 percent.

Source: *"A Private Matter," Institutional Investor (November 1994), p. 171. This copyrighted material is reprinted with permission from Institutional Investor, 488 Madison Avenue, New York, NY 10022.*

potential issuer of debt securities a firm bid to purchase a specified amount of the securities with a certain interest (coupon) rate and maturity. The issuer is given a day or so (it might even be a few hours) to accept or reject the bid. If the bid is accepted, the underwriting firm has "bought the deal." It can, in turn, sell the securities to other investment banking firms for distribution to their clients and/or distribute the securities to its own clients. Typically, the underwriting firm that buys the deal will have presold most of the issue to its institutional clients.

The bought deal appears to have found its way into the United States in mid-1985 when Merrill Lynch did a bond deal in which it was the only underwriter. The gross spread on the bond, a $50 million issue of Norwest Financial, was 0.268%. This is far less than the 0.7% gross spread indicated in Table 5-2 in Chapter 5. Merrill Lynch offered a portion of the securities to investors and the balance to other investment banking firms.

There are two reasons why some underwriting firms have found the bought deal attractive. First, prior to establishment of Rule 415, there was a lengthy period required before a security could be sold to the public. While Rule 415 gave certain issuers timing flexibility to take advantage of windows of opportunity in the global marketplace, it required that investment banking firms be prepared to respond on short notice to commit funds to a deal. This meant the underwriting firm had very little time to line up a syndicate, favoring the bought deal. However, a consequence of this is that underwriting firms needed to expand their capital so that they could commit greater amounts of funds to such deals.

Second, the risk of capital loss in a bought deal may not be as great as it may first appear. There are some deals that are so straightforward that a large underwriting firm may have enough institutional investor interest that the risks of distributing the issue at the reoffering price are small. Moreover, in the case of bonds, there are hedging strategies using the interest rate risk control tools, that we will discuss in Chapter 28, that reduce the risk of realizing a loss of selling the bonds at a price below the reoffering price.

Auction Process

Another variation for the issuance of securities is the auction process. In this method, the issuer announces the terms of the issue, and interested parties submit bids for the entire issue. The auction form is mandated for certain securities of regulated public utilities and many municipal debt obligations. It is commonly referred to as a **competitive bidding underwriting**. For example, suppose that a public utility wishes to issue $200 million of bonds. Various underwriters will form syndicates and bid on the issue. The syndicate that bids the lowest yield (i.e., the lowest cost to the issuer) wins the entire $200 million bond issue and then reoffers it to the public.

In a variant of the process, the bidders indicate the price they are willing to pay and the amount they are willing to buy. The security is then allocated to bidders on the basis of the highest bid price (lowest yield in the case of a bond) to lower bid prices (higher yield bids in the case of a bond) until the entire issue is allocated. For example, suppose that an issuer is offering $500 million of a bond issue, and nine bidders submitted the following yield bids:

Bidder	Amount (in millions)	Bid
A	$150	5.1%
B	110	5.2
C	90	5.2
D	100	5.3
E	75	5.4
F	25	5.4
G	80	5.5
H	70	5.6
I	85	5.7

Bidders A, B, C, and D will be allocated the amount of the issue for which they bid because they submitted the lowest yield bid. In total, they will receive $450 million of the $500 million to be issued. That leaves $50 million to be allocated to the next lowest bidders. Both E and F submitted the next lowest yield bid, 5.4%. In total, they bid for $100 million. Since the total they bid for exceeds the $50 million remaining to be allocated, they will receive an amount proportionate to the amount for which they bid. Specifically, E will be allocated three quarters ($75 million divided by $100 million) of the $50 million, or $37.5 million; and F will be allocated one quarter ($25 million divided by $100 million) of the $50 million, or $12.5 million.

The next question is the yield that all of the six winning bidders will have to pay for the amount of the issue allocated to them. One way in which a competitive bidding can occur is all bidders pay the highest winning yield bid (or, equivalently, the lowest winning price). In our example, all bidders would buy the amount allocated to them at 5.4%. This type of auction is referred to as a **single-price auction** or a **Dutch auction**. Another way is for each bidder to pay whatever they bid. This type of auction is called a **multiple-price auction**. As we explain in Chapter 20, both procedures are used in the auctioning of U.S. Treasury securities.

Using an auction allows corporate issuers to place newly issued debt obligations directly with institutional investors rather than using an underwriting firm. One step in this direction is the services provided by CapitaLink Securities, which links issuers directly to institutional investors using computerized auctions. In 1989, CapitaLink was successful in offering a new corporate bond issue directly to institutional investors via a computerized auction.[6] At the end of 1990, there were 125 major institutions and 16 prospective issuers that had joined the service.[7] In February 1988, Great Northern Nekoosa was able to place $75 million in publicly registered bonds directly with Metropolitan Life Insurance Company.[8]

Preemptive Rights Offering

A corporation can issue new common stock directly to existing shareholders via a **preemptive rights offering**. A preemptive right grants existing shareholders the right to buy some proportion of the new shares issued at a price below market value. The price at which the new shares can be purchased is called

---

[6] Beth Selby, "End-Running the Underwriters," *Institutional Investor* (June 1989), p. 27.

[7] Chris Welles and Monica Roman, "The Future of Wall Street," *Business Week* (November 5, 1990), p. 122.

[8] Beth Selby, "End-Running the Street," *Institutional Investor* (September 1989), p. 181.

the **subscription price**. A rights offering insures that current shareholders may maintain their proportionate equity interest in the corporation. In the United States, the practice of issuing common stock via a preemptive rights offering is uncommon. In other countries it is much more common; in some countries, it is the only means by which a new offering of common stock may be sold.

For the shares sold via a preemptive rights offering, the underwriting services of an investment banker are not needed. However, the issuing corporation may use the services of an investment banker for the distribution of common stock that is not subscribed to. A **standby underwriting arrangement** will be used in such instances. This arrangement calls for the underwriter to buy the unsubscribed shares. The issuing corporation pays a **standby fee** to the investment banking firm.

To demonstrate how a rights offering works, the effect on the economic wealth of shareholders, and how the terms set forth in a rights offering affect whether or not the issuer will need an underwriter, we will use an illustration. Suppose that the market price of the stock of ABC Corporation is $20 per share and that there are 30,000 shares outstanding. Thus, the capitalization of this firm is $600,000. Suppose that the management of ABC Corporation is considering a rights offering in connection with the issuance of 10,000 new shares. Each current shareholder would receive one right for every three shares owned. The terms of the rights offering are as follows: for three rights and $17 (the subscription price) a new share can be acquired. The subscription price must always be less than the market price or the rights will not be exercised. However, as we will see, the amount of the discount (i.e., the difference between the market price and subscription price) is relevant. In our illustration, the subscription price is 15% ($3/$20) below the market price.[9]

In addition to the number of rights and the subscription price, there are two other elements of a rights offering that are important. First is the choice to transfer the rights. This is done by selling the right in the open market. This is critical since, as we will see, the right has a value and that value can be captured by selling the right. The second element is the time when the right expires—when it can not longer be used to acquire the stock. Typically, the time period before a right expires is short.

The value of a right can be found by taking the price of a share before the rights offering and subtracting the price of a share after the rights offering.[10] That is,

value of a right = price before rights offering – price after rights offering

Or, equivalently ,

value of a right = share price rights on – share price ex rights

Table 6-1 shows the impact of the rights offering on the price of a share for the ABC Corporation. The price after the rights offering will be $19.25. Therefore, the value of a right is $0.75 ($20 – $19.25).

---

[9] Note that the same results can be achieved by issuing one right per share but requiring three rights plus the subscription price for a new share (except for rounding-off problems and implications for the value of one right discussed below).

[10] Alternatively, the value of a right can be found as follows:

$$\frac{\text{price after rights offering – subscription price}}{\text{number of rights required to buy a share}}$$

Table 6-1
Analysis of Rights Offering on the Market Price of ABC Corp.

Before rights issue	
Capitalization	$600,000
Number of shares	30,000
Share price (rights on)	$ 20.00
After issuance of shares via rights offering	
Number of shares	40,000 (= 30,000 + 10,000)
Capitalization	$ 770,000 (= $600,000 + 10,000 × $17)
Share price (ex rights)	$ 19.25 (= $770,000 / 40,000)
Value of one right	$ 0.75 (= $20.00 – $19.25)
Net gain or loss to initial stockholder	
Loss per share due to dilution	$ 0.75 (= 3.75% × $20)
Gain per share from selling or exercising a right	$ 0.75
Net gain or loss	$ 0

The difference between the price before the rights offering and after the rights offering expressed as a percentage of the original price is called the **dilution effect** of the rights issue. In the present case, the dilution effect is $0.75/$20, or 3.75%. The dilution is larger, the larger the ratio of old and new shares, and the larger the discount.[11]

The last section of Table 6-1 shows the net gain or loss to the initial shareholder as a result of the rights offering. The loss per share due to dilution is $0.75, but that is exactly equal to the value of a right which, if the shareholder desires, can be sold in the market. This result is important because it shows that the rights offering as such will not affect the sum of the value of the share without rights (referred to as ex rights) plus the value of the rights he receives, no matter how much the dilution or the initial discount offered. This is because a larger dilution is exactly compensated by the increase in the value of the rights.

However, this does not mean that the size of the discount and dilution is irrelevant for the welfare of the stockholders. On the contrary, the value of one right will, in general, not be constant during the period over which the rights may be exercised. In our example, it is $0.75 on the day the rights begin trading and are exercisable. However, for any successive day between this day and the last day that the rights may be exercised, the value of the rights will tend to be equal to the difference between the market price of the stock at that date and the subscription price.

---

[11] Specifically:

$$\text{dilution effect} = \frac{\text{discount\%}}{1 + (\text{ratio of old to new shares})}$$

In our illustration the discount is 15% and the ratio of old to new shares is 30,000/10,000 or 3, so the dilution effect is 15%/4, or 3.75%.

This is because in a perfect market, with no transaction costs, any difference can be arbitraged (risklessly), forcing the stock and the right to be priced consistently. Thus, suppose that just after the rights issuance the price of the stock is at $19.25 as expected, but at the same time the price of a right is underpriced selling at only $0.60. Then one can arbitrage by buying the "cheap" rights, exercising them by paying the subscription price of $17, and receiving shares at the cost of $18.80 which can be simultaneously sold at $19.25, for a gain of $0.45 per share. This arbitrage activity will drive the price of the shares and the rights to be priced consistently so as to not allow any arbitrage profit.

In reality, however, there are transaction costs in this arbitrage including at least the double commission. Therefore, the price of the right may remain somewhat lower than the difference between the market price of the shares and the subscription price.

This has two implications. First, if the market price of the stock were to fall by more than the initial value of the rights, then the rights would become worthless and remain worthless as long as the market price remained below that critical level. From the point of view of the issuing company, this would mean that some rights would fail to be exercised and therefore the firm would be unable to raise the amount of financing it sought. For this reason some would suggest that the firm should rely on the services of an investment banker who would commit to buy any unsold shares at the subscription price.

The risk of a rights offering failing will depend on the value of the right relative to the volatility of the stock price; but the value of the right (given the shares to be issued) depends on the discount chosen in designing the issue. Suppose that the subscription is to occur within one month and the monthly price volatility (as measured by the standard deviation) can be estimated. Then, by the choice of an appropriately high discount and resulting value of the right, the issuer can make the probability of failure as small as desired (if there are no other constraints on the discount). Therefore, we conclude that in general the rights offering can be so designed that the services of an investment banker are not needed, which can reduce substantially the cost of the issue to shareholders.[12]

There is another consideration which suggests the desirability of designing the rights offering with a relatively high discount. We have already seen that the value of the right will be unfavorably affected by transaction costs. In addition, these costs will reduce the net amount received by a stockholder who decides to sell his rights rather than exercise them. For both reasons it is desirable to keep transaction costs low. Since transaction cost per dollar transacted increases the smaller the share price, it is desirable to design the offering so that the right has a large unit value, which means a relatively high discount.

There is potential disadvantage, however, to designing a rights offering with a high discount. Some stockholders fail to either exercise or sell their rights. This may occur because they did not receive notice of the rights offering and its terms, or because they simply elected not to act. Stockholders who fail to act will suffer a net loss per share equal to the value of the right per share times the number of shares held. The loss, then, is equal to the dilution times the value

---

[12] The value of the rights is also affected by the choice described in the previous footnote. Clearly, the value of one right is three times larger if a shareholder is given one right per three shares larger than if the shareholder is given one right per share but requires three shares to buy one unit of the stock. In other words, the value of rights are enhanced by giving one right to each 1/y shares than one right per share and requiring 1/y rights to buy one new share.

of the holdings; the dilution is no longer compensated for from the sale of the rights and thus the loss increases with the value of the rights. It can be argued that when the rights have greater value, stockholders are more likely to make use of their opportunity, though there is no empirical evidence on this point.

It seems safe to conclude that there is a strong case for designing an offering that makes the value of the rights substantial, but the greater the value the more it behooves the board of directors to make efforts to ensure that stockholders are apprised of the economic value of their rights. The proportion of stockholders that are "hard to locate" will differ from one circumstance to the other and there are a variety of methods for reaching such stockholders. Each method has differential costs, making the problem of choice among alternatives somewhat important.

When there is no investment banker acting as the residual buyer, and there is the probability that at least some of the stockholders will fail to either exercise or sell their rights, the risk exists that some of the stock will remain unsold. This danger can be eliminated by making available more stock to those who will exercise the right through instituting the privilege of over subscribing—that is, allowing stockholders to buy more shares at the subscription price in proportion to their purchases. In this way, if there are some nonexercised rights, they are allocated to the oversubscribers.

There are various possible criterion for this allocation. One reasonable gauge may be to allocate what is available first to the stockholders of record before the issue, ensuring that at least a portion of the losses due to the nonexercisers will remain within the stockholder family. Because one oversubscription is worth as much as one right, there is a substantial possibility that the abundance of oversubscription will absorb the entire number of shares not exercised during the primary offering. (Warning: Oversubscription could cause the rights to be overpriced!)

WORLD CAPITAL MARKETS INTEGRATION AND FUND RAISING IMPLICATIONS

An entity may seek funds outside its local capital market with the expectation of doing so at a lower cost than if its funds are raised in its local capital market. Whether this is possible depends on the degree of integration of capital markets. At the two extremes, the world capital markets can be classified as either **completely segmented** or **completely integrated**.

In the former case, investors in one country are not permitted to invest in the securities issued by an entity in another country. As a result, in a completely segmented market, the required return of securities of comparable risk that are traded in different capital markets throughout the world will be different even after adjusting for taxes and foreign-exchange rates. This implies that an entity may be able to raise funds in the capital market of another country at a cost that is lower than doing so in its local capital market.

At the other extreme, in a completely integrated capital market there are no restrictions to prevent investors from investing in securities issued in any capital market throughout the world. In such an ideal world capital market, the required return on securities of comparable risk will be the same in all capital markets after adjusting for taxes and foreign-exchange rates. This implies that the cost of funds will be the same regardless of where in the capital markets throughout the world a fund-seeking entity elects to raise funds.

Real-world capital markets are neither completely segmented nor completely integrated, but fall somewhere in between. Such markets can be referred to as **mildly segmented** or **mildly integrated**. This implies that in a world capital market characterized in this way, there are opportunities to raise funds at a lower cost in some capital markets outside the local capital market.

It is important to emphasize that we are talking about capital markets in general. There are markets for different instruments. More specifically, there are equity (common stock) markets and debt markets. The degree of integration can be different for these two markets. In Chapter 13 we will discuss the evidence on the degree of integration of equity markets.

MOTIVATION FOR RAISING FUNDS OUTSIDE OF THE DOMESTIC MARKET

There are four reasons why a corporation may seek to raise funds outside of its domestic market. First, in some countries, large corporations seeking to raise a substantial amount of funds may have no other choice but to obtain financing in either the foreign-market sector of another country or the Euromarket. This is because the fund-raising corporation's domestic market is not fully developed to be able to satisfy its demand for funds on globally competitive terms. Governments of developing countries have used these markets in seeking funds for government-owned corporations that they are privatizing.

The second reason is that there may be opportunities for obtaining a reduced cost of funding (taking into consideration issuing costs) compared to that available in the domestic market. As explained in Chapter 16, in the case of debt the cost will reflect two factors: (1) the risk-free rate which is accepted as the interest rate on a U.S. Treasury security with the same maturity (called the **base rate;**) and (2) a **spread** to reflect the greater risks that investors perceive as being associated with the issue or issuer.

A corporate borrower who seeks reduced funding costs is seeking to reduce the spread. With the integration of capital markets throughout the world, such opportunities have diminished. Nevertheless, as discussed in the next chapter, there are imperfections in capital markets throughout the world that prevent complete integration and thereby may permit a reduced cost of funds. These imperfections, or market frictions, occur because of differences in: security regulations in various countries, tax structures, restrictions imposed on regulated institutional investors, and the credit risk perception of the issuer. In the case of common stock, a corporation is seeking to gain a higher value for its stock and to reduce the market impact cost of floating a large offering.

The third reason to seek funds in foreign markets is a desire by corporate treasurers to diversify their source of funding in order to reduce reliance on domestic investors. In the case of equities, diversifying funding sources may encourage foreign investors who have different perspectives of the future performance of the corporation. There are two additional advantages of raising foreign equity funds from the perspective of U.S. corporations: (1) some market observers believe that certain foreign investors are more loyal to corporations and look at long-term performance rather than short-term performance as do investors in the U.S.;[13] and (2) diversifying the investor base reduces the dominance of U.S. institutional holdings and its impact on corporate governance.

Finally, a corporation may issue a security denominated in a foreign currency as part of its overall foreign-currency management. For example, consider a U.S. corporation that plans to build a factory in a foreign country where the construction costs will be denominated in the foreign currency. Also assume that the corporation plans to sell the output of the factory in the same foreign country. Therefore, the revenue will be denominated in the foreign currency. The corporation then faces exchange-rate risk: the construction costs are uncertain in U.S. dollars because during the construction period the U.S. dollar may depreciate relative to the foreign currency. Also, the projected revenue is uncertain in U.S. dollars because the foreign currency may depreciate relative to the U.S. dollar. Suppose that the corporation arranges debt financing for the plant in which it receives the proceeds in the foreign currency and the liabilities are denominated in the foreign currency. This financing arrangement can reduce exchange-rate risk because the proceeds received will be in the foreign currency and will be used to pay the construction costs, and the projected revenue can be applied to service the debt obligation.

Corporate Financing Week asked the corporate treasurers of several multinational corporations why they used nondomestic markets to raise funds.[14] Their responses reflected one or more of the reasons cited above. For example, the director of corporate finance of General Motors said that the company uses the Eurobond market with the objective of "diversifying funding sources, attract new investors and achieve comparable, if not, cheaper financing." A managing director of Sears Roebuck stated that the company "has a long-standing policy of diversifying geographical [funding] sources and instruments to avoid reliance on any specific market, even if the cost is higher." He further stated that "Sears cultivates a presence in the international market by issuing every three years or so."

SUMMARY

The primary market involves the distribution to investors of newly issued securities. The SEC is responsible for regulating the issuance of newly issued securities, with the major provisions set forth in the Securities Act of 1933.

---

[13] "U.S. Firms Woo Investors in Europe and Japan," *Euromoney Corporate Finance* (March 1985), p. 45; and Peter O'Brien, "Underwriting International Corporate Equities," Chapter 4 in Robert L. Kuhn (ed.), *Capital Raising and Financial Structure*, Vol. II in The Library of Investment Banking (Homewood, IL: Dow Jones-Irwin, 1990), p. 120.

[14] Victoria Keefe, "Companies Issue Overseas for Diverse Reasons," *Corporate Financing Week* (November 25, 1991, Special Supplement), pp. 1 and 9.

The act requires that the issuer file a registration statement with the SEC and that the registration statement be approved by the SEC.

Rule 415, the shelf registration rule, permits certain issuers to file a single registration document indicating that it intends to sell a certain amount of a certain class of securities at one or more times within the next two years.

Variations in the underwriting process include the bought deal for the underwriting of bonds, the auction process for both stocks and bonds, and pre-emptive rights offering for underwriting common stock.

A private placement is different from the public offering of securities in terms of the regulatory requirements that must be satisfied by the issuer. If an issue qualifies as a private placement, it is exempt from the more complex registration requirements imposed on public offerings. Rule 144A will contribute to the growth of the private placement market by improving the liquidity of securities issued in this market.

World capital markets can be classified as either completely segmented or completely integrated. Real-world capital markets are neither completely segmented or completely integrated but are best described as mildly segmented or mildly integrated. In a world capital market that can be characterized in this way, there are opportunities to raise funds at a lower cost in some capital markets outside the local capital market.

A firm may seek to raise funds outside of its domestic capital market for one or more of the following reasons: (1) the amount sought can not be accommodated by its local market, (2) there is an opportunity to raise funds at a lower cost, (3) the diversification of its funding sources is sought, and (4) as part of its overall currency management it needs funds denominated in another currency.

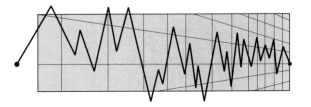

QUESTIONS

1. a. What is a registration statement?

   b. What is a prospectus?

   c. What is meant by the waiting period?

2. The Securities Act of 1933 and the Securities Exchange Act of 1934 require that all securities offered to the general public must be registered with the SEC, unless there is a specific exemption. The Securities Acts allow three exemptions from federal registration. What are the three exemptions?

3. What is meant by a bought deal?

4. Why do bought deals expose investment banking firms to greater capital risk than the traditional underwriting process?

5. How has Rule 415 encouraged investment banking firms to

underwrite issues using the bought deal rather than the traditional underwriting process?

6. An underwriter is responsible for performing due diligence before offering a security to investors. What does due diligence mean?

7. Suppose that a corporation is issuing a bond on a competitive bidding basis. The corporation has indicated that it will issue $200 million of an issue. The following yield bids and the corresponding amounts were submitted:

Bidder	Amount (in millions)	Bid
A	$ 20	7.4%
B	40	7.5
C	10	7.5
D	50	7.5
E	40	7.6
F	20	7.6
G	10	7.7
H	10	7.7
I	20	7.8
J	25	7.9
K	28	7.9
L	20	8.0
M	18	8.1

a. Who are the winning bidders?

b. How much of the security will be allocated to each winning bidder?

c. If this auction is a single-price auction, at what yield will each winning bidder pay the amount they will be awarded?

d. If this auction is a multiple-price auction, at what yield will each winning bidder pay the amount they will be awarded?

8. Indicate whether you agree or disagree with the following statement: "A preemptive rights

offering always requires the issuer to use the services of an investment banker to underwrite the unsubscribed shares."

9. The market price of the stock of the Bernstein Corporation is $50 per share and there are 1 million shares outstanding. Suppose that the management of this corporation is considering a rights offering in connection with the issuance of 500,000 new shares. Each current shareholder would receive one right for every two shares owned. The terms of the rights offering are as follows: for two rights and $30 (the subscription price) a new share can be acquired.

a. What would the share price be after the rights offering?

b. What is the value of one right?

c. Demonstrate the effect on the economic well-being of the initial shareholders as a result of the rights offering.

10. Suppose that the Bernstein Corporation in the previous question set the subscription price at $20 per share instead of $30.

a. What would the share price be after the rights offering?

b. What is the value of one right?

c. Demonstrate the effect on the economic well-being of the initial shareholders as a result of the rights offering.

11. Explain why the difference between the initial share price and the new share price is relevant in designing a rights offering.

12. The following statements come from the December 24, 1990, issue of *Corporate Financing Week:*

As in the public market, growth in the private placement market was slowed this year by a rise in interest rates that pushed many issuers to the sidelines, by the Mideast crisis and by a flight to quality by investors. . . . Foreign private placements saw a marked increase due to Rule 144A.

a. What are the key distinctions between a private placement and a public offering?

b. Why would Rule 144A have increased foreign private placements?

13. What is meant by a completely integrated world capital market?

14. How can the integration of world capital markets best be described and what are the implications for fund raising?

15. Why might a corporation seek to raise funds outside of its local capital market even if it results in a higher cost of funds?

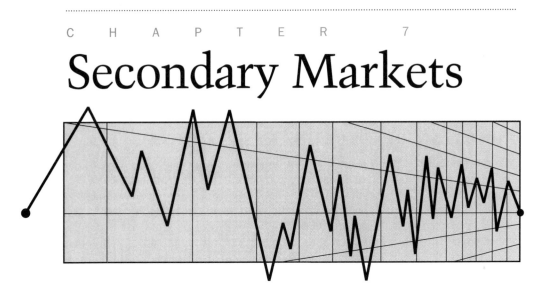

CHAPTER 7

Secondary Markets

LEARNING OBJECTIVES

After reading this chapter you will understand:

- the definition of a secondary market.

- the need for secondary markets for financial assets.

- the various trading locations for securities.

- the difference between a continuous and a call market.

- the requirements of a perfect market.

- frictions that cause actual financial markets to differ from a perfect market.

- trading mechanisms such as the types of orders.

- why brokers are necessary.

- the role of a dealer as a market maker and the costs associated with market making.

- what is meant by the operational efficiency of a market.

- what is meant by the pricing efficiency of a market and the different forms of pricing efficiency.

- the implications of pricing efficiency for market participants.

- transaction costs which include commissions, fees, execution costs, and opportunity costs.

The secondary market is where already-issued financial assets are traded. The key distinction between a primary market and a secondary market is that in the secondary market the issuer of the asset does not receive funds from the buyer. Rather, the existing issue changes hands in the secondary market, and funds flow from the buyer of the asset to the seller. In this chapter, we will explain the various features of secondary markets. These features are common to any type of financial instrument traded. We take a closer look at individual markets in later chapters.

FUNCTION OF SECONDARY MARKETS

It is worthwhile to review once again the function of secondary markets. It is in the secondary market where an issuer of securities, whether the issuer is a corporation or a governmental unit, may be provided with regular information about the value of the security. The periodic trading of the asset reveals to the issuer the consensus price that the asset commands in an open market. Thus, firms can discover what value investors attach to their stocks, and firms and noncorporate issuers can observe the prices of their bonds and the implied interest rates investors expect and demand from them. Such information helps issuers assess how well they are using the funds acquired from earlier primary market activities, and it also indicates how receptive investors would be to new offerings.

The other service a secondary market offers issuers is that it provides the opportunity for the original buyers of the asset to reverse their investment by selling it for cash. Unless investors are confident that they can shift from one financial asset to another as they may deem necessary, they would naturally be reluctant to buy any financial asset. Such reluctance would harm potential issuers in one of two ways: either issuers would be unable to sell new securities at all or they would have to pay a high rate of return, as investors would demand greater compensation for the expected illiquidity of the securities.

Investors in financial assets receive several benefits from a secondary market. Such a market obviously offers them liquidity for their assets as well as information about the assets' fair or consensus values. Further, secondary markets bring together many interested parties and so can reduce the costs of searching for likely buyers and sellers of assets. Moreover, by accommodating many trades, secondary markets keep the cost of transactions low. By keeping the costs of both searching and transacting low, secondary markets encourage investors to purchase financial assets.

TRADING LOCATIONS

One indication of the usefulness of secondary markets is that they exist throughout the world. Here, we give just a few examples of these markets.

In the United States, secondary trading of common stock occurs in a number of trading locations. Many shares are traded on major national stock exchanges and regional stock exchanges, which are organized and somewhat regulated markets in specific geographical locations. Additional significant trading in stocks takes place on the so-called over-the-counter (OTC) market, which is a geographically dispersed group of traders who are linked to one another via telecommunication systems. Some bonds are traded on exchanges; however, most trading in bonds in the United States and throughout the world occurs in the OTC market.

The London International Stock Exchange (ISE) is basically an over-the-counter market whose members are in various places but communicate directly with one another through sophisticated electronic and computer facilities. Assets traded on the ISE include stocks of domestic and international firms as well as a wide array of bonds and options. Germany has eight organized stock exchanges, the most important of which is the Frankfurt Stock Exchange which handles over half of the turnover on listed shares and also trades in bonds and currencies. The Paris Bourse, another organized exchange located in a specific place, is France's main secondary market for stocks, bonds, and some derivative securities. Japan has eight exchanges; the largest is the Tokyo Stock Exchange where trading in stocks, bonds, and futures takes place. The second largest is the Osaka Stock Exchange. The Stock Exchange of Hong Kong Limited (SEHK) is an organized secondary market for shares and bonds in that major Southeast Asian city.

MARKET STRUCTURES

Many secondary markets are **continuous,** which means that prices are determined continuously throughout the trading day as buyers and sellers submit orders. For example, given the order flow at 10 A.M., the market clearing price of a stock on some organized stock exchange may be $70; at 11 A.m. of the same trading day, the market clearing price of the same stock, but with different order flows, may be $70.75. Thus, in a continuous market, prices may vary with the pattern of orders reaching the market and not because of any change in the basic situation of supply and demand. We will return to this point later.

A contrasting market structure is the **call market**, in which orders are batched or grouped together for simultaneous execution at the same price. That is, at certain times in the trading day (or possibly more than once in a day), a market maker holds an auction for a stock. The auction may be oral or written. In either case, the auction will determine or "fix" the market-clearing price at a particular time of the trading day. This use of the word "fix" is traditional and not pejorative or suggestive of illegal activity. For example, the *Financial Times* reports on the activities of the London gold bullion market, which is a call market, and records prices set at the "morning fix" and the "afternoon fix." These fixes take place at the two call auctions which are held daily. Until the mid 1980s, the Paris Bourse was a call market, with auctions for large stocks being oral and auctions for smaller issues being written. It has since become a continuous market and trading takes place "en continu."

Currently, some markets are mixed, using elements of the continuous and the call frameworks. For example, the New York Stock Exchange begins trading (at 9:30 A.M.) with a call auction. With opening prices set in that manner, trading proceeds in a continuous way until closing. The Tokyo Stock Exchange also begins trading in large stocks with an auction. Exchanges in Germany and Switzerland still use the call market system to a significant extent.

PERFECT MARKETS

In order to explain the characteristics of secondary markets, we will first describe a "perfect market" for a financial asset. Then we can show how common occurrences in real markets keep them from being theoretically perfect.

In general, a perfect market results when the number of buyers and sellers is sufficiently large, and all participants are small enough relative to the market so that no individual market agent can influence the commodity's price. Consequently, all buyers and sellers are price takers, and the market price is determined where there is equality of supply and demand. This condition is more likely to be satisfied if the commodity traded is fairly homogeneous (for example, corn or wheat).

There is more to a perfect market than market agents being price takers. It is also required that there are no transactions costs or impediments that interfere with the supply and demand of the commodity. Economists refer to these various costs and impediments as "frictions." The costs associated with frictions generally result in buyers paying more than in the absence of frictions, and/or sellers receiving less.

In the case of financial markets, frictions would include:

- commissions charged by brokers.
- bid-ask spreads charged by dealers.
- order handling and clearance charges.
- taxes (notably on capital gains) and government-imposed transfer fees.
- costs of acquiring information about the financial asset.
- trading restrictions, such as exchange-imposed restrictions on the size of a position in the financial asset that a buyer or seller may take.
- restrictions on market makers.
- halts to trading that may be imposed by regulators where the financial asset is traded.

SECONDARY MARKET TRADING MECHANICS

In this chapter we describe the key features involved in secondary market trading of securities. In Chapter 13, we will discuss trading arrangements that developed specifically for coping with the trading needs of institutional investors.

Types of Orders

An investor must provide information to the broker about the conditions under which he will transact. The parameters that the investor must provide are the specific security, the number of shares in the case of common stock and the quantity in the case of bonds, and the type of order. We will now describe seven types of orders that an investor can place.

Market orders—When an investor wants to buy or sell a share of common stock, the price and conditions under which the order is to be executed must be communicated to a broker. The simplest type of order is the **market order**, an order executed at the best price available in the market. The best price is assured by requiring that when more than one buy order or sell order reaches the market at the same time, the order with the best price is given priority.

Thus, buyers offering a higher price are given priority over those offering a lower price; sellers asking a lower price are given priority over those asking a higher price.

In the case of common stock traded on an exchange, another priority rule is needed to handle the receipt of more than one order at the same price. Most often, the priority in executing such orders is based on the time of arrival of the order—first orders in are the first orders executed—although there may be a rule that gives higher priority to certain types of market participants over others who are seeking to transact at the same price. For example, an exchange may classify orders as either "public orders" or orders of those member-firms dealing for their own account. Exchange rules require that public orders be given priority over orders of member-firms dealing for their own account.

Limit orders—The danger of a market order is that an adverse move may take place between the time the investor places the order and the time the order is executed. For example, suppose Ms. Hieber wants to buy the stock of Walt Disney Corporation at $42, but not at $44. If she places a market order when the stock is trading at $42, Ms. Hieber faces the risk that the price will rise before her order is carried out, and she will have to pay an unacceptable price. Similarly, suppose Ms. Davis owns Ford Motors and wants to sell the stock at its current price of $65, but not at $63. If Ms. Davis places a market order to sell Ford at the same time Ford announces a major recall of one of its cars, the stock would be sold at the best available price, but the price might be unacceptable to Ms. Davis.

To avoid the danger of adverse unexpected price changes, an investor can place a **limit order** that designates a price threshold for the execution of the trade. The limit order is a conditional order—it is executed only if the limit price or a better price can be obtained. A **buy limit order** indicates that the security may be purchased only at the designated price or lower. A **sell limit order** indicates that the security may be sold at the designated price or higher. Using our earlier examples, Ms. Hieber, who wants to purchase Disney but will not want to pay more than $42, can place a buy limit order at $42; and Ms. Davis can place a sell limit order for $65.

The danger of a limit order is that there is no guarantee that it will be executed at all. The designated price may simply not be obtainable. On an exchange, a limit order that is not executable at the time it reaches the market is recorded in a **limit order book**. The orders recorded in this book are treated equally with other orders in terms of priority.

Stop orders—Another type of conditional order is the **stop order**, which specifies that the order is not to be executed until the market moves to a designated price, at which time it becomes a market order. A **stop order to buy** specifies that the order is not to be executed until the market rises to a designated price (i.e., trades or bids at or above the designated price). A **stop order to sell** specifies that the order is not to be executed until the market price falls below a designated price (i.e., trades or offers at or below the designated price). Once the designated price in the stop order is reached, the order becomes a market order.

A stop order is useful when an investor cannot watch the market constantly. Profits can be preserved or losses minimized on a security position by allowing market movements to trigger a trade. In a sell stop order, the designated price is less than the current market price of the security. By contrast, in a sell limit order the designated price is greater than the current market price of the security. In a buy stop order the designated price is greater than the current market price of the security. However, in a buy limit order the designated price is less than the current market price of the security. This is depicted in Figure 7-1.

For example, suppose Ms. Hieber is uncertain about buying the stock of Disney at its current price of $42 but wants to be sure that if the price moves up she does not pay more than $45. If she places a stop order to buy at $45, the order becomes a market order when the price reaches $45. In the case of the sale of Ford by Ms. Davis, if she wants to assure that she will not sell at less than $60 a share, she can place a stop order to sell at $60.

There are two dangers associated with stop orders. Security prices sometimes exhibit abrupt price changes, so the direction of a change in a security's price may be quite temporary, resulting in the premature trading of a security. Also, once the designated price is reached, the stop order becomes a market order and is subject to the uncertainty of the execution price noted earlier for market orders.

A stop-limit order is a hybrid of a stop order and a limit order, in that it is a stop order that designates a price limit. In contrast to the stop order, which becomes a market order if the stop is reached, the stop-limit order becomes a limit order if the stop is reached. The order can be used to cushion the market impact of a stop order. The investor may limit the possible execution price after the activation of the stop. As with a limit order, the limit price may never be reached after the order is activated, which therefore defeats one purpose of the stop order—to protect a profit or limit a loss.

Market-if-touched orders—An investor may also enter a **market-if-touched order**. This order becomes a market order if a designated price is reached. However, a market-if-touched order to buy becomes a market order if the

Figure 7-1
Comparison of Limit Orders and Stop Orders

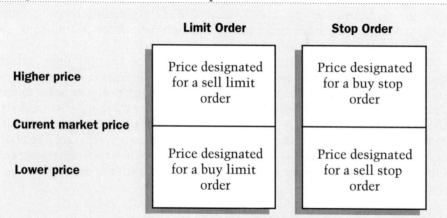

	Limit Order	Stop Order
Higher price	Price designated for a sell limit order	Price designated for a buy stop order
Current market price		
Lower price	Price designated for a buy limit order	Price designated for a sell stop order

market *falls* to a given price, while a stop order to buy becomes a market order if the market *rises* to a given price. Similarly, a market-if-touched order to sell becomes a market order if the market rises to a specified price, while the stop order to sell becomes a market order if the market falls to a given price. We can think of the stop order as an order designed to get out of an existing position at an acceptable price (without specifying the exact price), and the market-if-touched order as an order designed to get into a position at an acceptable price (also without specifying the exact price).

Time-specific orders—Orders may be placed to buy or sell at the open or close of trading for the day—that is, time-specific orders. An opening order indicates a trade to be executed only in the opening range for the day, and a closing order indicates a trade to be executed only within the closing range for the day.

An investor may enter orders that contain order cancellation provisions. A **fill-or-kill** order must be executed as soon as it reaches the trading floor or it is immediately canceled. Orders may designate the time period for which the order is effective—a day, week, or month, or perhaps by a given time within the day. An **open order**, or **good-till-canceled order**, is good until the order is specifically canceled.

Size-related orders—For common stock, orders are also classified by their size. A **round lot** is typically 100 shares of a stock. An **odd lot** is defined as less than a round lot; for example, an order of 75 shares of Digital Equipment Corporation (DEC) is an odd lot order. An order of 350 shares of DEC includes an odd lot portion of 50 shares. A **block trade** is defined on the NYSE as an order of 10,000 shares of a given stock or a total market value of $200,000 or more.

Short Selling

An investor who expects that the price of a security will increase can benefit from buying that security. However, suppose that an investor expects that the price of a security will decline and wants to benefit should the price actually decline. What can the investor do? The investor may be able to sell the security without owning it. There are various institutional arrangements by which an investor can borrow securities so that the borrowed security can be delivered to satisfy the sale.

This practice of selling securities that are not owned at the time of sale is referred to as **selling short**. The security is purchased subsequently by the investor and returned to the party that lent it. When the security is returned, the investor is said to have "covered the short position." A profit will be realized if the purchase price is less than the price that the investor sold short the security.

The ability of investors to sell short is an important mechanism in financial markets. In the absence of an effective short-selling mechanism, security prices will tend to be biased toward the view of more optimistic investors, causing a market to depart from the standards of a perfect price-setting situation.

To illustrate short selling with an example, suppose Ms. Stokes believes that Wilson Pharmaceuticals common stock is overpriced at $20 per share and wants to be in a position to benefit if her assessment is correct. Ms. Stokes calls her broker, Mr. Yats, indicating that she wants to sell 100 shares of Wilson Pharmaceuticals. Mr. Yats will do two things: sell 100 shares of Wilson Pharmaceuticals on behalf of Ms. Stokes, and arrange to borrow 100 shares of that stock. Suppose that Mr. Yats is able to sell the stock for $20 per share and arrange to borrow the stock from Mr. Jordan. The shares borrowed from Mr. Jordan will be delivered to the buyer of the 100 shares. The proceeds from the sale (ignoring commissions) will be $2,000. However, the proceeds will not be given to Ms. Stokes because she has not given her broker the 100 shares.

Now, suppose that one week later the price of Wilson Pharmaceuticals stock declines to $15 per share. Ms. Stokes may instruct her broker to *buy* 100 shares of Wilson Pharmaceuticals. The cost of buying the shares (once again ignoring commissions) is $1,500. The shares purchased are then delivered to Mr. Jordan, who loaned the original 100 shares to Ms. Stokes. At this point, Ms. Stokes has sold 100 shares and bought 100 shares, so she no longer has any obligation to her broker or Mr. Jordan—she has covered her short position. She is entitled to the funds in her account that were generated by the selling and buying activity. She sold the stock for $2,000 and bought it for $1,500. Thus, she realizes a profit of $500 before commissions and fees. The broker's commission and a fee charged by the lender of the stock are then subtracted from the $500. Furthermore, if any dividends were paid by Wilson Pharmaceuticals while the stock was borrowed, Ms. Stokes must return them to Mr. Jordan, who still owned the stock at the time.

If instead of falling, suppose the price of Wilson Pharmaceuticals stock rises. Ms. Stokes will realize a loss when she is forced to cover her short position. For example, if the price rises to $27, Ms. Stokes will lose $700, to which must be added commissions and the cost of borrowing the stock.

There are exchange-imposed restrictions as to when a short sale may be executed which are intended to prevent investors from destabilizing the price of a stock when the market price is falling. These are the so-called **tick-test rules**. A short sale can be made only when either (1) the sale price of the particular stock is higher than the last trade price (referred to as an **uptick trade**), or (2) there is no change in the last trade price of the particular stock, and the previous trade price must be higher than the trade price that preceded it (referred to as a **zero uptick**). For example, if Ms. Stokes wanted to "short" Wilson Pharmaceuticals at a price of $20, and the two previous trade prices were $20⅛ and then $20, she could not sell short at that time because of the uptick trade rule. If the previous trade prices were $19⅞, $19⅞, and then $20, she could short the stock at $20 because of the uptick trade rule. Suppose that the sequence of the last three trades is: $19⅞, $20, and $20. Ms. Stokes could short the stock at $20 because of the zero uptick rule.

Margin Transactions

Investors can borrow cash to buy securities and use the securities themselves as collateral. For example, suppose Mr. Boxer has $10,000 to invest and is considering buying Wilson Pharmaceuticals, which is currently selling for $20 per share. With his $10,000, Mr. Boxer can buy 500 shares. Suppose his broker can arrange for him to borrow an additional $10,000 so that Mr. Boxer can buy an additional 500 shares. Thus, with a $10,000 investment, he can purchase a total of 1,000 shares. The 1,000 shares will be used as collateral for the $10,000 borrowed, and Mr. Boxer will have to pay interest on the amount borrowed.

A transaction in which an investor borrows to buy additional securities using the securities themselves as collateral is called **buying on margin**. By borrowing funds, an investor creates financial leverage. Note that Mr. Boxer, for a $10,000 investment, realizes the consequences associated with a price change of 1,000 shares rather than 500 shares. He will benefit if the price rises but be worse off if the price falls (compared to not borrowing funds).

To illustrate what happens if the price subsequently changes, suppose the price of Wilson Pharmaceuticals rises to $29 per share. Mr. Boxer will then realize a profit of $9 per share on 1,000 shares, or $9,000, ignoring commissions and the cost of borrowing. Had Mr. Boxer not borrowed $10,000 to buy the additional 500 shares, his profit would have been only $4,500. Suppose, instead, that the price of Wilson Pharmaceuticals stock declines to $13 per share. Then by borrowing so that he could buy 500 additional shares, he lost $7,000 ($7 per share on 1,000 shares) instead of just $3,500 ($7 on 500 shares).

The funds borrowed to buy the additional stock will be provided by a broker, and the broker gets the money from a bank. The interest rate that banks charge brokers for these transactions is known as the **call money rate** (also called the **broker loan rate**). The broker charges the investor the call money rate plus a service charge.

Margin Requirements

The broker is not free to lend as much as it wishes to the investor to buy securities. The Securities and Exchange Act of 1934 prohibits brokers from lending more than a specified percentage of the market value of the securities. The **initial margin requirement** is the proportion of the total market value of the securities that the investor must pay for in cash. The 1934 act gives the Board of Governors of the Federal Reserve the responsibility to set initial margin requirements, under Regulations T and U. The initial margin requirement varies for stocks and bonds and is currently 50%, though it has been below 40%. The Fed also establishes a **maintenance margin requirement**. This is the minimum amount of equity needed in the investor's margin account as compared to the total market value. If the investor's margin account falls below the minimum maintenance margin, the investor is required to put up additional cash. The investor receives a **margin call** from the broker specifying the additional cash to be put into the investor's margin account. If the investor fails to put up the additional cash, the securities are sold.

As we will explain in Chapter 10, investors who take positions in the futures market are also required to satisfy initial and maintenance margin requirements. Margin requirements for the purchase of securities are different in concept from those in futures markets. In a margin transaction involving securities, the initial margin requirement is equivalent to a down payment; the balance is borrowed funds for which interest is paid (the call rate plus a service charge). In the futures market, the initial margin requirement is effectively "good faith" money, indicating that the investor will satisfy the obligation of the futures contract. No money is borrowed by the investor.

ROLE OF BROKERS AND DEALERS IN REAL MARKETS

Common occurrences in real markets keep them from being theoretically perfect. Because of these occurrences, brokers and dealers are necessary to the smooth functioning of a secondary market.

Brokers

One way in which a real market might not meet all the exacting standards of a theoretically perfect market is that many investors may not be present at all times in the marketplace. Further, a typical investor may not be skilled in the art of the deal or completely informed about every facet of trading in the asset. Clearly, most investors in even smoothly functioning markets need professional assistance. Investors need someone to receive and keep track of their orders for buying or selling, to find other parties wishing to sell or buy, to negotiate for good prices, to serve as a focal point for trading, and to execute the orders. The broker performs all of these functions. Obviously, these functions are more important for the complicated trades, such as the small or large trades, than for simple transactions or those of typical size.

A **broker** is an entity that acts on behalf of an investor who wishes to execute orders. In economic and legal terms, a broker is said to be an "agent" of the investor. It is important to realize that the brokerage activity does not require the broker to buy and hold in inventory or sell from inventory the financial asset that is the subject of the trade. (Such activity is termed "taking a position" in the asset, and it is the role of the dealer.) Rather, the broker receives, transmits, and executes investors' orders with other investors. The broker receives an explicit commission for these services, and the commission is a "transactions cost" of the capital markets.

Dealers as Market Makers

A real market might also differ from the perfect market because of the possibly frequent event of a temporary imbalance in the number of buy and sell orders that investors may place for any security at any one time. Such unmatched or unbalanced flow causes two problems. First, the security's price may change abruptly even if there has been no shift in either supply or demand for the security. Second, buyers may have to pay higher than market-clearing prices (or sellers accept lower ones) if they want to make their trade immediately.

For example, suppose the consensus price for ABC security is $50, which was determined in several recent trades. Also suppose that a flow of buy orders from investors who suddenly have cash arrives in the market, but there is no accompanying supply of sell orders. This temporary imbalance could be sufficient to push the price of ABC security to, say, $55. Thus, the price has changed sharply even though there has been no change in any fundamental financial aspect of the issuer. Buyers who want to buy immediately must pay $55 rather than $50, and this difference can be viewed as the price of "immediacy." By immediacy, we mean that buyers and sellers do not want to wait for the arrival of sufficient orders on the other side of the trade, which would bring the price closer to the level of recent transactions.

The fact of imbalances explains the need for the dealer or market maker, who stands ready and willing to buy a financial asset for its own account (add to an inventory of the security) or sell from its own account (reduce the inventory of the security). At a given time, dealers are willing to buy a security at a price (the bid price) that is less than what they are willing to sell the same security for (the ask price).

In the 1960s, economists George Stigler[1] and Harold Demsetz[2] analyzed the role of dealers in securities markets. They viewed dealers as the suppliers of immediacy—the ability to trade promptly—to the market. The bid-ask spread can be viewed in turn as the price charged by dealers for supplying immediacy, together with short-run price stability (continuity or smoothness) in the presence of short-term order imbalances. There are two other roles that dealers play: they provide better price information to market participants, and in certain market structures they provide the services of an auctioneer in bringing order and fairness to a market.[3]

The price-stabilization role relates to our earlier example of what may happen to the price of a particular transaction in the absence of any intervention when there is a temporary imbalance of order. By taking the opposite side of a trade when there are no other orders, the dealer prevents the price from materially diverging from the price at which a recent trade was consummated.

Investors are concerned with immediacy, and they also want to trade at prices that are reasonable, given prevailing conditions in the market. While dealers cannot know with certainty the true price of a security, they do have a privileged position in some market structures with respect to the flow of market orders. They also have a privileged position regarding "limit" orders, the special orders that can be executed only if the market price of the security changes in a specified way. (See Chapter 13 for more information on limit orders.)

Finally, the dealer acts as an auctioneer in some market structures, thereby providing order and fairness in the operations of the market. For example, as we will explain in Chapter 13, the market maker on organized stock exchanges in the United States performs this function by organizing trading to make sure that the exchange rules for the priority of trading are followed. The role of a market maker in a call market structure is that of an auctioneer. The market maker does not take a position in the traded security, as a dealer does in a continuous market.

What factors determine the price dealers should charge for the services they provide? Or equivalently, what factors determine the bid-ask spread? One of the most important is the order processing costs incurred by dealers, such as the costs of equipment necessary to do business and the administrative and operations staff. The lower these costs, the narrower the bid-ask spread. With the reduced cost of computing and better-trained personnel, these costs have declined since the 1960s.

Dealers also have to be compensated for bearing risk. A **dealer's position** may involve carrying inventory of a security (a *long* position) or selling a

[1] George Stigler, "Public Regulation of Securities Markets," *Journal of Business* (April 1964), pp. 117-34.

[2] Harold Demsetz, "The Cost of Transacting,," *Quarterly Journal of Economics* (October 1968), pp. 35-6.

[3] Robert A. Schwartz, *Equity Markets: Structure, Trading, and Performance* (New York: Harper & Row Publishers, 1988), pp. 389-97.

security that is not in inventory (a *short* position). There are three types of risks associated with maintaining a long or short position in a given security. First, there is the uncertainty about the future price of the security. A dealer who has a long position in the security is concerned that the price will decline in the future; a dealer who is in a short position is concerned that the price will rise.

The second type of risk has to do with the expected time it will take the dealer to unwind a position and its uncertainty. And this, in turn, depends primarily on the rate at which buy and sell orders for the security reaches the market (i.e., the thickness of the market). Finally, while a dealer may have access to better information about order flows than the general public, there are some trades where the dealer takes the risk of trading with someone who has better information.[4] This results in the better-informed trader obtaining a better price at the expense of the dealer. Consequently, in establishing the bid-ask spread for a trade, a dealer will assess whether the trader might have better information.[5]

MARKET EFFICIENCY

The term "efficient" capital market has been used in several contexts to describe the operating characteristics of a capital market. There is a distinction, however, between an *operationally* (or *internally*) *efficient market* and a *pricing* (or *externally*) *efficient capital market.*[6]

Operational Efficiency

In an operationally efficient market, investors can obtain transaction services as cheaply as possible, given the costs associated with furnishing those services. For example, in national equity markets throughout the world the degree of operational efficiency varies. At one time, brokerage commissions in the United States were fixed, and the brokerage industry charged high fees. That changed in May 1975, as the American exchanges were forced to adopt a system of competitive and negotiated commissions. Non-U.S. markets have been moving toward more competitive brokerage fees. France, for example, adopted a system of negotiated commissions for large trades in 1985. In its "Big Bang" of 1986, the London Stock Exchange abolished fixed commissions.

Commissions are only part of the cost of transacting as we noted above. The other part is the dealer spread. Bid-ask spreads for bonds vary by type of bond. For example, the bid-ask spread on U.S. Treasury securities are much smaller than for other bonds. Even with the U.S. Treasury securities market, certain issues have a narrower bid-ask spread than other issues. Other components of transaction costs are discussed later in this chapter.

Pricing Efficiency

Pricing efficiency refers to a market where prices at all times fully reflect all available information that is relevant to the valuation of securities. That is,

---

[4]Walter Bagehot, "The Only Game in Town," *Financial Analysts Journal* (March-April 1971), pp. 12-14, 22.

[5]Some trades that we will discuss in Chapter 13 can be viewed as "informationless trades." This means that the dealer knows or believes a trade is being requested to accomplish an investment objective that is not motivated by the potential future price movement of the security.

[6]Richard R. West, "Two Kinds of Market Efficiency," *Financial Analysts Journal* (November-December 1975), pp. 30-4.

relevant information about the security is quickly impounded into the price of securities.

In his seminal review article on pricing efficiency, Eugene Fama points out that in order to test whether a market is price efficient, two definitions are necessary. First, it is necessary to define what it means that prices "fully reflect" information. Second, the "relevant" set of information that is assumed to be "fully reflected" in prices must be defined.[7]

Fama, as well as others, defines "fully reflects" in terms of the expected return from holding a security. The expected return over some holding period is equal to expected cash distributions plus the expected price change, all divided by the initial price. The price formation process defined by Fama and others is that the expected return one period from now is a stochastic (i.e., random) variable that already takes into account the "relevant" information set.[8]

In defining the "relevant" information set that prices should reflect, Fama classified the pricing efficiency of a market into three forms: weak, semi-strong, and strong. The distinction between these forms lies in the relevant information that is hypothesized to be impounded in the price of the security. **Weak efficiency** means that the price of the security reflects the past price and trading history of the security. **Semi-strong efficiency** means that the price of the security fully reflects all public information (which, of course, includes but is not limited to historical price and trading patterns). **Strong efficiency** exists in a market where the price of a security reflects all information, whether or not it is publicly available.

A price-efficient market has implications for the investment strategy that investors may wish to pursue. Throughout this book, we shall refer to various active strategies employed by investors. In an active strategy, investors seek to capitalize on what they perceive to be the mispricing of a security or securities. In a market that is price efficient, active strategies will not consistently generate a return after taking into consideration transaction costs and the risks associated with a strategy that is greater than simply buying and holding securities. This has lead investors in certain markets that empirical evidence suggests are price efficient to pursue a strategy of **indexing**, which simply seeks to match the performance of some financial index. We will look at the pricing efficiency of the stock market in Chapter 13; it is in this market that the greatest amount of empirical evidence exists.

TRANSACTION COSTS[9]

In an investment era where one-half of one percentage point can make a difference when a money manager is compared against a performance benchmark, an important aspect of the investment process is the cost of implementing an investment strategy. Transaction costs are more than merely brokerage commissions—they consist of commissions, fees, execution costs, and opportunity costs.

---

[7] Eugene F. Fama, "Efficient Capital Markets: A Review of Theory and Empirical Work," *Journal of Finance* (May 1970), pp. 383-417.

[8] If it is assumed that investors will not invest in a security unless its expected return is greater than zero, then the price formation process is called a *submartingale process*.

[9] The discussion in this section draws from Bruce M. Collins and Frank J. Fabozzi, "A Methodology for Measuring Transactions Costs," *Financial Analysts Journal* (March-April 1991), pp. 27-36.

Commissions are the fees paid to brokers to trade securities. Since May 1975 commissions have been fully negotiable. According to a survey by Greenwich Associates, for common stock the trend of average commissions in cents per share has declined from $0.136 in 1977, to $0.087 in 1989.[10] Included in the category of fees are custodial fees and transfer fees. Custodial fees are the fees charged by an institution that holds securities in safekeeping for an investor.

Execution costs represent the difference between the execution price of a security and the price that would have existed in the absence of the trade. Execution costs can be further decomposed into **market (or price) impact** and **market timing costs**. Market impact cost is the result of the bid-ask spread and a price concession extracted by dealers to mitigate their risk that an investor's demand for liquidity is information-motivated.[11] Market timing cost arises when an adverse price movement of the security during the time of the transaction can be attributed in part to other activity in the security and is not the result of a particular transaction. Execution costs, then, are related to both the demand for liquidity and the trading activity on the trade date.

There is a distinction between **information-motivated trades** and **informationless trades**.[12] Information-motivated trading occurs when investors believe they possess pertinent information not currently reflected in the security's price. This style of trading tends to increase market impact because it emphasizes the speed of execution, or because the market maker believes a desired trade is driven by information and increases the bid-ask spread to provide some protection. It can involve the sale of one security in favor of another. Informationless trades are the result of either a reallocation of wealth or implementation of an investment strategy that utilizes only existing information. An example of the former is a pension fund's decision to invest cash in the stock market. Other examples of informationless trades include portfolio rebalances, investment of new money, or liquidations. In these circumstances, the demand for liquidity alone should not lead the market maker to demand the significant price concessions associated with new information.

The problem with measuring execution costs is that the true measure—which is the difference between the price of the security in the absence of the investor's trade and the execution price—is not observable. Furthermore, the execution prices are dependent on supply and demand conditions at the margin. Thus, the execution price may be influenced by competitive traders who demand immediate execution, or other investors with similar motives for trading. This means that the execution price realized by an investor is the consequence of the structure of the market mechanism, the demand for liquidity by the marginal investor, and the competitive forces of investors with similar motivations for trading.

---

[10] "Getting Down to Business," Greenwich Associates, Greenwich, CT, 1990.

[11] By a price concession we mean the investor will have to pay a higher price when buying and a lower price when selling.

[12] L. Cuneo and W. Wagner, "Reducing the Cost of Stock Trading," *Financial Analysts Journal* (November-December 1975), pp. 835-43.

The cost of not transacting represents an opportunity cost.[13] Opportunity costs may arise when a desired trade fails to be executed. This component of costs represents the difference in performance between an investor's desired investment and the same investor's actual investment after adjusting for execution costs, commissions, and fees.

Opportunity costs have been characterized as the hidden cost of trading, and it has been suggested that the shortfall in performance of many actively managed portfolios is the consequence of failing to execute all desired trades.[14] Measurement of opportunity costs is subject to the same problems as measurement of execution costs. The true measure of opportunity cost depends on knowing what the performance of a security would have been if all desired trades had been executed at the desired time across an investment horizon. As these are the desired trades that the investor could not execute, the benchmark is inherently unobservable.[15]

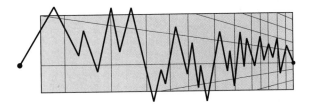

SUMMARY

A secondary market in financial assets is one where existing or outstanding assets are traded among investors. A secondary market serves several needs of the firm or governmental unit that issues securities in the primary market. The secondary market provides the issuer with regular information about the value of its outstanding stocks or bonds, and it encourages investors to buy securities from issuers because it offers them an ongoing opportunity for liquidating their investments in securities.

Investors also get services from the secondary market. The market supplies them with liquidity and prices for the assets they are holding or want to buy; and the market brings interested investors together, thereby reducing the costs of searching for other parties and of making trades.

Secondary markets for securities exist around the world. Such markets may be continuous, where trading and price determination go on throughout the day as orders to buy and sell reach the market. Some markets are call markets where prices are determined by executions of batched or grouped orders to buy and sell at a specific time (or times) within the trading day. Some secondary markets combine features of call and continuous trading.

---

[13] For discussion of opportunity cost, within the context of costs defined as the implementation shortfall of an investment strategy, see André F. Perold, "The Implementation Shortfall: Paper versus Reality," *Journal of Portfolio Management* (Summer 1988), pp. 4-9.

[14] See J. L. Treynor, "What Does It Take to Win the Trading Game?" *Financial Analysts Journal* (January-February 1981), pp. 55-60, for a discussion of the consequences of high opportunity costs.

[15] Methodologies have been proposed to estimate execution costs and opportunity costs. See, for example, Collins and Fabozzi, "A Methodology for Measuring Transactions Costs."

Even the most developed and smoothly functioning secondary market falls short of being "perfect" in the economically theoretical meaning of the term. Actual markets tend to have numerous "frictions" that affect prices and investors' behavior. Some key frictions are transaction costs.

Investors can place different types of orders with brokers. These include market orders, limit orders, stop orders, stop-limit orders, market-if-touched orders, and time-specific orders. There are also size-related orders.

An investor who expects that the price of a security will decline can benefit by selling a security short. A mechanism to allow investors to sell short is critical in financial markets because in the absence of such a mechanism, security prices will tend to be biased toward the view of more optimistic investors. There are exchange-imposed restrictions as to when a short sale can be executed.

Buying on margin is a transaction in which an investor borrows to buy additional securities, using the securities themselves as collateral. By borrowing funds to buy securities, an investor creates financial leverage. The funds borrowed to buy the additional securities will be provided by a broker. The call money rate is the interest rate that banks charge brokers for buying on margin. Margin requirements must be satisfied when buying on margin.

Because of imperfections in actual markets, investors need the services of two types of market participants: dealers and brokers. Brokers aid investors by collecting and transmitting orders to the market, by bringing willing buyers and sellers together, by negotiating prices, and by executing orders. The fee for these services is the broker's commission.

Dealers perform three functions in markets: (1) they provide the opportunity for investors to trade immediately rather than waiting for the arrival of sufficient orders on the other side of the trade (i.e., "immediacy"), and dealers do this while maintaining short-run price stability ("continuity"); (2) dealers offer price information to market participants; and (3) in certain market structures, dealers serve as auctioneers in bringing order and fairness to a market. Dealers buy for their own account and maintain inventories of securities, and their profits come from selling assets at higher prices than they purchased them.

A market is operationally efficient if it offers investors reasonably priced services related to buying and selling. A market is price efficient if at all times prices fully reflect all available information that is relevant to the valuation of securities. There are three forms of pricing efficiency according to what is hypothesized to be the relevant information set: weak form, semi-strong form, and strong form. In such a price-efficient market, pursuing active strategies will not consistently produce superior returns after adjusting for risk and transaction costs.

Transaction costs include commissions, fees, execution costs, and opportunity costs. Execution costs represent the difference between the execution price of a security and the price that would have existed in the absence of the trade, and arise out of the demand for immediate execution through both the demand for liquidity and the trading activity on the trade date. Opportunity costs arise when a desired trade fails to be executed.

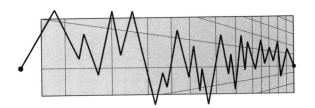

QUESTIONS

1. How do secondary markets benefit investors?

2. What is an organized exchange?

3. What is meant by an over-the-counter market?

4. What are the basic features of the call method of trading?

5. What is meant by a continuous market?

6. The following quote is taken from "The Taxonomy of Trading Strategies," by Wayne H. Wagner, which appears in *Trading Strategies and Execution Costs* published by The Institute of Chartered Financial Analysts in 1988:

   When a trader decides how to bring an order to the market, he or she must deal with some very important issues; to me, the most important is: What kind of trade is this? It could be either an active or a passive trade. The type of trade will dictate whether speed *of execution is more or less important than* cost *of execution. In other words, do I want immediate trading (a market order); or am I willing to forgo the immediate trade for the possibility of trading less expensively if I am willing to "give" on the* timing *of the trade (a limit order)?*

   a. What is meant by a market order and why would one be placed when a trader wants immediate trading?

   b. What is meant by a limit order and why may it be less expensive than a market order?

7. Suppose that Mr. Mancuso has purchased the stock of Harley Bike Company for $45 and that he sets a maximum loss that he will accept on this stock of $6. What type of order can Mr. Mancuso place?

8. a. A market can be perfect, in a theoretical sense, only if it meets certain conditions. What are those conditions?

   b. What is meant by a market friction?

9. a. Why would an investor sell short a security?

   b. What happens if the price of a security that is sold short rises in price?

   c. What are the restrictions on shorting common stock?

   d. What is the role of the broker in a short sale?

10. a. What is meant by buying on margin?

b. How does margin increase an investor's leverage?

c. Who determines margin requirements for purchasing securities on margin?

11. What is the difference between a broker and a dealer?

12. How does a dealer make a profit when making a market?

13. What are the risks that a dealer accepts in making a market?

14. What is meant by the bid-ask spread?

15. How does the rate of order flow (or thickness) of a market affect a dealer's bid-ask spread?

16. What are the benefits that a market derives from the actions of dealers?

17. The residential real estate market boasts many brokers but very few dealers. What explains this situation?

18. What makes a market operationally or internally efficient?

19. What is the key characteristic of a market that has pricing or external efficiency?

20. What is meant by the semi-strong form of market efficiency?

21. Indicate why you agree or disagree with the following statement: "An investor who believes a market is price efficient should pursue an active investment strategy."

22. The following statements are taken from Greta E. Marshall's article "Execution Costs: The Plan Sponsor's View," which appears in *Trading Strategies and Execution Costs* published by The Institute of Chartered Financial Analysts in 1988.

a. "There are three components of trading costs. First there are direct costs which may be measured—commissions. Second, there are indirect—or market impact—costs. Finally, there are the undefined costs of not trading." What are market impact costs, and what do you think the "undefined costs of not trading" represent?

b. "Market impact, unlike broker commissions, is difficult to identify and measure." Why is market impact cost difficult to measure?

23.a. What is meant by an information-motivated trade?

b. What is meant by an informationless trade?

Risk and Return Theories: I

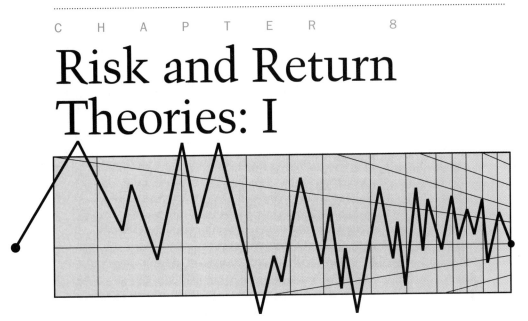

LEARNING OBJECTIVES

After reading this chapter you will understand:

- how to calculate the historical single-period investment return for a security or portfolio of securities.

- the different methods for calculating the return over several unit periods.

- what is meant by an efficient portfolio.

- how to calculate the expected return and risk of a single asset and a portfolio of assets.

- why the expected return of a portfolio of assets is a weighted average of the expected return of the assets included in the portfolio.

- how portfolio theory assumes that investors make investment decisions.

- the difference between systematic risk and unsystematic risk.

- the impact of diversification on total risk.

- the importance of the correlation of two assets in measuring a portfolio's risk.

- what is meant by a feasible portfolio and a set of feasible portfolios.

- what is the Markowitz efficient frontier.

- what is meant by an optimal portfolio and how an optimal portfolio is selected from all the portfolios available on the Markowitz efficient frontier.

As we explained in Chapter 1, valuation is the process of determining the fair value of a financial asset. The fundamental principle of valuation is that the value of any financial asset is the present value of the cash flow expected. The process requires two steps: estimating the cash flow and determining the appropriate interest rate that should be used to calculate the present value. The appropriate interest rate is the minimum interest rate plus a risk premium. The amount of the risk premium depends on the risk associated with realizing the cash flow. In this chapter and the next, theories about how to determine the appropriate risk premium are presented. This is done by demonstrating the theoretical relationship between risk and expected return that should prevail in capital markets.

The development of the theoretical relationship between risk and expected return is built on two economic theories: portfolio theory and capital market theory. Portfolio theory deals with the selection of portfolios that maximize expected returns consistent with individually acceptable levels of risk. Capital market theory deals with the effects of investor decisions on security prices. More specifically, it shows the relationship that should exist between security returns and risk, if investors constructed portfolios as indicated by portfolio theory.

Together, portfolio and capital market theories provide a framework to specify and measure investment risk and to develop relationships between risk and expected return (and hence between risk and the required return on an investment). These theories have revolutionized the world of finance, by allowing portfolio managers to quantify the investment risk and expected return of a portfolio and allowing corporate treasurers to quantify the cost of capital and risk of a proposed capital investment.

In this chapter, we begin with the basic concepts of portfolio theory and then build upon these concepts in the next chapter to develop the theoretical relationship between the expected return of an asset and risk. Because the risk and return relationship indicates how much an asset's expected return should be given its relevant risks, it also tells us how an asset should be priced. Hence the risk and return relationship is also referred to as an **asset pricing model**. In the next chapter we present three asset pricing models that dominate financial thinking today.

Prior to the development of the theories we present, investors would often speak of risk and return, but the failure to quantify these important measures made the goal of constructing a portfolio of assets highly subjective and provided no insight as to the return investors should expect. Moreover, investors would focus on the risks of individual assets without understanding how combining them into a portfolio can affect the portfolio's risk. The theories we present here quantify the relationship between risk and expected return. In October 1990, as confirmation of the importance of these theories, the Alfred Nobel Memorial Prize in Economic Science was awarded to Professor Harry Markowitz,[1] the developer of portfolio theory, and to Professor William Sharpe who is one of the developers of capital market theory.[2]

---

[1] Harry M. Markowitz, "Portfolio Selection," *Journal of Finance* (March 1952), pp. 77-91; and *Portfolio Selection,* Cowles Foundation Monograph 16 (New York: John Wiley & Sons, 1959).

[2] William F. Sharpe, *Portfolio: Theory and Capital Markets* (New York, McGraw-Hill, 1970).

MEASURING INVESTMENT RETURN

Before proceeding with the theories, we will explain how the actual investment return of a portfolio should be measured. The return on an investor's portfolio during a given interval is equal to the change in value of the portfolio plus any distributions received from the portfolio, expressed as a fraction of the initial portfolio value. It is important that any capital or income distributions made to the investor be included, or the measure of return will be deficient.

Another way to look at return is as the amount (expressed as a fraction of the initial portfolio value) that can be withdrawn at the end of the interval while maintaining the initial portfolio value intact. The return on the investor's portfolio, designated R_p, is given by:

$$R_p = \frac{V_1 - V_0 + D}{V_0} \tag{8.1}$$

where V_1 = the portfolio market value at the end of the interval
V_0 = the portfolio market value at the beginning of the interval
D = the cash distributions to the investor during the interval

The calculation assumes that any interest or dividend income received on the portfolio of securities and not distributed to the investor is reinvested in the portfolio (and thus reflected in V_1). Further, the calculation assumes that any distributions occur at the end of the interval, or are held in the form of cash until the end of the interval. If the distributions were reinvested prior to the end of the interval, the calculation would have to be modified to consider the gains or losses on the amount reinvested. The formula also assumes no capital inflows during the interval. Otherwise, the calculation would have to be modified to reflect the increased investment base. Capital inflows at the end of the interval (or held in cash until the end), however, can be treated as just the reverse of distributions in the return calculation.

Thus, given the beginning and ending portfolio values, plus any contributions from or distributions to the investor (assumed to occur at the end of an interval), Equation (8.1) lets us compute the investor's return. For example, if the XYZ pension fund had a market value of $100 million at the end of June, benefit payments of $5 million made at the end of July, and an end-of-July market value of $103 million the return for the month would be 8%.

$$R_p = \frac{103,000,000 - 100,000,000 + 5,000,000}{100,000,000} = 0.08$$

In principle, this sort of calculation of returns could be carried out for any interval of time, say, for one month or ten years. Yet there are several problems with this approach. First, it is apparent that a calculation made over a long period of time, say, more than a few months, would not be very reliable because of the underlying assumption that all cash payments and inflows are made and received at the end of the period. Clearly, if two investments have the same return as calculated by Equation (8.1), but one investment makes cash payment early and the other late, the one with early payment will be understated. Second, we cannot rely on the formula above to compare return on a one-month investment with that on a ten-year portfolio. For purposes of comparison the return must be expressed per unit of time—say, per year.

In practice, we handle these two problems by first computing the return over a reasonably short unit of time, perhaps a quarter of a year or less. The return over the relevant horizon, consisting of several unit periods, is computed by averaging the return over the unit intervals. There are three generally used methods of averaging: (1) the arithmetic average return, (2) the time-weighted rate of return (also referred to as the geometric rate of return), and (3) the dollar-weighted return. The averaging produces a measure of return per unit of time period. The measure can be converted to an annual or other period return by standard procedures.

Arithmetic Average Rate of Return

The **arithmetic average rate of return** is an unweighted average of the returns achieved during a series of such measurement intervals. The general formula is:

$$R_A = \frac{R_{P1} + R_{P2} + \dots + R_{PN}}{N}$$

R_A = the arithmetic average return
R_{Pk} = the portfolio return in interval k as measured by
　　　　Equation (8.1), $k = 1, \dots, N$
N = the number of intervals in the performance evaluation period

For example, if the portfolio returns were -10%, 20%, and 5% in July, August, and September, respectively, the arithmetic average monthly return is 5%.

The arithmetic average can be thought of as the mean value of the withdrawals (expressed as a fraction of the initial portfolio value) that can be made at the end of each interval while maintaining the initial portfolio value intact. In the example above, the investor must add 10% of the initial portfolio value at the end of the first interval and can withdraw 20% and 5% of the initial portfolio value per period.

Time-Weighted Rate of Return

The **time-weighted rate of return** measures the compounded rate of growth of the initial portfolio during the performance evaluation period, assuming that all cash distributions are reinvested in the portfolio. It is also commonly referred to as the "geometric rate of return." It is computed by taking the geometric average of the portfolio returns computed from Equation (8.1). The general formula is:

$$R_T = [(1 + R_{P1})(1 + R_{P2}) \dots (1 + R_{PN})]^{1/N} - 1$$

where R_T is the time-weighted rate of return and R_{Pk} and N are as defined earlier.

For example, if the portfolio returns were –10%, 20%, and 5% in July, August, and September, as in the example above, then the time-weighted rate of return is:

$$R_T = [(1 + (-0.10)) (1 + 0.20) (1 + 0.05)]^{1/3} - 1$$
$$= [(0.90) (1.20) (1.05)]^{1/3} - 1 = 0.043$$

As the time-weighted rate of return is 4.3% per month, one dollar invested in the portfolio at the end of June would have grown at a rate of 4.3% per month during the three-month period.

In general, the arithmetic and time-weighted average returns do not provide the same answers. This is because computation of the arithmetic average assumes the initial amount invested to be maintained (through additions or withdrawals) at its initial portfolio value. The time-weighted return, on the other hand, is the return on a portfolio that varies in size because of the assumption that all proceeds are reinvested.

We can use an example to show how the two averages fail to coincide. Consider a portfolio with a $100 million market value at the end of 1992, a $200 million value at the end of 1993, and a $100 million value at the end of 1994. The annual returns are 100% and –50%. The arithmetic return is 25%, while the time-weighted average return is 0%. The arithmetic average return consists of the average of the $100 million withdrawn at the end of 1993 and the $50 million replaced at the end of 1994. The rate of return is clearly zero, however, the 100% in 1993 being exactly offset by the 50% loss in 1994 on the larger investment base. In this example, the arithmetic average exceeds the time-weighted average return. This always proves to be true, except in the special situation where the returns in each interval are the same, in which case the averages are identical.

Dollar-Weighted Rate of Return

The **dollar-weighted rate of return** (also called the **internal rate of return**) is computed by finding the interest rate that will make the present value of the cash flows from all the interval periods plus the terminal market value of the portfolio equal to the initial market value of the portfolio. The internal rate of return calculation, as explained in Chapter 17, is calculated exactly the same way the yield to maturity on a bond is. The general formula for the dollar-weighted return is:

$$V_0 = \frac{C_1}{(1 + R_D)} + \frac{C_2}{(1 + R_D)^2} + ... + \frac{C_N + V_N}{(1 + R_D)^n}$$

where R_D = the dollar-weighted rate of return
V_0 = the initial market value of the portfolio
V_N = the terminal market value of the portfolio
C_k = the cash flow for the portfolio (cash inflows minus cash outflows) for interval k, $k = 1,..., N$

For example, consider a portfolio with a market value of $100 million at the end of 1990, capital withdrawals of $5 million at the end of 1991, 1992, and

1993, and a market value at the end of 1993 of \$110 million. Then $V_0 =$ \$100,000,000; $N = 3$; $C_1 = C_2 = C_3 =$ \$5,000,000; $V_3 =$ \$110,000,000; and R_D is the interest rate that satisfies the equation:

$$\$110,000,000 = \frac{\$5,000,000}{(1 + R_D)^1} + \frac{\$5,000,000}{(1 + R_D)^2} + \frac{\$5,000,000 + \$110,000,000}{(1 + R_D)^3}$$

It can be verified that the interest rate that satisfies this expression is 8.1%. This is the dollar-weighted return.

Under special conditions, both the dollar-weighted return and the time-weighted return produce the same result. This will occur when no further additions or withdrawals occur, and all dividends are reinvested.

Throughout this chapter we generally use rate of return to refer to an appropriately standardized measure.

PORTFOLIO THEORY

In constructing a portfolio of assets, investors seek to maximize the expected return from their investment given some level of risk they are willing to accept.[3] Portfolios that satisfy this requirement are called **efficient portfolios**. Portfolio theory tells us how this should be done. Because Markowitz is the developer of portfolio theory, efficient portfolios are sometimes referred to as "Markowitz efficient portfolios."

To construct an efficient portfolio of risky assets, it is necessary to make some assumption about how investors behave in making investment decisions. A reasonable assumption is that investors are **risk averse**. A risk-averse investor is one who, when faced with two investments with the same expected return but two different risks, will prefer the one with the lower risk. Given a choice of efficient portfolios from which an investor can select, an **optimal portfolio** is the one that is most preferred.

To construct an efficient portfolio, it is necessary to understand what is meant by "expected return" and "risk." The latter concept, risk, could mean any one of many types of risk. We shall be more specific about its meaning as we proceed in this chapter.

RISKY ASSETS VERSUS RISK-FREE ASSETS

It is important to distinguish between risky assets and risk-free assets. A **risky asset** is one for which the return that will be realized in the future is uncertain. For example, suppose an investor purchases the stock of General Motors today and plans to hold the stock for one year. At the time she purchased the stock, she does not know what return will be realized. The return will depend on the price of General Motors stock one year from now and the dividends that the company pays during the year. Thus, General Motors stock, and indeed the stock of all companies, is a risky asset.

Even securities issued by the U.S. government are risky assets. For example, an investor who purchases a U.S. government bond that matures in 30

[3] Alternatively stated, investors seek to minimize the risk that they are exposed to given some target expected return.

years does not know the return that will be realized if this bond is to be held for only one year. This is because, as we explain in Chapter 17, a change in interest rates will affect the price of the bond one year from now and therefore the return from investing in that bond for one year.

There are assets, however, in which the return that will be realized in the future is known with certainty today. Such assets are referred to as **risk-free** or **riskless assets.** The risk-free asset is commonly defined as short-term obligations of the U.S. government. For example, if an investor buys a U.S. government security that matures in one year and plans to hold that security for one year, then there is no uncertainty about the return that will be realized. The investor knows that in one year, on the maturity date of the security the government will pay a specific amount to retire the debt. Notice how this situation differs for the U.S. government security that matures in 30 years. While the one year and the 30-year securities are obligations of the U.S. government, the former matures in one year so that there is no uncertainty about the return that will be realized. In contrast, while the investor knows what the government will pay at the end of 30 years for the 30-year bond, he does not know what the price of the bond will be one year from now.

MEASURING PORTFOLIO RISK

The definition of investment risk leads us into less-explored territory. Not everyone agrees on how to define risk, let alone measure it. Nevertheless, there are some attributes of risk that are reasonably well accepted.

An investor holding a portfolio of Treasury securities until the maturity date faces no uncertainty about monetary outcome. The value of the portfolio at maturity of the securities will be identical with the predicted value; the investor bears no price risk. In the case of a portfolio composed of common stocks, however, it will be impossible to predict the value of the portfolio at any future date. The best an investor can do is to make a best-guess or most-likely estimate, qualified by statements about the range and likelihood of other values. In this case, the investor does bear price risk.

Defining risk in terms of price risk, one measure of risk is the extent to which future portfolio values are likely to diverge from the expected or predicted value. More specifically, risk for most investors is related to the chance that future portfolio values will be less than expected. That is, if the investor's portfolio has a current value of $100,000, and an expected value of $110,000 at the end of the next year, what matters is the probability of values less than $110,000.

Before proceeding to the quantification of risk, it is convenient to shift our attention from the terminal value of the portfolio to the portfolio rate of return, R_p, because the increase in portfolio value is related directly to R_p.[4]

Expected Portfolio Return

A particularly useful way to quantify the uncertainty about the portfolio return is to specify the probability associated with each of the possible future

---

[4] The transformation changes nothing of substance because:

$$\tilde{M}_T = (1 + \tilde{R}_p)M_0 = M_0 + M_0\,\tilde{R}_p,$$

where $\tilde{M}_T$ is the terminal portfolio value and $\tilde{R}_p$ is the portfolio return. (The tilde (~) above a variable indicates that it is a random variable.) Since $\tilde{M}_T$ is a linear function of $\tilde{R}_p$, any risk measures developed for the portfolio return will apply equally to the terminal market value.

returns. Assume, for example, that an investor has identified five possible outcomes for the portfolio return during the next year. Associated with each return is a subjectively determined probability, or relative chance of occurrence. The five possible outcomes are shown in Table 8-1.

Note that the probabilities sum to 1 so that the actual portfolio return is confined to assume one of the five possible values. Given this probability distribution, we can measure the expected return and risk for the portfolio.

The expected return is simply the weighted average of possible outcomes, where the weights are the relative chances of occurrence. In general, the expected return on the portfolio, denoted $E(R_p)$, is given by:

$$E(R_p) = P_1R_1 + P_2R_2 + \ldots + R_nP_n \tag{8.2}$$

$$E(R_p) = \sum_{j=1}^{n} P_jR_j$$

where the R_j's are the possible returns, the P_j's the associated probabilities, and n the number of possible outcomes.

The expected return of the portfolio in our illustration is:

$$E(R_p) = 0.1(50\%) + 0.2(30\%) + 0.4(10\%) + 0.2(-10\%) + 0.1(-30\%)$$
$$= 10\%$$

Variability of Expected Return

If risk is defined as the chance of achieving returns less than expected, it would seem logical to measure risk by the dispersion of the possible returns below the expected value. Risk measures based on below-the-mean variability are difficult to work with, however, and moreover are unnecessary as long as the distribution of future return is reasonably symmetric about the expected value. Figure 8-1 shows three probability distributions: the first symmetric, the second skewed to the left, and the third skewed to the right. For a symmetrical distribution, the dispersion of returns on one side of the expected return is the same as the dispersion on the other side of the expected return.

Table 8-1
Five Possible Outcomes for the Possible Return

Outcome	Possible Return	Probability
1	50%	0.1
2	30	0.2
3	10	0.4
4	−10	0.2
5	−30	0.1

Figure 8-1
Possible Shapes for Probability Distributions

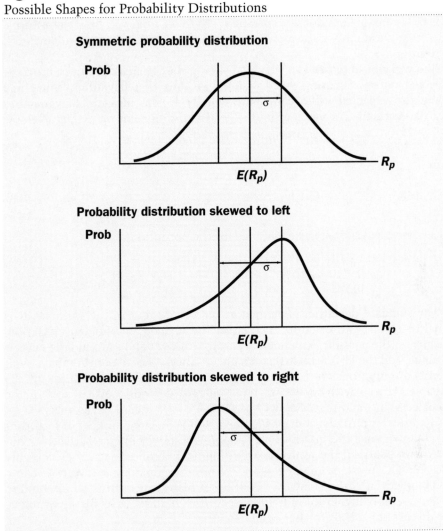

Empirical studies of realized rates of return on diversified portfolios consisting of more than 20 stocks show that skewness is not a significant problem.[5] If future distributions are shaped like historical distributions, it makes little difference whether we measure variability of returns on one or both sides of the expected return. If the probability distribution is symmetric, measures of the total variability of return will be twice as large as measures of the portfolio's variability below the expected return. Thus, if total variability is used as a risk surrogate, the risk ranking for a group of portfolios will be the same as when variability below the expected return is used. It is for this

---

[5] For example, see Marshall E. Blume, "Portfolio Theory: A Step Toward Its Practical Application," *Journal of Business* (April 1970), pp. 152-73.

reason that total variability of returns has been used so widely as a surro-gate for risk.

It now remains to choose a specific measure of total variability of returns. The most commonly used measures are the variance and standard deviation of returns.

The **variance of return** is a weighted sum of the squared deviations from the expected return. Squaring the deviations ensures that deviations above and below the expected value contribute equally to the measure of variability regardless of sign. The variance for the portfolio, designated $var(R_p)$, is given by:

$$var(R_p) = P_1[R_1 - E(R_p)]^2 + P_2[R_2 - E(R_p)]^2 + \ldots + P_n[R_n - E(R_p)]^2$$

or

$$var(R_p) = \sum_{j=1}^{n} P_j[R_j - E(R_p)]^2 \tag{8.3}$$

In the previous example, the variance for the portfolio is

$$var(R_p) = 0.1 \, (50\% - 10\%)^2 + 0.2(30\% - 10\%)^2$$
$$+ 0.4(10\% - 10\% \,)^2 + 0.2(-10\% - 10\%)^2 + 0.1(-30\% - 10\%)^2$$
$$= 480\%$$

The **standard deviation** is defined as the square root of the variance. It is equal to 22% in our example. The larger the variance or standard deviation, the greater the possible dispersion of future realized values around the expect-ed value, and the larger the investor's uncertainty. As a rule of thumb for sym-metric distributions, it is often suggested that roughly two-thirds of the possible returns will lie within one standard deviation either side of the expected value, and that 95% will be within two standard deviations.

Historical return distributions for a portfolio of a large number of securities have shown that the distribution is approximately, but not perfectly, sym-metric. In contrast, the return distribution for individual securities is highly skewed. The most interesting aspect of observed historical return distribu-tions, however, is the standard deviation of historical returns which tend to be considerably higher for individual securities than for diversified portfolios. We discuss this result further below.

Thus far we have confined our discussion of portfolio risk to a single-peri-od investment horizon such as the next year—that is, the portfolio is held unchanged and evaluated at the end of the year. An obvious question relates to the effect of holding the portfolio for several periods—say, for the next 20 years. Will the one-year risks tend to cancel out over time? The answer depends on the random process that security prices follows. Specifically, it has been observed that security prices follow a **random walk**. This means that the expected value of future price changes is independent of past price changes. Given the random-walk nature of security prices, the answer to this question is "no". If the risk level (standard deviation) is maintained during each year, the portfolio risk for longer horizons will increase with the horizon length. The standard deviation of possible terminal portfolio values after N years is equal to $\sqrt{N}$ times the standard deviation after one year.[6] Thus, the investor cannot rely on the "long run" to reduce the risk of loss.

DIVERSIFICATION

Often, one hears investors talking about diversifying their portfolio. By this an investor means constructing a portfolio in such as way as to reduce portfolio risk without sacrificing return. This is certainly a goal that investors should seek. However, the question is how does one do this in practice.

When the distribution of historical returns over a long period of time for a portfolio of diversified common stock is compared to the distribution for individual stocks, a curious relationship has been observed. While the standard deviation of returns for the stock alone can be significantly greater than that of the portfolio, the stock average return is less than the portfolio return! For example, for the period January 1989 to December 1993, the average monthly return of IBM stock was –0.61% and a standard deviation of 7.65%. Over the same time period, average monthly return and standard deviation of the Standard & Poor's 500 was 1.2% and 3.74%, respectively. Is the capital market so imperfect that over this period of time it rewarded substantially higher risk with lower stock return?

Not so. The answer lies in the fact that not all of a security's risk is relevant. Much of the total risk (standard deviation of return) of an individual security is diversifiable. That is, if that investment had been combined with other securities, a portion of the variation in its returns could have been smoothed or canceled by complementary variation in the other securities. The same portfolio diversification effect accounts for the low standard deviation of return for a diversified stock portfolio of 20 or more stocks. In fact, it would be found that the portfolio standard deviation is lower than that of the typical security in the portfolio. Much of the total risk of the component securities had been eliminated by diversification. As long as much of the total risk can be eliminated simply by holding a stock in a portfolio, there is no economic requirement for the return earned to be in line with the total risk. Instead, we should expect realized returns to be related to that portion of security risk that cannot be eliminated by portfolio combination—so-called **systematic risk**.

Diversification results from combining securities whose returns are less than perfectly correlated in order to reduce portfolio risk. As noted above, the portfolio return is simply a weighted average of the individual security returns, no matter the number of securities in the portfolio. Therefore, diversification will not

---

[6] This result can be illustrated as follows. The portfolio market value after N years, $\tilde{M}_N$, is equal to:

$$\tilde{M}_N = M_0[(1 + \tilde{R}_{p1})(1 + \tilde{R}_{p2}) \ldots (1 + \tilde{R}_{pN})],$$

where M_0 is the initial value, and $\tilde{R}_{pt}$ ($t = 1, \ldots, N$) is the return during year t (as given by Equation [8.1]). For reasonably small values of the annual returns, the above expression can be approximated by:

$$\tilde{M}_N = M_0[1 + \tilde{R}_{p1} + \tilde{R}_{p2} + \ldots + \tilde{R}_{pN}].$$

Now, if the annual returns, $\tilde{R}_{pt}$, are independently and identically distributed with variance σ^2, the variance of $\tilde{M}_N$ will equal $(M_0)^2 N \sigma^2$, or N times the variance after one year. Therefore, the standard deviation of the terminal value will equal $\sqrt{N}$ times the standard deviation after one year. The key assumption of independence of portfolio returns over time is realistic since security returns appear to follow a random walk through time.

A similar result could be obtained without the restriction on the size of the $\tilde{R}_{pt}$ if we had dealt with continuously, as opposed to annually, compounded rates of return. However, the analysis would be more complicated.

systematically affect the portfolio return, but it will reduce the variability (standard deviation) of return. In general, the less the correlation among security returns, the greater the impact of diversification on reducing variability. This is true no matter how risky the securities of the portfolio are when considered in isolation.

Theoretically, if we could find sufficient securities with uncorrelated returns, we could eliminate portfolio risk completely. Unfortunately, this situation is not typical in the capital market, where returns are positively correlated to a considerable degree because they tend to respond to the same set of influences (e.g., business cycles and interest rates). Thus, while portfolio risk can be reduced substantially by diversification, it cannot be eliminated entirely. This can be demonstrated very clearly by measuring the standard deviations of randomly selected portfolios containing various numbers of securities and the percentage of systematic risk to total risk. The latter ratio, called the correlation of coefficient and denoted by R^2, indicates the proportion of the portfolio return variability (variance) that is attributable to variability in market returns. The ratio can vary between 0 and 1.

Below we review the empirical studies for both common stocks and bonds of the effect of diversification on portfolio risk.

Empirical Evidence for Common Stock

Several studies have investigated the impact of portfolio diversification on risk and average return for common stock. In the first such study, Wayne Wagner and Sheila Lau divided a sample of 200 New York Stock Exchange (NYSE) stocks into six subgroups based on the Standard & Poor's stock quality ratings as of June 1960.[7] The highest-quality ratings (A+) formed the first group, the second-highest rating (A) the next group, and so on. Randomly selected portfolios containing from one to 20 securities were then formed from each of the subgroups. The month-by-month portfolio returns for the 10-year period through May 1970 were then computed for each portfolio (portfolio composition remaining unchanged). The exercise was repeated ten times to reduce the dependence on single samples. The values for the ten trials were then averaged.

Table 8-2 shows the average return and standard deviation for portfolios from the first subgroup (A+ quality stocks). The average return is unrelated to the number of issues in the portfolio. Yet the standard deviation of return declines as the number of holdings increases. On the average, approximately 40% of the single-security risk is eliminated by forming randomly selected portfolios of 20 stocks. It is also evident, however, that additional diversification yields rapidly diminishing reduction in risk. The improvement is slight when the number of securities held is increased beyond, say, ten. Figure 8-2 shows the results for all six quality groups. The figure shows the rapid decline in total portfolio risk as the portfolios are expanded from one to ten securities.

Returning to Table 8-2, note from the second-to-last column in the table that the return on a diversified portfolio follows the market very closely. The degree of association is measured by the correlation coefficient (R) of each portfolio with an unweighted index of NYSE stocks (perfect positive correlation results in a correlation coefficient of 1.0).[8] The 20-security portfolio has

---

[7] Wayne H. Wagner and Sheila Lau, "The Effect of Diversification on Risks," *Financial Analysts Journal* (November-December 1971), pp. 48-53.

[8] Two securities with perfectly correlated patterns will have a correlation coefficient of 1.0. Conversely, if the return patterns are perfectly inversely correlated, the correlation coefficient will equal −1.0. Two securities with uncorrelated (i.e., statistically unrelated) returns will have a correlation coefficient of zero.

Table 8-2

Risk versus Diversification for Randomly Selected
Portfolios of A+ Quality Securities (June 1960-May 1970)

Number of Securities in Portfolio	Average Return (%/mo.)	Standard Deviation of Return (%/mo.)	Correlation Coefficient with Market R	Coefficient of Determination with Market R^2
1	0.88	7.0	0.54	0.29
2	0.69	5.0	0.63	0.40
3	0.74	4.8	0.75	0.56
4	0.65	4.6	0.77	0.59
5	0.71	4.6	0.79	0.62
10	0.68	4.2	0.85	0.72
15	0.69	4.0	0.88	0.77
20	0.67	3.9	0.89	0.80

Figure 8-2

Standard Deviation versus Number of Issues in Portfolio.

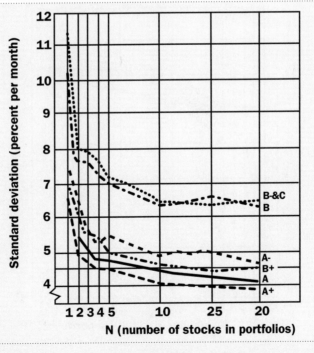

a correlation of 0.89 with the market. The implication is that the risk remaining in the 20-stock portfolio is predominantly a reflection of uncertainty about the performance of the stock market in general. Figure 8-3 shows the results for the six quality groups.

Also shown in Table 8-2 is the correlation coefficient squared, R^2. As explained earlier, this measure is called the coefficient of determination and possible values range from 0 to 1.0. The coefficient of determination has a useful interpretation: it measures the proportion of portfolio return variability (variance) that is attributable to variability in market returns. The remaining variability is risk that is unique to the portfolio and, as shown in Figure 8-2, that can be eliminated by proper diversification of the portfolio. Thus, the coefficient of determination, R^2, measures the degree of portfolio diversification. A poorly diversified portfolio will have a lower R^2 (0.30 – 0.40). A well-diversified portfolio will have a much higher R^2 (0.85 – 0.95). A perfectly diversified portfolio will have an R^2 of 1.0; that is, all the risk in such a portfolio is a reflection of market risk.

Figure 8-3 shows the rapid gain in diversification as each of the portfolios increases in size from one security to two securities and on up to ten securities. Beyond ten securities, the gains tend to be smaller. Note that increasing the number of issues tends to be less efficient at achieving diversification for the highest-quality A+ issues. Apparently the companies comprising this group are more homogeneous than the companies grouped under the other quality codes.

Figure 8-3
Correlation versus Number of Issues in Portfolio.

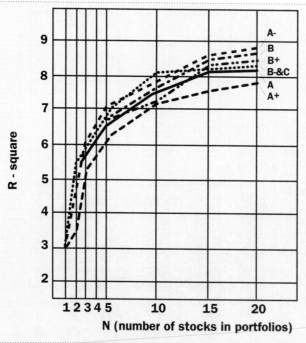

These results show that, while some common stock risks can be eliminated through diversification, others cannot. Thus we are led to distinguish between a security's "unsystematic" risk, which can be washed away by mixing the security with other securities in a diversified portfolio, and its "systematic" risk, which cannot be eliminated by diversification. This proposition is illustrated in Figure 8-4. It shows total portfolio risk declining as the number of holdings increases. Increasing diversification gradually tends to eliminate the unsystematic risk, leaving only systematic, i.e., market-related risk. The remaining variability results from the fact that the return on nearly every security depends to some degree on the overall performance of the market. Consequently, the return on a well-diversified portfolio is highly correlated with the market, and its variability or uncertainty is basically the uncertainty of the market as a whole. Investors are exposed to market uncertainty no matter how many stocks they hold.

To summarize, the major findings on the impact of diversification on the risk of a portfolio of common stock are:

1. The average return is unrelated to the number of issues in the portfolio, yet the standard deviation of return declines as the number of holdings increases.

2. At a portfolio size of about 20 randomly selected common stocks, the level of total portfolio risk is reduced such that all is left is systematic risk.

3. For individual stocks the average ratio of systematic risk to total risk is about 30%.

4. On the average, approximately 40% of the single-security risk is eliminated by forming randomly selected portfolios of 20 stocks.

Figure 8-4
Systematic and Unsystematic Portfolio Risk

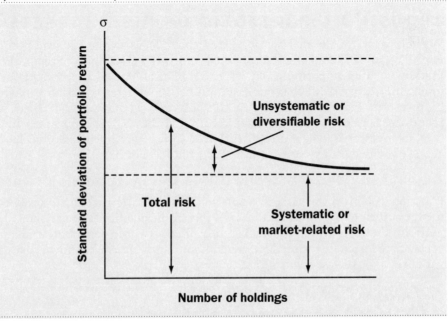

Additional diversification yields rapidly diminishing reduction in risk. The improvement is slight when the number of securities held is increased beyond, say, 10.

5. The return on a diversified portfolio follows the market very closely with the ratio of systematic risk to total risk exceeding 90%.

Empirical Evidence for Bonds

While most of the studies on the impact of diversification on portfolio risk has focused on common stock, one would expect that the findings should be similar in the bond market. A study by McEnally and Boardman found this to be so.[9] Their sample consisted of 515 corporate bonds with quality or credit ratings ranging from Aaa to Baa. (We will discuss bond ratings in Chapter 21.) For all the bonds in their sample and for each quality rating, they constructed 1,000 randomly selected bond portfolios for a given number of issues. They then computed the variance of monthly returns. The results of the McEnally-Boardman study are summarized in Table 8-3.

The first row of Table 8-3 shows the average variance of returns for the 515 issues. The last row presents the variance of returns for a portfolio consisting of all bond issues. The body of the table shows the average variance for the 1,000 randomly constructed portfolios as the number of issues in the portfolio increases. As can be seen, as the number of issues in the portfolio increases, the average variance of the portfolio return decreases and approaches the variance of returns of the portfolio consisting of all issues. Also shown in the table is the systematic return variation (that is, the variance of the return for the all-bond portfolio) as a proportion of the total return variation (that is, the average variation of return) for the random portfolios.

Thus, the McEnally-Boardman study suggests that the effect of portfolio size on diversification for bonds closely parallels the relationship found in common stocks.[10]

CHOOSING A PORTFOLIO OF RISKY ASSETS

Diversification in the manner suggested above leads to the construction of portfolios that have the highest expected return at a given level of risk, called **Markowitz efficient portfolios**. In order to construct Markowitz efficient portfolios, the theory requires some assumptions about asset selection behavior by investors. First, it assumes that the only two parameters that affect an investor's decision are the expected return and the risk. Second, it assumes that an investor is risk averse. Third, it assumes that an investor seeks to achieve the highest expected return at a given level of risk.

Calculating the Portfolio Risk Using Historical Data

Equation (8.3) gives the variance of an n-asset portfolio based on a probability for the return of the individual asset's return. In practice, the variance of a portfolio's return—which we shall simply refer to as the portfolio variance— is calculated from historical data, generally monthly. It can be shown that the variance of a two-asset portfolio is:

[9] Richard W. McEnally and Calvin M. Boardman, "Aspects of Corporate Bond Portfolio Diversification," *Journal of Financial Research* (Spring 1979), pp. 27-36.

[10] See John L. Evans and Stephen H. Archer, "Diversification and the Reduction of Dispersion: An Empirical Analysis," *Journal of Finance* (December 1968), pp. 761-67.

Table 8-3
Monthly Return Variance of Corporate Bond Portfolios, January 1973 to June 1976 ($\times 10^4$)

	All issues	Aaa	Aa	A	Baa
All bonds in universe, individually[a]	9.257	7.756	8.419	9.912	10.977
Random portfolios of bonds[b]					
1 bond	9.367(1.85)	7.737(1.21)	8.308(1.47)	9.721(2.10)	10.974(2.52)
2 bonds	7.469(1.48)	7.175(1.20)	7.234(1.28)	7.316(1.58)	7.557(1.73)
4 bonds	6.004(1.19)	6.777(1.06)	6.298(1.11)	5.827(1.26)	6.100(1.40)
6 bonds	5.782(1.15)	6.630(1.03)	6.096(1.08)	5.503(1.19)	5.446(1.25)
8 bonds	5.591(1.11)	6.644(1.04)	6.075(1.07)	5.309(1.15)	5.229(1.20)
10 bonds	5.376(1.07)	6.482(1.01)	5.965(1.05)	5.133(1.11)	4.982(1.14)
12 bonds	5.401(1.07)	6.537(1.02)	5.894(1.04)	5.050(1.09)	4.912(1.13)
14 bonds	5.341(1.06)	6.549(1.02)	5.871(1.04)	5.003(1.08)	4.845(1.11)
16 bonds	5.299(1.05)	6.484(1.02)	5.876(1.04)	4.940(1.07)	4.768(1.09)
18 bonds	5.266(1.05)	6.524(1.02)	5.784(1.02)	4.917(1.06)	4.760(1.09)
20 bonds	5.274(1.05)	6.410(1.00)	5.809(1.03)	4.928(1.06)	4.699(1.07)
40 bonds	5.155(1.02)	6.449(1.00)	5.767(1.02)	4.776(1.03)	4.513(1.03)
All bond portfolio[c]	5.039	6.416	5.661	4.633	4.362

[a] mean variance of individual issues
[b] mean variance of portfolios constructed by investing $1/n$ of the portfolio in each of n randomly selected securities. Based on 1,000 portfolios in each cell.
[c] mean systematic variance for the universe

Values in parentheses indicate ratio of mean variance of portfolio to mean market related variance. (Computed by authors)

Source: Richard W. McEnally and Calvin M. Boardman, "Aspects of Corporate Bond Portfolio Diversification," Journal of Financial Research, Spring 1979, p.31.

$$\text{var}(R_p) = w_i^2 \, \text{var}(R_i) + w_j^2 \, \text{var}(R_j)$$
$$+ \, 2 \; w_i \, w_j \, \text{std}(R_i) \, \text{std}(R_j) \, \text{cor}(R_i, R_j) \qquad (8.4)$$

where $\text{var}(R_p)$ = portfolio variance
$\quad\quad w_i$ = percentage of the portfolio's funds invested in asset i
$\quad\quad w_j$ = percentage of the portfolio's funds invested in asset j
$\quad\quad \text{var}(R_i)$ = variance of asset i
$\quad\quad \text{var}(R_j)$ = variance of asset j
$\quad\quad \text{std}(R_i)$ = standard deviation of asset i
$\quad\quad \text{std}(R_j)$ = standard deviation of asset j
$\quad\quad \text{cor}(R_i, R_j)$ = correlation between the return for assets i and j

In words, Equation (8.4) states that the portfolio variance is the sum of the weighted variances of the two assets plus the weighted correlation between the two assets. Given our earlier discussion, it should not be surprising that the correlation between the two assets affects the portfolio variance. Notice from Equation (8.4) that the lower the correlation between the return on two assets, the lower the portfolio variance. The portfolio variance is the lowest if the two assets have a correlation of –1.

The equation for the portfolio variance when there are more than two assets in the portfolio is more complicated. The extension to three assets— i, j, and k—is as follows:

$$\text{var}(R_p) = w_i^2 \, \text{var}(R_i) + w_j^2 \, \text{var}(R_j) + w_k^2 \, \text{var}(R_k)$$
$$+ \, 2 \; w_i \, w_j \, \text{std}(R_i) \, \text{std}(R_j) \, \text{cor}(R_i, R_j)$$
$$+ \, 2 \; w_i \, w_k \, \text{std}(R_i) \, \text{std}(R_k) \, \text{cor}(R_i, R_k)$$
$$+ \, 2 \; w_j \, w_k \, \text{std}(R_j) \, \text{std}(R_k) \, \text{cor}(R_j, R_k) \qquad (8.5)$$

where w_k = percentage of the portfolio's funds invested in asset k
$\quad \text{std}(R_k)$ = standard deviation of asset k
$\text{cor}(R_i, R_k)$ = correlation between the return for assets i and k
$\text{cor}(R_j, R_k)$ = correlation between the return for assets j and k

In words, Equation (8.5) states that the portfolio variance is the sum of the weighted variances of the individual assets plus the sum of the weighted correlations of the assets. Hence, the portfolio variance is the weighted sum of the individual variances of the assets in the portfolio plus the weighted sum of the degree to which the assets vary together. The formula for the portfolio variance of any size will involve the variances and standard deviations of all the assets and each pair of correlations.[11]

Constructing Markowitz Efficient Portfolios

An investor who is constructing a portfolio will calculate the portfolio risk (as measured by the portfolio variance) and expected return. For all of the

---

[11] In general, for a portfolio with G assets, the portfolio variance is:

$$\text{var}(R_p) = \sum_{g=1}^{G} w_g^2 \, \text{var}(R_g) + \sum_{g=1}^{G} \sum_{b=1}^{G} w_g \, w_b \text{cov}(R_g, R_b)$$
$$\text{for } b \neq g$$

portfolios with the same level of risk, there will be a large number of portfolios, each with its own expected return. The investor will select the portfolio with the greatest expected return for a given portfolio risk. This portfolio is the Markowitz efficient portfolio for that level of risk.

In practice, the procedure for determining the maximum expected return for a given level of portfolio risk can be found by using a management science technique called quadratic programming. A discussion of this technique is beyond the scope of this chapter. However, it is possible to illustrate the general idea of the construction of Markowitz efficient portfolios graphically by using Figure 8-5.

Figure 8-5 shows all possible portfolios that can be created from the assets that are available. Any portfolio that can be created is called a **feasible portfolio**. The collection of all feasible portfolios is called the **feasible set of portfolios**. In Figure 8-5, the feasible set of portfolios is the shaded area, including the boundaries of the shaded area.

In contrast to a feasible portfolio, a Markowitz efficient portfolio is one that gives the highest expected return of all feasible portfolios with the same risk. A Markowitz efficient portfolio is also said to be a **mean-variance efficient portfolio**. Thus, for each level of risk there is a Markowitz efficient portfolio. The collection of all efficient portfolios is called the **Markowitz efficient set of portfolios**.

In Figure 8-5, the Markowitz efficient set is the upper part of the boundary of the feasible set of portfolios. This is because every point on the upper part of the boundary of the feasible set of portfolios has the greatest expected return for a given level of risk. The Markowitz efficient set of portfolios is sometimes called the **Markowitz efficient frontier**, because graphically all the Markowitz efficient portfolios lie on the boundary of the set of feasible portfolios that have the maximum return for a given level of risk. Any portfolios above the Markowitz efficient

Figure 8-5
Feasible and Efficient Sets of Portfolios

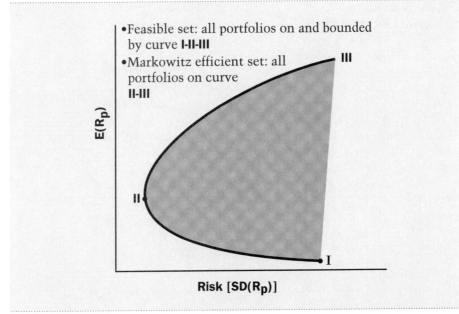

frontier can not be achieved. Any below the Markowitz efficient frontier are dominated by portfolios on the Markowitz efficient frontier.

Choosing a Portfolio in the Markowitz Efficient Set

Now that we have constructed the Markowitz efficient set of portfolios, the next step is to determine the optimal portfolio. An investor will want to hold one of the portfolios on the Markowitz efficient frontier. Notice that the portfolios on the Markowitz efficient frontier represent trade-offs in terms of risk and return. Moving from left to right on the Markowitz efficient frontier, the expected risk increases, but so does the expected return. The question is, which is the best portfolio to hold? The best portfolio to hold of all those on the Markowitz efficient frontier is called the **optimal portfolio**.

Intuitively, the optimal portfolio should depend on the investor's preference or utility as to the trade off between risk and expected return. A natural question is how to estimate an investor's utility function so that the optimal portfolio can be determined. Unfortunately, there is little guidance as to how to construct one. In general, economist have not been successful in measuring utility functions. However, the inability to measure utility functions does not mean that the theory is flawed. What it does mean is that once an investor constructs the Markowitz efficient frontier, an investor will subjectively determine which Markowitz efficient portfolio is appropriate given his or her tolerance to risk.

The Markowitz Efficient Frontier and Asset Correlations

As we explained earlier, the lower the correlation between assets, the lower the portfolio variance. Figure 8-6 shows the Markowitz efficient frontier for different correlations among assets. Notice that the lower the correlation, the higher the expected return for a given level of risk.

Figure 8-6
Markowitz Efficient Frontier for Different Correlations between Assets

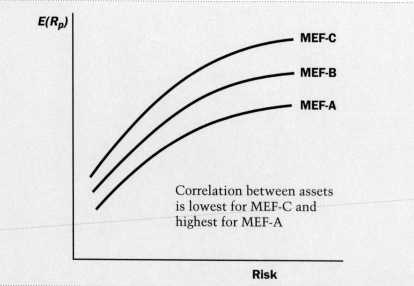

Studies attempting to support the diversification of investors into different types of assets use a figure such as Figure 8-6 to support their contention. For example, the correlation between the return on U.S. stocks and foreign stocks is less than one. Thus, the Markowitz efficient frontier if an investor limits his investments to only U.S. stocks is below that of the Markowitz efficient frontier if an investor expands his investments to foreign stocks.

In general, there are diversification benefits when an investor expands into different types of investments if the correlation with existing assets in which the investor already invests is less than one. The diversification benefits come in the form of shifting out the Markowitz efficient frontier.

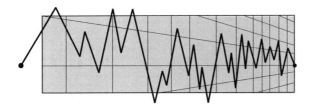

SUMMARY

In this chapter we have introduced portfolio theory. Developed by Harry Markowitz, this theory explains how investors should construct efficient portfolios and select the best or optimal portfolio from among all efficient portfolios. The theory differs from previous approaches to portfolio selection in that Markowitz demonstrated how the key parameters should be measured. These parameters include the risk and the expected return for an individual asset and a portfolio of assets.

The goal of diversifying a portfolio is to reduce a portfolio's risk without sacrificing expected return. This goal can be cast in terms of these key parameters plus the correlation between assets. A portfolio's expected return is simply a weighted average of the expected return of each asset in the portfolio. The weight assigned to each asset is the market value of the asset in the portfolio relative to the total market value of the portfolio. The risk of an asset is measured by the variance or standard deviation of its return. Unlike the portfolio's expected return, a portfolio's risk is not a simple weighting of the standard deviation of the individual assets in the portfolio. Rather, the portfolio risk is affected by the correlation between the assets in the portfolio. The lower the correlation, the smaller the portfolio risk.

Studies of both common stock and bond returns support the view that diversification can reduce portfolio variance. This is because the return of a portfolio can be divided into two types of risk: systematic and unsystematic risk. The former cannot be eliminated by diversification, while the latter can be. For common stock portfolios, studies have found that at a portfolio size of about 20 randomly selected common stocks, the level of total portfolio risk is reduced such that all that is left is systematic risk. The average ratio of systematic risk to total risk is about 30% for individual stocks while for a diversified portfolio it exceeds 90%.

Markowitz has set forth the theory for the construction of an efficient portfolio, which has come to be called a Markowitz efficient portfolio; it is a portfolio that has the highest expected return of all feasible portfolios with the same level of risk. The collection of all Markowitz efficient portfolios is called the Markowitz efficient set of portfolios or the Markowitz efficient frontier. The optimal portfolio is the one that maximizes an investor's preferences with respect to return and risk.

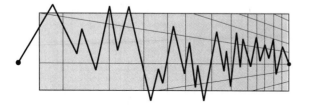

QUESTIONS

1. Calculate the historical rate of return for the months of January and February for the Minniefield Corporation.

Price on January 1: $20
    Cash dividends in January = $0

Price on February 1: $21
    Cash dividends in February= $2

Price on March 1: $24

2. Suppose that the monthly return for two investors is as follows:

Month	Investor I	Investor II
1	9%	25%
2	13%	13%
3	22%	22%
4	–18%	–24%

a. What is the arithmetic average monthly rate of return for the two investors?

b. What is the time-weighted average monthly rate of return for the two investors?

c. Why does the arithmetic average monthly rate of return diverge more from the time-weighted monthly rate of return for investor II than for investor I?

3. The Mabelle Company is a money management firm that manages the funds of pension plan sponsors. For one of its clients it manages $200 million. The cash flow for this particular client's portfolio for the past three months was $20 million, –$8 million, and $4 million. The market value of the portfolio at the end of three months was $208 million.

a. What is the dollar-weighted rate of return for this client's portfolio over the three-month period?

b. Suppose that the $8 million cash outflow in the second month was a result of withdrawals by the plan sponsor and that the cash flow after adjusting for this withdrawal is therefore zero. What would the dollar-weighted rate of return then be for this client's portfolio?

4. Suppose the probability distribution for the one-period return of some asset is as follows:

Return	Probability
0.20	0.10
0.15	0.20
0.10	0.30
0.03	0.25
−0.06	0.15

a. What is this asset's expected one-period return?

b. What is this asset's variance and standard deviation for the one-period return?

5. What statistical measures are used in calculating the risk of an asset or a portfolio?

6. "A portfolio's expected return and variance of return are simply the weighted average of the individual asset expected returns and variances." Do you agree with this statement?

7. Professor Harry Markowitz, core-cipient of the 1990 Nobel Prize in Economics, wrote the following:

   A portfolio with sixty differ-ent railway securities, for example, would not be as well diversified as the same size portfolio with some rail-road, some public utility, mining, various sort of man-ufacturing, etc.

   Why is this true?

8. Two portfolio managers are dis-cussing modern portfolio theory. Manager A states that the objective of Markowitz portfolio analysis is to construct a portfolio that maxi-mizes expected return for a given level of risk. Manager B disagrees, believing that the objective is to construct a portfolio that mini-mizes risk for a given level of return. Which portfolio manager is correct?

9. Explain what is meant by a risk-averse investor.

10. What is meant by a Markowitz efficient frontier?

11. Explain why all feasible portfolios are not on the Markowitz effi-cient frontier.

12. What is meant by an optimal portfolio and how is it related to an efficient portfolio?

13. a. How does an investor select the optimal portfolio?

    b. Explain the role of an investor's preference in selecting an opti-mal portfolio.

14. Explain the critical role of the cor-relation between assets in deter-mining the potential benefits from diversification.

15. "The maximum diversification benefits will be achieved if asset returns are perfectly correlated." Explain whether you agree or dis-agree with this statement.

16. Investment advisors who argue for investing in a portfolio consisting of both stocks and bonds point to the fact that the correlation of returns between these two asset classes is less than 1 and therefore there will be benefits to diversifying.

    a. What does the correlation of the returns between two asset classes measure?

    b. In what sense would a correla-tion of return of less than 1 between stocks and bonds sug-gest that there are potential diversification benefits?

17. The following excerpt is from Warren Bailey and Rene M. Stulz, "Benefits of International Diversification: The Case of

Pacific Basin Stock Markets," (*Journal of Portfolio Management*, Summer 1990).

> Recent international diversification literature uses monthly data from foreign stock markets to make the point that American investors should hold foreign stock to reduce the variance of a portfolio of domestic stocks without reducing its expected return.

a. Why would you expect that the justification of diversifying into foreign stock markets would depend on empirical evidence regarding the ability to "reduce the variance of a portfolio of domestic stocks without reducing its expected return."

b. Typically in research papers that seek to demonstrate the benefits of international diversification by investing in a foreign stock market, two efficient frontiers are compared. One is an efficient frontier constructed using only domestic stocks; the other is an efficient frontier constructed using both domestic and foreign stocks. If there are benefits to diversifying into foreign stocks, should the efficient frontier constructed using both domestic and foreign stocks lie above or below the efficient frontier constructed using only domestic stocks? Explain your answer.

18. The following excerpt is from John E. Hunter and T. Daniel Coggin, "An Analysis of the Diversification from International Equity Investment" (*Journal of Portfolio Management*, Fall 1990).

> The extent to which investment risk can be diversified depends upon the degree to which national markets were completely dominated by a single world market factor (i.e., if all cross-national correlations were 1.00), then international diversification would have no benefit. If all national markets were completely independent (that is, if all cross-national correlations were zero), then international diversification over an infinite number of countries would completely eliminate the effect of variation in national markets.

a. Why are the "cross-national correlations" critical in justifying the benefits from international diversification?

b. Why do Hunter and Coggin argue that there would be no benefit from international diversification if the these correlations are all 1.00?

19. Indicate why you agree or disagree with the following statement: "Because it is difficult to determine an investor's utility function, Markowitz portfolio theory can not be employed in practice to construct a Markowitz efficient portfolio."

20. The following is an excerpt from Marshall E. Blume, "The Capital Asset Pricing Model and the CAPM Literature," in Diana R. Harrington and Robert A. Korajczyk (eds.), *The CAPM Controversy: Policy and Strategy Implications for Investment Management* (Charlottesville, VA: Association for Investment

Management and Research, 1993), p. 5 (the first sentence was modified):

> *Implicit in Graham and Dodd's original theory (Security Analysis, 1934) was the idea that a stock has an intrinsic value. If an investor purchased an asset or stock at a price below its intrinsic value, the asset over time would move up to its intrinsic value without risk. Graham and Dodd recognized that people hold different expectations of the future, but they had little to say about diversification. The basic idea was that, if every stock bought was below its intrinsic value, the overall portfolio would be a good one and would make money as the values of the component stocks rose to their intrinsic values.*

> *The legal profession translated this intellectual idea into the Prudent Man rule for investing personal trusts. According to this rule, a trust manager must invest in each asset on its own merit. If each asset is safe, then the total portfolio will be safe.*

> *For example, futures cannot be used under the Prudent Man rule because they are inherently risky—even though investment managers now know that when futures are combined with other assets, they can reduce portfolio risk.*

> *Markowitz in 1959 then developed mathematics for the efficient set. . . . This concept of looking at the entire portfolio changed the way investors think about investing.*

> *Markowitz focused on the portfolio as a whole, not explicitly on the individual assets in the portfolio, which was clearly at odds with the Prudent Man rule for personal trusts. In fact, under the Employee Retirement Income Security Act passed in the mid-1970s, investing in derivatives to reduce the risk of a portfolio was, for the most part, legally imprudent.*

Why is the Prudent Man rule for investing personal trust in conflict with the way to construct a portfolio as suggested by Markowitz portfolio theory?

Risk and Return Theories: II

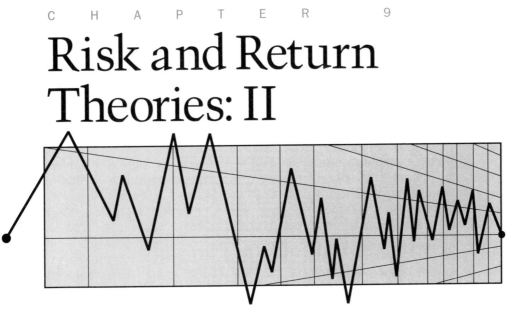

LEARNING OBJECTIVES

After reading this chapter you will understand:

- the assumptions underlying capital market theory.

- the capital market line and the role of a risk-free asset in its construction.

- why the capital market line dominates the Markowitz efficient frontier.

- what the security market line is.

- the difference between systematic and unsystematic risk.

- the capital asset pricing model, the relevant measure of risk in this model, and the limitations of the model.

- what the market model is.

- the findings of empirical tests of the capital asset pricing model and the difficulties of testing this model.

- the multifactor CAPM and the difficulties in applying it.

- the arbitrage pricing theory, the difficulties in empirically testing the arbitrage pricing theory model, and the difficulty in applying this model.

- the factors that researchers have found appear to affect the return on securities.

- some fundamental principles concerning risk and return that are valid regardless of the asset pricing model used.

Having introduced the principles of portfolio theory in Chapter 8, we will now describe capital market theory and the implications of both that theory and portfolio theory for the pricing of financial assets. This leads to one well-known asset pricing model called the capital asset pricing model (CAPM). We also discuss other asset pricing models.

The asset pricing models we describe in this chapter are equilibrium models. Given assumptions about the behavior and expectations of investors, and assumptions about capital markets, these models predict the expected return that an investor should require in order to acquire an asset. Thus, the models provide an answer to the question of what risk premium an investor should require. Knowing the expected cash flow and the expected return one can determine the theoretical value of an asset, therefore these models are referred to as asset pricing models.

ECONOMIC ASSUMPTIONS

Economic theories are an abstraction of the real world and, as such, are based upon some simplifying assumptions. These assumptions simplify matters a great deal and some of them may even seem unrealistic. However, these assumptions make economic theories more tractable from a mathematical standpoint.

Assumptions About Investor Behavior

Capital market theory makes assumptions about the behavior of investors in constructing a portfolio of risky assets. These assumptions are described below.

Behavioral assumption 1—Capital market theory assumes that investors make investment decisions based on two parameters: the expected return and the variance of returns. That is why portfolio theory described in the previous chapter is sometimes referred to as a **two-parameter model**.

The two-parameter assumption tells us what investors use as inputs in making their investment decisions. The specific behavior they are assumed to follow is that in order to accept greater risk, they must be compensated by the opportunity of realizing a higher return. We refer to such investors as risk averse. This is an oversimplified definition. Actually, a more rigorous definition of risk aversion is described by a mathematical specification of an investor's utility function. However, this complexity need not concern us here. What is important is that if an investor faces a choice between two portfolios with the same expected return, she will select the portfolio with the lower risk. Certainly, this is a reasonable assumption.

Behavioral assumption 2—Capital market theory assumes that the risk-averse investor will ascribe to the methodology of reducing portfolio risk by combining assets with counterbalancing correlations as explained in the previous chapter.

Behavioral assumption 3—Capital market theory assumes all investors make investment decisions over some single-period investment horizon. The length of that period (six months, one year, two years, etc.) is not specified. In reality, the investment decision process is more complex than that, with many investors having more than one investment horizon. Nonetheless, the assumption of a one-period investment horizon is necessary to simplify the mathematics of the theory.

Behavioral assumption 4—Capital market theory assumes that investors have the same expectations with respect to the inputs that are used to derive the Markowitz efficient portfolios: asset returns, variances, and correlations. This is called the **homogeneous expectations assumption.**

Assumptions About Capital Markets

The previous assumptions dealt with the behavior of investors in making investment decisions. It is also necessary to make assumptions about the characteristics of the capital market in which investors transact. There are three assumptions in this regard.

Capital market assumption 1—Capital market theory assumes that the capital market is perfectly competitive. In general, this means the number of buyers and sellers is sufficiently large, and all investors are small enough relative to the market, so that no individual investor can influence an asset's price. Consequently, all investors are price takers, and the market price is determined where there is equality of supply and demand.

Capital market assumption 2—Capital market theory assumes that there are no transaction costs or impediments that interfere with the supply and demand for an asset. Economists refer to these various costs and impediments as "frictions." The costs associated with frictions generally result in buyers paying more than in the absence of frictions and/or sellers receiving less. In the case of financial markets, frictions would include commissions charged by brokers and bid-ask spreads charged by dealers. They also include taxes and government-imposed transfer fees.

Capital market assumption 3—Capital market theory assumes that there is a risk-free asset in which investors can invest. Moreover, it assumes that investors can not only invest in such an asset but can borrow funds at the same interest rate offered on that risk-free asset. That is, it is assumed that investors can lend and borrow at some risk-free rate.

CAPITAL MARKET THEORY

In the previous chapter, we distinguished between a risky asset and a risk-free asset. We explained that an investor should create a portfolio with the highest expected return for a given level of risk, where risk is measured by the portfolio's variance. We did not consider the possibility of constructing efficient portfolios in the presence of a risk-free asset, that is, an asset where the return is known with certainty.

In the absence of a risk-free rate, portfolio theory tells us that Markowitz efficient portfolios can be constructed based on expected return and variance. Once a risk-free asset is introduced and assuming that investors can borrow and lend at the risk-free rate (Capital Market Assumption 3), the conclusion of portfolio theory can be qualified as illustrated in Figure 9-1. Every combination of the risk-free asset and the Markowitz efficient portfolio M is shown on the tangent line in the figure. This line is drawn from the vertical axis at the risk-free rate tangent to the Markowitz efficient frontier. The point of tangency is denoted by M. All of the portfolios on the line are feasible for the investor to construct. Portfolios to the left of M represent combinations of risky assets and the risk-free asset. Portfolios to the right of M include purchases of risky assets made with funds borrowed at the risk-free rate.

Now compare a portfolio on the line to the portfolio on the Markowitz efficient frontier with the same risk. For example, compare portfolio P_A, which is on the Markowitz efficient frontier with portfolio P_B, which is on the line and therefore has some combination of the risk-free rate and the Markowitz efficient portfolio M. Notice that for the same risk the expected return is greater for P_B than for P_A. A risk-averse investor will prefer P_B to P_A. That is, P_B will dominate P_A. In fact, this is true for all but one portfolio on the line: portfolio M which is on the Markowitz efficient frontier.

Recognizing this, we must modify the conclusion from portfolio theory that an investor will select a portfolio on the Markowitz efficient frontier, the particular portfolio depending on the investor's risk preference. With the introduction of the risk-free asset, we can now say that an investor will select a portfolio on the line, representing a combination of borrowing or lending at the risk-free rate and purchases of the Markowitz efficient portfolio M. The particular efficient portfolio that the investor will select on the line will depend on the investor's risk preference.

Figure 9-1
The Capital Market Line

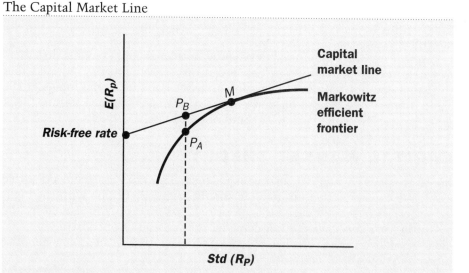

Portfolios to the right of M are leveraged portfolios (borrowing at a risk-free rate to buy a market portfolio)

Portfolios to the left of M are combinations of risk-free asset and market portfolio

It was William Sharpe,[1] John Lintner,[2] Jack Treynor,[3] and Jan Mossin[4] who demonstrated that the opportunity to borrow or lend at the risk-free rate implies a capital market where risk-averse investors will prefer to hold portfolios consisting of combinations of the risk-free asset and some portfolio M on the Markowitz efficient frontier. Sharpe called the line from the risk-free rate to portfolio M on the efficient frontier the **capital market line** (*CML*), and this is the name that has been adopted in the industry.

One more key question remains: How does an investor construct portfolio M? Eugene Fama answered this question by demonstrating that M must consist of all assets available to investors, and each asset must be held in proportion to its market value relative to the total market value of all assets.[5] So, for example, if the total market value of some asset is $500 million and the total market value of all assets is $X, then the percentage of the portfolio that should be allocated to that asset is $500 million divided by $X. Because portfolio M consists of all assets, it is referred to as the **market portfolio**.

Now we can restate how a risk-averse investor who makes investment decisions as suggested by portfolio theory and who can borrow and lend at the risk-free rate should construct efficient portfolios. This should be done by combining an investment in the risk-free asset and the market portfolio. The theoretical result that all investors will hold a combination of the risk-free asset and the market portfolio is known as the **two-fund separation theorem**[6]—one fund consists of the risk-free asset and the other is the market portfolio. While all investors will select a portfolio on the capital market line, the optimal portfolio for a specific investor is the one that will maximize that investor's risk preference.

Deriving the Formula for the Capital Market Line

Figure 9-1 shows us graphically the capital market line. But we can derive a formula for the capital market line algebraically as well. This formula will be key in our goal of showing how a risky asset should be priced.

To derive the formula for the capital market line, we combine the two-fund separation theorem with the assumption of homogeneous expectations (Behavioral Assumption 4). Suppose an investor creates a two-fund portfolio: a portfolio consisting of w_F invested in the risk-free asset and w_M in the market portfolio, where w represents the corresponding percentage (weight) of the portfolio allocated to each asset. Thus,

$$w_F + w_M = 1 \text{ or } w_F = 1 - w_M$$

What is the expected return and the risk of this portfolio? As we explained in the previous chapter, the expected return is equal to the weighted average

[1] William F. Sharpe, "Capital Asset Prices," *Journal of Finance* (September 1964), pp. 425-42.

[2] John Lintner, "The Valuation of Risk Assets and the Selection of Risky Investments in Stock Portfolio and Capital Budgets," *Review of Economics and Statistics* (February 1965), pp. 13-37.

[3] Jack L. Treynor, "Toward a Theory of Market Value of Risky Assets," Unpublished Paper, Arthur D. Little, 1961.

[4] Jan Mossin, "Equilibrium in a Capital Asset Market," *Econometrica* (October 1966), pp. 768-83.

[5] Eugene F. Fama, "Efficient Capital Markets: A Review of Theory and Empirical Work," *Journal of Finance* (May 1970), pp. 383-417.

[6] James Tobin, "Liquidity Preference as Behavior Towards Risks," *Review of Economic Studies* (February 1958), pp. 65-86.

of the two assets. Therefore, for our two-fund portfolio, the expected portfolio return, $E(R_p)$, is equal to:

$$E(R_p) = w_F R_F + w_M E(R_M)$$

Since we know that $w_F = 1 - w_M$, we can rewrite $E(R_p)$ as follows:

$$E(R_p) = (1 - w_M) R_F + w_M E(R_M)$$

This can be simplified to:

$$E(R_p) = R_F + w_M [E(R_M) - R_F] \qquad (9.1)$$

Now that we know the expected return of our hypothetical portfolio, we turn to the portfolio's risk as measured by the variance of the portfolio. We know from Equation (8.4) of the previous chapter how to calculate the variance of a two-asset portfolio. We repeat Equation (8.4) below:

$$var(R_p) = w_i^2 \, var(R_i) + w_j^2 \, var(R_j) + 2 \, w_i \, w_j \, std(R_i) \, std(R_j) \, cor(R_i, R_j)$$

We can use this equation for our two-fund portfolio. Asset i in this case is the risk-free asset F and asset j is the market portfolio M. Then,

$$var(R_p) = w_F^2 \, var(R_F) + w_M^2 \, var(R_M) + 2 \, w_F \, w_M \, std(R_F) std(R_M) \, cor(R_F, R_M)$$

We know that the variance of the risk-free asset, $var(R_F)$ is equal to zero. This is because there is no possible variation in the return since the future return is known. The correlation between the risk-free asset and the market portfolio, $cor(R_F, R_M)$, is zero. This is because the risk-free asset has no variability and therefore does not move at all with the return on the market portfolio which is a risky asset. Substituting these two values into the formula for the portfolio's variance we get:

$$var(R_p) = w_M^2 \, var(R_M)$$

In other words, the variance of the two-fund portfolio is represented by the weighted variance of the market portfolio. We can solve for the weight of the market portfolio by substituting standard deviations for variances.

Since the standard deviation is the square root of the variance, we can write:

$$std(R_p) = w_M \, std(R_M)$$

and therefore:

$$w_M = \frac{std(R_p)}{std(R_M)}$$

Now let's return to Equation (9.1) and substitute for w_M the result we just derived:

$$E(R_p) = R_F + \frac{std(R_p)}{std(R_M)} \, [E(R_M) - R_F]$$

Rearranging, we get:

$$E(R_p) = R_F + \frac{[E(R_M) - R_F]}{std(R_M)} \, std(R_p)$$

(9.2)

This is the equation for the capital market line (CML).

Interpreting the CML Equation

Capital market theory assumes that all investors have the same expectations for the inputs into the model (Behavioral Assumption 4). With homogeneous expectations, $std(R_M)$ and $std(R_p)$ are the market's consensus for the expected return distributions for the market portfolio and portfolio p. The slope of the CML is:

$$\frac{[E(R_M) - R_F]]}{std(R_M)}$$

Let's examine the economic meaning of the slope. The numerator is the expected return of the market beyond the risk-free return. It is a measure of the risk premium or the reward for holding the risky market portfolio rather than the risk-free asset. The denominator is the risk of the market portfolio. Thus, the slope measures the reward per unit of market risk. Since the CML represents the return offered to compensate for a perceived level of risk, each point on the line is a balanced market condition, or equilibrium. The slope of the line determines the additional return needed to compensate for a unit change in risk. That is why the slope of the CML is also referred to as the **market price of risk.**

The CML says that the expected return on a portfolio is equal to the risk-free rate plus a risk premium. As we noted in Chapter 1 and Chapter 8, we seek a measure of the risk premium. According to capital market theory, the risk premium is equal to the market price of risk times the quantity of risk for the portfolio (as measured by the standard deviation of the portfolio). That is:

$$E(R_p) = R_F + \text{Market price of risk} \times \text{Amount of portfolio risk}$$

THE CAPITAL ASSET PRICING MODEL

Up to this point, we know how a risk-averse investor who makes decisions based on two parameters (risk and expected return) should construct an efficient portfolio—by using a combination of the market portfolio and the risk-free rate. Based on this result, we can derive a model that shows how a risky asset should be priced. In the process of doing so, we can refine our thinking about the risk associated with an asset. Specifically, we can show that the appropriate risk that investors should be compensated for accepting is not the variance of an asset's return but some other quantity. In order to do this, we need to take a closer look at portfolio risk.

Systematic and Unsystematic Risk

In our discussion of portfolio theory in Chapter 8, we initially defined the variance of return as the appropriate measure of risk. We suggested, however, this risk measure can be decomposed into two general types of risk: systematic risk and unsystematic risk.

Systematic risk is the portion of an asset's return variability that can be attributed to a common factor. It is also called **undiversifiable risk** or **market risk**. Systematic risk is the minimum level of risk that can be obtained for a portfolio by means of diversification across a large number of randomly chosen assets. As such, systematic risk results from general market and economic conditions that cannot be diversified away.

The portion of an asset's return variability that can be diversified away is referred to as **unsystematic risk**. It is also sometimes called **diversifiable risk, residual risk**, or **company-specific risk**. This is the risk that is unique to a company such as a strike, the outcome of unfavorable litigation, or a natural catastrophe. As examples of this type of risk, one need only recall the case of product tampering involving Tylenol capsules (manufactured by Johnson & Johnson, Inc.) in October 1982, or the chemical accident at the Union Carbide plant in Bhopal, India in December 1984. Both of these unforecastable and hence unexpected tragedies had negative impacts on the stock prices of the two companies involved.

How diversification reduces unsystematic risk for portfolios was illustrated in Figure 8-4. As we indicated, at a portfolio size of about 20 randomly selected securities, the level of unsystematic risk is almost completely diversified away. Essentially, all that is left is systematic or market risk.

Therefore the total risk of an asset can be measured by its variance. However, the total risk can be decomposed into its systematic and unsystematic risk components. Next we will show how this can be done so as to be able to quantify both components.

Quantifying Systematic Risk

Quantification of systematic risk can be accomplished by dividing security return into two parts: one perfectly correlated with and proportionate to the market return, and a second independent from (uncorrelated with) the market. The first component of return is usually referred to as systematic, the second as unsystematic or diversifiable return. Thus we have:

$$\text{Security return} = \text{Systematic return} + \text{Unsystematic return} \qquad (9.3)$$

As the systematic return is proportional to the market return, it can be expressed as the symbol beta (ß) times the market return, R_M. The proportionality factor beta is a **market sensitivity index**, indicating how sensitive the security return is to changes in the market level. (How to estimate beta for a security or portfolio will be discussed later.) The unsystematic return, which is independent of market returns, is usually represented by the symbol epsilon (ε'). Thus, the security return, R, may be expressed as:

$$R = ßR_M + \varepsilon' \qquad (9.4)$$

For example, if a security has a ß of 2.0, then a 10% market return will generate a 20% systematic return for the stock. The security return for the period would be the 20% plus the unsystematic component. The unsystematic component depends on factors unique to the company, such as labor difficulties, higher-than-expected sales, and so on.

The security returns model given by Equation (9.4) is usually written in such a way that the average value of the residual term, ε', is zero. This is accomplished by adding a factor, alpha (α), to the model to represent the average value of the unsystematic returns over time. That is, we set $\varepsilon' = \alpha + \varepsilon$ so that:

$$R = \alpha + ßR_M + \varepsilon \tag{9.5}$$

where the average ε over time should tend to zero.

The model for security returns given by Equation (9.5) is usually referred to as the **market model.** Graphically, the model can be depicted as a line fitted to a plot of security returns against rates of return on the market index. This is shown for a hypothetical security in Figure 9-2.

The beta factor can be thought of as the slope of the line. It gives the expected increase in security return for a 1% increase in market return. In Figure 9-2, if a security has a beta of 1.0, a 10% market return will result, *on the average*, in a 10% security return.

The alpha factor is represented by the intercept of the line on the vertical security return axis. It is equal to the average value over time of the unsystematic returns (ε') on the stock. For most stocks, the alpha factor tends to be small and unstable.

Figure 9-2
Graphical Depiction of the Market Model

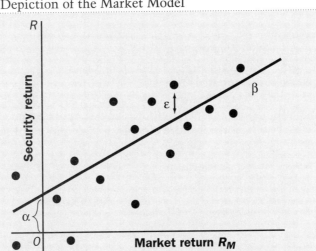

Beta (β), the market sensitivity index, is the slope of the line.
Alpha (α), the average of the residual returns, is the intercept of the line on the security axis.
Epsilon (ε), the residual returns, are the perpendicular distances of the points from the line.

Using the definition of security return given by the market model, the specification of systematic and unsystematic risk is straightforward—they are simply the standard deviations of the two return components.[7]

The systematic risk of a security is equal to ß times the standard deviation of the market return.

$$\text{Systematic risk} = \text{ß std}(R_M) \tag{9.6}$$

The unsystematic risk equals the standard deviation of the residual return factor ε:

$$\text{Unsystematic risk} = \text{std}(\varepsilon) \tag{9.7}$$

Given measures of individual-security systematic risk, we can now compute the systematic risk of the portfolio. It is equal to the beta factor for the portfolio, $ß_p$, times the risk of the market index, $\text{std}(R_M)$:

$$\text{Portfolio systematic risk} = ß_p \text{ std }(R_M) \tag{9.8}$$

The portfolio beta factor in turn can be shown to be simply an average of the individual security betas, weighted by the proportion of each security in the portfolio:

$$ß_p = w_1 ß_1 + w_2 ß_2 + \ldots + w_n ß_n$$

Or more concisely as:

$$ß_p = \sum_{i=1}^{n} w_i ß_i \tag{9.9}$$

where

w_i = the proportion of portfolio market value represented by security i
n = the number of securities

Thus, the systematic risk of a portfolio is simply the market value-weighted average of the systematic risk of the individual securities. It follows that the ß for a portfolio consisting of all securities is 1. If a stock's ß exceeds 1, it is above the average. If the portfolio is composed of an equal dollar investment in each security, the $ß_p$ is simply an unweighted average of the component security betas.

The unsystematic risk of the portfolio is also a function of the unsystematic security risks, but the form is more complex.[8] The important point is that with increasing diversification this risk approaches zero.

---

[7] The relationship between the risk components is given by

$$\text{var}(R_p) = ß^2 \text{ var}(R_M) + \text{var}(\varepsilon')$$

This follows directly from Equation (9.5) and the assumption of statistical independence of R_M and ε'. The R^2 term previously discussed is a ratio of systematic to total risk (both measured in terms of variance):

$$R^2 = \frac{ß^2 \text{ var}(R_M)}{\text{var}(\varepsilon')}$$

[8] Assuming the unsystematic returns (ε'_i) of securities to be uncorrelated (reasonably true in practice), the unsystematic portfolio risk is given by

$$\text{var}(\varepsilon'_p) = \sum_{i=1}^{n} w_i^2 \text{ var}(\varepsilon'_i)$$

where $\text{var}(\varepsilon'_i)$ is the unsystematic risk for stock i. Assume the portfolio is made up of an equal percentage invested in each security and $\text{var}(\varepsilon')$ is the average value of the $\text{var}(\varepsilon'_i)$. Then, $w_i = 1/n$ and:

$$\text{var}(\varepsilon'_p) = \frac{1}{n} \text{var}(\varepsilon')$$

which—assuming $\text{var}(\varepsilon')$ is finite—obviously approaches zero as the number of issues in the portfolio increases.

With these results for portfolio risk, it is useful to return to the studies of the impact of diversification on risk. One study compared the standard deviation for 20-stock portfolios with the predicted lower limits based on average security systematic risks. The lower limit is equal to the average beta for the portfolio times the standard deviation of the market return. The standard deviations in all cases studied were close to the predicted values. These results support the contention that portfolio systematic risk equals the average systematic risk of the component securities.

The implications of these results are substantial. First, we would expect realized rates of return over long periods of time to be related to the systematic as opposed to the total risk of securities. As the unsystematic risk is relatively easily eliminated, we should not expect the market to offer investors a "risk premium" for bearing such risk. Second, because security systematic risk is equal to the security beta times $std(R_M)$ (which is common to all securities), beta is useful as a *relative* risk measure. The ß gives the systematic risk of a security (or portfolio) relative to the risk of the market index. Thus, it is often convenient to speak of systematic risk in relative terms—that is in terms of beta rather than beta times $std(R_M)$.

Estimating Beta

The beta of a security or portfolio can be estimated only using statistical analysis. More specifically, we use regression analysis on historical data to estimate the market model given by Equation (9.5). The estimated slope for the market model is the estimate of beta. A series of returns is computed according to Equation (8.1), given in Chapter 8, over some time interval for some broad market index (such as the S&P 500 stock market index) and for the stock (or portfolio).[9] For example, monthly returns can be calculated for the past five years; thus, there would be 60 return observations for both the market index and the stock or portfolio. Or, weekly returns can be calculated for the past year. There is nothing in portfolio theory that indicates whether weekly, monthly, or even daily returns should be used. Nor does theory indicate any specific number of observations, except that statistical methodology requires that more observations will give a more reliable measure of beta.[10]

Table 9-1 gives estimates of beta using historical data plus systematic and unsystematic risk for 30 stocks estimated from 60 months of return data prior to July 31, 1992. For the values reported in Table 9-1 the Standard & Poor's 500, which is a broad market index, was used as a surrogate for the return on the market portfolio.

Another product of the statistical technique used to estimate beta is the percentage of systematic risk to total risk. In statistical terms, it is measured by the coefficient of determination from the regression which indicates the percentage of the variation in the return of the asset explained by the market

---

[9] We discuss several broad market indexes in Chapter 13.

[10] This assumes that the economic determinants that affect the beta of a stock do not change over the measurement period.

Table 9-1
Market Model Statistics for the 30 Stocks (July 31, 1992)

	Beta	Systematic Risk	Unsystematic Risk
Allied Signal	1.00	.42	.58
Alcoa	1.08	.42	.58
American Express	1.22	.44	.56
American Telephone	.80	.37	.63
Bethlehem Steel	1.44	.36	.64
Boeing	1.15	.49	.51
Caterpillar	.96	.28	.72
Chevron	.70	.30	.70
Coca Cola	.95	.53	.47
Disney	1.26	.59	.41
DuPont	1.13	.60	.40
Eastman Kodak	.76	.37	.63
Exxon	.58	.42	.58
General Electric	1.18	.72	.28
General Motors	1.00	.37	.63
Goodyear	1.10	.24	.76
IBM	.73	.30	.70
International Paper	1.19	.54	.46
McDonalds	.96	.51	.49
Merck	.84	.49	.51
Minnesota Mining	.91	.58	.42
J.P. Morgan	1.15	.48	.52
Philip Morris	1.00	.51	.49
Procter & Gamble	.87	.47	.53
Sears	1.15	.58	.42
Texaco	.61	.25	.75
Union Carbide	.93	.18	.82
United Technologies	1.38	.74	.26
Westinghouse	1.15	.47	.53
Woolworth	1.27	.46	.54

Note: Values estimated from 60 months of returns prior to July 31, 1992.

Source: Merrill Lynch Security Evaluation Service

portfolio return. The value of the coefficient ranges from 0 to 1. For example, a coefficient of determination of 0.3 for an asset means that 30% of the variation in the return of that asset is explained by the return of the market portfolio. Unsystematic or unique risk is then the amount not explained by the market portfolio's return. That is, it is one minus the coefficient of determination.

As we explained in the previous chapter, studies have shown that for the average NYSE common stock, systematic risk is about 30%, while unsystematic risk is about 70% of return variance. In contrast, the coefficient of determination for a well-diversified portfolio of stocks will typically exceed 90%, indicating that unsystematic risk is less than 10% of total portfolio return variance. This supports the point in Figure 8-2 that with a well-diversified portfolio, most of the portfolio risk is systematic risk.

Our purpose here is not to provide an explanation of the mechanics of calculating beta but to point out the practical problems in obtaining beta. (There are also many econometric issues, but we do not focus on these.)

There will be a difference in the calculated beta depending on the following factors:

1. the length of time over which a return is calculated (e.g., daily, weekly, monthly).

2. the number of observations used (e.g., three years of monthly returns or five years of monthly returns).

3. the specific time period used (e.g., January 1, 1985 to December 31, 1989, or January 1, 1983 to December 31, 1987).

4. the market index selected (e.g., the S&P 500 stock market index or an index consisting of all stocks traded on exchanges weighted by their relative market value).

Moreover, there is the question of the stability of beta over different time intervals—that is, does the beta of a stock or portfolio remain relatively unchanged over time, or does it change?[11]

The interesting question has to do with the economic determinants of the beta of a stock. The risk characteristics of a company should be reflected in its beta. Several empirical studies have attempted to identify these macroeconomic and microeconomic factors.[12]

The Security Market Line

The capital market line represents an equilibrium condition in which the expected return on a *portfolio* of assets is a linear function of the expected

---

[11] See Frank J. Fabozzi and Jack C. Francis, "Stability Tests for Alphas and Betas over Bull and Bear Markets," *Journal of Finance* (September 1977), pp. 1093-99; and "Beta as a Random Coefficient," *Journal of Financial and Quantitive Analysis* (March 1978), pp. 101-16.

[12] See, for example, Frank J. Fabozzi and Jack C. Francis, "Industry Effects and the Determinants of Beta," *Quarterly Review of Economics and Business* (Autumn 1979), pp. 61-74; Frank J. Fabozzi, Teresa Garlicki, Arabinda Ghosh, and Peter Kislowski, "Market Power as a Determinant of Systematic Risk: Empirical Evidence," *Review of Business and Economic Research* (Spring 1986), pp. 61-70; and Frank J. Fabozzi and Jack C. Francis, "The Effects of Changing Macroeconomic Conditions on the Parameters of the Single-Index Market Model," *Journal of Financial and Quantitative Analysis* (June 1979), pp. 351-56.

return on the market portfolio. A directly analogous relationship holds for *individual security* expected returns:

$$E(R_i) = R_F + \frac{[E(R_M) - R_F]}{std(R_M)} \, std(R_i) \tag{9.10}$$

Equation (9.10) simply uses risk and return variables for an individual security in place of the portfolio values in the equation for the CML given by Equation (9.2). This version of the risk-return relationship for individual securities is called the **security market line (SML)**. As in the case of the CML, the expected return for an asset is equal to the risk-free rate plus the product of the market price of risk and the quantity of risk in the security.

There is another more-common version of the SML relationship that uses the beta of a security. To see how this relationship is developed, look back at Equation (9.3). In a well-diversified portfolio (i.e., Markowitz diversified), the unique or unsystematic risk is eliminated. Consequently, it can be demonstrated that:

$$var(R_i) = \beta_i^2 \, var(R_M)$$

and the standard deviation as:

$$std(R_i) = \beta_i \, std(R_M)$$

Therefore,

$$\beta_i = \frac{std(R_i)}{std(R_M)}$$

If β_i is substituted into Equation (9.10), we have the beta version of the SML as shown in Equation (9.11), popularly referred to as the **capital asset pricing model (CAPM)**:[13]

$$E(R_i) = R_F + \beta_i \, [E(R_M) - R_F] \tag{9.11}$$

This equation states that, given the assumptions of capital market theory described earlier, the expected (or required) return on an individual asset is a positive linear function of its index of systematic risk as measured by beta. The higher the beta, the higher the expected return. Notice that it is only an asset's beta that determines its expected return.

Let's look at the prediction of the CAPM for several values of beta. The beta of a risk-free asset is zero. This is because the variability of the return of a

---

[13] The model is sometimes stated in risk premium form. Risk premiums, or excess returns, are obtained by subtracting the risk-free rate from the rate of return. The expected security and market risk premiums—designated $E(r_i)$ and $E(r_M)$, respectively—are given by:

$$E(r_i) = E(R_i) - R_F$$

$$E(r_M) = E(R_M) - R_F$$

Substituting these risk premiums into Equation (9.11), we obtain:

$$E(r_i) = \beta_i \, [E(r_M)]$$

In this form, the CAPM states that the expected risk premium for the investor's portfolio is equal to its beta value times the expected market risk premium. Or, equivalently stated, the expected risk premium should be equal to the quantity of risk (as measured by beta) and the market price of risk (as measured by the expected market risk premium).

risk-free is zero and therefore it does not covary with the market portfolio. So, if we want to know the expected return for a risk-free asset, we would substitute zero for ß$_i$ in Equation (9.11):

$$E(R_i) = R_F + 0 \, [E(R_M) - R_F] = R_F$$

Thus, the return on a risk-free asset is simply the risk-free return. Of course, this is what we expect.

The beta of the market portfolio is 1. If asset i has the same beta as the market portfolio, then substituting 1 into Equation (9.11) gives:

$$E(R_i) = R_F + 1 \, [E(R_M) - R_F] = E(R_M)$$

In this case, the expected return for the asset is the same as the expected return for the market portfolio. If an asset has a beta greater than the market portfolio (i.e., greater than 1), then the expected return will be higher than for the market portfolio. The reverse is true if an asset has a beta less than the market portfolio. A graph of the SML is presented in Figure 9-3.

The SML, CML, and Market Model

In equilibrium, the expected return of individual securities will lie on the SML and not on the CML. This is true because of the high degree of unsystematic risk that remains in individual securities that can be diversified out of portfolios of securities.

It follows that the only risk investors will pay a premium to avoid is market risk. Hence, two assets with the same amount of systematic risk will have

Figure 9-3
The Security Market Line

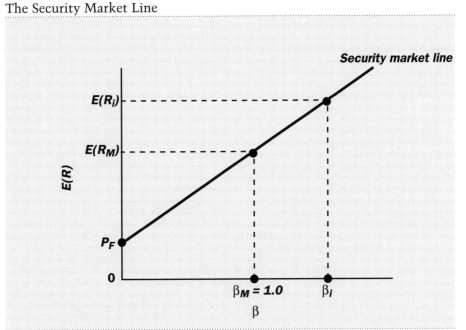

the same expected return. In equilibrium, only efficient portfolios will lie on both the CML and the SML. This underscores the fact that the systematic risk measure, beta, is most correctly considered as an *index* of the contribution of an individual security to the systematic risk of a well-diversified portfolio of securities.

It is important to point out the difference between the market model, and the CML and SML. The CML and the SML represent a predictive model for expected returns. The market model is a descriptive model used to describe historical data. Hence, the market model makes no prediction of what expected returns should be.

Tests of the Capital Asset Pricing Model

The CAPM is indeed a simple and elegant model, but these qualities do not in and of themselves guarantee that it will be useful in explaining observed risk/return patterns. Here we briefly review the empirical literature on attempts to verify the model.

The major difficulty in testing the CAPM is that the model is stated in terms of investors' expectations and not in terms of realized returns. To test the CAPM, it is necessary to convert the theoretical CAPM given by Equation (9.11) into a form that can be tested empirically. We will not go through this exercise here, but will simply provide the model that is typically tested.[14] Nor will we delve into the econometric problems associated with testing the CAPM, although we will discuss later an important theoretical issue that raises serious questions about the testability of the CAPM and therefore the empirical findings of researchers.

The empirical analogue of Equation (9.11) asserts that over the period of time analyzed: (1) there is a linear relationship between the average risk premium return on the market and the average risk premium return on a stock or portfolio, and its slope is $ß_j$; and (2) the linear relationship should pass through the origin. Moreover, according to the CAPM, beta is a complete measure of a stock's risk. Consequently, alternative risk measures that might be proposed, the most common being the standard deviation of return, should not be significant contributors to the explanation of a stock's return. Recall that the standard deviation measures a stock's total risk, which includes both systematic and unsystematic components.

The CAPM holds for both individual securities and portfolios. Therefore, the empirical tests can be based on either. Tests based on individual securities, however, are not the most efficient method of obtaining estimates of the magnitude of the risk/return trade-off for two reasons.

The first problem is called the "errors in variables bias;" it results from the fact that the beta of a stock typically is measured by correlating the stock's return over some sample of historical data. The slope of the resulting line (the regression coefficient) is the estimate of beta. It is subject to errors from various sources. These errors are random in their effect—that is, some stocks'

---

[14] The interested reader can find the procedure for developing the empirical model tested in Franco Modigliani and Gerald A. Pogue, "Introduction to Risk and Return: Concepts and Evidence: Part II," *Financial Analysts Journal* (May-June 1974), pp. 69-86.

betas are overestimated and some are underestimated. Nevertheless, when these estimated beta values are used in the test, the measurement errors tend to attenuate the relationship between average return and risk. By carefully grouping the securities into portfolios of securities with similar betas, much of this measurement error problem can be eliminated. The errors in individual stocks' betas cancel out so that the portfolio beta can be measured with much greater precision. This in turn means that tests based on portfolio returns will be more efficient than tests based on security returns.

The second problem relates to the obscuring effect of residual variation. Realized security returns have a large random component, which typically accounts for about 70% of the variation of return. (This is the diversifiable or unsystematic risk of the stock.) By grouping securities into portfolios, we can eliminate much of this "noise" and thereby get a much clearer view of the relationship between return and systematic risk.

It should be noted that grouping does not distort the underlying risk/return relationship. The relationship that exists for individual securities is exactly the same for portfolios of securities.

The major results of the empirical tests conducted in the early 1970s are summarized below:[15]

1. The evidence shows a significant positive relationship between realized returns and systematic risk as measured by beta. The average market risk premium estimated is usually less than predicted by the CAPM, however.

2. The relationship between risk and return appears to be linear. The studies give no evidence of significant curvature in the risk/return relationship.

3. Tests that attempt to discriminate between the effects of systematic and unsystematic risk do not yield definitive results. Both kinds of risk appear to be positively related to security returns, but there is substantial support for the proposition that the relationship between return and unsystematic risk is at least partly spurious—that is, partly a reflection of statistical problems rather than the true nature of capital markets.

Obviously, we cannot claim that the CAPM is absolutely right. On the other hand, the early empirical tests do support the view that beta is a useful risk measure and that high-beta stocks tend to be priced so as to yield correspondingly high rates of return.

In 1977, however, Richard Roll wrote a paper criticizing the previously published tests of the CAPM.[16] Roll argued that while the CAPM is testable in

---

[15] Some of the earlier studies are: Nancy Jacob, "The Measurement of Systematic Risk for Securities and Portfolios: Some Empirical Results," *Journal of Financial and Quantitative Analysis* (March 1971), pp. 815-34; Merton H. Miller and Myron S. Scholes, "Rates of Returns in Relation to Risk: A Reexamination of Recent Findings," and Fischer Black, Michael C. Jensen, and Myron S. Scholes, "The Capital Asset Pricing Model: Some Empirical Evidence," in Michael C. Jensen (ed.), *Studies in the Theory of Capital Markets* (New York: Praeger Books, 1972); Marshall E. Blume and Irwin Friend, "A New Look at the Capital Asset Pricing Model," *Journal of Finance* (March 1973), pp. 19-33; and Eugene F. Fama and James D. MacBeth, "Risk, Return and Equilibrium: Empirical Tests," Working Paper No. 7237, University of Chicago, Graduate School of Business, August 1972.

[16] Richard Roll, "A Critique of the Asset Pricing Theory: Part I. On the Past and Potential Testability of the Theory," *Journal of Financial Economics* (March 1977), pp. 129-76.

principle, no correct test of the theory had yet been presented. He also argued that there was practically no possibility that a correct test would ever be accomplished in the future.

The reasoning behind Roll's assertions revolves around his contribution that there is only one potentially testable hypothesis associated with the CAPM, namely, that the true market portfolio lies on the Markowitz efficient frontier (i.e., it is mean-variance efficient). Furthermore, because the true market portfolio must contain all worldwide assets, the value of most of which cannot be observed (e.g., human capital), the hypothesis is in all probability untestable.[17]

Since 1977 there have been a number of studies that purport either to support or reject the CAPM. These tests have attempted to examine implications of the CAPM other than the linearity of the risk/return relation as the basis of their methodology. Unfortunately, none provides a definitive test, and most are subject to substantial criticism, suffering from the same problem of identifying the "true" market portfolio. We mention two studies to provide a flavor of the post-Roll tests.

In 1980 Pao Cheng and Robert Grauer published the results of a test of the CAPM that they claimed were "free from the ambiguity imbedded in past tests."[18] Specifically, they made assumptions about the joint distribution of security returns so as to permit a test of the CAPM that circumvents the need to identify the "true" market portfolio. They then tested whether the predicted relationship holds among portfolio market values over various historical periods. The advantage of this approach is that the market portfolio is not required and betas do not have to be estimated. Unfortunately, the results of the Cheng and Grauer tests are inconclusive. Some results favor the CAPM; others reject it. The authors conclude that on balance their results provide evidence against the CAPM. Some have criticized these results on the basis that the assumptions are unwarranted, and, as the authors admit, their test is a joint test of the CAPM and the return distribution they assumed, rather than a pure test of the CAPM.

In 1982, Robert Stambaugh conducted a sensitivity analysis to determine whether changing the nature of the market proxy has a significant impact on the results of tests of the CAPM.[19] He expanded on the types of investments included in his proxy from stocks listed on the New York Stock Exchange to corporate and government bonds to real estate to durable goods such as house furnishings and automobiles. Results indicate that the nature of the conclusions is not materially affected as one expands the composition of the proxy for the market portfolio.

---

[17] The hypothesis tested in the traditional tests of the CAPM cited earlier—namely, that there is a linear relationship between average security returns and beta values—sheds no light on the question whatsoever. This follows because an approximately linear relation between risk and return would be achieved in tests involving large, well-diversified common stock portfolios, irrespective of whether securities were priced according to the CAPM or some totally different model. The result is tautological. The fact that a positive relationship between realized returns and betas is typically found simply indicates that the returns on the proxy indexes used for the true market portfolio were larger than the average return to the global minimum-variance portfolio.

[18] Pao L. Cheng and Robert R. Grauer, "An Alternative Test of the Capital Asset Pricing Model," *American Economic Review* (September 1980), pp. 660-71.

[19] Robert F. Stambaugh, "On the Exclusion of Assets from Tests of the Two-Parameter Model: A Sensitivity Analysis," *Journal of Financial Economics* (November 1982), pp. 237-68.

These results at first appear to be comforting until we realize that at the domestic level many investments, including human capital, are not included even in the broadest indexes examined. More importantly, the market portfolio—at least insofar as the public regards these markets as equivalent to the domestic one—should be internationally diversified, and the total invested capital of the United States is only a small fraction of invested capital worldwide. Moreover, many of these investments can be expected to exhibit a low degree of correlation with returns on investments in the United States. Stambaugh's results tell us only that when we move from using a market proxy that represents a small fraction of the market portfolio to a proxy that represents a larger but still small fraction, empirical results do not tend to change much.

THE MULTIFACTOR CAPM

The CAPM described above assumes that the only risk that an investor is concerned with is uncertainty about the future price of a security. Investors, however, usually are concerned with other risks that will affect their ability to consume goods and services in the future. Three examples would be the risks associated with future labor income, the future relative prices of consumer goods, and future investment opportunities.

Recognizing these other risks that investors face, Robert Merton has extended the CAPM based on consumers deriving their optimal lifetime consumption when they face these "extra-market" sources of risk.[20] These extra-market sources of risk are also referred to as "factors," hence the model derived by Merton is called a **multifactor CAPM** and is given below:

$$E(R_p) = R_F + \beta_{p,M}\, [E(R_M) - R_F] + \tag{9.12}$$
$$\beta_{p,F1}\, [E(R_{F1}) - R_F] + \beta_{p,F2}\, [E(R_{F2}) - R_F] + ... + \beta_{p,FK}\, [E(R_{FK}) - R_F]$$

where

R_F	= the risk-free return
$F1,\ F2,...,FK$	= factors or extra-market sources of risk, 1 to K
K	= number of factors or extra-market sources of risk
$\beta_{p,Fk}$	= the sensitivity of the portfolio to the k-th factor
$E(R_{Fk})$	= the expected return of factor k

The total extra-market sources of risk is equal to:

$$\beta_{p,F1}\, [E(R_{F1}) - R_F] + \beta_{p,F2}\, [E(R_{F2}) - R] +.. + \beta_{p,FK}\, [E(R_{FK}) - R_{FK}] \tag{9.13}$$

This expression says that investors want to be compensated for the risk associated with each source of extra-market risk, in addition to market risk. Note that if there are no extra-market sources of risk, then Equation (9.12) reduces to the expected return for the portfolio as predicted by the CAPM:

$$E(R_p) = R_F + \beta_p\, [E(R_M) - R_F]$$

---

[20] Robert C. Merton, "An Intertemporal Capital Asset Pricing Model," *Econometrica* (September 1973), pp. 867-888. A less technical version is published in "A Reexamination of the CAPM," in Irwin Friend and James Bicksler (eds.), *Risk and Return in Finance* (Cambridge, MA: Ballinger Publishing, 1976). Other papers on multifactor CAPMs are: John C. Cox, Jonathan E. Ingersoll, and Stephen A. Ross, "An Intertemporal Asset Pricing Model with Rational Expectations," *Econometrica* (1985), pp. 363-384, and Douglas Breeden, "An Intertemporal Asset Pricing Model with Stochastic Consumption and Investment Opportunities," *Journal of Financial Economics* (1979), pp. 265-96.

In the case of the CAPM, investors hedge the uncertainty associated with future security prices by diversification. This is done by holding the market portfolio, which can be thought of as a mutual fund that invests in all securities based on their relative capitalizations. In the multifactor CAPM, in addition to investing in the market portfolio, investors will also allocate funds to something equivalent to a mutual fund that hedges a particular extra-market risk. While not all investors are concerned with the same sources of extra-market risk, those that are concerned with a specific extra-market risk will basically hedge them in the same way.

We have just described the multifactor model for a portfolio. How can this model be used to obtain the expected return for an individual security? Since individual securities are nothing more than portfolios consisting of only one security, Equation (9.13) must hold for each security, i. That is:

$$E(R_i) = R_F + \beta_{i,M} [E(R_M) - R_F] + \beta_{i,F1} [E(R_{F1}) - R_F] + \qquad (9.14)$$
$$\beta_{i,F2} [E(R_{F2}) - R_F] + ... + \beta_{i,FK} [E(R_{FK}) - R_F]$$

The multifactor CAPM is an attractive model because it recognizes non-market risks. The pricing of an asset by the marketplace, then, must reflect risk premiums to compensate for these extra-market risks. Unfortunately, it may be difficult to identify all the extra-market risks and to value each of these risks empirically. Furthermore, when these risks are taken together, the multifactor CAPM begins to resemble the arbitrage pricing theory model described next.

ARBITRAGE PRICING THEORY MODEL

An alternative model to the CAPM and the multifactor CAPM was developed by Stephen Ross in 1976.[21] This model is based purely on arbitrage arguments, and hence is called the **arbitrage pricing theory (APT)** model.

Assumptions of the Arbitrage Pricing Theory

The APT model postulates that a security's expected return is influenced by a variety of factors, as opposed to just the single market index of the CAPM. Specifically, look back at Equation (9.5) which states that the return on a security is dependent on its market sensitivity index and an unsystematic return. The APT in contrast states that the return on a security is linearly related to H "factors." The APT does not specify what these factors are, but it is assumed that the relationship between security returns and the factors is linear.

To illustrate the APT model, assume a simple world with a portfolio consisting of three securities and with two factors (otherwise more complicated mathematical notation must be introduced). The following notation will be used:

---

[21] Stephen A. Ross, "The Arbitrage Theory of Capital Asset Pricing," *Journal of Economic Theory* (December 1976), pp. 343-62, and "Return, Risk and Arbitrage," in Friend and Bicksler (eds.), *Risk and Return in Finance*. Since the publication by Ross, there have been several studies that have refined the theory. See, for example, Gur Huberman, "A Simple Approach to Arbitrage Pricing Theory," *Journal of Economic Theory* (October 1982), pp. 183-191, and Jonathan E. Ingersoll, "Some Results in the Theory of Arbitrage Pricing," *Journal of Finance* (September 1984), pp. 1021-39.

$\tilde{R}_i$ = the random rate of return on security i (i = 1,2,3)

$E(R_i)$ = the expected return on security i (i = 1,2,3)

F_h = the h-th factor that is common to the returns of all three assets (h = 1,2)

$\beta_{i,h}$ = the sensitivity of the i-th security to the h-th factor

$\tilde{e}_i$ = the unsystematic return for security i (i = 1,2,3)

The APT model asserts that the random rate of return on security i is given by the following relationship:

$$\tilde{R}_i = E(R_i) + \beta_{i,1}F_1 + \beta_{i,2}F_2 + \tilde{e}_i \tag{9.15}$$

Derivation of the APT Model

For equilibrium to exist among these three assets, the following arbitrage condition must be satisfied: using no additional funds (wealth) and without increasing risk, it should not be possible, on average, to create a portfolio to increase return. In essence, this condition states that there is no "money machine" available in the market.

To see how this principle works, let V_i equal the *change* in the dollar amount invested in the i-th security as a percentage of the investor's wealth. For example, suppose that the market value of the investor's portfolio is initially $100,000, comprised of $20,000 in security 1, $30,000 in security 2, and $50,000 in security 3. Suppose an investor changes the initial portfolio to: $35,000 in security 1, $25,000 in security 2, and $40,000 in security 3; then the V_i's would be as follows:

$$V_1 = \frac{\$35,000 - \$20,000}{\$100,000} = 0.15$$

$$V_2 = \frac{\$25,000 - \$30,000}{\$100,000} = -0.05$$

$$V_3 = \frac{\$40,000 - \$50,000}{\$100,000} = -0.10$$

Note that the sum of the V_i's is equal to zero since no additional funds were invested. That is, rebalancing of the portfolio does not change the market value of the initial portfolio. Rebalancing does accomplish two things. First, it changes the future return of the portfolio. Second, it changes the total risk of the portfolio, both the systematic risk associated with the two factors and the unsystematic risk.

Consider the first consequence. Mathematically, the *change* in the portfolio's future return ($\Delta \tilde{R}_p$) can be shown to be as follows:

$$\Delta \tilde{R}_p = [V_1 E(R_1) + V_2 E(R_2) + V_3 E(R_3)] \tag{9.16}$$
$$+ [V_1 \beta_{1,1} + V_2 \beta_{2,1} + V_3 \beta_{3,1}] F_1$$
$$+ [V_1 \beta_{1,2} + V_2 \beta_{2,2} + V_3 \beta_{3,2}] F_2 + [V_1 \tilde{e}_1 + V_2 \tilde{e}_2 + V_3 \tilde{e}_3]$$

Equation (9.16) indicates that the change in the portfolio return will have a component that depends on systematic risk as well as unsystematic risk. While in our example we have assumed only three securities, when there are a large number of securities, the unsystematic risk can be eliminated by diversification as explained in Chapter 8. Thus, Equation (9.16) would reduce to:

$$\tilde{\Delta R}_P = [V_1\, E(R_1) + V_2\, E(R_2) + V_3\, E(R_3)] + \tag{9.17}$$
$$+ [V_1\, ß_{1,1} + V_2\, ß_{2,1} + V_3\, ß_{3,1}]\, F_1 + [V_1\, ß_{1,2} + V_2\, ß_{2,2} + V_3\, ß_{3,2}]\, F_2$$

Now look at the systematic risk with respect to each factor. The *change* in the portfolio risk with respect to factor 1 is just the betas of each security multiplied by their respective V_i's. Consequently, the change in the portfolio's sensitivity to systematic risk from factor 1 is:

$$V_1\, ß_{1,1} + V_2\, ß_{2,1} + V_3 ß_{3,1} \tag{9.18}$$

For factor 2, it is:

$$V_1\, ß_{1,2} + V_2\, ß_{2,2} + V_3 ß_{3,2} \tag{9.19}$$

One of the conditions that is imposed for no arbitrage is that the change in systematic risk with respect to each factor will be zero. That is, Equations (9.18) and (9.19) should satisfy the following:

$$V_1\, ß_{11} + V_2\, ß_{21} + V_3 ß_{31} = 0 \tag{9.20}$$
$$V_1\, ß_{12} + V_2\, ß_{22} + V_3 ß_{32} = 0 \tag{9.21}$$

If Equations (9.20) and (9.21) are satisfied, then Equation (9.17) reduces to:

$$\Delta E(\tilde{R}_P) = V_1\, E(R_1) + V_2\, E(R_2) + V_3\, E(R_3) \tag{9.22}$$

Now we can put all the conditions for no arbitrage together in terms of the equations above. As stated earlier, using no additional funds (wealth) and without increasing risk, it should not be possible, on average, to create a portfolio to increase return. No additional funds (wealth) means the following condition: $V_1 + V_2 + V_3 = 0$.

The condition that there be no change in the portfolio's sensitivity to each systematic risk is set forth in Equations (9.20) and (9.21). Finally, the expected additional portfolio return from reshuffling the portfolio must be zero. This can be expressed by setting Equation (9.22) equal to zero:

$$V_1\, E(R_1) + V_2\, E(R_2) + V_3\, E(R_3) = 0$$

Taken together, these Equations, as well as the condition that there be a sufficiently large number of securities so that unsystematic risk can be eliminated, describe mathematically the conditions for equilibrium pricing. These conditions can be solved mathematically, since the number of securities is greater than the number of factors, to determine the equilibrium value for the portfolio as well as the equilibrium value for each of the three securities. Ross has shown that the following risk and return relationship will result for each security *i*:

$$E(R_i) = R_F + ß_{i,F1}\, [E(R_{F1} - R_F)] + ß_{i,F2}\, [E(R_{F2}) - R_F] \tag{9.23}$$

where

$\beta_{i,Fj}$ = the sensitivity of security i to the j-th factor

$E(R_{i,Fj}) - R_F$ = the excess return of the j-th systematic factor over the risk-free rate, and can be thought of as the price (or risk premium) for the j-th systematic risk.

Equation (9.23) can be generalized to the case where there are H factors as follows:

$$E(R_i) = R_F + \beta_{i,F1}\,[E(R_{F1} - R_F)] + \beta_{i,F2}\,[E(R_{F2}) - R_F] \qquad (9.24)$$
$$+ \dots + \beta_{i,FH}\,[E(R_{FH}) - R_F]$$

Equation (9.24) is the APT model. It states that investors want to be compensated for all the factors that *systematically* affect the return of a security. The compensation is the sum of the products of the each factor's systematic risk $(\beta_{i,Fh})$, and the risk premium assigned to it by the market $[E(R_{Fh}) - R_F]$. As in the case of the two other risk and return models described earlier, an investor is not compensated for accepting unsystematic risk.

Comparison of APT Model and CAPM

Examining the equations, we can see that the CAPM Equation (9.11) and the multifactor CAPM Equation (9.14) are actually special cases of the APT model Equation (9.24).

CAPM: $E(R_i) = R_F + \beta_i\,[E(R_M) - R_F]$

Multifactor CAPM: $E(R_i) = R_F + \beta_{i,M}\,[E(R_M) - R_F] + \beta_{i,F1}\,[E(R_{F1}) - R_F] + \beta_{i,F2}\,[E(R_{F2}) - R_F] + \dots + \beta_{i,FH}\,[E(R_{FH}) - R_F]$

APT: $E(R_i) = R_F + \beta_{i,F1}\,[E(R_{F1}) - R_F] + \beta_{i,F2}\,[E(R_{F2}) - R_F] + \dots + \beta_{i,FK}\,[E(R_{FK}) - R_F]$

If the only factor is market risk, the APT model reduces to the CAPM. Contrast the APT with the multifactor CAPM. They look similar. Both say that investors are compensated for accepting all systematic risk and no unsystematic risk. The multifactor CAPM states that one of these systematic risks is market risk, while the APT model does not specify the systematic risks.

Advantages of APT

Supporters of the APT model argue that it has several major advantages over the CAPM or multifactor CAPM. First, it makes less-restrictive assumptions about investor preferences toward risk and return. As explained earlier, the CAPM theory assumes investors trade off between risk and return solely on the basis of the expected returns and standard deviations of prospective investments. The APT, on the other hand, simply requires some rather unobtrusive bounds be placed on potential investor utility functions.

Second, no assumptions are made about the distribution of security returns. Finally, since the APT does not rely on the identification of the true market portfolio, the theory is potentially testable.

Tests of the APT

The APT is a relatively new theory, and hence the financial literature continues to test its validity.[22] The research to date seems to indicate that the APT is a promising alternative to the single-factor CAPM in explaining asset returns. This research indicates that the APT may explain a significantly greater amount of the variance in common stock returns than the CAPM. However, there are some unresolved questions concerning the practical application of the APT.

There remains the question of how many factors explain security returns. One study by Nai-fu Chen, Richard Roll, and Stephen Ross suggests the following four plausible economic factors:[23]

1. unanticipated changes in industrial production.

2. unanticipated changes in the spread between the yield on low-grade and high-grade bonds.

3. unanticipated changes in interest rates and the shape of the yield curve.[24]

4. unanticipated changes in inflation.

Researchers at Salomon Brothers have developed a model similar to the general APT formulation, which posits seven macroeconomic factors systematically affecting common stock returns: long-run economic growth, short-run business cycle risk, long-term bond yield changes, short-term Treasury bill changes, inflation shocks, dollar changes versus trading partner currencies, and residual market beta.[25]

Thus, researchers continue to search for the factors that systematically explain returns. This research is carried out not only by researchers but practitioners.

SOME PRINCIPLES TO TAKE AWAY

In this chapter and in Chapter 8, we have covered the heart of what is popularly called modern portfolio theory and asset pricing theory. We have pointed out the assumptions and their critical role in the development of these theories and explained the empirical findings. While you may understand the topics covered, you may still be uncomfortable as to where we have progressed given the lack of theoretical and empirical support for the CAPM or the

---

[22] For a discussion of the issue of the number of factors in the APT, see Phoebus J. Dhrymes, "The Empirical Relevance of Arbitrage Pricing Models," *Journal of Portfolio Management* (Summer 1984), pp. 35-44; Stephen A. Ross, "Reply to Dhrymes: APT Is Empirically Relevant," *Journal of Portfolio Management* (Fall 1984), pp. 54-6; T. Daniel Coggin and John E. Hunter, "A Meta-Analysis of Pricing 'Risk' Factors in APT," *Journal of Portfolio Management* (Fall 1987), pp. 35-8; and Delores A. Conway and Marc R. Reinganum, "Stable Factors in Security Returns," *Journal of Business & Economic Statistics* (January 1988), pp. 1-15.

[23] Nai-fu Chen, Richard Roll and Stephen A. Ross, "Economic Forces and the Stock Market," *Journal of Business* (July 1986), pp. 383-403.

[24] The yield curve is discussed in Chapter 18.

[25] Eric H. Sorensen, Joseph J. Mezrich, and Chee Thum, "The Salomon Brothers U.S. Stock Risk Attribute Model," Salomon Brothers, New York, October 1989.

difficulty of identifying the factors in the multifactor CAPM and APT model. You are not alone—there are a good number of practitioners and academics who feel uncomfortable with these models, particularly the CAPM.

Nevertheless, what is comforting is that there are several general principles about risk and return that are derived from these theories that very few would question.

1. Investing has two dimensions, risk and return. Therefore, focusing only on the actual return that an investor has achieved without looking at the risk that had to be accepted to achieve that return is inappropriate.

2. It is inappropriate to look at the risk of an individual asset when deciding whether it should be included in a portfolio. What is important is how the inclusion of an asset into a portfolio will affect the risk of the portfolio.

3. Whether investors consider one risk or 1,000 risks, risk can be divided into two general categories: systematic risks that cannot be eliminated by diversification, and unsystematic risk which can be diversified.

4. Investors should only be compensated for accepting systematic risks. Thus, it is critical in formulating an investment strategy to identify the systematic risks.

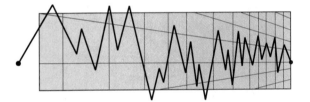

SUMMARY

This chapter explains the implications of portfolio theory, a theory that deals with the construction of efficient portfolios by rational risk-averse investors. Once a risk-free asset is introduced, the new efficient frontier is the capital market line, which represents a combination of a risk-free asset and the market portfolio.

The capital asset pricing model is an economic theory that describes the relationship between risk and expected return; or, equivalently, it is a model for the pricing of risky securities. The CAPM asserts that the only risk that is priced by rational investors is systematic risk, because that risk cannot be eliminated by diversification. Essentially, the CAPM says that the expected return of a security or a portfolio is equal to the rate on a risk-free security plus a risk premium. The risk premium in the CAPM is the product of the quantity of risk times the market price of risk.

The beta of a security or portfolio is an index of the systematic risk of the asset and is estimated statistically. Beta is calculated from historical data on both the asset's return and the market portfolio's return.

There have been numerous empirical tests of the CAPM and, in general, these have failed to fully support the theory. Richard Roll has criticized these studies because of the difficulty of identifying the true market portfolio. Furthermore, Roll asserts that such tests are not likely to appear soon, if at all.

The CAPM assumes that investors are concerned with only one source of risk: the risk having to do with the future price of a security. However, there are other risks, such as the capacity of investors to consume goods and services in the future. The multifactor CAPM assumes that investors face such extra-market sources of risk called factors. The expected return in the multifactor CAPM is the market risk (as in the case of the basic CAPM) plus a package of risk premiums. Each risk premium is the product of the beta of the security or portfolio with respect to the particular factor, times the difference between the expected return for the factor less the risk-free rate.

The arbitrage pricing theory is developed purely from arbitrage arguments. It postulates that the expected return on a security or a portfolio is influenced by several factors. Proponents of the APT model cite its less-restrictive assumptions as a feature that makes it more appealing than the CAPM or multifactor CAPM. Moreover, testing the APT model does not require identification of the "true" market portfolio. It does, however, require empirical determination of the factors because they are not specified by the theory. Consequently, the APT model replaces the problem of identifying the market portfolio in the CAPM with the problem of choosing and measuring the underlying factors.

Despite the fact that the theories presented are controversial or difficult to implement in practice, there are several principles that are not controversial and can be used in understanding how to value financial assets.

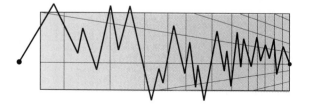

QUESTIONS

1. a. Explain how the capital market line is constructed on a graph.

   b. Explain why the capital market line assumes that there is a risk-free asset and that investors can borrow or lend at the risk-free rate.

   c. Using a graph, demonstrate why the capital market line dominates the Markowitz efficient frontier.

2. How should an investor construct an efficient portfolio in the presence of a risk-free asset?

3. a. What is meant by two-fund separation?

   b. What do the two funds consist of?

4. Indicate why you agree or disagree with the following statement: "As a percent of the total risk, the

unsystematic risk of a diversified portfolio is greater than that of an individual asset."

5. Why is systematic risk also called market risk?

6. Indicate why you agree or disagree with the following statement: "An investor should be compensated for accepting unsystematic risk."

7. In the January 25, 1991, issue of *The Value Line Investment Survey*, you note the following:

Company	Beta
IBM	0.95
Bally Manufacturing	1.40
Cigna Corp.	1.00
British Telecom	0.60

a. How do you interpret these betas?

b. Is it reasonable to assume that the expected return on British Telecom is less than that on IBM shares?

c. "Given that Cigna Corporation has a beta of 1.00, one can mimic the performance of the stock market as a whole by buying only these shares." Do you agree with this statement?

8. a. What is the market model?

b. What input into the CAPM is estimated from the market model?

9. Assume the following: expected market return equals 15%; risk-free rate equals 7%. If a security's beta is 1.3, what is its expected return according to the CAPM?

10. Following is an excerpt from an article, "Risk and Reward," in *The Economist* of October 20, 1990:

[I]s the CAPM supported by the facts? That is controversial, to put it mildly. It is a tribute to Mr. Sharpe [cowinner of the 1990 Nobel Prize in Economics] that his work, which dates from the early 1960s, is still argued over so heatedly. Attention has lately turned away from beta to more complicated ways of carving up risk. But the significance of CAPM for financial economics would be hard to exaggerate.

a. What are the general conclusions of studies that have empirically investigated the CAPM?

b. Summarize Roll's argument on the problems inherent in empirically verifying the CAPM.

11. What was the motivation for the development of the multifactor CAPM?

12. a. What is meant by the extra-market sources of risk in the multifactor CAPM?

b. If there are no extra-market sources of risk, explain why the multifactor CAPM reduces to the pure CAPM.

13. What are the fundamental principles underlying the APT model?

14. What are the advantages of the APT model relative to the CAPM?

15. What are the difficulties in practice of applying the arbitrage pricing theory model?

16. Does Richard Roll's criticism also apply to the arbitrage pricing theory model?

17. "In the CAPM, investors should be compensated for accepting systematic risk; for the APT model, investors are rewarded for accepting both systematic risk and unsystematic risk." Explain why you agree or disagree with this statement.

18. a. What factors have researchers found affect security returns?

    b. Explain why it is difficult to empirically distinguish between the multifactor CAPM and the APT model.

19. Indicate why you agree or disagree with the following statements.

    a. "There is considerable controversy concerning the theories about how assets are priced. Therefore, the distinction between systematic risks and unsystematic risk is meaningless."

    b. "The theories of the pricing of capital assets are highly questionable. Basically, there is only one type of risk and investors should seek to avoid it when they purchase individual securities."

Introduction to Financial Futures Markets

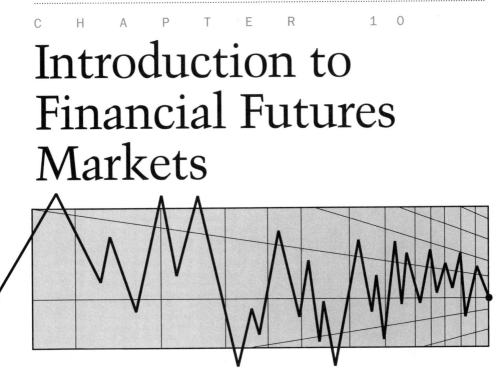

LEARNING OBJECTIVES

After reading this chapter you will understand:

- what a futures contract is.

- the basic economic function of a futures contract.

- the difference between futures and forward contracts.

- the role of the clearinghouse.

- the mark-to-market and margin requirements of a futures contract.

- the risk/return relationship of futures positions.

- how a futures contract is priced.

- why the actual futures price may differ from the theoretical futures price.

- the principles of hedging and the risks associated with hedging.

- the role of futures markets in the economy.

- the General Accounting Office study on derivatives.

A **futures contract** is an agreement that requires a party to the agreement either to buy or sell something at a designated future date at a predetermined price. The basic economic function of futures markets is to provide an opportunity for market participants to hedge against the risk of adverse price movements.

Futures contracts are products created by exchanges. To create a particular futures contract, an exchange must obtain approval from the Commodity Futures Trading Commission (CFTC), a government regulatory agency. When applying to the CFTC for approval to create a futures contract, the exchange must demonstrate that there is an economic purpose for the contract. While many futures contracts are approved for trading, not all succeed if there is lack of investor interest.

Prior to 1972, only futures contracts involving traditional agricultural commodities (such as grain and livestock), imported foodstuffs (such as coffee, cocoa, and sugar), or industrial commodities were traded. Collectively, such futures contracts are known as **commodity futures**.

Futures contracts based on a financial instrument or a financial index are known as **financial futures**. Financial futures can be classified as (1) stock index futures, (2) interest rate futures, and (3) currency futures. The first financial futures contracts were currency futures contracts, which were introduced in 1972 by the International Monetary Market (IMM) of the Chicago Mercantile Exchange (the "Merc" or CME). In October 1975, the Chicago Board of Trade (CBT) pioneered trading in a futures contract based on a fixed-income instrument. In 1982, three futures contracts based on broadly-based common stock indexes made their debut.

As the value of a futures contract is derived from the value of the underlying instrument, they are commonly called **derivative instruments**. Other derivative instruments are options (discussed in Chapter 11) and swaps (discussed in Chapter 12).

In Chapters 15, 28, and 31, we shall take a closer look at stock index futures, interest rate futures, and currency futures, respectively. Our purpose in this chapter is to provide an introduction to financial futures contracts, how they are priced, and how they can be used for hedging. More detailed strategies employing futures contracts will be discussed in later chapters.

MECHANICS OF FUTURES TRADING

A futures contract is a firm legal agreement between a buyer (seller) and an established exchange or its clearinghouse in which the buyer (seller) agrees to take (make) delivery of something at a specified price at the end of a designated period of time. The price at which the parties agree to transact in the future is called the **futures price**. The designated date at which the parties must transact is called the **settlement** or **delivery date**.

To illustrate, suppose there is a futures contract traded on an exchange where the something to be bought or sold is Asset XYZ, and the settlement is three months from now. Assume further that Bob buys this futures contract, and Sally sells this futures contract, and the price at which they agree to transact in the future is $100. Then $100 is the futures price. At the settlement date, Sally will deliver Asset XYZ to Bob; Bob will give Sally $100, the futures price.

Liquidating a Position

Most financial futures contracts have settlement dates in the months of March, June, September, or December. This means that at a predetermined time in the contract settlement month the contract stops trading, and a price is determined by the exchange for settlement of the contract. The contract with the closest settlement date is called the **nearby futures contract**. The next futures contract is the one that settles just after the nearby contract. The contract farthest away in time from settlement is called the **most distant futures contract**.

A party to a futures contract has two choices on liquidation of the position. First, the position can be liquidated prior to the settlement date. For this purpose, the party must take an offsetting position in the same contract. For the buyer of a futures contract, this means selling the same number of identical futures contracts; for the seller of a futures contract, this means buying the same number of identical futures contracts.

The alternative is to wait until the settlement date. At that time the party purchasing a futures contract accepts delivery of the underlying (financial instrument, currency, or commodity) at the agreed-upon price; the party that sells a futures contract liquidates the position by delivering the underlying at the agreed-upon price. For some futures contracts that we shall describe in later chapters in this book, settlement is made in cash only. Such contracts are referred to as **cash-settlement contracts**.

The Role of the Clearinghouse

Associated with every futures exchange is a clearinghouse, which performs several functions. One of these functions is guaranteeing that the two parties to the transaction will perform. To see the importance of this function, consider potential problems in the futures transaction described earlier from the perspective of the two parties—Bob the buyer and Sally the seller. Each must be concerned with the other's ability to fulfill the obligation at the settlement date. Suppose that at the settlement date the price of Asset XYZ in the cash market is $70. Sally can buy Asset XYZ for $70 and deliver it to Bob who, in turn, must pay her $100. If Bob does not have the capacity to pay $100 or refuses to pay, however, Sally has lost the opportunity to realize a profit of $30. Suppose, instead, that the price of Asset XYZ in the cash market is $150 at the settlement date. In this case, Bob is ready and willing to accept delivery of Asset XYZ and pay the agreed-upon price of $100. If Sally does not have the ability or refuses to deliver Asset XYZ, Bob has lost the opportunity to realize a profit of $50.

The clearinghouse exists to meet this problem. When an investor takes a position in the futures market, the clearinghouse takes the opposite position and agrees to satisfy the terms set forth in the contract. Because of the clearinghouse, the investor need not worry about the financial strength and integrity of the party taking the opposite side of the contract. After initial execution of an order, the relationship between the two parties ends. The clearinghouse interposes itself as the buyer for every sale and the seller for every purchase. Thus investors are free to liquidate their positions without involving the other party in the original contract, and without worry that the other party may default. This is the reason why we define a futures contract as an agreement between a party and a clearinghouse associated with an exchange.

Besides its guarantee function, the clearinghouse makes it simple for parties to a futures contract to unwind their positions prior to the settlement date. Suppose that Bob wants to get out of his futures position. He will not have to seek out Sally and work out an agreement with her to terminate the original agreement. Instead, Bob can unwind his position by selling an identical futures contract. As far as the clearinghouse is concerned, its records will show that Bob has bought and sold an identical futures contract. At the settlement date, Sally will not deliver Asset XYZ to Bob but will be instructed by the clearinghouse to deliver to someone who bought and still has an open futures position. In the same way, if Sally wants to unwind her position prior to the settlement date, she can buy an identical futures contract.

Margin Requirements

When a position is first taken in a futures contract, the investor must deposit a minimum dollar amount per contract as specified by the exchange. This amount is called the **initial margin** and is required as deposit for the contract.[1] The initial margin may be in the form of an interest-bearing security such as a Treasury bill. As the price of the futures contract fluctuates, the value of the investor's equity in the position changes. At the end of each trading day, the exchange determines the settlement price for the futures contract. This price is used to mark to market the investor's position, so that any gain or loss from the position is reflected in the investor's equity account.

Maintenance margin is the minimum level (specified by the exchange) by which an investor's equity position may fall as a result of an unfavorable price movement before the investor is required to deposit additional margin. The additional margin deposited is called **variation margin**, and it is an amount necessary to bring the equity in the account back to its initial margin level. Unlike initial margin, variation margin must be in cash not interest-bearing instruments. Any excess margin in the account may be withdrawn by the investor. If a party to a futures contract who is required to deposit variation margin fails to do so within 24 hours, the futures position is closed out.

Although there are initial and maintenance margin requirements for buying securities on margin as explained in Chapter 7, the concept of margin differs for securities and futures. When securities are acquired on margin, the difference between the price of the security and the initial margin is borrowed from the broker. The security purchased serves as collateral for the loan, and the investor pays interest. For futures contracts, the initial margin, in effect, serves as "good faith" money, an indication that the investor will satisfy the obligation of the contract. Normally no money is borrowed by the investor.

We illustrate futures margin requirements and the mark-to-market procedure more fully in Chapter 15 where we discuss stock index futures.

Market Structure

All futures exchanges in the United States trade more than one futures contract. On the exchange floor, each futures contract is traded at a designated

---

[1] Individual brokerage firms are free to set margin requirements above the minimum established by the exchange.

location in a polygonal or circular platform called a pit. The price of a futures contract is determined by open outcry of bids and offers in an auction market. Because of the large number of traders attempting to communicate to other traders the price and quantity that they wish to transact at, pit traders are often forced to communicate using a system of hand signals. There is no designated market maker in the futures market as there is on an exchange where common stock is traded.

Trading on the floor of the exchange is restricted to members of the exchange. A membership is said to be a seat on the exchange. The price of a seat is determined by supply and demand. Nonexchange members can lease a seat, which conveys to them the right to trade on an exchange. Floor traders include two types: **locals** and **floor brokers** (also called **pit brokers**). Locals buy and sell futures contracts for their own account, thereby risking their own capital. They are professional risk takers. Their presence in the futures market adds liquidity to the market and brings bid and offer prices closer together. Consequently, collectively they play the same effective role as a market maker. Most locals do not maintain an open position overnight. The number of locals and the amount of capital that they can commit to the market far exceeds that of the floor brokers.

Floor brokers, just like locals, buy and sell for their own account. They execute customer orders as well. These orders come through an authorized futures broker, called a **futures commissions merchant**, or in the form of orders requested by other floor traders. For trades that they execute on behalf of others, floor brokers receive a commission. While floor brokers can both execute orders for customers and trade for their own account, most of their trades involve the former. When floor brokers do trade for their own account, such trades must not conflict with the interests of customers for whom they are executing trades.

This system of trading in futures markets is not very different from what it was in the 1800s. Monitoring of this sort of system is difficult, which has led to allegations that floor traders profit at the expense of customers whose orders are to be executed.

Several approaches for improving the system of trading futures via electronic trading are at the experimental stage. One approach is a computerized automated system for executing routine trades. Another approach is to automate the entire competitive trading system that now takes place in the pit. The Chicago Mercantile Exchange in conjunction with Reuters Holdings have developed such a system (called the Globex system) for trading of futures contracts globally when a futures exchange is closed. Outside the United States, various forms of electronic trading of futures contracts have already been introduced.

Daily Price Limits

The exchange has the right to impose a limit on the daily price movement of a futures contract from the previous day's closing price. A daily price limit sets the minimum and maximum price at which the futures contract may trade that day. When a daily price limit is reached, trading does not stop but rather continues at a price that does not violate the minimum or maximum price.

The rationale offered for the imposition of daily price limits is that they provide stability to the market at times when new information may cause the futures price to exhibit extreme fluctuations. Those who support daily price limits argue that giving market participants time to digest or reassess such information when trading ceases at the point that price limits would be violated gives them greater confidence in the market. Not all economists agree with this rationale. The question of the role of daily price limits and whether they are necessary remains the subject of extensive debate.

FUTURES VERSUS FORWARD CONTRACTS

A **forward contract**, just like a futures contract, is an agreement for the future delivery of something at a specified price at the end of a designated period of time. Futures contracts are standardized agreements as to the delivery date (or month) and quality of the deliverable, and are traded on organized exchanges. A forward contract differs in that it is usually nonstandardized (that is, the terms of each contract are negotiated individually between buyer and seller), there is no clearinghouse, and secondary markets are often nonexistent or extremely thin. Unlike a futures contract, which is an exchange-traded product, a forward contract is an over-the-counter instrument.

Although both futures and forward contracts set forth terms of delivery, futures contracts are not intended to be settled by delivery. In fact, generally less than 2% of outstanding contracts are settled by delivery. Forward contracts, in contrast, are intended for delivery.

Futures contracts are marked to market at the end of each trading day. Consequently, futures contracts are subject to interim cash flows as additional margin may be required in the case of adverse price movements, or as cash is withdrawn in the case of favorable price movements. A forward contract may or may not be marked to market, depending on the wishes of the two parties. For a forward contract that is not marked to market, there are no interim cash flow effects because no additional margin is required.

Finally, the parties in a forward contract are exposed to credit risk because either party may default on the obligation. Credit risk is minimal in the case of futures contracts because the clearinghouse associated with the exchange guarantees the other side of the transaction.

Other than these differences, most of what we say about futures contracts applies equally to forward contracts.

RISK AND RETURN CHARACTERISTICS OF FUTURES CONTRACTS

When an investor takes a position in the market by buying a futures contract, the investor is said to be in a **long position** or to be **long futures**. If, instead, the investor's opening position is the sale of a futures contract, the investor is said to be in a **short position** or **short futures**.

The buyer of a futures contract will realize a profit if the futures price increases; the seller of a futures contract will realize a profit if the futures price decreases. For example, suppose one month after Bob and Sally take their positions in the futures contract, the futures price of Asset XYZ increases to $120. Bob, the buyer of the futures contract, could then sell the futures contract and realize a profit of $20. Effectively, at the settlement date he has agreed to buy Asset XYZ for $100 and agreed to sell Asset XYZ for $120. Sally, the seller of the futures contract, will realize a loss of $20.

If the futures price falls to $40 and Sally buys the contract, she realizes a profit of $60 because she agreed to sell Asset XYZ for $100 and now can buy it for $40. Bob would realize a loss of $60. Thus, if the futures price decreases, the buyer of the futures contract realizes a loss while the seller of a futures contract realizes a profit.

Leveraging Aspect of Futures

When a position is taken in a futures contract, the party need not put up the entire amount of the investment. Instead, only initial margin must be put up. Consequently, suppose Bob has $100 to invest in Asset XYZ because he believes its price will appreciate. If Asset XYZ is selling for $100, he can buy one unit of the asset. His payoff will then be based on the price action of one unit of Asset XYZ.

Suppose instead that the exchange where the futures contract for Asset XYZ is traded requires initial margin of $5. Then Bob can purchase 20 contracts with his $100 investment. (This example ignores the fact that Bob may need funds for variation margin.) His payoff will then depend on the price action of 20 units of Asset XYZ. Thus he can leverage the use of his funds. While the degree of leverage available in the futures market varies from contract to contract, the leverage attainable is considerably greater than in the cash market by buying on margin.

At first, the leverage available in the futures market may suggest that the market benefits only those who want to speculate on price movements. This is not true. As we shall see later in this chapter, futures markets can be used to reduce price risk. Without the leverage possible in futures transactions, the cost of reducing price risk using futures would be too high for many market participants.

PRICING OF FUTURES CONTRACTS

To understand what determines the futures price, consider once again the futures contract where the underlying instrument is Asset XYZ. The following assumptions will be made:

1. In the cash market Asset XYZ is selling for $100.
2. Asset XYZ pays the holder (with certainty) $12 per year in four quarterly payments of $3, and the next quarterly payment is exactly three months from now.
3. The futures contract requires delivery three months from now.
4. The current three-month interest rate at which funds can be loaned or borrowed is 8% per year.

What should the price of this futures contract be? That is, what should the futures price be? Suppose the price of the futures contract is $107. Consider this strategy:

- Sell the futures contract at $107
- Purchase Asset XYZ in the cash market for $100
- Borrow $100 for three months at 8% per year

The borrowed funds are used to purchase Asset XYZ, resulting in no initial cash outlay for this strategy. At the end of three months, $3 will be received from holding Asset XYZ. Three months from now, Asset XYZ must be delivered to settle the futures contract, and the loan must be repaid. This strategy produces an outcome as follows:

1. *From Settlement of the Futures Contract*

Proceeds from sale of Asset XYZ to settle the futures contract	=	107
Payment received from investing in Asset XYZ for 3 months	=	3
Total proceeds	=	110

2. *From the Loan*

Repayment of principal of loan	=	100
Interest on loan (2% for 3 months)	=	2
Total outlay	=	102
Profit	=	8

Notice that this strategy will guarantee a profit of $8. Moreover, this profit is generated with no investment outlay because the proceeds obtained to purchase Asset XYZ were borrowed. The profit will be realized regardless of what the futures price at the settlement date is. The profit is a riskless arbitrage profit. Obviously, in a well-functioning market, arbitrageurs would sell the futures and buy Asset XYZ, forcing the futures price down and bidding up Asset XYZ's price so as to eliminate this profit.

Suppose instead that the futures price is $92 and not $107. Consider the following strategy:

- Buy the futures contract at $92
- Sell (short) Asset XYZ for $100
- Invest (lend) $100 for three months at 8% per year[2]

Once again, there is no initial cash outlay for the strategy. Three months from now, Asset XYZ must be purchased to settle the long position in the futures contract. Asset XYZ accepted for delivery will then be used to cover the short position (i.e., to cover the short sale of Asset XYZ in the cash market). By shorting Asset XYZ, the short seller must pay the lender of Asset XYZ the proceeds that the lender would have earned for the quarter. Therefore, $3

---

[2] Technically, a short seller may not be entitled to the full use of the proceeds resulting from the sale. We shall discuss this later in this section.

must be paid to the lender of Asset XYZ. The outcome in three months would be as follows:

1. *From Settlement of the Futures Contract*

Price paid for purchase of Asset XYZ to settle the futures contract	=	92
Proceeds to lender of Asset XYZ in order to borrow the asset	=	3
Total outlay	=	95

2. *From the Loan*

Proceeds received from maturing of investment	=	100
Interest earned from the 3-month loan investment (2% for 3 months)	=	2
Total proceeds	=	102
Profit	=	7

The $7 profit from this strategy is a riskless arbitrage profit. It requires no initial cash outlay, and again a profit will be realized regardless of what the futures price is at the settlement date.

Is there a futures price that will eliminate the riskless arbitrage profit? Yes, there is. There will be no arbitrage profit if the futures price is $99. Look at what would happen if the two previous strategies are followed, assuming a futures price of $99. First, consider the strategy:

- Sell the futures contract at $99
- Purchase Asset XYZ for $100
- Borrow $100 for three months at 8% per year

In three months the outcome will be as follows:

1. *From Settlement of the Futures Contract*

Proceeds from sale of Asset XYZ to settle the futures contract	=	99
Payment received from investing in Asset XYZ for 3 months	=	3
Total proceeds	=	102

2. *From the Loan*

Repayment of the principal of loan	=	100
Interest (2% for 3 months)	=	2
Total outlay	=	102
Profit	=	0

There is no arbitrage profit with this strategy.

Next consider the strategy:

- Buy the futures contract at $99
- Sell (short) Asset XYZ for $100
- Invest (lend) $100 for 3 months at 8% per year

The outcome in three months would be as follows:

1. *From Settlement of the Futures Contract*

Price paid for purchase of Asset XYZ to settle futures contract	=	99
Proceeds to lender of Asset XYZ in order to borrow the asset	=	3
Total outlay	=	102

2. *From the Loan*

Proceeds received from maturing of investment	=	100
Interest earned from the 3-month loan investment (2% for 3 months)	=	2
Total proceeds	=	102
Profit	=	2

Thus, neither strategy results in an arbitrage profit. Hence, a futures price of $99 is the equilibrium price because any higher or lower futures price will permit riskless arbitrage profits. This equilibrium price is also called the **theoretical futures price**.

Theoretical Futures Price Based on Arbitrage Model

According to the arbitrage arguments just presented, we see that the theoretical futures price can be determined based on the following information:

1. The price of the asset in the cash market.
2. The cash yield earned on the asset until the settlement date. In our example, the cash yield on Asset XYZ is $3 on a $100 investment or 3% quarterly (12% annual cash yield).
3. The interest rate for borrowing and lending until the settlement date. The borrowing and lending rate is referred to as the **financing cost**. In our example, the financing cost is 2% for the three months.

We will assign the following:

r = financing cost
y = cash yield
P = cash market price ($)
F = futures price ($)

Now consider the strategy:

- Sell the futures contract at F
- Purchase Asset XYZ for P
- Borrow P until the settlement date at r

The outcome at the settlement date then is:

1. *From Settlement of the Futures Contract*

Proceeds from sale of Asset XYZ to settle the futures contract	= F
Payment received from investing in Asset XYZ for 3 months	= yP
Total proceeds	= $F + yP$

2. *From the Loan*

Repayment of the principal of loan	$= P$
Interest on loan	$= rP$
Total outlay	$= P + rP$

The profit will equal:

Profit = Total proceeds – Total outlay

Profit = $F + yP - (P + rP)$

The theoretical futures price is where the profit from this strategy is zero. Thus, to have equilibrium, the following must hold:

$$0 = F + yP - (P + rP)$$

Solving for the theoretical futures price, we have:

$$F = P + P\,(r - y) \tag{10.1}$$

Alternatively, consider the strategy:

- Buy the futures contract at F
- Sell (short) Asset XYZ for P
- Invest (lend) P at r until the settlement date

The outcome at the settlement date would be:

1. *From Settlement of the Futures Contract*

Price paid for purchase of Asset XYZ to settle futures contract	$= F$
Payment to lender of Asset XYZ in order to borrow the asset	$= yP$
Total outlay	$= F + yP$

2. *From the Loan*

Proceeds received from maturing of the loan investment	$= P$
Interest earned	$= rP$
Total proceeds	$= P + rP$

The profit will equal:

Profit = Total proceeds – Total outlay

Profit = $P + rP - (F + yP)$

Setting the profit equal to zero so that there will be no arbitrage profit and solving for the futures price, we would obtain the same equation for the futures price as given by Equation (10.1)

We shall apply this equation to our previous example to determine the theoretical futures price. Here:

$r = 0.02$
$y = 0.03$
$P = \$100$

Then, from Equation (10.1) the theoretical futures price is:

$$F = \$100 + \$100 \ (0.03 - 0.02)$$
$$= \$100 - \$1 = \$99$$

This agrees with the theoretical futures price we demonstrated earlier.

The theoretical futures price may be at a premium to the cash market price (higher than the cash market price) or at a discount from the cash market price (lower than the cash market price) depending on $P \ (r - y)$. The term $r - y$, which reflects the difference between the cost of financing and the asset's cash yield, is called the **net financing cost**. The net financing cost is more commonly called the **cost of carry** or, simply, carry. Positive carry means that the yield earned is greater than the financing cost; negative carry means that the financing cost exceeds the yield earned. Then the relationships shown in Table 10-1 hold.

Price Convergence at the Delivery Date

At the delivery date, the futures price must be equal to the cash market price. Thus, as the delivery date approaches, the futures price will converge to the cash market price. This can be seen by looking at Equation (10.1) for the theoretical futures price. As the delivery date approaches, the financing cost approaches zero, and the yield that can be earned by holding the investment approaches zero. Hence the cost of carry approaches zero, and the futures price will approach the cash market price.

A Closer Look at the Theoretical Futures Price

To derive the theoretical futures price as given by Equation (10.1) using the arbitrage argument, we made several assumptions. When the assumptions are violated, there will be a divergence between the actual futures price and the theoretical futures price as given by Equation (10.1); that is, the difference between the two prices will differ from carry. The implications of this for pricing will be discussed in more detail when we focus on stock index futures in Chapter 15 and interest rate futures in Chapter 28. For the time being we shall look at reasons for the deviation of the actual futures price from the theoretical futures price that are common to all financial futures contracts.

Interim cash flows—No interim cash flows due to variation margin are assumed. In addition, any dividends or coupon interest payments are assumed to be paid at the delivery date rather than at an interim date. However, we know that interim cash flows can occur for both of these reasons. Because we assume no variation margin, the theoretical price for the contract is technically the theoretical price for a forward contract that is not marked to market, not the theoretical price for a futures contract. This is because, unlike a

Table 10-1

Relationship between Carry and Futures Price

Carry	Futures Price
Positive $(y > r)$	will sell at a discount to cash price $(F < P)$
Negative $(y < r)$	will sell at a premium to cash price $(F > P)$
Zero $(r = y)$	will be equal to the cash price $(F = P)$

futures contract, a forward contract that is not marked to market at the end of each trading day does not require additional margin.

Differences between lending and borrowing rates—In deriving the theoretical futures price it is assumed that the borrowing rate and lending rate are equal. Typically, however, the borrowing rate is greater than the lending rate. Letting

r_B = borrowing rate
r_L = lending rate

and using the strategy:

- Sell the futures contract at F
- Purchase the asset for P
- Borrow P until the settlement date at r_B

the futures price that would produce no arbitrage profit is:

$$F = P + P\,(r_B - y) \tag{10.2}$$

For the strategy:

- Buy the futures contract at F
- Sell (short) the asset for P
- Invest (lend) P at r_L until the settlement date

the futures price that would produce no profit is:

$$F = P + P\,(r_L - y) \tag{10.3}$$

Equations (10.2) and (10.3) together provide boundaries between which the futures price will be in equilibrium. Equation (10.2) establishes the upper boundary, and Equation (10.3) the lower boundary. For example, assume that the borrowing rate is 8% per year, or 2% for three months, while the lending rate is 6% per year, or 1.5% for three months. According to Equation (10.2), the upper boundary for the theoretical futures price is:

F (upper boundary) = \$100 + \$100 (0.02 – 0.03) = \$99

The lower boundary for the theoretical futures price according to Equation (10.3) is:

F (lower boundary) = \$100 + \$100 (0.015 – 0.03) = \$98.50

Thus the theoretical futures price must satisfy the condition: 98.50 < F < 99.

Transactions costs—In determining the theoretical futures price, we have ignored transactions costs involved in establishing the positions. In actuality, there are transactions costs of entering into and closing the cash position as well as round-trip transactions costs for the futures contract that do affect the theoretical futures price. Transactions costs widen the boundaries for the theoretical futures price.

Proceeds from short-selling—In the strategy involving short-selling of Asset XYZ, it is assumed that the proceeds from the short sale are received and reinvested. In practice, for individual investors, the proceeds are not received, and, in fact, the individual investor is required to put up margin (securities margin not futures margin) to short-sell. For institutional investors, the asset may be borrowed, but there is a cost to borrowing. This cost of borrowing can be incorporated into the model by reducing the yield on the asset.

Deliverable asset and settlement date known—Our example assumes that only one asset is deliverable, and that the settlement date occurs three months from now. In Chapter 28 where we discuss Treasury bond futures contracts, we will see that there are several Treasury bond issues that can be delivered to satisfy the futures contract. The choice of which Treasury bond issue to deliver is given to the short. Thus, the buyer of this futures contract does not know what the deliverable asset will be. Also, for the same futures contract, the short is also given the choice of when in the settlement month to deliver the Treasury bond issue. As a result, the buyer does not know the specific settlement date. These factors influence the futures price.

Deliverable is a basket of securities—The underlying for some futures contracts is not a single asset but a basket of assets, or an index. Stock index futures, discussed in Chapter 15, and the municipal bond index futures contract, explained in Chapter 28, are examples. The problem in arbitraging these two futures contracts is that it is too expensive to buy or sell every asset included in the index. Instead, a portfolio containing a smaller number of assets may be constructed to "track" the index. The arbitrage, however, is no longer risk-free because there is the risk that the portfolio will not track the index exactly. All of this leads to higher transactions costs and uncertainty about the outcome of the arbitrage.

GENERAL PRINCIPLES OF HEDGING WITH FUTURES

The major function of futures markets is to transfer price risk from hedgers to speculators. That is, risk is transferred from those willing to pay to avoid risk to those wanting to assume the risk in the hope of gain. Hedging in this case is the employment of a futures transaction as a temporary substitute for a transaction to be made in the cash market. The hedge position locks in a value for the cash position. As long as cash and futures prices move together, any loss realized on one position (whether cash or futures) will be offset by a profit on the other position. When the profit and loss are equal, the hedge is called a **perfect hedge**. In a market where the futures contract is correctly priced, a perfect hedge should provide a return equal to the risk-free rate.

Risks Associated with Hedging

In practice, hedging is not that simple. The amount of the loss or profit on a hedge will be determined by the relationship between the cash price and the futures price when a hedge is placed and when it is lifted. The difference between the cash price and the futures price is called the **basis**. That is: Basis = Cash price – Futures price.

As we explained earlier, if a futures contract is priced according to its theoretical value, the difference between the cash price and the futures price should be equal to the cost of carry. The risk that the hedger takes is that the basis will change. This is called **basis risk**. Therefore, hedging involves the substitution of basis risk for price risk; that is, the substitution of the risk that the basis will change for the risk that the cash price will change.

When a futures contract is used to hedge a position where either the portfolio or the individual financial instrument is not identical to the instrument underlying the futures, it is called **cross-hedging**. **Cross-hedging** is common in asset/liability and portfolio management because there are no futures contracts on specific common stock shares and bonds. Cross-hedging introduces another risk—the risk that the price movement of the underlying instrument of the futures contract may not accurately track the price movement of the portfolio or financial instrument to be hedged. This is called **cross-hedging risk**. Therefore, the effectiveness of a cross-hedge will be determined by:

1. The relationship between the cash price of the underlying instrument and its futures price when a hedge is placed and when it is lifted.

2. The relationship between the market (cash) value of the portfolio and the cash price of the instrument underlying the futures contract when the hedge is placed and when it is lifted.

Short Hedge and Long Hedge

A **short hedge** is used to protect against a decline in the future cash price of a financial instrument or portfolio. To execute a short hedge, the hedger sells a futures contract (agrees to make delivery). Consequently, a short hedge is also known as a **sell hedge**. By establishing a short hedge, the hedger has fixed the future cash price and transferred the price risk of ownership to the buyer of the futures contract.

A **long hedge** is undertaken to protect against an increase in the price of a financial instrument or portfolio to be purchased in the cash market at some future time. In a long hedge, the hedger buys a futures contract (agrees to accept delivery). A long hedge is also known as a **buy hedge**.

Hedging Illustrations

To illustrate hedging, we shall present several numerical examples from the traditional commodities markets. It is better to start with the traditional commodities because they are simpler than most financial futures contracts. The principles we illustrate still are equally applicable to financial futures contracts but it is easier to grasp the sense of the commodities product example without involving financial contract nuances. In Chapter 15, we will illustrate hedging for a stock portfolio.

Assume that a gold mining company expects to sell 1,000 ounces of gold one week from now and that the management of a jewelry company plans to purchase 1,000 ounces of gold one week from now. The managers of both the gold mining company and the jewelry company want to lock in today's price—that is, they both want to eliminate the price risk associated with gold one week from now. The cash price for gold is currently $352.40 per ounce. The cash price is also called the **spot price**. The futures price for gold is currently $397.80 per ounce. Each futures contract is for 100 ounces of gold.

Because the gold mining company seeks protection against a decline in the price of gold, the company will place a short hedge. That is, the company will promise to make delivery of gold at the current futures price. The gold mining company will sell 10 futures contracts.

The management of the jewelry company seeks protection against an increase in the price of gold. Consequently, it will place a long hedge. That is, it will agree to accept delivery of gold at the futures price. Because it is seeking protection against a price increase for 1,000 ounces of gold, it will buy 10 contracts.

Let's look at what happens under various scenarios for the cash price and futures price of gold one week from now, when the hedge is lifted.

Perfect hedge—Suppose that at the time the hedge is lifted the cash price has declined to $304.20 and the futures price has declined to $349.60. Notice what has happened to the basis under this scenario. At the time the hedge is placed, the basis is – $45.40 ($352.40 – $397.80). When the hedge is lifted, the basis is still – $45.40 ($304.20 – $349.60).

The gold mining company wanted to lock in a price of $352.40 per ounce of gold, or $352,400 for 1,000 ounces. The company sold 10 futures contracts at a price of $397.80 per ounce or $397,800 for 1,000 ounces. When the hedge is lifted, the value of 1,000 ounces of gold is $304,200 ($304.20 × 1,000). The gold mining company realizes a decline in the cash market in the value of its gold of $48,200. However, the futures price has declined to $349.60, or $349,600 for 1,000 ounces. The mining company thus realizes a $48,200 gain in the futures market. The net result is that the gain in the futures market matches the loss in the cash market. Consequently, the gold mining company does not realize an overall gain or loss. This is an example of a perfect hedge. The results of this hedge are summarized in Table 10-2.

The outcome for the jewelry company of its long hedge is also summarized in Table 10-2. Because there was a decline in the cash price, the jewelry company would gain in the cash market by $48,200 but realize a loss of the same amount in the futures market. Therefore this hedge is also a perfect hedge.

This scenario illustrates two important points. First, for both participants there was no overall gain or loss. The reason for this was that the basis did not change when the hedge was lifted. Consequently, if the basis does not change, the effective purchase or sale price ends up being the cash price on the day the hedge is set. Second, note that the management of the jewelry company would have been better off if it had not hedged. The cost of the gold would have been $48,200 less. This, however, should not be interpreted as a sign of a bad decision. Managers are usually not in the business of speculating on the price of gold and hedging is the standard practice used to protect against an increase in the cost of doing business in the future. The "price" of obtaining this protection is the potential windfall that one gives up.

Suppose that when the hedge is lifted the cash price of gold has increased to $392.50 and that the futures price has increased to $437.90. Notice that the basis is unchanged at –$45.40. Because the basis is unchanged, the effective purchase and sale price will equal the price of gold at the time the hedge is placed.

The gold mining company will gain in the cash market because the value of 1,000 ounces of gold is $392,500 ($392.50 × 1,000). This represents a $40,100 gain compared to the cash value at the time the hedge was placed. However, the gold mining company must liquidate its position in the futures market by buying 10 futures contracts at a total price of $437,900, which is $40,100 more than the price when the contracts were sold. The loss in the

Table 10-2
A Hedge that Locks in the Current Price of Gold: Cash Price Decreases

Assumptions	
Cash price at time hedge is placed	$352.40 per oz
Futures price at time hedge is placed	397.80 per oz
Cash price at time hedge is lifted	304.20 per oz
Futures price at time hedge is lifted	349.60 per oz
Number of ounces to be hedged	1,000
Number of ounces per futures contract	100
Number of futures contracts used in hedge	10

Short (Sell) Hedge by Gold Mining Company

Cash Market	Futures Market	Basis
At time hedge is placed		
Value of 1,000 oz:	Sell 10 contracts:	–$45.40 per ounce
1,000 × $352.40 = $352,400	10 × 100 × $397.80 = $397,800	
At time hedge is lifted		
Value of 1,000 oz:	Buy 10 contracts	–$45.40 per ounce
1,000 × $304.20 = $304,200	10 × 100 × $349.60 = $349,600	
Loss in cash market = $48,200	Gain in futures market = $48,200	
	Overall gain or loss = $0	

Long (Buy) Hedge by Jewelry Company

Cash Market	Futures Market	Basis
At time hedge is placed		
Value of 1,000 oz:	Buy 10 contracts:-	–$45.40 per ounce
1,000 × $352.40 = $352,400	10 × 100 × $397,80 = $397,800	
At time hedge is lifted		
Value of 1,000 oz:	Sell 10 contracts	–$45.40 per ounce
1,000 × $304.20 = $304,200	10 × 100 × $349.60 = $349,600	
Gain in cash market= $48,200	Loss in futures market = $48,200	
	Overall gain or loss = $ 0	

futures market offsets the gain in the cash market. The results of this hedge are summarized in Table 10-3.

The jewelry company realizes a $40,100 gain in the futures market but will have to pay $40,100 more in the cash market to acquire 1,000 ounces of gold. The results of this hedge are also summarized in Table 10-3.

Notice that in this scenario the management of the jewelry company saved $40,100 by employing a hedge. The gold mining company, on the other hand, would have been better off if it had not hedged and had simply sold its product on the market one week later. However, it must be emphasized that the management of the gold mining company, just like the management of the jewelry company, employed a hedge to protect against unforeseen adverse price changes in the cash market, and the price of this protection is that one forgoes the favorable price changes enjoyed by those who do not hedge.

Basis risk—In the two previous scenarios we assumed that the basis does not change. There is no reason why this would necessarily be the case. In the real world the basis frequently changes between the time a hedge is placed and the time it is lifted.

Assume that the cash price of gold decreases to $304.20, just as in the first scenario; however, assume further that the futures price decreases to $385.80 rather than $349.60. The basis has now declined from –$45.40 to –$81.60 ($304.20 – $385.80). The results are summarized in Table 10-4. For the short hedge, the $48,200 loss in the cash market is only partially offset by the $12,000 gain realized in the futures market. Consequently, the hedge resulted in an overall loss of $36,200.

There are several points to note here. First, if the gold mining company did not hedge, the loss would have been $48,200, because the value of its 1,000 ounces of gold is $304,200 compared to the $352,400 one week earlier. Although the hedge is not perfect, the loss of $36,200 is less than the loss of $48,200 that would have occurred if no hedge had been placed. This is what we meant earlier by stating that hedging substitutes basis risk for price risk. Second, the management of the jewelry company faces the same problem from an opposite perspective. An unexpected gain for one participant results in an unexpected loss of equal dollar value for the other. That is, the participants face a zero-sum game since they have identically opposite cash and futures positions. Consequently, the jewelry company would realize an overall gain of $36,200 from its long (buy) hedge. This gain represents a gain in the cash market of $48,200 and a realized loss in the futures market of $12,000.

Suppose that the cash price increases to $392.50 per ounce, just as in the second scenario, but that the basis widens to –$81.60. That is, at the time the hedge is lifted the futures price has increased to $474.10. The results of this hedge are summarized in Table 10-5.

As a result of the long hedge, the jewelry company will realize a gain of $76,300 in the futures market but only a $40,100 loss in the cash market. Therefore, there is an overall gain of $36,200 for the jewelry company. For the gold mining company, there is an overall loss of $36,200.

In the two previous scenarios it was assumed that the basis widened. It can be demonstrated that if the basis narrowed, the outcome will not be a perfect hedge.

Table 10-3
A Hedge that Locks in the Current Price of Gold: Cash Price Increases

Assumptions

Cash price at time hedge is placed	$352.40 per oz
Futures price at time hedge is placed	397.80 per oz
Cash price at time hedge is lifted	392.50 per oz
Futures price at time hedge is lifted	437.90 per oz
Number of ounces to be hedged	1,000
Number of ounces per futures contract	100
Number of futures contracts used in hedge	10

Short (Sell) Hedge by Gold Mining Company

Cash Market	Futures Market	Basis
At time hedge is placed		
Value of 1,000 oz:	Sell 10 contracts:	–$45.40 per ounce
1,000 × $352.40 = $352,400	10 × 100 × $397.80 = $397,800	
At time hedge is lifted		
Value of 1,000 oz:	Buy 10 contracts	–$45.40 per ounce
1,000 × $392.50 = $392,500	10 × 100 × $437.90 = $437,900	
Gain in cash market = $40,100	Loss in futures market = $40,100	
	Overall gain or loss = $0	

Long (Buy) Hedge by Gold Mining Company

Cash Market	Futures Market	Basis
At time hedge is placed		
Value of 1,000 oz:	Buy 10 contracts:	–$45.40 per ounce
1,000 × $352.40 = $352,400	10 × 100 × $397.80 = $397,800	
At time hedge is lifted		
Value of 1,000 oz:	Sell 10 contracts	–$45.40 per ounce
1,000 × $392.50 = $392,500	10 × 100 × $437.90 = $437,900	
Loss in cash market = $40,100	Gain in futures market = $40,100	
	Overall gain or loss = $0	

Table 10-4
Hedge: Cash Price Decreases and Basis Widens

Assumptions	
Cash price at time hedge is placed	$352.40 per oz
Futures price at time hedge is placed	397.80 per oz
Cash price at time hedge is lifted	304.20 per oz
Futures price at time hedge is lifted	385.80 per oz
Number of ounces to be hedged	1,000
Number of ounces per futures contract	100
Number of futures contracts used in hedge	10

Short (Sell) Hedge by Gold Mining Company

Cash Market	Futures Market	Basis
At time hedge is placed		
Value of 1,000 oz:	Sell 10 contracts:	−$45.40 per ounce
1,000 × $352.40 = $352,400	10 × 100 × $397.80 = $397,800	
At time hedge is lifted		
Value of 1,000 oz:	Buy 10 contracts	−$81.60 per ounce
1,000 × $304.20 = $304,200	10 × 100 × $385.80 = $385,800	
Loss in cash market = $48,200	Gain in futures market = $12,000	
	Overall loss = $36,200	

Long (Buy) Hedge by Jewelry Company

Cash Market	Futures Market	Basis
At time hedge is placed		
Value of 1,000 oz:	Buy 10 contracts:	−$45.40 per ounce
1,000 × $352.40 = $352,400	10 × 100 × $397.80 = $397,800	
At time hedge is lifted		
Value of 1,000 oz:	Sell 10 contracts	−$81.60 per ounce
1,000 × $304.20 = $304,200	10 × 100 × $385.80 = $385,800	
Gain in cash market = $48,200	Loss in futures market = $12,200	
	Overall gain = $36,200	

Table 10-5
Hedge: Cash Price Decreases and Basis Widens

Assumptions

Cash price at time hedge is placed	$352.40 per oz
Futures price at time hedge is placed	397.80 per oz
Cash price at time hedge is lifted	392.50 per oz
Futures price at time hedge is lifted	474.10 per oz
Number of ounces to be hedged	1,000
Number of ounces per futures contract	100
Number of futures contracts used in hedge	10

Short (Sell) Hedge by Gold Mining Company

Cash Market	Futures Market	Basis
At time hedge is placed		
Value of 1,000 oz:	Sell 10 contracts:	–$45.40 per ounce
1,000 × $352.40 = $352,400	10 × 100 × $397.80 $397,800	
At time hedge is lifted		
Value of 1,000 oz:	Buy 10 contracts	–$81.60 per ounce
1,000 × $392.50 = $392,500	10 × 100 × $474.10 = $474,100	
Gain in cash market = $40,100	Loss in futures market = $76,300	
	Overall loss = $36,200	

Long (Buy) Hedge by Jewelry Company

Cash Market	Futures Market	Basis
At time hedge is placed		
Value of 1,000 oz:	Buy 10 contracts:	–$45.40 per ounce
1,000 × $352.40 = $352,400	10 × 100 × $397.80 = $397,800	
At time hedge is lifted		
Value of 1,000 oz:	Sell 10 contracts	–$81.60 per ounce
1,000 × $392.50 = $392,500	10 × 100 × $474.10 = $474,100	
Loss in cash market = $40,100	Gain in futures market = $76,300	
	Overall gain = $36,200	

Cross-hedging—Suppose that a mining company on a far-away planet plans to sell 2,500 ounces of kryptonite one week from now and that a jewelry company plans to purchase the same amount of kryptonite in one week. Both parties want to hedge against price risk.[3] However, kryptonite futures contracts are not currently traded. Both parties believe that there is a close relationship between the price of kryptonite and the price of gold. Specifically, both parties believe that the cash price of kryptonite will remain at 40% of the cash price of gold. The cash price of kryptonite is currently $140.96 per ounce, and the cash price of gold is currently $352.40 per ounce. The futures price of gold is currently $397.80 per ounce.

We shall examine various scenarios to see how effective the cross-hedge will be. In each scenario, the gold basis is held constant at –$45.40. We make this assumption so that we can focus on the importance of the relationship between the two cash prices at the two points in time.

Before proceeding, we must first determine how many gold futures contracts should be used in the cross-hedge. The value of 2,500 ounces of kryptonite at the cash price of $140.96 per ounce is $352,400. To protect the value of the kryptonite using gold futures, the cash value of 1,000 ounces of gold ($352,400/$352.40) must be hedged. Because each gold futures contract covers 100 ounces, 10 gold futures contracts will be used.

Suppose that the cash prices of kryptonite and gold decrease to $121.68 and $304.20 per ounce, respectively, and that the futures price of gold decreases to $349.60 per ounce. The relationship between the cash price of kryptonite and the cash price of gold when the cross-hedge was placed holds when the cross-hedge is lifted. That is, the cash price of kryptonite is 40% of the cash price of gold. The gold basis stays constant at –$45.40. The outcome for the short and long cross-hedge is summarized in Table 10-6.

The short cross-hedge produces a gain of $48,200 in the futures market and an exactly offsetting loss in the cash market. The opposite occurs for the long cross-hedge. There is neither an overall gain nor a loss from the cross-hedge for either hedger in this scenario. The same would occur if the cash prices of both commodities increase by the same percentage and the basis does not change.

Suppose that the cash price of both commodities decreases but the cash price of kryptonite falls by a greater percentage than the cash price of gold. For example, suppose that the cash price of kryptonite falls to $112.00 per ounce, while the cash price of gold falls to $304.20 per ounce. The futures price of gold falls to $349.60 so that the basis is not changed. The cash price of kryptonite at the time the cross-hedge is lifted is 37% of the cash price of gold, rather than the 40% when the cross-hedge was constructed. The outcome for the long and short cross-hedge is shown in Table 10-7.

For the short cross-hedge, the loss in the cash market exceeds the realized gain in the futures market by $24,200. For the long cross-hedge, the opposite is true. There is an overall gain of $24,200 from the cross-hedge.

If the cash price of kryptonite had fallen by a smaller percentage amount than the cash price of gold, the short cross-hedge would have produced an overall gain, while the long cross-hedge would have generated an overall loss.

---

[3] We will ignore interplanetary-exchange-rate risk in our illustrations.

Table 10-6
A Hedge that Locks in the Current Price of Kryptonite:
Cash Price Decreases by Same Percentage

Assumptions
Price of kryptonite

Cash price at time hedge is placed	$140.96 per oz
Cash price at time hedge is lifted	121.68 per oz
Price of gold	
Cash price at time hedge is placed	$352.40 per oz
Futures price at time hedge is placed	397.80 per oz
Cash price at time hedge is lifted	304.20 per oz
Futures price at time hedge is lifted	349.60 per oz
Number of ounces of Kryptonite to be hedged	2,500
Number of ounces of gold to be hedged	
assuming ratio of cash price of kryptonite to gold is 0.4	1,000
Number of ounces per futures contract for gold	100
Number of gold futures contracts used in hedge	10

Short (Sell) Cross-Hedge by Kryptonite Mining Company

Cash Market	Futures Market	Gold Basis
At time hedge is placed		
Value of 2,500 oz:	Sell 10 contracts:	
2,500 × $140.96 = $352,400	10 × 100 × $397.80 = $397,800	–$45.40 per ounce
At time hedge is lifted		
Value of 2,500 oz:	Buy 10 contracts:	
2,500 × $121.68 = $304,200	10 × 100 × $349.60 = $349,600	–$45.40 per ounce
Loss in cash market= $48,200	Gain in futures market = $48,200	
	Overall gain or loss = $0	

Long (Buy) Cross-Hedge by Jewelry Company

Cash Market	Futures Market	Gold Basis
At time hedge is placed		
Value of 2,500 oz:	Buy 10 contracts:	
2,500 × $140.96 = $352,400	10 × 100 × $397.80 = $397,800	–$45.40 per ounce
At time hedge is lifted		
Value of 2,500 oz:	Sell 10 contracts:	
2,500 × $121.68 = $304,200	10 × 100 × $349.60 = $349,600	–$45.40 per ounce
Gain in cash market = $48,200	Loss in futures market = $48,200	
	Overall gain or loss = $0	

Table 10-7
Cross-Hedge: Cash Price of Kryptonite to Be Hedged Falls
by a Greater Percentage than the Futures Used for the Hedge

Assumptions

Price of kryptonite	
Cash price at time hedge is placed	$140.96 per oz
Cash price at time hedge is lifted	112.00 per oz
Price of gold	
Cash price at time hedge is placed	$352.40 per oz
Futures price at time hedge is placed	397.80 per oz
Cash price at time hedge is lifted	304.20 per oz
Futures price at time hedge is lifted	349.60 per oz
Number of ounces of kryptonite to be hedged	2,500
Number of ounces of gold to be hedged	
assuming ratio of cash price of kryptonite to gold is 0.4	1,000
Number of ounces per futures contract for gold	100
Number of gold futures contracts used in hedge	10

Short (Sell) Cross-Hedge by Kryptonite Mining Company

Cash Market	Futures Market	Gold Basis
At time hedge is placed		
Value of 2,500 oz:	Sell 10 contracts:	
2,500 × $140.96 = $352,400	10 × 100 × $397.80 = $397,800	−$45.40 per ounce
At time hedge is lifted		
Value of 2,500 oz:	Buy 10 contracts:	
2,500 × $112.00 = $280,000	10 × 100 × $349.60 = $349,600	−$45.40 per ounce
Loss in cash market= $72,400	Gain in futures market = $48,200	
	Overall loss = $24,200	

Long (Buy) Cross-Hedge by Jewelry Company

Cash Market	Futures Market	Gold Basis
At time hedge is placed		
Value of 2,500 oz:	Buy 10 contracts:	
2,500 × $140.96 = $352,400	10 × 100 × $397.80 = $397,800	−$45.40 per ounce
At time hedge is lifted		
Value of 2,500 oz:	Sell 10 contracts:	
2,500 × $112.00 = $280,000	10 × 100 × $349.60 = $349,600	−$45.40 per ounce
Gain in cash market= $72,400	Loss in futures market = $48,200	
	Overall gain = $24,200	

Suppose that the cash price of kryptonite falls to $121.68 per ounce, while the cash and futures price of gold rise to $392.50 and $437.90, respectively. The results of the cross-hedge are shown in Table 10-8.

The short cross-hedge results in a loss in both the cash market and the futures market. The overall loss is $88,300. Had the kryptonite mining company not used the cross-hedge, its loss would have been limited to the decline in the cash price—$48,200 in this instance. The long hedger, on the other hand, realizes a gain in both the cash and futures market, and therefore an overall gain.

If, instead, the cash price of kryptonite increases to $189.10 per ounce, while the cash and futures price of gold decline to $304.20 and $349.60, respectively, it can be demonstrated that the long cross-hedge results in a loss in both the cash and futures markets. The total loss is $168,550. The loss would have been only $120,350, the loss in the cash market, had the management of the jewelry company not cross-hedged with gold.

These illustrations demonstrate the risks associated with cross-hedging.

THE ROLE OF FUTURES IN FINANCIAL MARKETS

Without financial futures, investors would have only one trading location to alter portfolio positions when they get new information that is expected to influence the value of assets—the cash market. If economic news that is expected to impact the value of an asset adversely is received, investors can reduce their price risk exposure to that asset. The opposite is true if the new information is expected to impact the value of that asset favorably: an investor would increase price-risk exposure to that asset. There are, of course, transactions costs associated with altering exposure to an asset—explicit costs (commissions), and hidden or execution costs (bid-ask spreads and market impact costs).[4]

Futures provide another market that investors can use to alter their risk exposure to an asset when new information is acquired. But which market—cash or futures—should the investor employ to alter a position quickly on the receipt of new information? The answer is simple: the one that is the more efficient to use in order to achieve the objective. The factors to consider are liquidity, transactions costs, taxes, and leverage advantages of the futures contract.

The market that investors feel is the one that is more efficient to use to achieve their investment objective should be the one where prices will be established that reflect the new economic information. That is, this will be the market where price discovery takes place. Price information is then transmitted to the other market. In many of the markets that we will discuss in this book, it is in the futures market that it is easier and less costly to alter a portfolio position. We give evidence for this when we discuss the specific contracts in later chapters. Therefore, it is the futures market that will be the market of choice and will serve as the price discovery market. It is in the futures market that investors send a collective message about how any new information is expected to impact the cash market.

---

[4] These are discussed in Chapters 7 and 13.

Table 10-8

Cross-Hedge: Cash Price of Kryptonite to Be Hedged Falls and the Price of Futures Used for the Hedge Rises

Assumptions

Price of kryptonite

Cash price at time hedge is placed	$140.68 per oz
Cash price at time hedge is lifted	121.68 per oz

Price of gold

Cash price at time hedge is placed	$352.40 per oz
Futures price at time hedge is placed	397.80 per oz
Cash price at time hedge is lifted	392.50 per oz
Futures price at time hedge is lifted	437.90 per oz
Number of ounces of kryptonite to be hedged	2,500
Number of ounces of gold to be hedged	
assuming ratio of cash price of kryptonite to gold is 0.4	1,000
Number of ounces per futures contract for gold	100
Number of gold futures contracts used in hedge	10

Short (Sell) Cross-Hedge by Kryptonite Mining Company

Cash Market	Futures Market	Gold Basis
At time hedge is placed		
Value of 2500 oz:	Sell 10 contracts:	
2,500 × $140.96 = $352,400	10 × 100 × $397.80 = $397,800	–$45.40 per ounce
At time hedge is lifted		
Value of 2,500 oz:	Buy 10 contracts:	
2,500 × $121.68 = $304,200	10 × 100 × $437.90 = $437,900	–$45.40 per ounce
Loss in cash market = $48,200	Loss in futures market = $40,100	
	Overall loss=$88,300	

Long (Buy) Cross-Hedge by Jewelry Company

Cash Market	Futures Market	Gold Basis
At time hedge is placed		
Value of 2,500 oz:	Buy 10 contracts:	
2,500 × $140.96 = $352,400	10 × 100 × $397.80= $397,800	–$45.40 per ounce
At time hedge is lifted		
Value of 2,500 oz:	Sell 10 contracts:	
2,500 × $121.68 = $304,200	10 × 100 × $437.90 = $437,900	–$45.40 per ounce
Gain in cash market = $48,200	Gain in futures market = $40,100	
	Overall gain = $88,300	

How is this message sent to the cash market? Recall our discussion on determination of the theoretical futures price, where we showed that the futures price and the cash market price are tied together by the cost of carry. If the futures price deviates from the cash market price by more than the cost of carry, arbitrageurs (in attempting to obtain arbitrage profits) would pursue a strategy to bring them back into line. Arbitrage brings the cash market price into line with the futures price. It is this mechanism that assures that the cash market price will reflect the information that has been collected in the futures market.

Effect of Futures on Volatility of Underlying Asset

Some investors and the popular press consider that the introduction of a futures market for an asset will increase the price volatility of the asset in the cash market. This criticism of futures contracts is referred to as the "destabilization hypothesis."[5]

There are two variants of the destabilization hypothesis: the liquidity variant and the populist variant. According to the liquidity variant, large transactions that are too difficult to accommodate in the cash market will be executed first in the futures markets because of better liquidity. The increased volatility that may occur in the futures contracts market is only temporary because volatility will return to its normal level once the liquidity problem is resolved. The implication is that there should be no long-term impact on the volatility of the underlying cash market asset.

The populist variant, in contrast, asserts that as a result of speculative trading in derivative contracts, the cash market instrument does not reflect fundamental economic value. The implication here is that the asset price would better reflect economic value in the absence of a futures market.

Whether the introduction of futures markets destabilizes prices is an empirical question. We will look at the evidence for the stock market in Chapter 15, but for now, it is worth noting that the analysis of one researcher concludes that in general it would take a substantial number of "irrational" speculators to destabilize cash markets.[6]

Is Increased Asset Price Volatility Bad?

Whether or not the introduction of futures contracts increases cash market price volatility, we might ask whether greater volatility has negative effects on markets. At first glance, it might seem that volatility has adverse effects from the points of view of allocative efficiency and market participation.

Actually, it has been pointed out that this inference may not be justified if, say, the introduction of new markets lets prices respond more promptly to changes in fundamentals, and if the fundamentals themselves are subject to large shocks.[7] Thus the greater volatility resulting from an innovation may simply more faithfully reflect the actual variability of fundamental values. In

---

[5] Lawrence Harris, "S&P 500 Futures and Cash Stock Price Volatility," University of Southern California, unpublished paper, 1987.

[6] Jerome L. Stein, "Real Effects of Futures Speculation: Rational Expectations and Diverse Opinions," working paper no. 88, Center for the Study of Futures Markets, Columbia University, 1984.

[7] Eugene F. Fama, "Perspectives on October 1987, or What Did We Learn from the Crash?" in Robert J. Barro et al. (eds.), *Black Monday and the Future of Financial Markets* (Homewood, IL: Dow Jones-Irwin, 1989), p. 72.

this case, "more" asset volatility need not be bad but rather may be a manifestation of a well-functioning market. Of course, to say that more volatility need not be bad does not mean that it is good. Clearly, price volatility greater than what can be justified by relevant new information or fundamentals (or by standard asset pricing models) is undesirable. By definition, it makes prices inefficient. This is referred to as "excess volatility."[8]

No one has been able to test whether recent financial innovations have increased or decreased excess volatility. Moreover, as Franklin Edwards points out, "Too little volatility is equally bad, although this concept does not seem to have generated enough interest to have been given the label of `deficient volatility.'"[9]

In any event, as Edwards notes in the case of stock index futures:

> *Investors are concerned about the present and future value of their investments (and wealth). Greater volatility leads to a perception of greater risk, which threatens investors' assets and wealth. When the stock market takes a sharp nose-dive, investors see the value of their assets rapidly dissipating. They are not consoled by being told that there is no social cost associated with this price change, only a redistribution of wealth. Even more fundamental, when asset prices exhibit significant volatility over very short periods of time (such as a day), investors "lose confidence in the market." They begin to see financial markets as the province of the speculator and the insider, not the rational.*[10]

THE GAO STUDY ON FINANCIAL DERIVATIVES

We have just explored our first derivative instrument and we shall look at other derivatives in the next two chapters, and several other chapters that focus on derivatives for specific products. Some of these products are exchange-traded, such as the futures contracts we discussed in this chapter; other products are created by commercial banks and investment banking firms, as we explained in Chapters 3 and 5. These customized derivative products are called **over-the-counter** or **OTC derivatives**. Forward contracts are an example of an OTC derivative product. Swaps are another example of an OTC derivative and there are also OTC options.

There is public concern that commercial banks are creating OTC derivative products that put them in a position that could result in severe financial problems. Since it is the larger commercial banks that are creating OTC derivatives, this could have a rippling effect on the U.S. financial system. Specifically, there is concern that banks creating OTC derivative products do not have the proper risk-management systems in place to effectively monitor their risk exposure. For example, a July 1993 report by a highly influential bank group—the Group of Thirty—recommended how to improve bank risk-management systems. However, the recommendations did not appear to be

---

[8] Franklin R. Edwards, "Futures Trading and Cash Market Volatility: Stock Index and Interest Rate Futures," *Journal of Futures Markets* 8, no. 4 (1988), p. 423

[9] Ibid.

[10] Franklin R. Edwards, "Does Futures Trading Increase Stock Price Volatility?" *Financial Analysts Journal* (January-February 1988), p. 64.

uniformly adopted since they did not carry the force of law. Moreover, end-users of derivatives—financial institutions and businesses—may not have the requisite skills and risk-management systems to use derivatives or might be using them for speculative purposes rather than controlling financial risk.

In May 1994, the General Accounting Office (GAO) prepared a report on *Financial Derivatives: Actions Needed to Protect the Financial System*. The study recognized the importance of derivatives for market participants. Page 6 of the report states:

> *Derivatives serve an important function of the global financial marketplace, providing end-users with opportunities to better manage financial risks associated with their business transactions. The rapid growth and increasing complexity of derivatives reflect both the increased demand from end-users for better ways to manage their financial risks and the innovative capacity of the financial services industry to respond to market demands.*

Despite the importance of derivatives, the study goes on to state:

> *However, Congress, federal regulators, and some members of the industry are concerned about these products and the risk they may pose to the financial system, individual firms, investors, and U.S. taxpayers. These concerns have been heightened by recent reports of substantial losses by some derivative end-users.*

The GAO study was undertaken because of these concerns. The cover letter to the GAO report stated that the objectives of the report were to determine:

> *. . . (1) what the extent and nature of derivatives use was, (2) what risks derivatives might pose to individual firms and to the financial system, (3) whether gaps and inconsistencies existed in U.S. regulation of derivatives, (4) whether existing accounting rules resulted in financial reports that provided market participants and investors with adequate information about firms' use of derivatives, and (5) what the implications of the international use of derivatives were for U.S. regulations.*

Here are some of the principal conclusions of the study. First, boards of directors and senior management have primary responsibility for managing derivative risks and therefore should have the necessary internal controls in place to carry out this responsibility. Moreover, regulations should provide a legal framework that would require OTC derivative product dealers to comply with a common set of basic standards to effectively manage risk.

Second, financial reporting requirements for derivative instruments are inadequate and the Financial Accounting Standards Board should implement comprehensive accounting rules for derivative products. Third, improving regulations for derivatives in the United States without coordinating with foreign regulators will reduce the effectiveness of the regulations. Finally, policymakers and regulators should not stifle the use of derivatives. Rather a proper balance should be struck between allowing the financial services to be innovative in creating products useful to end-users and protecting the safety and soundness of the financial system.

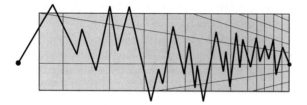

SUMMARY

This chapter has explained the basic features of financial futures markets. The traditional purpose of futures markets is to provide an important opportunity to hedge against the risk of adverse future price movements. Futures contracts are creations of exchanges, which require initial margin from parties. Each day positions are marked to market. Additional (variation) margin is required if the equity in the position falls below the maintenance margin. The clearinghouse guarantees that the parties to the futures contract will satisfy their obligations.

A forward contract differs in several important ways from a futures contract. In contrast to a futures contract, the parties to a forward contract are exposed to the risk that the other party to the contract will fail to perform. The positions of the parties are not necessarily marked to market, so there are no interim cash flows associated with a forward contract. Finally, unwinding a position in a forward contract may be difficult.

A buyer (seller) of a futures contract realizes a profit if the futures price increases (decreases). The buyer (seller) of a futures contract realizes a loss if the futures price decreases (increases). Because only initial margin is required when an investor takes a futures position, futures markets provide investors with substantial leverage for the money invested.

The theoretical futures price is determined by the cash market price and the cost of carry. At the delivery date, the futures price converges to the cash market price. There are reasons why the actual futures price will depart from the theoretical futures price. In practice, there is not one theoretical futures price but a band above and below it. The actual futures price tends to remain within the band through the operation of arbitrageurs.

The basis is the difference between the cash price and the futures price. The basis should equal the cost of carry. Basis risk occurs when the basis changes between the time a hedge is placed and the time it is lifted. Hedging eliminates price risk but substitutes basis risk. Cross-hedging occurs when the underlying instrument of the futures contract is different from the financial instrument or portfolio to be hedged, and most hedging in financial markets involves cross-hedging. The risk associated with cross-hedging is that the financial instrument or portfolio to be hedged will not be tracked exactly by the instrument underlying the futures contract.

Investors can use the futures market or the cash market to react to economic news that is expected to change the value of an asset. Futures markets are often the market of choice for altering asset positions and therefore represent the price discovery market, because of the lower transactions costs involved and the greater speed with which orders can be executed. The actions of arbitrageurs assure that price discovery in the futures markets will be transmitted to the cash market.

Critics of futures markets believe that they are the source of greater price volatility in the cash market for the underlying asset. Although this is an empirical question not fully discussed here, even if price volatility in the cash market were greater because of the introduction of futures markets, this does not necessarily mean that greater volatility is bad for the economy.

The General Accounting Office study cited in this chapter addresses the concerns of Congress and regulators regarding derivative products. There is concern that major banks and end-users do not have adequate risk-management systems in place. Inadequate accounting disclosure and the lack of coordination with foreign regulators were other concerns highlighted by the study.

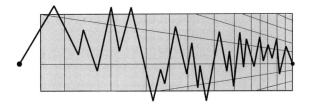

QUESTIONS

1. The chief financial officer of the corporation you work for recently told you that he had a strong preference to use forward contracts rather than futures contracts to hedge: "You can get contracts tailor-made to suit your needs." Comment on the CFO's statement. What other factors influence the decision to use futures or forward contracts?

2. You work for a conservative investment firm. You recently asked the firm's managing director for permission to open up a futures account so that you could trade financial futures as well as cash instruments. She replied, "Are you crazy? I might as well write you a check, wish you good luck, and put you on a bus to Atlantic City. The futures markets are nothing more than a respectable game of craps. Don't you think you're taking enough risk trading cash instruments?" How would you try to persuade the managing director to let you use futures?

3. Explain why you agree or disagree with the following statement: "Of course the futures are more expensive than the cash price—there's positive carry."

4. Suppose there is a financial asset ABC, which is the underlying asset for a futures contract with settlement six months from now. You know the following about this financial asset and futures contract: in the cash market ABC is selling for $80; ABC pays $8 per year in two semiannual payments of $4, and the next semiannual payment is due exactly six months from now; and the current six-month interest rate at which funds can be loaned or borrowed is 6%.

   a. What is the theoretical (or equilibrium) futures price?

   b. What action would you take if the futures price is $83?

   c. What action would you take if the futures price is $76?

d. Suppose that ABC pays interest quarterly instead of semiannually. If you know that you can reinvest any funds you receive three months from now at 1% for three months, what would the theoretical futures price for six-month settlement be?

e. Suppose that the borrowing rate and lending rate are not equal. Instead, suppose that the current six-month borrowing rate is 8% and the six-month lending rate is 6%. What is the boundary for the theoretical futures price?

5. You are a major producer of goat cheese. Concerned that the price of goat cheese might plummet, you are considering some kind of hedging strategy. Unfortunately, you discover that there are no exchange-traded futures on goat cheese. A business associate suggests a cross-hedge with orange juice futures. Specifically, your business associate suggests a short hedge using orange juice futures.

a. Before you commit to this hedging strategy, what other kinds of information would you like to know?

b. Why is it likely that this hedge will not turn out to be a perfect hedge?

6. Explain why you agree or disagree with the following statement: "Hedging with futures involves substituting basis risk for price risk."

7. Suppose that a corn farmer expects to sell 30,000 bushels of corn three months from now. Assume further that the management of a food-processing company plans to purchase 30,000 bushels of corn three months from now. Both the corn farmer and the management of the food-processing company want to lock in a price today. That is, each wants to eliminate the price risk associated with corn three months from now. The cash or spot price for corn is currently $2.75 per bushel.

A corn futures contract is available with the following terms: the settlement date for the contract is five months from now, and 5,000 bushels of corn must be delivered. Notice that the settlement date is two months after the parties expect to lift their hedge. Since each contract is for 5,000 bushels of corn, six corn futures contracts cover 30,000 bushels. The futures price for this futures contract is currently $3.20 per bushel.

a. Since the corn farmer seeks to lock in the price of corn to eliminate the risk of a decline in the price three months from now, will he place a long hedge or a short hedge?

b. Since the management of the food-processing company seeks to lock in the cost of corn to eliminate the risk of an increase in the price of corn three months from now, will it place a short hedge or long hedge?

c. What is the basis at the time of the hedge?

d. Suppose that when the hedge is lifted, the cash price declines to $2.00 and the futures contract price declines to $2.45. What has happened to the basis? What is the outcome for the corn farmer and the food-processing company?

e. Suppose that the cash price of corn when the hedge is lifted increases to $3.55, and that the futures price increases to $4.00. What has happened to the basis? What is the outcome for the corn farmer and the food-processing company?

f. Suppose that the cash price of corn decreases to $2.00 and that the futures price decreases to $2.70. What has happened to the basis? What is the outcome for the corn farmer and the food-processing company?

8. Suppose that a zucchini farmer plans to sell 37,500 bushels of zucchini three months from now and that a food-processing company plans to purchase the same amount of zucchini three months from now. Each party wants to hedge against price risk, but zucchini futures contracts are not traded. Both parties believe that there is a close price relationship between zucchini and corn. Specifically, both parties believe that the cash price of zucchini will be 80% of the cash price of corn. The cash price of zucchini is currently $2.20 per bushel, and the cash price of corn is currently $2.75 per bushel. Information about the futures contract is given in the previous question. The futures price of corn is currently $3.20 per bushel.

The parties must determine how many corn futures contracts must be used in the cross-hedge. The cash value of 37,500 bushels of zucchini at the cash price of $2.20 per bushel is $82,500. To protect a value of $82,500 using corn futures with a current cash price of $2.75, the price of 30,000 bushels of corn ($82,500/$2.75) must be hedged. Each corn futures contract involves 5,000 bushels, so six corn futures contracts are used.

a. Why is this a cross-hedge?

b. Suppose at the time the cross-hedge is lifted that the cash prices of zucchini and corn decrease to $1.60 and $2.00 per bushel; respectively, and the futures price of corn decreases to $2.45 per bushel; and that the relationship between the cash price for zucchini and corn assumed when the cross-hedge was placed holds at the time the cross-hedge is lifted. That is, the cash price of zucchini is 80% of the cash price of corn. What has happened to the basis between cash corn and futures corn? What is the outcome for the zucchini farmer and the food-processing company?

c. Suppose at the time the hedge is lifted that the cash price of zucchini falls to $1.30 per bushel while the cash price of corn falls to $2.00 per bushel; and that the futures price of corn falls to $2.45. What has happened to the basis between cash corn and futures corn? What is the outcome for the zucchini farmer and the food-processing company?

9. Explain why you agree or disagree with the following statement: "The futures market is where price discovery takes place."

10. Explain why you agree or disagree with the following statement: "The introduction of futures contracts creates greater price volatility for the underlying commodity or asset."

11. What is the destabilization hypothesis and what are the two variants of this hypothesis?

12. What is meant by an OTC derivative product?

13. What is the major concern with banks creating OTC derivative products?

Introduction to Options Markets

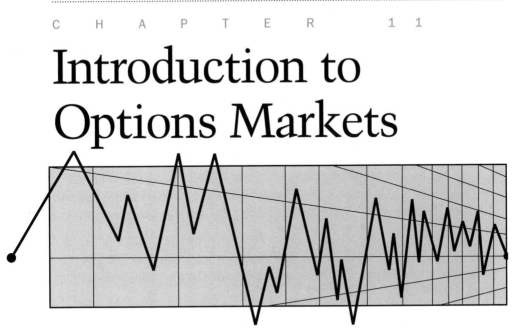

LEARNING OBJECTIVES

After reading this chapter you will understand:

- what an option contract is.

- the difference between a futures contract and an option contract.

- the risk/return characteristics of an option.

- the basic components of the option price.

- the factors that influence the option price.

- the fundamentals of option pricing models.

- the principles of the binomial option pricing model and how it is derived.

- the role of options in financial markets.

- two types of exotic options known as alternative options and outperformance options.

In Chapter 10 we introduced our first derivative instrument, a futures contract. In this chapter we introduce a second derivative contract, an options contract. Here, we will not look at specific options contracts, but instead focus on the general characteristics of the contract. We will discuss options on common stocks in Chapter 14, options on stock indexes in Chapter 15, options on bonds in Chapter 28, and options on currencies in Chapter 31.

In this chapter we discuss the differences between options and futures contracts and show how to determine the price of an option based on arbitrage arguments. In later chapters we will illustrate how investors can use options to create payoffs that can better satisfy their investment objectives.

OPTION CONTRACT DEFINED

An **option** is a contract in which the writer of the option grants the buyer of the option the right, but not the obligation, to purchase from or sell to the writer something at a specified price within a specified period of time (or at a specified date). The **writer**, also referred to as the **seller**, grants this right to the buyer in exchange for a certain sum of money, which is called the **option price** or **option premium**. The price at which the asset may be bought or sold is called the **exercise** or **strike price**. The date after which an option is void is called the **expiration date**. Our focus in this book is on options where the "something" underlying the option is a financial instrument, financial index, or financial futures contract. Our discussion of options on futures contracts (called futures options) is in Chapter 28.

When an option grants the buyer the right to purchase the designated instrument from the writer (seller), it is referred to as a **call option**, or **call**. When the option buyer has the right to sell the designated instrument to the writer, the option is called a **put option**, or **put**.

An option is also categorized according to when the option buyer may exercise the option. There are options that may be exercised at any time up to and including the expiration date. Such an option is referred to as an **American option**. There are options that may be exercised only at the expiration date. An option with this feature is called a **European option**.

To demonstrate the fundamental option contract, suppose that Jack buys a call option for $3 (the option price) with the following terms:

1. The underlying asset is one unit of Asset XYZ.
2. The strike price is $100.
3. The expiration date is three months from now, and the option can be exercised any time up to and including the expiration date (that is, it is an American option).

At any time up to and including the expiration date, Jack can decide to buy from the writer of this option one unit of Asset XYZ, for which he will pay a price of $100. If it is not beneficial for Jack to exercise the option, he will not, and will explain shortly how he decides when it will be beneficial. Whether Jack exercises the option or not, the $3 he paid for the option will be kept by the option writer. If Jack buys a put option rather than a call option, then he would be able to sell Asset XYZ to the option writer for a price of $100.

The maximum amount that an option buyer can lose is the option price. The maximum profit that the option writer can realize is the option price. The option buyer has substantial upside return potential, while the option writer has substantial downside risk. The risk/reward relationship for option positions will be discussed later in this chapter.

Margin Requirements

There are no margin requirements for the buyer of an option once the option price has been paid in full. Because the option price is the maximum amount that the investor can lose, no matter how adverse the price movement of the underlying asset, there is no need for margin. Because the writer of an option has agreed to accept all of the risk (and none of the reward) of the position in the underlying asset, the writer is generally required to put up the option price received as margin. In addition, as price changes occur that adversely affect the writer's position, the writer is required to deposit additional margin (with some exceptions) as the position is marked to market.

Exchange-Traded versus OTC Options

Options, like other financial instruments, may be traded either on an organized exchange or in the over-the-counter market. An exchange that wants to create an options contract must obtain approval from either the Commodities Futures Trading Commission or the Securities and Exchange Commission.[1] Exchange-traded options have three advantages. First, the exercise price and expiration date of the contract are standardized. Second, as in the case of futures contracts, the direct link between buyer and seller is severed after the order is executed because of the interchangeability of exchange-traded options. The clearinghouse associated with the exchange where the option trades performs the same function in the options market that it does in the futures market. Finally, the transactions costs are lower for exchange-traded options than for OTC options.

The higher cost of an OTC option reflects the cost of customizing the option for the many situations where an institutional investor needs to have a tailor-made option because the standardized exchange-traded option does not satisfy its investment objectives. As we explained in Chapters 3 and 5, some commercial and investment and banking firms act as principals as well as brokers in the OTC options market. OTC options are sometimes referred to as **dealer options.** While an OTC option is less liquid than an exchange-traded option, this is typically not of concern to an institutional investor—most institutional investors who use OTC options as part of an asset/liability strategy intend to hold them to expiration.

DIFFERENCES BETWEEN OPTIONS AND FUTURES CONTRACTS

Notice that, unlike in a futures contract, one party to an option contract is not obligated to transact—specifically, the option buyer has the right but not the obligation to transact. The option writer does have the obligation to perform. In the case of a futures contract, both buyer and seller are obligated to perform. Of course, a futures buyer does not pay the seller to accept the obligation, while an option buyer pays the seller an option price.

Consequently, the risk/reward characteristics of the two contracts are also different. In the case of a futures contract, the buyer of the contract realizes a dollar-for-dollar gain when the price of the futures contract increases and

---

[1] By an agreement between the CFTC and the SEC and pursuant to an act of Congress, options on futures are regulated by the former.

suffers a dollar-for-dollar loss when the price of the futures contract drops. The opposite occurs for the seller of a futures contract. Options do not provide this symmetric risk/reward relationship. The most that the buyer of an option can lose is the option price. While the buyer of an option retains all the potential benefits, the gain is always reduced by the amount of the option price. The maximum profit that the writer may realize is the option price; this is offset against substantial downside risk. This difference is extremely important because, as we shall see in subsequent chapters, investors can use futures to protect against symmetric risk and options to protect against asymmetric risk.

We shall return to the difference between options and futures for hedging at the end of the chapter.

RISK AND RETURN CHARACTERISTICS OF OPTIONS

Here we illustrate the risk and return characteristics of the four basic option positions—buying a call option, selling a call option, buying a put option, and selling a put option. The illustrations *assume that each option position is held to the expiration date and not exercised early.* Also, to simplify the illustrations, we ignore transactions costs.

Buying Call Options

The purchase of a call option creates a financial position referred to as a **long call position**. To illustrate this position, assume that there is a call option on Asset XYZ that expires in one month and has a strike price of $100. The option price is $3. Suppose that the current price of Asset XYZ is $100. What is the profit or loss for the investor who purchases this call option and holds it to the expiration date?

The profit and loss from the strategy will depend on the price of Asset XYZ at the expiration date. A number of outcomes are possible.

1. If the price of Asset XYZ at the expiration date is less than $100, then the investor will not exercise the option. It would be foolish to pay the option writer $100 when Asset XYZ can be purchased in the market at a lower price. In this case, the option buyer loses the entire option price of $3. Notice, however, that this is the maximum loss that the option buyer will realize regardless of how low Asset XYZ's price declines.

2. If Asset XYZ's price is equal to $100 at the expiration date, there is again no economic value in exercising the option. As in the case where the price is less than $100, the buyer of the call option will lose the entire option price, $3.

3. If Asset XYZ's price is more than $100 but less than $103 at the expiration date, the option buyer will exercise the option. By exercising, the option buyer can purchase Asset XYZ for $100 (the strike price) and sell it in the market for the higher price. Suppose, for example, that Asset XYZ's price is $102 at the expiration date. The buyer of the call option will realize a $2 gain by exercising the option. Of course, the cost of purchasing the call option was $3, so $1 is lost on this position. By failing to exercise the option, the investor loses $3 instead of only $1.

4. If Asset XYZ's price at the expiration date is equal to $103, the investor will exercise the option. In this case, the investor breaks even, realizing a gain of $3 that offsets the cost of the option, $3.

5. If Asset XYZ's price at the expiration date is more than $103, the investor will exercise the option and realize a profit. For example, if the price is $113, exercising the option will generate a profit on Asset XYZ of $13. Reducing this gain by the cost of the option ($3), the investor will realize a net profit from this position of $10.

Table 11-1 shows the profit and loss in tabular form for the buyer of the hypothetical call option, while Figure 11-1 graphically portrays the result. While the break-even point and the loss will depend on the option price and the strike price, the profile shown in Figure 11-1 will hold for all buyers of call options. The shape indicates that the maximum loss is the option price and that there is substantial upside potential.

It is worthwhile to compare the profit and loss profile of the call option buyer to taking a long position in one unit of Asset XYZ. The payoff from the position depends on Asset XYZ's price at the expiration date. Consider again the five price outcomes given above:

1. If Asset XYZ's price at the expiration date is less than $100, then the investor loses the entire option price of $3. In contrast, a long position in Asset XYZ will have one of three possible outcomes:

   a. if Asset XYZ's price is less than $100 but greater than $97, the loss on the long position in Asset XYZ will be less than $3.

   b. if Asset XYZ's price is $97, the loss on the long position in Asset XYZ will be $3.

   c. if Asset XYZ's price is less than $97, the loss on the long position in Asset XYZ will be greater than $3. For example, if the price at the expiration date is $80, the long position in Asset XYZ will result in a loss of $20.

Figure 11-1
Profit/Loss Profile for a Long Call Position

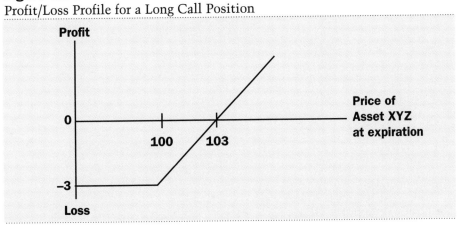

Table 11-1
Profit/Loss Profile for a Long Call Position

Assumptions:

Option price = $3
Strike price = $100
Time to expiration = 1 month

Price of Asset XYZ at Expiration Date	Net Profit/Loss*
$150	$47
140	37
130	27
120	17
115	12
114	11
113	10
112	9
111	8
110	7
109	6
108	5
107	4
106	3
105	2
104	1
103	0
102	−1
101	−2
100	−3
99	−3
98	−3
97	−3
96	−3
95	−3
94	−3
93	−3
92	−3
91	−3
90	−3
89	−3
88	−3
87	−3
86	−3
85	−3
80	−3
70	−3
60	−3

*Price at expiration − $100 − $3
Maximum loss = $3

2. If Asset XYZ's price is equal to $100, the buyer of the call option will realize a loss of $3 (option price). There will be no gain or loss on the long position in Asset XYZ.

3. If Asset XYZ's price is more than $100 but less than $103, the option buyer will realize a loss of less than $3, while the long position in Asset XYZ will realize a profit.

4. If the price of Asset XYZ at the expiration date is equal to $103, there will be no loss or gain from buying the call option. The long position in Asset XYZ, however, will produce a gain of $3.

5. If Asset XYZ's price at the expiration date is greater than $103, both the call option buyer and the long position in Asset XYZ will post a profit, but the profit for the buyer of the call option will be $3 less than that for the long position. If Asset XYZ's price is $113, for example, the profit from the call position is $10, while the profit from the long position in Asset XYZ is $13.

Table 11-2 compares the long call strategy and the long position in Asset XYZ. This comparison clearly demonstrates the way in which an option can change the risk/return profile for investors. An investor who takes a long position in Asset XYZ realizes a profit of $1 for every $1 increase in Asset XYZ's price. As Asset XYZ's price falls, however, the investor loses dollar-for-dollar. If the price drops by more than $3, the long position in Asset XYZ results in a loss of more than $3. The long call strategy, in contrast, limits the loss to only the option price of $3 but retains the upside potential, which will be $3 less than for the long position in Asset XYZ.

Which alternative is better, buying the call option or buying the asset? The answer depends on what the investor is attempting to achieve. This will become clearer in later chapters as we explain various strategies using either option positions or cash market positions.

We can also use this hypothetical call option to demonstrate the speculative appeal of options. Suppose an investor has strong expectations that Asset XYZ's price will rise in one month. At an option price of $3, the speculator can purchase 33.33 call options for each $100 invested. If Asset XYZ's price rises, the investor realizes the price appreciation associated with 33.33 units of Asset XYZ; while with the same $100, the investor could buy only one unit of Asset XYZ selling at $100, realizing the appreciation associated with one unit if Asset XYZ's price increases. Now, suppose that in one month the price of Asset XYZ rises to $120. The long call position will result in a profit of $566.50 [($20 × 33.33) − $100)] or a return of 566.5% on the $100 investment in the call option. The long position in Asset XYZ results in a profit of $20, for only a 20% return on $100.

It is this greater leverage that attracts investors to options when they wish to speculate on price movements. There are some drawbacks of leverage, however. Suppose that Asset XYZ's price is unchanged at $100 at the expiration date. The long call position results in this case in a loss of the entire investment of $100, while the long position in Asset XYZ produces neither a gain nor a loss.

Table 11-2

Comparison of Long Call Position and Long Asset Position

Assumptions:
  Price of Asset XYZ = $100
        Option price = $3
        Strike price = $100
  Time to expiration = 1 month

Price of Asset XYZ at Expiration Date	Net Profit/Loss Long Call	Net Profit/Loss Long Asset XYZ
$ 150	$ 47	$ 50
140	37	40
130	27	30
120	17	20
115	12	15
114	11	14
113	10	13
112	9	12
111	8	11
110	7	10
109	6	9
108	5	8
107	4	7
106	3	6
105	2	5
104	1	4
103	0	3
102	−1	2
101	−2	1
100	−3	0
99	−3	−1
98	−3	−2
97	−3	−3
96	−3	−4
95	−3	−5
94	−3	−6
93	−3	−7
92	−3	−8
91	−3	−9
90	−3	−10
89	−3	−11
88	−3	−12
87	−3	−13
86	−3	−14
85	−3	−15
80	−3	−20
70	−3	−30
60	−3	−40

Writing (Selling) Call Options

The writer of a call option is said to be in a **short call position**. To illustrate the option seller's (writer's) position, we use the same call option we used to illustrate buying a call option. The profit and loss profile of the short call position (that is, the position of the call option writer) is the mirror image of the profit and loss profile of the long call position (the position of the call option buyer). That is, the profit of the short call position for any given price for Asset XYZ at the expiration date is the same as the loss of the long call position. Consequently, the maximum profit that the short call position can produce is the option price. The maximum loss is not limited because it is the highest price reached by Asset XYZ on or before the expiration date, less the option price; this price can be indefinitely high. Figure 11-2 shows the profit/loss profile for a short call position.

Buying Put Options

The buying of a put option creates a financial position referred to as a **long put position**. To illustrate this position, we assume a hypothetical put option on one unit of Asset XYZ with one month to maturity and a strike price of $100. Assume the put option is selling for $2. The current price of Asset XYZ is $100. The profit or loss for this position at the expiration date depends on the market price of Asset XYZ. The possible outcomes are:

1. If Asset XYZ's price is greater than $100, the buyer of the put option will not exercise it because exercising would mean selling Asset XYZ to the writer for a price that is less than the market price. A loss of $2 (the option price) will result in this case from buying the put option. Once again, the option price represents the maximum loss to which the buyer of the put option is exposed.

2. If the price of Asset XYZ at expiration is equal to $100, the put will not be exercised, leaving the put buyer with a loss equal to the option price of $2.

Figure 11-2
Profit/Loss Profile for a Short Call Position

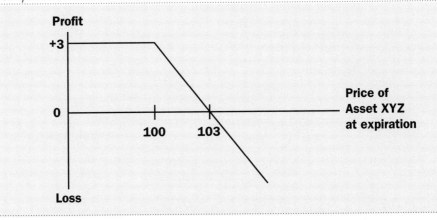

3. Any price for Asset XYZ that is less than $100 but greater than $98 will result in a loss; exercising the put option, however, limits the loss to less than the option price of $2. For example, suppose that the price is $99 at the expiration date. By exercising the option, the option buyer will realize a loss of $1. This is because the buyer of the put option can sell Asset XYZ, purchased in the market for $99, to the writer for $100, realizing a gain of $1. Deducting the $2 cost of the option results in a loss of $1.

4. At a $98 price for Asset XYZ at the expiration date, the put buyer will break even. The investor will realize a gain of $2 by selling Asset XYZ to the writer of the option for $100, offsetting the cost of the option ($2).

5. If Asset XYZ's price is below $98 at the expiration date, the long put position (the put buyer) will realize a profit. For example, suppose the price falls at expiration to $80. The long put position will produce a profit of $18: a gain of $20 for exercising the put option less the $2 option price.

The profit and loss profile for the long put position is shown in tabular form in the second column of Table 11-3 and in graphical form in Figure 11-3. As with all long option positions, the loss is limited to the option price. The profit potential, however, is substantial: the theoretical maximum profit is generated if Asset XYZ's price falls to zero. Contrast this profit potential with that of the buyer of a call option. The theoretical maximum profit for a call buyer cannot be determined beforehand because it depends on the highest price that can be reached by Asset XYZ before or at the option expiration date.

To see how an option alters the risk/return profile for an investor, we again compare it to a position in Asset XYZ. The long put position is compared to taking a short position in Asset XYZ because this is the position that would realize a profit if the price of the asset falls. Suppose an investor sells Asset XYZ short for $100. The short position in Asset XYZ would produce the profit or loss compared with the long put position as shown on the following page.

Figure 11-3

Profit/Loss Profile for a Long Put Position

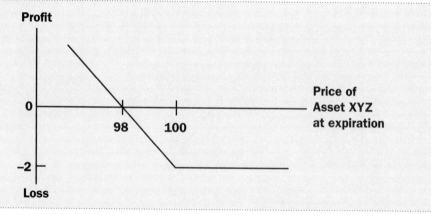

Table 11-3
Profit/Loss Profile for a Long Put Position and
Comparison with a Short Asset Position

Assumptions:
    Price of Asset XYZ = $100
            Option price = $2
            Strike price = $100
    Time to expiration = 1 month

Price of Asset XYZ at Expiration Date	Net Profit/Loss for	
	Long Put*	Short Asset XYZ**
$ 150	−$2	−$50
140	−2	−40
130	−2	−30
120	−2	−20
115	−2	−15
110	−2	−10
105	−2	−5
100	−2	0
99	−1	1
98	0	2
97	1	3
96	2	4
95	3	5
94	4	6
93	5	7
92	6	8
91	7	9
90	8	10
89	9	11
88	10	12
87	11	13
86	12	14
85	13	15
84	14	16
83	15	17
82	16	18
81	17	19
80	18	20
75	23	25
70	28	30
65	33	35
60	38	40

* $100 − Price at expiration − $2

   Maximum loss = $2
** $100 − Price of Asset XYZ

1. If Asset XYZ's price rises above $100, the long put option results in a loss of $2, but the short position in Asset XYZ realizes one of the following:

   a. if the price of Asset XYZ is less than $102, there will be a loss of less than $2.

   b. if the price of Asset XYZ is equal to $102, the loss will be $2, the same as the long put position.

   c. if the price of Asset XYZ is greater than $102, the loss will be greater than $2. For example, if the price is $125, the short position will realize a loss of $25, because the short-seller must now pay $125 for Asset XYZ that he sold short at $100.

2. If Asset XYZ's price at expiration is equal to $100, the long put position will realize a $2 loss, while there will be no profit or loss on the short position in Asset XYZ.

3. Any price for Asset XYZ that is less than $100 but greater than $98 will result in a loss of less than $2 for the long put position but a profit for the short position in Asset XYZ. For example, a price of $99 at the expiration date will result in a loss of $1 for the long put position but a profit of $1 for the short position.

4. At a $98 price for Asset XYZ at the expiration date, the long put position will break even, but the short position in Asset XYZ will generate a $2 profit.

5. At a price below $98, both positions will generate a profit; however, the profit will always be $2 less for the long put position.

Table 11-3 gives this comparison of the profit and loss profile for the long put position and short position in Asset XYZ. While the investor who takes a short position in Asset XYZ faces all the downside risk as well as the upside potential, the long put position limits the downside risk to the option price while still maintaining upside potential (reduced only by an amount equal to the option price).

Writing (Selling) Put Options

Writing a put option creates a financial position referred to as a **short put position**. The profit and loss profile for a short put option is the mirror image of the long put option. The maximum profit from this position is the option price. The theoretical maximum loss can be substantial should the price of the underlying asset fall; at the outside, if the price were to fall all the way to zero, the loss would be as large as the strike price less the option price. Figure 11-4 graphically depicts this profit and loss profile.

To summarize, buying calls or selling puts allows the investor to gain if the price of the underlying asset rises. Selling calls and buying puts allows the investor to gain if the price of the underlying asset falls.

Considering the Time Value of Money

Our illustration of the four option positions do not address the time value of money. Specifically, the buyer of an option must pay the seller the option price at the time the option is purchased. Thus, the buyer must finance the

Figure 11-4
Profit/Loss Profile for a Short Put Position

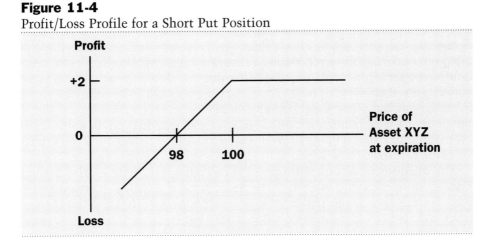

purchase price of the option or, assuming the purchase price does not have to be borrowed, the buyer loses the income that can be earned by investing the amount of the option price until the option is sold or exercised. In contrast, assuming that the seller does not have to use the option price amount as margin for the short position or can use an interest-earning asset as security, the seller has the opportunity to earn income from the proceeds of the option sale.

The time value of money changes the profit/loss profile of the option positions we have discussed. The break-even price for the buyer and the seller of an option will not be the same as in our illustrations. The break-even price for the underlying asset at the expiration date is higher (lower) for the buyer (seller) of a call option. The reverse is true for a put option.

Our comparisons of the option position with positions in the underlying instrument also ignore the time value of money. We have not considered the fact that the underlying asset may generate interim cash flows (dividends in the case of common stock, interest in the case of bonds). The buyer of a call option is not entitled to any interim cash flows generated by the underlying asset. The buyer of the underlying asset, however, would receive any interim cash flows and would have the opportunity to reinvest them. A complete comparison of the position of the long call option position and the long position in the underlying asset must take into account the additional dollars from reinvesting any interim cash flows. Moreover, any effect on the price of the underlying asset as a result of the distribution of cash must be considered. This occurs, for example, when the underlying asset is common stock and, as a result of a dividend payment, the stock declines in price. For simplicity, however, we continue to ignore the time value of money in the discussion to follow.

PRICING OF OPTIONS

So far, in our illustrations we have simply picked an option price as a given. The next question we ask is: How is the price of an option determined in the market?

Basic Components of the Option Price

The option price is a reflection of the option's intrinsic value and any additional amount over its intrinsic value. The premium over intrinsic value is often referred to as the **time value** or **time premium**. While the former term is more common, we will use the term time premium to avoid confusion between the time value of money and the time value of the option.

Intrinsic value—The intrinsic value of an option is the economic value of the option if it is exercised immediately, except that if there is no positive economic value that will result from exercising immediately then the intrinsic value is zero.

The intrinsic value of a call option is the difference between the current price of the underlying asset and the strike price if positive; it is otherwise zero. For example, if the strike price for a call option is $100 and the current asset price is $105, the intrinsic value is $5. That is, an option buyer exercising the option and simultaneously selling the underlying asset would realize $105 from the sale of the asset, which would be covered by acquiring the asset from the option writer for $100, thereby netting a $5 gain.

When an option has intrinsic value, it is said to be "in the money." When the strike price of a call option exceeds the current asset price, the call option is said to be "out of the money"; it has no intrinsic value. An option for which the strike price is equal to the current asset price is said to be "at the money." Both at-the-money and out-of-the-money options have an intrinsic value of zero because it is not profitable to exercise the option. Our call option with a strike price of $100 would be: (1) in the money when the current asset price is greater than $100, (2) out of the money when the current asset price is less than $100, and (3) at the money when the current asset price is equal to $100.

For a put option, the intrinsic value is equal to the amount by which the current asset price is below the strike price. For example, if the strike price of a put option is $100 and the current asset price is $92, the intrinsic value is $8. That is, the buyer of the put option who exercises the put option and simultaneously sells the underlying asset will net $8 by exercising. The asset will be sold to the writer for $100 and purchased in the market for $92. For our put option with a strike price of $100, the option would be: (1) in the money when the asset price is less than $100, (2) out of the money when the current asset price exceeds the strike price, (3) at the money when the strike price is equal to the asset's price.

Time premium—The time premium of an option is the amount by which the option price exceeds its intrinsic value. The option buyer hopes that, at some time prior to expiration, changes in the market price of the underlying asset will increase the value of the rights conveyed by the option. For this prospect, the option buyer is willing to pay a premium above the intrinsic value. For example, if the price of a call option with a strike price of $100 is $9 when the current asset price is $105, the time premium of this option is $4 ($9 minus its intrinsic value of $5). Had the current asset price been $90 instead of $105, then the time premium of this option would be the entire $9 because the option has no intrinsic value. Clearly, other things being equal, the time premium of an option will increase with the amount of time remaining to expiration.

There are two ways in which an option buyer may realize the value of a position taken in the option. First is to exercise the option. The second is by selling the call option for $9. In the first example above, selling the call is preferable because the exercise of an option will realize a gain of only $5—it will cause the immediate loss of any time premium. There are circumstances under which an option may be exercised prior to the expiration date; they depend on whether the total proceeds at the expiration date would be greater by holding the option or exercising and reinvesting any cash proceeds received until the expiration date.

Put-Call Parity Relationship

Is there a relationship between the price of a call option and the price of a put option on the same underlying instrument, with the same strike price and the same expiration date? There is. To see this relationship, which is commonly referred to as the **put-call parity relationship**, we will use an example.

In our previous illustrations we used a put and call option on the same underlying asset (Asset XYZ), with one month to expiration, and a strike price of $100. The price of the underlying asset was assumed to be $100. The call price and put price were assumed to be $3 and $2, respectively. Consider this strategy:

- Buy Asset XYZ at a price of $100
- Sell a call option at a price of $3
- Buy a put option at a price of $2

This strategy involves:

- Long Asset XYZ
- Short the call option
- Long the put option

Table 11-4 shows the profit and loss profile at the expiration date for this strategy. Notice that, no matter what Asset XYZ's price is at the expiration date, the strategy will produce a profit of $1.

The net cost of creating this position is the cost of purchasing Asset XYZ ($100) plus the cost of buying the put ($2) less the cost from selling the call ($3), which is $101. Suppose that the net cost of creating the position for one month is less than $1. Then, by borrowing $101 to create the position so that no investment outlay is made by the investor, this strategy will produce a net profit of $1 (as shown in the last column of Table 11-4) less the cost of borrowing $101 which is assumed to be less than $1. This situation cannot exist in an efficient market. In implementing the strategy to capture the $1 profit, the actions of market participants will have one or more of the following consequences that will tend to eliminate the $1 profit: (1) the price of Asset XYZ will increase, (2) the call option price will drop, and/or (3) the put option price will rise.

Table 11-4
Profit/Loss Profile for a Strategy Involving a Long Position in Asset XYZ, Short Call Option Position, and Long Put Option Position

Assumptions:
Price of Asset XYZ = $100
Call option price = $3
Put option price = $2
Strike price = $100
Time to expiration = 1 month

Price of Asset XYZ at Expiration Date	Profit from Asset XYZ*	Price Received for Call	Price Paid for Put	Overall Profit
$ 150	0	3	–2	1
140	0	3	–2	1
130	0	3	–2	1
120	0	3	–2	1
115	0	3	–2	1
110	0	3	–2	1
105	0	3	–2	1
100	0	3	–2	1
95	0	3	–2	1
90	0	3	–2	1
85	0	3	–2	1
80	0	3	–2	1
75	0	3	–2	1
70	0	3	–2	1
65	0	3	–2	1
60	0	3	–2	1

*There is no profit, because at a price above $100, Asset XYZ will be called from the investor at a price of $100; and at a price below $100, Asset XYZ will be put by the investor at a price of $100.

In our example, assuming Asset XYZ's price does not change, the call price and the put price must tend toward equality. This is true only when we ignore the time value of money (financing cost, opportunity cost, cash payments, and reinvestment income). Also, our illustration does not consider the possibility of early exercise of the options. Thus, we have been considering a put-call parity relationship for only European options.

It can be shown that the put-call parity relationship for an option where the underlying asset makes cash distributions is:

Put option price – Call option price =
Present value of strike price + Present value of cash distribution
– Price of underlying asset

This relationship is actually the put-call parity relationship for European options though it is approximately true for American options. If this relationship does not hold, arbitrage opportunities exist. That is, there will exist portfolios consisting of long and short positions in the asset and related options that will provide an extra return with (practical) certainty.

Factors that Influence the Option Price

There are six factors that influence the option price:

1. current price of the underlying asset.
2. strike price.
3. time to expiration of the option.
4. expected price volatility of the underlying asset over the life of the option.
5. short-term risk-free interest rate over the life of the option.
6. anticipated cash payments on the underlying asset over the life of the option.

The impact of each of these factors may depend on whether the option is a call or a put, and whether the option is an American option or a European option. A summary of the effect of each factor on put and call option prices is presented in Table 11-5.

Current price of the underlying asset—The option price will change as the price of the underlying asset changes. For a call option, as the price of the underlying asset increases (all other factors being constant, and the strike price in particular), the option price increases. The opposite holds for a put option: as the price of the underlying asset increases, the price of a put option decreases.

Strike price—The strike price is fixed for the life of the option. All other factors being equal, the lower the strike price, the higher the price of a call option. For put options, the higher the strike price, the higher the price of a put option.

Time to expiration of the option—An option is a "wasting asset." That is, after the expiration date the option has no value. All other factors being equal, the longer the time to expiration of the option, the greater the option price. This is because as the time to expiration decreases, less time remains for the underlying asset's price to rise (for a call buyer) or fall (for a put buyer)—that is, to compensate the option buyer for any time premium paid—and therefore the probability of a favorable price movement decreases. Consequently, for American options, as the time remaining until expiration decreases, the option price approaches its intrinsic value.

Expected price volatility of the underlying asset over the life of the option — All other factors being equal, the greater the expected volatility (as measured

Table 11-5
Summary of Factors that Affect the Price of an Option

Factor	Effect of an Increase of Factor on	
	Call Price	Put Price
Current price of underlying asset	increase	decrease
Strike price	decrease	increase
Time to expiration of option	increase	increase
Expected price volatility	increase	increase
Short-term interest rate	increase	decrease
Anticipated cash payments	decrease	increase

by the standard deviation or variance) of the price of the underlying asset, the more an investor would be willing to pay for the option, and the more an option writer would demand for it. This is because the greater the volatility, the greater the probability that the price of the underlying asset will move in favor of the option buyer at some time before expiration.

Notice that it is the standard deviation or variance, not the systematic risk as measured by beta,[2] that is relevant in the pricing of options.

Short-term risk-free interest rate over the life of the option—Buying the underlying asset ties up one's money. Buying an option on the same quantity of the underlying asset makes the difference between the asset price and the option price available for investment at (at least) the risk-free rate. Consequently, all other factors being constant, the higher the short-term risk-free interest rate, the greater the cost of buying the underlying asset and carrying it to the expiration date of the call option. Hence, the higher the short-term risk-free interest rate, the more attractive the call option will be relative to the direct purchase of the underlying asset. As a result, the higher the short-term risk-free interest rate, the greater the price of a call option.

Anticipated cash payments on the underlying asset over the life of the option—Cash payments on the underlying asset tend to decrease the price of a call option because the cash payments make it more attractive to hold the underlying asset than to hold the option. For put options, cash payments on the underlying asset tend to increase their price.

Option Pricing Models

In the Chapter 10, we illustrated that the theoretical price of a futures contract can be determined on the basis of arbitrage arguments. Theoretical boundary conditions for the price of an option also can be derived through arbitrage arguments. For example, using arbitrage arguments it can be shown that the minimum price for an American call option is its intrinsic value; that is:

Call option price ≥ Max (0, Price of asset – Strike price)

This expression says that the call option price will be greater than or equal to the difference between the price of the underlying asset and the strike price (intrinsic value), or zero, whichever is higher.

The boundary conditions can be "tightened" by using arbitrage arguments coupled with certain assumptions about the cash distribution of the asset.[3] The extreme case is an option pricing model that uses a set of assumptions to derive a single theoretical price, rather than a range. As we shall see below, deriving a theoretical option price is much more complicated than deriving a theoretical futures price, because the option price depends on the expected price volatility of the underlying asset over the life of the option.

Several models have been developed to determine the theoretical value of an option. The most popular one was developed by Fischer Black and Myron Scholes in 1973 for valuing European call options.[4] Several modifications to their model have followed since then. We shall discuss the Black-Scholes

---

[2] Beta is explained in Chapter 9.

[3] See John C. Cox and Mark Rubinstein, *Option Markets* (Englewood Cliffs, N.J.: Prentice-Hall, 1985), Chapter 4.

[4] Fischer Black and Myron Scholes, "The Pricing of Corporate Liabilities," *Journal of Political Economy* (May-June 1973), pp. 637-59.

model and its assumptions in Chapter 14. For now, we use another pricing model called the binomial option pricing model to see how arbitrage arguments can be used to determine a fair value for a call option.

Basically, the idea behind the arbitrage argument is that if the payoff from owning a call option can be replicated by purchasing the asset underlying the call option and borrowing funds, the price of the option is then (at most) the cost of creating the replicating strategy.

Deriving the Binomial Option Pricing Model

To derive a one-period binomial option pricing model for a call option, we begin by constructing a portfolio consisting of: (1) a long position in a certain amount of the asset, and (2) a short call position in the underlying asset. The amount of the underlying asset purchased is such that the position will be hedged against any change in the price of the asset at the expiration date of the option. That is, the portfolio consisting of the long position in the asset and the short position in the call option will produce the risk-free interest rate. A portfolio constructed in this way is called a hedged portfolio.

To illustrate, assume that there is an asset that has a current market price of $80 and only two possible future values one year from now:

State	Price
1	$100
2	70

Assume further that there is a call option on this asset with a strike price of $80 (the same as the current market price) that expires in one year. Suppose an investor forms a hedged portfolio by acquiring ⅔ of a unit of the asset and selling one call option. The ⅔ of a unit of the asset is the so-called hedge ratio (how we derive the hedge ratio will be explained later). Let us consider the outcomes for this hedged portfolio corresponding to the two possible outcomes for the asset.

If the price of the asset one year from now is $100, the buyer of the call option will exercise it. This means that the investor will have to deliver one unit of the asset in exchange for the strike price, $80. As the investor has only ⅔ of a unit of the asset, she has to buy ⅓ at a cost of $33⅓ (the market price of $100 times ⅓). Consequently, the outcome will equal the strike price of $80 received, minus the $33⅓ cost to acquire the ⅓ unit of the asset to deliver, plus whatever price the investor initially sold the call option for. That is, the outcome will be:

$80 – 33⅓ + Call option price = $46⅔ + Call option price

If, instead, the price of the asset one year from now is $70, the buyer of the call option will not exercise it. Consequently, the investor will own ⅔ of a unit of the asset. At the price of $70, the value of ⅔ of a unit is $46⅔. The outcome in this case is then the value of the asset plus whatever price the investor received when she initially sold the call option. That is, the outcome also will be $46⅔ plus the call option price.

It is apparent that, given the possible asset prices, the portfolio consisting of a short position in the call option and ⅔ of a unit of the asset will generate an outcome that hedges changes in the price of the asset; hence, the hedged portfolio is riskless. Furthermore, this will hold regardless of the price of the call, which affects only the magnitude of the outcome.

Deriving the hedge ratio—To show how the hedge ratio can be calculated, we will use the following notation:

S = current asset price

u = 1 plus the percentage change in the asset's price if the price goes up in the next period

d = 1 plus the percentage change in the asset's price if the price goes down in the next period

r = a risk-free one-period interest rate (the risk-free rate until the expiration date)

C = current price of a call option

C_u = intrinsic value of the call option if the asset price goes up

C_d = intrinsic value of the call option if the asset price goes down

E = strike price of the call option

H = hedge ratio, that is, the amount of the asset purchased per call sold

In the first illustration we started with, u, d, and H are:

u = 1.250 ($100/$80)
d = 0.875 ($70/$80)
$H = \frac{2}{3}$

State 1 in our illustration means that the asset's price goes up; State 2 means that the asset's price goes down.

The investment made in the hedged portfolio is equal to the cost of buying H amount of the asset minus the price received from selling the call option. Therefore, because the amount invested in the asset equals HS, then the cost of the hedged portfolio = $HS - C$.

The payoff of the hedged portfolio at the end of one period is equal to the value of the H amount of the asset purchased minus the call option price. The payoffs of the hedged portfolio for the two possible states are:

If the asset's price goes up:

$uHS - C_u$

If the asset's price goes down:

$dHS - C_d$

From our illustration:

If the asset's price goes up:

$1.250\ H\ \$80 - C_u$

or

$\$100\ H - C_u$

If the asset's price goes down:

0.875 H $80 – C_d

or

$70 H – C_d

Regardless of the state that occurs, we want the payoff of the hedged portfolio to be the same. That is, we want:

$$uHS - C_u = dHS - C_d \qquad (11.1)$$

Solving Equation (11.1) for H we have:

$$H = \frac{C_u - C_d}{(u - d) S} \qquad (11.2)$$

To determine the hedge ratio, H, we must know C_u and C_d. These two values are equal to the difference between the price of the asset and the strike price. Of course, the minimum value of the call option is zero. Mathematically, this can be expressed as follows:

If the asset's price goes up:

C_u = Max [0, (uS – E)]

If the asset's price goes down:

C_d = Max [0, (dS – E)]

As the strike price in our illustration is $80, uS is $100, and dS is $70. Then: If the asset's price goes up:

C_u = Max [0, ($100 – $80)] = $20

If the asset's price goes down:

C_d = Max [0, ($70 – $80)] = $0

For our illustration, we substitute the values of u, d, s, C_u, and C_d into Equation (11.2) to obtain the hedge ratio:

$$H = \frac{\$20 - \$0}{(1.25 - 0.875) \$80} = \frac{2}{3}$$

The value for H agrees with the amount of the asset purchased in our earlier illustration.

Now we can derive a formula for the call option price. Figure 11-5 diagrams the situation. The top left half of the figure shows the current price of the asset for the current period and at the expiration date. The lower left-hand portion of the figure does the same thing using the notation above. The upper right-hand side of the figure gives the current price of the call option and the value of the call option at the expiration date; the lower right-hand side does

Figure 11-5
One-Period Option Pricing Model

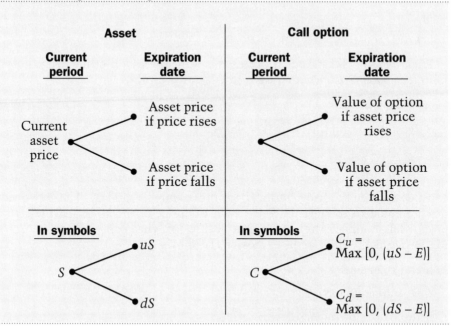

the same thing using our notation. Figure 11-6 uses the values in our illustration to construct the outcomes for the asset and the call option.

Deriving the price of a call option—To derive the price of a call option we can rely on the basic principle that the hedged portfolio, being riskless, must have a return equal to the riskless rate. Given that the amount invested in the hedged portfolio is HS – C, the amount that should be generated one period from now is:

$$(1 + r)\,(HS - C) \tag{11.3}$$

We also know what the payoff will be for the hedged portfolio if the asset's price goes up or goes down. Because the payoff of the hedged portfolio will be

Figure 11-6
One-Period Option Pricing Model Illustration

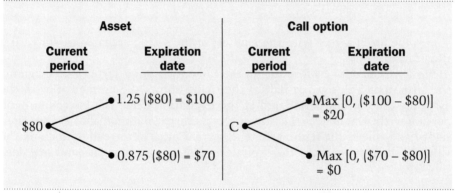

the same whether the asset's price goes up or down, we can use the payoff if it goes up, which is: $uHS - C_u$. The payoff of the hedged portfolio given above should be the same as the amount to be generated by investing the initial cost of the portfolio given by Equation (11.3). Equating the two, we have:

$$(1 + r)(HS - C) = uHS - C_u \qquad (11.4)$$

Substituting Equation (11.2) for H in Equation (11.4), and solving for the call option price, C, we find:

$$C = \left(\frac{1 + r - d}{u - d}\right) \frac{C_u}{(1 + r)} + \left(\frac{u - 1 - r}{u - d}\right) \frac{C_d}{(1 + r)} \qquad (11.5)$$

Equation (11.5) is the formula for the one-period binomial option pricing model. We would have derived the same formula if we had used the payoff if the asset's price goes down.

Applying Equation (11.5) to our illustration where:

$u = 1.250$
$d = 0.875$
$r = 0.10$
$C_u = \$20$
$C_d = \$0$

we get:

$$C = \left(\frac{1 - 0.10 - 0.875}{1.25 - 0.875}\right) \frac{\$20}{1 + 0.10} + \left(\frac{1.25 - 1 - 0.10}{1.25 - 0.875}\right) \frac{\$0}{1 + 0.10}$$

$$= \$10.90$$

This value agrees with our first finding for the call option price.

This approach to pricing options may seem oversimplified, given that we assume only two possible future states for the underlying asset. In fact, we can extend the procedure by making the periods smaller and smaller, so we can calculate a fair value for the option. To illustrate these basic principles we extend the original illustration to a two-period model.

Extension to two-period model—The extension to two periods requires that we introduce more notation. To help understand the notation, look at Figure 11-7. The left panel of the figure shows for the asset, the initial price, the price one period from now if the price goes up or goes down, and the price at the expiration date (two periods from now) if the price in the previous period goes up or goes down. The right panel of Figure 11-7 shows the value of the call option at the expiration date and the value one period prior to the expiration date.

The new notation has to do with the value of the call option at the expiration date. We now use two subscripts. Specifically, we will let:

C_{uu} = call value if the asset's price went up in both periods
C_{dd} = call value if the asset's price went down in both periods
$C_{ud} = C_{du}$ = call value if the asset's price went down in one period and up in one period

Figure 11-7
Two-Period Option Pricing Model

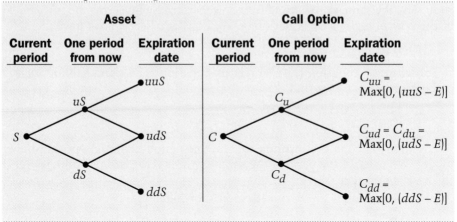

We solve for the call option price, C, by starting at the expiration date to determine the value of C_u and C_d. This can be done by using Equation (11.5) because that equation gives the price of a one-period call option. Specifically:

$$C_u = \left(\frac{1 + r - d}{u - d}\right) \frac{C_{uu}}{(1 + r)} + \left(\frac{u - 1 - r}{u - d}\right) \frac{C_{ud}}{(1 + r)} \tag{11.6}$$

$$C_d = \left(\frac{1 + r - d}{u - d}\right) \frac{C_{du}}{(1 + r)} + \left(\frac{u - 1 - r}{u - d}\right) \frac{C_{dd}}{(1 + r)} \tag{11.7}$$

Once C_u and C_d are known, we can solve for C using Equation (11.5)

To make this more concrete, substitute numbers. We will assume that the asset's price can go up by 11.8% per period or down by 6.46% per period. That is: $u = 1.118$ and $d = 0.9354$. Then, as shown in the top left panel of Figure 11-8, the asset can have three possible prices at the end of two periods:

Price goes up both periods: $uuS = (1.118)(1.118)\,\$80 = \$100$
Price goes down both periods: $ddS = (0.9354)(0.9354)\,\$80 = \$70$
Price goes up one period and down the other:

$$udS = (1.118)(0.9354)\,\$80 = duS = (0.9354)(1.118)\,\$80 = \$83.66$$

Notice that the first two prices are the same as in the one-period illustration. By extending the length of time until expiration to two periods rather than one, and adjusting the change in the asset price accordingly, we now have three possible outcomes. If we increase the number of periods, the number of possible outcomes that the asset price may take on at the expiration date will increase. Consequently, what seemed like an unrealistic assumption about two possible outcomes for each period becomes more realistic with respect to the number of possible outcomes that the asset price may take at the expiration date.

Now we can use the values in the top right panel of Figure 11-8 to calculate C. The riskless interest rate for one period is now 4.88% because when compounded this rate will produce an interest rate of 10% from now to the

Figure 11-8
Two-Period Option Pricing Model Illustration

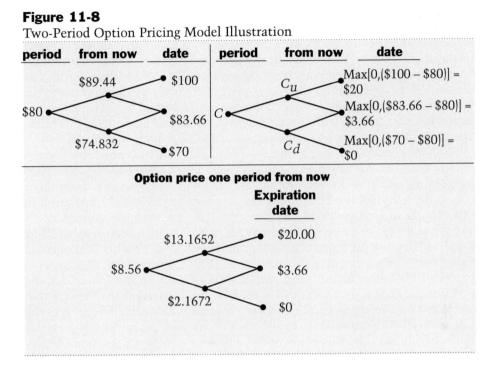

expiration date (two periods from now). First, consider the calculation of C_u using Equation (11.6). From Figure 11-8 we see that: $C_{uu} = \$20$ and $C_{ud} = \$3.66$. Therefore:

$$C_u = \left(\frac{1 + 0.0488 - 0.9354}{1.118 - 0.9354}\right)\frac{\$20}{1 + 0.0488}$$

$$+ \left(\frac{1.118 - 1 - 0.0488}{1.118 - 0.9354}\right)\frac{\$3.66}{1 + 0.0488} = \$13.1652$$

From Figure 11-8 $C_{dd} = \$0$ and $C_{du} = \$3.66$. Therefore:

$$C_d = \left(\frac{1 + 0.0488 - 0.9354}{1.118 - 0.9354}\right)\frac{\$3.66}{1 + 0.0488}$$

$$+ \left(\frac{1.118 - 1 - 0.0488}{1.118 - 0.9354}\right)\frac{\$0}{1 + 0.0488} = \$2.1672$$

We have inserted the values for C_u and C_d in the bottom panel of Figure 11-8 and can now calculate C by using Equation (11.5) as follows:

$$C = \left(\frac{1 + 0.0488 - 0.9354}{1.118 - 0.9354}\right)\frac{\$13.1652}{1 + 0.0488}$$

$$+ \left(\frac{1.118 - 1 - 0.0488}{1.118 - 0.9354}\right)\frac{\$2.1672}{1 + 0.0488} = \$8.58$$

ECONOMIC ROLE OF THE OPTION MARKETS

In the previous chapter, we explained the important role that futures play in our financial markets because they allow investors to hedge the risks associated with adverse price movements. Hedging with futures lets a market participant lock in a price, and thereby eliminates price risk. In the process, however, the investor gives up the opportunity to benefit from a favorable price movement. In other words, hedging with futures involves trading off the benefits of a favorable price movement for protection against an adverse price movement.

Hedging with options has a variety of potential benefits, which we discuss in later chapters. For now, we provide an overview of how options can be used for hedging, and how the outcomes of hedging with options differ from those of hedging with futures. To see this, let us return to the initial illustration in this chapter where the underlying instrument for the option is Asset XYZ.

First, consider an investor who owns Asset XYZ, which is currently selling for $100. The investor expects to sell it one month from now but is concerned that Asset XYZ's price may decline below $100 in that month. One alternative available to this investor is to sell Asset XYZ now. Suppose, however, the investor does not want to sell this asset now because either she expects that the price will rise in one month or there are some restrictions that prevent the sale of Asset XYZ now. Suppose also that an insurance company is aware of the situation faced by this investor and offers to sell her an insurance policy providing that, if at the end of one month Asset XYZ's price is less than $100, the insurance company makes up the difference between $100 and the market price. That is, if one month from now Asset XYZ's price is $80, the insurance company will pay the investor $20.

The insurance company naturally charges the investor a premium to write this policy. Let us suppose that the premium is $2. Holding aside the cost of the insurance policy, the payoff that this investor then faces is as follows. The minimum price for Asset XYZ that the investor is assured is $100 because if the price is less, the insurance company will make up the difference. If Asset XYZ's price is greater than $100, however, the investor will receive the higher price. Once we consider the premium of $2 to purchase this insurance premium, the investor is effectively assured a minimum price of $98 ($100 minus $2), but if the price is above $100 the investor realizes the benefits of a higher price (reduced always by the $2 for the insurance policy). By buying this insurance policy, the investor has purchased protection against an adverse price movement, while maintaining the opportunity to benefit from a favorable price movement reduced by the cost of the insurance policy.

Insurance companies do not offer such policies, but we have described a contract in this chapter that provides the same protection as this hypothetical insurance policy. Consider the put option on Asset XYZ with one month to expiration, a strike price of $100, and an option price of $2 that we used in our illustrations earlier in this chapter. The payoff is identical to the hypothetical insurance policy. The option price resembles the hypothetical insurance premium; this is the reason why the option price is referred to as the option premium. A put option can be used to hedge against a decline in the price of the underlying instrument.

This is quite a different payoff from a futures contract. Suppose that a futures contract with Asset XYZ as the underlying instrument is available with a futures price equal to $100 and a settlement date one month from now. By selling this futures contract, the investor would be agreeing to sell Asset XYZ for $100 one month from now. If Asset XYZ's price falls below $100, the investor is protected because she will receive $100 upon delivery of the asset to satisfy the futures contract. If Asset XYZ's price rises above $100, however, the investor will not realize the price appreciation because she must deliver the asset for an agreed-upon amount of $100. By selling the futures contract, the investor has locked in a price of $100, failing to realize a gain if the price rises but avoiding a loss if the price declines.

Call options, too, can be used to hedge. A call option can be used to protect against a rise in the price of the underlying instrument while maintaining the opportunity to benefit from a decline in the price of the underlying instrument. Suppose, for example, that an investor expects to receive $100 one month from now, and plans to use that money to purchase Asset XYZ, which is currently selling for $100. The risk that the investor faces is that Asset XYZ's price will rise above $100 one month from now. By purchasing the call option with a strike price of $100 and with an option price of $3 that we used earlier in this chapter, the investor has hedged the risk of a rise in the price of Asset XYZ.

The hedge outcome is as follows. If the price rises above $100 one month from now, the investor would exercise the call option and realize the difference between the market price of Asset XYZ and $100. Thus, holding aside the cost of the option, the investor is assuring a maximum price that she will have to pay for Asset XYZ of $100. Should the asset's price fall below $100, the call option expires worthless, but the investor benefits by being able to purchase Asset XYZ at a price less than $100. Once the $3 cost of the option is considered, the payoff is as follows. The maximum price that the investor will have to pay for Asset XYZ is $103 (the strike price plus the option price), but if the price of the asset declines below $100 the investor will benefit by the amount of the price decline less $3.

Compare this situation to a futures contract where Asset XYZ is the underlying instrument, settlement is in one month, and the futures price is $100. Suppose that the investor buys this futures contract. If one month from now the price of Asset XYZ rises above $100, the investor has contracted to buy the asset for $100, thereby eliminating the risk of a price rise; if the price falls below $100, however, the investor cannot benefit because she has contracted to pay $100 for the asset.

It should be clear by now how hedging with options differs from hedging with futures. This difference cannot be overemphasized. Options and futures are not interchangeable instruments.

Is it possible to create the same hedging payoff that an option provides against an adverse price movement in a world in which there are no option contracts? It should be obvious from our illustrations of how to price an option that the same payoff can be accomplished synthetically with an appropriate position in the cash market instrument and by borrowing funds. So why do we need option contracts? The reason is that an option contract is a more *efficient* vehicle to create the hedged position.

While our focus has been on hedging price risk, options also allow investors an efficient way to expand the range of return characteristics available. That is, investors can use options to "mold" a return distribution for a portfolio to fit particular investment objectives.[5]

EXOTIC OPTIONS

As we explained earlier in this chapter, OTC options can be customized in any manner sought by an institutional investor. Basically, if a dealer can reasonably hedge the risk associated with the opposite side of the option sought, it will create the option desired by a customer. OTC options are not limited to European or American types. An option can be created in which the option can be exercised at several specified dates as well as the expiration date of the option. Such options are referred to as **limited exercise options**, **Bermuda options**, and **Atlantic options**.

The more complex options created are called **exotic options**. There are several types of exotic options discussed throughout this book; here we examine two types: alternative options and outperformance options. An **alternative option**, also called an **either-or option**, has a payoff that is the best independent payoff of two distinct assets. For example, suppose that Donna buys an alternative call option with the following terms:.

1. The underlying asset is one unit of Asset M or one unit of Asset N.
2. The strike price for Asset M is $80.
3. The strike price for Asset N is $110.
4. The expiration date is three months from now.
5. The option can only be exercised three months from now (that is, it is a European option).

At the expiration date, Donna can decide to buy from the writer of this option *either* one unit of Asset M at $80 *or* Asset N at $110. Donna will buy the asset with the larger payoff. So, for example, if Asset M and Asset N at the expiration date are $84 and $140, respectively, then the payoff would be $4 if Donna elects to exercise to buy Asset M but $30 if she elects to exercise to buy Asset N. Thus, she will exercise to buy Asset N. If the price for either asset at the expiration date is below their strike price, Donna will let the option expire worthless.

An **outperformance option** is an option whose payoff is based on the relative payoff of two assets at the expiration date. For example, consider the following outperformance call option purchased by Karl.

---

[5] See Stephen A. Ross, "Options and Efficiency," *Quarterly Journal of Economics* (February 1976), pp. 75-89, and Fred Arditti and Kose John, "Spanning the State Space with Options," *Journal of Financial and Quantitative Analysis* (March 1980), pp. 1-9.

1. Portfolio A consists of the stock of 50 public utility companies with a market value of $1 million.

2. Portfolio B consists of the stock of 50 financial services companies with a market value of $1 million.

3. The expiration date is six months from now and is a European option.

4. The strike is equal to the market value of Portfolio B less the market value of Portfolio A.

At the expiration date, if the market value of Portfolio A is greater than the market value of Portfolio B, then there is no value to this option and it will expire worthless. The option will be exercised if the market value of Portfolio B exceeds the market value of Portfolio A at the expiration date.

The motivation for the use of exotic options such as alternative options and outperformance options will become evident when we discuss various investment and financing strategies in later chapters.

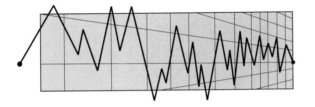

SUMMARY

In this chapter we have reviewed the fundamentals of options. An option grants the buyer of the option the right either to buy (in the case of a call option) or to sell (in the case of a put option) the underlying asset to the seller (writer) of the option at a stated price called the strike (exercise) price by a stated date called the expiration date. The price that the option buyer pays to the writer of the option is called the option price or option premium. An American option allows the option buyer to exercise the option at any time up to and including the expiration date; a European option may be exercised only at the expiration date.

The buyer of an option cannot realize a loss greater than the option price, and has all the upside potential. By contrast, the maximum gain that the writer (seller) of an option can realize is the option price; the writer is exposed to all the downside risk.

The option price consists of two components: the intrinsic value and the time premium. The intrinsic value is the economic value of the option if it is exercised immediately (except that if there is no positive economic value that will result from exercising immediately, then the intrinsic value is zero). The time premium is the amount by which the option price exceeds the intrinsic value. Six factors influence the option price: (1) the current price of the underlying asset, (2) the strike price of the option, (3) the time remaining to the expiration of the option, (4) the expected price volatility of the underlying asset, (5) the short-term risk-free interest rate over the life of the option, and (6) anticipated cash payments on the underlying asset.

Arbitrage arguments can be used to place a lower boundary on the option price. There is also a relationship between the call option price, the put option price, and the price of the underlying asset known as the put-call parity relationship. The theoretical option price can be calculated using the binomial option pricing model, also based on arbitrage arguments.

Dealer-created or OTC options can be customized to satisfy the desires of institutional investors. More complex OTC options are called exotic options; alternative and outperformance options being two types of exotic options.

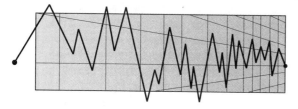

QUESTIONS

1. What is the difference between a put option and a call option?

2. What is the difference between an American option and a European option?

3. Why does an option writer need to post margin?

4. Identify two important ways in which an exchange-traded option differs from a typical over-the-counter option.

5. "There's no real difference between options and futures. Both are hedging tools, and both are derivative products. It's just that with options you have to pay an option premium, while futures require no upfront payment except for a `good faith' margin. I can't understand why anyone would use options." Do you agree with this statement?

6. Explain how this statement can be true: "A long call position offers potentially unlimited gains, if the underlying asset's price rises, but a fixed, maximum loss if the underlying asset's price drops to zero."

7. Suppose a call option on a stock has a strike price of $70 and a cost of $2, and suppose you buy the call. Identify the profit to your investment, at the call's expiration, for each of these values of the underlying stock: $25, $70, $100, $400.

8. Consider the situation in the previous question once more. Suppose you had sold the call option. What would your profit be at expiration for each of those stock prices?

9. Explain why you agree or disagree with this statement: "Buying a put is just like short-selling the underlying asset. You gain the same thing from either position, if the underlying asset's price falls. If the price goes up, you have the same loss."

10. You have just opened up the morning newspaper to check the

prices of call options on Asset ABC. It is now December, with the near contract maturing in one month's time. Asset ABC's price is currently trading at $50.

Strike	Jan.	March	June
$ 40	$11	$12	$11.50
50	6	7	8.50
60	7	8	9.00

Glancing at the figures, you note that two of these quotes seem to violate some of the rules you learned regarding option pricing.

a. What are these discrepancies?

b. How could you take advantage of the discrepancies? What is the minimum profit you would realize by arbitraging based on these discrepancies?

c. Suppose the price of the January $40 call were $9 rather than $11. The option would thus be selling for less than its intrinsic value. Why might it not be the case that an arbitrage profit were instantly available?

11. The payoff from a long position in a forward contract on the settlement date is the difference between the spot price of the underlying asset at the maturity of the forward contract and the forward price. For example, if you are long a forward contract to purchase an asset at $100, your payoff at the settlement date would be as follows:

Spot Price	Forward Price	Payoff
80	100	−20
90	100	−10
100	100	0
110	100	10
120	100	20

A forward contract is equivalent to being long a call option and short a put option, with the strike price such that the price of the call is equal to the price of the put.

a. For the five spot prices above, demonstrate that being long a forward is equivalent to being long a call and short a put.

b. Why do you think that the strike price has to be set such that the price of the call is equal to the price of the put?

12. Indicate whether you agree or disagree with the statements following.

a. "To determine the theoretical value of an option, we will need some measure of the volatility of the underlying asset. Because financial theorists tell us that the appropriate measure of risk is beta (i.e., systematic risk), then we should use this value."

b. "It does not make sense that the price of a call option should rise in value if the price of the underlying asset falls."

13. For an asset that does not make cash distributions over the life of an option, it does not pay to exercise a call option prior to the expiration date. Why?

14. Consider the following two strategies. *Strategy 1:* Purchase one unit of Asset M currently selling for $103. A distribution of $10 is expected one year from now. *Strategy 2:* Purchase a call option on Asset M with an expiration date one year from now and a strike price of $100; and place sufficient funds in a 10% interest-

bearing bank account sufficient to exercise the option at expiration ($100) and to pay the cash distribution that would be paid by Asset M ($10)

a. What is the investment required under Strategy 2?

b. What are the payoffs of Strategy 1 and Strategy 2, assuming that the price of Asset M one year from now is: $120; $103; $100; $80.

c. For the four prices of asset M one year from now, demonstrate that the following relationship holds:

Call option price > Max [0, (Price of underlying asset − Present value of strike price − Present value of cash distribution)]

15. The current price of Asset W is $25. There are no cash distributions expected for this asset for the next year. The one-year interest rate is 10%. The asset's price will be either $35 or $15 one year from now. What is the price of a European call option on Asset W with a strike price of zero that expires in one year's time?

16. a. Calculate the option value for a two-period European call option with the following terms:

Current price of the underlying asset equals $100.
Strike price equals $10.
One-period risk-free rate is 5%.
The stock price can either go up or down by 10% at the end of one period.

b. Recalculate the value for the option when the stock price can move either up or down by 50% at the end of one period.

Compare your answer with the calculated value in part (a). Why is the answer different from what you might have expected?

17. Suppose that you buy an alternative call option with the following terms:

The underlying asset is one unit of Asset G or one unit of Asset H.
The strike price for Asset G is $100.
The strike price for Asset H is $115.
The expiration date is four months from now.
The option can only be exercised at the expiration date.

a. What is the payoff from this option if at the expiration date the price of Asset G is $125 and price of Asset H is $135?

b. What is the payoff from this option if at the expiration date the price of Asset G is $90 and price of Asset H is $125?

c. What is the payoff from this option if at the expiration date the price of Asset G is $90 and price of Asset H is $105?

18. Suppose that you buy an outperformance call option with the following terms:

Portfolio X consists of bonds with a market value of $5 million.
Portfolio Y consists of stocks with a market value of $5 million.
The expiration date is nine months from now and is a European option.
The strike is equal to the market value of Portfolio X − market value of Portfolio Y.

What is the payoff of this option if at the expiration date the market value of Portfolio X is $10 million and the market value of Portfolio Y is $12 million?

Introduction to the Swaps, Caps, and Floors Markets

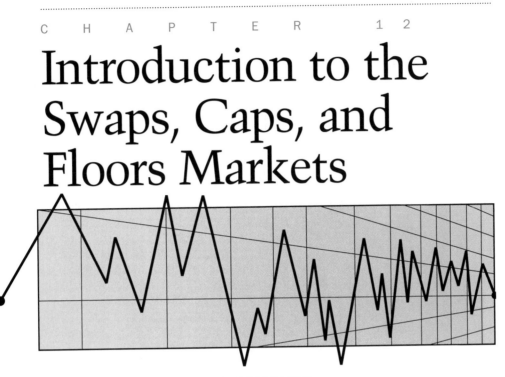

LEARNING OBJECTIVES

After reading this chapter you will understand:

- what a swap is.

- what is meant by the notional principal amount.

- the various types of swaps; including interest rate swap, interest rate-equity swap, equity swap, and currency swap.

- the relationship between a swap and forward contract.

- how swaps can be used for asset/liability management.

- how swaps can be used to create securities.

- what a cap and a floor are.

- the relationship between a cap and a floor and an option.

- how a cap can be used by a depository institution.

The newest derivative contracts that have been introduced into the financial markets are swaps, caps, and floors. As with futures and options, these derivative products can be used to control risks faced by borrowers and investors.

Moreover, particularly in the case of swaps, they have given investment bankers the ability to create a wide range of securities that meet the objectives of investors. All of these derivative contracts are currently traded in the over-the-counter market and not on any organized exchange.

In this chapter, we provide an overview of these contracts and some basic applications. In Chapters 15, 29, and 31, we shall take a closer look at these contracts and their mechanics. Our motivation for introducing them at this early stage is the key role that they have played in the development of a global financial market and the development of new financial instruments and strategies.

SWAPS

A **swap** is an agreement whereby two parties (called **counterparties**) agree to exchange periodic payments. The dollar amount of the payments exchanged is based on some predetermined dollar principal, which is called the **notional principal amount** or **notional amount**. The dollar amount each counterparty pays to the other is the agreed-upon periodic rate times the notional principal amount. The only dollars that are exchanged between the parties are the agreed-upon payments, not the notional principal amount.

To illustrate a swap and give you a flavor for the wide range of swaps, consider the following four swap agreements in which the payments are exchanged once a year for the next five years.

1. The counterparties to the swap are the First Renwick Bank and the General Manufacturing Corporation. The notional principal amount of this swap is $100 million. Every year for the next five years, First Renwick Bank agrees to pay General Manufacturing Corp. 8% per year, while General Manufacturing agrees to pay First Renwick the rate on a one-year Treasury security. This means that every year, First Renwick will pay $8 million (8% times $100 million) to General Manufacturing. The amount that General Manufacturing will pay the bank depends on the rate on a one-year Treasury security. For example, if this rate is 5%, General Manufacturing will pay the bank $5 million (5% times $100 million).

2. The counterparties to this swap agreement are the Brotherhood of Basket Weavers (a pension sponsor) and the Reliable Investment Management Corporation (a money management firm). The notional principal amount is $50 million. Every year for the next five years the Brotherhood agrees to pay Reliable the return realized on the Standard & Poor's 500 stock index for the year minus 200 basis points. (This index will be described in Chapter 13.) In turn, Reliable agrees to pay the pension sponsor 10%. So, for example, if over the past year the return on the S&P 500 stock index is 14%, then the pension sponsor pays Reliable 12% (14% minus 2%) of $50 million, or $6 million, and the money management firm agrees to pay the pension sponsor $5 million (10% times $50 million).

3. The counterparties to this swap agreement are the Beneficial Pension Fund (a pension fund sponsor) and the Investment Management Associates (a German money management firm). The notional principal amount is $80 million. Every year for the next five years Beneficial Pension agrees to pay Investment Management the return realized on the S&P 500 stock index for the year. In turn, Investment Management agrees to pay the pension fund sponsor the return realized on the German stock index (called the DAX index) for the year. So, for example, if over the past year the return on the S&P 500 stock index and the German stock index are 14% and 10%, respectively, then the pension fund sponsor pays Investment Management $11.2 million (14% times $80 million), and the German money management firm agrees to pay Beneficial Pension $8 million (10% times $80 million).

4. The two counterparties to this swap agreement are the Regency Electronics Corporation (a U.S. manufacturing firm) and the All-Swiss Watches Corporation (a Swiss manufacturing firm). The notional principal amount is $100 million and its Swiss franc equivalent at the time the contract was entered into was SF 127 million. Every year for the next five years the U.S. manufacturing firm agrees to pay All-Swiss Watches Swiss francs equal to 5% of the Swiss franc notional principal amount, or SF 6.35 million. In turn, the Swiss manufacturing firm agrees to pay Regency Electronics 7% of the U.S. notional principal amount of $100 million, or $7 million.

Types of Swaps

Swaps are classified based on the characteristics of the swap payments. There are four types of swaps: interest rate swaps, interest rate-equity swaps, equity swaps, and currency swaps.

In an **interest rate swap**, the counterparties swap payments in the same currency based on an interest rate. For example, one of the counterparties can pay a fixed interest rate and the other party a floating interest rate. The floating interest rate is commonly referred to as the **reference rate**. The swap between First Renwick Bank and General Manufacturing Corporation described above is an example of an interest rate swap. The payments made by both parties can be based on different reference rates. For example, one of the counterparties can pay an interest rate based on the one-year Treasury security rate and the other party can pay an interest rate based on the federal funds rate.

In an **interest rate-equity swap**, one party is exchanging a payment based on an interest rate and the other party based on the return of some equity index. The payments are made in the same currency. Our second illustrative swap above is an example of an interest rate-equity swap. While in this illustration one of the counterparties paid a fixed interest rate, interest rate-equity swaps also include agreements whereby one of the parties pays a floating interest rate.

In an **equity swap**, both parties exchange payments in the same currency based on some equity index. The third illustrative swap above is an example of an equity swap.

Finally, in a **currency swap**, two parties agree to swap payments based on different currencies. An example of this type of swap is the fourth illustrative swap above.

Interpretation of a Swap

If we look carefully at a swap, we can see that it is not a new derivative instrument. Rather, it can be decomposed into a package of derivative instruments that we have already discussed.

To see this, consider our first illustrative swap. Every year for the next five years Renwick Bank agrees to pay General Manufacturing Corp. 8% per year, while General Manufacturing agrees to pay First Renwick the rate on a one-year Treasury security. Since the notional principal amount is $100 million, General Manufacturing agrees to pay $8 million. Alternatively, we can rephrase this transaction as follows: Every year for the next five years, General Manufacturing agrees to deliver to First Renwick something (the rate on a one-year Treasury security) and to accept payment of $8 million. Looked at in this way, the two parties are entering into multiple forward contracts: One party is agreeing to deliver something at some time in the future, and the other party is agreeing to accept delivery. The reason we say that there are multiple forward contracts is that the agreement calls for making the exchange each year for the next five years.

While a swap may be nothing more than a package of forward contracts, it is not a redundant contract for several reasons. First, in many markets where there are forward and futures contracts, the longest maturity does not extend out as far as that of a typical swap. Second, a swap is a more transactionally efficient instrument. By this we mean that in one transaction an entity can effectively establish a payoff equivalent to a package of forward contracts. The forward contracts would each have to be negotiated separately. Third, the liquidity of the swap market has grown since its beginning in 1981; it is now more liquid than many forward contracts, particularly long-dated (i.e., long-term) forward contracts.

Applications

Now that we have described a swap and explained how a swap can be viewed as a package of forward contracts, the next question is how can a market participant use a swap to accomplish a financial objective. While we will provide more detailed applications in later chapters, for our purposes early in our exploration of capital markets, we will provide two simple ones. The first application will demonstrate how a swap, more specifically, an interest rate swap can be used by a depository institution for asset/liability management. In our second application, we will show how we can create a new financial instrument by using an interest rate-equity swap.

Application to asset/liability management—Suppose that the Buckingham Bank raises $100 million for three years at a fixed interest rate of 8% and then lends that money to Stay-a-Flight Airlines for three years. The loan calls for an interest rate that changes every year. The interest rate that the airline company agrees to pay is the London interbank offered rate (LIBOR) plus 250 basis points. Suppose LIBOR is 7.5% when the loan is initiated. This means that in the first year the airline company will pay 10% (LIBOR of 7.5% plus 2.5%). The bank locks in a spread of 2% for the first year.

The interest rate risk exposure for this bank is that LIBOR will decline. Should LIBOR fall below 5.5%, the interest rate for the loan for that one-year period would be less than Buckingham Bank must pay on the money it borrowed at 8%. Thus, the bank would realize a negative spread for that period.

Suppose that Buckingham Bank could find another party, say Bankers Trust, that would be willing to enter into an interest rate swap on the following terms: (1) the term of the swap is five years with a notional amount of $100 million; (2) every year Bankers Trust will pay Buckingham Bank 7.5% of $100 million; and (3) at the same time Buckingham Bank will pay Bankers Trust LIBOR plus 100 basis points of $100 million. Each year the outcome of this interest rate swap, coupled with the fixed interest rate that Buckingham Bank must pay on the money it borrowed, and the interest income it receives on the loan it made to the airline company, is as follows.

1. It earns LIBOR plus 250 basis points on the $100 million loan.

2. It pays 8% on the $100 million it has borrowed.

3. As part of the swap, it receives 7.5% of $100 million from Bankers Trust.

4. As part of the swap, it pays LIBOR plus 100 basis points of $100 million to Bankers Trust.

Buckingham Bank therefore earns LIBOR plus 250 basis points (from the loan) and pays LIBOR plus 100 basis point (as per the swap), resulting in a net inflow of 150 basis points. In addition, it pays 8% (to borrow funds) and receives 7.5% (as per the swap), resulting in a net outflow of 50 basis points. The net result is that it has locked in a spread of 1% (150 basis points minus 50 basis points) on the $100 million, regardless of how LIBOR changes.

This simple illustration demonstrates how an interest rate swap can be employed for asset/liability management. Probably you have questions such as: Who would be willing to take the other side of the swap (i.e., who would be the counterparty)? How does one find a counterparty? How are the terms of the swap determined? Why couldn't this depository institution just issue a floating-rate note rather than issue a fixed-rate note? These questions will be addressed in Chapter 28 when we discuss interest rate swaps more fully.

Application to creation of a security—Swaps can be used by investment bankers to create a security. To see how this is done, suppose the following. The Universal Information Technology Company (UIT) seeks to raise $100 million for the next five years on a fixed-rate basis. UIT's investment banker, the First Boston Corporation, indicates that if bonds with a maturity of five years are issued, the interest rate on the issue would have to be 8%. At the same time, there are institutional investors seeking to purchase bonds but are interested in making a play on the stock market. These investors are willing to purchase a bond whose annual interest rate is based on the actual performance of the S&P 500 stock market index.

The First Boston Corporation recommends to UIT's management that it consider issuing a five-year bond whose annual interest rate is based on the actual performance of the S&P 500. The risk with issuing such a bond is that UIT's annual interest cost is uncertain since it depends on the performance of the S&P 500. However, suppose that the following two transactions are entered into:

1. On January 1, UIT agrees to issue, using First Boston as the underwriter, a $100 million five-year bond issue whose annual interest rate is the actual performance of the S&P 500 that year minus 300 basis points. The minimum interest rate, however, is set at zero. The annual interest payments are made on December 31.

2. UIT enters into a five-year, $100 million notional principal amount interest rate-equity swap with First Boston in which each year for the next five years UIT agrees to pay 7.9% to First Boston, and First Boston agrees to pay the actual performance of the S&P 500 that year minus 300 basis points. The terms of the swap call for the payments to be made on December 31 of each year. Thus, the swap payments coincide with the payments that must be made on the bond issue. Also as part of the swap agreement, if the S&P 500 minus 300 basis points results in a negative value, First Boston pays nothing to UIT.

Consider what has been accomplished with these two transactions from the perspective of UIT. Specifically, focus on the payments that must be made by UIT on the bond issue and the swap and the payments that it will receive from the swap. These are summarized below.

Interest payments on bond issue:	S&P 500 return – 300 basis points
Swap payment from First Boston:	S&P 500 return – 300 basis points
Swap payment to First Boston:	7.9%
Net interest cost:	7.9%

Thus, the net interest cost is a fixed rate despite the bond issue paying an interest rate tied to the S&P 500. This was accomplished with the interest rate-equity swap.

There are several questions that should be addressed. First, what was the advantage to UIT to entering into this transaction? Recall that if UIT issued a bond, First Boston estimated that UIT would have to pay 8% annually. Thus, UIT has saved 10 basis points (8% minus 7.9%) per year. Second, why would investors purchase this bond issue? As explained in earlier chapters, there are restrictions imposed on institutional investors as to types of investment. For example, a depository institution may not be entitled to purchase common stock, however it may be permitted to purchase a bond of an issuer such as UIT despite the fact that the interest rate is tied to the performance of common stocks. Third, is First Boston exposed to the risk of the performance of the S&P 500? While it is difficult to demonstrate at this point, there are ways that First Boston can protect itself.

While this may seem like a far-fetched application, it is not. In fact, it is quite common and one of the reasons for discussing swaps so early in this book. Debt instruments created by using swaps are commonly referred to as **structured notes** (discussed in Section VI of this book).

Counterparty Risk

In a swap, two parties are exchanging payments. Consequently, there is the risk that one of the parties will fail to meet its obligation to make payments (default). This is referred to as **counterparty risk**.

CAP AND FLOOR AGREEMENTS

There are agreements available in the financial market whereby one party, for a fee (premium), agrees to compensate the other if a designated reference is different from a predetermined level. The party that will receive payment if the designated reference differs from a predetermined level and pays a premium to enter into the agreement is called the buyer. The party that agrees to make the payment if the designated reference differs from a predetermined level is called the seller.

When the seller agrees to pay the buyer if the designated reference exceeds a predetermined level, the agreement is referred to as a **cap**. The agreement is referred to as a **floor** when the seller agrees to pay the buyer if a designated reference falls below a predetermined level.

The designated reference could be a specific interest rate such as LIBOR or the prime rate, the rate of return on some domestic or foreign stock market index such as the S&P 500 or the DAX, or an exchange rate such as the exchange rate between the U.S. dollar and the Japanese yen. The predetermined level is called the **strike**. As with a swap, a cap and a floor have a notional principal amount. Only the buyer of a cap or a floor is exposed to counterparty risk.

In general, the payment made by the seller of the cap to the buyer on a specific date is determined by the relationship between the designated reference and the strike. If the former is greater that the latter, then the seller pays the buyer:

Notional principal amount × [Actual value of designated reference – Strike]

If the designated reference is less than or equal to the strike, then the seller pays the buyer nothing.

For a floor, the payment made by the seller to the buyer on a specific date is determined as follows. If the designated reference is less than the strike, then the seller pays the buyer:

Notional principal amount × [Strike – Actual value of designated reference]

If the designated reference is greater than or equal to the strike, then the seller pays the buyer nothing.

The following are two examples of these agreements and how they work.

Example 1. The Peterson Shipping Company enters into a five-year cap agreement with Citibank with a notional principal amount of $50 million. The terms of the cap specify that if LIBOR exceeds 8% on December 31 each year for the next five years, Citibank (the seller of the cap) will pay Peterson Shipping Company the difference between 8% (the strike) and LIBOR (the designated reference). The fee or premium Peterson Shipping agrees to pay Citibank each year is $200,000.

The payment made by Citibank to Peterson Shipping on December 31 for the next five years based on LIBOR on that date will be as follows. If LIBOR > 8%, then Citibank pays $50 million × [Actual value of LIBOR – 8%]. If LIBOR ≤ 8%, then Citibank pays nothing.

So, for example, if LIBOR on December 31 of the first year of the cap is 10%, Citibank pays Peterson Shipping Company $1 million as shown below:

$50 million × [10% – 8%] = $1 million

Example 2. The R&R Company, a money management firm, enters into a three-year floor agreement with Merrill Lynch with a notional principal amount of $100 million. The terms of the floor specify that if the S&P 500 is less than 3% on December 31 each year for the next three years, Merrill Lynch (the seller of the floor) will pay R&R Company the difference between 3% (the strike) and the return realized on the S&P 500 (the designated reference). The premium R&R Company agrees to pay Merrill Lynch each year is $600,000.

The payment made by Merrill Lynch to R&R Company on December 31 for the next three years based on the performance of the S&P 500 for that year will be as follows. If the actual return on S&P 500 < 3%, then Merrill Lynch pays: $100 million × [3% – Actual return on S&P 500]. If the actual return on S&P 500 ≥ 3%, then Merrill Lynch pays nothing.

For example, if the actual return on the S&P 500 in the first year of the floor is 1%, Merrill Lynch pays R&R Company $2 million as shown below:

$100 million × [3% – 1%] = $2 million

Interpretation of a Cap and Floor

In a cap or floor, the buyer pays a fee which represents the maximum amount that the buyer can lose and the maximum amount that the seller of the agreement can gain. The only party that is required to perform is the seller. The buyer of a cap benefits if the designated reference rises above the strike because the seller must compensate the buyer. The buyer of a floor benefits if the designated reference falls below the strike because the seller must compensate the buyer.

In essence the payoff of these contracts is the same as that of an option. A call option buyer pays a fee and benefits if the value of the option's underlying asset (or equivalently, designated reference) is higher than the strike price at the expiration date. A cap has a similar payoff. A put option buyer pays a fee and benefits if the value of the option's underlying asset (or equivalently, designated reference) is less than the strike price at the expiration date. A floor has a similar payoff. An option seller is only entitled to the option price. The seller of a cap or floor is only entitled to the fee.

Thus, a cap and a floor can be viewed as simply a package of options. As with a swap, a complex contract can be seen to be a package of basic contracts (forward contracts in the case of swaps and options in the case of caps and floors).

Application to Asset/Liability Management

To see how a cap can be used for asset/liability management, consider the problem faced by Buckingham Bank in our earlier illustration. Recall that the bank's objective is to lock in an interest rate spread over its cost of funds. Yet because it borrows short term, its cost of funds is uncertain. The Buckingham

Bank may be able to purchase a cap such that the cap rate plus the cost of purchasing the cap is less than the rate it is earning on its fixed-rate commercial loans. If short-term rates decline, Buckingham Bank does not benefit from the cap, but its cost of funds declines. The cap therefore allows the bank to impose a ceiling on its cost of funds while retaining the opportunity to benefit from a decline in rates.

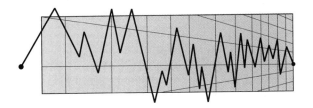

SUMMARY

In this chapter we have covered three relatively new types of derivative contracts: swaps, caps, and floors. In a swap the counterparties agree to exchange periodic payments. The dollar amount of the payments exchanged is based on the notional principal amount. There are four types of swaps: interest rate swaps, interest rate-equity swaps, equity swaps, and currency swaps. A swap has the risk/return profile of a package of forward contracts. Swaps can be used for asset/liability management and the creation of securities.

A cap is an agreement whereby the seller agrees to pay the buyer when a designated reference exceeds a predetermined level (the strike). A floor is an agreement whereby the seller agrees to pay the buyer when a designated reference is less than a predetermined level (the strike). The designated reference could be a specific interest rate, the rate of return on some stock market index, or an exchange rate. A cap is equivalent to a package of call options; a floor is equivalent to a package of put options.

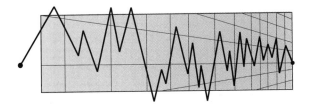

QUESTIONS

1. The Window Wipers Union (a pension sponsor) and the All-Purpose Asset Management Corp. (a money management firm) enter into a four-year swap with a notional principal amount of $150 million with the following terms: Every year for the next four years the Window Wipers Union agrees to pay All-Purpose Asset Management the return realized on the S&P 500 stock index for the year minus 400 basis points and receive from All-Purpose Asset Management 9%.

   a. What type of swap is this?

b. In the first year payments are to be exchanged, suppose that the return on the S&P 500 is 7%. What is the amount of the payment that the two parties must make to each other?

2. Burlingame Bank and the ABC Manufacturing Corp. enter into the following seven-year swap with a notional principal amount of $75 million and the following terms: Every year for the next seven years, Burlingame Bank agrees to pay ABC Manufacturing 7% per year and receive from ABC Manufacturing LIBOR.

   a. What type of swap is this?

   b. In the first year payments are to be exchanged, suppose that LIBOR is 4%. What is the amount of the payment that the two parties must make to each other?

   c. Suppose that the swap agreement called for ABC Manufacturing to pay the rate on a one-year Treasury security. What type of swap would this be?

3. The American Dishwashers Union (a pension sponsor) and the Nippon Investment Management Company (a Japanese money management firm) enter into the following three-year swap with a notional principal amount of $40 million: Every year for the next three years American Dishwashers Union agrees to pay Nippon the return realized on the S&P 500 stock index for the year minus 200 basis points and receive from Nippon the return realized on a Japanese stock index for the year.

   a. What type of swap is this?

b. In the first year payments are to be exchanged, suppose that the return realized on the S&P 500 and the Japanese stock index are 18% and 23%, respectively. What is the amount of the payment that the two parties must make to each other?

c. Explain why this swap allows the American Dishwashers Union to participate in the performance of the Japanese stock market without actually investing in any Japanese stocks.

4. Consider the following quotation from the March 25, 1991, issue of *Bank Letter:*

   > *Intense negotiations are underway involving regulatory officials, interested bank and brokerage industry representatives and Senate Staff to try to fashion a compromise floor amendment for a bill that would potentially put interest rate and currency swaps and forward foreign exchange agreements under the regulatory authority of the Commodity Futures Trading Commission, sources said . . . . Industry forces involved in the $2 trillion market are fighting to block Commodity Futures Trading Commission jurisdiction, arguing that the pending bill, if enacted, would scare the business overseas.*

   Explain why a swap is similar to a futures (or forward) contract?

5. The Ringwood Bank raised $30 million for four years at a fixed interest rate of 7% and then lent

the funds to Micro-Technology Inc. The loan calls for an interest rate that changes every year. The interest rate that Micro-Technology agreed to pay is LIBOR plus 400 basis points. At the same time, Ringwood Bank entered into a four-year interest rate swap with an investment banking firm, Goldman Sachs, with a notional principal amount of $30 million. The swap terms are as follows: every year Goldman Sachs pays Ringwood Bank 7.3%; and every year Ringwood Bank pays Goldman Sachs LIBOR plus 150 basis points.

a. What is the risk that Ringwood bank faces if it does not enter into the interest rate swap?

b. Suppose that LIBOR at a payment date is 3%, what is the interest rate spread that Ringwood Bank would realize?

c. What did Ringwood Bank accomplish by entering into this interest rate swap?

6. There are several depository institutions that offer certificates of deposit where the interest rate paid is based on the performance of the S&P 500 stock index.

a. What is the risk that a depository institution encounters by offering such certificates of deposit?

b. How do you think that a depository institution can protect itself against the risk you identified in part (a) of this question?

7. The Acme Insurance Company has purchased a five-year bond whose interest rate floats with LIBOR. Specifically, the interest rate in a given year is equal to LIBOR plus 200 basis points. At the same time the insurance company purchases this bond, it enters into a floor agreement with Bear Stearns in which the notional principal amount is $35 million with a strike of 6%. The premium Acme Insurance Company agrees to pay Bear Stearns each year is $300,000.

a. Suppose at the time that it is necessary to determine if a payment must be made by Bear Stearns, LIBOR is 9%. How much must Bear Stearns pay Acme Insurance Company?

b. Suppose at the time that it is necessary to determine if a payment must be made by Bear Stearns, LIBOR is 3%. How much must Bear Stearns pay Acme Insurance Company?

c. What is the minimum interest rate that Acme Insurance Company has locked in each year for the next five years by entering into this floor agreement and buying the five-year bond, ignoring the premium that Acme Insurance Company must make each year?

8. Rogers Asset Management, a money management firm, entered into a four-year agreement with the First Boston Corporation. The terms of the agreement specify that if the annual return realized by the German stock index, the DAX, is greater than 15% for the year ending December 31, Rogers Asset Management agrees to pay First Boston Corporation the excess over 15%. First Boston agrees to pay Rogers Asset Management $300,000 each year. The notional principal amount for this agreement is $90 million.

a. What type of agreement is this?

b. Who is the buyer of this agreement?

c. Who is the seller of this agreement?

d. What is the strike?

e. If the actual return on the DAX in the first year of this agreement is 24%, how much will Rogers Asset Management pay First Boston Corporation?

9. What is the relationship between a cap and an option?

10. The following excerpt is taken from an article entitled "IRS Rule to Open Swaps to Pension Funds," that appeared in the November 18, 1991 issue of *BondWeek*, (pp. 1 and 2):

> *A proposed Internal Revenue Service rule that gives tax-free status to income earned on swaps by pension funds and other tax-exempt institutions is expected to spur pension fund use of these products, say swap and pension fund professionals.* [Note: the proposal has subsequently been passed.]
>
> *UBS Asset Management has received permission from most of its pension fund clients to use interest rate and currency swaps in its fixed-income portfolios and is awaiting the IRS regulation before stepping into the market, says Kenneth Choie, v.p. and head of research and product development . . . "The IRS' proposed rule is great news for pension fund managers," as the use of swaps can enhance returns and lower transaction costs, Choie says.*
>
> *. . . While some pension funds are exploring the swap market, pension fund consultants underscore that the funds' entrance into the market is likely to be slow. Counterparty risk has been a more formidable obstacle than the ambiguity of the tax status of income from interest rate and currency swaps, says Paul Burik, director of research at Ennis, Knupp & Associates, a pension fund consulting firm.*

a. What is meant by counterparty risk?

b. Why would counterparty risk slow the growth of use of the swap market by pension funds?

Common Stock Market

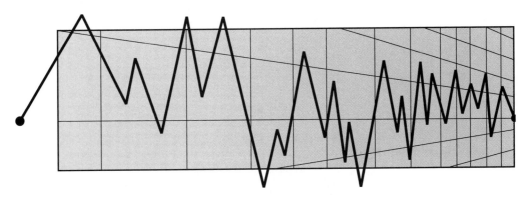

LEARNING OBJECTIVES

After reading this chapter you will understand:

- the reasons why the stock market has undergone significant structural changes since the 1960s.

- the various trading locations for stocks.

- the key structural difference between a stock exchange and an over-the-counter market.

- what is meant by a fragmented market, and why stock markets in the 1960s and early 1970s were characterized as fragmented markets.

- the key elements of the proposed national market system.

- the key elements of the *Market 2000* study.

- trading arrangements to accommodate institutional traders such as block trades and program trades.

- what the upstairs market is and its role in institutional trading.

- the various stock market indicators followed by market participants and how they are constructed.

- evidence on the pricing efficiency of the common stock market and its implications for common stock strategies.

- what an indexing strategy is, and how such a strategy can be implemented.

- the reasons offered for the market crash of October 1987.

- the market structures and trading procedures in non-U.S. stock markets.

- the Euroequity markets.

- the motivation for listing on foreign stock exchanges.

- the correlation of world equity markets.

Equity securities represent an ownership interest in a corporation. Holders of equity securities are entitled to the earnings of the corporation when those earnings are distributed in the form of dividends; they are also entitled to a prorata share of the remaining equity in case of liquidation. There are two types of equity securities: common stock and preferred stock. The key distinction between these two forms of equity securities is the degree to which they may participate in any distribution of earnings and capital and the priority given to each in the distribution of earnings. Typically, preferred stockholders are entitled to a fixed dividend that they receive before common stockholders may receive dividends. We refer therefore to preferred stock as a senior corporate security, in the sense that preferred stock interests are senior to the interests of common stockholders. We postpone an explanation of preferred stock to Chapter 22 where we discuss the market for senior corporate securities.

Our focus in this chapter is on the secondary market for common stock. It is in this market that the opinions of investors about the economic prospect of a company are expressed through the trades they execute. These trades together give the market consensus opinion about the price of the stock. In turn, the company's cost of common stock is determined. This market has undergone significant changes since the 1960s, reflecting primarily three interacting factors: (1) the institutionalization of the stock market as a result of a shift away from traditional small investors to large institutional investors, (2) changes in government regulation of the market, and (3) innovation, largely because of advances in computer technology.

Evidence of institutionalization of the stock market can be seen from the ownership distribution of stocks and the share of trading by individuals (referred to as "retail" trading) and institutions (pension funds, insurance companies, investment companies, bank trusts, and foundations). In 1949, institutional ownership of NYSE-listed stocks was 13%; in recent years, it has been almost 50%. Moreover, over 80% of the volume of trading on the NYSE is done by institutional investors.[1] This, of course, does not mean that indi-

---

[1] Securities Industry Association, *Trends* (March 16, 1989).

viduals' ownership of stocks has diminished. Instead, institutions trade on behalf of individuals, who hold stock through the instruments of mutual funds, pension funds, and so forth. The institutionalization of this market has had important implications for the design of trading systems because the demands made by institutional investors are different from those made by traditional small investors.

Besides describing the arrangements to accommodate institutional investors in the secondary market for common stocks, this chapter reviews evidence on how efficiently common stocks are priced and the implications of efficiency for investment strategies. An important issue is whether stock price volatility has increased in recent years and, if so, what institutional characteristics have caused it. As the culprit that is alleged to have increased stock price volatility is the introduction of stock index futures and stock index options, we shall postpone discussion of this question until we cover these contracts in Chapter 15. We also discuss the reasons offered for the stock market crash of October 1987. We conclude the chapter with a discussion of major non-U.S. equity markets.

SECONDARY MARKETS

In the United States, secondary trading of common stock occurs in a number of trading locations: major national stock exchanges, regional stock exchanges, and the over-the-counter market. In addition to these trading locations, independently-operated electronic trading systems are being developed.

In the United States, stock prices on exchanges and in the OTC market are determined continuously throughout the trading day as buyers and sellers submit orders. As explained in Chapter 7, this type of market structure is called a continuous market.

Stock Exchanges

Stock exchanges are formal organizations, approved and regulated by the Securities and Exchange Commission (SEC), that are made up of members that use the facilities to exchange certain common stocks.[2] Stocks that are traded on an exchange are said to be **listed stocks.** To be listed, a company must apply and satisfy requirements established by the exchange where listing is sought. Since August 1976, the listing of a common stock on more than one exchange has been permitted.

To have the right to trade securities on the floor of the exchange, firms or individuals must buy a "seat" on the exchange; that is, they must become a member of the exchange. The cost of a seat is market-determined. A member firm may trade for its own account or on behalf of a customer. In the latter case it is acting as a broker.

Each stock is traded at a specific location on the trading floor called a **post.** Firms that are members of an exchange and that are brokers trade stock on behalf of their customers. On an exchange the market maker role for a listed

---

[2] Securities other than common stock are traded on exchanges. We shall discuss some of these products in Chapter 14. Some exchanges trade derivative instruments, which we discuss in later chapters. While some bonds are traded on exchanges, the main market for such securities is the over-the-counter market.

stock is performed by a **specialist**. A member firm may be designated as a specialist for the common stock of more than one company, but only one specialist is designated for the common stock of a given company. An important difference between exchanges and the OTC market is the market structure design with respect to a single market maker or multiple market makers. This is a critical institutional difference underlying some controversy associated with secondary trading on an exchange versus over-the-counter, and we discuss it later in this chapter.

At one time stock exchanges fixed minimum commissions on transactions, according to the value and the volume of shares involved. The fixed commission structure did not allow the commission rate to decline as the number of shares in the order increased, thereby ignoring the economies of scale in executing transactions. For example, brokers incurred lower total costs in executing an order of 10,000 shares of one stock for one investor than in executing 100 orders for the same stock from 100 investors. The institutional investors who had come to dominate trading activity demanded larger order size, yet did not reap the benefits of the economies of scale in order execution that brokers did. Pressure from institutional investors led the SEC in April 1971 to permit negotiated commissions for that portion of trades with a market value in excess of $500,000; one year later, the market value that was negotiable was dropped to $300,000. By May 1975, fixed minimum commissions on stocks traded on an exchange were eliminated. Commissions are now fully negotiable between investors and their brokers.

Major national stock exchanges—The two major national stock exchanges are the New York Stock Exchange, popularly referred to as the "Big Board," and the American Stock Exchange (ASE or AMEX). The NYSE is the largest exchange in the United States, with about 2,300 companies listed. A highly controversial rule is the NYSE's Rule 390. This rule, applicable only to the NYSE, requires permission from the exchange for a member firm to execute a transaction of an NYSE-listed stock off the exchange.[3] The AMEX is the second largest exchange, with about 1,100. Several other products that we will discuss in later chapters are also traded on this exchange.

The major national exchanges have faced considerable competition for certain types of orders from the other trading locations discussed below (the NASDAQ, regional exchanges, the electronic trading systems), as well as foreign exchanges such as the London Stock Exchange. To meet this competition the NYSE established in 1990 an after-hours electronic trading, called Cross Networks. Moreover, the exchanges have sought regulatory action and other legal remedies against the electronic trading systems so as to have them treated as "exchanges" by regulators.

Regional exchanges—There are five regional stock exchanges including Midwest, Pacific, Philadelphia, Boston, and Cincinnati. On these exchanges there are two kinds of stocks listed: stocks of companies that could not qualify for listing (or do not wish to list) on one of the major national exchanges; and stocks that are also listed on one of the major national exchanges. The latter are called "dually listed stocks."

---

[3] Certain stocks listed on the NYSE are exempt from this rule.

The motivation for dual listing is that a local brokerage firm that purchases a membership on a regional exchange can trade these stocks without having to purchase a considerably more expensive membership on the major national stock exchange where the stock is also listed. A local brokerage firm, of course, could use the services of a member of a major national stock exchange to execute an order, if it were willing to give up part of its commission.

The regional stock exchanges themselves compete with the NYSE for the execution of smaller trades such as those for 5,000 shares or less. Major national brokerage firms have in recent years routed such orders to regional exchanges because of the lower cost they charge for executing orders.

Over-the-Counter Market

The over-the-counter (OTC) market is the market for unlisted stocks. The National Association of Securities Dealers (NASD), a private organization, represents and regulates the dealers in the OTC market under the supervision of the SEC. The National Association of Securities Dealers Automatic Quotation (NASDAQ) system is an electronic quotation system that provides price quotations to market participants about the more actively traded issues in the OTC market. There were about 3,800 common stocks included in the NASDAQ system.

A stock may be both listed on an exchange and traded in the OTC market. The **third market** refers to the trading of such listed stocks in the OTC market.[4] Dealers in this market are not members of an exchange, and therefore were not required to charge the fixed minimum commissions once set by the exchange. The third market grew as institutional investors used it in the early 1960s to avoid fixed minimum commissions.

Independent Electronic Trading Systems

It is not always necessary for two transactors to use the services of a broker or a dealer to execute a transaction. The direct trading of stocks between two transactors without the use of a broker is called the **fourth market**. This market grew for the same reasons as the third market—the excessively high minimum commissions established by the exchanges. Its growth was limited initially by the availability of information on other institutions that wanted to trade.

Today, systems have been developed that allow institutional investors to cross trades (i.e., match buyers and sellers) via computer. The two major systems that handle large institution-to-institution trades are Instinet and POSIT. Instinet, established by Reuters in 1987, is an interactive **hit and take** system. This means that participants search for counterparties electronically, negotiate, and execute trades. POSIT, which stands for Portfolio System for Institutional Investors, is a trading system developed by BARRA and Jefferies & Co. in 1987. POSIT is more than a simple order-matching system but rather

---

[4] The **first market** refers to the trading of listed stocks executed on the floor of the exchange. The **second market** refers to the execution of unlisted stocks in the over-the-counter market.

matches the purchase and sale of portfolios in such a way so as to optimize the liquidity of the system.[5]

The Arizona Stock Exchange in Phoenix, which commenced trading in March 1992, is an after-hours electronic marketplace where anonymous participants trade stocks via personal computers. It provides a call auction market. Bids and offers are accumulated and, at a designated time, a single price is derived which maximizes the number of shares that can be traded.

Automated Order Routing

Both the major national stock exchanges and the regional stock exchanges have systems for routing orders of a specified size that are submitted by brokers via computer directly to the specialists' posts where the order can be executed. On the NYSE, this system is called the SuperDOT (Super Designated Order Turnaround) system. The AMEX's Post Execution Reporting system allows orders up to 2,000 shares to be routed directly to specialists. The regional stock exchanges have computerized systems for routing small orders to specialists. The Small Order Execution system of the NASDAQ routes and executes orders up to 1,000 shares of a given stock.

Role of Dealers in Exchange and OTC Markets

There is an important structural difference between exchanges and the OTC market. In our discussion of secondary markets in Chapter 7, we explained the role of market makers or dealers. On the exchanges there is only one market maker or dealer per stock, known as the specialist. The specialist keeps the limit order book. Designation of who will be a specialist for a stock is determined by the exchange, taking numerous factors into account. Because capital is necessary to perform as a market maker, one requirement is satisfaction of the minimum capital requirement. Currently, the minimum capital requirement is $1 million.[6] Prior to the October 1987 market crash (called "Black Monday"), it was only $100,000. Specialists realize a profit only from those trades in which they are involved.

As there is only one specialist for a given stock, there is no competition from other market makers on the exchange. Does this mean that the specialist has a monopolistic position? Not necessarily, because specialists do face competition from several sources. The existence of public limit orders affects the bid-ask spread. There are brokers in the crowd who have public orders that compete with specialists. In the case of multiple-listed stocks there is competition from specialists on other exchanges where the stock is listed. For stocks that are exempt from Rule 390 (restricting member firms to execute trades on the exchange), there is competition from dealers in the OTC market (discussed below). Finally, as we discuss later in this chapter, when a block trade is involved, specialists compete with the "upstairs market."

---

[5] A description of the algorithm used to maximize the liquidity of POSIT is described in "An Inside Look at the POSIT Matching Algorithm," *POSITNEWS* (Summer/Fall 1990), p. 2.

[6] There is also a position assumption capability requirement. At the present time, it is 15,000 shares.

In the OTC market, in contrast, there may be more than one dealer for a stock. For example, at the time of this writing, there are more than 50 dealers for MCI Corporation. The number of dealers depends on the volume of trading in a stock. If a stock is not actively traded, there may be no need for more than one or two dealers. As trading activity increases in a stock, there are no barriers preventing more entities from becoming a dealer in that stock, other than satisfaction of capital requirements. Competition from more dealers—or the threat of new dealers—forces bid-ask spreads to more competitive levels. Moreover, the capital-raising ability of more than one dealer is believed to be more beneficial to markets than that of a single specialist in performing the role of a market maker.

The greater competition and greater potential capital arguments have been put forth by those citing the advantages of the OTC market. The exchanges, however, argue that the commitment of the dealers to provide a market in the OTC market is not the same obligation as that of the specialist on the exchange. On the NYSE, for example, Rule 104 sets forth the specialist's obligation to maintain fair and orderly markets. Failure to fulfill this obligation results in a loss of specialist status. In the aftermath of the October 1987 market crash, 11 stocks were taken away from member firms that had been specialists for those stocks because the NYSE's Market Surveillance Division interpreted their actions as failing to fulfill their responsibilities under Rule 104. A dealer in the OTC market is under no obligation to continue its market-making activity during volatile and uncertain market conditions. This became most apparent during Black Monday, when some dealers stopped making markets.

To what extent do trades from public orders meet other public orders, which therefore do not need the specialist to take the other side of the trade? That is, to what extent do specialists perform the function of stabilizing markets? Information provided by the NYSE indicates that, in 1988, 77% of all shares traded were public orders meeting public orders. Only 9% of shares traded involved specialist activity. The balance of trading, 14%, was by non-specialist member firms dealing for their own accounts.[7] The 9% participation by specialists, however, may understate the importance of the role played by the specialist because the activity may have occurred under difficult market conditions.

SEC STUDIES OF THE STRUCTURE OF THE EQUITY MARKETS

The SEC is concerned with the structure of the U.S. equity market. Specifically, it is concerned with the fairness, competitiveness, and efficiency of the market. The first serious look at the structure of the equity market came in the early 1970s and led to legislation promoting a "national market system." The market structure was revisited in the 1990s, leading to a study entitled *Market 2000*. Before we discuss the national market system and

---

[7] James E. Shapiro, "The NYSE Trading System: Background and Issues," a paper presented at the NYSE Academic Seminar on May 5, 1989.

Market 2000, let us look at the developments that led to the SEC initial investigation in the 1970s.

Fragmented Equity Market

In the 1960s and early 1970s, U.S. secondary markets for stocks became increasingly fragmented. By a "fragmented market" we mean one in which some orders for a given stock are handled differently from other orders.

Here are two examples of a fragmented stock market. First is the different handling of small orders versus large orders on the same exchange. Small orders typically are executed immediately without trying to work the order to obtain the best execution. Large orders are worked by the floor trader and, as explained later, in the case of block trades, are typically negotiated in the upstairs market.[8] A second example is stock that can be bought on several exchanges as well as in the over-the-counter market. An order to buy IBM stock, for example, could be executed on one of the exchanges where IBM is listed (i.e., on the specialist system) or in the third market using the multiple-dealer system. Thus, the treatment of the order differs, depending upon where it is ultimately executed.

National Market System

The concern of public policy makers has been that investors were not receiving the best execution. That is, transactions were not necessarily being executed by a broker on behalf of a customer at the most favorable price available. Another concern with the increased fragmentation of the secondary market for stocks was a growing number of completed transactions in listed stocks that were not reported to the public. This is because transactions in the third market and on the regional exchanges were not immediately disclosed on the major national exchange ticker tapes where the stock was listed.

Congress asked the SEC to investigate the situation. The investigation produced the *Institutional Investor Study Report,* which the SEC presented to Congress in 1971, substantiating the concerns we noted above. Prior to the study, the SEC had favored competing but separate markets for stock trading. In its letter accompanying the report, however, the SEC reversed its position by endorsing the development of a "central market system," which would link the various secondary markets to assure that investors realized the best execution. Such a system would maximize the market making capacity for a stock by putting the specialist on an exchange in competition not only with specialists for the same stock on other exchanges, but also with dealers in the OTC market. In subsequent years, the SEC issued several statements concerning the problems of fragmentation and the means by which a central market system could be developed.[9]

As a result of increased concerns in the equity markets, Congress enacted the Securities Act of 1975. The two basic principles of this act are that com-

---

[8] Robert A. Schwartz, *Equity Markets: Structure, Trading and Performance* (New York: Harper & Row, 1988), pp. 22-3.

[9] Securities and Exchange Commission, *Statement of the Future Structure of the Securities Market,* February 2, 1972; and *Policy Statement on the Structure of the Central Market System,* March 29, 1973.

petition and comprehensive disclosure of market information should be fostered in order to generate the best prices for investors, and that the interests of public investors should be placed ahead of the interests of broker-dealers.

A key provision of the Act is Section 11A(a)(2), which amended the Securities Exchange Act of 1934, directing the SEC to "facilitate the establishment of a national market system for securities..." The SEC in its efforts to implement a national market system (previously referred to by the SEC as a "central market system") targeted six elements, described as follows by N.S. Posner:

1. a system for public reporting of completed transactions on a consolidated basis (consolidated tape).

2. a composite system for the collection and display of bid and asked quotations (composite quotation system).

3. systems for transmitting orders to buy and sell securities and reports of completed transactions from one market to another (market linkage systems).

4. elimination of restrictions on the ability of exchange members to effect over-the-counter transactions in listed securities (off-board trading rules).

5. nationwide protection of limit price orders, against inferior execution in another market.

6. rules defining the securities that are qualified to be traded in the NMS.[10]

These six elements required either changes in technology or legislative initiative. A consolidated tape, a composite quotation system, a market linkage system, and a system for nationwide protection of limit price orders are examples of technology change; elimination of off-board trading rules and securities to be included in a national market system are examples of legislative change.

Overall, the general issue that the SEC faced was how to design the national market system. Should it be structured as an electronic linkage of existing exchange floors? Or should it be an electronic trading system that was not tied to any existing exchange?

After several pilot programs since the passage of the 1975 act,[11] the following is what has been implemented for listed stocks. The Intermarket Trading System (ITS), whose operations began in April 1978, was developed as an electronic system that displays the quotes posted on all the exchanges where a stock is listed, as well as in the OTC market, and provides for intermarket executions. A display system on trades on listed stocks in different market centers is provided by the Consolidated Quotation System.

---

[10] N.S. Posner, "Restructuring the Stock Markets: A Critical Look at the SEC's National Market System," *New York University Law Review* (November-December 1981), p. 916.

[11] For a discussion of these pilot programs see William C. Melton, "Corporate Equities and the National Market System," *Federal Reserve Bank of New York, Quarterly Review* (Winter 1978-79), pp. 13-25.

Market 2000

In 1992, the SEC released a study of the structure of the equity market. In this study, titled *Market 2000*, the SEC reiterates the basic principles of the 1975 Act in designing market structure and legislation and states that "today's equity markets are operating efficiently within the existing regulatory structure." However, the study goes on to focus on recent concerns about fragmentation, inadequate disclosure, and other issues.

In its overview of the *Market 2000* study in July 14, 1992, the SEC raised many issues.[12] In particular, the SEC discussed the following issues it faced in identifying what role it will play as a regulator in the presence of computer and communication advances in which there is competition between the exchanges and the electronic trading systems.

1. The central purpose of the equity markets is to raise capital for use by businesses. To what degree do developments affecting traders and competing trading systems enhance or detract from the attractiveness of the U.S. equity market to savers and investors providing capital? (page 50)

2. The Commission has been asked whether electronic trading system proliferation poses the potential for "balkanizing" our nation's securities markets into a two-tiered system—one for large institutional traders and another for individual investors. (page 28)

3. The Division [of Market Regulation] seeks to understand the costs and benefits of integrating individual and institutional traders in a system without harming either group. (page 30)

4. Does the attraction of trading volume away from the traditional exchanges by proprietary trading systems further fragment the market for listed securities?... Is "fragmentation" simply another word for "competition"? (page 37)

Some of the recommendation made by the study are:

1. The SEC should not take any action to impose a single structure on the equity markets or to expedite broad deregulation of the equity markets.

2. There should be greater information made available to investors of prices, volumes, and transactions by a more complete display of limit orders and better dissemination of NASDAQ orders and after-hours trading activities.

3. An oversight program for the trading of listed stock in the OTC market should be developed by the NASD.

4. The SEC should not regulate electronic trading systems since most do not function as an exchange; however, these trading systems should develop better reporting rules.

---

[12] Securities and Exchange Commission, *U.S. Equity Market Structure Study*, Release No. 34-30920, File No. S7-18-92, July 14, 1992.

5. Rules imposed by the NYSE on off-exchange trading by members should be loosened (Rule 390).

TRADING ARRANGEMENTS FOR INSTITUTIONAL INVESTORS

As we noted earlier in this chapter, the trading practices of institutional investors had to be accommodated with the increase in institutional trading. This has resulted in the evolution of special arrangements for the execution of certain types of orders commonly sought by institutional investors: (1) orders requiring the execution of a trade of a large number of shares of a given stock; and (2) orders requiring the execution of trades in a large number of different stocks at as near a time as possible. The former types of trades are called **block trades**; the latter are called **program trades**. An example of a block trade would be a mutual fund that seeks to buy 15,000 shares of IBM stock. An example of a program trade is a pension fund that seeks to buy shares of 200 names (by names we mean companies) at the end of a trading day.

The institutional arrangement that has evolved to accommodate these two types of institutional trades is development of a network of trading desks of the major investment banking firms and institutional investors that communicate with each other by means of electronic display systems and telephones. This network is referred to as the **upstairs market**. Participants in the upstairs market play a key role not only in providing liquidity to the market so that such institutional trades can be executed, but also through arbitrage activities that help to integrate the fragmented stock market.

Block Trades

Block trades are defined as trades of 10,000 shares or more of a given stock, or trades of shares with a market value of $200,000 or more.[13] In 1961, there were about nine block trades per day, which accounted for about 3% of trading volume; in recent years, by contrast, there have been about 3,000 block trades per day accounting for almost half the trading volume.[14]

As executing large numbers of block orders places strains on the specialist system, special procedures have been developed to handle them. An institutional customer contacts its salesperson at a brokerage firm, indicating that it wishes to place a block order. The salesperson then gives the order to the brokerage firm's block execution department.[15] Notice that the salesperson does not submit the order to be executed to the exchange where the stock might be traded or, in the case of an unlisted stock, try to execute the order on the NASDAQ system. The sales traders in the block execution department then contact other institutions in the hope of finding one or more institutions that would be willing to take the other side of the order. That is, they use the

---

[13] *New York Stock Exchange Guide* (CCH), Rule 127.10, sec. 2127.10.

[14] U.S. Congress, *Office of Technology Assessment, Electronic Bulls & Bears: U.S. Securities Markets & Information Technology,* OTA-CIT-469 (Washington, DC: U.S. Government Printing Office, September 1990), p. 8.

[15] Before a firm can do block trading, it must obtain permission from both the SEC and the exchanges.

upstairs market in their search to fill the block trade order. If this can be accomplished, the execution of the order is complete.

If, on the other hand, the sales traders cannot find enough institutions to take the entire block (e.g., if the block trade order is for 40,000 shares of IBM, but only 25,000 can be crossed with other institutions), then the balance of the block trade order is given to the firm's market maker. The market maker must then make a decision as to how to handle the balance of the block trade order. There are two choices: the brokerage firm can take a position in the stock, or the unfilled order can be executed by using the services of competing market makers. Remember that in the former case the brokerage firm is committing its own capital.

Program Trades

Program trades involve the buying and/or selling of a large number of names *simultaneously.* Such trades are also called basket trades, because effectively a "basket" of stocks is being traded. Some obvious examples of why an institutional investor may want to use a program trade are deployment into the stock market of new cash, implementation of a decision to move funds invested from the bond market to the stock market (or vice versa), rebalancing the composition of a stock portfolio because of a change in investment strategy, or liquidation of a stock portfolio of a pension fund money manager whose services a plan sponsor has terminated.

There are other reasons that an institutional investor may have a need to execute a program trade that will become apparent later in this chapter when we discuss an investment strategy called indexing. Another use, which we explain when we discuss stock index futures contracts in Chapter 15, is to arbitrage any price discrepancies between the stock market and the stock index futures market. This strategy is called **index arbitrage**. Unfortunately, the popular press tends to use the terms program trading and index arbitrage interchangeably, which is incorrect. One is an investment strategy (index arbitrage), and the other is an institutional trading arrangement (program trading). It is true that a program trade will be employed to implement an index arbitrage. Another confusion is that because computers are used to execute a program trade, the popular press has wrongly characterized program trading as "computerized trading."

There are several commission arrangements available to an institution for a program trade. Each has numerous variants. Considerations in selecting one (besides commission costs) are the risk of failing to realize the best execution price, and the risk that the brokerage firms to be solicited about executing the program trade will use their knowledge of the program trade to benefit from the anticipated price movement that might result (i.e., they will "frontrun" the transaction).

A program trade executed on an **agency basis** involves the selection of a brokerage firm solely on the basis of commission bids (cents per share) submitted by various brokerage firms. The brokerage firm selected uses its best efforts as an agent of the institution to obtain the best price. The disadvantage of the agency basis arrangement for a program trade is that, while commissions may be the lowest, the execution price may not be the best because of market impact costs (discussed in Chapter 7) and the potential frontrunning by the brokerage firms that were solicited to submit a commission bid.

In an **agency incentive arrangement**, a benchmark portfolio value is established for the portfolio that is the subject of the program trade. The price for each name in the program trade is determined as either the price at the end of the previous day or the average price of the previous day. If the brokerage firm can execute the trade on the next trading day such that a better-than-benchmark portfolio value results (i.e., a higher value in the case of a program trade involving selling, or a lower value in the case of a program trade involving buying), then the brokerage firm receives a specified commission plus some predetermined additional compensation.

What if the brokerage firm does not achieve the benchmark portfolio value? Here is where the variants come into play. One arrangement may call for the brokerage firm to receive just an agreed-upon commission. Other arrangements may involve sharing the risk of not realizing the benchmark portfolio value with the brokerage firm. That is, if the brokerage firm falls short of the benchmark portfolio value, it must absorb a portion of the shortfall. In these risk-sharing arrangements, the brokerage firm is risking its own capital. The greater the risk-sharing the brokerage firm must accept, the higher the commission it will charge.

One problem that remains is the possibility of frontrunning. If brokerage firms know that an institution will execute a program trade with the prices as determined the previous day, they can take advantage of the knowledge. To minimize the possibility of frontrunning, other types of program trade arrangements have been used. They call for a brokerage firm to be given not specific names and quantities, but only enough information about key portfolio parameters to allow several brokerage firms to bid on the entire portfolio. The winning bidder is then selected and given the details of the portfolio. This increases the risk to the brokerage firm of successfully executing the program trade, but the brokerage firm can use the derivative products described in Chapter 15 to protect itself if the characteristics of the portfolio in the program trade are similar to the general market.

Brokerage firms can execute the trade in the upstairs market or send orders electronically to exchange floors or the NASDAQ system through the automated order routing systems such as the NYSE SuperDOT System.

STOCK MARKET INDICATORS

Stock market indicators have come to perform a variety of functions, from serving as benchmarks for evaluating the performance of professional money managers to answering the question "How did the market do today?" Thus, stock market indicators (indexes or averages) have become a part of everyday

Capital Markets: Institutions and Markets

life. Even though many of the stock market indicators are used interchangeably, each measures a different facet of the "stock market."

The most commonly quoted stock market indicator is the Dow Jones Industrial Average. Other stock market indicators cited in the financial press are the Standard & Poor's 500 Composite, the New York Stock Exchange Composite Index, the American Stock Exchange Market Value Index, the NASDAQ Composite Index, and the Value Line Composite Index. Yet, there are a myriad of other stock market indicators such as the Wilshire stock indexes and the Russell stock indexes, which are followed primarily by institutional money managers.

In general, market indexes rise and fall in unison. Table 13-1 shows the correlation between the commonly cited market indexes. There are, however, important differences in the magnitude of these moves. To understand the reasons for these differences, it is necessary to understand how indicators are constructed. Three factors differentiate stock market indicators: the universe of stocks represented by the indicator, the relative weights assigned to the stocks, and the method of averaging used.

A stock market indicator can include all publicly traded stocks or a sample of publicly traded stocks. No stock market indicator currently available is based on all publicly traded stocks, however. Breadth of coverage is different for each market indicator.

The stocks included in a stock market indicator must be combined in certain proportions to construct the index or average. Each stock, therefore, must be assigned some relative weight. One of three approaches is used to assign relative weights to the stock market indicators: (1) weighting by the market value of the company (i.e., market capitalization, which is the price of the stock times the number of shares outstanding); (2) weighting by the price of

Table 13-1

U.S. Stock Index Correlations Based on
Monthly Price Changes: June 1988 to April 1993

	S&P 500	Dow	NASDAQ	AMEX	Wilshire 5000	Value Line	Russell 2000	NYSE
S&P 500	1.00							
Dow	0.96	1.00						
NASDAQ	0.84	0.80	1.00					
AMEX	0.85	0.83	0.90	1.00				
Wilshire 5000	0.99	0.95	0.91	0.90	1.00			
Value Line	0.89	0.87	0.96	0.95	0.94	1.00		
Russell 2000	0.80	0.79	0.97	0.93	0.88	0.97	1.00	
NYSE	1.00	0.96	0.86	0.87	0.99	0.91	0.83	1.00

Source: Merrill Lynch Quantitative Analysis Group

the company's stock; and (3) weighting each company equally regardless of its market value or price.

Given the stocks that will be used to create the sample and the relative weighting to be assigned to each stock, it is then necessary to average the individual components. Two methods of averaging are possible: arithmetic and geometric. An arithmetic mean is basically a simple average of the component stocks, calculated by summing the components after weighting them (if appropriate) and dividing by the sum of the weights. A geometric average involves multiplication of the components, after which the product is raised to the power of 1 divided by the number of components. All properly constructed stock market indicators are constructed using arithmetic averaging.

Stock market indicators can be classified into three groups: (1) those produced by stock exchanges based on all stocks traded on the exchange, (2) those produced by organizations that subjectively select the stocks to be included in the index, and (3) those where stock selection is based on an objective measure, such as the market capitalization of the company. In the first group we have the New York Stock Exchange Composite Index and the American Stock Exchange Market Value Index, which reflect the market value of all stocks traded on the respective stock exchange. While it is not an exchange, the NASDAQ Composite Index falls into this category.

The three most popular stock market indicators that fall into the second group are the Dow Jones Industrial Average (DJIA), the Standard & Poor's 500, and the Value Line Composite Average (VLCA). The DJIA is constructed from 30 of the largest blue-chip industrial companies traded on the NYSE. The companies included in the average are those selected by Dow Jones & Company, publisher of *The Wall Street Journal*. The composition of the average changes over time as companies are dropped because of merger or bankruptcy, or because of a low level of trading activity, or because a company not in the average becomes very prominent. When a company is replaced by another company, the average is readjusted in such a way as to provide comparability with earlier values.

The S&P 500 represents selected samples of stocks chosen from the two major national stock exchanges and the over-the-counter market. The stocks in the index at any given time are determined by a committee of Standard & Poor's Corporation, which may occasionally add or delete individual or entire industry groups. The aim of the committee is to capture present overall stock market conditions representing a very broad range of economic indicators. The VLCA, produced by Arnold Bernhard & Company, covers a broad range of widely held and actively traded NYSE, AMEX, and OTC issues selected by Value Line.

In the third group we have the Wilshire Indexes produced by Wilshire Associates (Santa Monica, California) and Russell Indexes produced by the Frank Russell Company (Tacoma, Washington), a consultant to pension funds and other institutional investors. The criterion for inclusion in each of these indexes is solely market capitalization. The most comprehensive is the Wilshire 5000, which actually includes almost 6,000 companies (at the outset it included 5,000 stocks). The Wilshire 4500 includes all the stocks in the

Wilshire 5000 except for those in the S&P 500. Thus, the Wilshire 4500 includes companies with smaller market capitalizations than the Wilshire 5000. The motivation for creating a stock market indicator that reflects a sector of the stock market with smaller market capitalization will be evident later when we discuss market anomalies. The Russell 3000 encompasses the 3,000 largest companies ranked by market capitalization, while the Russell 1000 includes the largest 1,000 market capitalization companies. The Russell 2000 includes the bottom two-thirds of the companies in the Russell 3000, so it too represents a small capitalization market index.

Besides the stock market indicators cited above, there are indexes developed by exchanges that are the underlying index for the stock index options and futures traded on these exchanges. The Standard & Poor's 100 and the Major Market Index (MMI) are two examples to be discussed further in Chapter 15 when we cover stock index options and futures contracts.

With the exception of the DJIA, VLCA, and MMI, the preeminent stock market indicators are market value-weighted. The DJIA is a price-weighted index, with the index adjusted for stock splits and stock dividends. The VLCA and MMI are equally-weighted indexes.

EMPIRICAL EVIDENCE ON PRICING EFFICIENCY AND IMPLICATIONS FOR PORTFOLIO STRATEGIES

In Chapter 7, we discussed the concept of pricing efficiency of a market and the three forms of pricing efficiency: weak form, semistrong form, and strong form. Weak efficiency means that the price of the security reflects the past price and trading history of the security. Semistrong efficiency means that the price of the security fully reflects all public information. Strong efficiency exists in a market where the price of a security reflects all information, whether or not it is publicly available. There have been numerous studies of the pricing efficiency of the stock market. While it is not our intent in this chapter to provide a comprehensive review of these studies, we can summarize their basic findings and the implications for investment strategies.[16]

Formulating Tests of Pricing Efficiency

Tests of pricing efficiency investigate whether it is possible to generate **abnormal returns.** An abnormal return is defined as the difference between the actual return and the expected return from an investment strategy. The expected return used in empirical tests is one generated from some pricing model. The most common models used in empirical tests are the capital asset pricing model (an equilibrium model) or the market model, which we discussed in Chapter 9. Consequently, expected return considers the risk associated with the investment. More specifically, it considers systematic risk as proxied by beta. Calculation of the actual return takes transactions

---

[16] For a detailed review of these studies, see Chapters 3-5 in Diana R. Harrington, Frank J. Fabozzi, and H. Russell Fogler, *The New Stock Market* (Chicago: Probus Publishing, 1990).

costs from commissions and fees into account. Execution and opportunity costs are typically not considered in these studies.To summarize, the abnormal return is calculated as follows: abnormal return equals the actual return (net of transactions costs) minus the expected return (from some pricing model).

This abnormal return is then tested to determine if it is statistically different from zero. If it is, it is not sufficient to conclude that the investment strategy that produced the positive abnormal return can outperform the market in the future and therefore there is a pricing inefficiency.[17] The empirical test depends critically on the expected return calculated from an assumed pricing model. If this model is misspecified because it either fails to consider the appropriate measure of risk (for example, if the arbitrage pricing model is the appropriate equilibrium pricing model) or the market risk parameter beta is not estimated properly, then the results are questionable.

Tests of weak form pricing efficiency—The preponderance of empirical evidence is that the common stock market is efficient in the weak form. These tests explore whether historical price movements can be used to project future prices in such a way as to produce positive abnormal returns. The implications are that investors who follow a strategy of selecting stocks on the basis of price patterns or trading volume (such investors are referred to as technical analysts or chartists) should not expect to do better than the market. In fact, they may fare worse because of higher transactions costs associated with frequent buying and selling of stocks.

Tests of semistrong form pricing efficiency—Evidence on semistrong pricing efficiency is mixed. There are studies suggesting that investors who select stocks on the basis of fundamental security analysis (i.e., analyzing financial statements, the quality of management, and the economic environment of a company) will not outperform the market. The reason is simply that there are many analysts undertaking basically the same sort of analysis, with the same publicly available data, so that the price of the stock reflects all the relevant factors that determine value.

While some studies question the usefulness of fundamental security analysis, a good number of other studies suggest that there are pockets of pricing inefficiency in the stock market. That is, there are some investment strategies that have historically produced statistically significant positive abnormal returns. These market anomalies are referred to as: the small-firm effect, the low price-earnings ratio effect, the neglected firm effect, and various calendar effects.

The **small-firm effect** emerges in several studies that have shown that portfolios of small firms (in terms of total market capitalization) have outperformed the stock market (consisting of both large and small firms).[18] Because of these findings, there has been increased interest in stock market indicators that monitor small capitalization firms.

---

[17] If a statistically significant negative abnormal return is found, an investment strategy involving shorting stock would be pursued.

[18] Marc R. Reinganum, "Misspecification of Capital Asset Pricing: Empirical Anomalies Based on Earnings Yields and Market Values," *Journal of Financial Economics* (March 1981), pp. 19-46; and Rolf W. Banz, "The Relationship between Return and Market Value of Stocks," *Journal of Financial Economics* (March 1981), pp. 103-26.

The **low price-earnings ratio effect** is based on studies showing that portfolios consisting of stocks with a low price-earnings ratio have outperformed portfolios consisting of stocks with a high price-earnings ratio.[19] However, another study finds that, after adjusting for transactions costs necessary to rebalance a portfolio as prices and earnings change over time, the superior performance of portfolios of low price-earnings ratio stocks no longer holds.[20] An explanation for the presumably superior performance is that stocks trade at low price-earnings ratios because they are temporarily out of favor with market participants. As fads do change, companies not currently in vogue will rebound at some indeterminate time in the future.[21]

Not all firms receive the same degree of attention from security analysts, and one school of thought is that firms that are neglected by security analysts will outperform firms that are the subject of considerable attention. One study has found that an investment strategy based on changes in the level of attention devoted by security analysts to different stocks may lead to positive abnormal returns.[22] This market anomaly is referred to as the **neglected firm effect**.

While some empirical work focuses on selected firms according to some criterion such as market capitalization, price-earnings ratio, or degree of analysts' attention, studies on **calendar effects** look at the best time to implement strategies. Examples of anomalies are the January effect, month-of-the-year effect, day-of-the-week effect, and the holiday effect. It seems from the empirical evidence that there are times when the implementation of a strategy will, on average, provide a superior performance relative to other calendar time periods.

One of the difficulties with all of these pricing efficiency studies is that the factors that are believed to give rise to market anomalies are interrelated. For example, small firms may be those that are not given much attention by security analysts and that trade at low price-earnings ratio. Current research has attempted to disentangle these effects.[23]

Aside from the various effects reviewed above, some authors[24] claim that the pricing of equities is not rational because the variability of stock prices, particularly that of broad indices, is too large to be consistent with rational prices (while it is consistent with the presence of "bubbles" which we discuss in the next section).

[19] Sanjoy Basu, "Investment Performance of Common Stocks in Relation to Their Price-Earnings Ratios: A Test of the Efficient Market Hypothesis," *Journal of Finance* (June 1977), pp. 663-82.

[20] Haim Levy and Zvi Lerman, "Testing P/E Ratio Filters with Stochastic Dominance," *Journal of Portfolio Management* (Winter 1985), pp. 31-40.

[21] David Dreman, *Contrarian Investment Strategy: The Psychology of Stock Market Success* (New York: Random house, 1979).

[22] Avner Arbel and Paul Strebel, "Pay Attention to Neglected Firms," *Journal of Portfolio Management* (Winter 1983), pp. 37-42.

[23] See Bruce I. Jacobs and Kenneth N. Levy, "Stock Market Complexity and Investment Opportunity," in Frank J. Fabozzi, ed. *Managing Institutional Assets* (New York: Harper & Row, 1990).

[24] Robert J. Shiller, "Do Stock Prices Move Too Much to Be Justified by Subsequent Changes in Dividends?" *American Economic Review* 71 (1981), pp. 421-35, and "The Probability of Gross Violations of a Present Value Variance Inequality," *Journal of Political Economy* 96 (1988), pp. 1089-92.

Other authors have called attention to periods of irrational over- or under-valuation of the market as a whole. In particular, Modigliani and Cohn[25] provide some evidence that the stock market was undervalued during the inflation of the 1970s because of the market's inability to value equity correctly in the presence of significant inflation.

Testing of strong form pricing efficiency—Empirical tests of strong form pricing efficiency fall into two groups: studies of the performance of professional money managers, and studies of the activities of "insiders" (individuals who are either company directors, major officers, or major stockholders). Studying the performance of professional money managers to test the strong form of pricing efficiency has been based on the belief that these managers have access to better information than the general public. Whether this is true is moot, because the empirical evidence suggests professional managers have not been able to outperform the market consistently. In contrast, evidence based on the activities of insiders has generally revealed that insiders consistently outperform the stock market.[26] Consequently, strong form pricing efficiency—where the relevant information set includes non-public information—is not supported with respect to insider trading activity.

Implications for Investing in Common Stock

Common stock investment strategies can be classified into two general categories: active strategies and passive strategies. **Active strategies** are those that attempt to outperform the market by one or more of the following: timing the selection of transactions, such as in the case of technical analysis; identifying undervalued or overvalued stocks using fundamental security analysis; or selecting stocks according to one of the market anomalies. Obviously, the decision to pursue an active strategy must be based on the belief that there is some type of gain from such costly efforts; for there to be a gain, pricing inefficiencies must exist. The particular strategy chosen depends on why the investor believes this is the case.

If investors believe that the market is efficient with respect to pricing stocks, then they should accept the implication that attempts to outperform the market cannot be successful systematically, except by luck. This does not mean that investors should shun the stock market, but rather that they should pursue a **passive strategy**, which is one that does not attempt to outperform the market. Is there an optimal investment strategy for someone who holds this belief in the pricing efficiency of the stock market? Indeed there is. Its theoretical basis is capital market theory that we discussed in Chapter 9. According to this theory, the "market" portfolio offers the highest level of return per unit of risk in a market that is price-efficient. A portfolio of financial assets with characteristics similar to those of a portfolio consisting of the entire market (i.e., the market portfolio) will capture the pricing efficiency of the market.

---

[25] Franco Modigliani and Richard A. Cohn, "Inflation, Rational Valuation and the Market," *Financial Analysts Journal* (March/April 1979), pp. 24-44.

[26] Researchers obtain information about the activities of insiders from reports they are required to file with the SEC. These reports are available to the public six weeks after filing.

How can such a passive strategy be implemented? More specifically, what is meant by a "market portfolio," and how should that portfolio be constructed? In theory, the market portfolio consists of all financial assets, not just common stock. The reason is that investors compare all investment opportunities, not just stock, when committing their capital. Thus, the principles of investing we accept are based on capital market theory, not stock market theory. When the theory has been followed by those investing in the stock market, the market portfolio has been defined as consisting of a large universe of common stocks. But how much of each common stock should be purchased when constructing the market portfolio? Theory states that the chosen portfolio should be an appropriate fraction of the market portfolio; hence the weighting of each stock in the market portfolio should be based on its relative market capitalization. Thus, if the aggregate market capitalization of all stocks included in the market portfolio is $T and the market capitalization of one of these stocks is $A, then the fraction of this stock that should be held in the market portfolio is $A/$T.

The passive strategy that we have just described is called **indexing**. Because pension fund sponsors increasingly believe that money managers have been unable to outperform the stock market, the amount of funds managed using an indexing strategy has increased since the 1980s. However, index funds are still a relatively small fraction of institutional stock investments. The stock market index whose performance the passive money manager attempts to replicate is called the **bogey**. There are currently several mutual funds with the investment objective to create an indexed portfolio to match some bogey, the most common being the S&P 500.

There are several methodologies for constructing an indexed portfolio.[27] The first is to buy each and every stock in the bogey. Another is to construct an indexed portfolio consisting of a sample of all the stocks in the bogey that is constructed in such a way as to minimize the risk of failing to replicate the performance of the bogey. This risk is referred to as **tracking error**. An indexed portfolio with less than the complete set of stocks in the bogey typically is constructed using mathematical optimization techniques. A third technique involves investing the whole portfolio in Treasury bills and buying a stock index futures contract (whose underlying stock index is the bogey) for an amount equal to the value of the portfolio. Stock index futures are discussed in Chapter 15. For the present it is necessary only to understand that if stock index futures are priced based on their theoretical price, then a package of a long position in stock index futures and Treasury bills will produce the same return as holding the stocks in the bogey. Moreover, this can be done without incurring the transactions costs associated with buying the stocks in the bogey.

When an indexing strategy is followed, it is critical that any new cash coming into the portfolio be invested in such a way within the indexed portfolio as to leave the relative proportion of each stock unchanged. For example, suppose that the bogey for an index strategy is the S&P 500, and the indexed portfolio is constructed using all 500 stocks. Suppose further that $10 million of additional funds are received and must be invested in the same portfolio.

---

[27] For a discussion of these techniques, see Frank J. Fabozzi, *Investment Management* (Englewood Cliffs, NJ: Prentice-Hall, 1995), Chapter 14.

Then the money manager must invest the $10 million in all 500 stocks, with an amount in each stock based on its relative market capitalization. Moreover, all stocks must be purchased at as close to one time as possible. Similarly, $10 million to be withdrawn from the portfolio would require selling a proportionate amount of each stock as close in time as possible. Both objectives are accomplished via program trading.

Before leaving the topic of indexing, it is worthwhile to note that there are strategies referred to as **enhanced indexing**. The objective of such strategies is to create a portfolio that is essentially an indexed portfolio but in which the money manager makes small bets by tilting the portfolio to a sector of the stock market that is believed will outperform the bogey or employs mispriced stock index futures. The difference between this strategy and pure active strategies depends on the size of the bets that the manager is placing— that is, the extent to which the portfolio created is expected to depart from the bogey. In the case of enhanced indexing, the deviation is small; in active strategies, the portfolio constructed may have little resemblance to a bogey.

THE MARKET CRASH OF 1987

The largest single-day decline in the history of the stock market occurred on Monday, October 19, 1987. On this day, popularly referred to as "Black Monday," the DJIA declined by 23%. Other countries besides the United States also saw a precipitous drop in their stock markets.

The aftermath saw several studies commissioned by the U.S. government, regulators, and exchanges to assess the causes of the crash and offer recommendations guarding against a reoccurrence. The four government-related studies include: a presidential task force commission study, popularly known as the Brady Report,[28] a General Accounting Office study,[29] an SEC study,[30] and a Commodity Futures Trading Commission study.[31] In addition, there were studies by the New York Stock Exchange (referred to as the Katzenbach Report),[32] and the Chicago Mercantile Exchange (referred to as the Miller Report).[33]

Explanations for Black Monday that these various studies offer include: presence or absence of institutional arrangements; overvaluation of stock prices prior to the crash; and overreaction to economic news. While an analysis of these explanations for Black Monday is beyond the scope of this chapter, we can note that a study by several well-respected university-affiliated researchers sponsored by The Mid-America Institute (MAI) for Public Policy Research seems to help us eliminate some misconceptions about the causes. The MAI task force study also evaluates some of the recommendations made

---

[28] Brady Report, *Presidential Task Force on Market Mechanisms*, 1988.

[29] U.S. Congress, General Accounting Office, *Preliminary Observations on the October 1987 Crash*, 1988.

[30] Securities and Exchange Commission, *The October 1987 Market Break*, Report by the Division of Market Regulation, 1988.

[31] Commodity Futures Trading Commission, *Final Report on Stock Index Futures and Cash Market Activity During October 1987*, Divisions of Economic Analysis and Trading and Markets, 1988.

[32] Nicholas Katzenbach, *An Overview of Program Trading and Its Impact on Current Market Practices*, December 21, 1987.

[33] *The Final and Preliminary Reports of the CME Committee of Inquiry*, 1988.

by the commissioned studies. Such an evaluation is needed because, as Alan Meltzer, one of the contributors to the MAI study, notes:[34]

> *A striking but generally disregarded feature of the recommendations made is that, often, no claim is made and no evidence offered that the events of October would have been different if the recommended changes had been in effect. Indeed, in some reports, there is little relation between the problems described and some of the solutions proposed.*

Institutional Arrangements

The six commissioned studies focus on institutional characteristics of the market such as (1) the presence of a specialist, (2) the existence of computer-directed trading, (3) the nature of price limits, (4) continuous versus call auctions, (5) the level of margin requirements, and (6) the existence of derivative instruments (futures and options).

Roll has since looked at the institutional arrangements in 23 countries with major stock markets.[35] He estimates a regression relating the change in the decline in a country's stock market to the presence or absence of ten institutional arrangements. His regression results do not provide support for the position that institutional arrangements can be used to explain the decline in stock prices in the 23 stock markets studied.

In Chapter 15, we shall focus on derivative instruments—stock index futures and stock index options—and additional empirical evidence challenging whether their existence may have caused the market crash, as many contend.

Overvaluation of Stock Prices Prior to Black Monday

Another argument is that the decline in stock prices in the United States was a result of a permanent return to fundamental values from which the market had progressively departed during the frenzied rise of the previous year or so. Support for this explanation has been documented by the Brady report, Bernstein and Bernstein,[36] and Fama.[37] As Bernstein and Bernstein state:

> *...careful studies of stock selection techniques published by Goldman Sachs & Co. and Zacks Investment Research during the summer of 1987 demonstrated that, for at least a year, sheer price momentum had been the only functioning model for selected stocks: The stocks that moved were the stocks that were moving. Valuation parameters of all kinds had been left far behind in the dust, a common complaint among managers all during 1987.*[38]

---

[34] Alan H. Meltzer, "Overview," in Robert J. Barro et al. (eds.), *Black Monday and the Future of Financial Markets* (Homewood, IL: Dow Jones-Irwin, 1989).

[35] Richard Roll, "The International Crash of October 1987," *Black Monday and the Future of Financial Markets*, op. cit.

[36] Peter L. Bernstein and Barbara S. Bernstein, "Where the Postcrash Studies Went Wrong," *Institutional Investor* (April 1988), pp. 173-77.

[37] Eugene F. Fama, "Perspectives on October 1987, or What Did We Learn From the Crash?" in *Black Monday and the Future of Financial Markets*, op. cit.

This formulation is consistent with a more specific explanation of the episode, namely, that it represented the bursting of a speculative bubble that had been developing throughout the year, carrying market prices well above fundamentals. The sharp decline brought the market back to values more nearly consistent with the fundamentals.

A **bubble** essentially occurs when prices rise progressively above fundamental values, and overvaluation continues to be supported by the continuing rise in prices along with expectations of further rises. Of course, holders can enjoy an attractive return only as long as the price rises exponentially, so the price itself must get farther and farther away from its fundamental value to provide remuneration for risk. As the rate of price increases slows down, this contributes to reducing the belief among market participants that the explosive process can continue, which makes continuation of the bubble more precarious. With the path becoming more and more unstable, almost any news can cause the bubble to burst. When it does, prices must go all the way back to the rationally warranted level (or initially even lower which is called overshooting).

The main difficulty with the bubble explanation is that, while it seems appealing, at least compared with other explanations offered, it is hard to support statistically. However, Richard Roll has reported an ingenious test that provides evidence in support of the bubble hypothesis. He argues that bubbles should be characterized by serial dependence (autocorrelation) in the returns. Relying on data from stock markets of 23 countries including nearly all the major markets, he is able to provide convincing evidence of such dependence for the precrash period from the beginning of January to August 1987.[39] At the same time, he acknowledges the need for further tests to check for the possibility of a statistical pitfall that could bias the test.

Overreaction to Economic News

Some market observers suggest that the crash was attributable to an overreaction to some economic news. Several candidates for such economic news include concern about the negative impact of the merchandise trade news, additional increases in interest rates, proposed tax legislation, and news over the preceding weekend about a further decline in the value of the dollar expressed by Treasury Secretary Baker. This argument, however, lacks support because the decline was not temporary.

Is There a Conclusion?

It is worth noting that even though more than 60 years have passed since the October 29, 1929, market crash (the largest to date), no consensus has been reached as to the reason for the 1929 decline. It should come as no surprise that there is no consensus explaining Black Monday after only a few years of investigation.

---

[38] Bernstein and Bernstein, op. cit., p. 175.

[39] Roll, "The International Crash of October 1987," op. cit.

NON-U.S. EQUITY MARKETS

Table 13-2 provides a comparative analysis of the size, measured in U.S. dollars, of the equity markets of the world. The stock markets of the United States and Japan are the largest in the world. As the markets are measured in U.S. dollars, the relative size of the U.S. and Japanese market varies as the value of the yen changes against the dollar—U.S. share increases when the yen depreciates, and decreases when the yen appreciates. The third largest market, but trailing considerably behind the U.S. and Japanese markets, is the U.K. market.

Estimated round-trip transactions costs as a percentage of the amount invested are higher in stock markets outside the United States, as can be seen in Table 13-3. These costs include commissions, market impact costs, and taxes. Deregulation in many countries, however, is reducing the gap between transactions costs in stock markets outside the U.S.

Stocks of some firms are listed for trading on stock exchanges in other countries as well as on the exchange in their own country. Arbitrage assures that the price is the same on all exchanges after adjusting for exchange rates and transaction costs. The readiness of an exchange to list and trade the shares of a foreign company varies among countries and exchanges.

In the United States, shares of some foreign companies can be traded through American Depository Receipts (ADRs), which are instruments denominated in U.S. dollars that pay dividends in U.S. dollars. ADRs are issued by banks as evidence of ownership of the underlying stock of a foreign corporation that the U.S. bank holds. ADRs are traded on the NYSE, AMEX, and OTC. Examples of ADRs listed on the New York Stock Exchange are Honda Motor Co. (a Japanese company listed since February 1977), Club Med (a British West Indies company listed since September 1984), Royal Dutch Petroleum Co. (a Netherlands company listed since July 1954), and British Petroleum Company (a U.K. company listed since March 1970). There may be more than one share of the foreign stock underlying an ADR.

Euroequities

Euroequity issues are those issued simultaneously in several national markets by an international syndicate. The Euroequity markets began in 1980. By 1986, issuance of Euroequities was between $8 and $10 billion.[40] This growth has been fueled by rising stock prices throughout the world, the desire of investors to diversify their portfolios internationally, the need for corporations to expand their sources of equity funding, and by governments seeking international investors for entities that have been privatized.

An increasing number of U.S. firms had equity offerings which included a Euroequity tranche. (In the international financial vocabulary, the word *"tranche"*, which is French for slice or segment or cut, means a distinctive portion of the issue of a financial security. In this context, the word means that some of the newly issued equity shares were reserved for sale in Euro-

---

[40] P. L. Gilibert, B. Lygum, and F. Wurtz, "The International Capital Market in 1986," *Cahiers BEI/EIB Papers*, European Investment Bank, Luxembourg, March 1987.

Table 13-2

Estimated Total Market Value of National Stock Markets Included in Morgan Stanley Capital International Indices as of December 31, 1994 (in billions of U.S. dollars)

Area and Country		Estimated Market Value
United States		$ 4,626.3
Canada		$ 288.0
Europe		$ 3,275.0
By country:		
Austria	$ 30.7	
Belgium	84.0	
Denmark	46.6	
Finland	36.8	
France	444.3	
Germany	476.9	
Ireland	19.5	
Italy	177.1	
Netherlands	224.4	
Norway	36.1	
Spain	151.3	
Sweden	118.3	
Switzerland	284.0	
United Kingdom	1,145.0	
Asia, and Far East		$ 4,425.9
By country:		
Australia	212.4	
Hong Kong	241.2	
Japan	3,624.5	
Malaysia	182.0	
New Zealand	26.4	
Singapore	139.4	
South African Gold Mines		$ 24.6
"World"		$ 12,639.8

Source: **Morgan Stanley Capital International Perspective,** *January 1995, p. 5. (Adapted by the author.)*

Table 13-3

Estimated Round-Trip Transactions Costs for Common
Stocks as a Percentage of Amount Invested*

	Country**				
	U.S.	**Japan**	**U.K.**	**France**	**Germany**
Commissions	0.20%	0.30%	0.10%	0.20%	0.20%
Market impact cost***	0.57	1.00	0.90	0.800	.60
Taxes	0.00	0.30	0.50	0.00	0.00
Total	0.77%	1.60%	1.50%	1.00%	0.80%
Avg Stock Price in U.S. dollars(**)	45	6.77	6.17	97.18	271

 * Assumes a $25 million cap weighted indexed portfolio executed as agent;
   does not include settlement and custody fees.

 ** Trader estimate

 *** Local index: S&P 500, Nikkei 225, FT-SE 100, CAC-40, DAX

markets.) Similarly, more European firms are offering equity securities with
a U.S. tranche. For example, in 1990, 84 issues were offered by European firms
with U.S. tranches having a market value of $3.85 billion compared to the
first three quarters of 1991 in which 154 equity offerings with a total market
value of $7.09 billion were made. [41]

Corporations have not limited their equity offerings to just their domestic
equity market and a foreign market of another country. Instead, the offerings
have been more global in nature. For example, the initial public offering (IPO)
of British Telecommunications (the United Kingdom's government-owned
telephone company) in 1984 was offered simultaneously in the United
Kingdom, the United States, Japan, and Canada. As a more recent example,
the Dutch Aircraft manufacturer Fokker expected to raise Dfls 500 million in
equity the first half of 1992. There were seven tranches that were planned: the
United States, the United Kingdom, Germany, Switzerland, Canada, Benelux,
and the rest of the world.[42]

The innovation in the Euroequities markets is not in terms of new equity
structures. Rather, it is in the development of an efficient international chan-
nel for distributing equities. This development can probably be traced back to
1984 and 1985 when issues of three non-U.S. corporations, Nestlè, British
Telecom, and Esselte, utilized the international market to raise equity. The
depth and breath of the market can be illustrated by Nestlè which was able to
use the international market to raise more than $400 million in equity funds
three separate times in 1985.[43]

---

[41] As reported in Janine Schultz, "International Equity Tranches to Shed Weak Sister Image," *Corporate Financing Week*
Special Supplement, November 25, 1991, pp. 1 and 8.

[42] *International Financial Review* Issue 902 (November 2, 1991), p. 39.

[43] Julian Walmsley, *The New Financial Instruments* (New York: John Wiley & Sons, 1988), p. 328.

Motivation for Listing on a Foreign Market

Euromoney surveyed several firms that either listed stock on a foreign stock exchange or had a stock offering in a foreign market to find out why they did so.[44] One corporation surveyed was Scott Paper, a U.S. corporation, which listed its stock on the London Stock Exchange in November 1984. The stock had already been listed on the NYSE and a regional stock exchange, the Philadelphia Stock Exchange. The following reason for listing was given by an official in the company's public relations department:

> We had no immediate need for extra equity, but may well do so at some time in the future. We would like a broader stockholder base, and felt there would be some interest in the company overseas. The London Stock Exchange has high visibility, so it best served the purpose of getting the company's name known.[45]

A second firm surveyed was Saatchi & Saatchi, a U.K. corporation that raised equity in the United States via an ADR offering traded in the over-the-counter market. Several reasons were given for Saatchi & Saatchi's raising of equity in the United States. The firm had considerable U.S. activities and therefore felt it necessary to establish a presence in the U.S. equity market and a higher profile in the U.S. in general. Also, the firm wanted to offer stock options to its U.S. employees and apparently felt that having stocks traded in the U.S. equity market would make the options more attractive to employees.

Yet another set of reasons which we discussed earlier was given by a third firm in the *Euromoney* survey, Norsk Data, a Norwegian firm. The firm is in the high technology industry and before it sought foreign listing had a history of earning per share growth of 60%. In 1981, the firm listed its stock on the London Stock Exchange and followed this several months later with an offering of new shares in London. In 1983, the firm raised funds in the U.S. equity market with the stock traded in the U.S. over-the-counter market. The chief executive officer of the firm gave the following reasons for listing:

> For major computer companies, the U.S. market is a very important source of funds, since it is alive to the possibility of high technology. However, we went to London first, since we felt a leap straight from Oslo to New York would be too great. Our major customers are in Germany, the U.K. and to a lesser extent, the U.S.[46]

In 1984, Norsk Data raised equity funds in a simultaneous U.S. and European offering. With respect to its various equity offerings, the chief executive officer stated:

> We have now brought equity up to the level of our competitors, and we have a natural balance sheet for a high growth, high technology company. That would have been very difficult if we had been limited to the Oslo stock market.[47]

---

[44] "Why Corporations Gain from Foreign Equity Listings," *Euromoney Corporate Finance* (March 1985), pp. 39-40.

[45] Ibid., p. 39.

[46] Ibid., p. 40.

[47] Ibid., p. 40

In addition, after these equity offerings on foreign markets, the firm was 60% owned by foreign investors, most of which was non-voting common stock. Thus, corporate control was not sacrificed.

In a survey conducted by the Economic Council of Canada of Canadian borrowers who raised funds outside of Canada, 85% cited the primary reason was the lower cost of funding.[48] The other reasons cited by the participants in the survey were: diversification of the investor base (50%); ease of borrowing funds (37%); the presence of a subsidiary, parent, or affiliate in the country of borrowing (43%); the ability to attract new investors (30%); and publicity for the corporation's name (30%).

A survey of corporate managers investigating why U.S. corporations list on the London, Frankfurt, and Tokyo stock exchanges found the following four major motives:[49]

1. increase visibility (awareness, name recognition or exposure).

2. broaden shareholder base (diversify ownership).

3. increase access to financial markets.

4. provide future market for products.

The most popular motive was the first.

National Market Structures

While the stock exchanges in the United States are regulated by the SEC, they are privately owned entities. Activities of members of the exchange are regulated by the exchanges, and commissions are fully negotiable. Thus, the United States equity markets can be characterized as private markets whose activities, while regulated at the federal level, are essentially self-regulated.

There are other countries that have a similar market structure: Japan, the United Kingdom, Canada, and Australia. In Japan, for example, there are eight major exchanges, three of which handle more than 98% of the trades (Tokyo Stock Exchange, Osaka Exchange, and Nagoya Exchange). In contrast, in the United Kingdom, the one dominant exchange is the London Stock Exchange. This exchange has predominated not because of any regulation but through absorption or attrition of its competitors. In many countries deregulation has resulted in commissions that are either fully or partially negotiable.

In some other countries, the stock exchange is a public institution. Brokers are selected by the government, and the commission rate structure is fixed by the government. Thus, the broker has a monopoly over all stock transactions. In some countries with this structure, all transactions are required to go through the exchange, even if they are consummated privately between a buyer and seller without the assistance of a broker. In such cases, a broker is paid a fee. European countries where the stock market is a public market include France, Belgium, Spain, Italy, and Greece. The last type of market structure is one where the majority of trading is done through banks. In

---

[48] A. Nigam, *Canadian Corporations and Governments, Financial Innovation and International Capital Markets*, a paper prepared for the Economic Council of Canada, 1989.

[49] H. Kent Baker, "Why U.S. Companies List on the London, Frankfurt and Tokyo Stock Exchanges," *The Journal of International Securities Markets* (Autumn 1992), pp. 219-27.

Germany the universal banks dominate securities transactions. Other countries with this type of structure include Switzerland and the Netherlands.

In Chapter 7 we explained the difference between continuous and call markets. In the former, prices are determined continuously throughout the trading day as buyers and sellers submit orders. U.S. equity markets are continuous markets. Equity markets in Canada, in the Far East, and in most of Europe have a continuous market structure. A call market is one in which orders are batched for simultaneous execution at the same price. The equity markets in Germany, Belgium, Austria, and Israel have a call market structure. In several countries, electronic technology is being used to incorporate a call market structure into a continuous market structure.[50]

The U.S. stock markets are continuous markets. On the stock exchanges, the specialist is the market maker or dealer who has the role of providing liquidity; in the over-the-counter market there may be more than one market maker or dealer. On the Amsterdam Stock Exchange there is also only one specialist, the *hoekman.* On the London Stock Exchange there are more than one specialist, called *jobbers.*

Stock Market Indexes

There are many indexes of stock prices that chart and measure the performance of foreign stock markets. In every country where stock trading takes place, there is at least one index that measures general share price movements. If a country has more than one stock exchange, each exchange usually has its own index. Also, news organizations and financial advisory services create indexes.

In Japan, there are two major indexes. The Tokyo Stock Exchange produces the *Tokyo Stock Price Index* or TOPIX. This is a composite index which is based on all the shares in the Tokyo market's First Section, a designation reserved for the established and large companies whose shares are the most actively traded and widely held. A financial information firm, Nihon Keizai Shimbun, Inc., calculates and publishes the *Nikkei 225 Stock Average.* This average is based on 225 of the largest companies in the First Section.

The United Kingdom's London Stock Exchange is covered by several widely followed indexes. *The Financial Times Industrial Ordinary Index* is based on the prices of shares of 30 leading companies and is known as the "FT30." A broader index is the *Financial Times-Stock Exchange 100*, commonly referred to as the "FTSE 100" (and pronounced "Footsie 100"). This index is based on the shares of the largest 100 U.K. firms, whose market value makes up a majority of the market value of all U.K. equities.[51] Indexes for different sectors and a composite index across sectors are produced by the *Financial Times* and the Institute for Actuaries. These "FT-A" indexes are very broadly based, with the composite including over 700 stocks.

---

[50] For a discussion of how this is being done and the advantages of this approach, see Chapter 10 of Robert A. Schwartz, *Reshaping the Equity Markets: A Guide for the 1990s* (N.Y.: HarperBusiness, 1991).

[51] Carolyn Moses, "U.K. Equity Market," in Jess Lederman and Keith K.H. Park (eds.), *The Global Equity Markets* (Chicago: Probus Publishing Company, 1991), p. 105.

The primary German stock index is the DAX, which stands for the "Deutscher Aktienindex," and it is produced by the Frankfurt Stock Exchange. (The German name for this exchange is the "Frankfurter Wertpapierbörse." Some financial services regularly refer to the exchange by its initials, FWB.) The DAX is based on the 30 most actively traded shares listed on the Frankfurt exchange. The *FAZ Index* is another popular German index. Compiled by the *Frankfurter Allgemeine Zeitung,* which is a daily newspaper, the FAZ Index is computed from the share prices of the 100 largest companies listed on the Frankfurt exchange. In France, a national association of stockbrokers and the Paris Bourse produce an index based on the shares of 40 large and prominent firms traded on the exchange. The index is known as the CAC 40 Index, with CAC standing for "Cotation Assistée en Continu," which is the name of the Bourse's electronic trading system. Given the increasing economic integration of Europe, the CAC 40, like the FT-SE 100 and possibly the DAX, may well be a reliable indicator of the overall performance of European stocks and markets. Other widely followed national stock indexes include the Hang Seng Index produced by the Stock Exchange of Hong Kong, the TSE 300 Composite of the Toronto Stock Exchange, and the Swiss Performance Index (SPI) which applies to almost 400 firms and is published by the stock exchanges in that country.

To meet the increased interest in global equity investing, financial institutions have crafted several respected international equity indexes. The international equity index that is followed the most by U.S. pension funds is the Morgan Stanley Capital International Europe, Australia, Far East Index (EAFE) Index. This index covers more than 2,000 companies in 21 countries. Relatively new international equity indexes include: *The Financial Times World Index* (a joint product of the Institute of Actuaries in the U.K., Goldman Sachs & Co., and Wood MacKenzie & Co.), the Salomon Brothers-Russell Global Equity Index (a joint product of Salomon Brothers, Inc and Frank Russell, Inc.), and the Global Index (a joint product of First Boston Corporation and London-based *Euromoney).*

Motivation for Global Investing

Numerous studies have documented the potential portfolio diversification benefits associated with global investing.[52] In particular, those studies have shown that the inclusion of securities from other countries can increase a portfolio's expected return without increasing its risk, as measured by variability in returns. Similarly, including securities from other countries might reduce the portfolio's risk with no fall in its expected return.

The cause of these benefits from diversification is that international capital markets are less than perfectly correlated. This degree of independence is not really surprising because the different countries in which the markets are located do not tend to have the same experiences in such important areas as taxation, monetary management, banking policies, political stability and

---

[52] For a review of these studies, see Chapter 2 of Bruno Solnik, *International Investments* (Addison-Wesley Publishing, 1994).

goals, population growth, and so on. Because the largest influences on stock prices are domestic or local events and policies, the prices of groups of stock from different areas tend to move up or down at somewhat different times and to somewhat different extents. As explained in Chapter 8, this pattern of dissimilar security price changes allows investors to diversify a certain amount of risk and creates the benefits of international or global investing.

Table 13-4 provides evidence regarding the degree of dissimilarity in the movement of stock prices of eight major equity markets. The table presents correlation coefficients for annual returns (in U.S. dollars), which measure the overall or general level of share prices on the exchanges in those countries, for the period from 1982 to 1992.

Table 13-4 reveals that these markets are quite different from one another and the correlations of their returns tend to be substantially less than unity. The highest coefficient is 0.81, for the U.S. and Canada, and many values are below 0.50. So, investors can diversify by spreading their portfolio across these various markets. It is interesting that all the correlations are positive and well above zero, a value which implies complete independence of action. The positive values mean that the world's stock prices are, like their economies, somewhat integrated. Thus, the benefit of international diversification has limits. In other words, the markets of the world are members of a somewhat loosely connected system of economies, and allocating funds among the various economies provides some, but not complete, reduction of variability in returns on securities.

Table 13-4

Annual Intermarket Return Correlations Between Country Equity Markets (1982-1992)

	U.S.	France	U.K.	Japan	Germany	Switzerland	Canada	Australia
U.S.	1.00	0.57	0.63	0.44	0.41	0.58	0.81	0.51
France		1.00	0.56	0.53	0.65	0.64	0.39	0.34
U.K.			1.00	0.51	0.38	0.45	0.52	0.53
Japan				1.00	0.30	0.30	0.30	0.30
Germany					1.00	0.75	0.27	0.22
Switzerland						1.00	0.43	0.35
Canada							1.00	0.56
Australia								1.00

Source: Gary Gastineau, Gordon Holterman, and Scott Beighley, "Equity Investment Across Borders: Cutting the Costs," SBC Research, Swiss Bank Corporation Banking Inc., January 1993, p. 24.

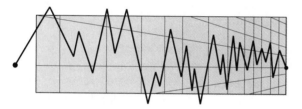

SUMMARY

Common stock represents an ownership interest in a corporation. Secondary trading of common stock occurs in one or more of the following trading locations: two major national stock exchanges (the NYSE and AMEX), five regional stock exchanges, and the OTC market (NASDAQ system). Independent electronic trading systems such as INSTINET and POSIT permit institution-to-institution trading without the use of a broker.

The secondary market has undergone significant changes since the 1960s. The major participants are now institutional investors rather than small (retail) investors. Elimination of fixed commissions and the government's mandate to develop a national market system to reduce the fragmentation of the stock market have fostered increased competition among market makers on the exchanges and in the OTC market. Advances in computer technology have ushered in developments for linking the various market locations and systems for institution-to-institution direct trading.

An important structural difference between exchanges and the OTC market is that on exchanges there is only one market maker or dealer per stock, the specialist, while there is no restriction on the number of dealers in the OTC market.

The SEC has studied the structure of the U.S. equity market, leading to the promotion of a national market system in the early 1970s and recommendations in its 1994 study, *Market 2000*. The basic principles embodied in the Securities Act of 1975 is that competition and comprehensive disclosure of market information should be fostered in order to generate the best prices for investors, and the interests of public investors should be placed ahead of the interests of broker-dealers. The same principles were expressed in the *Market 2000* study, with the SEC identifying the problems it faced in a world of advanced computer technology and independent trading systems.

To accommodate the trading needs of institutional investors who tend to place orders of larger sizes and with a large number of names, special arrangements have evolved. Block trades are trades of 10,000 shares or more of a given stock, or trades with a market value of $200,000 or more. Program trades, or basket trades, involve the buying and/or selling of a large number of names simultaneously. The institutional arrangement that has evolved to accommodate these needs is the upstairs market, which is a network of trading desks of the major investment banking firms and institutional investors that communicate with each other by means of electronic display systems and telephones.

Stock market indicators can be classified into three groups: (1) those produced by stock exchanges that include all stocks traded on the exchange, such as the New York Stock Exchange Composite Index, the American Stock Exchange Market Value Index, and the NASDAQ Composite Index; (2) those in which a committee subjectively selects the stocks to be included in the index, such as the Dow Jones Industrial Average, the Standard & Poor's 500, and the Value Line Composite Average; and (3) those in which the stocks selected are based solely on market capitalization, such as the Wilshire indexes (Wilshire 5000 and Wilshire 4500) and the Russell indexes (Russell 3000, Russell 2000, and Russell 1000).

Most of the empirical evidence suggests that markets are efficient in the weak form. The evidence on the semistrong form is mixed, as pockets of inefficiency have been observed. These market anomalies include the small-firm effect, the low price-earnings ratio effect, the neglected firm effect, and various calendar effects. Empirical tests of strong form pricing efficiency reveal two sets of results: studies of the performance of professional money managers suggest that they have not outperformed the market; and analysis of the activity of insiders generally finds that they consistently outperform the market.

Active strategies are pursued by investors who believe that markets are sufficiently mispriced so that it is possible to capitalize on strategies designed to exploit the perceived inefficiency. The optimal strategy to pursue when the stock market is perceived to be price-efficient is indexing, because it allows the investor to capture the efficiency of the market.

Black Monday (October 19, 1987) saw the largest single decline in the stock market. Despite several studies, there is no universally accepted conclusion as to the reasons for the crash, although we support the view that it represented the bursting of a speculative bubble.

In terms of value of listed shares, the United States and Japanese stock markets are the two largest stock markets in the world, followed by the U.K. stock market. Effective transactions costs (commissions and taxes) are lower for trades in the United States than in any other stock market of the world.

Stocks of large corporations may be listed in more than one country. Firms are in favor of multiple listings, because they boost the companies' image and, among other things, allow access to funding in many major financial centers. An American Depository Receipt (ADR) is the right to a foreign share (or set of shares) that is traded in the United States. The Euroequities market includes stocks issued simultaneously in several national markets by an international syndicate.

Every stock market in the world has an index, which is a measure of the general movement in the prices of shares on the market. Some indexes are produced by exchanges and some by financial news services. The largest markets have well-known and widely followed indexes: the TOPIX and the Nikkei 225 in Japan, the FT-SE 100 in the U.K., the DAX and FAZ indexes of Germany, and the CAC 40 in France. Popular international equity price indexes are based on several markets; a good example is the Morgan Stanley EAFE Index which covers Europe, Australia, and the Far East.

The prices of stocks on markets around the world do not move together in an exact way, because the economic systems in which those markets are located have dissimilar environments in terms of taxation, industrial growth, political stability, monetary policy, and so on. Low levels of simultaneous movement of stock prices offer investors a benefit from diversifying their holdings across the markets of countries. That is, an investor who allocates some of his or her portfolio to shares from other countries can reduce the portfolio's risk with no fall in expected return, or raise the portfolio's expected return with no increase in risk.

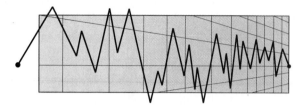

QUESTIONS

1. The following quotation is from an interview with William Donaldson, Chairman of the New York Stock Exchange, that appeared in *The New York Times* of January 30, 1990:

   There's a need to understand the advantages of an auction market versus a dealer market. The auction market allows a buyer and a seller to get together and agree on a price and the dealer is not involved at all. That's opposed to a dealer market where the house is on both sides of the trade and the dealer makes the spread rather than having the spread shared by the buyer and the seller.

   One of the things we're coming to the forefront on now is the whole idea of what makes a good market. I think the best market is where you have the maximum number of people coming together in a single location and bidding against each other...That is far superior to what we are getting now, which is a fractionalization of the market.

   Traders on machines, trades in the closet, trades in many areas where buyers and sellers don't have the opportunity to meet.

   Discuss Donaldson's opinion. In your answer be sure to address the pros and cons of the different trading locations and practices addressed in this chapter.

2. Following is a quotation from "The Taxonomy of Trading Strategies" by Wayne H. Wagner that appears in *Trading Strategies and Execution Costs*, published by The Institute of Chartered Financial Analysts in 1988. (The publication is the product of a conference held in New York City on December 3, 1987.)

   The NYSE is not the only operating market; there are ancillary markets that provide trading facilities beyond what is available on the Exchange floor. This suggests that some needs are not well served by the process as it occurs on the Exchange. Examples of how the NYSE is augmented by other trading facilities include the support-

ing specialists (particularly on the regional exchange); the upstairs brokers . . . ; the third market, the fourth market, and crossing networks; and the informal floor accommodations. All of these structures are intended to accommodate trading. Without these facilities, the NYSE as it exists today probably could not exist.

Describe what is meant by each of the following terms: the upstairs brokers; the third market; the fourth market; crossing networks?

3. What is the function of the NYSE's SuperDOT?

4. What is meant by a fragmented market?

5. What are the two basic principles of the Securities Act of 1975?

6. a. What was the recommendation of the SEC *Market 2000* study regarding the regulation of electronic trading systems?

   b. What did this study recommend regarding off-exchange trading imposed by the NYSE (Rule 390)?

7. a. What is a program trade?

   b. What are the various types of commission arrangements for executing a program trade and the advantages and disadvantages of each?

8. What is the difference between a market-value weighted index and an equally weighted index?

9. a. What is the most popular market index followed by institutional investors?

   b. "The stocks selected for the S&P 500 are the largest 500 companies in the United States." Indicate whether you agree or disagree with this statement.

   c. Explain how the companies in the Russell indexes and the Wilshire indexes are determined.

10. The following excerpts are from an interview with William Donaldson, Chairman of the New York Stock Exchange, that appeared in *The New York Times* of January 30, 1990:

    Sure it's possible to beat the market...By investing for the long term with an individual selection of stocks, it's quite possible to beat the market.

    My concern is that by simply buying an index, investors are not channeling their capital into the best investments, and that has long-term negative implications for the cost of capital in this country. The risk of indexing and treating all companies the same is to give in to a very mediocre goal.

    a. What is meant by "beating the market"?

    b. What can you infer about Donaldson's views on pricing efficiency from his comments?

    c. Assuming he is correct, why do you think so few professional stock pickers have been able to "beat the market"?

11. Why should an investor who believes that the market is efficient pursue an indexing strategy?

12. In every issue of *The Wall Street Journal*, information appears on the performance (measured in terms of total return) for mutual funds with the same stated objective. The top 15 performers and the bottom 10 performers are shown. This information is called the "Mutual Fund Scorecard." In the Monday, February 4, 1991, issue, the following ranking was reported for several of the top performers based on the 12-month period ending January 31, 1991, for mutual funds with capital appreciation as their objective:

Fund	12-Month Total Return
Seligman Capital	20.77
M-S Mainstay: Cap. Appre.	20.11
Janus Twenty Fund	20.09
Piper Jaffray: Sector	19.64
ABT Inv: Emerging Growth	19.13

a. On the basis of the figures reported above, can you determine if these mutual funds beat the market?

b. Should the total return figures reported above be used to provide a relative performance ranking?

13. What is the major reason for the market crash of October 1987 (Black Monday)?

14. In recent years, the Japanese stock market has sometimes been ranked as the largest and sometimes as second in size to the market in the United States. What accounts for this fairly frequent change in the size rankings of the two markets?

15. Some stocks are listed on several exchanges around the world. Give three reasons why a firm might want its stock to be listed on an exchange in the firm's home country as well as on exchanges in other countries.

16. a. What is the key feature of a so-called "Euroequity issue"?

b. What is the most important innovation that Euroeqities have achieved?

c. What does it mean that a U.S. firm's new stock offering might contain a Euroequity "tranche"?

17. a. Often, a news report will survey the day's trading in Europe with a statement like this: "The Footsie 100 rose 1.5% today, while the DAX dropped 0.25% and the CAC 40 finished unchanged." What are the formal names of the indexes that the reporter is citing and to which country do they apply?

b. What is the most popular international equity price index that is comprised of most equity markets?

18. a. In general, the correlations between stock indexes in two countries are positively correlated. Why does this occur?

b. Are the correlations between stock indexes in two countries perfectly positively correlated—that is, do they have a correlation close to 1?

19. What empirical evidence supports the position that U.S. investors can "benefit" by expanding into non-U.S. stocks?

Stock Options Market

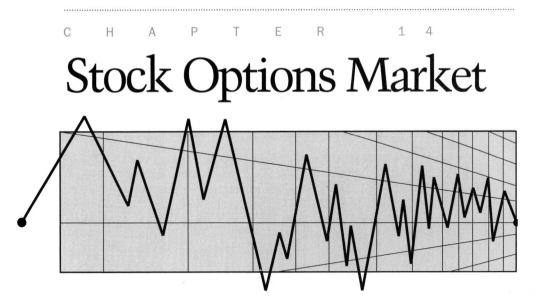

LEARNING OBJECTIVES

After reading this chapter you will understand:

- the basic features of stock options.

- how stock options can change the risk/return profile of a stock portfolio.

- the different stock option strategies that institutional investors use.

- the empirical evidence on whether there is a stock option strategy that consistently beats other strategies.

- the intuition behind the Black-Scholes option pricing model and its limitations.

- evidence on the pricing efficiency of the stock options market.

- what a warrant is.

Chapter 11 provided an introduction to options contracts. In this chapter, we will look at options on individual common stocks (or, simply, stock options). We will discuss strategies that institutional investors use, and we introduce a popular model used to determine the theoretical price of a stock option, the Black-Scholes option pricing model. We also discuss another stock option product, a warrant.

While the most important use of options is to alter return distributions to satisfy particular investment objectives, investors also have tried to use the options market to generate abnormal returns.[1] We review the evidence on stock option strategies, focusing on two critical empirical questions. First, is there (as often suggested in promotional literature) an option strategy that outperforms other option and stock strategies? Second, is the market for stock options efficient?

HISTORY OF EXCHANGE-TRADED OPTIONS

Options were traded only in the over-the-counter market until 1973, when the Securities and Exchange Commission authorized the establishment of a "pilot" program for the trading of options on organized exchanges. On February 1, 1973, the Chicago Board Options Exchange (CBOE) was granted permission by the SEC to register as a national securities exchange so that the CBOE could be used to "test the market" for the trading of listed options on common stock. CBOE began trading on call options on common stock in April 1973. Since then the SEC has granted permission to other exchanges to trade options: the American Stock Exchange in 1974, the Philadelphia Stock Exchange in 1975, the Pacific and the Midwest Stock Exchanges in 1976, and the New York Stock Exchange in 1982. SEC permission to trade put options on common stocks on organized exchanges was not granted until March 1977.

The SEC did not grant permission to trade options without extensive investigation. Public hearings were held in February of 1974 to address several questions concerning options: did they serve a useful economic role, are they in the public interest, and what impact would listed options have on the trading habits of the investing public. The evidence presented at the hearings supported the view that listed option trading would benefit the financial markets and the economy.

The SEC was concerned about the listing of options on the same common stock on more than one exchange, so it recommended that options terms and conditions be standardized, that a common clearing system be established, and that a common tape for recording transactions in listed options be developed. The SEC approved the creation of a national clearing system for options, the Options Clearing Corporation (OCC), established jointly at the time by the CBOE and the American Stock Exchange. Since its establishment in 1974, the OCC issues, guarantees, registers, clears, and settles all transactions involving listed options on all exchanges.

As the listed options market grew, evidence of manipulative practices and fraudulent and deceptive selling practices was found. In July 1977 the SEC imposed a moratorium on the listing of additional options until it could study the matter further. The *Options Study* began in October 1977 to "determine whether standardized options trading is occurring in a manner and in an environment which is consistent with fair and orderly markets, the public interest, the protection of investors, and other objectives of the Act."[2] The study

---

[1] Abnormal returns are defined in Chapter 13.

[2] Securities Exchange Act Release No. 14056 (October 17, 1977).

addresses what, if any, steps the SEC should take to protect investors from abusive practices. Among its key recommendations were procedures to improve market surveillance in order to detect manipulative practices and policies that the exchanges and brokerage firms should implement to improve the caliber of brokers selling options and prevent abusive selling practices. The SEC worked with several groups to implement its recommendations.

In March 1980, the SEC was satisfied that the major regulatory deficiency it cited in the *Options Study* had been adequately addressed, and it lifted the moratorium on expansion of the listed options markets and granted permission to list options on the other financial products discussed in Chapters 15, 28, and 30. While the ending of the moratorium did allow the four exchanges that were approved for trading options to list options on more companies, the SEC did not allow the multiple listing of options. That is, the SEC did not allow the listing of an option on the same underlying common stock on more than one exchange. Instead, the SEC worked out a mechanism for allocating options on stocks among the four exchanges. These rules on multiple listing were subsequently changed. Effective January 1990, any exchange could list any new stock and ten stocks from other exchanges. Effective January 1991, any exchange can list options on any stock eligible for option trading.

FEATURES OF EXCHANGE-TRADED STOCK OPTIONS

Exchange-traded stock options are for 100 shares of the designated common stock. While most underlying stocks are those of listed companies, stock options on a number of over-the-counter stocks are also available.

The Options Clearing Corporation has established standard strike price guidelines for listed options. For stocks with a price above $100, strike prices are set at $10 intervals; for stocks with a price below $100 and above $30, strike prices are set at $5 intervals; and for stocks priced between $10 and $30 the interval is $2.50. While the strike price is not changed because of cash dividends paid to common stockholders, for exchange-traded options the strike price is adjusted for stock splits, stock dividends, reorganization, and other recapitalizations.

All exchange-traded stock options in the United States may be exercised any time before the expiration date; that is, they are American options. They expire at 11:59 P.M. Eastern Standard Time on the Saturday following the third Friday of the expiration month. To exercise an expiring option, exchange rules provide that the owner of the option instruct his or her broker to do so no later than 5:30 P.M. Eastern time on the business day immediately preceding the expiration date. Notices to exercise a nonexpiring option (i.e., on a date other than the expiration date) must be made between 10 A.M. and 8:00 P.M. Eastern Standard Time. When a nonexpiring option is exercised, the OCC assigns it the next day to someone who has written the option; assignment is on a random basis.

Options are designated by the name of the underlying common stock, the expiration month, the strike price, and the type of option (put or call). Thus, an Exxon call option with a strike price of 60 and expiring in April is referred to as the "Exxon April 60 call."

The expirations dates are standardized. Each stock is assigned an option cycle—the three option cycles being January, February, and March. The expiration months for each option cycle are as follows:

Option cycle	Expiration months
January	January, April, July, October
February	February, May, August, November
March	March, June, September, December

In addition, the practice is to trade options with an expiration date of the current calendar month, the next calendar month, and the next two expiration months in the cycle. For example, suppose a stock is assigned the January option cycle. In February, options with the following expiration months would be traded: February (the current calendar month), March (the next calendar month), April (first next-expiration month in January option cycle), and July (second-next-option cycle month in January option cycle). In May the following expiration months would be traded for a stock assigned to the January option cycle: May (the current calendar month), April (the next calendar month), July (next first-expiration month in January option cycle), and October (second option-cycle-month in January option cycle).

Given that only the next two expiration months are traded, the longest time for an option on a stock is six months. There are exceptions. There are some stocks that have an expiration date up to three years in the future. These options are called **long-term equity anticipation securities**, commonly referred to as **LEAPS**. For example, IBM trades on the January option cycle. In February 1995, options with expiration dates of February 1995, March 1995, April 1995, and July 1995 were traded. In addition, there were put and call LEAPS with an expiration date of January 1997 traded.

STOCK OPTION PRICING MODELS

In the Chapter 11 introduction to option pricing, we explained the factors that influence the price of an option and that a lower boundary for the option price can be determined based only on arbitrage arguments. We also set forth the basic principle behind an option pricing model. Here we provide more detailed discussion of option pricing models.

Black-Scholes Option Pricing Model

Arbitrage conditions provide boundaries for option prices, but to identify investment opportunities and construct portfolios to satisfy their investment objectives, investors want an exact price for an option. By imposing certain assumptions (to be discussed later) and using arbitrage arguments, Black and Scholes developed the formula given below to compute the fair (or theoretical) price of a European call option on a nondividend-paying stock:[3]

---

[3] Fischer Black and Myron Scholes, "The Pricing of Options and Corporate Liabilities," *Journal of Political Economy* (May 1973), pp. 637-54.

$$C = S\ N(d_1) - X\ e^{-rt}\ N(d_2)$$

where

$$d_1 = \frac{ln\ (S/X\ ) + (r + 0.5\ s^2)\ t}{s\ \sqrt{t}}$$

$$d_2 = d_1 - s\sqrt{t}$$

C = call option price

S = current stock price

X = strike price

r = short-term risk-free interest rate over the life of the option

t = time remaining to the expiration date (measured as a fraction of one year)

s = standard deviation of the stock price

$N(.)$ = the cumulative probability density [the value for $N(.)$ is obtained from a normal distribution function that is tabulated in most statistics textbooks]

Notice that five of the factors that we said in Chapter 11 influence the price of an option are included in the formula. (The sixth factor, anticipated cash dividends, is not included because the model is for a nondividend-paying stock.) In the Black-Scholes model, the direction of the influence of each of these factors is the same as stated in Chapter 11. Four of the factors—strike price, stock price, time to expiration, and short-term risk-free interest rate—are easily observed. The standard deviation of the stock price must be estimated.

The option price derived from the Black-Scholes option pricing model is "fair" in the sense that if any other price existed, it would be possible to earn riskless arbitrage profits by taking an offsetting position in the underlying stock. That is, if the price of the call option in the market is higher than that derived from the Black-Scholes option pricing model, an investor could sell the call option and buy a certain number of shares in the underlying stock.[4] If the reverse is true, that is, the market price of the call option is less than the "fair" price derived from the model, the investor could buy the call option and sell short a certain number of shares in the underlying stock. This process of hedging by taking a position in the underlying stock allows the investor to lock in the riskless arbitrage profit. The number of shares necessary to hedge the position changes as the factors that affect the option price change, so the hedged position must be changed constantly.

Figures 14-1 and 14-2 provide illustrations to demonstrate calculation of the fair value of a call option using the Black-Scholes option pricing model. The two illustrations differ only in the assumption made about the volatility (variance) of the price of the underlying stock. Notice that with the higher

---

[4] The number of shares will not necessarily be equal to the number of shares underlying the call option. The reason is that the change in the value of the call price generally will be less than the change in the stock price. In the Black-Scholes model, the number of shares is given by the function $N(d_1)$.

Figure 14-1

First Illustration of Black-Scholes Option Pricing Model

Call option:

Strike price = $45

Time remaining to expiration = 183 days

Current stock price = $47

Expected price volatility = standard deviation = 25%

Short-term risk-free rate = 10%

Therefore:

$S = 47$

$X = 45$

$t = 0.5$ (183 days/365, rounded)

$s = 0.25$

$r = 0.10$

The call option price (C) is found as follows:

$$C = S \, N(d_1) - X \, e^{-rt} \, N(d_2)$$

$$d_1 = \frac{\ln (S/X) + (r + 0.5 \, s^2) \, t}{s \sqrt{t}}$$

Substituting:

$$d_1 = \frac{\ln (47/45) + (.10 + .5 \, [.25]^2) \, .5}{.25 \ \sqrt{.5}} = 0.61722$$

$$d_2 = d_1 - s \sqrt{t}$$

Substituting:

$$d_2 = .61722 - .25 \sqrt{.5} = .440443$$

From a normal distribution table:

$N(.6172) = .7315$ and $N(.4404) = .6702$

Then:

$$C = 47 \, (.7315) - 45 \, (e^{-(.10)(.5)}) \, (.6702) = \$ \, 5.69$$

assumed volatility, the price of the call option is greater. The higher the expected price volatility of the underlying stock price, the higher the price of a call option.

Table 14-1 shows the option value as calculated from the Black-Scholes option pricing model for different assumptions concerning (1) the standard deviation, (2) the risk-free rate, and (3) the time remaining to expiration. Notice that: (1) the lower (higher) the volatility, the lower (higher) the option price; (2) the lower (higher) the risk-free rate, the lower (higher) the option price; and (3) the shorter (longer) the time remaining to expiration, the lower (higher) the option price. All of this agrees with what we stated in Chapter 11 as to the effect of a change in one of the factors on the price of a call option.

We have been focusing our attention on call options. How do we value put options? Recall from Chapter 11 that the put-call parity relationship indicates

Figure 14-2
Second Illustration of Black-Scholes Option Pricing Model

Call option:
> Strike price = $45
> Time remaining to expiration = 183 days
> Current stock price = $47
> Expected price volatility = standard deviation = 40%
> Short-term risk-free rate = 10%

Therefore:
> $S = 47$
> $X = 45$
> $t = 0.5$ (183 days/365, rounded)
> $s = 0.40$
> $r = 0.10$

The call option price (C) is found as follows:

$$C = S\ N(d_1) - X\ e^{-rt}\ N(d_2)$$

$$d_1 = \frac{ln\ (S/X) + (r + 0.5\ s^2)\ t}{s\ \sqrt{t}}$$

Substituting:

$$d_1 = \frac{1n\ (47/45) + (.10 + .5\ [.40]^2)\ 0.5}{.40\ \sqrt{.5}} = 0.471941$$

$$d_2 = d_1 - s\ \sqrt{t}$$

Substituting:

$$d_2 = .471941 - .40\ \sqrt{.5} = .189098$$

From a normal distribution table:

$$N(.4719) = .6815 \text{ and } N(.1891) = .5750$$

Then:

$$C = 47\ (.6815) - 45\ (e^{-(.10)(.5)})\ (.5750) = \$7.42$$

the relationship among the price of the common stock, the call option price, and the put option price. If we can calculate the fair value of a call option, the fair value of a put with the same strike price and expiration on the same stock can be calculated from the put-call parity relationship.

Assumptions Underlying the Black-Scholes Model and Extensions

The Black-Scholes model is based on several restrictive assumptions. These assumptions were necessary to develop the hedge to realize riskless arbitrage profits if the market price of the call option deviates from the price obtained from the model. We shall look at these assumptions, along with extensions of the basic model.

Table 14-1

Comparison of Black-Scholes Call Option Price Varying One Factor at a Time

BASE CASE

Call option:

Strike price = $45

Time remaining to expiration = 183 days

Current stock price = $47

Expected price volatility = standard deviation = 25%

Short-term risk-free rate = 10%

HOLDING ALL FACTORS CONSTANT
EXCEPT EXPECTED PRICE VOLATILITY

Expected price Volatility	Call Option Price
15%	4.69
20	5.17
25 (base case)	5.69
30	6.26
35	6.84
40	7.42

HOLDING ALL FACTORS CONSTANT
EXCEPT THE SHORT-TERM RISK-FREE RATE

Risk-Free Interest Rate	Call Option Price
7%	5.27
8	5.41
9	5.50
10 (base case)	5.69
11	5.84
12	5.99
13	6.13

HOLDING ALL FACTORS CONSTANT
EXCEPT TIME REMAINING TO EXPIRATION

Time Remaining To Expiration	Call Option Price
30 days	2.85
60	3.52
91	4.15
183 (base case)	5.69
273	6.99

A European option—The Black-Scholes model assumes that the call option is a European call option. As the Black-Scholes model is based on a nondividend-paying stock, early exercise of an option will not be economic because by selling rather than exercising the call option, the option holder can recoup the option's time premium. The binomial option pricing model, also known as the Cox-Rubinstein-Ross model, can easily handle American call options.[5] (See Chapter 11 for the basic principle of this model.) The fair value of the option in the case of a binomial option pricing model cannot be given by a formula but requires an iterative process.

Variance of the stock price—The Black-Scholes model assumes two aspects regarding the variance of the stock price: that it is constant over the life of the option, and that it is known with certainty. If the first aspect does not hold, an option pricing model can be developed that allows the variance to change. Violation of the second aspect is more serious. As the Black-Scholes model depends on the riskless hedge argument, and, in turn, the variance must be known to construct the proper hedge, then if the variance is not known, the hedge will not be riskless.

Stochastic process generating stock prices—To derive an option pricing model, an assumption is needed about the way stock prices move. The Black-Scholes model is based on the assumption that stock prices are generated by one kind of stochastic (random) process called a **diffusion process**. In a diffusion process, the stock price can take on any positive value, but when it moves from one price to another, it must take on all values in between. That is, the stock price does not jump from one stock price to another, skipping over interim prices. An alternative assumption is that stock prices follow a **jump process**; that is, prices are not continuous and smooth but do jump from one price across intervening values to the next. Merton[6] and Cox and Ross[7] have developed option pricing models assuming a jump process, which is more realistic.

Short-term risk-free interest rate—In deriving the Black-Scholes model two assumptions were made about the short-term risk-free interest rate. First, it was assumed that the interest rates for borrowing and lending were the same. Second, it was assumed that the interest rate was constant and known over the life of the option. The first assumption is unlikely to hold because borrowing rates are higher than lending rates. The effect on the Black-Scholes model is that the option price will be bounded between the call price derived from the model using the two interest rates. The model can handle the second assumption by replacing the risk-free rate over the life of the option by the geometric average of the period returns expected over the life of the option.[8]

Dividends—The original Black-Scholes model is for a nondividend-paying stock. In the case of a dividend-paying stock, it may be advantageous for the holder of the call option to exercise the option early. To understand why,

---

[5] John C. Cox, Stephen A. Ross, and Mark Rubinstein, "Option Pricing: A Simplified Approach," *Journal of Financial Economics* 7 (1979), pp. 229-63.

[6] Robert Merton, "The Theory of Rational Option Pricing," *Bell Journal of Economics and Management Science* 4 (Spring 1973), pp. 141-83.

[7] John C. Cox and Stephen A. Ross, "The Valuation of Options for Alternative Stochastic Processes," *Journal of Financial Economics* 3 (March 1976), pp. 145-66.

[8] Returns on short-term Treasury bills cannot be known with certainty over the *long* term; only the *expected* return is known, and there is a variance around it. The effects of variable interest rates are considered in Merton, "The Theory of Rational Option Pricing."

suppose that a stock pays a dividend such that, if the call option is exercised, dividends would be received prior to the option's expiration date. If the dividends plus the accrued interest earned from investing the dividends from the time they are received until the expiration date are greater than the time premium of the option, then it would be optimal to exercise the option.[9] In the case where dividends are not known with certainty, it will not be possible to develop a model using the riskless arbitrage argument.

In the case of known dividends, a shortcut to adjust the Black-Scholes model is to reduce the stock price by the present value of the dividends. Black has suggested an approximation technique to value a call option for a dividend-paying stock.[10] A more accurate model for pricing call options in the case of known dividends has been developed by Roll,[11] Geske,[12] and Whaley.[13]

Taxes and transactions costs—The Black-Scholes model ignores taxes and transactions costs. The model can be modified to account for taxes, but the problem is that there is not one unique tax rate. Transactions costs include both commissions and the bid-ask spreads for the stock and the option, as well as other costs associated with trading options.

OPTION STRATEGIES

There are numerous strategies involving options that have been employed by investors. Below we discuss two types: naked strategies and covered (hedge) strategies. We then present evidence as to whether there is a superior option strategy.

Naked Strategies

There are four basic option strategies: (1) long call strategy (buying call options), (2) short call strategy (selling or writing call options), (3) long put strategy (buying put options), and (4) short put strategy (selling or writing put options). We illustrated the risk-reward characteristics of these four strategies in Chapter 11; they are usually referred to as "positions." By themselves these positions are called **naked strategies** because they do not involve an offsetting or risk-reducing position in either another option or the underlying common stock.

The profit and loss from each strategy depends on the price of the underlying asset, in our case common stock, at the expiration date (on the assump-

---

[9] Recall from Chapter 11 that the time premium is the excess of the option price over its intrinsic value.

[10] See Fischer Black, "Fact and Fantasy in the Use of Options," *Financial Analysts Journal* (July-August 1975), pp. 36-41, 61-72. The approach requires that the investor at the time of purchase of the call option and for every subsequent period specify the exact date the option will be exercised.

[11] Richard Roll, "An Analytic Formula for Unprotected American Call Options on Stocks with Known Dividends," *Journal of Financial Economics* (November 1977), pp. 251-8.

[12] Robert Geske, "A Note on an Analytical Formula for Unprotected American Call Options on Stocks with Known Dividends," *Journal of Financial Economics* (December 1979), pp. 375-80, and Robert Geske, "Comment on Whaley's Note," *Journal of Financial Economics* (June 1981), pp. 213-5.

[13] Robert Whaley, "On the Valuation of American Call Options on Stocks with Known Dividends," *Journal of Financial Economics* (June 1981), pp. 207-11.

tion that the option is not exercised or sold earlier). The most that the option buyer can lose with each strategy is the option price. At the same time, the option buyer preserves the benefits of a favorable price movement of the underlying asset (a price increase for a call option and a price decline for a put option) reduced by the option price. By contrast, the maximum profit that the option writer can realize is the option price, while remaining exposed to all the risks associated with an unfavorable price movement.

The long call strategy (buying call options) is the most straightforward option strategy for taking advantage of an anticipated increase in the stock price, while at the same time limiting the maximum loss to the option price. The speculative appeal of call options is that they provide an investor with the opportunity to capture the price action of more shares of common stock for a given number of dollars available for investment. An investor who believes that the price of some common stock will decrease or change very little can, if the expectation is correct, realize income by writing (selling) a call option (following a short call strategy). The profit and loss of the option writer is the mirror image of the option buyer's.

The most straightforward option strategy for benefiting from an expected decrease in the price of some common stock, while avoiding the unfavorable consequences should the price rise, is to follow a long put strategy (buying put options). The short put strategy (selling put options) is employed if the investor expects that the price of a stock will increase or stay the same. The maximum profit from this strategy is the option price. The maximum loss for the short put strategy will occur if the price of the stock declines to zero at or before the expiration date.

Individual investors and institutional investors use at least two other naked option strategies: (1) the long call/paper buying strategy, and (2) the cash-secured put writing strategy.

Long call/paper buying strategy—This naked strategy involves allocating a portion of a portfolio's funds to purchase a call option and investing the balance of the funds in a risk-free or low-risk money market instrument[14] such as Treasury bills or commercial paper.[15] This strategy is less risky than allocating all the portfolio's funds to stocks. The long call option allows the investor to participate in any stock price increase. The funds invested in the risk-free or low-risk money market instrument provide a cushion against any stock price decline.

Cash-secured put writing strategy—If an investor wants to purchase a stock at a price less than the prevailing market price, one way is to place a limit buy order—of course, the result may be that the order never gets placed.[16] Alternatively, the investor can use the options market to accomplish effectively the same thing: write a put option with a strike price near the desired price. Sufficient funds are then placed in escrow to satisfy the investor's obligation if the buyer of the put option exercises the option.

---

[14] Money market instruments are the subject of Chapter 19.

[15] While this strategy involves investing in some risk-free or low-risk money market instrument, it does not involve a long or short position in the stock. For this reason, it is still classified as a naked option strategy.

[16] Limit buy orders are explained in Chapter 13.

Covered (Hedge) Strategies

In contrast to naked option strategies, **covered** or **hedge strategies** involve a position in an option and a position in the underlying stock. The aim is for one position to help offset any unfavorable price movement in the other position. The two popular covered or hedge strategies that we discuss, and for which we give empirical evidence later in this chapter, are: (1) the covered call writing strategy, and (2) the protective put buying strategy.

Covered call writing strategy—A **covered call writing strategy** involves writing a call option on stocks in the portfolio. That is, the investor takes a short position in a call option and a long position in the underlying stock. If the price of the stock declines, there will be a loss on the long stock position. However, the income generated from the sale of the call option will either (1) fully offset, (2) partially offset, or (3) more than offset the loss in the long stock position so as to generate a profit.

To illustrate, suppose that a money manager holds 100 shares of XYZ Corporation and that the current price of a share is $100. The total value of the portfolio is $10,000. Also suppose that a call option on 100 shares of XYZ with a $100 a strike price that expires in three months can be sold for $700. (The option is at the money because the strike price is equal to the current price of the stock.) If the money manager has decided to hold the 100 shares and write one call option (each call option is for 100 shares of the underlying stock), the profit or loss for this strategy will depend on the price of XYZ stock at the expiration date. One of the following five outcomes will occur.

1. If the price of XYZ stock is greater than $100, the call option buyer will exercise the option and pay the option writer $100 per share. The 100 shares in the portfolio are exchanged for $10,000. The value of the portfolio at the expiration date is then $10,700 ($10,000 received from the option buyer exercising the option plus $700 received from writing the call option). In fact, more than $10,700 will be in the portfolio if the $700 is invested when it is received. At a minimum, though, the profit from this strategy if the price of XYZ stock is greater than $100 is $700, the option price. If the price of XYZ stock rises above $107, however, there will also be an opportunity loss equal to the excess of the value of the stock over $10,700.

2. If the price of XYZ stock is equal to $100 at the expiration date, the call option buyer will not exercise the option. The value of the portfolio will still be at least $10,700: 100 shares of XYZ with a market value of $100 per share and the proceeds of $700 received from writing the call option.

3. If the price of XYZ stock is less than $100 but greater than $93, there will be a profit but it will be less than $700. For example, suppose that the price of the stock is $96; the long stock position will have a value of $9,600 while the short call position will have a value of $700. The portfolio value is therefore $10,300, resulting in a profit of $300.

4. At a price of $93, the long stock position will have a value of $9,300 and the short call position will have a value of $700, resulting in no profit or loss, as the portfolio value is $10,000.

5. Should the price of XYZ stock be less than $93 at expiration, the portfolio will realize a loss. For example, suppose that the price of the stock at expiration is $88. The portfolio value will be $9,500: the long stock position will be worth $8,800 and the short call position will have produced $700. Hence, there is a loss of $500. The worst case is if the price of XYZ stock declines to zero. This would result in a portfolio value of $700 and a loss of $9,300.

The profit and loss profile for this covered call writing strategy is graphically portrayed in Figure 14-3. There are two important points to note in this illustration. First, this strategy has allowed the investor to reduce the downside risk for the portfolio. In this example, for the at-the-money call option, the risk is reduced by an amount equal to the option price. In exchange for this reduction of downside risk, the investor has agreed to cap the potential profit. For the at-the-money option used in our illustration, the maximum profit is the option price.

The second point can be seen by comparing Figure 11-4 with Figure 14-3. Notice that the shape of the two profit and loss profiles is the same. That is, the covered call writing strategy has the same profit and loss profile as a naked short put strategy. Indeed, in our example, the covered call writing strategy has the same profit and loss outcome as writing a put on 100 shares of XYZ stock with a strike price of $100 and three months to expiration (provided the price of the call and put options are the same). This is not an accident. As we explained in Chapter 11, portfolios with equivalent payoffs can be constructed with different positions in options and the underlying instrument. A covered call writing position is equivalent to a long position in the stock and a short

Figure 14-3
Profit/Loss Profile for a Covered Call Writing Strategy

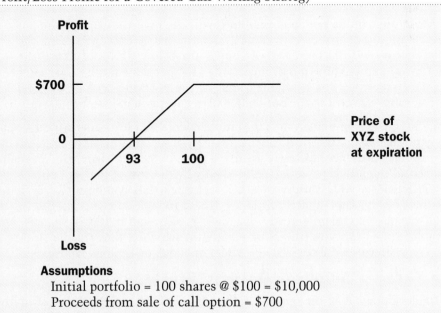

Assumptions
Initial portfolio = 100 shares @ $100 = $10,000
Proceeds from sale of call option = $700

call position, and a long position in a stock and a short position in a call will have a similar payoff to a short put position.

Protective put buying strategy—An investor may want to protect the value of a stock held in the portfolio against the risk of a decline in market value. A way of doing this with options is to buy a put option on that stock. By doing so, the investor is guaranteed the strike price of the put option less the cost of the option. Should the stock price rise rather than decline, the investor is able to participate in the price increase, with the profit reduced by the cost of the option. This strategy is called a **protective put buying strategy**; it involves a long put position (buying a put option) and a long position in the underlying stock that is held in the portfolio.

As an illustration, suppose that a money manager has 100 shares of XYZ stock in a portfolio and that the current market value of the stock is $100 per share (a portfolio value of $10,000). Assume further that a two-month put option selling for $500 can be purchased on 100 shares of XYZ stock with a strike price of $100. Two months from now at the expiration date the profit or loss can be summarized as follows:

1. If the price of XYZ stock is greater than $105, the investor will realize a profit from this strategy. For example, if the price is $112, the long stock position will have a value of $11,200. The cost of purchasing the put option was $500, so the value of the portfolio is $10,700, for a profit of $700.

2. If the price of XYZ stock is equal to $105, no profit or loss will be realized from this strategy.

3. There will be a loss if the price of XYZ stock is less than $105 but at least $100. For example, a price of $102 will result in a loss for this strategy of $300: a gain in the long stock position of $200 but a loss of $500 to acquire the long put position.

4. In none of the previous outcomes will the investor exercise the put option, but if the price of XYZ stock is below $100 per share, the option will be exercised. At any price below $100 per share, the investor will be assured of receiving $100 per share for the 100 shares of stock. In this case, the value of the portfolio will be $10,000 minus the cost of the option ($500), resulting in a loss of $500.

The graphical presentation of the profit and loss profile for this protective put buying strategy is shown in Figure 14-4. By implementing this strategy, the money manager has effectively assured a price of $95 per share. He has maintained all the upside potential, reduced only by the cost of the put option.

There are a wide variety of other strategies that combine two or more options on the same underlying stock. These include spread strategies (vertical spreads, horizontal spreads, diagonal spreads, and butterfly spreads) and combination strategies (the most popular of which is the straddle strategy). These strategies are discussed elsewhere in books on options strategies.

Is There a Superior Options Strategy?

The development of the options market brought with it a number of myths about strategies that were alleged to generate consistently superior returns

Figure 14-4
Profit/Loss Profile for a Protective Put Buying Strategy

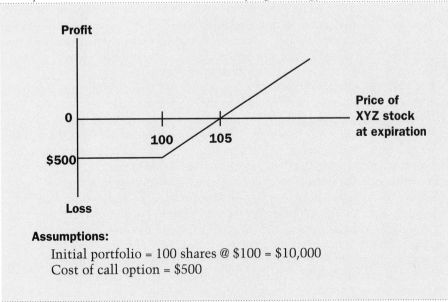

Assumptions:
  Initial portfolio = 100 shares @ $100 = $10,000
  Cost of call option = $500

over purchasing stocks. For example, the popular literature and advertising by the options industry has recommended that individual and institutional investors follow a covered call strategy that could be expected to generate "extra return" from the income received by selling (writing) a call option on stocks held in their portfolio. The proliferation of this popular literature and misleading advertisements led Fischer Black to write: "For every fact about options, there is a fantasy—a reason given for trading or not trading in options that doesn't make sense when examined carefully."[17]

Is there indeed an options strategy that has consistently outperformed a simple strategy of buying common stocks? Here we will examine the empirical evidence on this issue.

Call option strategies—There have been several studies that have empirically examined whether there are call option strategies that might provide superior risk-adjusted returns. The first major study was by Merton, Scholes, and Gladstein (MSG hereafter).[18] Using simulation analysis, they examined the risk and return patterns of the covered call writing and long call/paper buying strategies discussed earlier.[19] These strategies are examined not for a single stock option position but for portfolios of option positions.

The simulation analysis they performed is based on two samples of underlying stocks: (1) the 136 stocks on which listed options were available as of December 1975, and (2) the 30 stocks included in the Dow Jones Industrial Average (DJIA). The time period over which the simulations were performed was

---

[17] Black, "Fact and Fantasy in the Use of Options," p. 36.

[18] Robert C. Merton, Myron S. Scholes, and Matthew L. Gladstein, "The Return and Risk of Alternative Call Option Portfolio Investment Strategies," *Journal of Business* 51, no. 2 (1978), pp. 183-43.

[19] For a critique of the simulation approach and an alternative approach to testing performance of various option strategies, see Gary L. Gastineau, *The Options Manual* (New York: McGraw-Hill, 1988, Third Edition).

July 1, 1963, through December 31, 1975, an interval of 12.5 years. This time interval encompassed a variety of market environments (bull and bear markets, high and low volatility). The simulations were performed using six-month holding periods. For the two call option strategies investigated, the option prices used in the simulations were calculated from the Black-Scholes model adjusted for dividends. That is, the prices are theoretical prices not actual (observed) prices.[20] Transactions costs and taxes were ignored in all simulations.

The findings do not support the claims of those who preach that a covered call strategy can generate "extra return" for investors. As for the long call/paper buying strategy, there are instances where this strategy clearly outperformed the long stock strategy, as the average return was higher and the risk was lower. Consequently, for the period investigated and according to the assumptions employed, the MSG study suggests that it may have been possible to earn superior returns from a long call/paper buying strategy.[21]

While there have been no other comprehensive studies of the long call/paper buying strategy, there have been other studies of covered call writing strategies because this is the strategy most widely used by institutional investors. Henry Pounds studied the eight-year period from 1969 to 1976 for a sample of 43 stocks with listed call options.[22] Theoretical rather than actual prices again are used, but in this study commissions are considered.

Pounds finds that at-the-money and in-the-money covered call option strategies outperformed the long stock position.[23] Does this mean that a covered call strategy is superior to a long stock strategy? As Pounds points out, it is not possible to make this inference because the market did not rise during his study period. Consequently, a flat or declining market would favor a covered call writing strategy. When he investigated subperiods when the market increased within his eight-year study period, he found that the long stock portfolio outperformed all the covered call option strategies.

Is there a superior covered call option strategy according to Pounds's results? He argues that the out-of-the-money covered call strategy gives the best results and the in-the-money covered call strategy the worst results because there is a substantial reduction in risk. While this may be true for the entire period, for subperiods writing out-of-the-money call options resulted in better performance only when stock prices did not rise. Otherwise, the in-the-money covered call writing strategy performed better.

Yates and Kopprasch also investigated the covered call writing strategy, using actual call option prices for the July 1973-July 1980 period.[24] They constructed an index, Institutional Option Writers Index (IOWI), that institutions could use to measure their option-writing performance. The underlying port-

---

[20] For part of their study, MSG use actual rather than theoretical prices; results did not differ significantly.

[21] MSG do suggest several possible explanations for the superior performance of the long call/paper buying strategy.

[22] Henry M. Pounds, "Covered Call Options Writing: Strategies and Results," *Journal of Portfolio Management* (Winter 1978), pp. 31-42.

[23] The average return was greater and the standard deviation lower. The out-of-the-money call option had a slightly lower average return but a substantially lower standard deviation.

[24] James W. Yates and Robert W. Kopprasch, "Writing Covered Call Options: Profits and Risks," *Journal of Portfolio Management* (Fall 1978), pp. 74-9.

folio for the index was constructed by using all stocks with listed CBOE call options in the January, April, July, and October expiration cycle. Commissions were not considered.

The results of this study lend support to the position that the covered call writing strategy would have outperformed the S&P 500 and the underlying portfolio over the entire time period. While it is expected that the covered call strategy would have outperformed the long stock strategies during down markets, results indicate that the IOWI also performed well in up markets. These results, as well as others reported by Yates and Kopprasch, are at variance with those of MSG and Pounds.

Put option strategies—In a follow-up study to their call option strategies, Merton, Scholes, and Gladstein investigate the risk/return patterns of two put option strategies: (1) uncovered (or "naked") put option writing, and (2) protective put option buying strategies.[25] The simulation period for the second study was the 14-year period from July 1, 1963, through June 30, 1977. The same two stock samples used in their previous study were investigated. As theory would predict, they found that: (1) compared to the fully covered call writing strategy, the uncovered put writing is more conservative; and (2) both option strategies are more conservative than a long stock position. The average return for all the option strategies they report was less than that of the long stock position.

The second put option strategy simulated by MSG was the protective put strategy. In the case of protective put strategies, the standard deviation and range of returns were lower than for the long stock position. The higher the exercise price for the put option, the lower the volatility. The reduction in risk comes at the expense of a lower average return.

Summary of findings—With the exception of the Yates and Kopprasch study, none of the studies cited indicates that there is a superior option strategy. The empirical evidence suggests that option strategies have investment characteristics that are consistent with the familiar trade-off between risk and return: the higher the expected return, the more the expected risk as measured by return volatility. The relative risk characteristics of the strategies described by the simulations are consistent with those that would be expected from the risk/return characteristics of the portfolio. This view is best summarized by MSG in their conclusion to the first study:

> *The specific levels of the returns generated, however, are strongly dependent on the actual experience of the underlying stocks during the simulation period. To avoid the creation of new myths about option strategies, the reader is warned not to infer from our findings that any one of the strategies is superior to the others for all investors. Indeed, if options and their underlying stocks are correctly priced, then there is no single best strategy for investors.[26]*

The last sentence is particularly noteworthy. In a market that prices options fairly, there should be no options strategy that is superior. We turn next to the question of whether options are fairly priced.

[25] Robert C. Merton, Myron S. Scholes, and Matthew L. Gladstein, "The Return and Risk of Alternative Put Option Portfolio Investment Strategies," *Journal of Business* 55, no. 1 (1982), pp. 1-55.

[26] Merton, Scholes, and Gladstein, "The Return and Risk of Alternative Call Option Portfolio Investment Strategies," p. 184.

PRICING EFFICIENCY OF THE STOCK OPTIONS MARKET

A market is said to be efficient if investors cannot earn abnormal returns after accounting for risk and transactions costs. In Chapter 13 we discussed the problems associated with testing for the pricing efficiency of the stock market. Here we focus on tests of the pricing efficiency of the market for stock options.

A problem encountered by researchers in this area is that tests require information on the price of two instruments at the exact same time—the stock price and the option price. When prices are available on both assets at the same time, the data are said to be synchronous. In empirical tests, prices used may be nonsynchronous because of data availability limitations. That is, the stock price used in a study may be the closing price for the day, while the option price may be the price at the beginning of the same trading day. An empirical study that finds abnormal trading profits using nonsynchronous data does not necessarily indicate that the options market is inefficient.

Beyond the problem of nonsynchronous data, there is the problem of determining the fair price of an option to be used in the empirical tests. Thus, researchers must rely on some option pricing model, which makes the findings only as good as the option pricing model employed.

Tests of market efficiency fall into two categories. The first category is tests using no option pricing model. Instead, violations of boundary conditions or violations of put-call parity are examined to determine if abnormal trading profits are possible. The second set of tests employ various option pricing models to assess whether mispriced options can be identified and exploited using the riskless hedge strategy.

Tests Not Based on an Option Pricing Model

Boundary conditions for the price of an option can be determined. Violations of boundary conditions may permit an investor to earn abnormal profits. Also, there is a relationship between put and call prices that must hold. Violations of the put-call parity relationship may permit an investor to earn a return in excess of the riskless interest rate.

There are two studies that have examined pricing efficiency in the U.S. stock options market using boundary conditions for call option prices. A finding that a boundary condition is violated is not sufficient to argue that the market is inefficient. It is also necessary to test whether profits can be generated from trading strategies based on any violations.

The first is a study by Dan Galai based on daily closing prices of options traded on the Chicago Board Options Exchange between April and October 1973, the first six months of the operation of this exchange.[27] The empirical test was for the lower boundary for a call option of a dividend-paying stock. Galai does find violations of the lower boundary condition. Arbitrage trading based on these violations could have generated small profits. A study by Mihtu Bhattacharya using transactions data for options traded on the CBOE

---

[27] Dan Galai, "Tests of Market Efficiency and the Chicago Board Options Exchange," *Journal of Business* 50 (1970), pp 167-97.

finds that, when transactions costs are accounted for, profits resulting from arbitrage trading when boundary violations occurred disappear.[28]

If the put-call parity relationship is violated, it is possible for investors to create a riskless hedge to produce a return in excess of the riskless interest rate. There have been two studies of market efficiency based on violations of the put-call parity relationship for *listed* options.[29]

Klemkosky and Resnick examined 606 riskless hedges for 15 companies having both put and call options listed on the Chicago Board Options Exchange, American Stock Exchange, and Philadelphia Stock Exchange between July 1977 and June 1978.[30] Of the 606 hedges examined, 540 were riskless hedges in that conditions were such that there would be no rational early exercise of the call option. Of these riskless hedges, 306 were unprofitable *ex post,* while 234 where profitable *ex post.* After considering transactions costs of $20 for a member firm to obtain a round lot position in a hedge, only 147 turned out profitable. The authors conclude: "The empirical results of the models tests are consistent with put-call parity theory and thus support this aspect of efficiency for the registered options markets. The small degree of inefficiency detected appears to be the result of overpriced calls."[31]

In a follow-up study, Klemkosky and Resnick further investigate the hedges that produced profitable returns.[32] Specifically, they constructed hedges 5 and 15 minutes after a hedge was initially identified as having an *ex ante* return greater than $20. The purpose was to test the relationship on an *ex ante* basis by employing the *ex post* results as information from which to construct the hedge. They find that (1) *ex ante* profitability was less than the *ex post* profitability, and (2) the prices adjust rapidly enough to eliminate most if not all of the abnormal profit.

Tests Based on Option Pricing Models

Tests of market efficiency based on an option pricing model involve two steps. First, a model is used to identify under- or overvalued options. There are two approaches to identifying a mispriced option. Rather than computing a theoretical option price for comparison to the market price, an implied volatility can be calculated. How is this done? Recall from our discussion of the factors that determine the price of an option that, with the exception of expected price volatility, the other factors are known, and of course the market price of the option can be observed. The volatility consistent with the observations and the option pricing model can be calculated. This is called the **implied volatility.** The other approach to identifying a mispriced option calls for comparing the implied volatility to the historical volatility. An option is assumed

---

[28] Mihtu Bhattacharya, "Transactions Data Tests of Efficiency of the Chicago Board Options Exchange," *Journal of Financial Economics* 12 (August 1983), pp. 161-5.

[29] There have been two studies on over-the-counter options investigating put-call parity: Hans Stoll, "The Relationship between Put and Call Option Prices," *Journal of Finance* (December 1969), pp. 801-24; and J. Gould and Dan Galai, "Transactions Costs and the Relationship between Put and Call Prices," *Journal of Financial Economics* (July 1974), pp. 105-30.

[30] Robert C. Klemkosky and Bruce G. Resnick, "Put-Call Parity and Market Efficiency," *Journal of Finance* (December 1979), pp. 1141-55.

[31] Klemkosky and Resnick, ibid., p. 1154.

[32] Robert C. Klemkosky and Bruce G. Resnick, "An Ex Ante Analysis of Put-Call Parity," *Journal of Financial Economics,* 8 (1980), pp. 363-78.

to be overvalued (undervalued) if the implied volatility is greater (less) than historical volatility (assuming true volatility is constant).

The second step is to create a hedged position to exploit any option that is identified as mispriced and determine if it is sufficiently mispriced to produce a return greater than the risk-free rate. (Remember that the position created is a hedged portfolio, which means its return should be a risk-free rate.)

The first study examining market efficiency using an option pricing model is that performed by Black and Scholes.[33] Using the option pricing model they developed, they could not reject the hypothesis that the market is efficient. Galai, however, did detect evidence of market inefficiency.[34] Stronger evidence of market inefficiency was found by Trippi,[35] and Chiras and Manaster,[36] using implied volatility. Both studies found there were trading strategies that could produce abnormally high returns.

A criticism of the Trippi and Chiras and Manaster studies is that these researchers failed to take transactions costs into consideration. In the options market, transactions costs include: (1) floor trading and clearing costs, (2) any state transfer tax that might be imposed, (3) SEC transactions fee, (4) margin requirements, (5) net capital charges, and (6) bid-ask spreads. The magnitude of these costs needs to be considered in empirical studies that investigate market efficiency. These costs vary for market makers, arbitrageurs, and individuals in the options markets, so the market may be efficient for one type of market participant but not another.

Phillips and Smith have examined these transactions costs and then adjusted the Trippi and Chiras and Manaster studies to account for them.[37] After making the adjustment, they find that abnormally high returns were eliminated. Thus, the hypothesis that the option market is efficient is supported.

Finally, Blomeyer and Klemkosky used transaction-by-transaction option and price data (thereby overcoming the problem of nonsynchronous data) and two option pricing models to calculate implied volatility to test the efficiency of the market.[38] Unlike Trippi and Chiras and Manaster, Blomeyer and Klemkosky considered transactions costs as suggested by Phillips and Smith. In the absence of transactions costs, they found abnormal returns; after considering transactions costs, abnormal returns were eliminated.

All these empirical studies are based on either historical volatility or implied volatility. An investor who consistently does a better job of estimating volatility than other market participants can realize abnormal returns in the option markets.

WARRANTS

A **warrant** is a contract that gives the holder of the warrant the right but not the obligation to buy a designated number of shares of a stock at a specified

---

[33] Fischer Black and Myron Scholes, "The Valuation of Option Contracts and a Test Market Efficiency," *Journal of Finance* (May 1972), pp. 399-417.

[34] Dan Galai, "Empirical Tests of Boundary Conditions for CBOE Options," *Journal of Financial Economics* 6 (1978), pp. 187-211.

[35] Robert Trippi, "A Test of Option Market Efficiency Using a Random-Walk Valuation Model," *Journal of Economics and Business* 29 (1977), pp. 93-8.

[36] Donald Chiras and Steven Manaster, "The Information Content of Option Prices and a Test of Market Efficiency," *Journal of Financial Economics* 6 (1978) pp. 213-34.

[37] Susan M. Phillips and Clifford W. Smith, "Trading Costs for Listed Options: Implications for Market Efficiency," *Journal of Financial Economics* 8 (1980), pp. 179-201.

[38] Edward C. Blomeyer and Robert C. Klemkosky, "Tests of Market Efficiency for American Call Options," in Menachem Brenner (ed.) *Option Pricing* (Lexington, MA: D.C. Heath, 1983), pp. 101-21.

price before a set date. Consequently, a warrant is nothing more than a call option. As a warrant can be exercised at any time up to and including the expiration date of the warrant, it is an American call option.

There are several differences between the exchange-traded call options on common stocks that we have described in this chapter and warrants, however. First, the expiration date for an exchange-traded call option is much shorter than that for a warrant at the time of issuance. There are some warrants, for example, that have no expiration date; these are called perpetual warrants. Second, and most important, the issuer of a warrant is the company itself. That is, unlike exchange-traded options, which allow entities other than the issuer of the common stock to write a call option, the option writer in the case of a warrant is the company itself. Consequently, when a warrant is exercised, the number of shares of stock outstanding will increase accordingly. This will tend to result in a dilution of earnings. The fact that the exercise of a warrant dilutes earnings means that a model used to price warrants must take this into account. There are several warrant pricing models that do just that.[39]

When initially issued, a warrant is part of another type of security. Warrants are typically attached to a bond or preferred stock. Usually warrants may be detached from the host security that they were attached to and then be traded separately. There are warrants that trade in all the trading locations described in the previous chapter: the major national exchanges, regional exchanges, and the over-the-counter market.

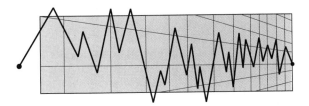

SUMMARY

Stock options permit investors to mold the shape of the return distribution to meet investment objectives better. Among the strategies that institutional investors use to control portfolio risk are basic naked option strategies, covered call writing, and protective put buying. The empirical evidence reviewed in this chapter suggests that there is no options strategy that dominates any other.

In 1973, Black and Scholes introduced a model that could be used to price a European call option on a nondividend-paying stock. Subsequent researchers have modified and extended the Black-Scholes model.

The empirical evidence on the pricing efficiency of the stock options market suggests that, after considering transactions costs, the market appears to be efficient. An investor who wishes to use this market should do so for its

---

[39] See George M. Constantides, "Warrant Exercise and Bond Conversion," *Journal of Financial Economics* (September 1984), pp. 371-98; David C. Emanuel, "Warrant Valuation and Exercise Strategy," *Journal of Financial Economics* (August 1983), pp. 211-35; Dan Galai and Meir Schneller, "The Pricing of Warrants and the Value of the Firm," *Journal of Finance* (December 1978), pp. 1333-42; and Eduardo S. Schwartz, "The Valuation of Warrants: Implementing a New Approach," *Journal of Financial Economics* (January 1977), pp. 79-93.

original purpose: to shape return distributions so that they are more consistent with investment objectives. It does seem, however, that astute investors can earn abnormal returns in an efficient market if they can predict volatility better than the market can.

Warrants are effectively long-term call options where the writer of the option is the company itself. The pricing of a warrant must take into consideration the potential dilution effect on earnings.

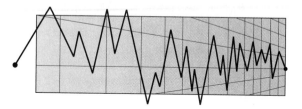

QUESTIONS

1. How many shares does an exchange-traded option involve?

2. What does the "IBM February 65 put" mean?

3. What is a LEAP?

4. "The option price depends on the volatility of the underlying stock. Since capital market theory asserts that the appropriate measure of volatility is a stock's beta, then the option price should depend on the stock's beta." Explain why you agree or disagree with this statement.

5. a. Assuming the values below for a European call option, calculate the theoretical option price using the Black-Scholes model.
   Strike price = $100
   Current stock price = $100
   Dividend = $0
   Short-term risk-free rate = 8%
   Expected price volatility = 20%
   Time to expiration = 91 days

   b. What is the intrinsic value and time premium for this call option?

6. For the call option in the previous question, what would be the theo-retical option price, intrinsic value, and time premium if:

   a. The current stock price is $55 instead of $100?

   b. The current stock price is $150 instead of $100?

7. a. Explain why it would not be economic for the buyer of an American call option on a non-dividend-paying stock to exercise the option prior to the expiration date?

   b. Is this true for an American call option on a dividend-paying stock? Under what circumstances (if any) would early exercise be economic?

   c. Would it be economic for the buyer of an American put option to exercise the option early? (Hint: Think about what happens if the price of the stock falls to zero before the expiration date.)

8. What is the difference between a naked strategy and a covered strategy?

9. What naked strategy or strategies would an investor pursue if she thought that a stock's price was going to rise?

10. What is the general conclusion of empirical studies that have investigated whether a superior option strategy exists?

11. Comment on the following statement: "Investors should pay closer attention to the options markets since option strategies offer risk and reward opportunities that are clearly superior to investing directly in common stock."

12. Suppose an investor wants to follow a protective put buying strategy for a stock she owns that has a market price of $60. She is told that there are three 180-day put options available on that stock with strike prices of $56, $58, and $60.

    a. Which put option will give her the greatest price protection?

    b. Which put option will be the most expensive?

    c. Which put option should be selected?

13. You are meeting with a pension plan sponsor who has asked you for advice on several investment policy guidelines that it has formulated for its money managers. One of the guidelines involves the use of options for hedging:

    Protective put buying and covered call writing strategies are recognized by the investment community as means for hedging a stock position. The former will not be permitted by any of our fund managers because it involves a cost that may not be recouped if the put option is not exercised. We will permit covered call writing because there is no cost generated to protect the portfolio.

    What advice would you give the plan sponsor concerning this investment policy guideline?

14. The quote following is from the June 22, 1992 issue of *Derivatives Week*, p. 4:

    Aetna Investment Management, the London-based fund management arm of U.S. insurer Aetna Life & Casualty, expects to start using derivatives within weeks in more than £200 million of U.K. equity holdings, according to Tom Chellew, director. The firm has not used derivatives before in its total of £700 million under management in the U.K.

    Aetna is talking to trustees over the next two weeks and expects to get approval to start dealing thereafter, he said. Initially, it will only use derivatives in its more than £200 million of U.K. holdings in its £250 million of unit trusts under management.

    Chellew said initial strategies are likely to include writing covered calls and writing puts on stock Aetna doesn't mind buying. The firm will likely be interested in both U.K. index and individual stock options.

    Subsequently, Aetna expects to expand use into other holdings—specifically, equity and later possibly fixed income—and into pension and life insurance money under management, he said. Aetna will use derivatives to enhance yields and for risk reduction, and will trade futures for asset allocation.

What does Mr. Chellew mean by "writing puts on stock Aetna doesn't mind buying"?

15. The following was overheard at a party:

   You have to be foolish not to sell a call option on stock you own. You don't really lose anything because if the stock is called, you own it and just have to give it up. In return, you receive fee income that you get to keep no matter what the buyer of the call option does. This is a no-lose proposition in my opinion.

   a. What type of strategy is this person suggesting?

   b. Is this view of call options correct?

16. The following is from an article entitled "Analytic Uses Options to Protect Tenneco Position," that appeared in the November 16, 1992 issue of *Derivatives Week*, p. 7:

   Analytic Investment Management in Irvine, Ca., last Monday sold 70 Nov. 40 puts and bought 70 Feb. 35 puts on Tenneco for its Analytic Optioned Equity Fund—a derivatives-driven mutual fund, according to Chuck Dobson, the fund's executive v.p. By selling and buying an equal number of exchange-traded puts, the firm maintained a fully-hedged position while using profits on its

options to counterbalance paper losses on the 7,000 Tenneco shares it owns for a net gain of 1-7/8 per option, Dobson said.

Though Dobson could not give the price at which the stock was bought, he noted that since Tenneco was trading around $35 last Monday, the 7,000 shares were worth roughly $245,000, or about 0.27% of the total $91 million portfolio. Dobson explained that the firm takes a non-directional approach to picking stock, relying instead on the stock's volatility, option premium and dividends.

Dobson explained that the fund, which contains 130-140 mostly high capitalization stocks, is governed by four basic derivatives-linked strategies: 1) buy a stock and sell a call on the stock; 2) buy a stock and a put on the stock; 3) sell a put and place the exercise price in a cash reserve fund and 4) buy a call and place the exercise price in a money market fund.

   a. Explain the option strategy cited in the first paragraph of this excerpt. Be sure to explain what Mr. Dobson meant by the "firm maintained a fully-hedged position."

   b. Explain the first two strategies listed in the third paragraph.

17. What is the difference between a stock option and a stock warrant?

18. Explain why you agree or disagree with the following statement: "As a warrant is nothing more than a European call option, the

Black-Scholes option pricing model can be used to value it."

19. Two option-type products that were issued in the market are "Primes" and "Scores." Primes and Scores separate the cash flow components of certain stocks into two components: dividend income and capital appreciation. Specifically, a Prime entitles the holder of the security to receive (1) the dividends of the underlying stock, and (2) the market value of the stock at a specified future date up to a preset amount, called the "termination value." The term Prime stands for "prescribed right to income." A Score entitles the instrument holder to all the appreciation above the termination value. Usually, the termination value is 20% to 25% above the current stock price. The term "Score" stands for "special claim on residual income."

There were 25 trusts issued and all matured some time in 1992.

Primes and Scores on individual stocks are not issued originally as securities. Instead, a trust is created in which the stock of a specific company is placed. The trust then issues a Prime and a Score for each share of stock placed in the trust. The trust has a maturity of five years, with its size restricted to no more than 5% of the total number of shares of the outstanding stock of the company. At the end of five years, the trust is terminated, and the Prime and Score holders receive the agreed-upon amount. Before the termination .date, the Prime and Score created are traded separately on the American Stock Exchange. At any time during a trading day, a combi-

nation of one unit of a Prime and one unit of a Score may be redeemed from the trust for one share of the underlying stock. There is no charge for the redemption.

While probably no new Primes and Scores will be created in the future because of adverse tax circumstances, it is still interesting to examine these instruments in order to understand that there are instruments that have option features even though they are not labeled options.

a. Explain why the Score has the payoff profile of a call option.

b. Explain why the Prime has the payoff profile of a covered call option.

c. In an efficient market, a package of a Prime and a Score should sell for the same price as the underlying stock after adjusting for transactions costs. However, in a study on the pricing of Primes and Scores, one study found that they were mispriced relative to the underlying stock (Robert A. Jarrow and Maureen O'Hara, "Primes and Scores: An Essay on Market Imperfections," *Journal of Finance* (December 1989), pp. 1263-87). More specifically, they found that a package of Primes and Scores often exceeded the price of the underlying stock by a considerable amount. They explain the discrepancy as arising from market imperfections with respect to short-selling and transactions costs. Explain why these two factors could cause the discrepancy.

Stock Index Derivative Markets

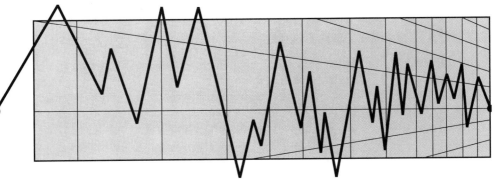

LEARNING OBJECTIVES

After reading this chapter you will understand:

- the investment features of stock index options and futures.

- institutional strategies that employ stock index options and futures.

- why stock index futures prices may diverge from their theoretical price based on a simple cost-of-carry model.

- the empirical evidence on the pricing efficiency of the stock index options and futures market.

- the role of stock index options and futures in the financial market.

- how alternative options and outperformance options can be used by money managers.

- what an equity swap is and its potential applications.

- the role, if any, that these contracts may have played in the stock market crash of October 19, 1987.

In Chapter 14 we covered options on individual stocks. In this chapter we will discuss equity index derivatives. These include stock index options, stock index futures, and equity swaps. The underlying instrument for these contracts is a stock index.

For each contract, we discuss (1) its basic characteristics, (2) how it can be employed by institutional investors, and (3) empirical evidence on market efficiency. As we have reviewed the pricing of futures and options in previous chapters, our focus here will be on the pricing nuances associated with index derivative products. We also look at the empirical evidence on the role of stock index futures and options in the U.S. financial market and the role these contracts played in the October 19, 1987, stock market crash.

STOCK INDEX OPTIONS

In March 1983, trading in an option whose underlying instrument was a stock index, the S&P 100 (originally called the CBOE 100), began on the Chicago Board Options Exchange. It was followed by options trading on the American Stock Exchange on an index designed by that exchange called the Major Market Index (MMI).[1] As in the case of options on individual stocks, stock index options are regulated by the Securities and Exchange Commission.

Basic Features of Stock Index Options

Table 15-1 lists the major stock index options currently traded in the United States and the key features common to all of these contracts. The most successful stock index futures contract has been the S&P 100 contract traded on the Chicago Board Options Exchange.

In addition to the contracts shown in Table 15-1, which are based on broad-based indexes, there are options traded on narrow-based indexes. These include the Pharmaceutical Index and the Biotech Index traded on the AMEX, and the Utilities Index traded on the Philadelphia Stock Exchange. There are also options on non-U.S. stock indexes traded on U.S. stock exchanges. Table 15-2 lists all the stock index options traded on U.S. stock exchanges as of February 1995.

The level of trading volume for each contract differs. A useful statistic measuring the liquidity of a contract is the number of contracts that have been entered into but not yet liquidated. This figure is called the contract's **Open interest**. An open interest figure is reported for all listed contracts. For example, on February 16, 1995 the open interest for the call and put options on the S&P 100 index was 566,041 contracts and 832,635 contracts, respectively; in contrast, open interest on the S&P Bank Index was 612 contracts for the call options and 2,298 contracts for the put options.

Unlike stock options, where a stock can be delivered if the option is exercised, it would be extremely complicated to settle a stock index option by delivering all the stocks that comprise the index. Instead, stock index options are **cash settlement contracts**. This means that if the option is exercised, the option writer pays cash to the option buyer. There is no delivery of any stock.

---

[1] The index includes 20 stocks and was constructed to be similar to the Dow Jones Industrial Average.

The dollar value of the stock index underlying an option is equal to the current cash index value multiplied by $100. The $100 is referred to as the **multiple** for the contract. That is,

Dollar value of the underlying stock index = Cash index value × $100

For example, if the cash index value for the S&P 100 is 420, then the dollar value of the S&P 100 contract is: 420 × $100 = $42,000.

A one-point movement in the index value, say, from 420 to 421, is therefore equal to $100.

For an option on an individual stock, the price at which the buyer of the option can buy or sell the stock is the strike price. For an option on a stock index, the **strike index** is the index value at which the buyer of the option can buy or sell the underlying stock index. The strike index is converted into a dollar value by multiplying the strike index by the multiple for the contract. For example, if the strike index is 410, the dollar value is $41,000 (410 × $100). If an investor purchases a call option on the S&P 100 with a strike index of 410, and exercises the option when the index value is 420, then the investor has the right to purchase the index for $41,000 when the market value of the index is $42,000. The buyer of the call option would then receive $1,000 from the option writer.

The price that the investor who wants to buy a stock index option must pay is found by multiplying the quoted option price by $100. For example, if the quoted option price is 4¼, then the dollar price is $425 (4.25 × $100).

As can be seen from Table 15-1, exercise provisions for stock index options come in both the American and European variety. Institutional investors find writing European options attractive because they need not fear that the option they write in order to accomplish an investment objective will be exercised early.

There are also options on stock index futures; however, these options are not as widely used as options on stock indexes. Options on futures contracts are the contracts of choice in the interest rate options market. We will postpone our discussion of options on futures until Chapter 28.

Pricing Efficiency of the Stock Index Options Markets

Empirical tests of the pricing of index options are subject to the same problems as stock options discussed in Chapter 14. Moreover, there is the added problem of estimating the amount and timing of dividends for the stocks in the index.

Two studies have examined the pricing efficiency of the stock index options market. Evnine and Rudd looked at the S&P 100 and Major Market Index (MMI) options.[2] Their data base consisted of prices from a real-time pricing service for the period between June 26 and August 30, 1984. For each trading day prices for every hour were included, for a total of 1,798 observations. For every hour, the information in the data base contained essentially the same information that would be displayed on screens on the exchange

---

[2] Jeremy Evnine and Andrew Rudd, "Index Options: The Early Evidence," *Journal of Finance* (July 1985), pp. 743-56.

Table 15-1

Summary of Major Stock Index Option Contracts Traded in the U.S. (as of January 1993)

Contract	Exchange	Exercise Provision	Delivery Months
S&P 100 Index (OEX)	CBOE	American	Nearest 4 months
S&P 500 Index (SPX)	CBOE	European	Nearest 3 months + next month in Mar. cycle
S&P 500 Index (NSX)	CBOE	European	Mar., June, Sept., Dec.
NYSE Index (NYA)	NYSE	American	Nearest 3 months
Major Market Index (XMI)	AMEX	American	Nearest 3 months
Value Line Index (VLE)	Phil.	European	Nearest 3 months

- The contract size is the futures price × the multiple. The multiple for each contract is $100.
- All contracts settle in cash.
- The expiration day is the Saturday after the third Friday of the expiration month. For the S&P 500 NSX it is at the open.
- The minimum price change is ⅛ of a point ($12.50) for option prices greater than $3; and 1/16 of a point ($6.25) for option prices less than $3.

Table 15-2

Stock Index Options Traded in the U.S. (as of February 1995)

Chicago Board Options Exchange
S&P 100 Index (OEX)
S&P 500 Index (SPX)
Russell 2000 Index (RUT)
NASDAQ 100 (NDX)
S&P Bank Index (BIX)
CB Mexico Index (MEX)

American Stock Exchange
Institutional Index (XII)
Major Market Index (XMI)
S&P Midcap Index (MID)
Biotech Index (TBK)
MS Consumer Index (CMR)
MS Cyclical Index (CYC)
Pharmaceutical Index (DRG)
Hong Kong Index (HKO)
AM Mexico Index (MXY)
Japan Index (JPN)

New York Stock Exchange
New York Stock Exchange Index (NYA)

Continued on next page

Table 15-2 *Continued from previous page*

Philadelphia Stock Exchange
Value Line Index (VLE)
Big Cap Index (MKT)
OTC Index (XOC)
Phlx KBW Bank Index (BKX)
Utility Index (UTY)

floor. There was still the problem that the last option trade recorded for the hour was not synchronized with the last value recorded for the index. The index option prices included bid-ask prices, so part of the cost of transacting was considered in the analysis.

Don Chance investigated the S&P 100 index options for the period January 3 through April 27, 1984, using a data base supplied by a regional brokerage and investment banking firm.[3] The final daily bid and ask quotes and their update times were included in his data base. The prices were market makers' quotes as the market closed and the final index level. As the prices are quotes rather than the closing transaction price, the problem of nonsynchronicity of the option and the index is not present. While there are problems in updating both the option quotes and the index, Chance argues that all quotes reflect transactions that could have been executed.

As we explained in Chapter 11, arbitrage arguments can be used to put a lower boundary on the price of a call option. Evnine and Rudd tested for violations of the lower boundary; that is, instances where the ask price of the call was below the difference between the value of the cash index and the strike price. They found 30 instances when the lower boundary for the call option on the S&P 100 was violated, 11 instances for the MMI. Evnine and Rudd report occasions when the size of the violation became so large that even "upstairs traders" would have been capable of taking advantage of these violations.[4]

A possible explanation for the large size of these violations, as Evnine and Rudd note, is that during the week when these violations were observed (August 1 to August 6), there was a dramatic rise in the market. Consequently, the value of the cash index was being updated faster than the bid-ask prices, possibly causing the observed violations.

Both Evnine and Rudd and Chance tested for violations of the put-call parity relationship. The Evnine and Rudd results suggest that if stock index options are treated as European, significant profit opportunities are possible. The violations suggest that the S&P 100 index call options were underpriced (which means that the puts were overpriced). The reverse is true for the MMI options. Even if the options are considered American options, these results suggest that there were profit opportunities. When Chance tested the put-call parity relationship, he found a significant number of violations in the 1,690 portfolios examined.

---

[3] Don M. Chance, "Parity Tests of Index Options," *Advances in Futures and Options Research* 2 (1987), pp. 47-64.

[4] As explained in Chapter 13, block trades (trades of 10,000 shares or more) typically are negotiated between traders and institutional investors using a network that links them together. This market is referred to as the upstairs market.

Why do we observe these violations? The reason is more than likely attributable to the difficulty of arbitraging between the index option market and the cash market. Two problems in arbitraging are: the difficulty and expense of creating a portfolio to replicate the performance of the cash market index, and estimating dividends for the stocks in the index. We shall elaborate on this when we discuss stock index futures later in this chapter.

Portfolio Strategies with Stock Index Options

In Chapter 14, we explained how stock options can be used to take advantage of the anticipated price movement of individual stocks. Alternatively, they can be used to protect current or anticipated positions in individual stocks. For example, an investor can protect against a decline in the price of a stock held in her portfolio by buying a put option on that stock. By doing so, the investor is guaranteed a minimum price equal to the strike price minus the option price. Also, if an investor anticipates buying a stock in the future but fears that the stock price will rise making it more expensive to buy the stock, she can buy a call option on the stock. By pursuing this strategy, the investor has guaranteed that the maximum price that will be paid in the future is the strike price plus the option price.

Consider an institutional investor that holds a portfolio consisting of a large number of stock issues. To protect against an adverse price movement, the institutional investor would have to buy a put option on every stock issue in the portfolio, which would be quite costly. By taking an appropriate position in a suitable stock index option, an institutional investor with a diversified portfolio can protect against adverse price movements.[5] For example, suppose that an institutional investor holding a diversified portfolio of common stock that is highly correlated with the S&P 100 is concerned that the stock market will decline in value over the next three months. Suppose that a three-month put option on the S&P 100 is available. Because the put option buyer gains when the price of the underlying stock index declines, if an institutional investor purchases this put option (i.e., follows a protective put buying strategy) rather than liquidating the portfolio, adverse movements in the value of the portfolio due to a decline in the stock market will be offset (in whole or in part) by the gain in the put option.

When stock options or stock index options are used to protect an existing or anticipated position, the investor need not exercise the option if there is a favorable price movement. This is an important characteristic of options compared to futures in attempting to protect a position. An institutional investor can obtain downside protection using options at a cost equal to the option price, but preserve upside potential (reduced by the option price).

Exotic Options

In Chapter 11 we discussed exotic options. These are complex OTC options created by dealer firms for their clients. The two options described in Chapter 11 were alternative options and outperformance options.

---

[5] The appropriate number of stock index options to buy depends on the beta of the portfolio with respect to the underlying stock. The procedure for calculating the appropriate position in a stock index option is beyond the scope of this chapter.

An alternative option gives a money manager the opportunity to obtain the best performing of either two asset classes in the same market (e.g., U.S. common stock and U.S. Treasury bonds), or the same asset class in two different markets (e.g., U.S. common stock and Japanese common stock). The money manager need not pick the better-performing asset class. The payoff of an alternative option at the expiration date is equal to the notional amount times the positive percentage change from the strike of the better-performing of the two assets. For example, suppose that an alternative call option is based on the performance of the S&P 500 and the Japanese Nikkei 225 stock average. The terms might be as follows:

1. the option expires in one year.
2. the notional amount is $10 million.
3. the strike for the S&P 500 is 410.
4. the strike for the Nikkei 225 is 17860.

Suppose at the expiration date the S&P 500 is 480 and the Nikkei 225 is 18500. Ignoring dividends for purposes of this illustration, the return on the S&P 500 and Nikkei 225 is 17.07% and 3.58%, respectively. The better-performing of the two stock indexes is the S&P 500. The payoff is the return of the S&P 500 of 17.07% times the notional amount of $10 million, or $170,070. The profit or loss from this alternative option is found by subtracting the option cost from the $170,070.

An outperformance option gives a manager the opportunity to benefit from expectations of the relative performance of either two asset classes in the same market, or the same asset class in two different markets. The manager must select the asset class or market that is expected to perform better. The payoff at the expiration date is the notional amount multiplied by the difference in performance of the two asset classes. If the difference is negative, there is no payoff. For example, suppose that an outperformance call option is based on the relative performance of the S&P 500 and the Japanese Nikkei 225 stock average. The money manager believes the S&P 500 will outperform the Nikkei 225. The terms of an outperformance option might be as follows:

1. the option expires in one year.
2. the notional amount is $10 million.
3. the strike is the difference between the S&P 500 and the Nikkei 225.

Suppose at the expiration date the return on the S&P 500 and Nikkei 225 is 17.07% and 3.58%, respectively. The difference in the two returns is 13.49% (17.07% minus 3.58%). Since the difference is positive, the payoff is 13.49% times the notional amount of $10 million, or $134,900. The profit or loss from this outperformance option is found by subtracting the option cost from the $134,900.

Index Warrants

In Chapter 11 we described warrants on common stock. There has been an explosion in warrants on stock indexes. These warrants are called **index warrants.** As with a stock index option, the buyer of an index warrant can purchase the underlying stock index. Index warrants are issued by either corporate or sovereign entities as part of a security offering, and they are guaranteed by an option clearing corporation.

STOCK INDEX FUTURES MARKET

Chapter 10 covers the fundamental characteristics of futures contracts. A futures contract is a firm legal agreement between a buyer and an established exchange or its clearinghouse in which the buyer agrees to take delivery of something at a specified price at a designated time (called the settlement date). On the other side of the contract is a seller who agrees to deliver the "something." A stock index futures contract is a futures contract where the underlying "something" is a stock index.

In 1982, three futures contracts on broad-based common stock indexes made their debut: the S&P 500 futures contract traded on the International Monetary Market of the Chicago Mercantile Exchange, the NYSE Composite futures contract traded on the New York Futures Exchange, and the Value Line Average traded on the Kansas City Board of Trade. Since then broad-based and specialized stock index futures contracts have been introduced. Table 15-3 lists the stock index futures contracts traded in the United States. The most actively traded contract is the S&P 500 futures contract. There are no contracts on individual stocks. Table 15-4 lists the countries with stock index futures as of January 1993 and indicates those approved for trading by U.S. investors.

Stock index futures contracts are regulated by the Commodity Futures Trading Commission (CFTC), although in recent years there have been proposals to shift regulatory authority to the SEC or to combine the SEC and CFTC.

Table 15-3
Stock Index Futures Contracts Traded in the U.S. (as of February 1995)

Contract	Multiple	Exchange
S&P 500 Index	$500	CME
S&P Midcap 400	$500	CME
Major Market Index	$500	CME
NYSE Composite Index	$500	NYSE
KC Value Line Index	$500	KC
Russell 2000 Index	$500	CME
Nikkei 225 Stock Average	$ 5	CME
EuroTop 100 Index	$100	CMX

Exchange symbols:
CME = Chicago Mercantile Exchange
NYSE = New York Stock Exchange
KC   = Kansas City Board of Trade
CMX = COMEX (Division of the New York Mercantile Exchange)

Table 15-4

Countries with Stock Index Futures Contracts (as of January 1993)

Country	Approved for use by U.S. investors
Australia	yes
Canada	yes
Denmark	no
France	yes
Germany	no
Hong Kong	no
Japan	yes
Netherlands	no
New Zealand	no
Spain	no
Sweden	no
Switzerland	no
United Kingdom	yes

Table 15-5 shows the estimated round-trip transaction costs (commissions, market impact cost, and taxes) as a percentage of the amount invested for five countries. As can be seen, transaction costs are less for stock index futures than in the cash market. The largest cost differential is in the United States.

Like the commissions on common stock transactions, the commissions on stock index futures trades are fully negotiable. The commissions charged on stock index futures contracts are based on a round trip (i.e., they cover buying and selling the contract). For individual investors, the commissions range from $40 to $100 per contract at a full-service brokerage firm. For institutional investors, the typical commission per contract is less than $15. The cost of transacting is typically less than 0.1% (0.001) of the contract value. A round-trip commission for a portfolio consisting of the underlying stocks would be roughly 1% of the value of the stocks.

Basic Features of Stock Index Futures

The dollar value of a stock index futures contract is the product of the futures price and the contract's **multiple**. The multiple is indicated in Table 15-3. The dollar value of a stock index futures contract is then:

Dollar value of a stock index futures contract = Futures price × Multiple

For the major U.S. stock index futures contracts, the multiple is $500. To illustrate, if the futures price for the S&P 500 is 400, the dollar value of the stock index futures contract is: 400 × $500 = $200,000. If an investor buys an

Table 15-5

Estimated Round-Trip Transaction Costs as a Percentage of Amount Invested for Stocks and Stock Index Futures*

Stocks

	U.S.	Japan	Country** U.K.	France	Germany
Commissions	0.20%	0.30%	0.10%	0.20%	0.20%
Market impact cost***	0.57	1.00	0.90	0.80	0.60
Taxes	0.00	0.30	0.50	0.00	0.00
Total	0.77%	1.60%	1.50%	1.00%	0.80%

Futures****

	U.S.	Japan	Country U.K.	France	Germany
Commissions	0.01%	0.11%	0.03%	0.03%	0.03%
Market impact cost***	0.10	0.30	0.40	0.40	0.30
Taxes	0.00	0.00	0.00	0.00	0.00
Total	0.11%	0.41%	0.43%	0.43%	0.33%

* Assumes a $25 million portfolio; does not include settlement and custody fees.

** Local index: S&P 500, Nikkei 225, FT-SE 100, CAC-40, DAX

*** Trader estimate

**** All contracts are quarterly except for the CAC-40

Source: **Structured International Investment,** *Goldman Sachs & Co., June 1992, p. 22.*

S&P 500 futures contract at 400 and sells it at 420, the investor realizes a profit of 20 times $500, or $10,000. If the futures contract is sold instead for 350, the investor will realize a loss of 50 times $500, or $25,000.

As in the case of stock index options, stock index futures contracts are cash settlement contracts. This means that at the settlement date, cash will be exchanged to settle the contract. For example, suppose an investor buys an S&P 500 futures contract at 400 and the futures settlement price is 420. Settlement would be as follows. The investor has agreed to buy the S&P 500 for 400 times $500, or $200,000. The S&P 500 value at the settlement date is 420 times $500, or $210,000. The seller of this futures contract must pay the investor $10,000 ($210,000 – $200,000). Had the futures price at the settlement date been 390 instead of 420, the dollar value of the S&P 500 futures contract would be $195,000 (390 × $500). The investor must pay the seller of the contract $5,000 ($200,000 – $195,000).

The minimum price fluctuation or "tick" for all stock index futures contracts is .05. The dollar value of a tick is found by multiplying .05 by the contract's multiple. For stock index futures contracts with a multiple of $500, the dollar value of a tick is $25 (.05 × $500).

As we explained in Chapter 10, there are margin requirements (initial, maintenance, and variation) for futures contracts. Margin requirements are revised periodically. The exchanges classify users of contracts as speculators or hedgers, with the margin for the former being less than that for the latter.[6] The S&P 500 futures contract initial requirement is $22,000 per contract. If the futures price for the contract is 400, the dollar value of the contract is $200,000. The initial margin is therefore about 11% of the contract value and the maintenance margin is 4%. For a speculator who purchases stock on margin, however, the initial margin requirement is 50% of the stock position, and the maintenance margin requirement is 25%.

An Illustration of Margin Requirements

As explained in Chapter 10, futures positions are marked to market at the end of each trading day. An illustration will demonstrate the mechanics of margin requirements and the mark-to-market procedure.[7] First we will give the particulars of the illustration.

1. A hedger purchases 193 S&P 500 futures contracts on April 14, 1988. The actual closing settlement price for the contract on that day was 259.

2. The closing settlement prices for the nine trading days following April 14, 1988, are shown in the second column of Table 15-6.

3. The initial and maintenance margin requirements at that time were $10,000 per contract for hedgers.

The dollar value of each S&P 500 futures contract when the settlement index was 259 was $129,500. As the hedger purchased 193 contracts, the total dollar value of the contracts was $24,993,500. The third column of Table 15-6 shows the dollar value for each of the nine trading days following April 14, 1988. The initial margin requirement is $1,930,000 for the 193 contracts; maintenance margin is $1,930,000 for the 193 contracts. The last column in Table 15-6 shows the variation margin for the nine trading days following April 14, 1988. A negative number (i.e., a number in parentheses) means that there will be a margin call; a positive number means that funds can be withdrawn.

On Day 1, the hedger must put up initial margin of $1,930,000, which may be in the form of a Treasury bill. Once the equity in the account falls below the maintenance margin (which in the case of a hedger is the same as the initial margin of $1,930,000), additional margin (variation margin) will be required. This must be in cash (Treasury bills are not acceptable to satisfy variation margin) and must be supplied in 24 hours.

On Day 2 of our illustration, the settlement price falls to 258.60, reducing the value of the 193 contracts to $24,954,900. The decrease in the contract value is subtracted from the equity in the account. This is what is meant by

---

[6] As explained later in this chapter, investors commonly use stock index futures to hedge a position. The clearinghouse requires less margin for investors who are using contracts for this purpose.

[7] This illustration is taken from Bruce M. Collins and Frank J. Fabozzi, "Mechanics of Trading Stock Index Futures," Chapter 5 in Frank J. Fabozzi and Gregory M. Kipnis (eds.), *The Handbook of Stock Index Futures and Options* (Homewood, IL: Dow Jones-Irwin, 1989).

Table 15-6

Illustration of Margin Requirements and Marking to Market

Day 1 is August 14, 1988
Initial margin per S&P 500 contract = $10,000*
Initial margin for 193 S&P 500 contracts = $1,930,000 (193 × $10,000)
Maintenance margin per S&P 500 contract = $10,000*
Maintenance margin for 193 S&P 500 contracts = $1,930,000

Day	Settlement Price	Value For 193 Contracts	Equity In Account	Variation Margin
1	259.00	$24,993,500	$1,930,000	—
2	258.60	24,954,900	1,891,400	$(38,600)
3	259.25	25,017,625	1,992,725	62,725
4	257.30	24,829,450	1,804,550	(188,175)
5	257.90	24,887,350	1,987,900	57,900
6	256.20	24,723,300	1,823,850	(164,050)
7	261.85	25,268,525	2,475,225	545,225
8	263.85	25,461,525	2,668,225	193,000
9	264.80	24,553,200	2,759,900	91,675
10	264.00	25,476,000	2,682,700	(77,200)

* Margin requirements at the time.

marking to market. The equity therefore declines to $1,891,400. As the equity on Day 2 is below the maintenance margin of $1,930,000, there will be a margin call of $38,600 ($1,930,000 minus $1,891,400).

When the equity in the account exceeds the maintenance margin, the hedger can withdraw the excess. On Day 3, for example, the settlement price for the index was 259.25, increasing the value of the contracts to $25,017,625. The resulting equity in the account was $1,992,725, which is $62,725 greater than the maintenance margin requirement. The hedger can withdraw the $62,725.

This example surely shows that anyone using the stock index futures market to pursue some strategy must have sufficient funds to satisfy margin calls.

Pricing of Stock Index Futures

In Chapter 10 we demonstrated that arbitrage arguments can be used to determine the theoretical futures price. In the case of stock index futures, we need the following information:

1. the value of the cash (spot) market index.
2. the dividend yield on the stocks in the index that would be earned until the settlement date.
3. the interest rate for borrowing and lending until the settlement date. (The borrowing and lending rate is referred to as the financing cost.)

The theoretical futures price that will prevent arbitrage profits can be shown to be equal to:

Futures price = Cash market price
+ Cash market price (Financing cost – Dividend yield)

where "Financing cost" is the cost of financing a position until the settlement date of the futures contract, and "Dividend yield" is the dividends over the same period. Moreover, it is assumed that dividends are received only at the settlement date. The difference between the financing cost and the dividend yield is called the **net financing cost** because it adjusts the financing cost for the yield earned. The net financing cost is more commonly called the cost of carry or, simply, carry. *Positive* carry means that the yield earned is greater than the financing cost; *negative* carry means that the financing cost exceeds the yield earned.

This equation for the theoretical futures price indicates that it may sell at a premium to the cash market price (higher than the cash market price) or at a discount from the cash market price (lower than the cash market price), depending on the financing cost and the dividend yield.

Recall from Chapter 10 that to derive the theoretical futures price using the arbitrage argument, also called the cost of carry model, several assumptions must be made. When these assumptions do not hold, there will be a divergence between the actual futures price and the theoretical futures price. We discussed several of these assumptions for futures contracts in general in Chapter 10. Here we highlight the six assumptions that are unique to stock index futures.

1. No interim cash flows from dividend payments are assumed in the futures pricing model. We know that interim cash flows do occur, and incorporating interim dividend payments into the futures pricing model is not difficult. The problem is that the value of the dividend payments at the settlement date will depend on the interest rate at which the dividend payments can be reinvested. The lower the dividend and the closer the dividend payments to the settlement date of the futures contract, the less important the reinvestment income is in determining the futures price.

2. In determining the cost of carry, both the financing cost and the dividend yield must be known. While the financing cost may be known, the dividend rate and the pattern of dividend payments are not known with certainty. They must be projected from the historical dividend payments of firms in the index.

3. For the arbitrage to work when the futures price is below its theoretical value, the investor must be able to use the proceeds from selling the cash index short. In practice, for individual investors, the proceeds are not received, and, in fact, the individual investor is required to put up margin (securities margin, not futures margin) to short-sell. For institutional investors, the securities may be borrowed, but there is a cost to borrowing them.

4. In the case of a short sale of the stocks in the index, all stocks must be sold simultaneously. The stock exchange rule for the short-selling of stock may prevent the arbitrage strategy from bringing the actual futures price in line with the theoretical futures price. The

short-selling rule for stocks specifies that a short sale can be made only at a price that is higher than the previous trade (referred to as an up-tick), or at a price that is equal to the previous trade but higher than the last trade at a different price (referred to as a zero-tick). If the arbitrage requires selling the stocks in the index simultaneously, and the last transaction for some of the stocks is not an up-tick, the stocks cannot be shorted simultaneously.

5. Another difficulty in arbitraging the cash and futures market is that it is too expensive to buy or sell every stock included in the index. Instead, a portfolio containing a smaller number of stocks may be constructed to "track" the index. The arbitrage, however, is no longer risk-free because we have introduced the risk that the portfolio will not track the index exactly. This is referred to as **tracking-error risk**.

6. The basic arbitrage model ignores not only taxes but also the differences between the tax treatment of cash market transactions and futures transactions.

Violation of the assumptions made in developing the cost of carry pricing model means that there will be discrepancies between the actual price and the theoretical futures price from a simple cost-of-carry model. Basically, there will be boundaries around which the futures price can trade that will not permit arbitrage profits. Researchers have derived upper and lower bounds for the theoretical futures prices that take into consideration several of the factors discussed above.[8]

Pricing Efficiency of the Stock Index Futures Market

Using theoretical futures prices and their bounds, several studies have examined the pricing efficiency of the stock index futures market. The first study to examine this issue empirically was by Cornell and French.[9] In this study they compare actual futures prices to theoretical futures prices for the S&P 500 futures contract and the NYSE futures contract on the first days of trading of June, July, August, and September 1982. In all but two of the cases they examine, the theoretical (predicted) futures price was higher than the actual futures price. The discrepancy they find was attributable to the difference in the tax treatment of futures and cash market transactions.

After deriving upper and lower bounds for the theoretical futures price, Modest and Sundaresan examine the June 1982 S&P futures contract from April 21 to June 16, 1982, and the December 1982 S&P 500 futures contracts from April 21, to September 15, 1982, to determine if the actual futures prices were outside the bounds.[10] Recall from our discussion of the theoretical futures price that the futures pricing model assumes that short-sellers have the

---

[8] David M. Modest and Mahadevan Sundaresan, "The Relationship between Spot and Futures Prices in Stock Index Futures: Some Preliminary Evidence," *Journal of Futures Markets* (Spring 1983), pp. 15-42.

[9] Bradford Cornell and Kenneth R. French, "Taxes and the Pricing of Stock Index Futures," *Journal of Finance* (June 1983), pp. 675-94.

[10] Modest and Sundaresan, "The Relationship between Spot and Futures Prices in Stock Index Futures: Some Preliminary Evidence."

use of the proceeds from selling the cash index short. Three sets of theoretical bounds are tested by Modest and Sundaresan assuming: (1) no use of the proceeds by short-sellers, (2) use of half the proceeds by short-sellers, and (3) use of all the proceeds by short-sellers. Recall also that the theoretical futures price is dependent on the expected dividend yield. Modest and Sundaresan construct theoretical bounds with and without adjusting for dividends. Thus, a total of six theoretical bounds are constructed for the two S&P 500 futures contracts investigated: theoretical bounds constructed with and without dividend adjustments for each of the three assumptions about how much of the proceeds short-sellers of the cash index would have available to use.

Modest and Sundaresan find that the actual futures prices for both futures contracts are within the theoretical bounds constructed when the investor has no use of the proceeds from short-selling the cash index when dividends are considered. Thus, under these conditions, no arbitrage profits were possible during the time frame studied. While there were sporadic instances when the theoretical bounds were violated, under realistic assumptions Modest and Sundaresan find few opportunities to generate arbitrage profits (i.e., few violations of the theoretical bounds) even at the inception of stock index futures trading.

While the Cornell and French, and Modest and Sundaresan studies examined pricing efficiency when the contracts started trading, Ed Peters looks at whether the stock index futures market became more efficient over time.[11] He examines market efficiency for the S&P 500 futures contract and the NYSE futures contract from the September 1982 contract to the December 1983 contract to determine if the actual prices moved closer to the theoretical prices. Results show that the market became more efficient in pricing futures, a finding that he attributes to better estimation of the dividend stream for each index contract.

Bruce Collins tests the pricing efficiency of the futures market by examining whether an investment strategy of buying the cash market index and selling the futures could have generated an abnormal return.[12] In an efficient market, the return on this strategy should be approximately equal to the return on a Treasury security with a maturity equal to the maturity of the futures contract. An abnormal return occurs if the return realized from this strategy exceeds the yield on a comparable-maturity Treasury security. Selected S&P 500 futures contracts were examined beginning with the December 1982 contract and extending to the September 1985 contract. Transactions costs were considered. His results suggest that, while there were instances of pricing inefficiency, the market has become more efficient. Other statistical tests performed by Collins lead to the same conclusion.

Portfolio Strategies with Stock Index Futures

We will examine seven investment strategies for which institutional investors can use stock index futures:

---

[11] Ed Peters, "The Growing Efficiency of Index-Futures Markets," *Journal of Portfolio Management* (Summer 1985), pp. 52-6.

[12] Bruce M. Collins, "An Empirical Analysis of Stock Index Futures Prices," unpublished doctoral dissertation, Fordham University, 1987.

1. speculating on the movement of the stock market.

2. controlling the risk of a stock portfolio (altering beta).

3. hedging against adverse stock price movements.

4. constructing indexed portfolios.

5. index arbitrage.

6. creating portfolio insurance.

7. asset allocation.

Speculating on the movement of the stock market—Prior to development of stock index futures, an investor who wanted to speculate on the future course of stock prices had to buy or short individual stocks. Now, the stock index can be bought or sold in the futures market. But making speculation easier for investors is not the main function of stock index futures contracts. The other strategies discussed below show how institutional investors can effectively use stock index futures to meet investment objectives.

Controlling the risk of a stock portfolio—An institution that wishes to alter its exposure to the market can do so by revising the portfolio's beta. This can be done by rebalancing the portfolio with stocks that will produce the target beta, but there are transaction costs associated with rebalancing a portfolio. Because of the leverage embedded in futures, institutions can use stock index futures to achieve a target beta at a considerably lower cost. Buying stock index futures will increase a portfolio's beta, and selling will reduce it.

Hedging against adverse stock price movements—Hedging is a special case of controlling a stock portfolio's exposure to adverse price changes. In a hedge, the objective is to alter a current or anticipated stock portfolio position so that its beta is zero. A portfolio with a beta of zero should generate a risk-free interest rate. This is consistent with the capital asset pricing model discussed in Chapter 9, and also consistent with our discussion of futures contracts in Chapter 10.

Remember that using stock index futures to hedge locks in a price, although the hedger cannot then benefit from a favorable movement in the portfolio's value. With stock index options, the hedger has downside protection but retains the upside potential reduced by the cost of the option.

An illustration will show how stock index futures can be used to hedge the risk of a portfolio against an adverse price movement.[13] Suppose that a portfolio manager owns all the stocks in the Dow Jones Industrial Average on July 1, 1986, and the market value of the portfolio held is $1 million. Also assume that the portfolio manager wants to hedge the position against a decline in stock prices from July 1 to August 31, 1986, using the September 1986 S&P 500 futures contract. As the S&P 500 futures September contract is used here to hedge a portfolio of Dow Jones Industrials to August 31, this is a cross-hedge, as explained in Chapter 10.

The first step in the hedge is to determine whether to buy or sell the futures contract. Because the portfolio manager wants to protect against a decline in

---

[13] This illustration is adapted from Frank J. Fabozzi and Edgar E. Peters, "Hedging with Stock Index Futures," Chapter 13 in *The Handbook of Stock Index Futures and Options*.

the portfolio's value, he will sell stock index futures contracts. The second step is to determine the appropriate number of contracts to sell. While computation is beyond the scope of this chapter, it can be demonstrated that for our illustration six is the approximate number of contracts to sell to obtain the same market risk exposure with the futures as with the portfolio of Dow Jones Industrial stocks.

Table 15-7 summarizes the actual outcome of this hedge, assuming that it is lifted on August 31, 1986. The hedge results in a loss of $11,100. And assuming commissions of $20 per contract, commissions for six futures contracts would be $120, for an overall loss of $11,220. The reason for the loss is the adverse change in the basis (which is the difference between the cash price and futures price), as shown in the last column of the lower panel of Table 15-7. Had the hedge not been employed, however, the loss would have been $72,500—the loss in the cash market. This is what we meant in Chapter 10 when we say that hedging substitutes basis risk for price risk.

This hedge is called a short or sell hedge. A long or buy hedge can be used in anticipation of the purchase of stocks at some future date. In this case, stock index futures contracts are purchased. For example, shortly after stock

Table 15-7
Hedging a $1 Million Dow Jones Industrial Index Fund Using S&P 500 Futures

Own $1 million worth of Dow Jones Industrial stocks on 7/1/86.

Need to hedge against an adverse market move.

Hedge is lifted 8/31/86.

Facts	July 1, 1986	August 31, 1986
Value of portfolio	$1,000,000	$927,500
Cash price of S&P 500	252.04	234.91
Price of Sept. 1986 S&P futures	253.95	233.15

Outcome		
Cash Market	**Futures Market**	**Basis**
Time hedge is placed		
Own $1,000,000 portfolio	Sell six Sept. 1986 S&P 500 futures contracts at 253.95	–1.91
Time hedge is lifted		
Own $927,500 portfolio	Buy six Sept. 1986 S&P 500 futures contracts at 233.15	+1.76
Loss in cash market = $72,500	Gain in futures market = $62,400	
	Overall loss = $11,000	

index futures began trading, Westinghouse Electric Corporation's pension fund bought 400 stock index contracts between July 29 and August 11, 1982. The reason cited by a company source for purchasing these contracts, which were worth over $20 million, was that the company was not "ready to buy individual stocks in such a short period of time." A company source stated that stock index futures gave the pension fund "a quick way of putting money into the market," and one "much cheaper" than if the fund had purchased stock in the cash market.[14] This Westinghouse hedging strategy can be viewed as a long hedge.

Two examples of how investment banking firms can use stock index futures to hedge their activities were reported shortly after stock index futures began trading. In the first example in June 1982, International Harvester traded its stock portfolio to Goldman Sachs in exchange for a bond portfolio.[15] As recipient of the stock portfolio, Goldman Sachs was exposed to market risk. To protect itself against a decline in the value of the stock portfolio, Goldman Sachs placed a short hedge on a "significant" portion of the stock portfolio, using all three stock index futures trading at the time to implement the hedge.

In the second example, Salomon Brothers used stock index futures to protect itself against a decline in stock prices in a transaction involving $400 million of stock. In that transaction, the New York City Pension Fund switched $400 million of funds that were being managed by Alliance Capital to Bankers Trust so that the latter could manage the funds using an indexing approach. Salomon Brothers guaranteed prices at which the city and Bankers Trust could purchase or sell the stocks in the portfolio being transferred. To do this, Salomon Brothers used options on individual stocks to protect certain stock prices, but also used stock index futures to protect itself against broad market movements that would decrease the value of the stocks in the portfolio.

Constructing indexed portfolios—As we explained in Chapter 13, an increasing number of institutional equity funds are indexed to some broad-based stock market index. There are management fees and transaction costs associated with creating a portfolio to replicate a stock index that has been targeted to be matched. The higher these costs, the greater the divergence between the performance of the indexed portfolio and the target index. Moreover, because a fund manager creating an indexed portfolio will not purchase all the stocks that comprise the index, the indexed portfolio is exposed to tracking-error risk. Instead of using the cash market to construct an indexed portfolio, the manager can use stock index futures. In fact, one trade publication, *Pensions and Investments*, reports that of the 60 or so largest pension funds that are indexed, about one-third use stock index futures in managing the fund.

We will now illustrate how and under what circumstances stock index funds can be used to create an indexed portfolio. If stock index futures are priced according to their theoretical value, a portfolio consisting of a long position in stock index futures and Treasury bills will produce the same portfolio return as that of the underlying cash index. To see this, suppose that an

---

[14] "Stock Futures Used in Rally," *Pension & Investment Age* (October 25, 1982), pp. 1, 52.

[15] Kimberly Blanton, "Index Futures Contracts Hedge Big Block Trades," *Pension & Investments Age* (July 19, 1982), pp. 1, 38.

index fund manager wishes to index a $9 million portfolio using the S&P 500 as the target index. Also assume the following:

1. The S&P 500 is currently 300.
2. The S&P 500 futures index with six months to settlement is currently selling for 303.
3. The expected dividend yield for the S&P 500 for the next six months is 2%.
4. Six-month Treasury bills are currently yielding 3%.
5. The theoretical futures price is 303.[16]

Consider two strategies that the index fund manager may choose to pursue:

Strategy 1: Purchase $9 million of stocks in such a way as to replicate the performance of the S&P 500.

Strategy 2: Buy 60 S&P 500 futures contracts with settlement six months from now at 303, and invest $9 million in six-month Treasury bills.[17]

How will the two strategies perform under various scenarios for the S&P 500 value when the contract settles six months from now? We shall investigate three scenarios in which the S&P 500: increases to 330, remains at 300, and declines to 270. At settlement, the futures price converges to the value of the index. Table 15-8 shows the value of the portfolio for both strategies for each of the three scenarios. As can be seen, for a given scenario, the performance of the two strategies is identical.

This result should not be surprising because a futures contract can be replicated by selling the instrument underlying the futures contract and buying Treasury bills. In the case of indexing, we are replicating the underlying instrument by buying the futures contract and investing in Treasury bills. Therefore, if stock index futures contracts are properly priced, index fund managers can use stock index futures to create an index fund.

There are several points that should be noted. First, in Strategy 1 the ability of the portfolio to replicate the S&P 500 depends on how well the portfolio is constructed to track the index. On the other hand, assuming that the expected dividends are realized and that the futures contract is fairly priced, the futures/Treasury bill portfolio (Strategy 2) will mirror the performance of the S&P 500 exactly. Thus, tracking error is reduced. Second, the cost of transacting is less for Strategy 2. For example, if the cost of one S&P 500 futures is $15, then the transactions costs for Strategy 2 would be only $900 for a $9 million fund. This would be considerably less than the transactions costs associated with the acquisition and maintenance of a broadly diversified stock portfolio designed to replicate the S&P 500. In addition, for a large fund that wishes to index, the market impact cost is less by using stock index futures rather than using the cash market to create an index. The third point is that

---

[16] The theoretical futures price is found using the formula presented earlier:

Cash market price + Cash market price (Financing cost – Dividend yield)

The financing cost is 3% and the dividend yield is 2%. Therefore, 300 + 300 (0.03 – 0.02) = 303.

[17] There are two points to note here. First, this illustration ignores margin requirements; the Treasury bills can be used for initial margin. Second, 60 contracts are selected in this strategy because with the current market index at 300 and a multiple of $500, the cash value of 60 contracts is $9 million.

Table 15-8

Comparison of Portfolio Value from Purchasing Stocks to Replicate an Index and a Futures/Treasury Bill Strategy When the Futures Contract Is Fairly Priced

Assumptions:

Amount to be invested = $9 million
Current value of S&P 500 = 300
Current value of S&P futures contract = 303
Expected dividend yield = 2%
Yield on Treasury bills = 3%
Number of S&P 500 contracts to be purchased = 60

Strategy 1: Direct purchase of stocks

	Index value at settlement*		
	330	300	270
Change in index value	10%	0%	–10%
Market value of portfolio that mirrors the index	$ 9,900,000	$9,000,000	$8,100,000
Dividends 0.02 × $9,000,000	$ 180,000	$ 180,000	$ 180,000
Value of portfolio	$10,080,000	$9,180,000	$8,280,000
Dollar return	$ 1,080,000	$ 180,000	$ (720,000)

Strategy 2: Futures/T-bill portfolio

	Index value at settlement*		
	330	300	270
Gain for 60 contracts 60 × $500 × gain per contract	$ 810,000	$ (90,000)	$ (999,000)
Value of Treasury bills $9,000,000 × 1.03	$ 9,270,000	$9,270,000	$9,270,000
Value of portfolio	$10,080,000	$9,180,000	$8,280,000
Dollar return	$ 1,080,000	$ 180,000	$ (720,000)

* Because of convergence of cash and futures price, the S&P 500 cash index and stock index futures price will be the same.

custodial costs are obviously less for an index fund created using stock index futures. The fourth point is that the performance of the synthetically created index fund will depend on variation margin. Finally, in the analysis of the performance of each strategy, the dollar value of the portfolio at the end of the six-month period is the amount in the absence of taxes. For Strategy 1, no taxes will be paid if the securities are not sold, though taxes will be paid on dividends. For Strategy 2, taxes must be paid on the interest from the Treasury bills and on any gain from the liquidation of the futures contract.

Therefore, if stock index futures contracts are properly priced, index fund managers can use stock index futures to create an index fund. Suppose instead that the futures price is less than the theoretical futures price (i.e., the futures contracts are cheap). If that situation occurs, the index fund manager can enhance the indexed portfolio's return by buying the futures and buying Treasury bills. That is, the return on the futures/Treasury bill portfolio will be greater than that on the underlying index when the position is held to the settlement date.

To see this, suppose that in our previous illustration the current futures price is 301 instead of 303, so that the futures contract is cheap (undervalued). For all three scenarios shown in Table 15-8 the value of the portfolio would be $60,000 greater by buying the futures contract and Treasury bills rather than buying the stocks directly.

Alternatively, if the futures contract is expensive based on its theoretical price, an index fund manager who owns stock index futures and Treasury bills will swap that portfolio for the stocks in the index. An index manager who swaps between the futures/Treasury bills portfolio and a stock portfolio based on the value of the futures contract relative to the cash market index is attempting to enhance the portfolio's return. This strategy, referred to as a **stock replacement strategy**, is one of several strategies used to attempt to enhance the return of an indexed portfolio.[18]

Index abitrage—Opportunities to enhance returns as a result of the mispricing of the futures contract are not restricted to index fund management. Money managers and arbitrageurs monitor the cash and futures market to see when the differences between the theoretical futures price and actual futures price are sufficient so that an arbitrage profit can be attained: selling the futures index if it is expensive and buying stocks, or buying the futures index if it is cheap and selling the stocks. Program trading is used to execute the buy and sell orders.[19]

Creating portfolio insurance—In Chapter 11, we explained how a put option can protect the value of an asset. At the expiration date of the put option, the minimum value for the asset will be the strike price minus the cost of the put option. Put options on stock indexes can do the same for a diversified portfolio of stocks.

Alternatively, an institutional investor can create a put option synthetically by using either (1) stock index futures, or (2) stocks and a riskless asset. Allocation of the portfolio's funds to stock index futures or between stocks and a riskless asset is adjusted as market conditions change.[20] A strategy that seeks to insure the value of a portfolio using a synthetic put option strategy is called **dynamic hedging**.

Given that put options on stock indexes are available to portfolio managers, why should they bother with dynamic hedging? There are four reasons.

---

[18] For a further discussion of this strategy, see Bruce M. Collins, "Index Fund Investment Management," Chapter 10 in Frank J. Fabozzi (ed.), *Portfolio and Investment Management* (Chicago: Probus Publishing, 1989).

[19] Program trading is discussed in Chapter 13.

[20] For a more detailed explanation of this strategy, see Mark Rubinstein and Hayne Leland, "Replicating Options with Positions in Stock and Cash," *Financial Analysts Journal* (July-August 1981), pp. 63-72; or Hayne Leland, "Portfolio Insurance," Chapter 12 in *The Handbook of Stock Index Futures and Options*.

First, the size of the market for options on stock indexes is not as large as that for stock index futures and therefore may not easily accommodate a large portfolio insurance program without moving the price of the option substantially. Second, exchanges impose position limits on the amount of contracts in which an investor can have a position.[21] In the case of institutions that want to protect large equity portfolios, position limits may effectively prevent them from using exchange-traded index options to protect their portfolio.

Third, existing exchange-traded index options contracts are of shorter maturity than the period over which some investors sought protection. Finally, the cost of a put option may be higher than the transactions costs associated with dynamic hedging. Yet while the cost of a put option is known (and is determined by expected price volatility), the cost of creating portfolio insurance by using stock index futures or stocks will be determined by actual price volatility in the market. The greater the actual price volatility in the market, the more rebalancing of the portfolio is necessary, and the higher the cost of creating portfolio insurance.

How does dynamic hedging work using stocks and a riskless asset? Recall that the buyer of a put option establishes a floor for the value of an asset but retains the opportunity to benefit if the asset's price rises. A dynamic hedging strategy seeks to reproduce the payoff of a long put option position by changing the allocation of the portfolio's funds between the risky asset and a riskless asset. In this case, the risky asset is the equity portfolio, and the riskless asset may be a money market instrument such as Treasury bills. When stock prices decline, the investor must reduce the exposure to the stock market and increase the holding of the riskless asset. Placing more funds in the riskless asset will help to insure the floor value for the portfolio. Thus, when stock prices decline, a commensurate amount of stocks are sold and the proceeds are invested in a riskless asset such as Treasury bills. When stock prices rise, a commensurate amount of stocks are purchased with the proceeds obtained from selling a portion of the riskless asset. This action increases the exposure of the portfolio to the equity market so that the investor can capture the benefits of a rising market. Fewer funds need be placed in the riskless asset, because the likelihood of achieving the floor value for the portfolio declines in a rising equity market. To execute the orders to buy or sell stocks, program trading is used.

Instead of implementing dynamic hedging by changing the allocation of the portfolio between stocks and a riskless asset, stock index futures can be used. When stock prices decline, stock index futures are sold. This is equivalent to selling stocks and investing the funds in a riskless asset. When stock prices rise, stock index futures are purchased, which is equivalent to buying stocks and reducing the portfolio's allocation to a riskless asset.[22]

Asset allocation—The decision on how to divide funds across the major asset classes (for example, equities, bonds, foreign securities, real estate) is referred to as the **asset allocation decision**. Futures and options can be used to

---

[21] Regulators will grant approval for contract trading only if the exchange imposes a position limit because it is believed such a limit will stabilize the option price.

[22] Determination of the amount of stock to buy or sell is based on an option pricing model.

implement an asset allocation decision more effectively than transacting in the cash markets.

For example, suppose that a pension fund sponsor with assets of $1 billion has allocated $300 million to the bond market and $700 million to the stock market. Suppose further that the sponsor has decided to alter that bond/stock mix to $600 million in bonds and $400 million in stock. Liquidation of $300 million in stock will involve significant transaction costs—both commissions and execution (market impact) costs.[23] Moreover, the external money managers who are managing the stock portfolios will face disruption as funds are withdrawn by the sponsor. Rather than liquidating the stock portfolio immediately, the sponsor can sell an appropriate number of stock index futures contracts. This effectively decreases the exposure of the pension fund to the stock market. To increase the fund's exposure to the bond market, the sponsor can buy interest rate futures contracts.[24]

EQUITY SWAPS

In Chapter 12 we introduced swaps. In recent years, the concept of swapping cash flows has been applied to the equity area. In an **equity swap**, the cash flows that are swapped are based on the total return on some stock market index and an interest rate (either a fixed rate or a floating rate). Moreover, the stock market index can be a non-U.S. stock market index and the payments could be nondollar-denominated. For example, a money manager can enter into a two-year quarterly reset equity swap based on the German DAX market index versus some money market index in which the money manager receives the market index in deutchemarks and pays the floating rate in deutchemarks.

The notional principal amount of the contract is not exchanged by the counterparties, but both parties are exposed to counterparty risk. An important difference between an equity swap and an interest rate swap (discussed in Chapter 29) is that it is possible for one of the parties in an equity swap—specifically, the party receiving the stock market index—to realize a negative total return. This means that party must pay to the counterparty the amount of the negative total return plus the payment on the reference interest rate.

Applications

As explained in Chapter 12, a swap is nothing more than a package of forward contracts. The advantage of the swap is that it is more transactionally efficient for accomplishing many investment objectives.

Two uses have been suggested for equity swaps. The first is to create a portfolio that replicates an index. An indexed portfolio can be created by buying all or some of the stocks that comprise the index. Alternatively, this can be done more efficiently—in terms of cost and speed of execution—by buying stock index futures contracts and investing funds in Treasury bills. The stock index futures position must then be rolled over before the settlement date

---

[23] These costs are described in Chapter 7.

[24] These contracts are explained in Chapter 27.

into a new futures position. Equity swaps provide a third alternative which has three advantages: (1) there are quarterly cash flows, (2) the money manager can specify the maturity of the contract so that frequent rolling of a futures position is unnecessary, and (3) there is no concern with the mispricing of the futures contract. Another distinct advantage of an equity swap is that since they are customized, a money manager can use a swap to index a non-U.S. stock market index. We saw this in our earlier illustration of swapping the DAX market index for DM LIBOR. Moreover, an equity swap can be used to hedge the currency risk. For example, an equity swap can be structured in which the money manager receives in U.S. dollars the DAX market index total return and pays in U.S. dollars LIBOR. There are two disadvantages of using an equity swap rather than stock index futures: (1) there is counterparty risk and (2) there is less liquidity in swaps compared to the very liquid stock index futures contract.

The second way in which it has been suggested that equity swaps can be used is to enhance return.[25] For example, suppose a pension plan sponsor has allocated a small portion of the portfolio to a specialty equity manager who has exhibited on a fairly consistent basis superior investment performance relative to some stock market benchmark; yet diversification and other constraints may prevent more funds from being allocated to this manager. Also suppose that the plan sponsor has established an asset-allocation policy fixing the amount in three-year Treasury securities. Using an equity swap, the pension plan sponsor can enter into a swap in which it receives over the next three years a fixed coupon rate based on three-year Treasuries and agrees to pay the total return on the stock market benchmark that the specialty equity manager has outperformed. The amount then allocated to this manager can be increased. Then, if the manager can outperform the benchmark, the excess return over the benchmark is retained by the pension plan sponsor. The total return for the pension plan would then be the three-year Treasury fixed coupon rate plus the excess return over the benchmark. The risk, of course, is that the specialty equity manager underperforms the index. The plan's return is then reduced by the amount of underperformance. Depending on the actual performance of the specialty equity manager, it is possible for the fund's return to be negative.

Market Quotation Conventions

In the case of interest rate and currency swaps that we discuss in later chapters, the market convention for quoting swap terms is now standardized. Because the equity swap market is in its infancy, no standardization for quoting these swaps exists at the time of this writing. This makes it difficult to compare swap terms among the various dealer firms that are making markets in these swaps. For example, there are some dealers that quote swaps in terms of the change in the stock market index without including dividends. That is, the return being received or paid just considers price changes. Other dealers will quote the total return (price change and dividends) for the index. In the

---

[25] Gary Gastineau, "Swaps and the Division of Labor," SBC Research, Swiss Bank Corporation Investment Banking Inc. (January 1993), p. 2.

case of non-U.S. stock market indexes, a dealer may quote the swap in terms of the total return after deducting foreign withholding taxes.

STOCK INDEX CONTRACTS, STOCK PRICE VOLATILITY, AND BLACK MONDAY

A great deal of debate surrounds the introduction of stock index options and futures. In this section, we will discuss the arguments at issue and review the empirical evidence. The first question is whether the introduction of stock index futures and options trading, and strategies employing these contracts, adds value to our financial markets, or whether index futures and options merely provide a form of legalized gambling for market participants. The second controversy is whether stock price volatility has increased as a result of futures and options trading. Finally, we will focus on the extent to which the existence of these contracts may have contributed to the October 1987 market crash, popularly known as Black Monday.

Are Derivative Index Markets Beneficial to the Financial Markets?

In the absence of stock index futures and options markets, investors have only one market in which to alter portfolio positions when new information is received—the cash market. If there is economic news that investors expect might impact the cash flow of all stocks adversely, they can reduce their equity exposure by selling stocks. The opposite is true if investors expect the new information to increase the cash flow of all stocks: in that case, an investor would increase the equity exposure of the portfolio. There are, of course, transaction costs associated with altering equity risk exposure—explicit costs (commissions), and hidden or execution costs (bid-ask spreads and market impact costs).

Stock index futures provide another market that institutional investors can use to alter equity risk exposure when new information is acquired. But which market—cash or futures—should the investor employ to alter a position *quickly* upon receipt of new information? As we explained in Chapter 10, it will be the one that is the more efficient to use to achieve the objective. The factors to consider are commissions, bid-ask spreads, market impact costs (hence the importance of market liquidity), and the leverage offered.

The market that investors feel is the one that is more efficient to use to achieve their investment objective will be the one where price discovery takes place. Price information will then be transmitted to the other market. So, for example, if the futures market is the market of choice, it will serve as the price discovery market. That is, it will be the market where investors send their collective message about how any new information is expected to impact the cash market. Then, there must be a mechanism for transmitting that message to the cash market. That mechanism is index arbitrage.

A comparison of transaction costs indicates that they are substantially lower in the stock index futures market. Typically, transactions cost in this market are between 5% to 10% of transactions cost in the cash market. For example, the firm of Morgan Stanley estimates that the transactions costs associated with trading a $120 million portfolio of stocks would be about $161,000, compared to only $10,000 using S&P 500 stock index futures. The corresponding execution costs (market impact costs), according to Morgan Stanley, would be $520,000 for the portfolio of stocks and $20,000 for stock index futures.[26]

The speed at which orders can be executed also gives the advantage to the futures market. It has been estimated that to sell a block of stock at a reasonable price would take about two to three minutes, while a futures transaction can be accomplished in 30 seconds or less.[27] The advantage is also on the side of the futures market when it comes to the amount of money that must be put up in a transaction (i.e., leverage). As we explained earlier, margin requirements for transactions in the stock market are considerably higher than in the stock index futures market. Thus, a study by the SEC's Division of Market Regulation concludes:

> [Institutions can] sell portions of their equity positions in a faster, less expensive manner by using index futures than by selling directly on stock exchanges . . . .

> Futures are used instead of stocks because of the increased speed and reduced transaction costs entailed in trading a single product in the futures market . . . . As a result of the futures market's liquidity, investors can execute large transactions with much smaller market effects than is possible in the separate stocks.

Which market is the one that investors have selected to employ to alter their risk exposure? John Merrick found that, prior to 1985 the cash market dominated the price discovery process, relative to the stock index futures market.[28] Since 1985, however, the S&P 500 futures market has played the dominant price discovery role. This reversal of the dominant market was not an accident. It followed the pattern of trading volume. When trading volume in the futures market surpassed that on the cash market, the futures market dominated.

How does the existence of competing markets with the attributes that we described above affect the stock market? In her testimony before Congress on July 23, 1987, Susan Phillips, then the Chairperson of the Commodity Futures Trading Commission, stated that: "The depth and liquidity of the futures markets facilitate the absorption of new fundamental information quickly, thus improving the efficiency of the stock markets . . . ."[29]

Is it possible for the futures market to take on a life of its own, so that the futures price does not reflect the economic value of the underlying instrument? It could be, if there were not a mechanism to bring futures prices and cash market prices in line. This mechanism is index arbitrage, which we described earlier.

---

[26] "Program Trading" (Morgan Stanley, October 8, 1987).

[27] Thomas Byrne, "Program Trading—A Trader's Perspective," *Commodities Law Letter* VI, nos. 9 and 10, p. 9.

[28] John J. Merrick, Jr., "Price Discovery in the Stock Market," Federal Reserve Bank of Philadelphia Working Paper No. 87-4, March 1987.

[29] Testimony before the Subcommittee on Telecommunications and Finance, Committee on Energy and Commerce, U.S. House of Representatives, July 23, 1987, p. 1.

Critics of stock index futures point to program trading, index arbitrage, and dynamic hedging (portfolio insurance) when there is a substantial decline in the cash market and/or increased stock price volatility. As we explained in Chapter 13, program trading is a technique for trading lists of stocks as close in time as possible. It is not, as is often stated in the popular press, a trading strategy. Program trades typically are implemented electronically using the automated order-execution facilities of the exchanges (e.g., the SuperDOT of the New York Stock Exchange) that allow orders to be transmitted simultaneously to the appropriate specialist post.

Why is it important for an institution to execute a list of orders as close in time as possible? There are several investment strategies that depend on this: indexing, index arbitrage, and portfolio insurance. The question is whether any of these strategies that rely on program trading and stock index futures are disruptive to the stock market.

Indexing—Indexing, as we explained in Chapter 13, is not a strategy that attempts to trade on information. Indexing is a strategy that theory tells us investors should employ in an efficient market in order to capture the efficiency embodied in the market. Yet the theory tells us nothing about how to implement the strategy. To manage an indexed portfolio, a money manager first constructs an initial portfolio that it is hoped will replicate the performance of the market. The money manager must rebalance the portfolio, however, as new monies are added to or withdrawn from an indexed portfolio. Program trading is used so that all stocks in the portfolio can be sold or purchased by simultaneous order at the closing prices, so that the performance of the indexed portfolio will do a good job tracking the index. Therefore, indexing should not be a disruptive market force.

Index arbitrage—As we just explained, there must be a mechanism to transmit the message about investor expectations from the price discovery market to the other market. Only if the cost of carry is zero will the futures price and the cash price be the same. Otherwise, the futures price will differ from the cash price by an amount equal to the cost of carry. Because of transaction costs and other factors, there are boundaries around the theoretical futures price limiting generation of arbitrage profits if the futures price trades within the bounds. In an attempt to capture arbitrage profits, those who follow an index arbitrage are simply tying the futures and cash markets together. This link prevents futures contracts from taking on a life of their own, and thereby allows hedgers to use stock index futures to carry out strategies to protect portfolio values at a fair price.

What happens if the futures price is outside the boundaries? An investor can generate arbitrage profits by selling the more expensive instrument and buying the cheaper instrument, driving the price of the expensive one down and driving the price of the cheaper one up until the futures price is within the theoretical boundaries. Suppose that the cash market is cheap relative to the futures market. An investor will borrow funds and buy the stocks while simultaneously selling the futures contract. At the expiration of the contract, the stocks will be sold in order to provide cash to cover the loan. The investor will liquidate the stock position by submitting market-on-close sell orders at the expiration of the futures contract.[30] If, in contrast, the futures price is

---

[30] A market-on-close order is a market order executed on the day it was entered at the official closing of the market.

cheap relative to the stocks, the investor will buy the futures and sell the stocks. At the settlement date, the investor must cover the short sale of the stock and therefore must buy the stocks. The short position would be covered by submitting market-on-close orders to buy the stocks.

What might happen on the settlement date when the stock portfolio in an index arbitrage must be liquidated in the case of a long stock position and stocks purchased in the case of a short position? There will certainly be an increase in orders but what will happen to stock prices? It depends on the composition of the orders. If they are balanced between arbitrageurs who have created long positions and short positions, then we should not expect any significant price movement. If orders are not balanced, the action should result in a significant change in prices. Thus, it is possible that stock price volatility will increase at settlement dates. We will look at the empirical evidence later.

Critics of index arbitrage argue that arbitrageurs consider only the relationship between cash and futures and the cost of transacting rather than making decisions based on the economic value of the underlying market. The response to these critics is that there must be a movement in at least one of the markets for arbitrage trading to be profitable. As long as nonarbitrageurs are pricing in at least one of the markets according to economic information, price changes capture assessments of this information. Arbitrage then irons out the inconsistency between the markets.

We can also see the importance of program trading in this strategy. An index arbitrage strategy requires program trading to implement the buy or sell orders so that trades will occur as close in time as possible. Without program trading, the theoretical bounds for the futures price would be much greater.

Dynamic hedging—Recall that dynamic hedging (portfolio insurance) involves buying stocks or futures when the market is rising and selling when the market is falling. The concern with this strategy that is expressed by the SEC Division of Market Regulation and other critics is that it may have a "cascade" effect when stock prices decline. To understand this argument, consider what would happen if stock prices decline and dynamic hedging is employed using stocks and a riskless asset. The strategy requires that stocks be sold. But if there are many institutional investors following a dynamic strategy, this will mean a substantial number of stocks will be sold, causing further decline in stock prices. In turn, more stocks must be sold, leading to a further decline in stock prices.

The same would happen if stock index futures are used to implement a dynamic hedging program. Their sales in the futures market would depress futures. What would arbitrageurs do? They would take offsetting positions in futures (by buying futures) and in stocks (by selling stocks). This action, it is argued, would lower cash prices further, and cause portfolio insurers to sell futures, resulting in a spiraling effect.

Proponents of dynamic hedging argue that the cascade effect is unlikely. At some point, value-oriented investors would step in when stocks are priced below their value based on economic fundamentals. However, Sanford Grossman (in a paper published several months before Black Monday) presented theoretical arguments that suggest that the imbalance of buyers and sellers of portfolio insurance could change stock market volatility. Specifically, if the demand for portfolio insurance exceeds the amount that market participants are willing to supply of portfolio insurance (that is, the amount of put options that market participants are willing to sell), volatility will increase; it would decrease if supply exceeded demand.[31]

SEC study of the September 11-12, 1986, market decline—We do have some evidence about index-related strategies during periods of sharp market declines. The Dow Jones Industrial Average dropped 86.61 points (a 4.61% decline) on September 11, 1986. The next day it dropped by another 34.17 points (1.91%). The Division of Market Regulation of the SEC investigated this two-day decline in stock prices to determine the role index-related strategies may have played.[32] It concluded that: "The magnitude of the September decline was a result of changes in investors' perception of fundamental economic conditions, rather than artificial forces arising from index-related strategies." The SEC study further states that: "Index-related futures trading was instrumental in the rapid transmission of these changed investor perceptions to individual stock prices, and may have condensed the time period in which the decline occurred."

The SEC study was also concerned with (1) the "cascade" effect resulting from the implementation of portfolio insurance strategies, and (2) potential manipulative uses employing stock index futures. The SEC did not find either present on September 11 and 12. Moreover, with respect to the "cascade effect," the SEC study concludes that there were sufficient economic forces to counteract it. As for potential manipulation, the SEC study notes that manipulation would be too costly and more risky than other potential manipulation targets.

The SEC study concludes that "Analysis of this particular market decline does not provide an independent basis to conclude that radical regulatory or structural changes are necessary at this time . . . . However, close monitoring should be maintained." The SEC study therefore exonerates index-related strategies.

What Has Been the Effect on Stock Price Volatility?

The view held by some investors and the popular press is that stock index futures and options, program trading, and index-related strategies (index arbitrage and dynamic hedging) have resulted in an increase in the volatility of stock prices. This criticism of futures contracts is not confined to stock index futures, but as we explained in Chapter 10, it has been leveled at all futures contracts. In Chapter 10 we also questioned whether greater price volatility for a market was necessarily bad.

Several studies have empirically investigated the effect of the introduction of futures trading, and the effect of index-related strategies on stock price volatility. The difficulty in carrying out the empirical tests is determining what the volatility of the cash market price would have been in the absence of futures trading. A simple comparison of price volatility before and after the

---

31 Sanford J. Grossman, "An Analysis of the Implications for Stock and Futures Price Volatility of Program Trading and Dynamic Hedging Strategies," presented at the Conference on the Impact of Stock Index Futures Trading at the Center for the Study of Futures Markets, Columbia University, June 8, 1987. The paper was subsequently published in the July 1988 issue of the Journal of Business. A less technical version of this paper is "Insurance Seen and Unseen: The Impact of Markets," *Journal of Portfolio Management* (Summer 1988), pp. 5-8.

32 Securities and Exchange Commission, Division of Market Regulation, "The Role of Index-Related Trading in the Market Decline on September 11 and 12, 1986," March 1987.

introduction of futures trading, while informative, is not sufficient. The pitfall of this approach is that there are other factors that will influence volatility—the variability of economic information that affects stock price volatility. Thus, an increase in price volatility may be due to an increase in the variability of economic information that affects stock market prices. Or, failure to observe an increase in price volatility may be due to a decrease in the variability of economic information, masking any increase in price volatility. Thus, studies must control for the other factors that impact stock price volatility.

Studies have examined *inter*day (i.e., day-to-day) price volatility[33] and *intra*day price volatility[34] using a wide range of measures. A fair conclusion of all of these studies is that the introduction of stock index options and futures and index-related strategies has not increased stock price volatility except, possibly, during periods when stock index futures and options expire.

Did Stock Index Contracts Cause Black Monday?

On Monday, October 19, 1987 ("Black Monday"), the DJIA declined by 23%, the largest single-day decline in its history. The decline was not unique to the United States—every major stock market in the world suffered a decline in local currency units. In response to the crash, six studies were commissioned in the United States to assess the cause of the crash and make recommendations on reducing the likelihood of another crash. Studies were commissioned by: President Reagan (Presidential Task Force on Market Mechanisms, popularly known as the Brady Report), the General Accounting Office, the Securities and Exchange Commission, the New York Stock Exchange, the Chicago Mercantile Exchange, and the Commodity Futures Exchange.

According to the popular press and many market observers, no study was needed; the culprits were well known to be the market participants who employed index-related strategies. For example, the day following the crash *The Wall Street Journal* reported: "In a nightmarish fulfillment of some traders' and academicians' worst fears, the five year old index futures for the first time plunged into a panicky, unlimited free-fall, fostering a sense of crisis throughout United States capital markets."[35] The evidence that has accumulated since, however, does not confirm that index-related trading was the culprit. We review the evidence below. (Other possible causes for the crash are discussed in Chapter 13.)

Index-related trading and the crash—Program trading was severely limited on October 19 and the morning of October 20 because the unavailability of the NYSE Designated Order Turnaround (DOT) system made it difficult to

---

[33] Studies that have looked at the impact of the introduction of stock price volatility are: Carolyn D. Davis and Alice P. White, "Stock Market Volatility," Staff Study, Board of Governors of the Federal Reserve System, August 1987; John J. Merrick, Jr., "Volume Determination in Stock and Stock Index Futures Markets: An Analysis of Volume and Volatility Effects," *The Journal of Futures Markets* (October 1987), pp. 483-96; Lawrence Harris, "S&P 500 Cash Stock Price Volatilities," *Journal of Finance* (December 1989), pp. 1155-76; and Franklin R. Edwards, "Does Futures Trading Increase Stock Price Volatility?" *Financial Analysts Journal* (January-February 1988), pp. 63-9.

[34] Studies of intraday price volatility include: Laszlo Birinyi, Jr., and H. Nicholas Hanson, "Market Volatility: An Updated Study" (Salomon Brothers, July 1986), and Hans R. Stoll and Robert E. Whaley, "Expiration Day Effects of Index Options and Futures," *Financial Analysts Journal* (March-April 1987), pp. 16-28.

[35] Scott McMurray and Robert L. Rose, "Chicago's Shadow Markets' Led Free-Fall in a Plunge that Began Right at Opening," *The Wall Street Journal* (October 20, 1987), p. 28.

execute trades. Suspension of the DOT system, however, gave the impression that it was program trading that caused the chaotic market. The actual motivation for suspension was the fear that the specialist system could not execute all the program trades.

Index arbitrage traders could not operate in the chaotic market environment even before suspension of the DOT system. At the outset on October 19, index arbitrageurs could not transact in the cash market because many of the major issues in the S&P 500 did not open for trading until 11 A.M. or later. It was difficult to execute the program trades necessary to implement an index arbitrage strategy in the futures market, with prices too volatile and bid-ask spreads too wide. Later in the day, the execution of an index arbitrage strategy became even more difficult. Delays in reporting trades in the cash market meant that identifying profitable arbitrage opportunities between the cash and futures market could not be done. Delays in executing orders in the cash market, particularly after suspension of the DOT system, meant that even if a profitable arbitrage could be identified there would be no assurance that one could execute at the prices used to identify the arbitrage opportunity. Thus, index arbitrage was not the culprit. It may be argued, on the contrary, that the impediments to index arbitraging made matters worse because this reduced demand in the stock index futures market.

Dynamic hedging (portfolio insurance) and the crash—Recall that Grossman argued that an imbalance between the demand for portfolio insurance and the supply of portfolio insurance will alter the volatility of the market. When the demand exceeds supply, volatility will increase, causing a dramatic decline in prices when the market is declining. It is interesting to note that on the morning of October 19, 1987, several options exchanges did begin trading in long-term index options that were designed to satisfy the needs of the portfolio insurance market.[36] A supply of long-term put index options—that is, actual exchange-traded put options—it is argued, could have satisfied the demand from portfolio insurers. Two things probably prevented that from happening. First, the new exchange-traded contracts did not have sufficient time to develop so that market participants could be comfortable with using them. Second, even if market participants did want to use these new contracts, as we explained earlier in this chapter, there were position limits imposed on investors by the exchange that may have prevented them from doing so. In discussing Black Monday, SEC Commissioner Joseph Grundfest in an article published in mid-1989 wrote:

> *Had all investors involved in portfolio insurance found it possible, and desirable, to satisfy their demand for "insurance" by buying puts instead of relying on dynamic hedges, the market would have had more information about the intensity of investor concern about a downside move. Under those circumstances, there's reason to believe that prices might not have fallen as low on the downside had the market simply been better informed of investors' own concerns. Thus, to the extent position limits on index options forced investors away from the options market and*

---

[36] Gary L. Gastineau, "Eliminating Option Position Limits: A Key Structural Reform" (New York: Salomon Brothers Inc, August 30, 1988), p. 3.

> *into secret dynamic hedging strategies, the government's position limit restrictions may have unwittingly exacerbated the market's decline.*[37]

Thus, the culprit might not be dynamic hedging/portfolio insurance but, instead (1) the inability to develop a long-term exchange-traded index option market, and (2) government imposition of the regulatory position limits that impeded the use of the exchange-traded market. Whether or not one is willing to accept this hypothesis, it should be understood that it is entirely untested and therefore has no empirical underpinning.

Index trading volume and the crash—By looking at trading volume statistics, Joanne Hill provides some additional evidence on the size of the role that the stock index futures market played on October 19 and 20.[38] On that Monday, S&P 500 futures trading volume was 162,022 contracts, approximately 1.5 times the average daily number of contracts traded in the previous week. In contrast, trading volume on the NYSE was 2.7 times greater than the average daily number of shares traded in the previous week (604 million versus 224 million shares). Based on normal levels of S&P 500 futures trading to NYSE stock trading, approximately 250,000 to 300,000 contracts would have been traded. Thus, actual futures trading was considerably below normal trading according to the number of shares traded. This low level of futures trading continued on Tuesday, with NYSE trading remaining at 600 million shares, and futures trading volume down to 126,462 contracts.

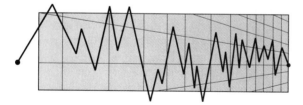

SUMMARY

Stock index options and futures were introduced in the early 1980s. The underlying stock market index may be a broad-based index or a narrow-based index. The dollar value of a contract is determined by the product of the index value and the contract's multiple. Unlike options on individual common stock, stock index products are cash settlement contracts. That is, the contracts are settled in cash at the expiration or settlement date. There are also complex OTC options, or exotic options, in which the underlying is a stock index.

Stock index options can be used to bet on the movement of stock prices (speculating) or to protect a portfolio position against an adverse price movement (hedging). In addition, the following index-related strategies can be employed by institutional investors: controlling market risk exposure, con-

---

[37] Joseph A. Grundfest, "Perestroika on Wall Street: The Future of Securities Trading," *Financial Executive* (May-June 1989), p. 25.

[38] Joanne M. Hill, "Program Trading, Portfolio Insurance, and the Stock Market Crash" (Kidder, Peabody, January 1988), pp. 27-8.

structing an index fund, enhancing returns via index arbitrage, dynamic hedging, and implementing an asset allocation decision. Dynamic hedging is related to replicating a put option with stocks or stock index futures.

Studies of the efficiency of the stock index options market suggest that mispricing was present when these contracts began trading. The reason may be that it is difficult to arbitrage an option where the underlying instrument is an index. More recent studies suggest that although stock index futures were occasionally mispriced when trading commenced in 1983, they are now fairly priced.

In equity swaps, the counterparties agree to exchange the return on some stock index for an interest rate (fixed or floating). Equity swaps can be used to create an indexed portfolio to match some U.S. or non-U.S. stock index.

Critics of stock index options and futures contracts believe that index-related trading has increased stock price volatility and is responsible for Black Monday. A closer examination suggests that the stock index futures market provides a less expensive and more speedy transaction market for investors to alter their exposure to economic information expected to impact stock prices. The stock index futures market has become the price discovery market. The evidence cited in this chapter suggests that index-related trading has not increased stock market price volatility, nor was it responsible for Black Monday.

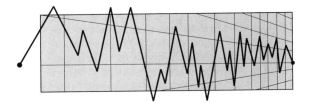

QUESTIONS

1. Suppose you bought an index call option for 5.50 with a strike index of 400 and that, at expiration, you exercised it. Also suppose that at the time you exercised the call option, the index had a value of 440.

   a. If the index option has a multiple of $100, how much money does the writer of this option pay you?

   b. What profit did you realize from buying this call option?

2. The following excerpt is from an article entitled "Scudder Writes Covered Calls on S&P 500," in the July 13, 1992 issue of *Derivatives Week*, p. 7:

   Scudder, Stevens & Clark writes covered calls on the S&P 500 Index to enhance the return of some of its equity portfolios, according to Harry Hitch, principal at Scudder. Hitch, who advises Scudder's equity portfolio managers on derivatives use, said that the S&P 500 has been in a trading range since the beginning of the year, making it a good candidate for covered call writing. Half of the index is made up of growth stocks, a group that Scudder sees as overbought, whereas the other half is probably increasing in price. The combination of one half appreciating with the other half depreciating creates the range, rather than a decided one-way movement.

The goal is to write calls at the top of the trading range, take the premium and wait for the options to expire worthless . . . . Typically, Scudder takes 1,000 contract positions, worth around $42 million.

Explain the risks and rewards of the strategy discussed in this excerpt.

3. Suppose that an alternative call option is based on the performance of the S&P 500 and the return on a particular U.S. Treasury bond. The terms are as follows: the option expires in one year; the notional amount is $20 million; the strike for the S&P 500 is 430; and the strike for the Treasury bond is 100.

a. Suppose at the expiration date the return on the S&P 500 is 9% and the return on the Treasury bond is 11%. What is the payoff of this option?

b. Suppose at the expiration date the return on S&P 500 is –4% and the return on the Treasury bond is –2%. What is the payoff of this option?

4. Explain how a money manager would use an alternative call option.

5. Explain how a money manager would use an outperformance call option.

6. The following statement comes from the September 1989 issue of *Institutional Investor:* "Two years ago Osaka became the first Japanese exchange to come out with a financial future—a stock-index future known as the Osaka 50. It was only a modest success, mainly because it had to be delivered in shares rather than cash."

Explain why cash settlement is preferred for stock index futures.

7. On February 16, 1995, open interest for the S&P 500 March 1995 futures contract was 199,447. Open interest for the December 1995 contract was 1,956. What is open interest, and why would the open interest figures for the March and December contracts be of concern to a portfolio manager considering using stock index futures?

8. What is the dollar value of the S&P 500 if the futures price is 343?

9. Suppose you know the following facts: the S&P 500 Index is 380; the dividend yield for the stocks comprising the index is 4%; the interest rate for 12 months is 12%; and the S&P 500 futures contract for settlement in 12 months' time is currently selling at 412.

a. Is there an arbitrage opportunity? If so, how would you take advantage of it?

b. What considerations would you want to address before executing this trade?

10. Donald Singleton is an investment banker for a regional firm. One of his clients, Dolby Manufacturing, Inc., is a private company that will be making an initial public offering of 20 million shares of common stock. Mr. Singleton's firm will buy the issue at $10 per share. He has suggested to the managing director of the firm, John Wilson, that the firm should hedge the position using stock index futures contracts. What should Mr. Wilson's response be?

11. This quotation is from the June 8, 1987, issue of *Business Week*:

    The idea sounds almost un-American. Instead of using your smarts to pick stocks that will reach the sky, you put money in a fund that merely tracks a broad market index. But that is precisely what institutional investors are doing . . . . Indexing is a new force in the stock market . . . . But the impact of index-funds reaches far beyond stock price.

    Discuss how indexing may have contributed to the growth of the stock index derivatives markets.

12. This quotation is from the December 1988 issue of *Euromoney*:

    The proliferation of futures and options markets has created new opportunities for international investors. It is now possible to change investment exposure from one country to another through the use of derivative instruments, augmented by a limited number of individual securities. Asset allocation in most major markets is now feasible using futures and options.

    Discuss the reasons for using derivative rather than cash instruments to facilitate asset-allocation decisions.

13. The following statement from an article entitled "Program Trading Spreads from Just Wall Street Firms" appeared in the August 18, 1989, issue of *The Wall Street Journal*: "Brokerage firms in the business, which tiptoed back into program trading after the post-crash furor died down, argue that such strategies as stock-index arbitrage—rapid trading between stock index futures and stocks to capture fleeting price differences—link two related markets and thus benefit both." A second quotation in the article is from a senior vice-president at Twenty-First Securities Corp.: "Program trading is a product that is here, links markets, and it is not going to disappear. It is a function of the computerization of Wall Street."

    Explain why you agree or disagree with these statements.

14. The following excerpt appeared in the December 7, 1992 issue of *Derivatives Week* entitled "Prudential Reduces FT-SE Futures Exposure in Favour of CAC-40":

    Prudential Portfolio Managers in London, which manages over £10 billion in pension fund assets, recently used futures to reduce an overweight position in U.K. equi-

*ties while increasing its expo-
sure to French equities,
according to Martin Bookes,
assistant director. Last June,
Prudential used LIFFE-
traded FT-SE futures to over-
weight U.K. equities by 2-3%
compared to benchmark
indices which have a 60%
exposure.*

   a. Explain how this money manager was able to increase its
exposure to French equities
using futures.

   b. Explain how this money manager was able to decrease its
exposure to U.K. equities using
futures.

15. The following excerpt is from an
article "Salomon Downplays
Japan Stock Index Arbitrage" that
appeared June 22, 1992 issue of
Derivatives Week, p. 2:

   *Salomon Brothers Asia is
deemphasizing Japanese
equity index arbitrage,
according to a spokesman for
the firm. The increasing efficiency of the Tokyo market
made index arbitrage less
attractive, he explained. "It's
a brokerage's work to find a
market's inefficiency and
earn profit, but [stock index
arbitrage offers] less now,"
the Salomon spokesman
said. The past two years, during which foreign firms dominated the business, were
unusual, he added.*

   a. What is stock index arbitrage?

   b. Based on the comments in the
excerpt, why is the experience
with stock index arbitrage in
Japan the same as in the United
States?

16. Explain how equity swaps can be
used by a money manager to create an index fund.

17. Explain why it is possible that in
an equity swap the party receiving the stock index may to have
to pay the counterparty more
than the reference interest rate.

18. Consider the following testimony
given by Alan Greenspan,
Chairman of the Board of
Governors of the Federal Reserve,
before a subcommittee in the U.S.
Senate:

   *In a more fundamental sense,
we believe it is counter-
productive to lay blame on
one sector, in this case the
market for stock index derivatives, for increasing occurrence of wide and rapid price
swings in equity markets . . . .
Rather, the volatility we
observe reflects more basic
changes in economic and
financial processes prompted
by technological advances
and the increasing concen-
tration of assets in institutional portfolios.*

   a. Do you agree with Mr.
Greenspan's view?

   b. Do you think that stock index
derivatives were responsible for
increased volatility and the
October 1987 crash?

The Theory and Structure of Interest Rates

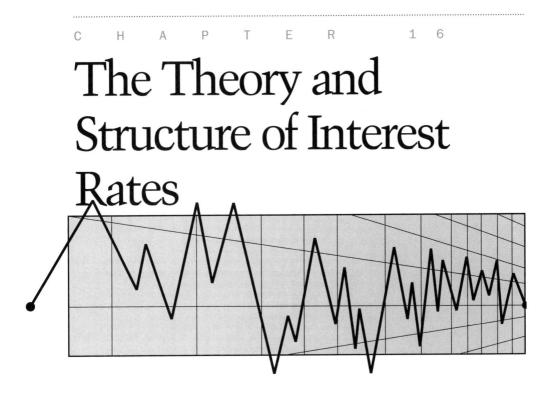

LEARNING OBJECTIVES

After reading this chapter you will understand:

- the role of individual preference in choosing current and future consumption in the determination of interest rates.

- what is meant by the marginal rate of time preference.

- the role of the loan market in the determination of interest rates.

- the role of production opportunities in the determination of interest rates.

- what is meant by the real rate of interest.

- the factors that determine the real rate of interest in an economy.

- how the market equilibrium interest rate is determined.

- what is meant by Pareto optimality.

- the relationship between the real rate of interest and the nominal rate of interest and inflation (Fisher's Law).

- why the yield on a Treasury security is the base interest rate.

• what is meant by a risk premium.

• what factors affect the yield spread between two bonds.

Interest rates are a measure of the price paid by a "borrower" (or "debtor") to a "lender" (or "creditor") for the use of resources during some time interval. The sum transferred from the lender to the borrower is referred to as the **principal** and the price paid for the use is usually expressed as a percentage of the principal per unit of time (mostly per year).

The transfer from savers to investors occurs through a variety of financial instruments, and the price paid may differ between one sort of instrument and another. Indeed, at any one time there is a bewildering array of rates offered on different instruments. The spread between the lowest and the highest rate in the market might run as high as 1500 basis points (15 percentage points).[1]

In this chapter we develop the theory of interest rates. In doing so, we focus on the one interest rate that can be said to provide the anchor for other rates—the short-term, riskless, real rate. By the **real rate** we mean the rate that would prevail in the economy if price levels remain constant, and are expected to be constant indefinitely. We then look at how all other rates differ from it by looking at the structure of interest rates. The yield offered on a particular bond depends on a myriad of factors having to do with the type of issuer, the characteristics of the bond issue, and the state of the economy. We will look at the factors that affect the yield offered in the bond market.

THE THEORY OF INTEREST RATES

To understand what determines the basic rate we must inquire why some people might decide not to consume all their current resources (i.e., to save), and why some others would want to invest. It should be noted that those desirous to borrow might want to use the proceeds either to make further loans (i.e., acquire financial assets) or to invest (i.e., acquire income-yielding physical assets such as plant, equipment, and residential structures). In this chapter we abstract from financial intermediaries and assume that all loans, directly or indirectly, end up being transferred to an investor.

Saving reflects primarily the choice between current consumption and future consumption. To understand that choice (and all consumer choices) we need to consider two fundamental concepts: preference and opportunity.

Description of Preferences between Current and Future Consumption

Consider first the representation of preferences. Suppose that our consumer is to choose among a variety of "baskets" (or "bundles"), where each basket consists of a certain quantity of current consumption and a certain quantity of future consumption.

Preferences (or tastes) can then be described fully by a complete preference ranking of all the relevant baskets. Given that the amount of current and

---

[1] It is common in the bond market to refer to differences or changes in interest rates in terms of basis points. A basis point is equal to 0.0001, or 0.01%, and 100 basis points represent 1%. So, for example, the difference between 10% and 11% is said to be 100 basis points. If the interest rate increases from 10% to 10.35%, it is said to have increased by 35 basis points.

future consumption can vary by any small dose, some choices among the possible baskets will be ranked equally; that is, the consumer will be indifferent as to certain choices among baskets.

This consideration makes it possible to obtain a very effective representation of preference, as shown in Figure 16-1. The figure measures current consumption (C_1), along the horizontal axis, and future consumption (C_2), along the vertical. Hence any point in the diagram represents a commodity basket, such as H. There will be some other point, H^*, representing an indifferent choice to H; more generally, there will be a curve going from H to $H^*$and beyond, consisting of baskets indifferent to both H and H^*. Such a curve is called an **indifference curve**. We have labeled the indifference curve in Figure 16-1 as u.

Note that an indifference curve will go through every point in the diagram, although they cannot intersect because that would imply that a given basket is ranked both higher and lower than another—a clear inconsistency. The indifference curve u has been drawn falling from left to right; this is because both consumption now and later can be taken to be desirable. As basket H in Figure 16-1 includes more current consumption than basket H^*, in order for it to be indifferent from basket H^*, basket H must have less future consumption, C_2. The reason the curve is drawn convex to the origin is the assumption that, as the consumer gives up successive equal amounts of current consumption, it will take growing quantities of future consumption to make up for the loss of an additional unit. This assumption appears reasonable, although complete justification of it is beyond the scope of this chapter.

Figure 16-1
Indifference Curve between Current and Future Consumption

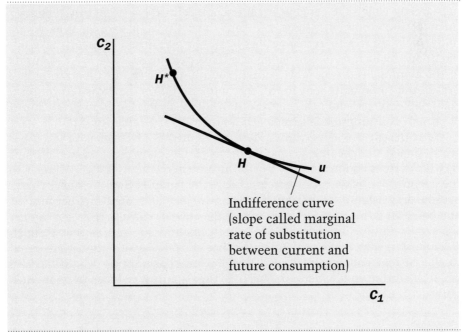

Indifference curve (slope called marginal rate of substitution between current and future consumption)

At any point on an indifference curve, we can draw a tangent to the curve. The slope of the tangent has been called by Irving Fisher, the father of the theory of interest rates, the **marginal rate of time preference**.[2] It measures how much additional consumption next period is needed to compensate the consumer for the loss of a unit of consumption now. That is, the slope of the tangent measures the marginal rate of substitution between current and future consumption. We might conjecture that a particular person would be impatient to consume now rather than later, and therefore that it would take more than one unit tomorrow to induce that person to give up the enjoyment of one unit today. In other words, the marginal rate of time preference, or the slope of the indifference curve, would be larger than one. It is for this reason that Fisher proposed labeling the excess of the slope over unity a "measure of impatience."

It turns out, however, that this conjecture about the slope is wrong. It is easy to verify that the slope of the indifference curve changes as we move along it, and therefore that it is most unlikely to be everywhere more than unity. On the left side of the diagram where today's endowment is small, the slope can be counted on to be larger than unity. However, as we move to the right, and the current endowment grows larger relative to the future one, the slope must become smaller than one, meaning that the consumer may very well be willing to give up a unit of today's abundant supply for less than one unit to add to tomorrow's scarce supply. This is an important insight behind understanding why interest rates can in principle be negative.

Opportunity in the Loan Market

To understand saving behavior, we need to look at how preferences interact with opportunities. Let us consider first a case where the opportunities or baskets among which the person can choose are defined by: (1) an initial endowment of the commodity now and later, and (2) by a loan market where individuals are free to exchange this initial or current endowment for a different one by lending or borrowing at a fixed exchange rate of $R = 1 + r$ units of the commodity in the next period (i.e., the future in our illustration) per unit of the commodity lent in the current period. R is the gross return (principal plus interest) and r the net return or interest rate. For example, if a unit of current consumption is loaned at 5%, then r is 0.05 and R is 1.05.

We represent this opportunity locus in Figure 16-2 by means of the negatively sloped straight line *mm* going through the endowment basket at point B (with current endowment as Y_1 and future endowment as Y_2). We refer to the opportunity locus in the loan market as the "market line." It slopes down, because to get more C_1 you must reduce C_2. It is a straight line because, at any point on it, by giving up one unit of the current consumption we can get the same additional amount, R, of future consumption. And it goes through B, because if there were no lending so that current consumption were equal to the current endowment of Y_1, then future consumption would have to equal the future endowment of Y_2. Thus, the opportunity locus must include point B.

---

[2] Irving Fisher, *The Theory of Interest Rates* (New York: Macmillan, 1930).

Figure 16-2

Representation of Opportunity Locus in the Loan Market (the Market Line)

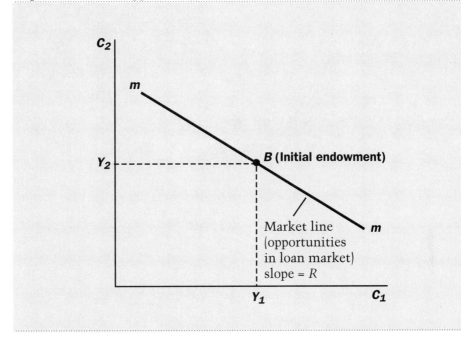

Now let us add to the diagram a family of indifference curves, as shown in Figure 16-3. There will be one curve in the diagram that is tangent to the market line, such as curve u_4 at point D. The consumption basket corresponding to point D can be shown to be the preferred one among all those available, given the market line; hence it will be the chosen basket.

To see this, suppose the consumer started by considering point H on indifference curve u_2, where current consumption is greater than at D. Suppose next he considered giving up some current consumption in favor of more future consumption along his market opportunity line. He would first reach point F and would find it a preferable choice, being on a higher indifference curve, u_3. Continuing, he would reach point D on u_4, offering yet higher utility. But beyond D he immediately starts reaching lower and lower utility curves, such as curves u_2 and u_3. We see that the point of tangency of the market line with an indifference curve provides the best of all feasible choices.

Recalling that the slope of an indifference curve at any point measures the marginal rate of substitution between current and future consumption, we see that at the chosen point the marginal rate of substitution is equal to the market rate R (or the marginal rate of impatience equal to r). It is an important property of a perfect market that, because everybody is confronted with the same market rate r, everybody at the chosen point must exhibit the same degree of impatience. In particular, if r is positive, as it generally is in our type of economy, everybody will be "impatient"; that is, they will be willing to give up a unit of current consumption to lend more only if they can get $1 + r$ units later, with $r > 0$, because that opportunity is offered by the market.

Figure 16-3
Family of Indifference Curves and the Market Line

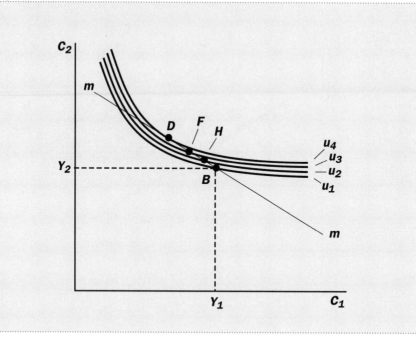

Economic Forces Affecting the Market Rate

So far we have taken the market rate r as a given. But what does in fact determine r in this simple economy? The answer, of course, is demand and supply. For any given R, each person will decide how much to consume now and how much to save or dissave (the difference between the current endowment and consumption). In this simple economy, saving or dissaving is the same as lending or borrowing. By summing up the net lending of each participant, for each R, we obtain a supply curve for loans, such as is graphed in Figure 16-4. We have drawn it as initially rising from left to right, on the commonly held assumption that net lending will rise as R rises. For sufficiently low R, net lending is shown as negative because borrowing would exceed lending. Suppose at first there is no investment. Then market equilibrium requires that net lending be zero. It therefore occurs at point E where the curve cuts the horizontal axis. (Note that we have drawn the net lending curve as declining in the rightmost section. We discuss the reason for this later.)

R will reflect two major forces, namely, the time preferences of participants and their endowments. More impatience will tend to make for a smaller supply of loans (saving) at any given R and to lower the supply curve in Figure 16-4, thereby shifting E to the right. A large endowment of the current commodity relative to the future will make people more eager to lend, raise the curve, and thus reduce R. If this situation is sufficiently prevailing, E may be pushed to the left to the point where it is less than unity and therefore r is negative! This may seem paradoxical, but it is important to understand that

Figure 16-4
Supply Curve for Loans

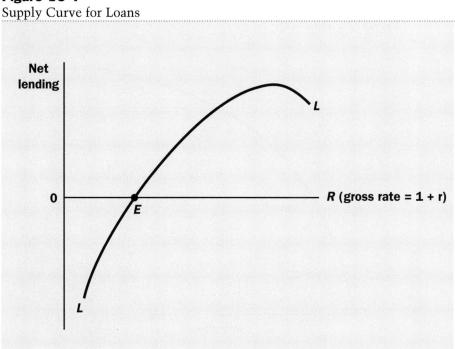

there is no opportunity of transferring resources to the future through invest-ment (or money, which is disregarded) outside of lending and borrowing.

Carryover Through Investment

It is instructive to enlarge the model to allow for the possibilities of invest-ments—a productive process through which, by using current resources as an input, we can obtain an output of future commodities. An investment oppor-tunity locus might look something like the curve *tt* of Figure 16-5, which is referred to as the **transformation curve** or the **production function**. It rises from left to right on the assumption that, the more invested, the more will be the resulting future output. It is convex from below on the customary assumption of decreasing returns to scale (although increasing returns are pos-sible in some regions without changing the argument). The slope of the trans-formation curve measures the **marginal productivity of capital**.

Consumer Choices

The consumer has several decisions to make regarding (1) how much to invest, (2) how much to lend (or borrow), and (3) how much to consume now and later. But only two of these choices are independent: because current resources are given, once the person has decided how much to consume and invest, net lending will be determined uniquely by income minus the two other expenditures. Similarly, net borrowing and investment, together with the future endowment, uniquely fix future consumption.

Figure 16-5

Representation of Opportunity Locus from Investment (Transformation Curve or Production Function)

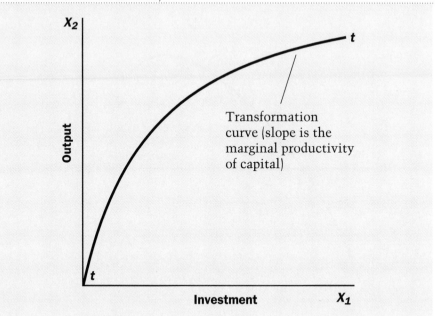

Consider first the decision as to how much to invest. As the consumer's "income," or what she has available to spend on consumption now and later, is limited by the sum of her endowment and any profits she may derive from her production opportunity, a necessary condition to achieve the best feasible consumption is to insure for herself as large a profit as possible. To see how this result can be achieved, look again at Figure 16-5. Recall that profit at any output (or input) is the difference between the output produced with the input (or investment) and the cost of the input. The output for any investment is given by the curve *tt* in Figure 16-5.

What about the cost? Let us suppose initially that the owner of a firm has to borrow the entire amount that is needed to finance the investment. In that case clearly the cost of any given investment will be what is to be repaid next period, namely, the amount borrowed times the gross market rate R. This cost can be represented in Figure 16-5 by a straight line going through the origin with a slope R, and as shown in Figure 16-6 by the line *MM*. Profit for any output, then, is the difference between the curve *tt* and the line *MM*. This is illustrated in Figure 16-6 for an assumed investment of X_1^*. We refer to the line *MM* in the figure as the "cost line." As it represents the cost of borrowing, however, it has the same slope as the market line in Figure 16-2.

As the consumer increases investment from an investment of zero (at the origin), we can see from the graph that profits will initially rise (provided there are profits at all). The additional profit attributable to increased investment gets smaller and smaller, though, until a point in the figure is reached at

Figure 16-6

Measuring the Profit from Investing

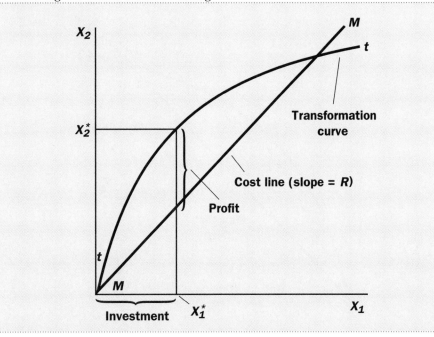

which there is no more incremental profit. This point is shown as *A* in Figure 16-7. If the consumer continues to expand investment still further, the profit (as measured by the vertical distance between the cost line *MM* and the transformation curve *tt*) becomes smaller and smaller. Point *A* has one distinguishing characteristic, which is that at this point the curve *tt* has precisely the same slope *R* as the cost curve *MM*. This is shown in Figure 16-8, where we have drawn through *A* a line *mm* with the same slope as *R* (and hence parallel to *MM*). This line is seen to be tangent to *tt* at *A*.

Because the slope of *tt* represents the **marginal productivity of capital**, we can conclude that the optimum rate of investment for the firm is where the marginal productivity of capital equals the market gross rate *R* or, equivalently, where the additional output that can be obtained from an additional unit of input is just equal to the cost of borrowing that additional unit of input (and the amount obtained by further increases in investment is less than the cost of borrowing).

We can now proceed to examine the consumption decision and its interaction with the investment decision. To this end, we first show how the transformation curve, curve *tt* in Figure 16-5, would be represented if graphed on the earlier Figures 16-1 through 16-3. This is what we have done in Figure 16-9. We obtain the transformation curve (production function), curve *tt*, in Figure 16-9 by rotating the curve *tt* in Figure 16-5 180 degrees and shifting the origin to point *B*, which represents the initial endowment as in Figure 16-2. The resulting curve is the locus of all achievable baskets of the current and

Figure 16-7
Profit Maximization Point

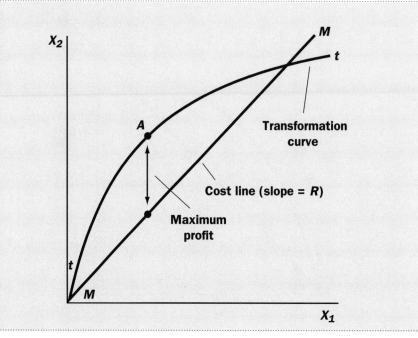

Figure 16-8
Profit Maximization and the Cost Line

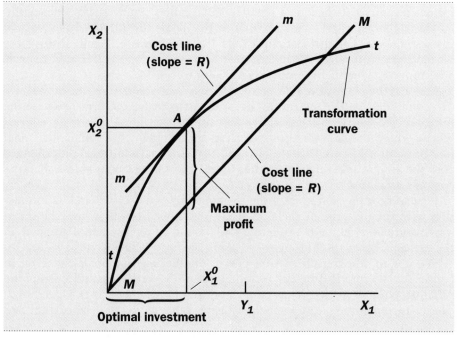

Figure 16-9

Transformation Curve Imposed on Current and Future Consumption Graph

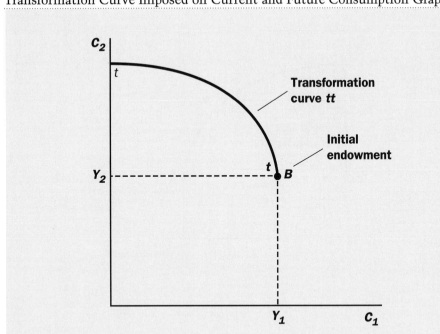

future commodity that are available to the person through a combination of the initial endowment with the transformation opportunity.

The amount invested is shown in Figure 16-9 along the horizontal axis by the difference between the current endowment Y_1 and the point on the horizontal axis corresponding to any point on the transformation curve. This is illustrated in Figure 16-10. At point W in that figure, the corresponding value on the horizontal axis is I^W and the amount of the investment is the difference between Y_1 and I^W. Future consumption corresponding to the point W on the transformation curve is C_2^W, which consists of the future endowment Y_2 plus the profit from the investment as measured by the difference between C_2^W and Y_2.

Suppose for a moment that there were no market for exchanging C_1 with C_2. Then the curve tt in Figure 16-10 would represent the household opportunity locus. The person's best choice, the basket (C_1,C_2), would then be found at a point of tangency of that curve with an indifference curve. But in a market economy the budget constraint does not come from the initial endowment B in Figure 16-2, or by the initial endowment enlarged by the transformation function as in Figure 16-9, but instead from the endowment plus the profit that can be earned through the production and sale of C_2. It follows that to maximize satisfaction the agent should, to begin with, maximize the profits obtained from the transformation activity. This will yield a new budget equation that will include the best choice of the basket (C_1,C_2).

This can be shown graphically in Figure 16-11. Here point A on the transformation function tt is such that the slope there is equal to the slope of the

Figure 16-10

Measuring Investment and Profit from Investment

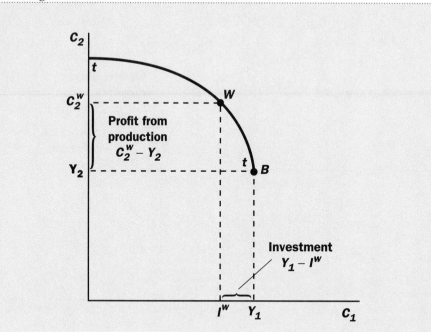

market line *mm*. We know that this point, which corresponds to point *A* in Figure 16-8, represents the amount of investment $(Y_1 - X_1^0)$ and output (X_2^0) that will maximize profits. Through point *A* there goes a new budget line *mm* (again tangent to *tt* at *A*) which represents the outcome of adding maximum profits to the endowment. The utility-maximizing basket will then be at a point of tangency of this profit-augmented budget line with an indifference curve, such as point C^0.

A most important property resulting from the existence of a perfect loan market, together with a transformation, is that it separates the current consumption decision from current income by opening the possibility to saving and dissaving through transformation and net lending. Similarly, it frees the investment from the saving decision, as the person can bridge the gap between saving and investment through lending and borrowing. In the specific case of Figure 16-11, we find that the chosen consumption C_1^0 is less than the initial endowment Y_1, so the person saves an amount shown in the figure. But that is not sufficient to finance an optimal investment that is equal to the distance between Y_1 and I_A of the chosen production. Hence, the difference $(C_1^0 - I_A)$ is made up by borrowing, as indicated in the figure.

This illustrates how a rational person can both save and borrow. There are many other combinations that we can work out by varying the position of the chosen points *A* and C^0 relative to each other and to the endowment basket *B*. If *A* falls between C^0 and *B*, the person will end up saving more than she needs for her investment, and thus she will save, invest, and lend. If on the

Figure 16-11

Optimal Investment and Borrowing Decisions

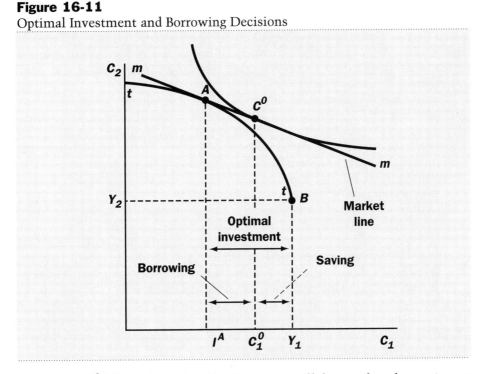

other hand C^0 falls to the right of B, the person will dissave, but she can invest at the same time by borrowing the sum of her investment and dissaving.

Incidentally, it should be apparent by now that we can drop our initial assumption that the investment is financed entirely by borrowing, for should it be financed by the owner's own saving, the cost to the investor of the funds would still be R per unit, which is the amount of interest that would have to be forgone in order to shift funds from making loans in the market to financing the investment (the opportunity cost).

Market Equilibrium

So far we have discussed how a person responds in terms of saving, investing, and borrowing to a given market R. But what determines R itself? The answer, once again, is demand and supply; that is, the price must be such as to clear the market. In the situation we have described there are two markets to clear. The first market for loans R must be such that gross lending equals gross borrowing; or, equivalently, that net borrowing is zero. The second market is the market for the current commodity. There are two sources of demand for it, namely, consumption and investment, and R must be such that aggregate consumption (C) plus aggregate investment (I) will equal the given endowment (Y). Thus: $C + I = Y$, or equivalently, $I = Y - C = S$.

So, R must be such that the demand for investment equals the economy's net saving, denoted by S. But how can R clear two markets at the same time? One variable cannot satisfy two equations at the same time, *unless* one is redundant in the sense that the two have an identical solution. Indeed it happens that the two market-clearing conditions here are redundant. To see this, recall that the decisions of each individual must satisfy a "budget constraint"; that is, a person's net lending must equal the excess of her saving over her investment. If we sum up this constraint over the entire market we get: $L = S - I$, where L is net lending.

It is apparent from this equation that if an interest rate clears the commodity market by making $S = I$, then that same rate will make $L = 0$, or clear the loan market. Thus we can conclude that the equilibrium R must equate the supply of saving and the demand for investment or, equivalently, the demand for and supply of loanable funds. If we want to graph the mechanism determining R, it will be more enlightening to use the commodity market (i.e., saving equals investment).

Equilibrium in this market is represented graphically in Figure 16-12, where the rising curve is the supply of saving, analogous to LL in Figure 16-4. The investment function is drawn to decline uniformly with R. The justification for this choice can be found in Figure 16-8: we have shown that the investment chosen is at the point where the transformation curve has slope R. If R rises to R_1, the investment must shift to a point where the slope is R_1; because R_1 is larger than R, the transformation curve at R_1 must be steeper. But given the convexity of the transformation curve, this can occur only if investment is to the left of the initial level—i.e., smaller. The market-clearing interest rate is then at the intersection of the saving and investment function, where the two are equal.

Figure 16-12
Market Equilibrium

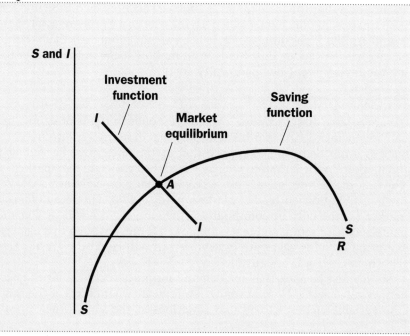

It is also apparent from Figure 16-12 that as long as the intersection occurs in a region where the saving rises with R, the market-clearing interest rate will be higher, the higher the investment function. As can be seen in Figure 16-13, a shift of the investment function up and to the right (meaning more demand for investment at any given R) will raise the interest rate, and result in increased saving and investment. Similarly, an increased propensity to save—a shift of the saving curve up and to the left as shown in Figure 16-14— will reduce the interest rate and result in saving and investment, although by less than the shift because the lower R will have a depressing effect on saving.

The basic conclusion is that the interest rate reflects the complex set of forces that control the demand for investment and the supply of saving. These are discussed extensively elsewhere, and we do not examine them here except for setting out a representative catalog of relevant factors: the rate of growth of population and productivity; fiscal policy, including incentives to save and invest; demographic variables; the role of bequests; the nature of technological progress; and the openness of international capital markets.

By way of illustrating how some of these forces work out, we discuss briefly the effect of fiscal investment incentives on saving, investment, and interest rates. This is a subject much discussed in recent years. If such incentives are effective, they will shift the curve II upward and to the right. If the initial intersection is at point A in Figure 16-12, the effect will certainly be that of raising interest rates (see Figure 16-3); but how nearly will it succeed in achieving the intended purpose of increasing investment? In the end, investment

Figure 16-13
Change in L, S and R if Investment Function Increases

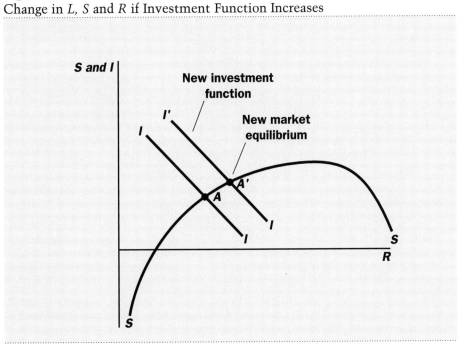

Figure 16-14

Change in *I*, *S* and *R* if Saving Function Increases

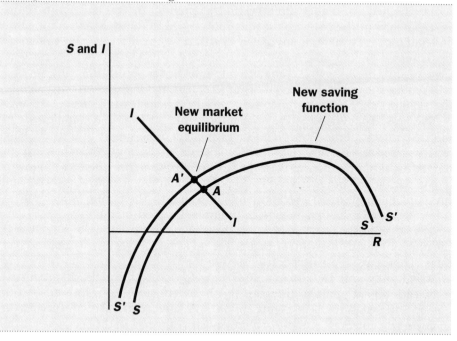

can rise only if and as far as savings rise; and the rise in saving depends on the extent to which saving responds to the higher rate. If the response is strong, there will be a relatively large rise in saving and investment, while the rise in interest rates will be contained. But in the opposite case the incentives will mostly increase interest rates and have little effect on investment.

To complete the picture, we consider the case in which the two curves intersect at a point like *G'* in Figure 16-15, where saving decreases in response to higher interest rates. Is such a response conceivable? If people get paid more for saving, could they possibly respond by saving less? The answer is that this is entirely possible; indeed, according to one school of thought, it is very likely. The reason is simple. Suppose that initially you own a portfolio of loans. An increasing *R* will have two effects influencing your response. First, future consumption is cheaper in terms of current consumption, which should encourage you to consume more later and save more now. But there is a second effect. As long as you are a creditor, a higher interest rate will make you richer and push you toward consuming more now and later. It is entirely possible that the second effect may predominate. In this case the supply of saving will decline with higher *R*, as shown by the terminal portion of the *SS* curve in Figure 16-15. If the intersection is in that region, the result of incentives can be quite perverse, as we can see if we shift the curve *II* up to the right from *I'I'* to *I"I"* and the equilibrium point from *G'* to *G"*. The effect is again to increase *R*, but now that increase will reduce saving and hence investment.

In other words, the fiscal incentive has the opposite effect from the intended one. The situation is made worse if the incentives are financed not

Figure 16-15
Possibility of Saving Decreasing in Response to Higher Interest Rate

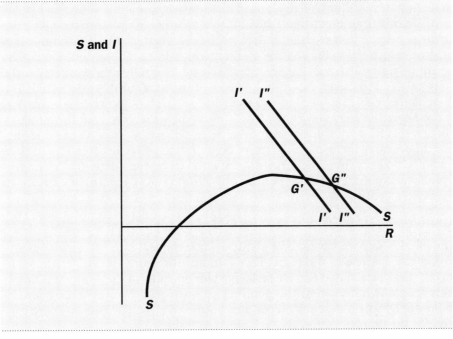

by new taxes but by increased deficit, which reduces investment further by cutting net national saving directly and through a higher interest rate. Some think that these considerations may help explain the catastrophic decline of saving during the years of Reaganomics. To be sure, net investment did not decline much, but that was because of the huge borrowing from non-U.S. savers made attractive by the high domestic interest rates, which has had the effect of making the country permanently poorer.

Efficiency Properties of Markets

The equilibrium achieved with the intermediation of the loan markets has an important property from the point of view of the efficiency of the economy in producing and allocating resources—a property that economists refer to as **Pareto optimality**. Instinctively we think of economic efficiency as implying the absence, or minimization, of waste. Pareto optimality makes that notion precise and conceptually operational: an allocation is Pareto optimal if it is not possible to reallocate the goods (inputs and outputs) in such a way that some will be better off while nobody will lose.

It is clear that if an allocation is not Pareto optimal there must be some slack or waste; conversely, if there is slack, the allocation cannot be Pareto optimal. Pareto optimality in our simplified economy is assured by profit maximization, plus the fact that, at market equilibrium, both the marginal productivity of capital and the marginal rate of time preference equals R for every firm and for every consumer. This means that there is no way of increasing output by reshuffling inputs among firms; the additional output by those who would gain inputs will be offset precisely by the output lost by those losing inputs. By similar reasoning, we can infer that no welfare gain can come from reshuffling the given output among consumers.

While this is an important logical result, it turns out we cannot make too much of it in respect to existing free market economies. First, the result presupposes a perfectly competitive market, which free competition may fail to assure because of restrictive practices. Second, it ignores transactions costs, information costs, and the consequences of incomplete information. Third, there is the whole problem of externalities or effects—negative or positive—that production may have on people other than the buyer of the product. Finally, society may value things other than efficiency, such as the distribution of welfare; there may therefore be some non-Pareto optimal solution, trading efficiency for some other property. All these considerations are incentives to make markets more perfect and allow valuing externalities through the price mechanism.

Real and Nominal Interest Rates: Fisher's Law

The interest rate we have talked about so far is the real rate, which would prevail in the absence of inflation. This rate measures the amount of the commodity next period that can be exchanged for one unit of the commodity now. This generally differs from the nominal rate, which measures the amount of money to be repaid next period per unit borrowed now. The two rates are connected by a simple relation that is known as **Fisher's Law**. It rests on the principle that an exchange of money now for money later must imply the same rate of exchange between the commodity now and later, as implied by the real rate.

Suppose the real rate is $1 + r$; then by delivering one unit of the commodity now, we can obtain $(1 + r)$ units next period. But we could, alternatively, sell the commodity now at the spot price, p_1, and invest the proceeds in a loan at the nominal rate $(1 + i)$, obtaining $p_1 (1 + i)$ units of money next period.

How many units of the next-period commodity does that represent? To find the answer we must divide by the second-period price of the commodity, p_2. Thus the second-period quantity is $p_1 (1 + i)/(p_2)$. This quantity must equal the real rate $(1 + r)$. Thus:

$$(1 + r) = \frac{1 + i}{1 + \dot{p}} \tag{16.1}$$

Where the denominator in Equation (16.1) follows from the fact that:

$$\frac{p_1}{p_2} = \frac{1}{p_2/p_1} = \frac{1}{1 + [(p_2 - p_1)/p_1]}$$

and that $(p_2 - p_1)/p_1) = \dot{p}$ = the percentage rise in the price level over the period of the loan.

Equation (16.1) can be restated in the form:

$$(1 + i) = (1 + r)(1 + \dot{p})$$

This means that the nominal gross rate is the product of the gross real rate and 1 plus the rate of inflation. The equation above, in turn, implies that, $i = r + \dot{p} + r\dot{p}$.

For the more common values of r and $\dot{p}$, the product of r and $\dot{p}$ is small enough to be neglected, and the equation can be written as:

$$i \approx r + \dot{p},$$

or:

$$r \approx i - \dot{p} \tag{16.2}$$

Equation (16.2) is the formula commonly used to compute the ex post real rate of interest, which cannot be observed directly in the market. It is equally common to measure the anticipated or ex ante real rate of interest by replacing $\dot{p}$ by anticipated inflation. The ex ante rate will differ from the ex post rate as a result of errors of expectation. It should be clear that the real rate so computed is not necessarily the same as the rate that would clear markets in the economy without inflation, because as a result of market imperfections, including taxation and possibly inflation illusion, inflation can alter the real rate. For instance, in the early phase of unanticipated inflation, the real rate typically falls. In other words, besides reflecting fundamental forces such as saving and productivity, the real rate may also be affected by other forces such as inflation, especially in the short run.

THE STRUCTURE OF INTEREST RATES

Thus far we have explained how the short-term, riskless interest rate is determined in a simple economy. However, there is not just one interest rate in any economy, rather there is a structure of interest rates. The interest rate that a borrower has to pay will depend on a myriad of factors, which we will describe in this section. We begin with a discussion of the base interest rate, which is the interest rate on U.S. government securities. Next we explain the factors that affect the yield spread or risk premium for non-Treasury securities. Throughout this section we refer to the yield on a security; this is the interest rate offered on a security. The procedure for computing a security's yield is described in Chapter 17.

The Base Interest Rate

The securities issued by the Department of the Treasury are backed by the full faith and credit of the U.S. government. Consequently, market participants throughout the world view them as having no credit risk. As such, interest rates on Treasury securities are the benchmark interest rates throughout the U.S. economy, as well as in international capital markets. The large size of any single issue has contributed to making the Treasury market the most active and hence the most liquid market in the world.

The minimum interest rate or **base interest rate** that investors will demand for investing in a debt obligation other than a Treasury security (referred to as a non-Treasury security), is the yield offered on a comparable-maturity Treasury security. As we explain in Chapter 20, Treasury securities are auctioned on a regularly scheduled basis. The most recently auctioned Treasury security for a given maturity is called the **on-the-run issue**. Table 16-1 shows the on-the run Treasury issues on January 13, 1994. So, for example, if an investor wanted to purchase a bond on January 13, 1994 that matures in ten

Table 16-1

Yields for On-the-Run Treasuries for January 13, 1994

Maturity	Yield
3-Month	3.02%
6-Month	3.22
1-Year	3.52
2-Year	4.11
3-Year	4.42
5-Year	5.05
7-Year	5.22
10-Year	5.67
20-Year	5.84
30-Year	6.26

Source: **Weekly Market Update, Goldman Sachs & Co., Fixed Income Research, New York, January 14, 1994, p. A-1. Copyright 1994 by Goldman Sachs.**

years, the minimum yield the investor would seek is 5.67%, the on-the-run Treasury yield reported in Table 16-1. The base interest rate is also called the **benchmark interest rate**.

Risk Premium

Market participants talk of interest rates on non-Treasury securities as trading at a spread to a particular on-the-run Treasury security. For example, if the yield on a ten-year non-Treasury security is 6.67% and the yield on a ten-year Treasury security is 5.67%, the spread is 100 basis points. This spread reflects the additional risks the investor faces by acquiring a security that is not issued by the U.S. government and therefore can be called a **risk premium**. We can express the interest rate offered on a non-Treasury security as:

base interest rate + spread

or equivalently

base interest rate + risk premium

The factors that affect the spread include:

1. the type of issuer.
2. the issuer's perceived creditworthiness.
3. the term or maturity of the instrument.
4. provisions that grant either the issuer or the investor the option to do something.
5. the taxability of the interest received by investors.
6. the expected liquidity of the issue.

Types of Issuers

A key feature of a debt obligation is the nature of the issuer. In addition to the U.S. government there are agencies of the government, municipal governments, corporations (domestic and foreign), and foreign governments that issue bonds.

The bond market is classified by the type of issuer. These are referred to as **market sectors**. The spread between the interest rate offered in two sectors of the bond market with the same maturity is referred to as an **intermarket sector spread**.

Excluding the Treasury market sector, other market sectors have a wide range of issuers, each with different abilities to satisfy their contractual obligation. For example, within the corporate market sector, issuers are classified as: (1) utilities, (2) transportations, (3) industrials, and (4) banks and finance companies. The spread between two issues within a market sector is called an **intramarket sector spread**.

Perceived Creditworthiness of Issuer

Default risk or credit risk refers to the risk that the issuer of a bond may be unable to make timely principal or interest payments. Most market participants rely primarily on commercial rating companies to assess the default risk of an issuer. We will discuss these rating companies in Chapter 22. The spread between Treasury securities and non-Treasury securities that are identical in all respects except for quality is referred to as a **quality spread** or **credit spread**.

Term to Maturity

A key feature of any bond is its term to maturity, the number of years during which the borrower has promised to meet the conditions of the debt obligation. A bond's term to maturity is the date on which the debt will cease to exist and the borrower will redeem the issue by paying the amount borrowed. In practice, the words **maturity, term**, and **term to maturity** are used interchangeably to refer to the number of years remaining in the life of a bond. Technically, however, maturity denotes the date the bond will be redeemed, and term or term to maturity denotes the number of years until that date.

A bond's maturity is crucial for several reasons. First, maturity indicates the expected life of the instrument or the number of periods during which the holder of the bond can expect to receive the coupon payments, and the number of years before the principal will be paid. Second, the yield on a bond depends substantially on its maturity. More specifically, at any given point in time, the yield offered on a long-term bond may be greater than, less than, or equal to the yield offered on a short-term bond. As explained in Chapter 18, how maturity affects the yield will depend on the shape of the yield curve. Finally, as explained in Chapter 17, the volatility of a bond's price is closely associated with maturity. Therefore, changes in the market level of rates will have a greater impact on the price of long-maturity debt than on otherwise similar debt of shorter maturity.[3]

---

[3] Chapter 17 discusses this point in detail.

Generally, bonds with a maturity of between one to five years are considered "short term"; bonds with a maturity between five and 12 years are viewed as "intermediate term," and "long-term" bonds are those with a maturity greater than 12 years. The spread between any two maturity sectors of the market is called a **maturity spread**. The relationship between the yields on comparable securities but different maturities is called the **term structure** of interest rates. This term structure is of such importance that we have devoted Chapter 18 to this topic.

Inclusion of Options

It is not uncommon for a bond issue to include a provision that gives the bondholder and/or the issuer an option to take some action against the other party. An option that is included in a bond issue is referred to as an **embedded option**. We will discuss the various types of embedded options in later chapters.

The most common type of option in a bond issue is the call provision that grants the issuer the right to retire the debt, fully or partially, before the scheduled maturity date. The inclusion of a call feature benefits issuers by allowing them to replace an old bond issue with a lower-interest-cost issue, should interest rates in the market decline. Effectively, a call provision allows the issuer to alter the maturity of a bond. A call provision is detrimental to the bondholder because the bondholder must reinvest the proceeds received at a lower interest rate.

The presence of an embedded option has an effect on the spread of an issue relative to a Treasury security, and the spread relative to otherwise comparable issues that do not have an embedded option. In general, market participants will require a larger spread to a comparable Treasury security for an issue with an embedded option which is favorable to the issuer (e.g., a call option) than for an issue without such an option. In contrast, market participants will require a smaller spread to a comparable Treasury security for an issue with an embedded option which is favorable to the investor (e.g., put option and conversion option). In fact, for a bond with an option that is favorable to an investor, the interest rate on an issue may be less than that on a comparable Treasury security.

Taxability of Interest

Unless exempted under the federal income tax code, interest income is taxable at the federal level. In addition, there may be state and local taxes on interest income.

The federal tax code specifically exempts the interest income from qualified municipal bond issues. (We discuss municipal bonds in Chapter 23.) Because of the tax-exempt feature of municipal bonds, their yield is less than that of Treasuries with the same maturity. Table 16-2 shows this relationship on January 13, 1994, for high-grade, tax-exempt securities. The difference in yield between tax-exempt securities and Treasury securities is typically measured not in basis points but in percentage terms. More specifically, it is measured as the percentage of the yield on a tax-exempt security relative to a comparable Treasury security.

Table 16-2
Yield on High-Grade, Tax-Exempt Securities for January 13, 1994

Maturity	Yield	Yield as a percent of Treasury yield
1-year	2.50%	71.1%
3-year	3.50	79.3
5-year	4.00	79.2
10-year	4.50	79.3
20-year	5.15	88.2
30-Year	5.20	83.1

Source: **Weekly Market Update,** *Goldman Sachs & Co., Fixed Income Research, New York, January 14, 1994, p. A-5. Copyright 1994 by Goldman Sachs.*

The yield on a taxable bond issue after federal income taxes are paid is equal to:

$$\text{after-tax yield} = \text{pre-tax yield} \times (1 - \text{marginal tax rate})$$

For example, suppose a taxable bond issue offers a yield of 6% and is acquired by an investor facing a marginal tax rate of 36%. The after-tax yield would then be:

$$\text{after-tax yield} = 0.06\ (1 - .36) = 0.0384 = 3.84\%.$$

Alternatively, we can determine the yield that must be offered on a taxable bond issue to give the same after-tax yield as a tax-exempt issue. This yield is called the **equivalent taxable yield** and is determined as follows:

$$\text{equivalent taxable yield} = \frac{\text{tax–exempt yield}}{(1 - \text{marginal tax rate})}$$

For example, consider an investor facing a 36% marginal tax rate who purchases a tax-exempt issue with a yield of 3.84%. The equivalent taxable yield is then:

$$\text{equivalent taxable yield} = \frac{.0384}{(1 - .36)} = .06$$

Notice that the higher the marginal tax rate, the higher the equivalent taxable yield. For example, if the marginal tax rate is 39% rather than 36%, the equivalent taxable yield would be 6.3% rather than 6%, as shown below:

$$\text{equivalent taxable yield} = \frac{.0384}{(1 - .39)} = .063$$

State and local governments may tax interest income on bond issues that are exempt from federal income taxes. Some municipalities exempt interest income from all municipal issues, others do not. Some states exempt interest income from bonds issued by municipalities within the state, but tax the interest income from bonds issued by municipalities outside of the state. The implication is that two municipal securities of the same quality rating and the same maturity may trade at some spread because of the relative demand for bonds of municipalities in different states. For example, in a high income tax state such as New York, the demand for bonds of municipalities will drive down their yield relative to municipalities in a low income tax state such as Florida, holding all credit issues aside.

Municipalities are not permitted to tax the interest income from securities issued by the U.S. Treasury. Thus, part of the spread between Treasury securities and taxable non-Treasury securities of the same maturity reflects the value of the exemption from state and local taxes.

Expected Liquidity of an Issue

Bonds trade with different degrees of liquidity. The greater the expected liquidity that an issue will trade, the lower the yield that investors would require. As noted earlier, Treasury securities are the most liquid securities in the world. The lower yield offered on Treasury securities relative to non-Treasury securities reflects the difference in liquidity as well as perceived credit risk. Even within the Treasury market, on-the-run issues have greater liquidity than other Treasury issues referred to as off-the-run issues.

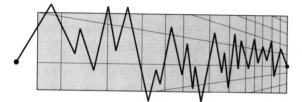

SUMMARY

In this chapter we have presented the theory of interest rates. We showed how consumers' choices between current and future consumption affect saving, relying on two fundamental concepts: preference and opportunity (in the loan market and production market).

An important property that results from the existence of a perfect loan market, together with production opportunities, is that it separates the current consumption decision from current income by creating the possibility to save or dissave through production and net lending. Our conclusion is that the equilibrium interest rate reflects a complex set of forces that control the demand for investment and the supply of savings.

The market equilibrium achieved with the intermediation of the loan markets has an important property with respect to the efficiency of the economy in producing and allocating resources. It will not be possible to reallocate resources in such a way that some will be better off while nobody will be worse off. Economists refer to this as Pareto optimality.

The real rate of interest is the interest rate that would prevail in the absence of inflation. It can be shown that the nominal rate of interest is approximately equal to the real rate of interest plus anticipated inflation, a relationship referred to as Fisher's Law.

In all economies, there is not just one interest rate but a structure of interest rates. The difference between the yield on any two bonds is called the yield spread. The base interest rate is the yield on a Treasury security. The yield spread between a non-Treasury security and a comparable on-the-run Treasury security is called a risk premium. The factors that affect the spread include: (1) the type of issuer (e.g., agency, corporate, municipality); (2) the issuer's perceived creditworthiness as measured by the rating system of commercial rating companies; (3) the term or maturity of the instrument; (4) the embedded options in a bond issue (e.g., call, put, or conversion provisions); (5) the taxability of interest income at the federal and municipal levels; and (6) the expected liquidity of the issue.

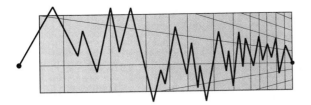

QUESTIONS

1. Why is the indifference curve between current and future consumption convex to the origin?

2. What is meant by the marginal rate of time preference?

3. a. What is the market line?

   b. Explain why the market line slopes downward.

4. What determines the market rate in a simple economy?

5. What is the transformation curve?

6. What is meant by the marginal productivity of capital?

7. How is the equilibrium market rate determined?

8. What is meant by the real rate of interest?

9. What is meant by the nominal rate of interest?

10. According to Fisher's Law, what is the relationship between the real rate and the nominal rate?

11. What is the difficulty of measuring an economy's real rate of interest?

12. In the May 29, 1992 *Weekly Market Update* published by Goldman Sachs & Co., the following information was reported in various exhibits for the Treasury market as of the close of business Thursday, May 28, 1992.

On-the-Run Treasuries.

Maturity	Yield
3-Month	3.77%
6-Month	3.95
1-Year	4.25
2-Year	5.23
3-Year	5.78
5-Year	6.67
7-Year	7.02
10-Year	7.37
20-Year	7.65
30-Year	7.88

Key off-the-run Treasuries

Issue	Yield
Old 10-Year	7.42%
Old 30 Year	7.90

a. What is the credit risk associated with a Treasury security?

b. Why is the Treasury yield considered the base interest rate?

c. What is meant by "on-the-run Treasuries"?

d. What is meant by "off-the-run Treasuries"?

e. What is the yield spread between: (i) the off-the-run 10-year Treasury issue and the on-the-run 10-year Treasury issue; and (ii) the off-the-run 30-year Treasury issue and the on-the-run 30-year Treasury issue?

f. What does the yield spread between the off-the-run Treasury issue and the on-the-run Treasury issue reflect?

13. In the May 29, 1992 *Weekly Market Update* published by Goldman Sachs & Co., the table below contains information that was reported in various exhibits for certain corporate bonds as of the close of business Thursday, May 28, 1992.

a. What is meant by "spread"?

b. What is meant by "Treasury benchmark"?

c. Using the information for the Treasury market reported for May 29, 1992 in question 12, explain how each of the spreads reported above was determined?

d. Why do each of the spreads reflect a risk premium?

14. a. The yield spread between the Mobil Corp. and General Electric Capital Co. issues reported in question 13 reflects more than just credit risk. What other factors could the spread reflect?

b. The Mobil Corp. issue is not callable. However, the General Electric Capital Co. issue is callable. How does this information help you in understanding the spread between these two issues?

Issuer	Rating	Yield	Spread	Treasury Benchmark
General Electric Cap. Co.	Triple A	7.87%	50	10
Mobil Corp.	Double A	7.77	40	10
Southern Bell Tel & Teleg	Triple A	8.60	72	30
Bell Tel Co Pa	Double A	8.66	78	30
AMR Corp	Triple B	9.43	155	30

15. Referring to the corporate bond issues reported in question 13, answer the following questions.

    a. What is the yield spread between the Southern Bell Telephone and Telegraph bond issue and the Bell Telephone Company (Pennsylvania) bond issue?

    b. The Southern Bell Telephone and Telegraph bond issue is not callable but the Bell Telephone Company (Pennsylvania) bond issue is callable. What does the yield spread in the previous question reflect?

    c. AMR Corp. is the parent company of American Airlines and is therefore classified in the transportation industry. The issue is not callable. What is the yield spread between AMR Corp. and Southern Bell Telephone and Telegraph bond issues, and what does this spread reflect?

16. In the May 29, 1992 *Weekly Market Update* published by Goldman Sachs & Co., the following information was reported in an exhibit for high-grade, tax-exempt securities as of the close of business Thursday, May 28, 1992.

Maturity	Yield	Yield as a percent of Treasury yield
1-Year	3.20%	76.5%
3-Year	4.65	80.4
5-Year	5.10	76.4
10-Year	5.80	78.7
30-Year	6.50	82.5

    a. What is meant by a tax-exempt security?

    b. Why is the yield on a tax-exempt security less than the yield on a Treasury security of the same maturity?

    c. What is meant by the equivalent taxable yield?

    d. In the same issue of the Goldman Sachs report is information on "Intra Market Yield Spreads." What does this term mean?

17. a. What is meant by an embedded option in a bond?

    b. Give three examples of an embedded option that might be included in a bond issue.

    c. Does an embedded option increase or decrease the risk premium relative to the base interest rate?

•

Valuation of Debt Contracts and Their Price Volatility Characteristics

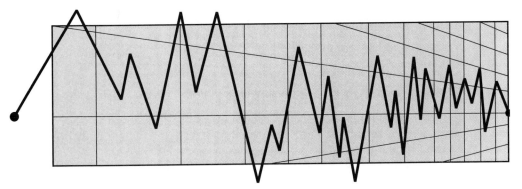

LEARNING OBJECTIVES

After reading this chapter you will understand:

- the cash flow characteristics of a bond.

- how the price of a bond is determined.

- why the yield to maturity is used as a measure of a bond's return.

- the importance of the reinvestment rate in realizing the yield to maturity.

- why the price of a bond changes.

- that the price/yield curve of an option-free bond is convex.

- that the two characteristics of a bond that affect its price volatility are its coupon and its maturity.

- what duration is and how it is calculated.

- the limitations of duration as a measure of price volatility of a bond when interest rates change.

- what the convexity measure of a bond is and how it is related to bond price volatility.

- how to approximate the duration of any bond.

In Chapter 16 we focused on determinants of the one-period rate on debt instruments and the structure of interest rates in any economy. Our concern in this chapter is the valuation of debt contracts. We will concentrate on one special case, namely, debt contracts that (1) are free of risk of default by the issuer, (2) enjoy no advantage from taxes, and (3) contain no embedded options (i.e., are not callable, putable, or convertible). Federal government debt, the subject of Chapter 20, is an example of this kind of obligation.[1] The rate earned on federal government debt instruments is usually characterized as the "riskless," meaning that there is no risk that the U.S. government will default on its obligation to pay interest and repay principal. After describing how debt obligations are valued, we look at the factors that affect the price volatility of a debt obligation and how to measure the price volatility of a debt obligation when interest rates change.

FEATURES OF DEBT CONTRACTS

In later chapters we will describe the various features of debt contracts. Here we will provide enough information about debt contracts to understand the basic principles for valuing them.

The term to maturity or maturity of a debt contract is the number of years during which the borrower has promised to meet the conditions of the debt. The amount that will be repaid by the borrower is called the principal. The entire principal can be repaid at the maturity date, in which case the debt contract is said to have a **bullet maturity**. Or, various amounts of the principal can be paid over the life of the debt contract in which case the remaining principal repaid at the maturity date is called a **balloon payment**. A special type of debt contract is a bond, and the amount paid at maturity is called the **par value, maturity value**, or **face value**.

A debt contract's **coupon** is the periodic interest payment made to owners during the life of the contract. The coupon is in fact the **coupon rate** or rate of interest that, when multiplied by the unpaid outstanding principal provides the dollar amount of the coupon payment. Typically, but not universally, for bonds issued in the United States the coupon payments are made every six months.

There are debt contracts in which no periodic coupon interest is paid over the life of the contract. Instead, both the principal and the interest are paid at the maturity date. Such debt contracts are called **zero-coupon instruments**.

The price of most debt contracts are quoted as percentages of par value. To convert the price quote into a dollar figure, one simply multiplies the price by the par value. The following table will illustrate the matter:.

---

[1] Federal government bond returns actually do have a minor tax advantage because they are exempt from state and local taxes.

Par value	Price quote	Price as a Percentage of par	Price in dollars
$1,000	91 ¾	91.75%	$ 917.50
5,000	102 ½	102.50	5,125.00
10,000	87 ¼	87.25	8,725.00
25,000	100 ⅞	108.875	25,218.75
100,000	71 ⁹⁄₃₂	71.28125	71,281.25

BASIC VALUATION PRINCIPLES

A useful way of understanding the valuation of longer-term debt contracts and how this relates to interest rates is to use the principle that, in perfect markets, all riskless instruments have the same short-term return, and it must coincide with the riskless short-term rate for that period. This condition may be expected to be enforced through arbitrage. The one-period rate of return from, say, an instrument with maturity n and a cash flow denoted by $(a_1, ..., a_n)$, consists of the cash payment, a_1, plus the capital gain, or the difference between the next-period price and the current price of the security, expressed as a percentage of initial value.

Let us denote by $_nP_j$ the price j periods $(j < n)$ from the present of an instrument maturing n periods later; the capital gain for the current period is: $_{n-1}P_1 - {_nP_0}$. Hence the condition that the one-period return from holding the instrument must be equal to the short-term rate for the forthcoming period, denoted by r_1, can be written as:

$$\frac{a_1 + ({_{n-1}P_1} - {_nP_0})}{{_nP_0}} = r_1 \tag{17.1}$$

Solving for $_nP_0$,

$$_nP_0 = \frac{a_1 + {_{n-1}P_1}}{1 + r_1} \tag{17.2}$$

The reason why the right-hand side of Equation (17.2) must be the equilibrium price of the n-period asset is that, as can be verified, if the current price, $_nP_0$, were larger than the right-hand side of Equation (17.2), then the one-period return of the instrument, given by Equation (17.1), would be smaller than the return r_1 obtainable by investing in the one-period instrument. As a result, no one would want to hold it, causing its price to drop. Similarly, if $_nP_0$ is smaller than the right-hand side of Equation (17.2), this yield for the instrument would be larger than r_1, and everyone would want to hold it.

Next we observe that $_{n-1}P_1$ must satisfy an equation like Equation (17.2), or:

$$_{n-1}P_1 = \frac{a_2 + {_{n-2}P_2}}{1 + r_2}$$

Substituting this equation into Equation (17.2), we get

$$_nP_0 = \frac{a_1}{(1 + r_1)} + \frac{a_2 + {_{n-2}P_2}}{(1 + r_1)(1 + r_2)}$$

Repeating the same substitution recursively, up to the maturity of the instrument, we find

$$_nP_0 = \frac{a_1}{(1 + r_1)} + \frac{a_2}{(1 + r_1)(1 + r_2)} + \tag{17.3}$$

$$\frac{a_{3n}}{(1 + r_1)(1 + r_2)(1 + r_3)} + \dots +$$

$$\frac{a_n}{(1 + r_1)(1 + r_2)(1 + r_3)\dots(1 + r_n)}$$

Each term on the right-hand side of the above equation is the present value of the cash flow at each successive time. Thus the price of a debt instrument must equal the sum of the present value of the payments that the debtor is required to make until maturity.

Let us illustrate the principles to this point. Assume that the length of a period is one year. Suppose that an investor purchases a four-year debt instrument with the following payments promised by the borrower.

Year	Interest payment	Principal repayment	Cash flow
1	$100	0	$100
2	120	0	120
3	140	0	140
4	150	$1,000	1,150

In terms of our notation: $a_1 = \$100$; $a_2 = \$120$; $a_3 = \$140$; $a_4 = \$1,150$. Assume that the one-year rates for the next four years are: $r_1 = .07$; $r_2 = .08$; $r_3 = .09$; $r_4 = .10$. The current value or price of this debt instrument today, denoted $_4P_0$, using Equation (17.3) is then:

$$_4P_0 = \frac{100}{(1.07)} + \frac{120}{(1.07)(1.08)} + \frac{140}{(1.07)(1.08)(1.09)} +$$

$$\frac{1,150}{(1.07)(1.08)(1.09)(1.10)}$$

$$= \$1,138.43$$

RETURN FROM A BOND: YIELD-TO-MATURITY MEASURE

Next we must consider how to construct a measure that will permit us to compare the rate of return of instruments having different cash flows and different maturities. For one-period instruments, the measure is clear; it is provided by the left-hand side of Equation (17.1). But that approach cannot be generalized readily to long-term debt instruments. For instance, for an instrument with a cash flow (a_1, a_2), the measure $(a_1 + a_2)/P_0$ would not be a useful measure of yield. In the first place, if we seek a measure that can be used to compare instruments of different maturities, it must measure return per unit of time. And second, the proposed measure ignores the timing of receipts, thus failing to reflect the time value of money.

The widely accepted solution to this problem is provided by a measure known as the **yield to maturity**. It is defined as the interest rate that makes the present value of the cash flow equal to the market value (price) of the instrument. Thus for the debt instrument in Equation (17.3), the yield to maturity is the interest rate y that satisfies Equation (17.4), which must generally be found by trial and error.

$$_nP_0 = \frac{a_1}{(1 + y)} + \frac{a_2}{(1 + y)^2} + \frac{a_3}{(1 + y)^3} + \ldots + \frac{a_n}{(1 + y)^n} \tag{17.4}$$

If the debt instrument is a bond, the cash flow $(a_1 \ldots a_n)$ can be written as $(C, C, \ldots, C + M)$, where C is the coupon payment and M the maturity value. Equation (17.4) can be rewritten as

$$P = \frac{C}{(1 + y)} + \frac{C}{(1 + y)^2} + \frac{C}{(1 + y)^3} + \ldots + \frac{C + M}{(1 + y)^n} \tag{17.5}$$

After dividing both sides of Equation (17.5) by M, to obtain the price per dollar of maturity value, and factoring C, we obtain

$$\frac{P}{M} = \frac{C}{M} \sum_{t=1}^{n} \frac{1}{(1 + y)^t} + \frac{1}{(1 + y)^n} \tag{17.6}$$

Recognizing that the summation on the right-hand side of Equation (17.6) is the sum of a geometric progression,[2] we can rewrite the equation) as:

$$\frac{P}{M} = \frac{C}{M} \left[\frac{1 - (1 + y)^{-n}}{y} \right] + \frac{1}{(1 + y)^n} \tag{17.7}$$

The yield to maturity is the solution to Equation (17.7) for y, the yield of an n-period bond. In Equation (17.7) P/M is the so-called **par value relation**, usually expressed as a percentage. If it is equal to one, the bond sells "at par"; if it is larger than one, it sells at a "premium"; and if it is less than one, it sells at a "discount." C/M is the coupon rate expressed as a ratio.

So far we have not specified the unit of time for measuring the frequencies with which interest is computed and the coupons are paid. Interest rates (and maturity) customarily are quoted per year (e.g., 7% per year), and we shall follow this convention; this means that in Equation (17.7) it is implicitly assumed that the coupon rate is C per year and paid once a year. In fact, in the United States almost all bonds pay interest twice a year. Each coupon payment therefore amounts to $C/2$, which must be discounted twice a year at half the annual yield or $y/2$. As a result, Equation (17.7) is changed to:

$$\frac{P}{M} = \frac{C}{2M} \left[\frac{1 - (1 + y/2)^{-2n}}{y/2} \right] + \frac{1}{(1 + y/2)^{2n}} \tag{17.8}$$

To illustrate calculation of the yield to maturity of a bond with semiannual coupon payments, consider a 7%, 20-year bond with a maturity or par value

---

[2] The sum of a geometric progression is:

$$\sum_{t=1}^{n} \frac{1}{(1 + k)^t} = \frac{1 - (1 + k)^{-n}}{k}$$

of $100, and selling for 74.26%, or 74.26 cents per $1 of par value. The cash flow for this bond per dollar of par value is: 40 six-month payments of $0.035, and $1 received in 40 six-month periods from now. The present value at various semiannual interest rates $(y/2)$ is:

Interest rate $(y/2)$:	3.5%	4.0%	4.5%	5.0%	5.5%	6.0%	6.5%
Present value (P/M):	1.0000	0.9010	0.8160	0.7426	0.6791	0.6238	0.5756

When a 5.0% semiannual interest rate is used, the present value of the cash flows is equal to 0.7426 per $1 of par value, which is the price of the bond. Hence, 5.0% is the semiannual yield to maturity.

The annual yield to maturity should, strictly speaking, be found by compounding 5.0% for one year. That is, it should be 10.25.[3] But the accepted convention in the market is to double $y/2$, the semiannual yield to maturity. Thus, the yield to maturity for the bond above is 10% (two times 5.0%). The yield to maturity computed using this convention—doubling the semiannual yield—is called the **bond equivalent yield**.

REASONS WHY A BOND'S PRICE WILL CHANGE

One can infer from Equation (17.7) or Equation (17.8) that the value of a bond depends on three things: its coupon, its maturity, and interest rates. Hence the price of a bond can change over time for any one of the following reasons.

1. *A change in the level of interest rates in the economy.* For example, if interest rates in the economy increase because of Fed policy, the price of a bond will decrease; if interest rates fall, the price of a bond will rise.

2. *A change in the price of a bond selling at a price other than par as it moves toward maturity without any change in the required yield.* Over time the price of a discount bond rises if interest rates do not change; the price of a premium bond declines over time if interest rates do not change.

3. *For a non-Treasury security, a change in the required yield because of a change in the yield spread between non-Treasury and Treasury securities.* If the Treasury rate does not change, but the yield spread between Treasury and non-Treasury securities changes (narrows or widens), the price of non-Treasury securities will change.

4. *A change in the perceived credit quality of the issuer.* Assuming interest rates in the economy and yield spreads between non-Treasury and Treasury securities do not change, the price of non-Treasury securities will increase if the issuer's perceived credit quality has improved; the price will drop if perceived credit quality deteriorates.

---

[3] The return at the end of the year is:

$(1.050)^2 - 1 = 1.1025 - 1 = 0.1025$

WHAT DETERMINES THE PREMIUM-PAR YIELD

In general, Equation (17.7) and Equation (17.8) cannot be solved explicitly for y (for $n > 2$); these equations must be solved by trial and error—with one important exception. It is apparent from Equation (17.7) that the par value, P/M, increases as the coupon rate, C/M, increases. Now consider a bond whose coupon rate is such that the corresponding value of P/M is one—that is, the bond sells at par. Then Equation (17.7) becomes:

$$1 = \frac{C}{M}\left[\frac{1 - (1 + y)^{-n}}{y}\right] + \frac{1}{(1 + y)^n} \tag{17.9}$$

Equation (17.9) can be solved explicitly for y; the solution is $y = C/M$. In other words, if a bond sells at par, its yield to maturity is the same as its coupon rate; for example, if a 7.75%, 20-year bond sells at par, its yield to maturity is 7.75%. This means that, for a bond to be issued at par, the coupon rate offered must be the same as the market-required yield for that maturity. The coupon rate of an n-period bond selling at par may be labeled the n-period par yield.

It can also be verified from Equation (17.9) that if the coupon rate on a bond is less than the required yield to maturity, or par yield, the bond will sell at a discount; the converse is true for a bond with a coupon above par yield. The explanation for this relation is self-evident: if the cash payment per period—namely, the coupon—is below the required yield per period, the difference must be made up by an increase in price, or capital gain, over the life of the instrument. This requires that the price of the bond be lower than its maturity value. In the United States, debt contracts (other than zero-coupon issues) customarily are issued with a yield to maturity as to insure that the issue sells at close to par.[4]

REINVESTMENT OF CASH FLOW AND YIELD

The yield to maturity takes into account the coupon income and any capital gain or loss that the investor will realize by holding the bond to maturity. The measure has its shortcomings, however. We might think that if we acquire for P a bond of maturity n and yield y, then at maturity we can count on obtaining a terminal value equal to $P(1 + y)^n$. This inference is not justified. By multiplying both sides of Equation (17.5) by $(1 + y)^n$, we obtain:

$$P(1 + y)^n = C(1 + y)^{n-1} + C(1 + y)^{n-2} + C(1 + y)^{n-3} + C + M$$

For the terminal value to be $P(1 + y)^n$, each of the coupon payments must be reinvested until maturity at an interest rate equal to the yield to maturity. If the coupon payment is semiannual, then each semiannual payment must be reinvested at the yield y.

An illustration demonstrates this point. Consider a 7%, 20-year bond that makes semiannual coupon payments of $3.50, and sells for $74.26 per $100

---

[4] This custom has been reinforced by tax laws discouraging tax arbitrage by the substitution of low coupon payments for capital gains from a low issue price. This is because interest income is taxed as ordinary income at the full tax rate, while capital gains are taxed at a preferential (lower) tax rate. The provisions in the tax code that discourage this are the "original issue discount" (OID) rules.

par value. As we demonstrated earlier, the yield to maturity for this bond is equal to 10%. If an investor can invest $74.26 in a certificate of deposit that pays 5% every six months for 20 years, or 10% per year (on a bond equivalent basis), at the end of 20 years (40 six-month periods), the $74.26 investment will have grown to $522.79—that is: $74.26 $(1.05)^{40}$ = $522.79. The terminal value represents a return of the amount invested of $74.26 with interest earned over the 40 years of $448.53 ($522.79 minus $74.26).

Now we shall see what the investor will receive by investing in the bond. There will be 40 semiannual interest payments of $3.50, which will total $140. When the bond matures, the investor will receive $100. Thus, the total dollars that the investor will receive is $240 if the bond is held to maturity. This is $282.79 less than the terminal value of $522.79 necessary to produce a yield of 10% on a bond equivalent basis ($522.79 minus $240). How is this deficiency to be made up? If the investor reinvests the coupon payments at a semiannual interest rate of 5% (or a 10% annual rate on a bond equivalent basis), then the interest earned on the coupon payments will be $282.79. Consequently, of the return on investment of $448.53 needed to generate a dollar return that gives a yield of 10%, about 63% ($282.79 divided by $448.53) must be generated by reinvesting the coupon payments.

Clearly, as the equation and the example demonstrate, the investor will realize the yield to maturity that is calculated at the time of purchase only if (1) all the coupon payments can be reinvested at the yield to maturity, and (2) the bond is held to maturity. With respect to the first assumption, the risk that an investor faces is that future interest rates at which the coupon can be reinvested will be less than the yield to maturity at the time the bond is purchased. This risk is referred to as **reinvestment risk**. And if the bond is not held to maturity, it may have to be sold for less than its purchase price, resulting in a return that is less than the yield to maturity. The risk that a bond will have to be sold at a loss is referred to as **interest rate risk** or **price risk**.

Our focus in this section has been on coupon-bearing bonds. In the special case of a debt instrument that produces only one cash flow, the maturity value, the yield to maturity does measure the rate at which the initial investment rises. We can see this if we substitute zero for the coupon payments in the last equation. Bonds that do not make coupon payments are called zero-coupon bonds. The advantage of these bonds is that they do not expose the investor to reinvestment risk. At the same time, they deprive the investor of the opportunity to reinvest the coupon at a rate higher than y.

BOND PRICE VOLATILITY

The return from holding a bond over some time period less than the maturity of the bond is uncertain because of the uncertainty about the future price of a bond, due to the stochastic nature of future interest rates. When interest rates rise, the price of a bond will fall. Maturity is one of the characteristics of a bond that we said will determine the responsiveness of a bond's price to a change in yields. In this section, we demonstrate this with hypothetical bonds. We will also show other characteristics that influence a bond's price volatility, and how to measure a bond's price volatility.

Review of Price/Yield Relationship

As explained earlier in this chapter, a fundamental characteristic of an option-free bond (that is, a bond that is not callable, putable, or convertible) is that its price changes in the opposite direction from the change in yield. This behavior follows from the fact that the price of a bond is equal to the present value of its cash flow.

Table 17-1 illustrates this property for four hypothetical bonds: a 9% coupon bond with 5 years to maturity, a 9% coupon bond with 20 years to maturity, a 5% coupon bond with 5 years to maturity, and a 5% coupon bond with 20 years to maturity.

The graph of the price/yield relationship for any of these bonds would exhibit the shape shown in Figure 17-1. Notice that the shape of this relationship for any option-free bond is not linear, but rather is convex. Keep in mind that the price/yield relationship that we have discussed is appropriate only at a given point in the life of the bond.

Price Volatility Properties

Although the prices of all (option-free) bonds move in the opposite direction of the change in yields, neither dollar price changes nor percentage price changes are the same for all bonds. For our four hypothetical bonds, this can be seen in Table 17-2. The top panel of the table shows the dollar price change

Table 17-1
Price/Yield Relationship for Four Hypothetical Bonds

Yield	9%/5-yr	Price at given yield * 9%/20-yr	5%/5-yr	5%/20-yr
6.00%	112.7953	134.6722	95.7349	88.4426
7.00	108.3166	121.3551	91.6834	78.6449
8.00	104.0554	109.8964	87.8337	70.3108
8.50	102.0027	104.7693	85.9809	66.6148
8.90	100.3966	100.9267	84.5322	63.8593
8.99	100.0396	100.0921	84.2102	63.2626
9.00	100.0000	100.0000	84.1746	63.1968
9.01	99.9604	99.9081	84.1389	63.1311
9.10	99.6053	99.0865	83.8187	62.5445
9.50	98.0459	95.5592	82.4132	60.0332
10.00	96.1391	91.4205	80.6957	57.1023
11.00	92.4624	83.9539	77.3871	51.8616
12.00	88.9599	77.4306	74.2397	47.3380

*Par = 100

Figure 17-1
Shape of the Price/Yield Relationship for an Option-Free Bond

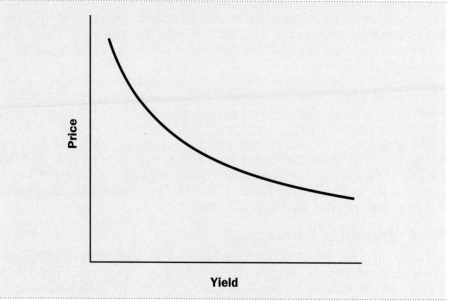

and the bottom panel the percentage price change for various changes in the yield assuming that initially all four bonds are priced to yield 9%.

Note from Table 17-2 that for a given bond the absolute dollar price change and the absolute percentage price change are not the same for an equal increase and decrease in the yield, except for very small changes in the yield. Even for a small change in yield, the absolute dollar price change is less symmetric than the absolute percentage price change. In general, the dollar price increase and the percentage price increase when the yield declines are greater than the dollar price decrease and percentage price decrease when the yield increases.

These two observations—that the absolute and percentage price change are not equal for all bonds, and that the absolute and percentage price change are asymmetric for equal changes in yield—are due to the characteristics of bonds that determine the shape of the price/yield relationship depicted in Figure 17-1. Later in this section we will provide an explanation for the second observation. First we look at the particular characteristics of a bond that affect its price volatility.

Characteristics of a Bond That Affect Price Volatility

There are two characteristics of a bond that are the primary determinants of its price volatility: coupon and term to maturity. First, we will look at price volatility in terms of percentage price change for a change in yields. For a given term to maturity and initial market yield, percentage price volatility is greater the lower the coupon rate. This property can be seen by comparing the

Table 17-2
Instantaneous Dollar and Percentage Price Changes
for Four Hypothetical Bonds

Bonds priced initially to yield 9%:

9% coupon, 5 years to maturity, price = 100.0000

9% coupon, 20 years to maturity, price = 100.0000

5% coupon, 5 years to maturity, price = 84.1746

5% coupon 20 years to maturity, price = 63.1968

Yield changes to	Change in basis points	Dollar price change per $100 par			
		9%/5-yr	9%/20-yr	5%/5-yr	5%/20-yr
6.00%	−300	12.7953	34.6722	11.5603	25.2458
7.00	−200	8.3166	21.3551	7.5088	15.4481
8.00	−100	4.0554	9.8964	3.6591	7.1140
8.50	− 50	2.0027	4.7693	1.8063	3.4180
8.90	− 10	0.3966	0.9267	0.3576	0.6625
8.99	− 1	0.0396	0.0921	0.0356	0.0658
9.01	1	− 0.3960	− 0.0919	− 0.0357	− 0.0657
9.10	10	− 0.3947	− 0.9135	− 0.3559	− 0.6523
9.50	50	− 1.9541	− 4.4408	− 1.7614	− 3.1636
10.00	100	− 3.8609	− 8.5795	− 3.4789	− 6.0945
11.00	200	− 7.5376	−16.0461	− 6.7875	−11.3352
12.00	300	− 11.0401	−22.5694	− 9.9349	−15.8588

Yield changes to	Change in basis points	Percentage price change			
		9%/5-yr	9%/20-yr	5%/5-yr	5%/20-yr
6.00%	−300	12.80%	34.67%	13.73%	39.95%
7.00	−200	8.32	21.36	9.92	24.44
8.00	−100	4.06	9.90	4.35	11.26
8.50	− 50	2.00	4.77	2.15	5.41
8.90	− 10	0.40	0.93	0.42	1.05
8.99	− 1	0.04	0.09	0.04	0.10
9.01	1	− 0.04	− 0.09	− 0.04	− 0.10
9.10	10	− 0.40	− 0.91	− 0.42	− 1.03
9.50	50	− 1.95	− 4.44	− 2.09	− 5.01
10.00	100	− 3.86	− 8.58	− 4.13	− 9.64
11.00	200	− 7.54	−16.05	− 8.06	−17.94
12.00	300	−11.04	−22.57	−11.89	−25.09

9% and 5% coupon bonds with the same maturity (lower panel of Table 17-2). The second characteristic of a bond that affects its price volatility is its term to maturity. For a given coupon rate and initial yield, the longer the term to maturity, the greater the price volatility, in terms of percentage price change.[5] This can be seen in the lower panel of Table 17-2 by comparing the 5-year bonds to the 20-year bonds with the same coupon.

Now we can ask if the same properties hold when volatility is measured in terms of dollar price change rather than percentage price change. The upper panel of Table 17-2 demonstrates that, holding all other factors constant, the dollar price change is greater, the longer the term to maturity. However, the first characteristic concerning the effect of the coupon rate does not hold when volatility is measured in terms of dollar price change instead of percentage price change. In terms of dollar price change, for a given maturity and initial market yield, the lower the coupon rate, the smaller the dollar price change.

Measure of Price Volatility: Duration

Participants in the bond market need to have a way to measure a bond's price volatility in order to measure interest rate risk and to implement portfolio and hedging strategies. The price sensitivity of a bond to a change in yield, y, can be measured by taking the derivative of bond price to a change in yield and then normalizing by the price of the bond. The price of a bond is given by Equation (17.5). Taking the first derivative of that equation with respect to y and dividing both sides by P, we get:

$$\frac{dP}{dy}\frac{1}{P} = -\frac{1}{(1+y)}D \tag{17.10}$$

where

$$D = \frac{\dfrac{(1)C}{(1+y)} + \dfrac{(2)\,C}{(1+y)^2} + \dfrac{(3)C}{(1+y)^3} + ... + \dfrac{(n)\,(C+M)}{(1+y)^n}}{P} \tag{17.11}$$

Equation (17.11) is called the **Macaulay duration** of a bond. It is named in honor of Frederick Macaulay who used this measure in a study published in 1938.[6] Duration is a weighted-average term to maturity of the components of a bond's cash flows, in which the time of receipt of each payment is weighted by the present value of that payment. The denominator is the sum of the weights, which is precisely the price of the bond. What makes Macaulay duration a valuable indicator is that, as can be seen from Equation (17.10), it is related to the responsiveness of a bond's price to changes in yield. The larger the Macaulay duration, the greater the price sensitivity of a bond to a change in yield.

---

[5] There are exceptions for certain deep-discount, long-term *coupon* bonds.

[6] Frederick R. Macaulay, *Some Theoretical Problems Suggested by the Movement of Interest Rates, Bond Yields, and Stock Prices in the U.S. Since 1856* (National Bureau of Economic Research, New York, 1938). Hicks used the same measure in his study of the properties of cash flows that made the ratio of their values invariant with respect to changes in interest. He called his measure "average maturity." See John R. Hicks, *Value and Capital* (Oxford: Clarendon Press, 1946, Second Ed.) In a study of the impact of a rise in interest rates on the banking system, Samuelson used a similar concept which he called the "average time period" of the cash flow. See Paul A. Samuelson, "The Effects of Interest Rate Increases on the Banking System," *American Economic Review* (March 1945), pp. 16-27.

Equation (17.11) is the formula for a bond that pays interest annually. As the bonds we are discussing pay interest semiannually, the formula for Macaulay duration must be adjusted to use a semiannual rather than annual yield and a semiannual interest payment. The number of periods used also should be double the number of years. These adjustments are made in the illustrations throughout this chapter.

Table 17-3 shows how Macaulay duration is calculated for the hypothetical 9%, 5-year bond selling at 100 to yield 9%. Notice that we made adjustments to C, y, and n because we assume that the bond pays interest semiannually. We also divide the Macaulay duration measure given in Equation (17.11) by 2 to convert a measure given in semiannual periods to an annual measure. The Macaulay duration for the four bonds in Table 17-1 is given below, assuming a yield to maturity of 9% for each:

Coupon	**Maturity**	**Macaulay duration**
9%	5 years	4.13years
9%	20 years	9.61years
5%	5 years	4.43years
5%	20 years	10.87years

There are two characteristics that affect the Macaulay duration of a bond, and therefore its price volatility. First, the Macaulay duration for a coupon bond is less than its maturity. For a zero-coupon bond, the Macaulay duration is equal to its maturity.[7] Therefore, for bonds with the same maturity and selling at the same yield, the lower the coupon rate, the greater a bond's Macaulay duration and volatility. Second, for two bonds with the same coupon rate and selling at the same yield, the longer the maturity, the larger the Macaulay duration and price sensitivity.[8] These properties are consistent with our earlier observations with respect to Table 17-2.

From Equation (17.10) we have:

$$\frac{dP}{P} = -\frac{1}{(1 + y)} \, D \, (dy) \qquad (17.12)$$

Equation (17.12) shows how to calculate the percentage change in a bond's price for a given change in yield (dy). Bond market participants commonly combine the first two terms on the right-hand side of this equation and refer to this measure as the **modified duration** of a bond. That is:

---

[7] This can be seen by substituting zero for the coupon payments in Equation (17.11) to obtain

$$D = \frac{\dfrac{(1)0}{(1 + y)} + \dfrac{(2)0}{(1 + y)^2} + \dfrac{(3)0}{(1 + y)^3} + \ldots + \dfrac{(n)(0 + M)}{(1 + y)^n}}{P}$$

so,

$$D = \frac{\dfrac{n\,M}{(1 + y)^n}}{P}$$

But since $M/(1 + y)^n$ is just the price of the bond,

$$D = \frac{n\,P}{P} = n$$

[8] This property does not necessarily hold for long-maturity deep-discount coupon bonds.

Table 17-3
Calculation of Macaulay Duration for a 9%, 5-Year Bond Selling at Par

Formula for Macaulay duration:

$$\frac{\dfrac{(1)C}{(1+y)}+\dfrac{(2)\,C}{(1+y)^2}+\dfrac{(3)C}{(1+y)^3}+\ldots+\dfrac{(n)\,(C+M)}{(1+y)^n}}{P}$$

Information about bond per $100 par:
    annual coupon = $0.09 \times \$100 = \$9.00$
    yield to maturity = 0.09
    number of years to maturity = 5 years
    price = $P = 100$

Values adjusting for semiannual payments:
    $C = \$9.00/2 = \$4.5$
    $y = .09/2 = .045$
    $n = 5 \times 2 = 10$

t	C	$\dfrac{C}{(1.045)^t}$	$t \times \dfrac{C}{(1.045)^t}$
1	$ 4.5	4.306220	4.30622
2	4.5	4.120785	8.24156
3	4.5	3.943335	11.83000
4	4.5	3.773526	15.09410
5	4.5	3.611030	18.05514
6	4.5	3.455531	20.73318
7	4.5	3.306728	23.14709
8	4.5	3.164333	25.31466
9	4.5	3.028070	27.25262
10	104.5	67.290443	672.90442
Total		100.000000	826.87899

$$\frac{(1)C}{(1+y)}+\frac{(2)\,C}{(1+y)^2}+\frac{(3)C}{(1+y)^3}+\ldots+\frac{(n)\,(C+M)}{(1+y)^n}=826.87899$$

Macaulay duration in six-month periods: $\dfrac{826.87899}{100}=8.27$

Macaulay duration in years: $\dfrac{8.27}{2}=4.13$

$$\text{modified duration} = \frac{\text{Macaulay duration}}{(1 + y)} \tag{17.13}$$

Substituting for modified duration into Equation (17.12), and substituting yield change for dy, we obtain:

$$\text{Percentage price change} = -\text{Modified duration} \times \text{Yield change} \tag{17.14}$$

To illustrate the relationship, consider the 5%, 20-year bond selling at 63.1968 to yield 9%. As the annual yield is 9%, y is 4.5%. The Macaulay duration for this bond is 10.87 years. Modified duration is 10.40 as shown below:

$$\text{Modified duration} = \frac{10.87}{1.045} = 10.40$$

Suppose yields increase instantaneously from 9.00% to 9.10%. The yield change is +0.10 (9.10 – 9.00); then: –10.40 × (+0.10) = –1.04%. Notice from the lower panel of Table 17-2 that the actual percentage price change is –1.03%. Similarly, if yields decrease instantaneously from 9.00% to 8.90% (a 10 basis point decrease), the formula indicates that the percentage change in price would be +1.04%. From the lower panel of Table 17-2, the actual percentage price change would be +1.05%. This example illustrates that for small changes in yield, duration provides a good approximation of the percentage price change.

Instead of a small change in yield, let's assume that yields increase by 200 basis points, from 9% to 11% (a yield change of +2.00). The percentage change in price estimated using duration would be: –10.40 × (+2.00) = –20.80%.

How good is this approximation? As can be seen from the lower panel of Table 17-2, the actual percentage change in price is only –17.94%. Moreover, if the yield decreases by 200 basis points, from 9% to 7%, the approximate percentage price change based on duration would be +20.80%, compared to an actual percentage price change of +24.44%. Not only is the approximation off, but we also can see that duration estimates a symmetric percentage change in price, which, as we pointed out earlier, is not a property of the price/yield relationship for an option-free bond.

Notice that the estimated new price based on duration in both instances where the yield changes by 200 basis points is less than the actual price change. For example, for a decline in yield of 200 basis points, the estimated percentage price decline is more than the actual percentage price decline. Similarly, for the same decline in yield, the estimated percentage price rise is less than the actual percentage price rise.

A useful interpretation of modified duration can be obtained by substituting 100 basis points into Equation (17.14). The percentage price change would then be:

$$-\text{Modified duration} \times (+1.00) = -\text{Modified duration}$$

Thus, modified duration can be interpreted as the approximate percentage price change for a 100 basis point change in yields. For example, a bond with a modified duration of 6 would change in price by approximately 6% for a 100 basis point change in yield. Institutional investors adjust the duration of a portfolio to increase (decrease) their interest rate risk exposure if interest rates are expected to fall (rise).

While modified duration measures the percentage price change, the *dollar duration* of a bond measures the dollar price change. The dollar duration can be easily obtained given the bond's modified duration. For example, if the modified duration of a bond is 5 and its price is 90, this means that its price will change by approximately $4.5 (5% times $90) for a 100 basis point change in yield. Thus, the dollar price change, or dollar duration, is $4.5 for a 100 basis change in yield.

We are now ready to tie together the price/yield relationship and several of the properties of bond price volatility that we discussed earlier. Recall the convex shape of the price/yield relationship shown in Figure 17-1. In Figure 17-2, a line is drawn tangent to the price/yield relationship at yield y^*. The tangent shows the rate of change of price with respect to a change in interest rates at that point (yield level). The tangent is closely related to the modified duration (which tells us about the rate of percentage price changes).[9] The steeper the tangent line, the greater the modified duration; the flatter the tangent line, the lower the modified duration. Thus, for a given starting price, the tangent line and the modified duration can be used interchangeably, and can be thought of as one and the same method of estimating the rate of price changes. Below we use the term "duration" to refer to modified duration.

Notice what happens to duration (steepness of the tangent line) as yield changes: as yield increases (decreases), duration decreases (increases). This property holds for all option-free bonds.

Figure 17-2
Tangent to Price/Yield Relationship

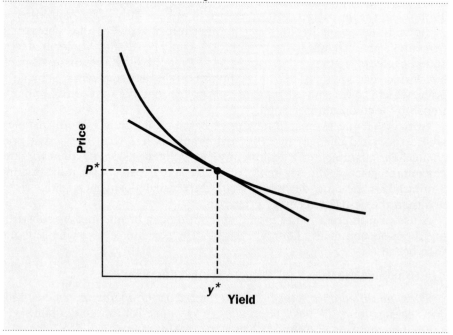

<hr>

[9] Technically, for the tangent line to be equal to modified duration, the axes in Figures 17-1 and 17-2 must be scaled to logarithms.

If we draw a vertical line from any yield (on the horizontal axis), the distance between the horizontal axis and the tangent line represents the price approximated by using duration starting with the initial yield y^*. The approximation will always understate the actual price. This agrees with our illustration earlier of the relationship between duration and the approximate price change.

For small changes in yield, the tangent line and duration do a good job in estimating the actual price, but the farther the distance from the initial yield, y^*, the worse the approximation. It should be apparent that the accuracy of the approximation depends on the convexity (bowedness) of the price/yield relationship.

Misconception about Duration

Unfortunately, market participants often confuse the main purpose of duration by constantly referring to it as some measure of the weighted average life of a bond. This is because of the original use of duration by Macaulay. If you rely on this interpretation of duration, it will be difficult for you to understand why a bond with a maturity of 20 years can have a duration greater than 20 years. For example, in Chapter 26 we will discuss collateralized mortgage obligation (CMO) bond classes. Certain CMO bond classes have a greater duration than the underlying mortgage loans. That is, a CMO bond class can have a duration of 50 while the underlining mortgage loans from which the CMO is created can have a maturity of 30 years. Also, some CMO bond classes have a negative duration.

This can happen because duration is the approximate percentage change in price for a small change in interest rates. In fact, a good way to remember duration is that it is the approximate percentage change in price for a 100 basis point change in interest rates.

Certain CMO bond classes are leveraged instruments whose price sensitivity or duration, as a result, is a multiple of the underlying mortgage loans from which they were created. Thus, a CMO bond class with a duration of 50 does not mean it has some type of weighted average life of 50 years. Instead, it means that for a 100 basis point change in yield, that bond's price will change by roughly 50%.

Approximating a Bond's Duration

Once we understand that the duration is related to percentage price change, a simple formula can be used to calculate the approximate duration of a bond, or any of the other more-complex derivative securities described throughout this book. All we are interested in is the percentage price change of a bond when interest rates change by a small amount. This can be found quite easily with the following procedure:

1. Increase the yield on the bond by a small number of basis points and determine the new price at this higher yield level. We denote this new price by P_+.

2. Decrease the yield on the bond by the same number of basis points and calculate the new price. We will denote this new price by P_-.

3. Letting P_0 be the initial price, then duration can be approximated using the following formula:

$$\text{Approximate duration} = \frac{P_- - P_+}{2\ (P_0)(\Delta y)} \tag{17.15}$$

where Δy is the change in rate used to calculate the new prices (in decimal form).

What the formula is measuring is the average percentage price change (relative to the initial price) per one basis point change in yield. To see how good this approximation is, we will apply it to the 5% coupon 20-year bond trading at 9%. All the necessary information is provided in Table 17-1. The initial price (P_0) is 63.1968. The steps are given below:

1. Increase the yield on the bond by 10 basis points from 9% to 9.1%. Thus, Δy is .001. The new price (P_+) is 62.5445.

2. Decrease the yield on the bond by 10 basis points from 9% to 8.9%. The new price (P_-) is 63.8593.

3. Since the initial price, P_0, is 63.1968 the duration can be approximated as follows:

$$\text{Approximate duration} = \frac{63.8593 - 62.5445}{2\ (63.1968)\ (0.001)} = 10.4$$

How good is the approximation? The modified duration as calculated by using Equation (17.11) to calculate Macaulay duration and then Equation (17.13) is 10.4.

If an investor is interested in the duration of any financial instrument, Equation (17.15) can be used. However, to use the equation, it is necessary to have a good pricing model to get the new prices. What is important to emphasize here is that duration is a byproduct of a pricing model. If the pricing model is poor, the resulting duration estimate is poor.

Curvature and Convexity

Mathematically, duration is a first approximation of the price/yield relationship. That is, duration attempts to estimate a convex relationship with a straight line (the tangent line).

A fundamental property of calculus is that a mathematical function can be approximated by a Taylor series. The more terms a Taylor series uses, the better the approximation. For example, the first two terms of a Taylor series for the price function given by Equation (17.5) would be:

$$\frac{dP}{P} = \frac{dP}{dy}\frac{1}{P}\ dy + \frac{1}{2}\ \frac{d^2P}{dy^2}\frac{1}{P}\ dy^2 \tag{17.16}$$

The fact that duration is the first term of the Taylor series can be seen by comparing the first term on the right-hand side of Equation (17.16) with Equation (17.12). The second term of the Taylor series requires the calculation of the second derivative of the price function, Equation (17.5). The second derivative of Equation (17.5) normalized by price (i.e., divided by price) is:

$$\frac{d^2P}{dy^2} \frac{1}{P} = \qquad (17.17)$$

$$\frac{\dfrac{(1)(2)C}{(1+y)} + \dfrac{(2)(3)C}{(1+y)^2} + \dfrac{(3)(4)C}{(1+y)^3} + \cdots + \dfrac{(n)(n+1)(C+M)}{(1+y)^n}}{(1+y)^2} \quad \frac{1}{P}$$

The measure in Equation (17.17) when divided by 2 is referred to popularly as the convexity of a bond. That is:

$$\text{Convexity} = \frac{1}{2} \frac{d^2P}{dy^2} \frac{1}{P} \qquad (17.18)$$

This is an unfortunate misuse of terminology because it suggests that the convexity measure conveys the curvature of the convex shape of the price/yield relationship for a bond. It does not. It is simply an approximation of the curvature.

Table 17-4 sets forth the calculations for the convexity of the 9%, five-year bond selling at 100 to yield 9%. Once again, notice that C, y, and n are adjusted as we discussed earlier. Also note that we divide the convexity measure as given by Equation (17.18) by 2 in order to convert convexity measured in semiannual periods into convexity measured in years.

The second term on the right-hand side of Equation (17.16) is the incremental percentage change in price due to convexity. From Equation (17.18), it can be expressed as:

Percentage change in price due to correction for convexity = $\qquad$ (17.19)
Convexity × (Change in yield)^2

For example, convexity for the 5% coupon bond maturing in 20 years is 80.43. Then the approximate percentage price change due solely to correct for convexity if the yield increases from 9% to 11% (+2.00 yield change) is: $80.43 \times (+0.02)^2$ = 3.22%. If the yield decreases from 9% to 7% (–2.00 yield change), the approximate percentage price change due solely to convexity would also be 3.22%.

The approximate total percentage price change based on both duration and convexity is found by simply adding the two estimates. For example, if yields change from 9% to 11%, we have an approximate percentage price change due to:

Duration $\qquad$ = –20.80%
Convexity Correction = + 3.22%

Total $\qquad$ = –17.58%

From Table 17-2, the actual percentage price change would be –17.94%.

For a decrease of 200 basis points, from 9% to 7%, we have an approximate percentage price change due to:

Duration $\qquad$ = +20.80
Convexity Correction = + 3.22

Total $\qquad$ = +24.02

The actual percentage price change would be +24.44%.

Table 17-4

Calculation of Convexity for a 9%, 5-Year Bond Selling at Par

Formula for convexity:

$$\frac{\dfrac{(1)(2)C}{(1 + y)} + \dfrac{(2)(3)C}{(1 + y)^2} + \dfrac{(3)(4)C}{(1 + y)^3} + \ldots + \dfrac{(n)(n+1)(C + M)}{(1 + y)^n}}{2\,(1 + y)^2\,P}$$

Information about bond per $100 par:

   annual coupon $= 0.09 \times \$100 = \$9.00$

   yield to maturity $= 0.09$

   number of years to maturity $= 5$ years

   price $= P = 100$

Values adjusting for semiannual payments:

   $C = \$9.00/2 = \$4.5$

   $y = .09/2 \quad = .045$

   $n = 5 \times 2 \quad = 10$

t	C	$\dfrac{C}{(1.045)^t}$	$t\,(t + 1)\,\dfrac{C}{(1.045)^t}$
1	$ 4.5	4.306220	8.6124
2	4.5	4.120785	24.7242
3	4.5	3.943335	47.3196
4	4.5	3.773526	75.4700
5	4.5	3.611030	108.3300
6	4.5	3.455531	145.1310
7	4.5	3.306728	185.1752
8	4.5	3.164333	227.8296
9	4.5	3.028070	272.5290
10	104.5	67.290443	7,401.9440
Total		100.000000	8,497.0650

$$\frac{\dfrac{(1)(2)C}{(1 + y)} + \dfrac{(2)(3)C}{(1 + y)^2} + \dfrac{(3)(4)C}{(1 + y)^3} + \ldots + \dfrac{(n)(n+1)(C + M)}{(1 + y)^n}}{2\,(1 + y)^2\,P} = 8{,}497.0650$$

Convexity in six-month periods: $\dfrac{8{,}497.0650}{2\,(1.045)^2\,100} = 38.90$

Convexity in years: $\dfrac{38.90}{2} = 19.45$

Consequently, for large yield movements, a better approximation for bond price movements when interest rates change is obtained by using both duration and convexity.

Convexity is actually measuring the rate of change of dollar duration as yields change. For all option-free bonds, modified and dollar duration increase as yields decline. This is a positive attribute of any option-free bond, because as yields decline, price appreciation accelerates. When yields increase, the duration for all option-free bonds will decrease. Once again, this is a positive attribute, because as yields decline, this feature will decelerate the price depreciation. This is the reason why we observed that the absolute and percentage price change is greater when yields decline compared to when they increase by the same number of basis points. Thus, an option-free bond is said to have **positive convexity**.

One final but important note. Duration and convexity are measures of price volatility assuming the yield curve is initially flat and that if there are any yield shifts they are parallel ones. That is, the Treasury yields of all maturities are assumed to change by the same number of basis points. To see where we assume to, look back at the price function we analyzed for changes in yield in [Equation (17.5)]. Each cash flow is discounted at the same yield. If the yield curve does not shift in a parallel fashion, duration and convexity will not do as good a job of approximating the percentage price change of a bond.

Approximating Convexity

Earlier the formula for approximating duration was presented. An approximation for convexity can be obtained from the following formula:

$$\text{Approximate convexity} = \frac{P_+ + P_- - 2\,P_0}{2\,P_0(\Delta y)^2} \qquad (17.20)$$

Using the 5%, 20-year bond, the approximate convexity is:

$$\text{Approximate convexity} = \frac{63.8593 + 62.5445 - 2\,(63.1968)}{2\,(63.1968)\,(.001)^2} = 80.7$$

Using Equation (17.18), the convexity is 80.43. Thus, Equation (17.20) does a fine job.

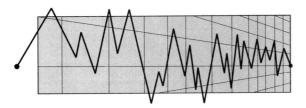

SUMMARY

The cash flow from a bond consists of periodic coupon payments (semiannual payments in the U.S.) and the repayment of the principal. The value of a bond is the present value of the cash flow it provides until maturity. The yield-to-maturity measure is used as an index to compare the rate of return of instruments having different cash flows and different maturities. As the yield to maturity assumes that the investor will hold the bond to the maturity date, and that all cash flows can be reinvested at the calculated yield to maturity, it has limited value in determining the relative value of two bonds with different maturities over some investment horizon. The risk that cash flows will have to be reinvested at an interest rate lower than the calculated yield to maturity is called reinvestment risk. The risk that a bond will have to be sold at a price less than the purchase price is called interest rate risk, or price risk.

A bond's price will change over time for several reasons. First, the level of interest rates in the economy may change. Second, a bond selling at a price above par will decrease in price as its maturity date approaches if interest rates in the economy do not change; the price of a bond selling below par will increase if interest rates in the economy do not change. For non-U.S. Treasury securities there are two additional reasons why a bond's price may change: a change in the yield spread between Treasury and non-Treasury securities, or a change in the perceived credit quality of the issuer.

Finally, we explore the sensitivity of bond prices to changes in interest rates. A graph of the relationship between price and yield for any option-free bond will have a convex shape. Not all bonds change by the same percentage or dollar amount if interest rates change. Two characteristics of a bond that affect its price volatility and therefore its interest rate risk exposure are maturity and coupon rate. For a given yield and coupon rate, the longer the maturity, the greater the price volatility. While there are exceptions, for a given yield and maturity, price volatility is greater, the lower the coupon rate.

A measure of price volatility that relates coupon and maturity is Macaulay duration, defined as the average time to maturity of the cash flow that is found by weighting the time of receipt of a cash flow by the present value of that cash flow. Modified duration is the approximate percentage price change of a bond for a 100 basis point change in interest rates. Dollar duration measures the dollar price change when interest rates change. The best way to think about duration is as a measure of price sensitivity rather than some weighted time measure. The duration of any bond can be approximated by changing the bond's yield up and down by a small number of basis points and looking at how its price would change.

Convexity is another measure of price volatility to be used in conjunction with modified duration to improve the estimate for price volatility for large changes in interest rates. The convexity measure of a bond shows the rate of change of the dollar duration of a bond as interest rates change.

In the next chapter we continue our study of the theory of the determinants of bond prices and long-term interest rates, focusing on the relationship between interest rates on bonds of the same issuer (the U.S. government) but with different maturities.

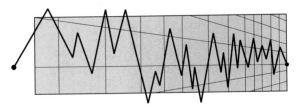

QUESTIONS

1. Determine the value of the following risk-free debt instrument, which promises to make the respective payments when the appropriate annual rates are as shown in the last column:

Year	Cash payment	Appropriate annual rate
1	$15,000	8.0%
2	17,000	8.5
3	20,000	9.0
4	21,000	9.5

2. For each of the bonds below calculate the price per $1,000 of par value assuming semiannual coupon payments.

Bond	Coupon rate	Years to maturity	Required yield
A	8%	9	7%
B		9	20 9
C	6	15	10
D	0	14	8

3. What is the maximum price of a bond?

4. Consider a bond selling at par ($100) with a coupon rate of 6% and 10 years to maturity.

    a. What is the price of this bond if the required yield is 15%?

    b. What is the price of this bond if the required yield increases from 15% to 16%, and by what percentage did the price of this bond change?

    c. What is the price of this bond if the required yield is 5%?

    d. What is the price of this bond if the required yield increases from 5% to 6%, and by what percentage did the price of this bond change?

    e. From your answers to parts (b) and (d) what can you say about the relative price volatility of a bond in high compared to low interest rate environments?

5. Suppose you purchased a debt obligation three years ago at its par value of $100,000. The market price of this debt obligation today is $90,000. What are some of the reasons why the price of this debt obligation could have declined since you purchased it three years ago?

6. What is meant by the "yield to maturity" of a bond?

7. What is meant by the yield to maturity calculated on a bond-equivalent basis?

8. a. Show the cash flows for the four bonds below, each of which has a par value of $1,000 and pays interest semiannually:

Bond	Coupon rate	Years to maturity	Price
W	7%	5	$884.20
X	8	7	948.90
Y	9	4	967.70
Z	0	10	456.39

b. Calculate the yield to maturity for the four bonds.

9. A portfolio manager is considering buying two bonds. Bond A matures in three years and has a coupon rate of 10% payable semiannually. Bond B, of the same credit quality, matures in 10 years and has a coupon rate of 12% payable semiannually. Both bonds are priced at par.

a. Suppose the portfolio manager plans to hold the bond that is purchased for three years. Which would be the best bond for the portfolio manager to purchase?

b. Suppose the portfolio manager plans to hold the bond that is purchased for six years instead of three years. In this case, which would be the best bond for the portfolio manager to purchase?

c. Suppose that the portfolio manager is managing the assets of a life insurance company that has issued a five-year guaranteed investment contract (GIC). The interest rate that the life insurance company has agreed to pay is 9% on a semiannual basis. Which of the two bonds should the portfolio manager purchase to assure that the GIC payments will be satisfied and that a profit will be generated by the life insurance company?

10. What is meant by reinvestment risk when purchasing a bond?

11. Can you tell from the information below which of the following three bonds will have the greatest price volatility, assuming each is trading to offer the same yield to maturity?

Bond	Coupon rate	Maturity
X	8%	9 years
Y	10	11
Z	11	12

12. Calculate the requested measures for bonds A and B (assume each bond pays interest semiannually):.

	A	B
Coupon	8%	9%
Yield to maturity	8%	8%
Maturity (in years)	2	5
Par	100.00	100.00
Price	100.000	104.055

a. Macaulay duration

b. modified duration

c. convexity

13. For bonds A and B in the previous question:

a. Calculate the actual price of the bonds for a 100 basis point increase in interest rates.

b. Using duration, estimate the price of the bonds for a 100 basis point increase in interest rates.

c. Using both duration and convexity, estimate the price of the bonds for a 100 basis point increase in interest rates.

d. Comment on the accuracy of your results in (b) and (c), and state why one approximation is closer to the actual price than the other.

e. Without working through calculations, indicate whether the duration of the two bonds would be higher or lower if the yield to maturity is 10% rather than 8%.

14. Approximate the duration and convexity of bonds A and B in question (12) by changing the yield by 20 basis points up and down and compare your answer to parts 12(b) and 12(c).

15. State why you would agree or disagree with the following statement: As the duration of a zero-coupon bond is equal to its maturity, the responsiveness of a zero-coupon bond to interest rate changes is the same regardless of the level of interest rates.

16. The November 26, 1990, issue of *Bondweek* includes an article, "Van Kampen Merritt Shortens." The article begins as follows: "Peter Hegel, first v.p. at Van Kampen Merritt Investment Advisory, is shortening his $3 billion portfolio from 110% of his normal duration of 6 1/2 years to 103-105% because he thinks that in the short run the bond rally is near an end."

Explain Hegel's strategy and the use of the duration measure in this context.

17. Which of the following bonds will have the larger price change for a 50 basis point change in yield?

Bond	Modified duration	Price
E	7	50
F	5	100

18. State why you would agree or disagree with the following statement: When interest rates are low, there will be little difference between the Macaulay duration and modified duration measures.

19. You are a portfolio manager who has presented a report to a client. The report indicates the duration of each security in the portfolio. One of the securities has a maturity of 15 years but a duration of 25. The client believes that there is an error in the report because he believes that the duration cannot be greater than the security's maturity. What would be your response be to this client?

20. A strategy called immunization is used by institutional investors to protect a portfolio against an adverse change in interest rates. Basically this strategy seeks to offset interest rate risk and reinvestment risk. Why do these two risks offset each other to a certain extent when interest rates change?

The Term Structure of Interest Rates

LEARNING OBJECTIVES

After reading this chapter you will understand:

- what is meant by the term structure of interest rates.

- what the yield curve is.

- the different shapes that the term structure can take.

- what is meant by a spot rate and a spot rate curve.

- how a theoretical spot rate curve can be determined from the Treasury yield curve.

- what is meant by an implied forward rate and how it can be calculated.

- the importance of knowing forward rates.

- why forward rates can be viewed as hedgeable rates.

- how long-term rates are related to the current short-term rate and short-term forward rates.

- the different theories about the determinants of the shape of the term structure; including pure expectations theory, the liquidity theory, the preferred habitat theory, and the market segmentation theory.

The relationship between yield and maturity is referred to as the **term structure of interest rates**. The term structure of interest rates plays a key role in the valuation of bonds because it is these rates that should be used to discount the cash flows of a bond. In this chapter we look at how the term structure of interest rates can be estimated and applied to value bonds. If bonds are not valued using the term structure of interest rates, arbitrage opportunities are possible. We also introduce the concept of forward rates and their importance in investment decisions.

THE YIELD CURVE

The graphical depiction of the relationship between the yield on bonds of the same credit quality but different maturities is known as the **yield curve**. Market participants typically construct yield curves from observations of prices and yields in the Treasury market. Two reasons account for this tendency. First, Treasury securities are free of default risk, and differences in creditworthiness do not affect yield estimates. Second, as the largest and most active bond market, the Treasury market offers the fewest problems of illiquidity or infrequent trading. Figure 18-1 shows the shape of four hypothetical Treasury yield curves that have been observed from time to time in the United States.

From a practical viewpoint, the key function of the Treasury yield curve is to serve as a benchmark for pricing bonds and setting yields in all other sectors of

Figure 18-1
Four Hypothetical Yield Curves

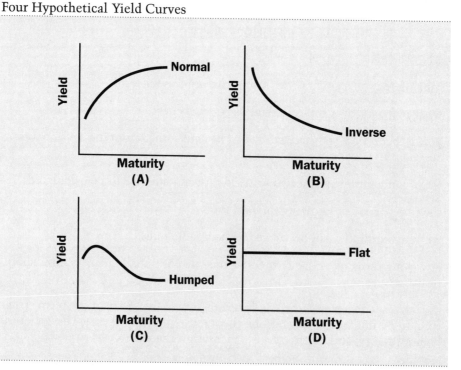

the debt market—bank loans, mortgages, corporate debt, and international bonds. However, market participants are coming to realize that the traditionally constructed Treasury yield curve is an unsatisfactory measure of the relation between required yield and maturity. The key reason is that securities with the same maturity may actually carry different yields. As we will explain below, this phenomenon reflects the role and impact of differences in the bonds' coupon rates. Hence, it is necessary to develop more accurate and reliable estimates of the term structure of interest rates. We will show how this is done later in this chapter. Basically, the approach consists of identifying yields that apply to "zero-coupon" bonds and, therefore, eliminates the problem of non-uniqueness in the yield-maturity relationship.

Limitations of Using the Yield Curve to Price a Bond

The price of a bond is the present value of its cash flow. However, in our illustrations and our discussion of the pricing of a bond in Chapter 17, we assume that one interest rate should be used to discount all the bond's cash flows. The appropriate interest rate is the yield on a Treasury security, with the same maturity as the bond, plus an appropriate risk premium or spread.

To illustrate the problem with using the Treasury yield curve to determine the appropriate yield at which to discount the cash flow of a bond, consider the following two hypothetical five-year Treasury bonds, A and B. The difference between these two Treasury bonds is the coupon rate, which is 12% for A and 3% for B. The cash flow for these two bonds per $100 of par value for the ten six-month periods to maturity would be:

Period	Cash flow for A	Cash flow for B
1-9	$ 6.00	$ 1.50
10	106.00	101.50

Because of the different cash flow patterns, it is not appropriate to use the same interest rate to discount all cash flows. Instead, each cash flow should be discounted at a unique interest rate that is appropriate for the time period in which the cash flow will be received. But what should be the interest rate for each period?

The correct way to think about bonds A and B is not as bonds but as packages of cash flows. More specifically, they are packages of zero-coupon instruments. Thus, the interest earned is the difference between the maturity value and the price paid. For example, bond A can be viewed as ten zero-coupon instruments: one with a maturity value of $6 maturing six months from now; a second with a maturity value of $6 maturing one year from now; a third with a maturity value of $6 maturing 1.5 years from now, and so on. The final zero-coupon instrument matures ten six-month periods from now and has a maturity value of $106. Likewise, bond B can be viewed as ten zero-coupon instruments: one with a maturity value of $1.50 maturing six months from now; one with a maturity value of $1.50 maturing one year from now; one with a maturity value of $1.50 maturing 1.5 years from now, and so on. The final zero-coupon instrument matures 10 six-month periods from now and has a maturity value of $101.50. Obviously, in the case of each coupon bond, the value or price of the bond is equal to the total value of its component zero-coupon instruments.

Valuing a Bond as a Package of Cash Flows

In general, any bond can be viewed as a package of zero-coupon instruments. That is, each zero-coupon instrument in the package has a maturity equal to its coupon payment date or, in the case of the principal, the maturity date. The value of the bond should equal the value of all the component zero-coupon instruments. If this does not hold, it is possible for a market participant to generate riskless profits by stripping the security and creating stripped securities. We will demonstrate this later in this chapter.

To determine the value of each zero-coupon instrument, it is necessary to know the yield on a zero-coupon Treasury with that same maturity. This yield is called the **spot rate**, and the graphical depiction of the relationship between the spot rate and its maturity is called the **spot rate curve**. Because there are no zero-coupon Treasury debt issues with a maturity greater than one year, it is not possible to construct such a curve solely from observations of market activity. Rather, it is necessary to derive this curve from theoretical considerations as applied to the yields of actual Treasury securities. Such a curve is called a *theoretical* spot rate curve.

CONSTRUCTING THE THEORETICAL SPOT RATE CURVE

We will now explain the process of creating a theoretical spot rate curve from the yield curve that is based on the observed yields of Treasury securities. This process is called **bootstrapping**.[1] To explain this process, we use the data for the price, annualized yield (yield to maturity) and maturity of the 20 hypothetical Treasury securities shown in Table 18-1.

Throughout the analysis and illustrations to come, it is important to remember that the basic principle of bootstrapping is that the value of the Treasury security should be equal to the value of the package of zero-coupon Treasury securities that duplicates the coupon bond's cash flow.

Consider the six-month Treasury bill in Table 18-1. As explained in Chapter 19, a Treasury bill is a zero-coupon instrument; therefore, its annualized yield of 8% is equal to the spot rate. Similarly, for the one-year Treasury, the cited yield of 8.3% is the one-year spot rate. Given these two spot rates, we can compute the spot rate for a theoretical 1.5-year zero-coupon Treasury. The price of a theoretical 1.5-year Treasury should equal the present value of three cash flows from an actual 1.5-year coupon Treasury, where the

---

[1] In practice, the Treasury securities that are used to construct the theoretical spot rate curve are the most recently auctioned Treasury securities of a given maturity. Such issues are the on-the-run Treasury issues. As we explain in Chapter 20, there are actual zero-coupon Treasury securities with a maturity greater than one year that are outstanding in the market. These securities are not issued by the U.S. Treasury but are created by certain market participants from actual coupon Treasury securities. It would seem logical that the observed yield on zero-coupon Treasury securities can be used to construct an actual spot rate curve. However, there are problems with this approach. First, the liquidity of these securities is not as great as that of the coupon Treasury market. Second, there are maturity sectors of the zero-coupon Treasury market that attract specific investors who may be willing to trade-off yield in exchange for an attractive feature associated with that particular maturity sector, thereby distorting the term structure relationship.

Table 18-1
Maturity and Yield to Maturity for 20 Hypothetical Treasury Securities

Maturity	Coupon rate	Yield to maturity	price
0.50 years	0.0000	0.0800	$ 96.15
1.00	0.0000	0.0830	92.19
1.50	0.0850	0.0890	99.45
2.00	0.0900	0.0920	99.64
2.50	0.1100	0.0940	103.49
3.00	0.0950	0.0970	99.49
3.50	0.1000	0.1000	100.00
4.00	0.1000	0.1040	98.72
4.50	0.1150	0.1060	103.16
5.00	0.0875	0.1080	92.24
5.50	0.1050	0.1090	98.38
6.00	0.1100	0.1120	99.14
6.50	0.0850	0.1140	86.94
7.00	0.0825	0.1160	84.24
7.50	0.1100	0.1180	96.09
8.00	0.0650	0.1190	72.62
8.50	0.0875	0.1200	82.97
9.00	0.1300	0.1220	104.30
9.50	0.1150	0.1240	95.06
10.00	0.1250	0.1250	100.00

yield used for discounting is the spot rate corresponding to the cash flow. Using $100 as par, the cash flow for the 1.5-year coupon Treasury is:

0.5 years:	$0.085 \times \$100 \times 0.5$	= $ 4.25
1.0 years:	$0.085 \times \$100 \times 0.5$	= $ 4.25
1.5 years:	$0.085 \times \$100 \times 0.5 + 100$	= $104.25

The present value of the cash flow is then:

$$\frac{4.25}{(1+z_1)^1} + \frac{4.25}{(1+z_2)^2} + \frac{104.25}{(1+z_3)^3}$$

where
z_1 = one-half the annualized six-month theoretical spot rate
z_2 = one-half the one-year theoretical spot rate
z_3 = one-half the annual value of the 1.5-year theoretical spot rate

Since the six-month spot rate and one-year spot rate are 8.0% and 8.3%, respectively, we know that: $z_1 = 0.04$ and $z_2 = 0.0415$. We can compute the present value of the 1.5-year coupon Treasury security as:

$$\frac{4.25}{(1.0400)^1} + \frac{4.25}{(1.0415)^2} + \frac{104.25}{(1 + z_3)^3}$$

Since the price of the 1.5-year coupon Treasury security (from Table 18-1) is $99.45, the following relationship must hold:

$$99.45 = \frac{4.25}{(1.0400)^1} + \frac{4.25}{(1.0415)^2} + \frac{104.25}{(1 + z_3)^3}$$

We can solve for the theoretical 1.5-year spot rate as follows:

$$99.45 = 4.08654 + 3.91805 + \frac{104.25}{(1 + z_3)^3}$$

$$91.44541 = \frac{104.25}{(1 + z_3)^3}$$

$$(1 + z_3)^3 = 1.140024$$

$$z_3 = .04465$$

Doubling this yield we obtain the bond-equivalent yield of 0.0893 or 8.93%, which is the theoretical 1.5-year spot rate. That rate is the rate that the market would apply to a 1.5-year zero-coupon Treasury security if, in fact, such a security existed.

Given the theoretical 1.5-year spot rate, we can obtain the theoretical two-year spot rate. The cash flow for the two-year coupon Treasury in Table 18-1 is:

0.5 years:	$0.090 \times \$100 \times 0.5$	=	$ 4.50
1.0 years:	$0.090 \times \$100 \times 0.5$	=	$ 4.50
1.5 years:	$0.090 \times \$100 \times 0.5$	=	$ 4.50
2.0 years:	$0.090 \times \$100 \times 0.5 + 100$	=	$ 104.50

The present value of the cash flow is then:

$$\frac{4.50}{(1 + z_1)^1} + \frac{4.50}{(1 + z_2)^2} + \frac{4.50}{(1 + z_3)^3} + \frac{104.50}{(1 + z_4)^4}$$

where z_4 = one-half of the two-year theoretical spot rate

Since the six-month spot rate, one-year spot rate, and 1.5-year spot rate are 8.0%, 8.3%, and 8.93%, respectively, then: $z_1 = 0.04$, $z_2 = 0.0415$ and $z_3 = 0.04465$. Therefore, the present value of the two-year coupon Treasury security is:

$$\frac{4.50}{(1.0400)^1} + \frac{4.50}{(1.0415)^2} + \frac{4.50}{(1.04465)^3} + \frac{104.50}{(1 + z_4)^4}$$

Since the price of the two-year coupon Treasury security is \$99.64, the following relationship must hold:

$$99.64 = \frac{4.50}{(1.0400)^1} + \frac{4.50}{(1.0415)^2} + \frac{4.50}{(1.04465)^3} + \frac{104.50}{(1 + z_4)^4}$$

We can solve for the theoretical two-year spot rate as follows:

$$99.64 = 4.32692 + 4.14853 + 3.94730 + \frac{104.50}{(1 + z_4)^4}$$

$$87.21725 = \frac{104.50}{(1 + z_4)^4}$$

$$(1 + z_4)^4 = 1.198158$$

$$z_4 = 0.046235$$

Doubling this yield, we obtain the theoretical two-year spot rate bond equivalent yield of 9.247%.

One can follow this approach sequentially to derive the theoretical 2.5-year spot rate from the calculated values of z_1, z_2, z_3, z_4 (the six-month, one-year, 1.5-year, and two-year rates), and the price and coupon of the bond with a maturity of 2.5 years. Further, one could derive theoretical spot rates for the remaining 15 half-yearly rates. The spot rates thus obtained are shown in Table 18-2. They represent the term structure of interest rates for maturities up to ten years, at the particular time to which the bond price quotations refer.

Why Treasuries Must Be Priced Based on Spot Rates

Financial theory tells us that the theoretical price of a Treasury security should be equal to the present value of the cash flow where each cash flow is discounted at the appropriate theoretical spot rate. What we did not do, however, is demonstrate what economic force will assure that the actual market price of a Treasury security will not depart significantly from its theoretical price.

To demonstrate this, we will use the 20 hypothetical Treasury securities given in Table 18-1. The longest maturity bond given in that table is the 10-year, 12.5% coupon bond selling at par and therefore with a yield to maturity of 12.5%. Suppose that a government dealer buys the issue at par and then immediately sells separately each coupon payment and the principal payment. This process is referred to as **stripping the security**. Each security created has a maturity value and maturity date equal to the date when the corresponding coupon payment or maturity value is due. Each is a zero-coupon bond. The process of coupon stripping is illustrated in Figure 18-2. Government dealers will follow this process if they can sell the zero-coupon Treasury securities created at the yields to maturity indicated in Table 18-1 for the corresponding maturity. (We will discuss zero-coupon Treasury securities creating by stripping coupon Treasury securities in more detail in Chapter 20.)

Table 18-2

Theoretical Spot Rates

Maturity	Yield to maturity	Theoretical spot rate
0.50	0.0800	0.08000
1.00	0.0830	0.08300
1.50	0.0890	0.08930
2.00	0.0920	0.09247
2.50	0.0940	0.09468
3.00	0.0970	0.09787
3.50	0.1000	0.10129
4.00	0.1040	0.10592
4.50	0.1060	0.10850
5.00	0.1080	0.11021
5.50	0.1090	0.11175
6.00	0.1120	0.11584
6.50	0.1140	0.11744
7.00	0.1160	0.11991
7.50	0.1180	0.12405
8.00	0.1190	0.12278
8.50	0.1200	0.12546
9.00	0.1220	0.13152
9.50	0.1240	0.13377
10.00	0.1250	0.13623

Table 18-3 shows the price that would be received for each zero-coupon Treasury security created. The price for each is just the present value of the cash flow from the stripped Treasury discounted at the yield to maturity corresponding to the maturity of the security (from Table 18-1). The total proceeds received from selling the zero-coupon Treasury securities created would be $104.1880 per $100 of par value of the Treasury issue purchased by the dealer. This would result in an arbitrage profit of $4.1880 per $100 of the 10-year, 12.5% coupon Treasury security purchased.

To understand why the government dealer has the opportunity to realize this profit, look at the third column of Table 18-3, which shows how much the government dealer paid for each cash flow by buying the entire package of cash flows (i.e., by buying the bond). For example, consider the $6.25 coupon payment in four years. By buying the 10-year Treasury bond priced to yield 12.5%, the dealer effectively pays a price based on 12.5% (6.25% semiannual)

Figure 18-2
Process of Coupon Stripping

Dealer purchases $500 million par of a 6% 10-year Treasury

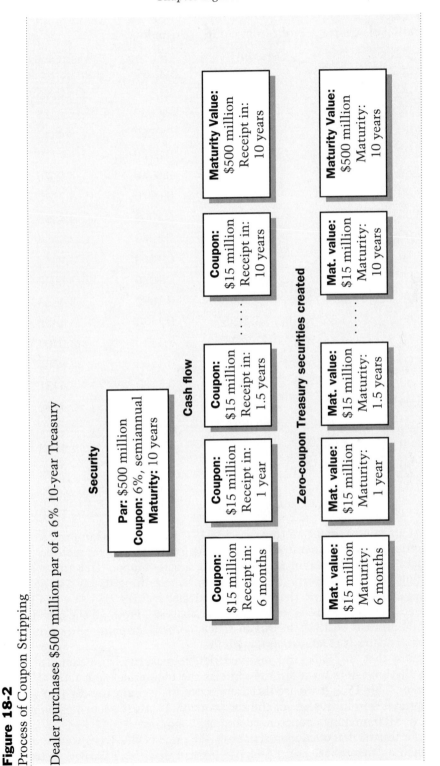

Table 18-3

Illustration of Arbitrage Profit from Coupon Stripping

Maturity	Cash flow	Present value at 12.5%	Yield to maturity	Present value at yield to maturity
0.50	6.25	5.8824	0.0800	6.0096
1.00	6.25	5.5363	0.0830	5.7618
1.50	6.25	5.2107	0.0890	5.4847
2.00	6.25	4.9042	0.0920	5.2210
2.50	6.25	4.6157	0.0940	4.9676
3.00	6.25	4.3442	0.0970	4.7040
3.50	6.25	4.0886	0.1000	4.4418
4.00	6.25	3.8481	0.1040	4.1663
4.50	6.25	3.6218	0.1060	3.9267
5.00	6.25	3.4087	0.1080	3.6938
5.50	6.25	3.2082	0.1090	3.4863
6.00	6.25	3.0195	0.1120	3.2502
6.50	6.25	2.8419	0.1140	3.0402
7.00	6.25	2.6747	0.1160	2.8384
7.50	6.25	2.5174	0.1180	2.6451
8.00	6.25	2.3693	0.1190	2.4789
8.50	6.25	2.2299	0.1200	2.3210
9.00	6.25	2.0987	0.1220	2.1528
9.50	6.25	1.9753	0.1240	1.9930
10.00	106.25	31.6046	0.1250	31.6046
Total		100.0000		104.1880

for that coupon payment, in this case $3.8481. Under the assumptions of this illustration, however, investors were willing to accept a lower yield to maturity, 10.4% (5.2% semiannual), to purchase a zero-coupon Treasury security with four years to maturity. Thus investors were willing to pay $4.1663. On this one coupon payment, the government dealer realizes a profit equal to the difference between $4.1663 and $3.8481 (or $0.3182). From all the cash flows, the total profit is $4.1880. In this instance, coupon stripping shows that the sum of the parts is greater than the whole.

Suppose that, instead of the observed yield to maturity from Table 18-1, the yields that investors want are the same as the theoretical spot rates that are shown in Table 18-2. If we use these spot rates to discount the cash flows, the total proceeds from the sale of the zero-coupon Treasury securities would be equal to $100, making coupon stripping uneconomic.

In our illustration of coupon stripping, the price of the Treasury security is less than its theoretical price. Suppose instead that the Treasury security is greater than its theoretical price. In such cases, investors can purchase in the market a package of zero-coupon Treasury securities such that the cash flow of the package of securities replicates the cash flow of the mispriced coupon Treasury security. By doing so, the investor will realize a yield higher than the yield on the coupon Treasury security. For example, suppose that the market price of the 10-year Treasury security we used in our illustration (Table 18-3) is $106. By buying the 20 zero-coupon bonds shown in Table 18-3 with a maturity value identical to the cash flow shown in the second column, the investor is effectively purchasing a 10-year Treasury coupon security at a cost of $104.1880 instead of $106.

It is the process of coupon stripping and synthetically creating a Treasury security by buying the zero-coupon bonds that will drive the price of a Treasury security to its value as determined by the spot rates.

FORWARD RATES

Thus far we have seen that from the Treasury yield curve we can extrapolate the theoretical spot rates. In addition, we can extrapolate what some market participants refer to as the **market's consensus for future interest rates**. To see the importance of knowing the market's consensus for future interest rates, consider the following two investment alternatives for an investor who has a one-year investment horizon:

Alternative 1: investor buys a one-year instrument, or
Alternative 2: investor buys a six-month instrument and when it matures in six months buys another six-month instrument.

With Alternative 1, the investor will realize the one-year spot rate and that rate is known with certainty. In contrast, with Alternative 2, the investor will realize the six-month spot rate, but the six-month rate six months from now is unknown. Therefore, for Alternative 2, the rate that will be earned over one year is not known with certainty. This is illustrated in Figure 18-3.

Suppose that this investor expects that six months from now the six-month rate will be higher than it is today. The investor might then think that Alternative 2 would be the better investment—but this is not necessarily true. To understand why and to appreciate the need to understand why it is necessary to know what the market's consensus for future interest rates is, we continue with our illustration.

The investor will be indifferent to the two alternatives if they produce the same total dollars over the one-year investment horizon. Given the one-year spot rate, there is some rate on a six-month instrument six months from now that will make the investor indifferent between the two alternatives. We will denote that rate by f.

The value of f can be readily determined given the theoretical one-year spot rate and the six-month spot rate. If an investor placed $100 in a one-year instrument (Alternative 1), the total dollars that will be generated at the end of one year is:

$$\text{Total dollars at end of year for Alternative 1} = \$100 \, (1 + z_2)^2 \qquad (18.1)$$

Figure 18-3
Two Alternative One-Year Investments

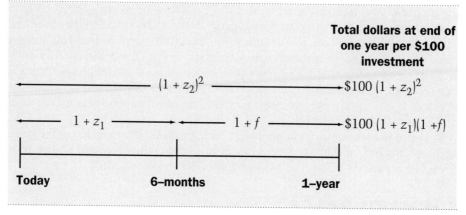

In this equation z_2 is the one-year spot rate. (Remember we are working in six-month periods, so the subscript 2 represents two six-month periods, or one year.)

The proceeds from investing at the six-month spot rate will generate the following total dollars at the end of six months:

Total dollars at end of six month for Alternative 2 = $100 $(1 + z_1)$ (18.2)

where z_1 is the six-month spot rate. If the amount in Equation (18.2) is reinvested at the six-month rate six months from now, which we denoted f, then the total dollars at the end of one year would be:

Total dollars at end of year for Alternative 2 = $100 $(1 + z_1)(1 + f)$ (18.3)

The investor will be indifferent between the two alternatives if the total dollars are the same. This will occur if Equation (18.1) is equal to Equation (18.3). Setting these two equations to equal each other we get:

$$\$100 \, (1 + z_2)^2 = \$100 \, (1 + z_1)(1 + f) \qquad (18.4)$$

Solving Equation (18.4) for f, we get:

$$f = \frac{(1 + z_2)^2}{(1 + z_1)} - 1 \qquad (18.5)$$

Doubling f gives the bond-equivalent yield for the six-month rate six months from now that we are interest in.

We can illustrate the use of Equation (18.5) with the theoretical spot rates shown in Table 18-2. From that table, we know the following.

six-month bill spot rate = 0.080, therefore z_1 = 0.0400
one-year bill spot rate   = 0.083, therefore z_2 = 0.0415

Substituting into the formula, we have:

$$f = \frac{(1.0415)^2}{1.0400} - 1 = .043$$

Therefore, the value of f quoted on a bond-equivalent basis is 8.6% (0.043×2).

Here is how we use this rate of 8.6%. If the six-month rate six months from now is less than 8.6%, then the total dollars at the end of one year would be higher by investing in the one-year instrument (Alternative 1). If the six-month rate six months from now is greater than 8.6%, then the total dollars at the end of one year would be higher by investing in the six-month instrument and reinvesting the proceeds six months from now at the six-month rate at the time (Alternative 2). Of course, if the six-month rate six months from now is 8.6%, the two alternatives gives the same total dollars at the end of one year.

Now that we have the rate for f that we are interested in and we know how that rate can be used, we return to the question posed at the outset. From Table 18-2, the six-month spot rate is 8%. Suppose that the investor expects that six months from now the six-month rate will be 8.2%, that is, the investor expects that the six-month rate will be higher than its current level. Should the investor select Alternative 2 because the six-month rate six months from now is expected to be higher? The answer is no. As we explained in the previous paragraph, if the rate is less than 8.6%, then Alternative 1 is the better alternative. Since this investor expects a rate of 8.2%, then he should select Alternative 1 despite the fact that he expects the six-month rate to be higher than it is today.

This is a somewhat surprising result for some investors. But the reason for this is that the market prices its expectations of future interest rates into the rates offered on investments with different maturities. This is why knowing the market's consensus for future interest rates is critical. The rate that we determined for f is the market's consensus for the six-month rate six months from now. A future interest rate calculated from either the spot rates or the yield curve is called a **forward rate** or an **implied forward rate**.

We can take this sort of analysis much further. It is not necessary to limit ourselves to implied forward rates six months from now. The yield curve can be used to calculate the implied forward rate for any time in the future for any investment horizon. As examples, the following can be calculated:

- the two-year implied forward rate five years from now
- the six-year implied forward rate ten years from now
- the seven-year implied forward rate three years from now

Relationship Between Spot Rates and Short-Term Forward Rates

Suppose an investor purchases a five-year zero-coupon Treasury security for $58.42 with a maturity value of $100. The investor could instead buy a six-month Treasury bill and reinvest the proceeds every six months for five years.

The number of dollars that will be realized will depend on the six-month forward rates. Suppose that the investor can actually reinvest the proceeds maturing every six months at the implied six-month forward rates. Let us see how many dollars would accumulate at the end of five years. The implied six-month forward rates were calculated for the yield curve given in Table 18-2. Letting f_t denote the six-month forward rate beginning t six-month periods from now, then the semiannual implied forward rates using the spot rates shown in Table 18-2 are:

$$f_1 = 0.043000 \quad f_2 = 0.050980 \quad f_3 = 0.051005 \quad f_4 = 0.051770$$
$$f_5 = 0.056945 \quad f_6 = 0.060965 \quad f_7 = 0.069310 \quad f_8 = 0.064625$$
$$f_9 = 0.062830$$

By investing the $58.48 at the six-month spot rate of 4% (8% on a bond-equivalent basis) and reinvesting at the above forward rates, the number of dollars accumulated at the end of five years would be:

$58.48 (1.04) (1.043) (1.05098) (1.051005) (1.05177) (1.056945)
(1.060965) (1.069310) (1.064625) (1.06283) = $100

Therefore, we see that if the implied forward rates are realized, the $54.48 investment will produce the same number of dollars as an investment in a five-year zero-coupon Treasury security at the five-year spot rate. From this illustration, we can see that the five-year spot rate is related to the current six-month spot rate and the implied six-month forward rates.

In general, the relationship between a t-period spot rate, the current six-month spot rate, and the implied six-month forward rates is as follows:

$$z_t = [(1 + z_1) (1 + f_1) (1 + f_2) (1 + f_3) \ldots (1 + f_{t-1})]^{1/t} - 1 \tag{18.6}$$

To illustrate how to use Equation (18.6), look at how the five-year (ten-period) spot rate is related to the six-month forward rates. Substituting into Equation (18.6) the relevant forward rates given above and the one-period spot rate of 4% (one half the 8% annual spot rate), we obtain:

$$z_{10} = [(1.04) (1.043) (1.05098) (1.051005) (1.05177) (1.056945)$$
$$(1.060965) (1.069310) (1.064625) (1.06283)]^{1/10} - 1$$
$$= 5.51\%$$

Doubling 5.51% gives an annual spot rate of 11.02%, which agrees with the spot rate given in Table 18-2.

Forward Rate as a Hedgeable Rate

A natural question to ask about forward rates is how well they do at predicting future interest rates. Studies have demonstrated that forward rates do not perform well in predicting future interest rates.[2] Then, why the big deal about understanding forward rates? The reason as we demonstrated in our illustration of how to select between two alternative investments is that the forward

---

[2] Eugene F. Fama, "Forward Rates as Predictors of Future Spot Rates," *Journal of Financial Economics* 3, no. 4, (1976), pp. 361-77.

rates indicate how an investor's expectations must differ from the market consensus in order to make the correct the decision.

In our illustration, the six-month forward rate may not be realized. That is irrelevant. The fact is that the six-month forward rate indicated to the investor that if his expectation about the six-month rate six months from now is less than 8.6%, he would be better off with Alternative 1.

For this reason, as well as others explained later, some market participants prefer not to talk about forward rates as being market consensus rates. Instead, they refer to forward rates as being **hedgeable rates**. For example, by buying the one-year security, the investor was able to hedge the six-month rate six months from now.

DETERMINANTS OF THE SHAPE OF THE TERM STRUCTURE

If we plot the term structure—the yield to maturity, or the spot rate, at successive maturities against maturity—what is it likely to look like? Figure 18-1 shows the four shapes that have appeared with some frequency over time. Panel *A* of the figure shows an upward-sloping yield curve; that is, yield rises steadily as maturity increases. This shape is commonly referred to as a "normal" or "positive" yield curve. Panel *B* shows a downward-sloping or "inverted" yield curve, where yields decline as maturity increases. Panel *C* shows a "humped" yield curve. Finally, panel *D* shows a "flat" yield curve. Two major theories have evolved to account for these observed shapes of the yield curve: **expectations theory** and **market segmentation theory**.

There are three forms of the expectations theory, including the **pure expectations theory, liquidity theory**, and **preferred habitat theory**. All share a hypothesis about the behavior of short-term forward rates and also assume that the forward rates in current long-term bonds are closely related to the market's expectations about future short-term rates. These three theories differ, however, on whether other factors also affect forward rates, and how. The pure expectations theory postulates that no systematic factors other than expected future short-term rates affect forward rates; the liquidity theory and the preferred habitat theory assert that there are other factors. Accordingly, the last two forms of the expectations theory are sometimes referred to as **biased expectations theories**. Figure 18-4 depicts the relationship between these three theories.

The Pure Expectations Theory

According to the pure expectations theory, the forward rates exclusively represent the expected future rates. Thus, the entire term structure at a given time reflects the market's current expectations of the family of future short-term rates. Under this view a rising term structure, as in Panel *A* of Figure 18-1, must indicate that the market expects short-term rates to rise throughout the relevant future. Similarly, a flat term structure reflects an expectation that future short-term rates will be mostly constant, while a falling term structure must reflect an expectation that future short rates will decline steadily.

Figure 18-4

Term Structure Theories

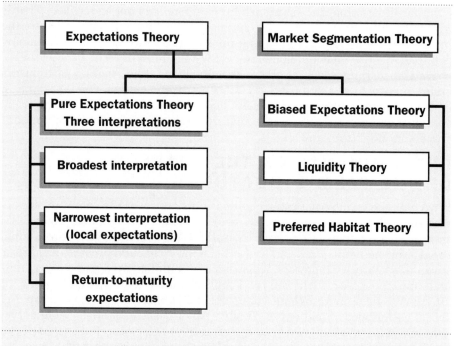

Source: Frank J. Fabozzi, **Valuation of Fixed Income Securities and Derivatives** *(New Hope, PA:*
Frank J. Fabozzi Associates, 1995).

We can illustrate this theory by considering how an expectation of a rising
short-term future rate would affect the behavior of various market participants, so as to result in a rising yield curve. Assume an initially flat term
structure, and suppose that economic news subsequently leads market participants to expect interest rates to rise.

1. Those market participants interested in a long-term investment
   would not want to buy long-term bonds because they would expect
   the yield structure to rise sooner or later, resulting in a price decline
   for the bonds and a capital loss on the long-term bonds purchased.
   Instead, they would want to invest in short-term debt obligations
   until the rise in yield had occurred, permitting them to reinvest
   their funds at the higher yield.

2. Speculators expecting rising rates would anticipate a decline in the
   price of long-term bonds and therefore would want to sell any long-
   term bonds they own and possibly to "short-sell" some they do not
   now own. (Should interest rates rise as expected, the price of longer-
   term bonds will fall. Since the speculator sold these bonds short and
   can then purchase them at a lower price to cover the short sale, a
   profit will be earned.) The proceeds received from the selling of long-
   term debt issues the speculators now hold or the shorting of longer-
   term bonds will be invested in short-term debt obligations.

3. Borrowers wishing to acquire long-term funds would be pulled toward borrowing now, in the long end of the market, by the expectation that borrowing at a later time would be more expensive.

All these responses would tend either to lower the net demand for, or to increase the supply of, long-maturity bonds, and two responses would increase demand for short-term debt obligations. This would require a rise in long-term yields in relation to short-term yields; that is, these actions by investors, speculators, and borrowers would tilt the term structure upward until it is consistent with expectations of higher future interest rates. By analogous reasoning, an unexpected event leading to the expectation of lower future rates will result in the yield curve sloping down.

Unfortunately, the pure expectations theory suffers from one shortcoming, which is qualitatively, quite serious. It neglects the risks inherent in investing in bonds and like instruments. If forward rates were perfect predictors of future interest rates, then the future prices of bonds would be known with certainty. The return over any investment period would be certain and independent of the maturity of the instrument initially acquired and of the time at which the investor needed to liquidate his instrument. However, with uncertainty about future interest rates and hence about future prices of bonds, these instruments become risky investments in the sense that the return over some investment horizon is unknown.

There are two risks that cause uncertainty about the return over some investment horizon. The first is the uncertainty about the price of the bond at the end of the investment horizon. For example, an investor who plans to invest for five years might consider the following three investment alternatives: (1) invest in a five-year bond and hold it for five years; (2) invest in a 12-year bond and sell it at the end of five years; and, (3) invest in a 30-year bond and sell it at the end of five years. The return that will be realized for the second and third alternatives is not known because the price of each long-term bond at the end of five years is not known. In the case of the 12-year bond, the price will depend on the yield on seven-year bonds five years from now; and the price of the 30-year bond will depend on the yield on 25-year bonds five years from now. Since forward rates implied in the current term structure for a future 12-year bond and a future 25-year bond are not perfect predictors of the actual future rates, there is uncertainty about the price for both bonds five years from now. Thus, there is price risk, that is, the risk that the price of the bond will be lower than currently expected at the end of the investment horizon. As explained in Chapter 17, an important feature of price risk is that it is greater the longer the maturity of the bond.

The second risk has to do with the uncertainty about the rate at which the proceeds from a bond that matures prior to the maturity date can be reinvested until the maturity date—that is, reinvestment risk. For example, an investor who plans to invest for five years might consider the following three alternative investments: (1) invest in a five-year bond and hold it for five years; (2) invest in a six-month instrument and, when it matures, reinvest the proceeds in six-month instruments over the entire five-year investment horizon; and, (3) invest in a two-year bond and, when it matures, reinvest the proceeds in a three-year bond. The risk in the second and third alternatives is that the return over the five-year investment horizon is unknown because rates at which the proceeds can be reinvested until maturity are unknown.

There are several interpretations of the pure expectations theory that have been put forth by economists. These interpretations are not exact equivalents nor are they consistent with each other, in large part because they offer different treatments of the two risks associated with realizing a return that we have just explained.[3]

The **broadest interpretation** of the pure expectations theory suggests that investors expect the return for any investment horizon to be the same, regardless of the maturity strategy selected.[4] For example, consider an investor who has a five-year investment horizon. According to this theory, it makes no difference if a five-year, 12-year, or 30-year bond is purchased and held for five years since the investor expects the return from all three bonds to be the same over five years. A major criticism of this very broad interpretation of the theory is that, because of price risk associated with investing in bonds with a maturity greater than the investment horizon, the expected returns from these three very different bond investments should differ in significant ways.[5]

A second interpretation, referred to as the **local expectations** form of the pure expectations theory, suggests that the return will be the same over a short-term investment horizon starting today. For example, if an investor has a six-month investment horizon, buying a five-year, 10-year, or 20-year bond will produce the same six-month return. It has been demonstrated that the local expectations formulation, which is narrow in scope, is the only one of the interpretations of the pure expectations theory that can be sustained in equilibrium.[6]

The third and final interpretation of the pure expectations theory suggests that the return that an investor will realize by rolling over short-term bonds to some investment horizon will be the same as holding a zero-coupon bond with a maturity that is the same as that investment horizon. (A zero-coupon bond has no reinvestment risk, so that future interest rates over the investment horizon do not affect the return.) This variant is called the **return-to-maturity expectations** interpretation. For example, once again assume that an investor has a five-year investment horizon. By buying a five-year, zero-coupon bond and holding it to maturity, the investor's return is the difference between the maturity value and the price of the bond, all divided by the price of the bond. According to the return-to-maturity expectations, the same return will be realized by buying a six-month instrument and rolling it over for five years. At this time, the validity of this interpretation is subject to considerable doubt.

Liquidity Theory

We have explained that the drawback of the pure expectations theory is that it does not consider the risks associated with investing in bonds. Nonetheless,

---

[3] These formulations are summarized by John Cox, Jonathan Ingersoll, Jr., and Stephen Ross, "A Re-examination of Traditional Hypotheses about the Term Structure of Interest Rates," *Journal of Finance* (September 1981), pp. 769-99.

[4] F. Lutz, "The Structure of Interest Rates," *Quarterly Journal of Economics* (1940-41), pp. 36-63.

[5] Cox, Ingersoll, and Ross, "A Re-examination of Traditional Hypotheses about the Term Structure of Interest Rates." pp. 774-5.

[6] Cox, Ingersoll, and Ross, "A Re-examination of Traditional Hypotheses about the Term Structure of Interest Rates."

we have just shown that there is indeed risk in holding a long-term bond for one period, and that risk increases with the bond's maturity because maturity and price volatility are directly related.

Given this uncertainty, and the reasonable consideration that investors typically do not like uncertainty, some economists and financial analysts have suggested a different theory. This theory states that investors will hold longer-term maturities if they are offered a long-term rate higher than the average of expected future rates by a risk premium that is positively related to the term to maturity.[7] Put differently, the forward rates should reflect both interest rate expectations and a "liquidity" premium (really a risk premium), and the premium should be higher for longer maturities.

According to this theory, which is called the liquidity theory of the term structure, the implied forward rates will not be an unbiased estimate of the market's expectations of future interest rates because they embody a liquidity premium. Thus, an upward-sloping yield curve may reflect expectations that future interest rates either (1) will rise, or (2) will be flat or even fall, but with a liquidity premium increasing fast enough with maturity so as to produce an upward-sloping yield curve.

Preferred Habitat Theory

Another theory, known as the preferred habitat theory, also adopts the view that the term structure reflects the expectation of the future path of interest rates as well as a risk premium. However, the preferred habitat theory rejects the assertion that the risk premium must rise uniformly with maturity.[8] Proponents of the preferred habitat theory say that the latter conclusion could be accepted if all investors intend to liquidate their investment at the shortest possible date while all borrowers are anxious to borrow long. This assumption can be rejected since institutions have holding periods dictated by the nature of their liabilities.

The preferred habitat theory asserts that, to the extent that the demand and supply of funds in a given maturity range do not match, some lenders and borrowers will be induced to shift to maturities showing the opposite imbalances. However, they will need to be compensated by an appropriate risk premium whose magnitude will reflect the extent of aversion to either price or reinvestment risk.

Thus, this theory proposes that the shape of the yield curve is determined by both expectations of future interest rates and a risk premium, positive or negative, to induce market participants to shift out of their preferred habitat. Clearly, according to this theory, yield curves sloping up, down, flat, or humped are all possible.

Market Segmentation Theory

The market segmentation theory also recognizes that investors have preferred habitats dictated by the nature of their liabilities. This theory also proposes

---

[7] John R. Hicks, *Value and Capital* (London: Oxford University Press, 1946), second ed., pp. 141-5.

[8] Franco Modigliani and Richard Sutch, "Innovations in Interest Rate Policy," *American Economic Review* (May 1966), pp. 178-97.

that the major reason for the shape of the yield curve lies in asset/liability management constraints (either regulatory or self-imposed) and/or creditors (borrowers) restricting their lending (financing) to specific maturity sectors.[9] However, the market segmentation theory differs from the preferred habitat theory in that it assumes that neither investors nor borrowers are willing to shift from one maturity sector to another to take advantage of opportunities arising from differences between expectations and forward rates. Thus, for the segmentation theory, the shape of the yield curve is determined by supply of and demand for securities within each maturity sector.

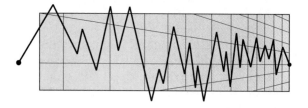

SUMMARY

The relationship between yield and maturity is referred to as the term structure of interest rates. There is a problem with using the Treasury yield curve to determine the one yield at which to discount all the cash payments of any bond. Each cash flow should be discounted at a unique interest rate that is applicable to the time period when the cash flow is to be received. Since any bond can be viewed as a package of zero-coupon instruments, its value should equal the value of all the component zero-coupon instruments. The rate on a zero-coupon bond is called the spot rate. The theoretical spot rate curve for Treasury securities can be estimated from the Treasury yield curve using a methodology known as bootstrapping.

Under certain assumptions, the market's expectation of future interest rates can be extrapolated from the theoretical Treasury spot rate curve. The resulting rate is called the implied forward rate. Spot rates include the current six-month spot rate and the implied six-month forward rates.

Several theories have been proposed about the determination of the term structure: pure expectations theory; biased expectations theory (liquidity theory and preferred habitat theory); and market segmentation theory. All the expectation theories hypothesize that the one-period forward rates represent the market's expectations of future actual rates. The pure expectations theory asserts that it is the only factor; the biased expectations theories assert that there are other factors.

---

[9] This theory was suggested in J.M. Culbertson, "The Term Structure of Interest Rates," *Quarterly Journal of Economics* (November 1957), pp. 489-504.

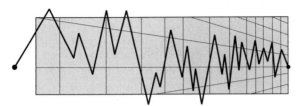

QUESTIONS

1. a. What is a yield curve?

   b. Why is the Treasury yield curve the one that is most closely watched by market participants?

2. What is meant by a spot rate?

3. Explain why it is inappropriate to use one yield to discount all the cash flows of a financial asset.

4. Explain why a financial asset can be viewed as a package of zero-coupon instruments.

5. How are spot rates related to implied forward rates?

6. Suppose you are a financial consultant who has heard the following comments on interest rates from a client. How would you respond to each comment?

   a. "The yield curve is upward-sloping today. This suggests that the market consensus is that interest rates are expected to increase in the future."

   b. "I can't make any sense out of today's term structure. For short-term yields (up to three years) the spot rates increase with maturity; for maturities greater than three years but less than eight years, the spot rates decline with maturity; and for maturities greater than eight years the spot rates are virtually the same for each maturity. There is simply no

theory that explains a term structure with this shape."

   c. "When I want to determine the market's consensus of future interest rates, I calculate the implied forward rates."

7. Suppose you observe the Treasury yield curve below (all yields are shown on a bond-equivalent basis):

Year	Yield to maturity	Spot rate
0.5	5.25%	5.25%
1.0	5.50	5.50
1.5	5.75	5.76
2.0	6.00	?
2.5	6.25	?
3.0	6.50	?
3.5	6.75	?
4.0	7.00	?
4.5	7.25	?
5.0	7.50	?
5.5	7.75	7.97
6.0	8.00	8.27
6.5	8.25	8.59
7.0	8.50	8.92
7.5	8.75	9.25
8.0	9.00	9.61
8.5	9.25	9.97
9.0	9.50	10.36
9.5	9.75	10.77
10.0	10.00	11.20

All the securities maturing from 1.5 years on are selling at par. The 0.5-year and 1-year securities are zero-coupon instruments.

   a. Calculate the missing spot rates.

   b. What should the price of a six-year Treasury security be?

c. What is the implied six-month forward rate starting in the sixth year?

8. You observe the following Treasury yield curve (all yields are shown on a bond-equivalent basis):

Year	Yield to maturity	spot rate
0.5	10.00%	10.00%
1.0	9.75	9.75
1.5	9.50	9.48
2.0	9.25	9.22
2.5	9.00	8.95
3.0	8.75	8.68
3.5	8.50	8.41
4.0	8.25	8.14
4.5	8.00	7.86
5.0	7.75	7.58
5.5	7.50	7.30
6.0	7.25	7.02
6.5	7.00	6.74
7.0	6.75	6.46
7.5	6.50	6.18
8.0	6.25	5.90
8.5	6.00	5.62
9.0	5.75	5.35
9.5	5.50	?
10.0	5.25	?

All the securities maturing from 1.5 years on are selling at par. The 0.5-year and 1-year securities are zero-coupon instruments.

a. Calculate the missing spot rates.

b. What should the price of a four-year Treasury security be?

9. What actions force a Treasury's bond price to be valued in the market at the present value of the cash flows discounted at the Treasury spot rates?

10. a. What is meant by stripping a Treasury security?

b. Show the instruments created if a dealer purchases $400 mil-lion of an 8%, 20-year Treasury security.

11. Explain the role that forward rates play in making investment decisions?

12. "Forward rates are poor predictors of the actual future rates that are realized. Consequently, they are of little value to an investor." Explain why you agree or disagree with this statement.

13. A client is considering two alternative investments. The first alternative is to invest in an instrument that matures in two years. The second alternative is to invest in an instrument that matures in one year and at the end of one year, reinvest the proceeds in a one-year instrument. The client believes that one-year interest rates one year from now will be higher than they are today and therefore is leaning in favor of the second alternative. What would you recommend to this client?

14. What is the common hypothesis about the behavior of short-term forward rates shared by the various forms of the expectations theory?

15. What are the types of risks associated with investing in bonds and how do these two risks affect the pure expectations theory?

16. Give three interpretations of the pure expectations theory.

17. What are the two biased expectations theories about the term structure of interest rates?

18. What are the underlying hypotheses of the two biased expectation theories of interest rates?

Money Markets

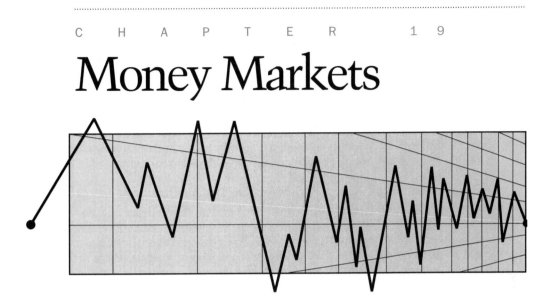

LEARNING OBJECTIVES

After reading this chapter you will understand:

• what the money market is.

• what a Treasury bill is.

• the auction process for Treasury bills.

• what commercial paper is and why it is issued.

• the types of issuers and major buyers of commercial paper.

• the credit ratings of commercial paper and why they are important.

• the difference between directly-placed and dealer-placed commercial paper.

• what a bankers acceptance is and how it is created.

• what a certificate of deposit is and the different types of certificates of deposit.

• what a repurchase agreement is and how it can be used to finance a security position.

• the factors that influence the interest rate on repurchase agreements.

• what the federal funds market is.

In this section of the book we turn our attention to debt securities—instruments that obligate the debtor to make a contractually fixed series of payments, generally in nominal dollars, up to some terminal maturity date. This chapter focuses on debt instruments that at the time of issuance have a maturity of one year or less. These instruments are referred to as **money market instruments**, and the market they trade in is called the **money market**. In Chapters 20 through 27 we deal with debt instruments with longer-term maturities.

The assets traded in the money market include Treasury bills, commercial paper, medium-term notes, bankers acceptances, short-term federal agency securities, short-term municipal obligations, certificates of deposit, repurchase agreements, floating-rate instruments, and federal funds. Short-term municipal securities are discussed in Chapter 23; medium-term notes are reserved for Chapter 22. Medium-term notes are corporate debt instruments with maturities ranging from 9 months to 30 years.

TREASURY BILLS

Treasury securities are issued by the U.S. Department of the Treasury and backed by the full faith and credit of the U.S. government. As a result, market participants perceive Treasury securities to carry no risk of default.

The U.S. Treasury issues three types of securities—bills, notes, and bonds. At issuance, bills have a maturity of one year or less, notes more than two years but no more than 10 years to maturity, and bonds more than 10 years to maturity. In Chapter 20 we cover Treasury securities in greater detail, but here we limit our discussion of Treasury securities to bills because they fall into the category of money market instruments—that is, instruments with one year or less to maturity. The market for Treasury bills is the most liquid market in the world.

A Treasury bill is a discount security. Such securities do not make periodic interest payments. The security holder receives interest instead at the maturity date, when the amount received is the face value (maturity value or par value) which is larger than the purchase price. For example, suppose an investor purchases a six-month Treasury bill that has a face value of $100,000 for $96,000. By holding the bill until the maturity date, the investor will receive $100,000; the difference of $4,000 between the proceeds received at maturity and the amount paid to purchase the bill represents the interest. Treasury bills are only one example of a number of money market instruments that are discount securities.

Bid and Offer Quotes on Treasury Bills

Bids and offers on Treasury bills are quoted in a special way. Unlike bonds that pay coupon interest, Treasury bills are quoted on a bank discount basis, not on a price basis. The yield on a bank discount basis is computed as follows:

$$Y_D = \frac{D}{F} \times \frac{360}{t}$$

where

Y_D = yield on a bank discount basis (expressed as a decimal)
D = dollar discount, which is equal to the difference between the face value and the price
F = face value
t = number of days remaining to maturity

As an example, a Treasury bill with 100 days to maturity, a face value of $100,000, and selling for $97,569 would be quoted at 8.75% on a bank discount basis:

$$D = \$100,000 - \$97,569 = \$2,431.$$

Therefore:

$$Y_D = \frac{\$2,431}{\$100,000} \times \frac{360}{100} = 8.75\%$$

Given the yield on a bank discount basis, the price of a Treasury bill is found by first solving the formula for Y_D for the dollar discount (D), as follows:

$$D = Y_D \times F \times \frac{t}{360}$$

The price is then:

Price = $F - D$, or equivalently:

$$\text{Price} = F\left(1 - Y_D \frac{t}{360}\right)$$

For our 100-day Treasury bill with a face value of $100,000, if the yield on a bank discount basis is quoted as 8.75%, D is equal to:

$$D = .0875 \times \$100,000 \times \frac{100}{360} = \$2,431$$

Therefore: Price = $100,000 - $2,431 = $97,569

The quoted yield on a bank discount basis is not a meaningful measure of the return from holding a Treasury bill for two reasons. First, the measure is based on a face value investment rather than on the actual dollar amount invested. Second, the yield is annualized according to a 360-day rather than 365-day year, making it difficult to compare Treasury bill yields with Treasury notes and bonds, which pay interest on a 365-day basis. The use of 360 days for a year is a money market convention for some money market instruments, however. Despite its shortcomings as a measure of return, this is the method dealers have adopted to quote Treasury bills. Many dealer quote sheets and some reporting services provide two other yield measures that attempt to make the quoted yield comparable to that for a coupon bond and other money market instruments.

The measure that seeks to make the Treasury bill quote comparable to Treasury notes and bonds is called the **bond equivalent yield**, which we explained in Chapter 17. The **CD equivalent yield** (also called the **money market**

equivalent yield) makes the quoted yield on a Treasury bill more comparable to yield quotations on other money market instruments that pay interest on a 360-day basis. It does this by taking into consideration the price of the Treasury bill rather than its face value. The formula for the CD equivalent yield is:

$$\text{CD equivalent yield} = \frac{360\ Y_D}{360 - t\,(\,Y_D\,)}$$

As an illustration, consider once again the hypothetical 100-day Treasury bill with a face value of $100,000, selling for $97,569, and offering a yield on a bank discount basis of 8.75%. The CD-equivalent yield is:

$$\frac{360\,(.0875)}{360 - 100\,(.0875)} = 8.97\%$$

The Primary Market for Treasury Bills

Treasury securities typically are issued on an auction basis according to regular cycles for specific maturities. Three-month and six-month Treasury bills are auctioned every Monday. The amounts to be auctioned are ordinarily announced the previous Tuesday afternoon. The one-year (52-week bill) Treasury bills are auctioned in the third week of every month, with announcement on the preceding Friday. When the Treasury is temporarily short of cash, it issues **cash management bills**. The maturities of cash management bills coincide with the length of time that the Treasury anticipates the shortfall of funds.

The auction for Treasury bills is conducted on a yield basis. Competitive bids for Treasury bills must be submitted on a bank discount basis, as we have explained. Noncompetitive tenders may also be submitted for up to a $1 million face amount. Such tenders are based only on quantity, not yield. The yield received by noncompetitive bidders is the average yield determined by competitive bidders.

The auction results are determined by first deducting the total noncompetitive tenders and nonpublic purchases (such as purchases by the Federal Reserve itself) from the total securities being auctioned. The remainder is the amount to be awarded to the competitive bidders. The lowest-yield (i.e., highest price) bidders are awarded securities at their bid price. Successively higher-yielding bidders are awarded securities at their bid price until the total amount offered (less noncompetitive tenders) is awarded. The highest yield accepted by the Treasury is referred to as the "stop yield," and bidders at that price are awarded a percentage of their total tender offer. The difference between the average yield of all the bids accepted by the Treasury and the stop yield is called the "tail."

For example, the auction result for an actual 364-day Treasury bill offering was as follows:

Total issue	= $9.00 billion
Less noncompetitive bids	= 0.64
Less Federal Reserve	= 2.80
Left for competitive bidders	= $5.56 billion

Total competitive bids might have been received as follows:

Amount (in Billions)	Bid
$0.20	7.55% (lowest yield/highest price)
0.26	7.56
0.33	7.57
0.57	7.58 (average yield/average price)
0.79	7.59
0.96	7.60
1.25	7.61
1.52	7.62 (stop or largest yield/stop or lowest price)

The Treasury would allocate bills to competitive bidders from the low-yield bid to the high-yield bid until $5.56 billion is distributed. Those who bid 7.55% to 7.61% will be awarded the entire amount for which they bid. The total that would be awarded to these bidders is $4.36 billion, leaving $1.2 billion to be awarded, less than the $1.52 billion bid at 7.62%. Each of the bidders at 7.62% would be awarded 79% ($1.2/$1.52) of the amount they bid. For example, if a financial institution bid for $100 million at 7.62%, it would be awarded $79 million. The results of the auction would show 7.55% high, 7.58% average, and 7.62% the stop yield, with 79% awarded at the stop. Bidders higher in yield than 7.62% "missed" or were "shut out." This auction would have a tail of 0.04 (7.62 minus 7.58).

The auction of Treasury bills results in different yields (prices) for different winning bidders. Thus, the auction is referred to as a **multiple-price auction**. The procedure for the auction of some Treasury coupon securities is identical to that for Treasury bills. There are some Treasury coupon securities that are issued on a **single-price auction** basis; that is, all winning bidders pay the same price. This is described in Chapter 20 where we will also discuss the secondary market for Treasury bills.

COMMERCIAL PAPER

Commercial paper is a short-term unsecured promissory note that is issued in the open market and represents the obligation of the issuing corporation. The U.S. commercial paper market has grown from $112.8 billion at year-end 1979 to $545 billion by August 1993.[1] Since 1988, there have been some years in which the size of the commercial paper market has exceeded that of the Treasury bill market.

The types of corporate issuers of commercial paper have changed since 1980. In the 1970s, large high-credit quality corporations were the principal issuers of commercial paper. For reasons described later, in the 1980s medium- and low-quality corporate issuers were able to raise funds via the commercial paper market; however, since 1989 such issuers have not found a receptive market for their issues and therefore withdrew from the market. The issuance of commercial paper is an alternative to bank borrowing for large corporations (nonfinancial and financial) with strong credit ratings.

---

[1] *Federal Reserve Bulletins.*

The original purpose of commercial paper was to provide short-term funds for seasonal and working capital needs. Basically, it provided a less expensive form of short-term borrowing for high credit-quality corporations than from borrowing at the bank. As the U.S. economy expanded in the 1980s, corporations sought to increase their short-term borrowing to finance high production levels. Commercial paper became even more attractive to those who could access the market because the cost of borrowing by issuing commercial paper was considerably cheaper than bank borrowing in the early 1980s. For example, using the 30-day London interbank offered rate (LIBOR) as a gauge for the cost of borrowing by high-quality corporations, the spread between LIBOR and commercial paper rates ranged between 0 and 60 basis points from 1975 to 1980. Between 1980 and 1985 that spread widened, exceeding 150 points at times. This encouraged medium- and low-quality corporate issuers into the market.

In the 1980s, corporations also began to use commercial paper for other purposes. It has been used quite often for "bridge financing." For example, suppose that a corporation needs long-term funds to build a plant or acquire equipment. Rather than raising long-term funds immediately, the corporation may elect to postpone the offering until more favorable capital market conditions prevail. The funds raised by issuing commercial paper are used until longer-term securities are sold. As merger and acquisition activity increased in the 1980s, commercial paper was sometimes used as bridge financing to finance corporate takeovers. Moreover, the interest rate swaps market encouraged the use of the commercial paper market. As explained in the description of the fundamental features of an interest rate swap in Chapter 12, one party exchanges a fixed rate for a floating rate. Corporate issuers issue commercial paper and use the interest rate swap to effectively convert the floating interest rate on commercial paper into a fixed interest rate. The motivation for this will be discussed in Chapter 29.

Money market mutual funds purchase roughly one-third of all the commercial paper issued. Retail investors, trusts, and nonprofit corporations purchase about 30% and nonfinancial corporations seeking short-term investments purchase about 10%.[2] The balance is purchased by private and public pension funds, life insurance companies, and commercial banks. The minimum round-lot transaction is $100,000, though some issuers will sell commercial paper in denominations of $25,000. There is very little secondary trading of commercial paper. Typically, an investor in commercial paper is an entity that plans to hold it until maturity. This is understandable since an investor can purchase commercial paper in a direct transaction with the issuer, who will issue paper with the specific maturity the investor desires.

Characteristics of Commercial Paper

In the United States, the maturity of commercial paper is typically less than 270 days and the most common maturity range is 30 to 50 days or less.[3] There are reasons for this. First, as explained in Chapter 6, the Securities Act

---

[2] Taken from various issues of the *Federal Reserve Bulletin*.

[3] *Money Market Instruments* (NY: Merrill Lynch Money Markets Inc., 1989), p. 16.

of 1933 requires that securities be registered with the SEC. Special provisions in the 1933 act exempt commercial paper from registration so long as the maturity does not exceed 270 days. Hence to avoid the costs associated with registering issues with the SEC, firms rarely issue commercial paper with maturities exceeding 270 days. Another consideration in determining the maturity is whether the commercial paper would be eligible collateral for a bank that wanted to borrow from the Federal Reserve Bank's discount window. In order to be eligible, the maturity of the paper may not exceed 90 days. Since eligible paper trades at a lower cost than paper that is not eligible, issuers prefer to issue paper whose maturity does not exceed 90 days.

To pay off holders of maturing paper, issuers generally use the proceeds obtained by selling new commercial paper. This process is often described as "rolling over" short-term paper. The risk that the investor in commercial paper faces is that the issuer will be unable to issue new paper at maturity. As a safeguard against this roll-over risk, commercial paper is typically backed by unused bank credit lines. Since there is a commitment fee charged by a bank for providing a credit line, this safeguard increases the effective cost of issuing commercial paper.

Issuers of Commercial Paper

As of the early 1990s, there were about 1,250 corporate and other entities issuing commercial paper in the United States.[4] Corporate issuers of commercial paper can be divided into financial companies and nonfinancial companies. Of the $545 billion of commercial paper outstanding as of August 1993, $398 billion have been issued by financial companies.

There are three types of financial companies: captive finance companies, bank-related finance companies, and independent finance companies. Captive finance companies are subsidiaries of equipment manufacturing companies. Their primary purpose is to secure financing for the customers of the parent company. For example, the three major U.S. automobile manufacturers—General Motors Acceptance Corporation (GMAC), Ford Credit, and Chrysler Financial—have captive finance companies. GMAC is by the far the largest issuer of commercial paper in the United States. A bank holding company may have a subsidiary finance company which provides loans to individuals and businesses who wish to acquire a wide range of products. Independent finance companies are those that are not subsidiaries of equipment-manufacturing firms or bank-holding companies.

As we noted earlier, while the issuers of commercial paper typically have high credit ratings, smaller and less, well-known companies with lower credit ratings were able to issue paper in the 1980s. They have been able to do so by means of credit support from a firm with a high credit rating or by collateralizing the issue with high-quality assets. The former type of commercial paper is called **credit-supported commercial paper** and the latter type is called **asset-backed commercial paper**. An example of credit-supported commercial paper is one supported by a letter of credit. A letter of credit specifies that the bank issuing the letter guarantees that if the issuer fails to pay off the paper when

---

[4] *Handbook of Securities of the United States Government and Agencies* (NY: First Boston Corporation, 1988), p. 140.

it comes due, the bank will do so. The bank will charge a fee for the letter of credit. From the issuer's perspective, the fee enables it to enter the commercial paper market and obtain funding at a lower cost than that of bank borrowing. Commercial paper issued with this credit enhancement is referred to as **LOC paper**. The credit enhancement may also take the form of a surety bond from an insurance company.[5] The key innovation that gave lower rated and lesser-known corporations access to the commercial paper market is the asset-backed structure. Basically, as explained in our discussion of asset securitization in Chapter 27, the collateral for an asset-backed security is a pool of assets. In the case of asset-backed commercial paper, the assets are pools of receivables.[6]

Both domestic and foreign corporations issue commercial paper in the United States. Commercial paper issued by foreign entities is called **Yankee commercial paper**.

Default Risk and Credit Ratings

With one exception, between 1971 and mid-1989, there were no defaults on commercial paper.[7] With the weakening economy in the late 1980s, three defaults occurred in 1989 and four in 1990. This and two other factors caused corporate medium- and lower-quality rated issuers out of the commercial paper market. The first factor was that banks became reluctant to provide backup facilities for these issuers. The introduction of the risk-based capital requirements for commercial banks, described in Chapter 3, made these commitments less attractive. Second, the demand for medium-grade commercial paper by money market mutual funds, the major buyer of commercial paper, was reduced by several SEC rulings in 1991. Specifically, at one time there were no restrictions on medium-grade commercial paper that money market mutual funds could hold; now there are.

There are four companies that evaluate the risk of default of issuers and summarize their evaluation in the form of a rating. The four rating companies are Moody's Investors Service, Standard & Poor's Corporation, Duff & Phelps Credit Rating Co., and Fitch Investors Service. These companies also assign ratings to other debt obligations, as we will see when we discuss other corporate obligations and municipal securities in later chapters.

The ratings assigned by these four rating companies are shown in Table 19-1. Commercial paper ratings, as the ratings on other securities, are categorized as either investment grade and noninvestment grade.

These ratings are used by money market mutual funds in determining the amount of commercial paper that they are permitted to hold. The SEC requirements establish two categories of eligible commercial paper: first-tier paper and second-tier paper. In general, to be categorized as first-tier paper the

---

[5] A surety bond is a policy written by an insurance company to protect another party against loss or violation of a contract.

[6] For a further discussion of asset-backed commercial paper, see Barbara Kavanaugh, Thomas R. Boemio, and Gerald A. Edwards, Jr., "Asset-Backed Commercial Paper," *Federal Reserve Bulletin* (February 1992), pp. 107-16.

[7] Mitchell A. Post, "The Evolution of the U.S. Commercial Paper Market since 1980," *Federal Reserve Bulletin* (December 1992), p. 888. The one exception was Manville Corporation in August 1982, which defaulted after filing in bankruptcy court for protection against potential liability from law suits related to injuries and deaths from asbestos.

Table 19-1
Commercial Paper Ratings*

Category	Duff & Phelps	Fitch	Moody's	S&P
Investment grade	Duff 1+	F-1+		A-1+
	Duff 1	F-1	P-1	A-1
	Duff 1-			
	Duff 2	F-2	P-2	A-2
	Duff 3	F-3	P-3	A-3
Noninvestment grade	Duff 4	F-S	NP(Not Prime)	B
				C
In default	Duff 5	D		D

* The definition of ratings varies by rating agency.

Source: Mitchell A. Post, "The Evolution of the U.S. Commercial Paper Market since 1980,"
Federal Reserve Bulletin *(December 1992), p. 882.*

SEC requires that two of the rating companies rate the issue as "1" (see Table 19-1). To be categorized as two-tier paper, requires that one rating company rate the issue as "1" and at least one other rate it as "2," or two companies rate it at "2". It is the second-tier paper that is considered medium-grade and for which there are restrictions on the amount that can be held by money market mutual funds.

Directly-Placed versus Dealer-Placed Paper

Commercial paper is classified as either **direct paper** or **dealer paper**. Direct paper is sold by the issuing firm directly to investors without the help of an agent or an intermediary. A large majority of the issuers of direct paper are financial companies. These entities require continuous funds in order to provide loans to customers. As a result, they find it cost-effective to establish a sales force to sell their commercial paper directly to investors.

With dealer-placed commercial paper, the issuer uses the services of an agent to sell its paper. The agent distributes the paper on a "best efforts" underwriting basis as discussed in Chapter 5. Historically, the dealer paper market was dominated by securities houses because commercial banks were prohibited from underwriting commercial paper by the Glass-Steagall Act. However, in June 1987, the Fed granted subsidiaries of bank-holding companies permission to underwrite commercial paper. While securities houses still dominate the dealer market, commercial banks are making inroads.[8] This seems natural since, for the most part, the funds being raised in the commercial

---

[8] As of this writing, the four largest commercial paper dealers are Merrill Lynch, Goldman Sachs, Lehman Brothers, and First Boston. The three largest commercial banks that underwrite commercial paper are Bankers Trust, Citicorp, and Morgan Guaranty.

paper market represent those previously raised via short-term bank loans. Banks are seeking to generate underwriting fees associated with commercial paper underwriting in order to recoup part of the lost interest income from borrowers who have increasingly favored commercial paper market rather than short-term bank loans.

The Secondary Market

Despite the fact that the commercial paper market is larger than markets for other money market instruments, secondary trading activity is much smaller. The typical investor in commercial paper is an entity that plans to hold it until maturity, given that an investor can purchase commercial paper with the specific maturity desired. Should an investor's economic circumstances change so that there is a need to sell the paper, it can be sold back to the dealer or, in the case of directly-placed paper, the issuer will repurchase it.

Yields on Commercial Paper

Commercial paper, like Treasury bills, is a discount instrument—that is, it is sold at a price that is less than its maturity value. The difference between the maturity value and the price paid is the interest earned by the investor, although there is some commercial paper that is issued as an interest-bearing instrument. For commercial paper, a year is treated as having 360 days.

The yield offered on commercial paper tracks that of other money market instruments. Table 19-2 shows the yield on commercial paper for selected weeks in 1992 and 1993. The commercial paper rate is higher than that on Treasury bills for the same maturity. There are three reasons for this. First, the investor in commercial paper is exposed to credit risk. Second, interest earned from investing in Treasury bills is exempt from state and local income taxes; as a result, commercial paper has to offer a higher yield to offset this tax advantage. Finally, commercial paper is less liquid than Treasury bills. The liquidity premium demanded is probably small, however, because investors typically follow a buy-and-hold strategy with commercial paper and so are less concerned with liquidity.

It can also be seen from Table 19-2 that the yield on commercial paper is higher by a few basis points than the yield on certificates of deposit (discussed later in this chapter) for the same maturity. The higher yield available on commercial paper is attributable to the poorer liquidity relative to certificates of deposit.

Non-U.S. Commercial Paper Markets

Other countries have developed their own commercial paper markets. For example, in November 1987, the Japanese Ministry of Finance (MOF) approved the issuance of commercial paper by Japanese corporations in its domestic market. A few months latter, the MOF approved the issuance of yen-denominated commercial paper in Japan by non-Japanese entities. Such paper is referred to as **Samurai commercial paper**.

Eurocommercial paper is issued and placed outside the jurisdiction of the currency of denomination. There are several differences between U.S. commercial

Table 19-2

Interest Rates on Money Market Instruments
for Selected Weeks in 1992 and 1993

Money market instrument	Week ending 1/31/92	1/29/93	9/24/93
U.S. Treasury bills, secondary market			
1-month	3.84	2.92	2.93
3-month	3.92	3.07	3.06
6-month	4.02	3.26	3.26
Commercial paper			
1-month	4.08	3.14	3.15
2-month	4.09	3.18	3.16
3-month	4.09	3.29	3.26
Finance paper, directly placed			
1-month	4.00	3.18	3.08
2-month	4.01	3.27	3.09
3-month	3.98	3.23	3.11
Bankers acceptances			
3-month	4.00	3.08	3.08
6-month	4.02	3.15	3.17
Certificates of deposit, secondary market			
1-month	4.06	3.08	3.10
3-month	4.08	3.16	3.11
6-month	4.11	3.26	3.24
Eurodollar deposits, 3-month	4.08	3.18	3.06
Federal funds	4.01	2.94	3.12

Source: Selected issues of the **Federal Reserve Bulletin.**

paper and Eurocommercial paper with respect to the characteristics of the paper and the market itself. First, as stated earlier, commercial paper issued in the United States usually has a maturity of less than 270 days; the most common maturity range is 30 to 50 days or less. The maturity of Eurocommercial paper can be considerably longer. Second, in the U.S. an issuer must have unused bank credit lines, while it is possible to issue commercial paper without such backing in the Eurocommercial paper market. Third, while in the U.S. commercial paper can be directly-placed or dealer-placed, Eurocommercial paper is almost always dealer-placed. The fourth distinction is the greater diversity of dealers in the Eurocommercial paper market. In the U.S., only a few dealers dominate the market. Finally, because of the longer maturity of Eurocommercial paper, that paper is traded more often in the secondary market than U.S. commercial paper. In the U.S., investors of commercial paper are typically buy-and-hold, and the secondary market is thin and illiquid.

BANKERS ACCEPTANCES

Simply put, a **bankers acceptance** is a vehicle created to facilitate commercial trade transactions. The instrument is called a bankers acceptance because a bank accepts the ultimate responsibility to repay a loan to its holder. The use of bankers acceptances to finance a commercial transaction is referred to as "acceptance financing."

The transactions in which bankers acceptances are created include (1) importing goods into the U.S., (2) exporting goods from the U.S. to foreign entities, (3) storing and shipping goods between two foreign countries where neither the importer nor the exporter is a U.S. firm,[9] and (4) storing and shipping goods between two entities in the U.S.

As of August 1993, the dollar amount of bankers acceptances outstanding was $32.5 billion.[10] Of this amount, $10.4 billion was created in transactions involving the importing of goods into the U.S. and $7.5 billion in the exporting of goods from the U.S. The balance, $14.6 billion, mostly covers transactions involving the storing and shipping of goods between two foreign countries. Little use is made of acceptance financing by two parties within the U.S. Unlike the commercial paper market, the bankers acceptance market has been shrinking since 1984, when it reached a peak of $78 billion.

Bankers acceptances are sold on a discounted basis just as Treasury bills and commercial paper. The major investors in bankers acceptances are money market mutual funds and municipal entities.

Illustration of the Creation of a Bankers Acceptance

The best way to explain the creation of a bankers acceptance is by an illustration. Several entities are involved in our transaction:

- Car Imports Corporation of America ("Car Imports"), a firm in New Jersey that sells automobiles
- Germany Fast Autos Inc. ("GFA"), a manufacturer of automobiles in Germany
- First Hoboken Bank ("Hoboken Bank"), a commercial bank in Hoboken, New Jersey
- West Berlin National Bank ("Berlin Bank"), a bank in Germany

---

[9] Bankers acceptances created from these transactions are called "third country acceptances."

[10] *Federal Reserve Bulletin.*

- High-Caliber Money Market Fund, a mutual fund in the U.S. that invests in money market instruments

Car Imports and GFA are considering a commercial transaction. Car Imports wants to import 15 cars manufactured by GFA. GFA is concerned with the ability of Car Imports to make payment on the 15 cars when they are received.

Acceptance financing is suggested as a means for facilitating the transaction. Car Imports offers $300,000 for the 15 cars. The terms of the sale stipulate payment to be made to GFA 60 days after it ships the 15 cars to Car Imports. GFA determines whether it is willing to accept the $300,000. In considering the offering price, GFA must calculate the present value of the $300,000, because it will not be receiving payment until 60 days after shipment. Suppose that GFA agrees to these terms.

Car Imports arranges with its bank, Hoboken Bank, to issue a letter of credit. The letter of credit indicates that Hoboken Bank will make good on the payment of $300,000 that Car Imports must make to GFA 60 days after shipment. The letter of credit, or time draft, will be sent by Hoboken Bank to GFA's bank, Berlin Bank. Upon receipt of the letter of credit, Berlin Bank will notify GFA, who will then ship the 15 cars. After the cars are shipped, GFA presents the shipping documents to Berlin Bank and receives the present value of $300,000. GFA is now out of the picture.

Berlin Bank presents the time draft and the shipping documents to Hoboken Bank. The latter will then stamp "accepted" on the time draft. By doing so, the Hoboken Bank has created a bankers acceptance. This means that Hoboken Bank agrees to pay the holder of the bankers acceptance $300,000 at the maturity date. Car Imports will receive the shipping documents so that it can procure the 15 cars once it signs a note or some other type of financing arrangement with Hoboken Bank.

At this point, the holder of the bankers acceptance is the Berlin Bank. It has two choices: it can continue to hold the bankers acceptance as an investment in its loan portfolio, or it can request that the Hoboken Bank make a payment of the present value of $300,000. We will assume that Berlin Bank requests payment of the present value of $300,000.

Now the holder of the bankers acceptance is the Hoboken Bank. It has two choices: retain the bankers acceptance as an investment as part of its loan portfolio, or sell it to an investor. Suppose that Hoboken Bank chooses the latter, and that High-Caliber Money Market Fund is seeking a high-quality investment with the same maturity as that of the bankers acceptance. The Hoboken Bank sells the bankers acceptance to the money market fund at the present value of $300,000. Rather than sell the instrument directly to an investor, Hoboken Bank could sell it to a dealer who would then resell it to an investor such as a money market fund. In either case, at the maturity date, the money market fund presents the bankers acceptance to Hoboken Bank, receiving $300,000, which the bank in turn recovers from Car Imports.

Accepting Banks

Banks that create bankers acceptances are called accepting banks. Major money center banks that issue bankers acceptances include Bankers Trust,

Bank of America, Chase Manhattan, Citibank, and Morgan Guaranty. They maintain their own sales forces to sell bankers acceptances rather than using the services of a dealer.

The larger regional banks such as Harris Trust and Pittsburgh National Bank are accepting banks. They maintain their own sales forces to sell the bankers acceptances they create but will use dealers to unload those they cannot sell. Japanese city banks are now major issuers of bankers acceptances. Because they do not have the sales force to distribute the bankers acceptances they create directly to investors, Japanese accepting banks use the services of dealers.

Eligible bankers acceptance—An accepting bank that has decided to retain a bankers acceptance in its portfolio may be able to use it as collateral for a loan at the discount window of the Federal Reserve. The reason we say "may" is that, to be used as collateral bankers acceptances must meet certain eligibility requirements established by the Federal Reserve. One requirement for eligibility is that maturity cannot exceed six months, with a few exceptions. While the other requirements for eligibility are too detailed to review here, [11] the basic principle is simple: the bankers acceptance should be financing a self-liquidating commercial transaction.

Eligibility is also important because the Federal Reserve imposes a reserve requirement on funds raised via bankers acceptances that are ineligible. Bankers acceptances sold by an accepting bank are potential liabilities of the bank, but no reserve requirements are imposed for eligible bankers acceptances. Consequently, most bankers acceptances satisfy the various eligibility criteria. Finally, the Federal Reserve also imposes a limit on the amount of eligible bankers acceptances that may be issued by a bank.[12]

Rates banks charge on acceptances—To calculate the rate to be charged the customer for issuing a bankers acceptance, the bank determines the rate for which it can sell its bankers acceptance in the open market. To this rate it adds a commission. It is here that competition from Japanese banks has significantly affected the bankers acceptance business. Japanese banks have been willing to accept lower commissions than U.S. banks. For a high-credit-rated customer, for example, a commercial bank may charge 25 to 30 basis points, while a Japanese bank may charge 10 to 15 basis points.[13] In the case of ineligible bankers acceptances, a bank will add an amount to offset the cost of the reserve requirements imposed.

Dealers

We mentioned that banks may sell their bankers acceptances directly to investors, or may sell all or part to dealers. When the bankers acceptance market was growing in the early 1980s, there were over 25 dealers. By 1989, the decline in the amount of bankers acceptances issued drove many one-time

---

[11] The eligibility requirements are described in Jean M. Hahr and William C. Melton, "Bankers' Acceptances," *Quarterly Review,* Federal Reserve Bank of New York, Summer 1981.

[12] It may not exceed 150% of a bank's capital and surplus.

[13] Marcia Stigum, *The Money Market* (Homewood, IL: Dow Jones-Irwin, 1990), p. 1007.

major dealers, such as Salomon Brothers, out of the business. Today, the major dealer is Merrill Lynch. Lehman Brothers, is another dealer in bankers acceptances. The other key dealers are commercial banks such as Bankers Trust and Morgan Guaranty.

Credit Risk

Investing in bankers acceptances exposes the investor to credit risk. This is the risk that neither the borrower nor the accepting bank will be able to pay the principal due at the maturity date. The market interest rates that acceptances offer investors reflect this risk—bankers acceptances have higher yields than risk-free Treasury bills. Table 19-2 reports yields for selected weeks in 1992 and 1993. The higher yield relative to Treasuries also includes a premium for relative illiquidity. The bankers acceptance yield has such a premium because its secondary market is much less-developed than that of Treasury bills. Hence, the spread between bankers acceptance rates and Treasury bill rates in the table represents a combined reward to investors for bearing the higher credit risk and relative illiquidity of acceptances.

LARGE-DENOMINATION NEGOTIABLE CDs

A certificate of deposit (CD) is a financial asset issued by a bank or thrift that indicates a specified sum of money has been deposited at the issuing depository institution. CDs are issued by banks and thrifts to raise funds for financing their business activities. A CD bears a maturity date and a specified interest rate, and can be issued in any denomination. CDs issued by banks are insured by the Federal Deposit Insurance Corporation but only for amounts up to $100,000. As for maturity, there is no limit on the maximum, but by Federal Reserve regulations CDs cannot have a maturity of less than seven days.

A CD may be non-negotiable or negotiable. In the former case, the initial depositor must wait until the maturity date of the CD to obtain the funds. If the depositor chooses to withdraw funds prior to the maturity date, an early withdrawal penalty is imposed. In contrast, a negotiable CD allows the initial depositor (or any subsequent owner of the CD) to sell the CD in the open market prior to the maturity date.

Negotiable CDs were introduced in the early 1960s. At that time the interest rate banks could pay on various types of deposits was subject to ceilings administered by the Federal Reserve (except for demand deposits defined as deposits of less than one month, which by law could pay no interest). For complex historical reasons, these ceiling rates started very low, rose with maturity, and remained below market rates up to some fairly long maturity. Before introduction of the negotiable CD, those with money to invest for, say, one month had no incentive to deposit it with a bank for they would get a below-market rate unless they were prepared to tie up their capital for a much longer period of time. When negotiable CDs came along, they could buy a three-month or longer negotiable CD yielding a market interest rate, and recoup all or more than the investment (depending on market conditions) by selling it in the market.

This innovation was critical in helping banks to increase the amount of funds raised in the money market, a position that had languished in the earlier postwar period. It also motivated competition among banks, ushering in a new era. There are now two types of negotiable CDs. The first is the large-denomination CD, usually issued in denominations of $1 million or more. These are the negotiable CDs whose history we described above.

In 1982, Merrill Lynch entered the retail CD business by opening up a primary and secondary market in small-denomination (less than $100,000) CDs. While it made the CDs of its numerous banking and savings institution clients available to retail customers, Merrill Lynch also began to give these customers the negotiability enjoyed by institutional investors by standing ready to buy back the CDs prior to maturity. Today, several retail-oriented brokerage firms offer CDs that can be sold in a secondary market. These are the second type of negotiable CD. Our focus in this chapter, though, is on the large-denomination negotiable CD and we refer to them simply as CDs throughout the chapter.

The largest group of CD investors is investment companies, and money market funds make up the bulk of them. Far behind are banks and bank trust departments, followed by municipal entities and corporations. One indication of the size of the market available to these investors is the Federal Reserve Board's data series for "Time deposits over $100,000." As of August 25, 1993, the amount outstanding was $332 billion.

CD Issuers

CDs can be classified into the following four types, based on the issuing bank: (1) CDs issued by domestic banks; (2) CDs that are denominated in U.S. dollars but are issued outside of the U.S., called **Eurodollar CDs** or **Euro CDs**; (3) **Yankee CDs**, which are denominated in U.S. dollars and issued by a foreign bank with a branch in the U.S; and (4) **thrift CDs**, which are issued by savings and loan associations and savings banks.

Money center banks and large regional banks are the primary issuers of domestic CDs. Most CDs are issued with a maturity of less than one year. Those issued with a maturity greater than one year are called **term CDs**.

Unlike Treasury bills, commercial paper, and bankers acceptances, yields on domestic CDs are quoted on an interest-bearing basis. CDs with a maturity of one year or less pay interest at maturity. For purposes of calculating interest, a year is treated as having 360 days. Term CDs issued in the U.S. normally pay interest semiannually, again with a year taken to have 360 days.

A **floating-rate CD** (FRCD) is one whose coupon interest rate changes periodically in accordance with a predetermined formula that indicates the spread (or margin) above some index at which the coupon will reset periodically. There are FRCDs that reset the coupon daily, weekly, monthly, quarterly, or semiannually. Typically FRCDs have maturities from 18 months to 5 years.

Euro CDs are U.S.-dollar-denominated CDs issued primarily in London by U.S., Canadian, European, and Japanese banks. Branches of large U.S. banks once were the major issuers of Euro CDs. In 1982, of the $93 billion Euro CDs issued, $50 billion were issued by branches of U.S. banks.[14] Since 1982,

---

[14] As reported in *Quarterly Bulletin* published by the Bank of England.

however, the share of Euro CDs issued by branches of U.S. banks has declined, and Japanese banks have become the major issuers of Euro CDs.

Yields on CDs

Table 19-2 shows the yield on CDs in the secondary market for selected weeks in 1992 and 1993. The yields posted on CDs vary depending on three factors: (1) the credit rating of the issuing bank, (2) the maturity of the CD, and (3) the supply and demand for CDs. With respect to the third factor, banks and thrifts issue CDs as part of their liability-management strategy, so the supply of CDs will be driven by the demand for bank loans and the cost of alternative sources of capital to fund these loans. Moreover, bank loan demand will depend on the cost of alternative funding sources such as commercial paper. When loan demand is weak, CD rates decline. When demand is strong, rates rise. The effect of maturity depends on the shape of the yield curve.

Credit risk has become more of an issue. At one time domestic CDs issued by money center banks traded on a no-name basis. Recent financial crises in the banking industry, however, have caused investors to take a closer look at issuing banks. Prime CDs (those issued by high-rated domestic banks) trade at a lower yield than nonprime CDs (those issued by lower-rated domestic banks). Because of the unfamiliarity investors have with foreign banks, generally Yankee CDs trade at a higher yield than domestic CDs.

Euro CDs offer a higher yield than domestic CDs for the same maturity, as shown in Table 19-2. There are three reasons for this. First, there are reserve requirements imposed by the Federal Reserve on CDs issued by U.S. banks in the United States that do not apply to issuers of Euro CDs. The reserve requirement effectively raises the cost of funds to the issuing bank because it cannot invest all the proceeds it receives from the issuance of a CD, and the amount that must be kept as reserves will not earn a return for the bank. Because it will earn less on funds raised by selling domestic CDs, the domestic issuing bank will pay less on its domestic CD than a Euro CD. Second, the bank issuing the CD must pay an insurance premium to the FDIC, which again raises the cost of funds. Finally, Euro CDs are dollar obligations that are payable by an entity operating under a foreign jurisdiction, exposing the holders to a risk (referred to as sovereign risk) that their claim may not be enforced by the foreign jurisdiction. As a result, a portion of the spread between the yield offered on Euro CDs and domestic CDs reflects what can be termed a sovereign risk premium. This premium varies with the degree of confidence in the international banking system.

CD yields are higher than yields on Treasury securities of the same maturity. The spread is due mainly to the credit risk that a CD investor is exposed to and the fact that CDs offer less liquidity. The spread due to credit risk will vary with both economic conditions and confidence in the banking system, increasing when there is a flight to quality or when there is a crisis in the banking system.

At one time, there were more than 30 dealers who made markets in CDs. The presence of that many dealers provided good liquidity to the market. Today, fewer dealers are interested in making markets in CDs, and the market can be characterized as an illiquid one.

REPURCHASE AGREEMENTS

A **repurchase agreement** is the sale of a security with a commitment by the seller to buy the security back from the purchaser at a specified price at a designated future date. Basically, a repurchase agreement is a collateralized loan, where the collateral is a security. The agreement is best explained with an illustration.

Suppose a government securities dealer has purchased $10 million of a particular Treasury security. Where does the dealer obtain the funds to finance that position? Of course, the dealer can finance the position with its own funds or by borrowing from a bank. Typically, however, the dealer uses the repurchase agreement or "repo" market to obtain financing. In the repo market the dealer can use the $10 million of the Treasury security as collateral for a loan. The term of the loan and the interest rate that the dealer agrees to pay (the "repo rate") are specified. When the term of the loan is one day, it is called an "overnight repo;" a loan for more than one day is called a "term repo."

The transaction is referred to as a repurchase agreement because it calls for the sale of the security and its repurchase at a future date. Both the sale price and the purchase price are specified in the agreement. The difference between the purchase (repurchase) price and the sale price is the dollar interest cost of the loan.

In our illustration the dealer needs to finance $10 million of a Treasury security that it purchased and plans to hold overnight. Suppose that a customer of the dealer has excess funds of $10 million. (The customer might be a municipality with tax receipts that it has just collected, and no immediate need to disburse the funds.) The dealer would agree to deliver ("sell") $10 million of the Treasury security to the customer for an amount determined by the repo rate and buy ("repurchase") the same Treasury security from the customer for $10 million the next day. Suppose that the overnight repo rate is 6.5%. Then, as will be explained below, the dealer would agree to deliver the Treasury securities for $9,998,194 and repurchase the same securities for $10 million the next day. The $1,806 difference between the sale price of $9,998,194 and the repurchase price of $10 million is the dollar interest on the financing. From the customer's perspective, the agreement is called a "reverse repo."

The following formula is used to calculate the dollar interest on a repo transaction:

$$\text{Dollar interest} = (\text{Dollar principal}) \times (\text{Repo rate}) \times \frac{\text{Repo term}}{360}$$

Notice that the interest is computed on a 360-day basis. In our example, at a repo rate of 6.5% and a repo term of one day (overnight), the dollar interest is $1,806:

$$\$10,000,000 \times 0.065 \times \frac{1}{360} = \$1,806$$

The advantage to the dealer of using the repo market for borrowing on a short-term basis is that the rate is less than the cost of bank financing. We will explain why later in this section. From the customer's perspective, the repo market offers an attractive yield on a short-term secured transaction that is highly liquid.

While the example illustrates financing a dealer's long position in the repo market, dealers can also use the market to cover a short position. For example, suppose a government dealer sold $10 million of Treasury securities two weeks ago and must now cover the position—that is, deliver the securities. The dealer can do a reverse repo (agree to buy the securities and sell them back). Of course, the dealer eventually would have to buy the Treasury security in the market in order to cover its short position.

There is a good deal of Wall Street jargon describing repo transactions. To understand it, remember that one party is lending money and accepting security as collateral for the loan; the other party is borrowing money and giving collateral to borrow money. When someone lends securities in order to receive cash (i.e., borrows money), that party is said to be "reversing out" securities. A party that lends money with the security as collateral is said to be "reversing in" securities. The expressions "to repo securities" and "to do repo" are also used. The former means that someone is going to finance securities using the security as collateral; the latter means that the party is going to invest in a repo. Finally, the expressions "selling collateral" and "buying collateral" are used to describe a party financing a security with a repo on the one hand, and lending on the basis of collateral, on the other.

The collateral in a repo is not limited to government securities. Money market instruments, federal agency securities, and mortgage-backed securities are also used. No official statistics are available on the size of the repo market.

Credit Risks

Despite the fact that there may be high-quality collateral underlying a repo transaction, both parties to the transaction are exposed to credit risk. The failure of a few small government securities dealer firms involving repo transactions in the 1980s has made market participants more cautious about the creditworthiness of the counterparty to a repo.[15]

Why does credit risk occur in a repo transaction? Consider our initial example where the dealer used $10 million of government securities as collateral to borrow. If the dealer cannot repurchase the government securities, the customer may keep the collateral; if interest rates on government securities have increased subsequent to the repo transaction, however, the market value of the government securities will decline, and the customer will own securities with a market value less than the amount it loaned to the dealer. If the market value of the security rises instead, the dealer firm will be concerned with the return of the collateral, which then has a market value higher than the loan.

Repos are now more carefully structured to reduce credit risk exposure. The amount loaned is less than the market value of the security used as collateral, which provides the lender with some cushion should the market value

---

[15] Failed firms include Drysdale Government Securities, Lion Capital, RTD Securities, Inc., Belvill Bressler & Schulman, Inc., and ESM Government Securities, Inc.

of the security decline. The amount by which the market value of the security used as collateral exceeds the value of the loan is called "margin" or "haircut." The amount of margin is generally between 1% and 3%. For borrowers of lower creditworthiness and/or when less liquid securities are used as collateral, the margin can be 10% or more.

Another practice to limit credit risk is to mark the collateral to market on a regular basis. Recall that the practice of marking to market, which we first discussed when we explained futures contracts in Chapter 10, means recording the value of a position at its market value. When market value changes by a certain percentage, the repo position is adjusted accordingly. Suppose that a dealer firm has borrowed $20 million using collateral with a market value of $20.4 million—the margin is 2%. Suppose further that the market value of the collateral drops to $20.1 million. A repo agreement can specify either a margin call, or repricing of the repo. In the case of a margin call, the dealer firm is required to put up additional collateral with a market value of $300,000 in order to bring the margin up to $400,000. If repricing is agreed upon, the principal amount of the repo will be changed from $20 million to $19.7 million (the market value of $20.1 million divided by 1.02). The dealer would then send the customer $300,000.

One concern in structuring a repo is delivery of the collateral to the lender. The most obvious procedure is for the borrower to deliver the collateral to the lender. At the end of the repo term, the lender returns the collateral to the borrower in exchange for the principal and interest payment. This procedure may be too costly, though, particularly for short-term repos, because of the costs associated with delivering the collateral. The cost of delivery would be factored into the transaction by a lower repo rate offered by the borrower. The risk of the lender not taking possession of the collateral is that the borrower may sell the security or use the same security as collateral for a repo with another party.

As an alternative to delivering the collateral, the lender may agree to allow the borrower to hold the security in a segregated customer account. Of course, the lender still faces the risk that the borrower uses the collateral fraudulently by offering it as collateral for another repo transaction.

Another method is for the borrower to deliver the collateral to the lender's custodial account at the borrower's clearing bank. The custodian then has possession of the collateral that it holds on behalf of the lender. This practice reduces the cost of delivery because it is merely a transfer within the borrower's clearing bank. If, for example, a dealer enters into an overnight repo with Customer A, the next day the collateral is transferred back to the dealer. The dealer can then enter into a repo with Customer B for, say, five days without having to redeliver the collateral. The clearing bank simply establishes a custodian account for Customer B and holds the collateral in that account.

Participants in the Market

Because it is used by dealer firms (investment banking firms and money center banks acting as dealers) to finance positions and cover short positions, the repo market has evolved into one of the largest sectors of the money market. Financial and nonfinancial firms participate in the market as both sellers and buyers, depending on the circumstances they face. Thrifts and commercial banks are typically net sellers of collateral (i.e., net borrowers of funds); money market funds, bank trust departments, municipalities, and corporations are typically net buyers of collateral (i.e., providers of funds).

While a dealer firm uses the repo market as the primary means for financing its inventory and covering short positions, it will also use the repo market to run a **matched book** where it takes on repos and reverse repos with the same maturity. The firm will do this to capture the spread at which it enters into the repo and reverse repo agreements. For example, suppose that a dealer firm enters into a term repo of 10 days with a money market fund and a reverse repo with a thrift for 10 days in which the collateral is identical. This means that the dealer firm is borrowing funds from the money market fund and lending money to the thrift. If the rate on the repo is 7.5% and the rate on the reverse repo is 7.55%, the dealer firm is borrowing at 7.5% and lending at 7.55%, locking in a spread of 0.05% (five basis points).

Another participant is the repo broker. To understand the role of the repo broker, suppose that a dealer firm has shorted $50 million of a security. It will then survey its regular customers to determine if it can borrow via a reverse repo the security it shorted. Suppose that it cannot find a customer willing to do a repo transaction (repo from the customer's point of view, reverse repo from the dealer's). At that point, the dealer firm will use the services of a repo broker. When the collateral is difficult to acquire, it is said to be a "hot" or "special" issue.

The Federal Reserve is also involved in the repo market. The Fed influences short-term interest rates through its open market operations—that is, by the outright purchase or sale of government securities. This is not the common practice followed by the Fed, however. Instead it uses the repo market to implement monetary policy by purchasing or selling collateral. By buying collateral (i.e., lending funds), the Fed injects money into the financial markets, thereby exerting downward pressure on short-term interest rates. When the Fed buys collateral for its own account, this is called a "system repo." The Fed also buys collateral on behalf of foreign central banks in repo transactions that are referred to as "customer repos." It is primarily through system repos that the Fed attempts to influence short-term rates. By selling securities for its own account, the Fed drains money from the financial markets, thereby exerting upward pressure on short-term interest rates. This transaction is called a **matched sale**.

Note the language that is used to describe the transactions of the Fed in the repo market. When the Fed lends funds based on collateral, we call it a system or customer repo, not a reverse repo. Borrowing funds using collateral is called a matched sale, not a repo. The jargon is confusing, which is why we used the terms of "buying collateral" and "selling collateral" to describe what parties in the market are doing.

Determinants of the Repo Rate

There is no one repo rate; rates vary from transaction to transaction depending on the following factors.

- *Quality*: The higher the credit quality and liquidity of the collateral, the lower the repo rate.

- *Term of the repo*: The effect of the term of the repo on the rate depends on the shape of the yield curve.

- *Delivery requirement*: As noted earlier, if delivery of the collateral to the lender is required, the repo rate will be lower. If the collateral can be deposited with the bank of the borrower, a higher repo rate is paid.

- *Availability of collateral*: The more difficult it is to obtain the collateral, the lower the repo rate. To understand why this is so, remember that the borrower (or equivalently the seller of the collateral) has a security that is a hot or special issue. The party that needs the collateral will be willing to lend funds at a lower repo rate in order to obtain the collateral.

While these factors determine the repo rate on a particular transaction, the federal funds rate determines the general level of repo rates. The repo rate will be below the federal funds rate because a repo involves collateralized borrowing, while a federal funds transaction is unsecured borrowing.

FEDERAL FUNDS

The last market we will discuss is the federal funds market. The rate determined in this market is the major factor that influences the rate paid on all the other money market instruments described in this chapter.

As we explained in Chapter 3, depository institutions (commercial banks and thrifts) are required to maintain reserves. The reserves are deposits at their district Federal Reserve Bank, which are called **federal funds**. The level of the reserves that a bank must maintain is based on its average daily deposits over the previous 14 days.

No interest is earned on federal funds. Consequently, a depository institution that maintains federal funds in excess of the amount required incurs an opportunity cost—the loss of interest income that could be earned on the excess reserves. At the same time, there are depository institutions whose federal funds are less than the amount required. Typically, smaller banks have excess reserves, while money center banks find themselves short of reserves and must make up the shortfall. Banks maintain federal funds desks whose managers are responsible for the bank's federal funds position.

One way that banks with less than the required reserves can bring reserves to the required level is to enter into a repo with a nonbank customer. An alternative is for the bank to borrow federal funds from a bank that has excess reserves. The market in which federal funds are bought (borrowed) by banks that need these funds, and sold (lent) by banks that have excess federal funds is called the **federal funds market**.

Commercial banks are by far the largest investors in federal funds. For example, for the week ending August 29, 1993, commercial banks in the United States invested $52.4 billion in the $87.7 billion of total federal funds sold. Nonbank brokers and dealers bought $29.7 billion, with the balance bought by others.

The equilibrium interest rate, which is determined by the supply and demand for federal funds, is the **federal funds rate**.

The federal funds rate and the repo rate are tied together because both are a means for a bank to borrow. The federal funds rate is higher because the lending of federal funds is done on an unsecured basis; this differs from the repo, in which the lender has a security as collateral. The spread between the two rates varies depending on market conditions; typically the spread is around 25 basis points. Table 19-2 shows the federal funds rate for selected weeks in 1992 and 1993.

While the term of most federal funds transactions is overnight, there are longer-term transactions that range from one week to six months. Trading typically takes place directly between the buyer and seller—usually between a large bank and one of its correspondent banks. Some federal funds transactions require the use of a broker.

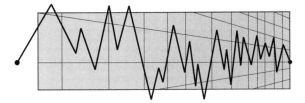

SUMMARY

Money market instruments are debt obligations that at issuance have a maturity of one year or less. Treasury securities with a maturity of one year or less when they are issued are called Treasury bills. Interest is not paid periodically, but Treasury bills are issued at a discount from their face value. The interest the investor earns is the difference between the face value received at the maturity date and the price paid to purchase the Treasury bill. Bids and offers on Treasury bills are quoted on a bank discount basis. Treasury bills are auctioned on a regularly scheduled cycle.

Commercial paper is a short-term unsecured promissory note issued in the open market that represents the obligation of the issuing entity. It is sold on a discount basis. To avoid SEC registration, the maturity of commercial paper is less than 270 days. Generally, commercial paper maturity is less than 90 days so that it will qualify as eligible collateral for the bank to borrow from the Federal Reserve Bank's discount window. Financial and nonfinancial corporations issue commercial paper, with the majority issued by the former. The commercial paper market was limited to entities with strong credit ratings, but lower-rated issuers have used credit enhancements to enter the market. Direct paper is sold by the issuing firm directly to investors without using a securities dealer as an intermediary; with dealer-placed commercial paper, the issuer uses the services of a securities firm to sell its paper. There is little liquidity in the commercial paper market.

A bankers acceptance is a vehicle created to facilitate commercial trade transactions, particularly international transactions. They are called bankers acceptances because a bank accepts the responsibility to repay a loan to the holder of the vehicle created in a commercial transaction in case the debtor fails to perform. Bankers acceptances are sold on a discounted basis as are Treasury bills and commercial paper. Accepting banks are money center banks, larger regional banks, and Japanese banks.

Certificates of deposit are issued by banks and thrifts to raise funds for financing their business activities. Unlike other bank deposits, these are negotiable in the secondary market. CDs can be classified into four types: domestic CDs, Eurodollar CDs (or Euro CDs), Yankee CDs, and thrift CDs. Japanese banks have now become major issuers of Euro CDs. Unlike Treasury bills, commercial paper, and bankers acceptances, yields on domestic CDs are quoted on an interest-bearing basis. A floating-rate CD is one whose coupon interest rate changes periodically in accordance with a predetermined formula.

A repurchase agreement is a lending transaction in which the borrower uses a security as collateral for the borrowing. The transaction is referred to as a repurchase agreement because it specifies the sale of a security and its subsequent repurchase at a future date. The difference between the purchase (repurchase) price and the sale price is the dollar interest cost of the loan. An overnight repo is for one day; a loan for more than one day is called a term repo. The collateral in a repo may be a Treasury security, money market instrument, federal agency security, or mortgage-backed security. The parties to a repo are exposed to credit risk, limited by margin and mark-to-market practices included in a repo agreement. Dealers use the repo market to finance positions and cover short positions, and to run a matched book so that they can earn spread income. The Fed uses the repo market to implement monetary policy. Factors that determine the repo rate are the federal funds rate, the quality of the collateral, the term of the repo, the delivery requirement, and the availability of the collateral.

The federal funds market is the market where depository institutions borrow (buy) and sell (lend) federal funds. The federal funds rate, which is the rate at which all money market interest rates are anchored, is determined in this market. The federal funds rate is higher than the repo rate because borrowing done in the federal funds market is unsecured borrowing.

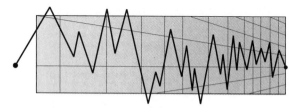

QUESTIONS

1. Suppose that the price of a Treasury bill with 90 days to maturity and a $1 million face value is $980,000.

   a. What is the yield on a bank discount basis?

   b. Why is the yield on a bank discount basis not a meaningful measure of the return from holding a Treasury bill?

2. The bid and ask yields for a Treasury bill maturing on January 16, 1992 were quoted by a dealer as 5.91% and 5.89%, respectively. Shouldn't the bid yield be less than the ask yield, because the bid yield indicates how much the dealer is willing to pay, and the ask yield is what the dealer is willing to sell the Treasury bill for?

3. In a Treasury auction, as the dollar amount of noncompetitive bids submitted increases, what happens to the average yield bid?

4. Why is commercial paper an alternative to short-term bank borrowing for a corporation?

5. a. Why does commercial paper have a maturity of less than 270 days?

   b. Why does paper typically have a maturity of less than 90 days?

6. What is the difference between directly-placed paper and dealer-placed paper?

7. What does the yield spread between commercial paper and Treasury bills of the same maturity reflect?

8. How does Eurocommercial paper differ from commercial paper issued in the United States?

9. a. Why is a bank that creates a bankers acceptance referred to as an accepting bank?

   b. Why is the "eligibility" of a bankers acceptance important?

10. How does a bank determine the rate it will charge its customer for issuing a bankers acceptance?

11. What are the four types of negotiable CDs?

12. How can a repurchase agreement be used by a dealer firm to finance a long position in a Treasury security?

13. One party in a repo transaction is said to "buy collateral," the other party to "sell collateral." Why?

14. Why would the lender of funds in a repo transaction be exposed to credit risk?

15. What is meant by a repo dealer running a "matched book"?

16. When there is a shortage of a specific security for a repo transaction, will the repo rate increase or decrease?

17. a. What is a system repo?

    b. What is a customer repo?

18. In a repo transaction, what is meant by a "haircut"?

19. Suppose the dollar principal in a repo transaction is $40 million and the repo rate is 5%.

    a. What is the dollar interest if the term of the repo is one day?

    b. What is the dollar interest if the term of the repo is five days?

20. a. What is the federal funds market?

    b. Which rate should be higher: the overnight repo rate, or the overnight federal funds rate?

Treasury and Agency Securities Markets

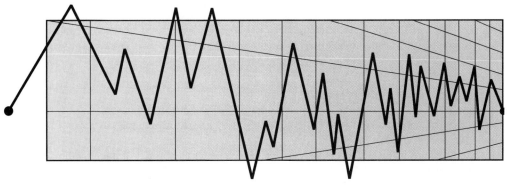

LEARNING OBJECTIVES

After reading this chapter you will understand:

- the importance of the Treasury market.

- the different types of securities issued by the Treasury.

- the auction process for Treasury securities.

- the role of government dealers and government brokers.

- the secondary market for Treasury securities.

- how Treasury securities are quoted in the secondary market.

- the different types of zero-coupon Treasury securities outstanding.

- the difference between government-sponsored enterprises and federally related institutions.

- the major government-sponsored enterprises.

• the methods of distribution that are being used by central governments to issue government bonds.

• the government bond markets of Japan and Germany.

Treasury securities are issued by the United States Department of the Treasury and are backed by the full faith and credit of the United States government. Consequently, market participants view them as having no credit risk. Interest rates on Treasury securities are the benchmark interest rates throughout the U.S. economy as well as in international capital markets. In Chapter 16, we briefly described this important role played by Treasury securities. In this chapter, we will discuss the Treasury securities market and the market for U.S. agency securities. We also take a look at how government bonds are issued in other countries and the structure of two major government bond markets, Japan and Germany.

TREASURY SECURITIES

Two factors account for the prominent role of U.S. Treasury securities: volume (in terms of dollars outstanding), and liquidity. The Department of the Treasury is the largest single issuer of debt in the world, with Treasury securities accounting for $2.3 trillion (represented by over 180 different Treasury note and bond issues and 30 Treasury bill issues). By contrast, the entire U.S. corporate bond market accounts for about $1.4 trillion and over 10,000 issues; the U.S. municipal bond market accounts for about $802 billion, with more than 70,000 separate issuers and millions of individual issues.

The large volume of total debt and the large size of any single issue have contributed to making the Treasury market the most active and hence the most liquid market in the world. The spread between bid and ask prices is considerably narrower than in other sectors of the bond market, and most issues can be purchased easily. Many issues in the corporate and municipal markets are illiquid by contrast, and cannot be traded readily.

Treasury securities are available in book-entry form at the Federal Reserve Bank. This means that the investor receives only a receipt as evidence of ownership instead of an engraved certificate. An advantage of book entry is ease in transferring ownership of the security.

Interest income from Treasury securities is subject to federal income taxes but is exempt from state and local income taxes.

Types of Treasury Securities

There are two categories of government securities—**discount** and **coupon securities**. The fundamental difference between the two types lies in the form of the stream of payments that the holder receives, which is reflected in turn in the prices at which the securities are issued. Coupon securities pay interest every six months, plus principal at maturity. Discount securities pay only a contractually fixed amount at maturity, called maturity value or face value.

Discount instruments are issued below maturity value, and return to the investor the difference between maturity value and issue price.

Current Treasury practice is to issue all securities with maturities of one year or less as discount securities. These securities are called **Treasury bills**, which we discussed in Chapter 19. All securities with maturities of two years or longer are issued as coupon securities. Treasury coupon securities issued with original maturities between 2 and 10 years are called **Treasury notes**; those with original maturities greater than 10 years are called **Treasury bonds**. While there is a distinction between Treasury notes and bonds, in this chapter we refer to both as Treasury bonds.

When the issuer of a bond has the option but not the obligation to retire an issue prior to the maturity date, the issue is said to be "callable." Although Treasury notes are not callable, many outstanding Treasury bond issues are callable within five years of maturity. Treasury bonds issued since February 1985 are not callable.

The Primary Market

The primary market is the market for newly issued Treasury securities. Treasury securities typically are issued on an auction basis with regular cycles for securities of specific maturities. Treasury bills with three and six months to maturity are auctioned every Monday, and one-year Treasury bills are auctioned on the third week of every month.

The Treasury regularly issues coupon securities with maturities of 2, 3, 5, 10, and 30 years.[1] Two- and 5-year notes are auctioned each month. At the beginning of the second month of each calendar quarter (February, May, August, and November) the Treasury conducts its regular refunding operations. At this time, it auctions 3-year, 10-year, and 30-year Treasury securities. The Treasury announces on the Wednesday of the month preceding: (1) the amount that will be auctioned, (2) what portion of that amount is to replace maturing Treasury debt, (3) what portion of that amount is to raise new funds, and (4) the estimated cash needs for the balance of the quarter and how it plans to obtain the funds. Table 20-1 summarizes the months that Treasury coupon securities are issued.

The auction for Treasury securities is conducted on a competitive bid basis, and the bids must be submitted on a yield basis. Noncompetitive tenders may also be submitted for up to a $1 million face amount. Such tenders are based only on quantity, not yield. The auction results are determined by first deducting the total noncompetitive tenders and nonpublic purchases (such as purchases by the Federal Reserve itself) from the total securities being auctioned. The remainder is the amount to be awarded to the competitive bidders.

At the time of this writing, there are two types of auctions held to determine the yield bidders will pay for the auctioned security: multiple-price auctions and single-price auctions. Single-price auctions are held for the 2-year and 5-year notes. In a single-price auction, all bidders are awarded securities at the highest yield of accepted competitive tenders.

---

[1] At one time the Treasury offered a 7-year and a 20-year issue.

Table 20-1

Treasury Coupon Securities Auctioned by Month

Month	\multicolumn{5}{c}{Number of Years to Maturity}
	2	3	5	10	30
January	x		x		
February	x	x	x	x	x
March	x		x		
April	x		x		
May	x	x	x	x	x
June	x		x		
July	x		x		
August	x	x	x	x	x
September	x		x		
October	x		x		
November	x	x	x	x	x
December	x		x		

x = auctioned in month indicated.

All other Treasury securities are issued using a multiple-price auction. Here the lowest-yield (i.e., highest-price) bidders are awarded securities at their bid price. Successively higher-yielding bidders are awarded securities at their bid price until the total amount offered (less noncompetitive tenders) is awarded. As explained in Chapter 19, the highest yield accepted by the Treasury is referred to as the "stop yield," and bidders at that price are awarded a percentage of their total tender offer. The price paid by noncompetitive bidders is the average price of the competitive bids. We illustrated this auction in Chapter 19, in our discussion of Treasury bills.

The difference between the average yield of all the bids accepted by the Treasury and the stop yield is called the "tail." Market participants use the tail as a measure of the success of the auction. The larger the tail, the less successful the auction. This is because the average price at which accepted bidders realize securities is considerable lower than the highest price paid.

Any firm can deal in government securities, but in implementing its open market operations, the Federal Reserve will deal directly only with dealers that it designates as **primary** or **recognized dealers**. Basically, the Federal Reserve wants to be sure that firms requesting status as primary dealers have adequate capital relative to positions assumed in Treasury securities and do a reasonable amount of volume in Treasury securities (at least 1% of Treasury market activity). Table 20-2 lists the primary government dealers as of June 1994.

When a firm requests status as a primary dealer, the Federal Reserve requests first that the applying firm informally report its positions and trading volume. If these are acceptable to the Federal Reserve, it gives the firm status as a **reporting dealer**. This means that the firm will be put on the Federal Reserve's regular reporting list. After the firm serves for some time as a reporting dealer, the Federal Reserve will make it a primary dealer if it is convinced that the firm will continue to meet the criteria established.

Until 1991, primary dealers and large commercial banks that were not primary dealers would submit bids for their own account and for their customers. Others who wished to participate in the auction process could only submit competitive bids for their own account, not their customers. Consequently, a broker-dealer in government securities that was not a primary dealer could not submit a competitive bid on behalf of its customers. Moreover, unlike primary dealers, nonprimary dealers had to make large cash deposits or provide guarantees to assure that they could fulfill their obligation to purchase the securities for which they bid.

Well-publicized violations of the auction process by Salomon Brothers in the summer of 1991 forced Treasury officials to more closely scrutinize the activities of primary dealers and also to reconsider the procedure by which Treasury securities are auctioned.[2] Specifically, the Treasury announced it would allow qualified broker-dealers to bid for their customers at Treasury auctions. If a qualified broker-dealer establishes a payment link with the Federal Reserve system, no deposit or guaranty would be required. Moreover, the auction would no longer be handled by the submission of hand-delivered sealed bids to the Federal Reserve. The new auction process will be a computerized auction system which can be electronically accessed by qualified broker-dealers.

The Secondary Market

The secondary market for Treasury securities is an over-the-counter market where a group of U.S. government securities dealers offer continuous bid and ask prices on specific outstanding Treasuries.[3] The secondary market is the most liquid financial market in the world. Daily average trading volume for all Treasury securities by primary dealers for the week ending December 28, 1994 was $166.69 billion, with the distribution among Treasury securities as follows:[4]

Treasury bills	$ 58.271 billion
Coupon securities:	
due in 5 years or less	79.665
due in more than 5 years	28.754

As we explained in Chapter 16, the most recently auctioned Treasury issues for each maturity are referred to as "on-the-run" or "current-coupon" issues.

---

[2] Salomon Brothers admitted it had repeatedly violated a restriction that limited the amount any one firm could purchase at the Treasury auction. The firm also admitted it had submitted unauthorized bids for some of its customers.

[3] Some trading of Treasury coupon securities does occur on the New York Stock Exchange, but the volume of these exchange-traded transactions is very small when compared to over-the-counter transactions.

[4] This figure represents immediate transactions of purchases and sales in the market as reported to the Federal Reserve Bank of New York. Immediate transactions are those scheduled for delivery in five days or less. The figure excludes all transactions under purchase and reverse repurchase agreements.

Table 20-2

Primary Government Securities Dealers

BA Securities, Inc.
Barclays de Zoete Wedd Securities Inc.
Bear, Stearns & Co., Inc.
BT Securities Corp.
Chase Securities, Inc.
Chemical Securities, Inc.
Citicorp Securities, Inc.
CS First Boston Corp.
Daiwa Securities America, Inc.
Dean Witter Reynolds, Inc.
Deutsche Bank Government Securities, Inc.
Dillon, Read & Co., Inc.
Donaldson, Lufkin & Jenrette Securities Corp.
Eastbridge Capital, Inc.
First Chicago Capital Markets, Inc.
Fuji Securities, Inc.
Goldman, Sachs & Co.
Greenwich Capital Markets, Inc.
Harris Nesbitt Thomson Securities, Inc.
HSBC Securities, Inc.
Kidder, Peabody & Co., Inc.
Aubrey G. Lanston & Co., Inc.
Lehman Government Securities, Inc.
Merrill Lynch Government Securities, Inc.
J.P. Morgan Securities, Inc.
Morgan Stanley & Co., Inc.
NationsBanc Capital Markets, Inc.
The Nikko Securities Co. International, Inc.
Nomura Securities International, Inc.
PaineWebber, Inc.
Prudential Securities, Inc.
Salomon Brothers, Inc.
Sanwa Securities (USA) Co., L.P.
Smith Barney, Inc.
SBC Government Securities, Inc.
UBS Securities, Inc.
S.G. Warburg & Co., Inc.
Yamaichi International (America), Inc.
Zions First National Bank

Source: Market Reports Division, Federal Reserve Bank of New York, June 23, 1994.

Issues auctioned prior to the current-coupon issues typically are referred to as "off-the-run" issues; they are not as liquid as on-the-run issues. That is, the bid-ask spread is larger for off-the-run issues relative to on-the-run issues.

Treasury securities are traded prior to the time they are issued by the Treasury. This component of the Treasury secondary market is called the "when-issued market," or "wi market." When-issued trading for both Treasury bills and Treasury coupon issues extends from the day the auction is announced until the issue day. All deliveries on when-issued trades occur on the issue day of the Treasury security traded.

As we explained in Chapter 19, Treasury bill bids and offers are computed on a bank discount basis (in basis points), not on a price basis. Treasury coupon securities are quoted differently. They trade on a dollar-price basis in price units of ½₂ of 1% of par (par is taken to be $100). For example, a quote of 92-14 refers to a price of 92 and ¹⁴⁄₃₂. On the basis of $100,000 par value, a change in price of 1% equates to $1,000, and ½₂ equates to $31.25. A plus sign following the number of 32nds means that a 64th is added to the price. For example, 92-14+ refers to a price of 92 and ²⁹⁄₆₄, or 92.453125% of par value. On quote sheets and screens, the price quote is followed by some "yield to maturity" measure.

When an investor purchases a bond between coupon payments, if the issuer is not in default, the investor must compensate the seller of the bond for the coupon interest earned from the time of the last coupon payment to the settlement date of the bond. This amount is called **accrued interest**, computed as follows:

$$\frac{C}{2} \times \frac{\text{Number of days from last coupon payment to settlement date}}{\text{Number of days in coupon period}}$$

Market conventions determine the number of days in a coupon period and the number of days from the last coupon payment to the settlement date. For a Treasury coupon security, both are equal to the actual number of days. (This is referred to as the "actual over actual" basis.)[5] The accrued interest for a Treasury coupon security is therefore determined as follows:

$$\frac{C}{2} \times \frac{\text{Actual number of days from last coupon payment to settlement date}}{\text{Actual number of days in coupon period}}$$

The total proceeds that the buyer of the bond pays the seller is equal to the price agreed upon by the buyer and the seller plus accrued interest.

Government-securities dealers generate profit from one or more of three sources: (1) the bid-ask spread, (2) appreciation in the securities held in inventory or depreciation in the securities sold short, and (3) the difference between the interest earned on the securities held in inventory and the cost of financing that inventory. The last source of profits is referred to as **carry**. Dealers obtain funds to finance inventory or to borrow securities to cover short positions in the repo market, which we described in Chapter 16.

Treasury dealers trade with the investing public and with other dealer firms. When they trade with each other, it is through intermediaries known as **government brokers**. Dealers leave firm bids and offers with brokers who display the highest bid and lowest offer in a computer network tied to each trading desk and displayed on a monitor. The dealer responding to a bid or offer by "hitting" or "taking" pays a commission to the broker. The size and prices of these transactions are visible to all dealers at once.

---

[5] For corporate and municipal bonds, the day count convention is "30/360" which means a year is treated as having 360 days and a month as having 30 days. Therefore, the number of days in a coupon period is 180.

Treasury dealers use brokers because of the speed and efficiency with which trades can be accomplished. Brokers never trade for their own account, and they keep the names of the dealers involved in trades confidential. Five major brokers handle the bulk of daily trading volume. They include Cantor, Fitzgerald Securities Corp.; Garban Ltd.; Liberty; RMJ Securities Corp.; and Hill Farber (Treasury bills only). These five firms service the primary government dealers and a dozen or so other large government dealers aspiring to be primary dealers.

The quotes provided on the government dealer screens represent prices in the "inside" or "interdealer" market, and the primary dealers have resisted attempts to allow the general public to have access to them. In 1989, when one government broker offered to disseminate quotes to some large institutional investors, pressure from the primary dealers persuaded the broker to withdraw its offer. However, pressure from the General Accounting Office and Congress in 1991 has forced government brokers to disseminate some information to nonprimary dealers.

As explained in Chapter 13, Congressional and SEC actions have resulted in a movement toward a consolidated tape for reporting trades on exchanges and the over-the-counter market and a composite quotation system for the collection and display of bid and ask quotations. In the Treasury market, however, despite the fact that trading activity is concentrated in the over-the-counter market, and that daily trading volume exceeds $100 billion, reporting of trades does not exist. Nor is there a display of bid and ask quotations that provides reliable price quotes at which the general public can transact. Such quotations do exist in the interdealer market on government broker screens, and though nonprimary dealers can subscribe to the government broker screens, the information they can obtain on these screens is limited. In particular, the government dealers that permit access to their screens only provide information on the best bid and offer quotation but not the size of the transaction.

Moreover, the rules for the sale of U.S. government securities have been exempt from most SEC provisions and rules.[6] Thus, government broker-dealers are not required to disclose the bid-ask spread on the Treasury securities that they buy from or sell to customers. There are guidelines established by the National Association of Security Dealers for reasonable bid-ask spreads; however, lack of disclosure to customers makes it difficult for customers to monitor the pricing practice of a broker-dealer. Congress is considering legislation which would regulate the pricing practices of broker-dealers who sell Treasury securities and would increase reporting requirements so that the Treasury market can be more closely monitored by regulators.

Stripped Treasury Securities

The Treasury does not issue zero-coupon notes or bonds. In August 1982, however, both Merrill Lynch and Salomon Brothers created synthetic zero-coupon Treasury receipts. Merrill Lynch marketed its Treasury receipts as "Treasury Income Growth Receipts" (TIGRs), and Salomon Brothers marketed its as "Certificates of Accrual on Treasury Securities" (CATS). The pro-

---

[6] Broker-dealers who sell government securities are still subject to the general fraud provisions of the Securities Act of 1933.

cedure was to purchase Treasury bonds and deposit them in a bank custody account. The firms then issued receipts representing an ownership interest in each coupon payment on the underlying Treasury bond in the account and a receipt for ownership of the underlying Treasury bond's maturity value. This process of separating each coupon payment, as well as the principal (called the **corpus**), and selling securities against them is referred to as "coupon stripping." Although the receipts created from the coupon stripping process are not issued by the U.S. Treasury, the underlying bond deposited in the bank custody account is a debt obligation of the U.S. Treasury, so the cash flow from the underlying security is certain.

To illustrate the process, suppose $100 million of a Treasury bond with a 20-year maturity and a coupon rate of 10% is purchased to create zero-coupon Treasury securities. The cash flow from this Treasury bond is 40 semiannual payments of $5 million each ($100 million times 0.10 divided by 2) and the repayment of principal (corpus) of $100 million 20 years from now. This Treasury bond is deposited in a bank custody account. Receipts are then issued, each with a different single-payment claim on the bank custody account. As there are 41 different payments to be made by the Treasury, a receipt representing a single-payment claim on each payment is issued, which is effectively a zero-coupon bond. The amount of the maturity value for a receipt on a particular payment, whether coupon or corpus, depends on the amount of the payment to be made by the Treasury on the underlying Treasury bond. In our example, 40 coupon receipts each have a maturity value of $5 million, and one receipt, the corpus, has a maturity value of $100 million. The maturity dates for the receipts coincide with the corresponding payment dates by the Treasury.

Other investment banking firms followed the lead of Merrill Lynch and Solomon Brothers by creating their own receipts.[7] They all are referred to as "trademark" zero-coupon Treasury securities because they are associated with particular firms.[8] Receipts of one firm were rarely traded by competing dealers, so the secondary market was not liquid for any one trademark. Moreover, the investor was exposed to the risk—as small as it may be—that the custodian bank may go bankrupt.

To broaden the market and improve liquidity of these receipts, a group of primary dealers in the government market agreed to issue generic receipts that would not be directly associated with any of the participating dealers. These generic receipts are referred to as "Treasury Receipts" (TRs). Rather than representing a share of the trust as the trademarks do, TRs represent ownership of a Treasury security. A common problem with both trademark and generic receipts was that settlement required physical delivery, which is often cumbersome and inefficient.

In February 1985, the Treasury announced its Separate Trading of Registered Interest and Principal of Securities (STRIPS) program to facilitate the stripping of designated Treasury securities. Specifically, all new Treasury

---

[7] Lehman Brothers offered "Lehman Investment Opportunities Notes" (LIONs); E.F. Hutton offered "Treasury Bond Receipts" (TBRs); and Dean Witter Reynolds offered "Easy Growth Treasury Receipts" (ETRs). There were also GATORs, COUGARs, and—you'll like this one—DOGS (Dibs on Government Securities).

[8] They are also called "animal products" for obvious reasons.

bonds and all new Treasury notes with maturities of 10 years and longer are eligible. The zero-coupon Treasury securities created under the STRIPS program are direct obligations of the U.S. government. Moreover, the securities clear through the Federal Reserve's book-entry system.[9] Creation of the STRIPS program ended the origination of trademarks and generic receipts.

The profit potential for a government dealer who strips a Treasury security lies in arbitrage resulting from the mispricing of the security, as illustrated in Chapter 18.

FEDERAL AGENCY SECURITIES

The federal agency securities market can be divided into two sectors—the **government-sponsored enterprises market** and the **federally related institution securities market**. Government-sponsored enterprises (GSEs) are privately owned and publicly chartered entities. They were created by Congress to reduce the cost of capital for certain borrowing sectors of the economy deemed to be important enough to warrant assistance. The entities in these privileged sectors include farmers, homeowners, and students. Government-sponsored enterprises issue securities directly in the marketplace. The market for these securities, while smaller than that of Treasury securities, has in recent years become an active and important sector of the bond market.

Federally related institutions are arms of the federal government and generally do not issue securities directly in the marketplace (although they did prior to 1973). Instead, they typically obtain all or part of their financing by borrowing from the Federal Financing Bank, an entity created in 1973. The relatively small size of these issues made the borrowing cost for individual issues significantly greater than that of Treasury securities. Creation of the Federal Financing Bank was intended to consolidate and reduce the borrowing cost of federally related institutions.

Federally related institutions include the following:

- Export-Import Bank of the United States
- Commodity Credit Corporation
- Farmers Housing Administration
- General Services Administration
- Government National Mortgage Association
- Maritime Administration
- Private Export Funding Corporation
- Rural Electrification Administration
- Rural Telephone Bank
- Small Business Administration
- Tennessee Valley Authority
- Washington Metropolitan Area Transit Authority

All federally related institutions are exempt from SEC registration. With the exception of securities of the Private Export Funding Corporation and the

---

[9] In 1987, the Treasury permitted the conversion of stripped coupons into book-entry form under its Coupons Under Book-Entry Safekeeping (CUBES) program.

Tennessee Valley Authority, the securities are backed by the full faith and credit of the U.S. government.

Average daily trading in GSEs is a small fraction of that of Treasury securities. For example, while average daily trading of Treasury securities for the week ending December 28, 1994 was $166.69 billion, the corresponding trading for federal agency securities (excluding federal agency mortgage-backed securities) was only $22.369 billion.

Government-Sponsored Enterprise Securities

There are eight government-sponsored enterprises. The enabling legislation dealing with GSEs is amended periodically. The Federal Farm Credit Bank System is responsible for the credit market in the agricultural sector of the economy. The Farm Credit Financial Association Corporation was created in 1987 to address problems in the existing Farm Credit System. The Federal Home Loan Bank, Federal Home Loan Mortgage Corporation, and Federal National Mortgage Association are responsible for providing credit to the mortgage and housing sectors. The Student Loan Marketing Association provides funds to support higher education. The Financing Corporation was created in 1987 to recapitalize the Federal Savings and Loan Insurance Corporation. Because of continuing difficulties in the savings and loan industry, the Resolution Trust Corporation was created in 1989 to liquidate or bail out insolvent institutions.

GSEs issue two types of securities: discount notes and bonds. Discount notes are short-term obligations, with maturities ranging from overnight to 360 days. Bonds are sold with maturities greater than 2 years.

With the exception of the securities issued by the Farm Credit Financial Assistance Corporation, GSE securities are not backed by the full faith and credit of the U.S. government, as is the case with Treasury securities. Consequently, investors purchasing GSEs are exposed to some potential credit risk. The yield spread between these securities and Treasury securities of comparable maturity reflects differences in perceived credit risk and liquidity. The spread attributable to credit risk reflects financial problems faced by the issuing GSE and the likelihood that the federal government will allow the GSE to default on its outstanding obligations.

Federal Farm Credit Bank System—The purpose of the Federal Farm Credit Bank System (FFCBS) is to facilitate adequate, dependable credit and related services to the agricultural sector of the economy. The Farm Credit System consists of three entities: the Federal Land Banks, Federal Intermediate Credit Banks, and Banks for Cooperatives. Before 1979, each entity issued securities in its own name. Starting in 1979, they began to issue debt on a consolidated basis as "joint and several obligations" of the FFCBS. All financing for the FFCBS is arranged through the Federal Farm Credit Banks Funding Corporation, which issues consolidated obligations through a selling group consisting of approximately 150 members. For discount notes, the selling group consists of only four dealers.

Farm Credit Financial Assistance Corporation—In the 1980s, the FFCBS faced financial difficulties because of defaults on loans made to farmers. The defaults were caused largely by high interest rates in the late 1970s and early 1980s and by depressed prices on agricultural products. To recapitalize the

Federal Farm Credit Bank System, Congress created the Farm Credit Financial Assistance Corporation (FACO) in 1987. This GSE is authorized to issue debt to assist the FFCBS. FACO bonds, unlike the debt of other GSEs, are backed by the Treasury.

Federal Home Loan Bank System—The Federal Home Loan Bank System (FHLBS) consists of the 12 district Federal Home Loan Banks (which are instrumentalities of the U.S. government) and their member banks. An independent federal agency, the Federal Home Loan Bank Board, was originally responsible for regulating all federally chartered savings and loan associations and savings banks, as well as state-chartered institutions insured by the Federal Savings and Loan Insurance Corporation. These responsibilities have been curtailed since 1989. The major source of debt funding for the Federal Home Loan Banks is the issuance of consolidated debt obligations, which are joint and several obligations of the 12 Federal Home Loan Banks.

Financing Corporation—The deposits of savings and loans were once insured by the Federal Savings and Loan Insurance Corporation (FSLIC), overseen by the Federal Home Loan Bank Board. When difficulties encountered in the savings and loan industry raised concerns about FSLIC's ability to meet its responsibility to insure deposits, Congress passed the Competitive Equality and Banking Act in 1987. This legislation included provisions to recapitalize FSLIC and establish a new government-sponsored enterprise, the Financing Corporation (FICO), to issue debt in order to provide funding for FICO.

FICO is capitalized by the nonvoting stock purchased by the 12 regional Federal Home Loan Banks. FICO issued its first bonds in September 30, 1987, a 30-year noncallable $500 million issue. The issue was priced 90 basis points over the 30-year Treasury security at the time. The principal of these bonds is backed by zero-coupon Treasury securities. The legislation permits FICO to issue up to $10.825 billion but not more than $3.75 billion in any one year. FICO is legislated to be dismantled in 2026, or after all securities have matured, whichever comes sooner.

Resolution Trust Corporation—The 1987 legislation that created FICO did not go far enough to resolve the problems facing the beleaguered savings and loan industry. In 1989, Congress passed more comprehensive legislation, the Financial Institutions Reform, Recovery and Enforcement Act (FIRREA). This legislation has three key elements. First, it transfers supervision of savings and loans to a newly created Office of Thrift Supervision. Second, it shifts the FSLIC insurance function to a Savings Association Insurance Fund, placed under the supervision of the Federal Deposit Insurance Corporation. Third, it establishes the Resolution Trust Corporation (RTC) as an agency charged with the responsibility of liquidating or bailing out insolvent savings and loan institutions. RTC obtains its funding from the Resolution Funding Corporation (REFCORP), which is authorized to issue up to $40 billion of long-term bonds. The principal of this debt is backed by zero-coupon Treasury bonds. REFCORP has issued *both* 30-year and 40-year bonds.[10]

Student Loan Marketing Association—Popularly known as "Sallie Mae," the Student Loan Marketing Association provides liquidity for private lenders

---

[10] The 40-year bonds represent the first offering of such a government or government agency bond since the Treasury issued 40-year bonds in the 1950s. The auction for the $5 billion, 40-year bond offering in January 1990 was not a successful undertaking.

participating in the Federal Guaranteed Student Loan Program, the Health Education Assistance Loan Program, and the PLUS loan program (a program that provides loans to the parents of undergraduate students). Sallie Mae is permitted to purchase and offer investor participation in student loans. Sallie Mae issues unsecured debt obligations in the form of discount notes. In January 1982, Sallie Mae first issued floating-rate securities based on the bond equivalent yield on 91-day Treasury bills. Sallie Mae also has long-term fixed-rate securities and zero-coupon bonds outstanding. The Higher Education Amendments of 1992 established minimum statutory capital requirements for Sallie Mae (contingent upon a credit downgrade below some level).

Future Regulation of GSEs

The U.S. bailout of the savings and loan industry raised increasing concerns in Congress over the potential cost of bailing out government-sponsored enterprises. The Financial Institutions Reform, Recovery and Enforcement Act of 1989 mandated the General Accounting Office and the Secretary of the Treasury to study the issues and prepare reports for Congress. Specifically, both the GAO and the Treasury were to investigate whether each government-sponsored enterprises maintained appropriate capital levels, given the risks associated with their activities. The Treasury was also charged with assessment of the impact of the activities of government-sponsored enterprises on federal borrowing.

The Treasury interim report recommended that a government-sponsored enterprises be required to maintain a triple-A credit rating from two nationally recognized rating companies.[11] The rating must be achieved in the absence of government sponsorship (i.e., as a stand-alone private entity). Failure to obtain such a credit rating would result in the loss of sponsorship by the federal government. The GAO interim report puts forth two possible forms of regulation. One is the same as that recommended by the Treasury. The alternative is to require government-sponsored enterprises to maintain a specified level of risk-weighted capital similar to the risk-weighted capital requirements for commercial banks discussed in Chapter 3. At the time of this writing, Congress has not settled upon the form of regulation, if any, to implement.

NON-U.S. GOVERNMENT BOND MARKETS

Table 20-3 shows the size of the 20 largest central government bond markets as of the end of 1993. The values reported are in nominal dollars outstanding, not market value. The U.S. government bond market is by far the largest government bond market in the world, followed by Japan, Italy, and then Germany. We review the Japanese and German government bond markets later.

Most central governments issue fixed-rate coupon bonds just as issued by the U.S. Department of the Treasury. Non-U.S. central governments also offer bonds with other characteristics. For example, the British government, whose bonds are referred to as **gilts**, offer bonds called **convertibles**. These gilts have short maturities that give the holder the option to convert into a specified amount of a longer-maturity gilt (or more than one gilt) for a number of years.

---

[11] Credit ratings are discussed in Chapter 21.

Table 20-3

Size of Major Government Bond Markets at Year-End 1993

Country	Outstanding (in billions of U.S. dollars)*
United States	$ 2,274.8
Japan	1,554.6
Italy	620.3
Germany	500.9
France	331.5
United Kingdom	282.2
Belgium	159.2
Canada	149.8
Netherlands	142.0
Spain	100.9
Denmark	72.9
Sweden	61.8
Australia	50.2
Austria	32.5
Ireland	20.0
Portugal	20.0
Switzerland	17.3
Norway	13.2
Finland	12.7
New Zealand	10.2

* Exchange rates prevailing as of December 31, 1993.

Adapted from the data reported in Rosario Benevides, "How Big is the World Bond Market?—1994 Update," Economic & Market Analysis (New York: Salomon Brothers Inc., August 1994), Figure 1, p. 1.

The British government also offers **index-linked gilts**. These gilts have coupons and final redemption amounts linked to the General Index of Retail Price (RPI), an index which is released each month by the Central Statistical Office. Index-linked gilts have low coupons, 2% to 2 ½%, which, in effect, reflect the real rate of return. Maturities of index-linked gilts vary from short-term to the year 2024.

Other central governments have offered bonds linked to inflation. For example, in 1991, the Canadian government issued its first issue of real return bonds ($700 million, due in 2021). The issue was priced to yield a real return equal to 4.25%. The Australian government has small amounts of index-linked Treasury bonds that have either interest payments or capital linked to the Australian Consumer Price Index. Interest-indexed securities pay a fixed coupon every six months plus an arrears adjustment that amounts to the increase in the CPI. Capital-indexed securities also pay a fixed coupon (usually 4%) with the increase in the CPI added to the capital value of the bond and paid on maturity.

Methods of Distribution of New Government Securities

There are four methods of distribution that have been used by central governments in issuing government bonds: the regular auction calendar/Dutch style system; the regular calendar auction/minimum-price offering system; the ad hoc auction system; and the tap system.

In the **regular auction calendar/Dutch style system**, winning bidders are allocated securities at the yield (price) they bid. In the United States, this distribution method is used for all but the 2-year and 5-year Treasury notes; we referred to this method as the multiple-price auction.

With the **regular calendar auction/minimum-price offering system** there is a regular calendar of offerings. The determination of the winners and the amount they will receive is determined in the same manner as in the regular calendar auction/Dutch style system—however, the price (yield) at which winning bidders are awarded the securities is different. Rather than awarding a winning bidder at yield (price) they bid, all winning bidders are awarded securities at the highest yield accepted by the government (i.e., the stop-out yield). The 2-year and 5-year Treasury notes in the United States are issued using this auction system, which we refer to as the single-price auction. The regular calendar auction/minimum-price offering method is used in Germany and France.

In the **ad hoc auction system**, governments announce auctions when prevailing market conditions appear favorable. It is only at the time of the auction that the amount to be auctioned and the maturity of the security to be offered is announced. This is one of the methods used by the Bank of England in distributing British government bonds. There are two advantages of an ad hoc auction system rather than a regular calendar auction from the issuing government's perspective. First, a regular calendar auction introduces greater market volatility than an ad hoc auction since yields tend to rise as the announced auction date approaches and then fall afterwards. Second, there is reduced flexibility is raising funds with a regular calendar auction. After the election of the Conservative Party in England in 1992, there was a significant drop in the yields on British government bonds. The Bank of England used that window to obtain almost a third of the government's funding needs for fiscal year 1992-93 in just the first two months of its fiscal year.

In a **tap system** additional bonds of a previously outstanding bond issue are auctioned. The government periodically announces that it is adding this new supply. The tap system has been used in the United Kingdom and the Netherlands.

Japanese Government Bond Market

There are three types of Japanese government bonds (JGBs) issued publicly: (1) medium-term bonds, (2) long-term bonds, and (3) super long-term bonds. There are two types of medium-term bonds: bonds with coupons and zero-coupon bonds. Ten-year bonds are coupon bearing and are referred to as long-term bonds. During October 1986, 20-year fixed-rate bonds, referred to as super long-term bonds, were issued publicly for the first time.

Long-term bonds and super long-term bonds are noncallable, but the government can repurchase bonds in the secondary market. Both long-term bonds and super long-term bonds are numbered serially and referred to by number rather than maturity and coupon. For example, the No. 129 10-year is the 6.4% of March 20, 2000, and the No. 16 super-long is the 6.8% of September 20, 2011. All coupon bonds pay semiannual interest, just as in the U.S. Treasury coupon market.

There are two methods of issuance of government bonds: syndicate and auction. The syndicate method is used for 10-year bonds and 5-year discount bonds. A new government bond issue is authorized by the Ministry of Finance (MOF), with issuance implemented by the Bank of Japan. A fixed syndicate of more than 700 financial firms, made up of city banks, long-term-credit banks, securities houses, and other financial institutions, is used. The MOF determines the coupon and the size of the issue in consultation with representatives from the underwriting syndicate. Subscriptions are then allocated via a quota system. The members of the underwriting syndicate must also accept and pay for any issues unsubscribed for at the offering. Except for 10-year issues, JGBs are now issued through public auction. Currently, 60% of 10-year JGBs are issued by public auction, with the rest underwritten by the government syndicate at the average auction price.

Once the borrowing authority has been established through the parliamentary process, the MOF has considerable discretion in deciding the composition of new government bond issues, although there are some restrictions on how maturing debt may be refinanced. The overall composition is determined in consultation with representatives of the government bond underwriting syndicate.

For coupon issues, the MOF sets the coupon ahead of the auction after consulting with representatives of the government bond syndicate. An attempt is made to set the coupon at a level that will result in an average auction price below par. Accordingly, bond market conditions, particularly yields on the most recently issued comparable JGB, are a key focus of attention just prior to the auctions.

JGB auctions are conventional price auctions. Since the spring of 1991, all auctions have been carried out in one day. Under present practice, the MOF announces the terms of the issue at 8:30 A.M., bids are accepted between 11:30 A.M.. and 1:30 P.M., and the result is announced at 4:30 P.M. the same day. As the coupon is known, bids are made in terms of bond price, to two decimal places. For example, a bid might be yen 99.75. Bids are filled at the price bid beginning with the highest price, until the entire auction amount is sold. If the entire auction amount is sold before all bids can be filled completely, a bid might be filled only partially. Noncompetitive bids are permitted for some JGBs.

Beginning in October 1987, a hybrid auction was used for 10-year JGBs. Eighty percent of new issues were allocated through the standard syndicate, with 20% available from a hybrid auction. In the hybrid auction, investors could bid for up to 1% of the total auction each; no price, however, was bid. The subscription price, coupon rate, and size of the issue were negotiated by the syndicate as usual. If bids for more than 20% of the auction were received, the amounts bid for were reduced proportionally. If bids for less than 20% were received, the remaining amount was allocated to the syndicate. Bidders, according to this method, accepted the results of the syndicate.

A unique feature of the secondary market for JGBs has to do with the benchmark or bellwether bond issue. It is this issue that is the most actively traded and therefore has the greatest liquidity of all issues of similar maturity. In the U.S. Treasury market, the on-the-run issues (the most recently auctioned issue for a given maturity) are the benchmark issues for each maturity. The on-the-run 30-year Treasury issue is the issue in which there is the most trading activity because investors use it to speculate on interest rates in the long-term end of the bond market.

In Japan, the benchmark issue is basically the issue that the four largest securities houses designate as such. The process of determining the benchmark from among the 10-year bonds is an informal one, usually taking place over a number of weeks. The most important factor in the selection is acceptance by the key market makers. Benchmark issues tend to have certain characteristics: (1) a coupon that is near the prevailing rate; (2) a large outstanding amount (usually yen 1.5 trillion or greater); (3) a wide distribution or placement after its issue; and (4) a remaining maturity as close to ten years as possible. Many observers maintain that the preeminence of the benchmark in the JGB market will decline, and that we will see an evolution toward more issues trading with approximately equal liquidity, although so far there is little indication that such an evolution is underway.

German Government Bond Market

The Federal Republic of Germany issues three types of bonds: (1) Federal government notes called *Bundeskassenobligationen*, or *Kassens*; (2) *Bundesobligationen*, often called *OBLEs*; and (3) government bonds called *Bundasanleihen*, also referred to as *Bunds*. With the unification of West and East Germany in October 1990, the German Unity Fund began to issue Unity Fund bonds (called *Unities*), which are fully guaranteed by the federal government.

Kassens are notes issued to satisfy short- and medium-term needs of the German government and its agencies. Maturities range from 2 to 6 years. They are noncallable. Kassens are issued irregularly several times a year by tender. OBLEs are five-year federal government debt issues. Bunds have original maturities from 6 to 30 years, although recently no issues have been longer than 10 years. Ten-year bunds are the largest sector of the German government securities market in terms of amount outstanding and secondary market turnover. While 10-year Bunds typically have been issued on a monthly basis, this schedule has not been rigid.

More than in any other country with a well-developed capital market, the German capital market is more interdependent with its banking system. This is because most intermediation of funds is via banks. Consequently, in the German capital markets, banks are the largest group of investors. There are two types of banks in Germany: universal banks and "special" banks. The activities of universal banks include the usual commercial banking business and any kind of securities business. The latter activity includes the underwriting, trading, and investing in securities. Thus, there is no separation of the banking and securities businesses in Germany. As a result, the secondary market for both stocks and bonds is mainly an interbank market. The three major universal banks are Deutsche Bank, Dresdner Bank, and Commerzbank. Special banks are institutions that provide financing for specific needs such as mortgage financing and consumer financing.

The issuing group for Bunds is the Federal Bond Syndicate (Konsortium), which is composed of 190 financial institutions (including foreign banks). A new issuance procedure for Bunds and Unities was initiated in July 1990 to promote a more global distribution of government bonds. It combines the traditional underwriting procedure and a multiple-price auction system.

Two tranches are auctioned. The first tranche has fixed terms, including issue price, and is allocated along traditional guidelines among syndicate members. In this traditional system of issue, all members are allocated a fixed percentage of total issue size, irrespective of the issue terms. Up to 25% of the initial offering is retained by the central bank (the Bundesbank) for intervention and market-making purposes. The second tranche is auctioned on the next day with bid prices made by eligible members in 0.05 increments in deutche marks for bonds with the same terms as the first tranche (except price). No selling commissions are paid on this tranche. Bids may be placed until the morning (from 10:00 A.M. to 11:30 A.M.) after the underwriting date, with allocation by the Bundesbank taking place within two hours thereafter. The two tranches plus the Bundesbank quota form one issue with identical terms and one security code. The total issue volume is announced by the Bundesbank after allocation. The proportions of total volume raised via the two tranches are flexible in order to suit market conditions at the same time of issuance.

Although there is no strict benchmark issue in Germany (as there is in the United States and Japan), a benchmark system has been evolving. The benchmark has typically been the most recently issued ten-year Bund.

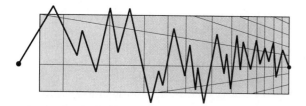

SUMMARY

The U.S. Treasury market is closely watched by all participants in the financial markets because interest rates on Treasury securities are the benchmark interest rates throughout the world. The Treasury issues three types of securities: bills, notes, and bonds. Treasury bills have a maturity of one year or less, are sold at a discount from par, and do not make periodic interest payments. Treasury notes and bonds are coupon securities.

Treasury securities are issued on a competitive-bid auction basis, according to a regular auction cycle. The auction process relies on the participation of the primary government securities dealers, with which the Federal Reserve deals directly. The auction process has been revised to allow greater participation by eligible nonprimary dealers.

The secondary market for Treasury securities is an over-the-counter market, where dealers trade with the general investing public and with other dealers. In the secondary market, Treasury coupon securities are quoted on a price basis. Government brokers are used by primary dealers to trade amongst themselves. Pressure has been placed on primary dealers to provide greater access to prices of Treasury securities.

While the Treasury does not issue zero-coupon Treasury securities, government dealers have created these instruments synthetically by a process called coupon stripping. Zero-coupon Treasury securities include trademarks, generic receipts, and STRIPS. Creation of the first two types of zero-coupon Treasury securities has ceased; STRIPS now dominate the market.

Government-sponsored enterprise securities and federally related institution securities comprise the federal agency securities market. The former are privately owned, publicly chartered entities created to reduce the cost of borrowing for certain sectors of the economy. Federally related institutions are arms of the federal government whose debt is guaranteed by the U.S. government. While government-sponsored enterprises issue their own securities, federally related institutions obtain all or part of their financing by borrowing from the Federal Financing Bank.

The U.S. government bond market is the largest in the world, followed by the Japanese, Italian, and then German government bond markets. Some central governments offer bonds indexed to the country's inflation. There are four methods of distribution that have been used by central governments in issuing bonds: the regular auction calendar/Dutch style system, the regular calendar auction/minimum-price offering system, the ad hoc auction system, and the tap system.

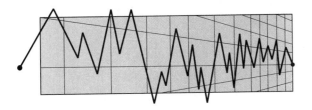

QUESTIONS

1. What is the difference between a Treasury note and a Treasury bond?

2. What is the when-issued market?

3. a. What is a primary dealer?

   b. What role does a primary dealer play in the Treasury market?

   c. What is a recognized dealer?

4. a. Why do government dealers use government brokers?

   b. Who are the major government brokers?

5. Calculate the dollar price for the following Treasury coupon securities:

	Price Quoted	Par
A.	95-4	$ 100,000
B.	87-16	1,000,000
C.	102-10	10,000,000
D.	116-30	10,000
E.	102-4+	100,000

6. The following excerpt is from the March 1991 monthly report published by *BlackRock Financial Management*:

   > The Treasury also brought $34.5 billion in new securities to the market in February as part of the normal quarterly refunding . . . . the auctions went slightly better than expected given the significant size and the uncertainties surrounding the duration of the war. The 3-year was issued at a 6.98% average yield, the 10-year at a 7.85% average yield, and the 30-year at a 7.98% average yield. All bids were accepted at the average yield or better (i.e., with no tail), indicating ample demand for the securities.

   a. What is meant by the average yield and the "tail"?

   b. Why does the absence of a tail indicate ample demand for the Treasuries auctioned?

7. Does the U.S. Department of the Treasury use a single-price or multiple-price auction in the issuance of Treasury coupon securities?

8. How is the yield of winning bidders determined in:

   a. a single-price auction?

   b. a multiple-price auction?

9. a. What is the difference between a STRIP, a trademark Treasury zero-coupon security, and a Treasury receipt?

   b. What is the most common type of Treasury zero-coupon security?

10. What is the difference between a government-sponsored enterprise and a federally related institution?

11. Are government-sponsored enterprise securities backed by the full faith and credit of the U.S. government?

12. What is a "gilt"?

13. What are the different methods for the issuance of government securities?

14. a. What are the three types of bonds issued by the Japanese government?

    b. How is the benchmark government issue determined in the Japanese bond market?

15. What are Bunds and Unities?

Corporate Bond Market

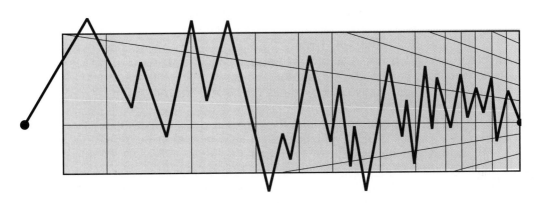

LEARNING OBJECTIVES

After reading this chapter you will understand:

- the key provisions of a corporate bond issue.

- provisions for paying off a bond issue prior to the stated maturity date.

- corporate bond ratings.

- what is meant by an investment-grade bond and a noninvestment-grade (or high-yield) bond.

- what event risk is.

- the general characteristics of the high-yield corporate bond market.

- bond structures that have been used in the high-yield bond market.

- the general characteristics of the secondary market for corporate bonds.

- the changing character of the private placement market for corporate debt.

- empirical evidence concerning the historical risk and return pattern in the corporate bond market.

- what a Eurobond is and the different types of Eurobond structures.

513

Corporate senior instruments are financial obligations of a corporation that have priority over its common stock in the case of bankruptcy. They include debt obligations and preferred stock. The market for corporate debt obligations can be classified into four sectors: (1) the commercial paper market, (2) the bond market, (3) medium-term note market, and (4) the bank loan market.

In Chapter 16, we discussed the commercial paper market. Chapter 22 covers the preferred stock market, medium-term note market, and the bank loan. In this chapter our focus is on the corporate bond market. One sector within the corporate bond market that has been the subject of considerable discussion is the high-yield or junk bond market. We will discuss this specific market sector by examining the issuers, the investors, and various bond structures. We will also look at an increasingly popular market used by corporations to issue bonds—the Eurobond market.

As the name indicates, corporate bonds are issued by corporations. As of the third quarter of 1993, there were $1.9 trillion of domestic corporate bonds outstanding, 63% of which was issued by nonfinancial corporations. The largest investor group is life insurance companies, followed by pension funds, both public and private. Historically, these institutional investors hold more than half of outstanding corporate bonds. The balance is held by households, foreign investors, depository institutions, non-life insurance companies, and mutual funds and securities brokers and dealers.

Corporate bonds are classified by the type of issuer. The four general classifications used by bond information services are: (1) utilities, (2) transportations, (3) industrials, and (4) banks and finance companies. Finer breakdowns are often made to create more homogeneous groupings. For example, utilities are subdivided into electric power companies, gas distribution companies, water companies, and communication companies. Transportations are divided further into airlines, railroads, and trucking companies. Industrials is the catchall class, and the most heterogeneous of the groupings with respect to investment characteristics. Industrials include all kinds of manufacturing, merchandising, and service companies.

FEATURES OF A CORPORATE BOND ISSUE

The essential features of a corporate bond are relatively simple. The corporate issuer promises to pay a specified percentage of par value on designated dates (the coupon payments) and to repay par or principal value of the bond at maturity. Failure to pay either the principal or interest when due constitutes legal default, and investors can go to court to enforce the contract. Bondholders, like creditors, have a prior legal claim over common and preferred stockholders as to both income and assets of the corporation for the principal and interest due them.

The promises of corporate bond issuers and the rights of investors who buy them are set forth in great detail in contracts called **bond indentures**. If bondholders were handed the complete indenture they would have trouble understanding the language and even greater difficulty in determining from time to time whether the corporate issuer were keeping all the promises made. These problems are solved for the most part by bringing in a corporate trustee as a third party to the contract. The indenture is made out to the corporate trustee as a representative of the interests of bondholders; that is, a trustee acts in a fiduciary capacity for investors who own the bond issue. A corporate trustee is a bond or trust company with a corporate trust department whose officers are experts in performing the functions of a trustee.

Most corporate bonds are **term bonds**—they run for a term of years, then become due and payable. Any amount of the liability that has not been paid off prior to maturity must be paid off at that time. The term may be long or short. Generally, obligations due in under 10 years from the date of issue are called **notes**. (However, the word "notes" has been used to describe particular types of securities that can have maturities considerably longer than 10 years.) Most corporate borrowings take the form of **bonds** due in 20 to 30 years. Term bonds may be retired by payment at final maturity or retired prior to maturity if provided for in the indenture. Some corporate bond issues are arranged so that specified principal amounts become due on specified dates. Such issues are called **serial bonds**. Equipment trust certificates (discussed later) are structured as serial bonds.

Prior to the 1970s, the securities issued in the U.S. bond market had a simple structure. They had a fixed coupon rate and a fixed maturity date. The only option available to the issuer was the right to call all or part of the issue prior to the stated maturity date. However, the historically high interest rates that prevailed in the United States in the late 1970s and early 1980s, in addition to the volatile interest rates since the 1970s ushered in new structures or increased use of special features that made issues more attractive to both borrowers and investors. These include zero-coupon bonds and floating-rate notes.

Security for Bonds

Either real property (using a mortgage) or personal property may be pledged to offer security beyond the issuer's general credit standing. A **mortgage bond** grants the bondholders a lien against the pledged assets, that is, a legal right to sell the mortgaged property to satisfy unpaid obligations to the bondholders. In practice, foreclosure and sale of mortgaged property is unusual. Usually in the case of default a financial reorganization of the issuer provides for settlement of the debt to bondholders. The mortgage lien is important, though, because it gives the mortgage bondholders a strong bargaining position relative to other creditors in determining the terms of any reorganization.

Some companies do not own fixed assets or other real property, and so have nothing on which they can give a mortgage lien to secure bondholders. Instead, they own securities of other companies; they are holding companies, and the other companies are subsidiaries. To satisfy the desire of bondholders for security, they will pledge stocks, notes, bonds, or whatever other kind of obligations they own. These assets are termed collateral (or personal property); bonds secured by such assets are called **collateral trust bonds**.

Many years ago the railway companies developed a way of financing the purchase of cars and locomotives (rolling stock) that enabled them to borrow at just about the lowest rates in the corporate bond market. Railway rolling stock has for a long time been seen as excellent security for debt. The equipment is sufficiently standardized so that it can be used by one railroad as well as another. It can be readily moved from the tracks of one railroad to another's, and there is generally a good market for lease or sale of cars and locomotives. The railroads have taken advantage of these characteristics of rolling stock by developing a legal arrangement for giving investors a claim that is different from, and generally superior to, a mortgage lien. The legal arrangement vests legal title to railway equipment in a trustee.

The procedure works like this. A railway company orders cars and locomotives from a manufacturer. The manufacturer then transfers legal title to the equipment to a trustee, who in turn leases it to the railroad, and at the same time sells equipment trust certificates to obtain the funds to pay the manufacturer. The trustee collects lease payments from the railroad and uses the money to pay interest and principal on the certificates. The principal is therefore paid off on specified dates. Although the railway companies developed the equipment trust arrangement, it has since been used by companies engaged in providing other kinds of transportation. For example, trucking companies finance the purchase of huge fleets of trucks in the same manner; airlines use this kind of financing to purchase transport planes; and international oil companies use it to buy huge tankers.

Debenture bonds are debt securities not secured by a specific pledge of property, but that does not mean that they offer no claim on property of issuers or on their earnings. Debenture bondholders have the claim of general creditors on all assets of the issuer not pledged specifically to secure other debt. And they have a claim on pledged assets even to the extent that these assets have more value than necessary to satisfy secured creditors. **Subordinated debenture bonds** rank after secured debt, after debenture bonds, and often after some general creditors in their claim on assets and earnings.

The type of security issued determines the cost to the corporation. For a given corporation, mortgage bonds will cost less than debenture bonds, and debenture bonds will cost less than subordinated debenture bonds.

Guaranteed bonds are obligations guaranteed by another entity. The safety of a guaranteed bond depends upon the guarantor's financial capability, as well as the financial capability of the issuer. The terms may call for the guarantor to guarantee the payment of interest and/or repayment of the principal.

It is important to recognize that the superior legal status of any debt security will not prevent bondholders from suffering financial loss when the issuer's ability to generate cash flow adequate to pay its obligations is seriously eroded.

Provisions for Paying Off Bonds

Most corporate issues have a call provision allowing the issuer an option to buy back all or part of the issue prior to the stated maturity date. Some issues specify that the issuer must retire a predetermined amount of the issue periodically. Various types of corporate call provisions are discussed below.[1]

---

[1] For a more detailed explanation of corporate call provisions, see Richard S. Wilson and Frank J. Fabozzi, *Corporate Bonds: Structures and Analysis* (New Hope, PA: Frank J. Fabozzi Associates, 1995).

Call and refund provisions—An important question in negotiating the terms of a new bond issue is whether the issuer shall have the right to redeem the entire amount of bonds outstanding on a date before maturity. Issuers generally want this right because they recognize that at some time in the future the general level of interest rates may fall sufficiently below the issue's coupon rate, at which time redeeming the issue and replacing it with another issue with a lower coupon rate would be attractive. This right is a disadvantage to the bondholder.

The usual practice is a provision that denies the issuer the right to redeem bonds during the first 5 to 10 years following the date of issue with proceeds received from issuing lower-cost debt obligations ranking equal or superior to the debt to be redeemed. This type of redemption is called **refunding**. While most long-term issues include these refunding restrictions, they may be callable immediately, in whole or in part, if the source of funds comes from other than lower-interest cost money. Cash flow from operations, proceeds from a common stock sale, or funds from the sale of property are examples of such sources.

Investors often confuse refunding protection with call protection. Call protection is much more absolute, in that bonds cannot be redeemed for any reason. Refunding restrictions provide protection only against the one type of redemption mentioned above.

As a rule, corporate bonds are callable at a premium above par. Generally, the level of the premium declines as the bond approaches maturity, often reaching par a number of years after issuance. The initial amount of the premium may be as much as one year's coupon interest or as little as coupon interest for half a year. When less than the entire issue is called, the specific bonds to be called are selected randomly or on a pro rata basis. When bonds are selected randomly, the serial number of the certificates selected is published in *The Wall Street Journal* and major metropolitan dailies.

Sinking fund provision—Corporate bond indentures may require the issuer to retire a specified portion of an issue each year. This is referred to as a **sinking fund requirement**. This kind of provision for repayment of corporate debt may be designed to liquidate all of a bond issue by the maturity date, or it may be arranged to pay only a part of the total by the end of the term. If only a part is paid, the remainder is called a balloon maturity. The purpose of the sinking fund provision is to reduce credit risk.

Generally, the issuer may satisfy the sinking fund requirement by either (1) making a cash payment of the face amount of the bonds to be retired to the corporate trustee, who then calls the bonds for redemption using a lottery; or (2) delivering to the trustee bonds purchased in the open market that have a total face value equal to the amount that must be retired. If the bonds are retired using the first method, interest payments stop at the redemption date.

Usually, the periodic payments required for sinking fund purposes will be the same for each period. A few indentures might permit variable periodic payments, where payments change according to certain prescribed conditions set forth in the indenture. Many corporate bond indentures include a provision that grants the issuer the option to retire more than the amount stipulated for sinking fund retirement. This is referred to as an **accelerated sinking fund provision**.

Usually, the sinking fund call price is the par value if the bonds were originally sold at par. When issued at a price in excess of par, the call price generally starts at the issuance price and scales down to par as the issue approaches maturity.

Conversion Provision

Some issues have a conversion provision. This provision grants the bondholder the right to convert the bond to a predetermined number of shares of common stock of the issuer. Such issues are called **convertible bonds**. A convertible bond is therefore a corporate bond with a call option to buy the common stock of the issuer. **Exchangeable bonds** grant the bondholder the right to exchange the bonds for the common stock of a firm other than the issuer of the bond. For example, some Ford Motor Credit bonds are exchangeable for the common stock of the parent company, Ford Motor Company.

The number of shares of common stock that the bondholder will receive from exercising the call option of a convertible bond or exchangeable bond is called the **conversion ratio**. The conversion privilege may be permitted for all or only some portion of the bond's life, and the conversion ratio may decline over time. It is always adjusted proportionately for stock splits and stock dividends.

Convertible issues are callable by the issuer. This is a valuable feature for the issuer, since an important reason for using convertibles is when a firm seeking to raise additional capital would prefer to raise equity funds but deems the current market price of its stock too undervalued so that selling stock would dilute the equity of current stockholders. So it issues a convertible setting the conversion ratio on the basis of a price it regards as acceptable. Once the market price reaches the acceptable conversion point, the firm wants to see the conversion occur in view of the risk that the price may decline again. The issuing firm therefore has an interest in forcing conversion, even though this is not in the interest of the owners of the security as its price is likely to be adversely affected by the call.

The price of a convertible bond should reflect the value of the embedded options. The two embedded options are (1) the call option on the stock that the investor has effectively purchased, and (2) the call option on the convertible bond that the investor has effectively sold to the corporate issuer.[2] That is, the convertible bondholder is in a long call position with respect to the common stock and in a short call position with respect to the bond issue.

Corporate takeovers add another risk to investing in convertible bonds. If an issuer is acquired by another company or by its own management (as in the case of a management-led leveraged buyout), the stock price may not appreciate sufficiently for the holders of the convertible bond to benefit from the conversion feature. As the stock of the acquired company may no longer trade after a takeover, the investor can be left with a bond that pays a lower coupon rate than comparable risk corporate bonds.

---

[2] A number of articles present models for valuing convertible bonds using an options approach. See Michael Brennan and Eduardo Schwartz, "Convertible Bonds: Valuation and Optimal Strategies for Call and Conversion," *Journal of Finance* (December 1977), pp. 1699-715; Jonathan Ingersoll, "A Contingent-Claims Valuation of Convertible Securities," *Journal of Financial Economics* (May 1977), pp. 289-322; Michael Brennan and Eduardo Schwartz, "Analyzing Convertible Bonds," *Journal of Financial and Quantitative Analysis* (November 1980), pp. 907-29; and George M. Constantinides, "Warrant Exercise and Bond Conversion in Competitive Markets," *Journal of Financial Economics* (September 1984), pp. 371-98.

Issues of Debt with Warrants

A bond may be issued with warrants attached as part of the offer. A warrant grants the holder the right to purchase a designated security at a specified price. Therefore, as we explain in Chapter 14, a warrant is simply a call option that permits the holder to purchase the common stock of the issuer of the debt or the common stock of a firm other than the issuer's. Alternatively, the warrant may grant the holder the right to purchase a debt obligation of the issuer. Warrants generally can be detached from the host bond and sold separately. The typical warrant can be exercised with cash or by exchanging the debt at par. In the case of convertible and exchangeable bonds, only the bond may be used to exercise the option.

The warrant may permit the bondholder to buy common stock of the issuer, as does a convertible bond. The embedded call option in the convertible bond, however, cannot be sold separately from the bond, while a warrant can be. Thus, the holder of a bond and a warrant has a long position in the corporate bond of the issuer and a long position in a call option on the common stock of the issuer. The same is true of a unit of debt with warrants to buy common stock of a firm other than the issuer. The holder of a bond and a warrant in this case has a long position in the corporate bond of the issuer and a long position in a call option on the common stock of some other firm.

CORPORATE BOND RATINGS

Professional money managers use various techniques to analyze information on companies and bond issues in order to estimate the ability of the issuer to live up to its future contractual obligations.[3] This activity is known as **credit analysis**.

Some large institutional investors and many investment banking firms have their own credit analysis departments. Few individual investors and institutional bond investors, though, do their own analysis. Instead, they rely primarily on nationally recognized rating companies that perform credit analysis and issue their conclusions in the form of ratings. The four commercial rating companies are (1) Duff and Phelps Credit Rating Co., (2) Fitch Investors Service, (3) Moody's Investors Service, and (4) Standard & Poor's Corporation. The rating systems use similar symbols, as shown in Table 21-1.

In all systems the term "high-grade" means low credit risk, or conversely, high probability of future payments. The highest-grade bonds are designated by Moody's by the letters Aaa, and by the others by AAA. The next highest grade is Aa or AA; for the third grade all rating agencies use A. The next three grades are Baa or BBB, Ba or BB, and B, respectively. There are also C grades. All but Moody's use plus or minus signs to provide a narrower credit quality breakdown within each class, and Moody's uses 1, 2, or 3 for the same purpose. Bonds rated triple A (AAA or Aaa) are said to be prime; double A (AA or Aa) are of high quality; single A issues are called upper medium grade, and triple B are medium grade. Lower-rated bonds are said to have speculative elements or be distinctly speculative.

---

[3] For an in-depth discussion of credit analysis, see Jane Tripp Howe, "Credit Analysis for Corporate Bonds," Chapter 18 in Frank J. Fabozzi and T. Dessa Fabozzi (eds.), *The Handbook of Fixed Income Securities* (Burr Ridge IL: Irwin, 1995).

Table 21-1

Summary of Corporate Bond Rating Systems and Symbols

Moody's	S&P	Fitch	D&P	Brief Definition
Investment Grade—High Creditworthiness				
Aaa	AAA	AAA	AAA	Gilt edge, prime, maximum safety
Aa1	AA+	AA+	AA+	
Aa2	AA	AA	AA	Very high grade, high quality
Aa3	AA–	AA–	AA–	
A1	A+	A+	A+	
A2	A	A	A	Upper medium grade
A3	A–	A–	A–	
Baa1	BBB+	BBB+	BBB+	
Baa2	BBB	BBB	BBB	Lower medium grade
Baa3	BBB–	BBB–	BBB–	
Distinctly Speculative—Low Creditworthiness				
Ba1	BB+	BB+	BB+	
Ba2	BB	BB	BB	Low grade, speculative
Ba3	BB–	BB–	BB–	
B1	B+	B+	B+	
B2	B	B	B	Highly speculative
B3	B–	B–	B–	
Predominantly Speculative—Substantial Risk in Default				
	CCC+			
Caa	CCC	CCC	CCC	Substantial risk, in poor standing
	CCC–			
Ca	CC	CC		May be in default, extremely speculative
C	C	C		Even more speculative than those above
	C1			C1= Income bonds—no interest is being paid
		DDD		Default
		DD	DD	
	D	D		

Bond issues that are assigned a rating in the top four categories are referred to as **investment-grade bonds**. Issues that carry a rating below the top four categories are referred to as **noninvestment-grade bonds**, or more popularly as **high-yield bonds** or **junk bonds**. Thus, the corporate bond market can be divided into two sectors: the investment-grade and noninvestment-grade markets.

EVENT RISK

Occasionally the ability of an issuer to make interest and principal payments changes seriously and unexpectedly because of (1) a natural or industrial accident or some regulatory change, or (2) a takeover or corporate restructuring. These risks are referred to generically as **event risk**. Examples of the first type of event risk would be a change in the accounting treatment of loan losses for commercial banks or cancellation of nuclear plants by public utilities.

A good example of the second type of event risk is the 1988 takeover of RJR Nabisco for $25 billion through a financing technique known as a leveraged buyout (LBO). The new company took on a substantial amount of debt incurred to finance the acquisition of the firm.[4] In the case of RJR Nabisco, the debt and equity after the leveraged buyout were $29.9 and $1.2 billion, respectively. Because the corporation must service a larger amount of debt, its bond quality rating was reduced; RJR Nabisco's quality rating as assigned by Moody's dropped from A1 to B3. To see how much more investors demanded because of the company's new capital structure with a greater proportion of debt, look at Figure 21-1. The figure shows the impact of the initial LBO bid announcement on yield spreads for RJR Nabisco's debt. The yield spread to a benchmark Treasury increased from about 100 basis points to 350 basis points.

Event risk can also have spillover effects on other firms. A nuclear accident, for example, will affect all utilities producing nuclear power. And in the case of takeovers, consider once again the RJR Nabisco LBO. An LBO of $25 billion was considered impractical prior to the RJR Nabisco LBO, but the Nabisco transaction showed that size was not an obstacle, and other large firms previously thought to be unlikely candidates for an LBO became fair game. To see the spillover effect, look at Figure 21-2, which shows how event risk fears caused yield spreads to widen for three large firms.

HIGH-YIELD CORPORATE BOND MARKET

As we have noted, high-yield bonds, commonly called junk bonds, are issues with quality ratings below triple B. Bond issues in this sector of the market may have been rated investment grade at the time of issuance and subsequently downgraded to noninvestment grade, or they may have been rated noninvestment grade at the time of issuance, called **original-issue high yield bonds**.

---

[4] For a discussion of event risk associated with takeovers, see N.R. Vijayarghavan and Randy Snook, "Takeover Event Risk and Corporate Bond Portfolio Management," in Frank J. Fabozzi (ed.), *Advances and Innovations in Bond and Mortgage Markets* (Chicago: Probus Publishing, 1989).

Figure 21-1

RJR Nabisco—Impact of the Initial LBO Bid Announcement on Yield Spreads

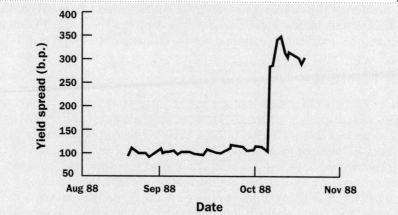

*RJR Nabico 9 3/8 due April 2016— U.S. Treasury 8 7/8 due August 2017.

Source: N. R. Vijayarghavan and Randy Snook, "Takeover Event Risk and Corporate Bond
    Portofolio Management," in Frank J. Fabozzi (ed.), Advances and Innovations in Bond
    and Mortgage Markets (Chicago: Probus Publishing, 1989), p. 55.

Figure 21-2

Anheuser Busch, Sara Lee, and Union Pacific—
Event Risk Fears and Widening Yield Spreads

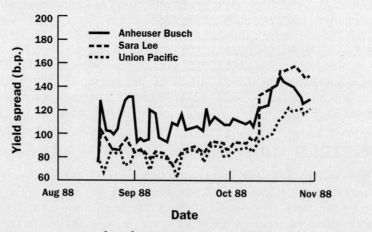

*Corporates are spread to the U.S. Treasuty 8 7/8 due August 2017.

Source: N. R. Vijayarghavan and Randy Snook, "Takeover Event Risk and Corporate Bond
    Portofolio Management," in Frank J. Fabozzi (ed.), Advances and Innovations in Bond
    and Mortgage Markets (Chicago: Probus Publishing, 1989), p. 55.

Bonds that have been downgraded fall into two groups: (1) issues that have been downgraded because the issuer voluntarily significantly increased their debt as a result of a leveraged buyout or a recapitalization, and (2) issues that have been downgraded for other reasons. The latter issues are commonly referred to as "fallen angels." As of year-end 1992, 14% of the high-yield market was made up of issues downgraded because of leveraged buyouts and recapitalizations, 16% were fallen angels, and 70% were original-issue high-yield bonds.[5]

The modern high-yield market began in the later half of the 1970s.[6] The high-yield market grew from approximately $24 billion at year-end 1977 to approximately $199 billion by year-end 1992, reaching $215 billion in 1990.[7] Due to the market's dramatic successes (such as the $1.5 billion LBO of Metromedia by John Kluge in 1984, and Kolberg Kravis Roberts & Company's 1986 LBO of Beatrice, a company with many well-known brand names) the media began to report stories helping to bring to a peak investors' appetites. The market's early growth was dominated by a single investment bank, Drexel Burnham Lambert, and it was not until the mid-1980s that this firm began to experience serious competition from other investment banks, namely Merrill Lynch, Morgan Stanley, and First Boston.[8] Also, as of that time, the high-yield sector represented about 23% of the total corporate bond market. Also as of that time, the largest holders of high-yield bonds were mutual funds and independent money managers who owned 43% of outstanding issues, followed by insurance companies (25%) and pension funds (15%).[9]

The Role of High-Yield Bonds in Corporate Finance

The introduction of original-issue high-yield bonds has been a very important financial innovation with wide impact throughout the financial system. There was a common view that high default risk bonds would not be attractive to the investing public, at least at interest rates that would be acceptable to the borrower. The view rested on the skewed nature of the outcomes offered by the instrument: The maximum return that an investor may obtain is capped by the coupon and face value, but the loss could be as large as the principal invested. It was the merit of Drexel Burnham Lambert, and particularly of Michael Milken of that firm, to disprove that view as evidenced by the explosive growth of that market.

Before development of the high-yield market, U.S. corporations that could not issue securities in the public debt market would borrow from commercial banks or finance companies on a short-term to intermediate-term basis or

---

[5] Joseph C. Bencivenga, "The High-Yield Corporate Bond Market," Chapter 15 in Fabozzi and Fabozzi (eds.), *The Handbook of Fixed Income Securities*, Exhibit 15-8.

[6] The evolution of the high-yield market since the early 1900s is described in J. Thomas Madden and Joseph Balestrino, "Evolution of the High-Yield Market," Chapter 2 in Frank J. Fabozzi (ed.), *The New High-Yield Debt Market* (New York: Harper & Row, 1991).

[7] Bencivenga, "The High-Yield Corporate Bond Market," p. 307.

[8] Drexel Burnham Lambert underwrote more than 45% of new high-yield issues.

[9] Bencivenga, The High-Yield Corporate Bond Market, Exhibit 15-9, p. 314.

would be shut off from credit. With the advent of the high-yield bond structure, financing shifted from commercial banks to the public market. One study estimated that about two-thirds of the $90 to $100 billion of the high-yield bonds issued simply represent a replacement of commercial bank borrowing.[10] The same study concluded that high-yield bonds are "no more a threat to the stability of the financial system than that bank debt itself was."

In essence, the high-yield bond market shifts the risk from commercial banks to the investing public in general. There are several advantages to such a shift. First, when commercial banks lend to high-credit-risk borrowers, that risk is accepted indirectly by all U.S. citizens, who may not wish to accept the risk. The reason is that commercial bank liabilities are backed by the federal deposit insurance. If high-credit-risk corporations default on their loans, causing a government bailout, all taxpayers eventually may have to pay. The liabilities of other investors (excluding thrifts that have invested in high-yield bonds) are not backed by the U.S. government (and therefore U.S. citizens). The risks of this investing are accepted by the specific investor group willing to accept them.

The second advantage is that commercial bank loans are typically short-term floating-rate loans, which make debt financing less attractive to corporations. High-yield bond issues give corporations the opportunity to issue long-term, fixed-rate debt. Third, commercial banks set interest rates based on their credit analysis. When high-yield bonds are traded in a public market, the investing public establishes the interest rate. Finally, the high-yield market opens the possibility of credit for some firms that previously had no means to it.

Corporate bond issuers use the proceeds from a bond sale for a number of purposes. These include working capital, expansion of facilities, refinancing of outstanding debt, and financing takeovers (mergers and acquisitions). In the case of noninvestment-grade bonds, it is the use of the proceeds to finance takeovers (particularly hostile takeovers) that has aroused some public concern over the excessive use of debt by U.S. corporations.[11] Table 21-2 shows the use of proceeds for new-issue high-yield bonds for the years 1987 through 1992. Notice that while just over half the proceeds raised in 1987 were used for either a leveraged buyout, to repay LBO debt, or for recapitalization, only 6% was used for that purpose in 1992. Instead, about 80% of the proceeds raised in 1992 was applied toward debt retirement.

High-Yield Bond Structures

In the early years of the high-yield market, all the issues had a conventional structure—that is, the issues paid a fixed coupon rate and were term bonds. Today, however, there are more complex bond structures in the junk bond area, particularly for bonds issued for LBO financing and recapitalizations producing higher debt. The structures we describe below have features that are more attractive to issuers.

---

[10] November 1986 speech by John Paulus, chief economist at Morgan Stanley, at a conference sponsored by *Citizens for a Sound Economy*.

[11] A hostile takeover is one in which the targeted firm's management resists the merger or acquisition.

Table 21-2
Use of Proceeds for New-Issue High-Yield Bonds, 1987-1992 (Dollars in millions)

	1987 Amount	%	1988 Amount	%	1989 Amount	%	1990 Amount	%	1991 Amount	%	1992 Amount	%
Acquisition	$2,571	7%	$4,805	14%	$959	3%	—	—	$546	6%	$1,651	4%
Repay acquisition debt	6,074	18	6,170	17	7,351	23	$1,000	80%	633	7	5,106	14
General refinancing	4,477	13	5,481	15	4,155	13	250	20	5,924	64	24,865	66
Internal growth	2.572	8	615	2	1,598	5	—	—	607	7	3,740	10
Leveraged buyout (LBO)	6,708	20	4,134	12	959	3	—	—	—	—	—	—
Repay LBO debt	7,597	22	9,781	28	12,146	38	—	—	1,506	16	—	—
Recapitalization	3,792	11	3,759	11	4,794	15	—	—	—	—	2,440	6
Troubled recapitalization	500	1	513	1	—	—	—	—	—	—	—	—

Note: Debt at face value.

Source: Indepth Data Inc.

In an LBO or a recapitalization, the heavy interest payment burden that the corporation assumes places severe cash flow constraints on the firm. To reduce this burden, firms involved in LBOs and recapitalizations have issued bonds with deferred coupon structures that permit the issuer to avoid using cash to make interest payments for a period of three to seven years. There are three types of deferred coupon structures: (1) deferred-interest bonds, (2) step-up bonds, and (3) payment-in-kind bonds.

Deferred-interest bonds are the most common type of **deferred coupon structure**. These bonds sell at a deep discount and do not pay interest for an initial period, typically from three to seven years. (Because no interest is paid for the initial period, these bonds are sometimes referred to as zero-coupon bonds.) **Step-up bonds** do pay coupon interest, but the coupon rate is low for an initial period and then increases ("steps up") to a higher coupon rate. Finally, **payment-in-kind (PIK) bonds** give the issuer an option to pay cash at a coupon payment date or give the bondholder a similar bond (i.e., a bond with the same coupon rate and a par value equal to the amount of the coupon payment that would have been paid). The period during which the issuer can make this choice varies from five to ten years.

In late 1987, a junk bond came to market with a structure allowing the issuer to reset the coupon rate so that the bond will trade at a predetermined price.[12] The coupon rate may reset annually or even more frequently, or reset only one time over the life of the bond. Generally, the coupon rate at reset time will be the average of rates suggested by two investment banking firms. The new rate will then reflect: (1) the level of interest rates at the reset date, and (2) the credit spread the market wants on the issue at the reset date. This structure is called an **extendable reset**.

Notice the difference between an extendable reset bond and a floating-rate issue as described earlier. In a floating-rate issue, the coupon rate resets according to a fixed spread over some benchmark, with the spread specified in the indenture. The amount of the spread reflects market conditions at the time the issue is offered. The coupon rate on an extendable reset bond by contrast is reset based on market conditions (as suggested by several investment banking firms) at the time of the reset date. Moreover, the new coupon rate reflects the new level of interest rates and the new spread that investors seek.

The advantage to issuers of extendable reset bonds is again that they can be assured of a long-term source of funds based on short-term rates. For investors, the advantage of these bonds is that the coupon rate will reset to the market rate—both the level of interest rates and the credit spread, in principle keeping the issue at par. In fact, experience with reset bonds has not been favorable during the recent period of difficulties in the high-yield bond market. The sudden substantial increase in default risk has meant that the rise in the rate needed to keep the issue at par was so large that it would have insured the bankruptcy of the firm. As a result, the rise in the coupon rate has been insufficient to keep the issue at the stipulated price.

Finally, there are high-yield structures collateralized by a pool of high-yield corporate bonds and with multiple classes of bondholders. These are called

---

[12] Most of the bonds have a coupon reset formula that requires the issuer to reset the coupon so that the bond will trade at a price of $101.

collateralized bond obligations. The bond structure in this case is similar to the collateralized mortgage obligations discussed in Chapter 26.[13]

SECONDARY MARKET

There are really two secondary corporate bond markets: the exchange market (the New York and American Stock Exchanges) and the over-the-counter (OTC) market. The great bulk of trading volume takes place in the OTC market, which is the market used by institutional investors and professional money managers. The corporate bond market is subject to the same problems with respect to the public reporting of completed transactions and public information on reliable bid and ask prices as the Treasury securities market is.

There are services that provide information on actively traded or bellwether issues. Figure 21-3 shows quotes for bellwether long industrial investment-grade bonds as of December 30, 1993 as reported on the Reuters Terminal.[14] Notice how the quotes are shown. Rather than a dollar price, a spread (in basis points) to an equivalent maturity U.S. Treasury is reported. For example, look at the Coca-Cola issue where the bid is 80. This means that a dealer would pay 80 basis points over the yield on an equivalent maturity Treasury to buy the issue. The ask is 72 which means the dealer would sell the issue for 72 basis points over the yield on an equivalent Treasury issue. Since the higher the yield, the lower the price, as expected the bid price is lower than the ask price.

Figure 21-4 shows quotes for bellwether high-yield issues. Notice for these issues that the quotes are in terms of price rather than a spread over an equivalent maturity Treasury.

As we explained in Chapter 16, in addition to the agreed-upon price, the buyer must pay the seller accrued interest. Market convention for determining the number of days in a corporate bond coupon period and the number of days from the last coupon payment to settlement date differs from that for a Treasury coupon security. While a calendar year has 365 days (366 days in the case of a leap year), corporate bond interest is computed as if the year were 360 days. Each month in a corporate bond year is 30 days whether it is February, April, or August. A 12% coupon corporate bond pays $120 per year per $1,000 par value, accruing interest at $10 per month or $0.33333 per day. The accrued interest on a 12% corporate bond for three months is $30; for three months and 25 days, $38.33, and so forth. The corporate calendar is referred to as "30/360."

PRIVATE PLACEMENT MARKET FOR CORPORATE BONDS

As explained in Chapter 6, securities privately placed are exempt from registration with the SEC because they are issued in transactions that do not

---

[13] For a detailed explanation of collateralized bond obligations, see Robert Gerber, "Collateralized Bond Obligations," Chapter 6 in Fabozzi (ed.), *The New High-Yield Debt Market*.

[14] The reporting source for the page is MKI, a corporate bond broker located in New York. Benchmark bonds are reported for eight different sectors of the corporate bond market. The benchmark bonds are those that MKI brokers "feel best represent their sectors" and are reviewed daily to determine the most active issues in each sector.

Figure 21-3

Quotes on Reuters Terminal for Long Industrial Investment-Grade Bellwether Issues (December 30, 1993)

MKI Corporate Bonds – Long Industrials   Index <1MKI>   1MKN

CUSIP	Issuer	Coupon	Maturity	PX Type	Bid	Ask
048825AZ6	ARCO	09.125	01-Aug-2031	S	080.000	075.000
097023AD7	BOEING	08.750	15-Aug-2021	S	070.000	065.000
099599AJ1	BORDEN	07.875	15-Feb-2023	S	140.000	135.000
149123BD2	CAT	08.000	15-Feb-2023	S	080.000	075.000
191219AP9	COCA COLA	08.500	01-Feb-2022	S	080.000	072.000
247361WH7	DELTA	09.750	15-May-2021	S	290.000	275.000
263534AW9	DUPONT	08.250	15-Jan-2022	S	092.000	088.000
263534BA6	DUPONT	07.950	15-Jan-2023	S	093.000	088.000
345370BL3	FORD	08.875	15-Nov-2022	S	107.000	102.000
362320AU7	GTE	07.830	01-May-2023	S	110.000	100.000
370442AD7	GM	08.125	15-Apr-2016	S	120.000	110.000
373298BG2	GA PAC	09.500	15-May-2022	S	188.000	178.000
482584AQ2	KMART	07.950	01-Feb-2023	S	087.000	083.000
494368AP8	KIM CLARK	07.875	01-Feb-2023	S	077.000	070.000
573275AP9	MARTIN MERE	07.750	15-Apr-2023	S	105.000	095.000
607059A25	MOBIL	07.625	23-Feb-2033	S	070.000	065.000
751277AR5	RALSTON	08.125	01-Feb-2023	S	160.000	150.000
812387BA5	SEARS	09.375	01-Nov-2011	S	095.000	085.000
88168BB6	TEXACO	08.000	01-Aug-2032	S	078.000	073.000
887315AK5	TIME	09.125	15-Jan-2013	S	185.000	175.000
DD5280142	WEYERHAUSER	07.500	01-Mar-2013	S	060.000	050.000

Source: Reuters Terminal, page 1MKN

Figure 21-4
Quotes on Reuters Terminal for High-Yield Bellwether Issues
(December 30, 1993)

				PX		
CUSIP	Issuer	Coupon	Maturity	Type	Bid	Ask
029717AG0	AMER STD	11.375	15-May-2002	D	111.000	111.750
099733AA5	BORG	09.125	01-May-2003	D	102.500	104.000
170032AJ5	CHIQUITA	09.625	15-Nov-2004	D	102.000	102.500
210741AF1	CONTAINER CO	13.500	01-Dec-1999	D	110.000	111.000
210741AJ3	CONTAINER	09.750	01-Apr-2003	D	103.250	104.000
211177AC4	CONT CABLE	12.875	01-Nov-2004	D	112.000	113.000
297015AB5	ESSEX	10.000	01-May-2003	D	100.000	100.750
347460AD9	FT HOWARD	12.625	01-Nov-2000	D	104.750	105.250
386532AD7	GRAND UNION	12.250	15-Jul-2002	D	105.250	106.000
465642AM8	ITEL	13.000	15-Jan-1999	D	104.000	104.500
486168AC1	KAUFMAN BRD	09.375	01-May-2003	D	102.750	103.250
501044AX9	KROGER	10.000	01-May-1999	D	108.000	109.500
556141AA7	MACY	14.500	15-Nov-2001	D	018.500	019.250
579468AA7	MCCAW CELL	12.950	30-Mar-2000	D	105.500	106.250
690768AU0	OWENS ILL	11.000	01-Dec-2003	D	115.250	118.750
747633AH8	QUANTUM	13.000	15-Mar-2004	D	108.000	108.875
747633AJ4	QUANTUM	10.375	01-Jun-2003	D	121.000	122.000
74960HAD7	RJR	15.000	15-May-2001	D	103.750	104.500
786514AC3	SAFEWAY	10.000	01-Dec-2001	D	111.000	112.000
812139AA1	SEALY	09.500	01-May-2003	D	103.500	104.250
861589AC3	STONE CONTAI	11.500	01-Sep-1999	D	084.000	085.000
862099AA6	STOP&SHOP	09.750	01-Feb-2002	D	112.000	113.000
90026AN6	TURNER	12.000	15-Oct-2001	D	108.500	109.000

MKI Corporate Bonds – High Yield   Index <1MKI>   1MKQ

Source: Reuters Terminal, page 1MKQ

involve a public offering. The private placement market has undergone a major change since the adoption of SEC Rule 144A in 1990, which allows the trading of privately placed securities among qualified institutional buyers. Not all private placements are Rule 144A private placement. Consequently, the private placement market can be divided into two sectors: the traditional market that includes non-144A securities, and the market for 144A securities. According to IDD Information Services, in 1991, Rule 144A private placements were $17 billion compared to $76 billion traditional private placements.[15]

Rule 144A private placement are now underwritten by investment bankers on a firm commitment basis, just as with publicly issued bonds. The features in these issues are similar to those of publicly issued bonds described at the outset of this chapter. For example, the restrictions imposed on the borrower are less onerous than for traditional private placement issues. For underwritten issues, the size of the offering is comparable to that of publicly offered bonds.

Unlike publicly issued bonds, the issuers of privately placed issues tend to be less well known. In this way, the private placement market shares a common characteristic with the bank loan market that we will discuss in Chapter 22. Borrowers in the publicly issued bond market are typically large corporations. Issuers of privately placed bonds tend to be medium-size corporations. Those corporations that borrow from banks tend to be small-size corporations.

To see how important the private placement market is as a source of funds for nonfinancial corporations, Table 21-3 shows the issuance of publicly offered and privately placed bonds for the years 1975 through 1991. At year-end 1991, there was $250 billion of outstanding privately placed debt of non-financial corporations compared to $800 billion of publicly offered bonds. Outstanding bank loans to nonfinancial corporations as of year-end 1991 were $530 billion.[16]

While the liquidity of issues has increased since Rule 144A became effective, it is still not comparable to that of publicly offered issues. Yields on privately placed debt issues are still higher than those on publicly offered bonds.

Table 21-3

Issuance of Publicly Offered and Privately Placed Bonds by Nonfinancial Corporations, 1975-1991 (billions of dollars, annual rate)

Type of bonds	1975-1980	1981-1985	1986-1991
Public	21.0	35.6	87.6
Private	14.7	19.8	64.8

Source: Mark S. Carey, Stephen D. Prose, John D. Reas, and Gregory Udell, "Recent Developments in the Market for Privately Placed Debt," Federal Reserve Bulletin (February 1993), p. 78.

---

[15] Mark S. Carey, Stephen D. Prose, John D. Reas, and Gregory Udell, "Recent Developments in the Market for Privately Placed Debt," *Federal Reserve Bulletin* (February 1993), p. 90.

[16] Carey, Prose, Reas, and Udell, "Recent Developments in the Market for Privately Placed Debt," p. 78.

However, one market observer reports that the premium that must be paid by borrowers in the private placement market has decreased as investment banking firms have committed capital and trading personnel to making markets for securities issued under Rule 144A.[17]

RISK AND RETURN IN THE CORPORATE BOND MARKET

Because of the credit risk associated with corporate bonds, it is expected that the performance of this sector of the market would outperform Treasury securities. Moreover, within the corporate bond market, because of the greater credit risk associated with high-yield bonds compared to investment-grade bonds, it is expected that the former would outperform the latter. Below we discuss the several empirical studies that address these questions.

Performance of Investment-Grade Corporate Bonds

A study by Thomas Bennett, Stephen Esser, and Christian Roth reported the risk and reward relationship in the corporate bond market.[18] Figure 21-5 shows the actual yield spread over U.S. Treasuries from 1983 to 1992 for the four investment-rate ratings and the first two noninvestment grade ratings. Also shown in the figure is the yield spread required to offset credit losses for each quality rating. As indicated in Figure 21-5, investors have been rewarded for accepting corporate credit risk.

Figure 21-5
Actual versus Required Corporate Bond Yield Premium, 1983-1992

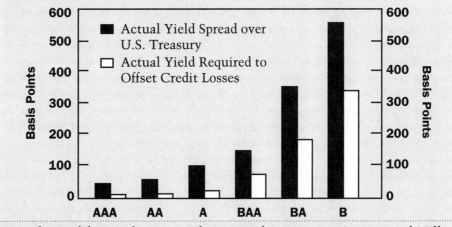

Data obtained from Salomon Brothers, Moody's Investors Service, and Miller Anderson & Sherrerd

Source: Thomas L. Bennett, Stephen F. Esser, and Christian G. Roth, Corporate Credit Risk and Reward, Miller Anderson & Sherrerd, 1993.

---

[17] Victoria Keefe, "Underwritten 144A Deals Surge," *Corporate Financing Week* (August 31, 1992), pp. 1 and 10.

[18] Thomas L. Bennett, Stephen F. Esser, and Christian G. Roth, *Corporate Credit Risk and Reward,* Miller Anderson & Sherrerd, 1993.

Table 21-4 shows the annualized total returns and return spreads versus U.S. Treasuries for investment-grade corporates and the Standard & Poor's 500 for various periods ending 1992. The two key findings reported in Table 21-4 are (1) corporate bonds outperformed Treasuries, and (2) the lower the credit rating the better the performance relative to Treasuries. Thus, the ratings appear to do a good job of differentiating the credit risk associated with investing in corporate bonds.

Performance of High-Yield Bonds

There have been several studies of the risk and return in the high-yield bond market. Historically, the promised yields offered on high-yield bonds have been substantial. For example, the yield spread over Treasury bonds between 1980 and 1989 ranged from 300 to 650 basis points, at least according to the Drexel Burnham Lambert 100 Bond Index. In late 1989 and 1990, a turbulent time for the high-yield sector, the yield spread increased to 700 to 800 basis points. Is this spread justified by a higher potential default rate? This intriguing question has been extensively investigated.

Table 21-4

Annualized Total Returns and Return Spreads for U.S. Treasuries, Investment-Grade Corporates, and S&P 500 for Periods Ended December 1992

	20 Years	10 Years	5 Years
Treasuries	9.13%	11.63%	10.85%
Corporates	9.64%	12.53%	11.46%
Spread vs. Treasuries	+51 basis points	+90 basis points	+61 basis points
AAA	9.20%	11.89%	11.04%
Spread vs. Treasuries	+7 basis points	+27 basis points	+27 basis points
AA	9.35%	12.18%	11.33%
Spread vs. Treasuries	+23 basis points	+55 basis points	+48 basis points
A	9.63%	12.58%	11.54%
Spread vs. Treasuries	+50 basis points	+95 basis points	+69 basis points
BBB	10.37%	13.45%	11.68%
Spread vs. Treasuries	+124 basis points	+182 basis points	+83 basis points
S&P 500	11.33%	16.18%	15.88%

Data obtained from Lehman Brothers and Miller Anderson & Sherrerd.

Source: Thomas L. Bennett, Stephen F. Esser, and Christian G. Roth, Corporate Credit Risk and Reward, Miller Anderson & Sherrerd, 1993.

Most of the research on the high-yield bond sector focuses on default rates.[19] From an investment perspective, default rates by themselves are not of paramount significance: it is perfectly possible for a portfolio of high-yield bonds to suffer defaults and to outperform Treasuries at the same time, provided the yield spread of the portfolio is sufficiently high to offset the losses from default. Furthermore, because holders of defaulted bonds typically recover at least 30% of the face amount of their investment, the default loss rate is substantially lower than the default rate.[20] Therefore, focusing exclusively on default rates merely highlights the worst possible outcome that a diversified portfolio of high-yield bonds would suffer, assuming all defaulted bonds would be totally worthless. Assessing the potential rewards from investing in this market sector requires understanding not only default and default loss rates, but also total returns offered over various investment horizons.

First, we will look at what research has found for the default rate experience of low-quality corporate bonds. In their 1987 study, Altman and Nammacher found that the annual default rate for low-rated corporate debt was 2.15%, a figure that Altman has updated since then to 2.40%. Drexel Burnham Lambert's (DBL) estimates have also shown default rates of about 2.40% per year. Asquith, Mullins, and Wolff, however, found that nearly one out of every three junk bonds defaults. The large discrepancy arises because the researchers use three different definitions of "default rate"; even if applied to the same universe of bonds (which they are not), all three results could be valid simultaneously.[21]

Altman and Nammacher define the default rate as the par value of all high-yield bonds that defaulted in a given calendar year, divided by the total par value outstanding during the year. Their estimates (2.15% and 2.40%) are simple averages of the annual default rates over a number of years. DBL takes the cumulative dollar value of all defaulted high-yield bonds, divides by the cumulative dollar value of all high-yield issuance, and further divides by the

---

[19] See, for example, Edward I. Altman, "Measuring Corporate Bond Mortality and Performance," *Journal of Finance* (September 1989), pp. 909-22; Edward I. Altman, "Research Update: Mortality Rates and Losses, Bond Rating Drift," unpublished study prepared for a workshop sponsored by Merrill Lynch Merchant Banking Group, High-Yield Sales and Trading, 1989; Edward I. Altman and Scott A. Nammacher, *Investing in Junk Bonds* (New York: John Wiley, 1987); Paul Asquith, David W. Mullins, Jr., and Eric D. Wolff, "Original Issue High-Yield Bonds: Aging Analysis of Defaults, Exchanges, and Calls," *Journal of Finance* (September 1989), pp. 923-52; Marshall Blume and Donald Keim, "Risk and Return Characteristics of Lower-Grade Bonds 1977-1987," Working Paper (8-89), Rodney L. White Center for Financial Research, Wharton School, University of Pennsylvania, 1989; Marshall Blume and Donald Keim, "Realized Returns and Defaults on Lower-Grade Bonds," Rodney L. White Center for Financial Research, Wharton School, University of Pennsylvania, 1989; Bond Investors Association, "Bond Investors Association Issues Definitive Corporate Default Statistics," press release dated August 15, 1989; Gregory T. Hradsky and Robert D. Long, "High-Yield Default Losses and the Return Performance of Bankrupt Debt," *Financial Analysts Journal* (July-August 1989), pp. 38-49; "Historical Default Rates of Corporate Bond Issuers 1970-1988," *Moody's Special Report*, July 1989 (New York: Moody's Investors Service); "High-Yield Bond Default Rates," Standard & Poor's *Creditweek*, August 7, 1989, pp. 21-3; David Wyss, Christopher Probyn, and Robert de Angelis, "The Impact of Recession on High-Yield Bonds," DRI-McGraw-Hill (Washington, D.C.: Alliance for Capital Access, 1989); and the 1984-1989 issues of *High-Yield Market Report: Financing America's Futures* (New York and Beverly Hills: Drexel Burnham Lambert, Inc.).

[20] For instance, a default rate of 5% and an average recovery rate of 30% imply a default loss rate of only 3.5% (70% of 5%).

[21] As a parallel, we know that the mortality rate in the United States is currently less than 1% per year, but we also know that 100% of all humans (eventually) die.

weighted-average number of years outstanding to obtain an average annual default rate. Asquith, Mullins, and Wolff use a cumulative default statistic. For all bonds issued in a given year, the default rate is the total par value of defaulted issues as of the date of their study, divided by the total par amount originally issued to obtain a cumulative default rate. Their result (that about one in three high-yield bonds defaults) is not normalized by the number of years outstanding.

While all three measures are useful indicators of bond default propensity, they are not directly comparable. Even when restated on an annualized basis, they do not all measure the same quantity. The default statistics from all studies, however, are surprisingly similar once cumulative rates have been annualized. A majority of studies place the annual default rates for all original-issue high-yield bonds between 3% and 4%.[22]

However, as we indicated earlier, default rates do not tell us how the securities in this market sector have performed. While there have been a number of studies on total returns, the findings have not been uniform, as the periods and the bonds studied differ substantially among researchers. Furthermore, each study employs different assumptions about a broad range of important factors, including reinvestment rates, treatment of defaults, and accrued interest. Recent studies by Cheung, Bencivenga, and Fabozzi,[23] Blume, Keim, and Patel,[24] and Cornell and Green[25] provide empirical evidence on the performance of the high-yield bond market. The first two studies examine originalissue high-yield bonds. Both find that from 1977 (the start of the modern high-yield bond market) to December 31, 1989, the actual return on originalissue high-yield bonds was greater than that on Treasuries and high-grade corporate bonds, but less than that on common stock. As a result, both studies conclude that there is no evidence that this sector of the bond market is systematically mispriced.

Cornell and Green do not look at individual bonds. Instead, for the period 1977 to 1989, they investigate the performance of mutual funds specializing in high-yield bonds. There are several drawbacks to this approach. First, there is an implicit assumption that the high-yield market is efficient so that fund managers cannot systematically find undervalued bonds. Second, fund managers are given the discretion to not fully allocate their funds to the high-yield market. To the extent that mutual fund managers pursue an active assetallocation strategy between the money market and long-term debt markets, performance will be misleading because it encompasses the timing ability of managers. The third disadvantage is that mutual fund managers are not restricted to original issue high-yield bonds (i.e., they can invest in fallen

---

[22] The Altman and Nammacher and Hradsky and Long studies cite significantly lower default rates, but they employ a definition of default rate that ignores the effect of aging on the propensity to default.

[23] Rayner Cheung, Joseph C. Bencivenga, and Frank J. Fabozzi, "Original Issue High-Yield Bonds: Historical Return and Default Experiences 1977-1989," *Journal of Fixed Income* (September 1992), pp. 58-76.

[24] Marshall E. Blume, Donald B. Keim, and Sandeep A. Patel, "Returns and Volatility of Low-Grade Bonds 1977-1989," *Journal of Finance* (March 1991), pp. 49-74.

[25] Bradford Cornell and K. Green, "The Investment Performance of Low-Grade Bond Funds," *Journal of Finance* (March 1991), pp. 29-48.

angels). Finally, there are management fees, administrative fees, and custodial fees that reduce returns. Despite these drawbacks, the Cornell and Green approach provides useful information about this sector of the bond market. They conclude that high-yield bonds are fairly priced relative to high-grade bonds, after adjusting for risk.

Consequently, none of the studies seem to suggest that investing in the high-yield market offers exceptional value. Rather, long-run returns are in line with what capital market theory would suggest: in the long run, high-yield bonds have outperformed both high-grade corporate bonds and Treasuries but have been outperformed by common stock. Therefore, any claim of superior performance by high-yield bonds must be taken with the greatest caution.

EUROBOND MARKET

As explained in Chapter 2, the external market is commonly called the Euromarket. It includes securities with the following distinguishing features: (1) they are underwritten by an international syndicate, (2) at issuance they are offered simultaneously to investors in a number of countries, (3) they are issued outside the jurisdiction of any single country, and (4) they are in unregistered form. A Eurobond refers to bonds issued with these characteristics. Corporations in the United States and other countries, as well as government entities, have raised funds in this market.

The Eurobond market is divided into sectors depending on the currency in which the issue is denominated. For example, when Eurobonds are denominated in U.S. dollars, they are referred to as **Eurodollar bonds**. Likewise, Eurobonds denominated in Japanese yen are referred to as **Euroyen bonds**.

Although Eurobonds are typically registered on a national stock exchange, the most common being the Luxembourg, London, or Zurich exchanges, the bulk of all trading is in the over-the-counter market. Listing is purely to circumvent restrictions imposed on some institutional investors who are prohibited from purchasing securities that are not listed on an exchange. Some of the stronger issuers privately place issues with international institutional investors.

The Eurobond market has been characterized by new and innovative bond structures to accommodate particular needs of issuers and investors. There are the "plain vanilla," fixed-rate coupon bonds, referred to as **Euro straights**. Because these are issued on an unsecured basis, they are usually issued by high-quality entities. Coupon payments are made annually, rather than semiannually, because of the higher cost of distributing interest to geographically dispersed bondholders. There are also zero-coupon bond issues, deferred-coupon issues, and step-up issues, all of which were described earlier in this chapter.

Dual currency bonds—There are three types of dual currency bonds that pay coupon interest in one currency but pay the principal in a different currency. For the first type, the exchange rate that is used to convert the principal and coupon payments into a specific currency is specified at the time the bond is issued. The second type differs from the first in that the applicable exchange rate is the rate that prevails at the time a cash flow is made (i.e., at the spot exchange rate at the time a payment is made). The third type is one that offers to either the investor or the issuer the choice of currency. These bonds are commonly referred to as **option currency bonds**. A specific example is the Index Currency Option Note (ICON) introduced by the Long-Term Credit Bank of Japan in 1985.

Convertible Bonds and Bonds with Warrants

A convertible Eurobond is one that can be converted into another asset. Bonds with attached warrants represent a large part of the Eurobond market. A warrant grants the owner of the warrant the right to enter into another financial transaction with the issuer if the owner will benefit as a result of exercising. Most warrants are detachable from the host bond so that the bondholder may detach the warrant from the bond and sell it.

There are a wide array of bonds with warrants. An **equity warrant** permits the warrant owner to buy the common stock of the issuer at a specified price. A **debt warrant** entitles the warrant owner to buy additional bonds from the issuer at the same price and yield as the host bond. The debt warrant owner will benefit if interest rates decline because a bond with a higher coupon can be purchased from the same issuer. A **currency warrant** permits the warrant owner to exchange one currency for another at a set price (i.e., a fixed exchange rate). This feature protects the bondholder against a depreciation of the foreign currency in which the bond's cash flows are denominated. There are also **gold warrants**, which allow the warrant holder to purchase gold from the issuer of the bond.

Floating-Rate Notes

There are a wide variety of floating-rate Eurobond notes. In the Eurobond market, almost all floating-rate notes are denominated in U.S. dollars with non-U.S. banks being the major issuers. The coupon rate on a Eurodollar floating-rate note is some stated margin over the London interbank offered rate (LIBOR), the bid on LIBOR (referred to as LIBID), or the arithmetic average of LIBOR and LIBID (referred to as LIMEAN). The size of the spread reflects the perceived credit risk of the issuer, margins available in the syndicated loan market, and the liquidity of the issue. Typical reset periods for the coupon rate are either every six months or every quarter, with the rate tied to six-month or three-month LIBOR, respectively. That is, the length of the reset period and the maturity of the index used to establish the rate for the period are matched.

Many issues have either a minimum coupon rate (or floor) that the coupon rate cannot fall below and a maximum coupon rate (or cap) that the coupon rate cannot rise above. An issue that has both a floor and a cap is said to be "collared". There are some issues that grant the borrower the right to convert the floating coupon rate into a fixed coupon rate at some time. There are some issues referred to as **drop-lock bonds**, which automatically change the floating coupon rate into a fixed coupon rate under certain circumstances.

A floating-rate note issue may have a stated maturity date, or it may be a **perpetual** or **undated issue**, with no stated maturity date. The perpetual issue was introduced into the Eurobond market in 1984. For floating-rate notes that do mature, the term is usually greater than 5 years, with the typical maturity being between 7 and 12 years. There are callable and putable floating-rate notes; some issues are both callable and putable.

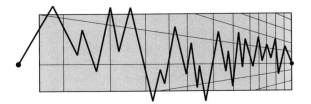

SUMMARY

Corporate bonds are debt obligating a corporation to pay periodic interest with full repayment at maturity. The promises of the corporate bond issuer and the rights of the investors are set forth in the bond indenture. Provisions to be specified include call and sinking fund provisions, as well as limitations on further debt and on management powers.

Security for bonds may be real or personal property. A mortgage bond grants the bondholders a lien against the pledged assets. Collateral trust bonds are secured by securities owned by the issuer. Debenture bonds are not secured by a specific pledge of property; bondholders have the claim of general creditors on all assets of the issuer not pledged specifically to secure other debt. Subordinated debenture bonds are issues that rank after secured debt, after debenture bonds, and often after some general creditors in their claim on assets and earnings.

Special corporate bond features include convertible and exchangeable bonds, units of debt with warrants, putable bonds, zero-coupon bonds, and floating-rate securities.

The credit risk of a corporate borrower can be gauged by the quality rating assigned by the commercial rating companies. The four rating companies are Duff and Phelps Credit Rating Co., Fitch Investors Service, Moody's Investors Service, and Standard & Poor's Corporation. Issues rated in the top ratings of all raters are referred to as investment-grade bonds; those below the top four ratings are called noninvestment-grade bonds, high-yield bonds, or junk bonds.

Event risk refers to the possibility of an event that leads investors to doubt the ability of an issuer to make interest and principal payments. Event risk can occur because of a natural or industrial accident, or a takeover or corporate restructuring.

The high-yield sector of the corporate bond market has permitted the shifting of corporate borrowing from commercial banks to the public bond market. Several complex bond structures are issued in the high-yield sector of the corporate bond market. These include deferred-coupon bonds (deferred-interest bonds, step-up bonds, and payment-in-kind bonds) and extendable reset bonds.

While corporate bond trading takes place both on exchanges and in the OTC market, the real market is the OTC market. Trading volume in this market swamps that of exchange trading.

The private placement market for corporate debt is an important source of financing for nonfinancial corporations. As a result of Rule 144A, the liquidity of privately placed securities has improved and the spread between publicly offered and privately placed issues has narrowed.

Studies of the historical risk and return of the corporate bond market indicate that long-run returns for are in line with what capital market theory would suggest. That is, in the long-run, investment-grade corporate bonds have outperformed Treasury securities and high-yield bonds have outperformed both investment-grade corporate bonds and Treasuries, but have been outperformed by common stock,

The Eurobond market is divided into sectors based on the currency in which the issue is denominated. Many innovative bond structures have been introduced in the Eurobond market, such as dual-currency issues and various types of convertible bonds and bonds with warrants. The floating-rate sector of the Eurobond market is dominated by U.S.-dollar-denominated issues.

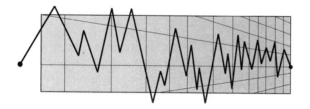

QUESTIONS

1. What is meant by an industrial bond?

2. a. What is the difference between refunding protection and call protection?

   b. Which provides the investor with greater protection that the bonds will be acquired by the issuer prior to the stated maturity date?

3. What is a sinking fund requirement in a bond issue?

4. "A sinking fund provision in a bond issue benefits the investor."
Do you agree with this statement?

5. What is the difference between a convertible bond and an exchangeable bond?

6. a. What role do rating companies play in financial markets?

   b. Who are the companies that assign ratings to debt obligations?

7. What is the difference between a fallen angel and an original-issue high-yield bond?

8. What is event risk?

9. Give two examples of event risk.

10. Indicate why you agree or disagree with the following statement: "Today, the proceeds from most original-issue high-yield bonds are used for leveraged buyouts and recapitalizations."

11. a. "A floating-rate note will always trade in the market at par value." Do you agree with this statement?

    b. "A floating-rate note and an extendable reset bond both have coupon rates readjusted periodically. Therefore, they are basically the same instrument." Do you agree with this statement?

12. a. What is a payment-in-kind bond?

    b. An investor who purchases a payment-in-kind bond will find that increased interest rate volatility will have an adverse economic impact. If interest rates rise substantially, there will be an adverse consequence. So too will a substantial decline in interest rates have adverse consequences. Why?

13. Indicate why you agree or disagree with the following statements pertaining to the private placement corporate debt market.

    a. Since Rule 144A became effective, all privately placed issues can be bought and sold in the market.

    b. Traditional privately placed issues now are similar to publicly offered securities.

    c. Rule 144A securities are not underwritten by an investment banking firm.

14. Indicate why you agree or disagree with the following statement: "Investing in the junk bond market offers the opportunity to realize superior investment returns compared to other debt instruments and common stock."

15. a. What is meant by a Eurobond?

    b. How are the sectors of the Eurobond market classified?

16. What is a dual-currency bond?

17. What type of warrants can be attached to a host Eurobond?

Medium-Term Note, Bank Loan, and Preferred Stock Markets

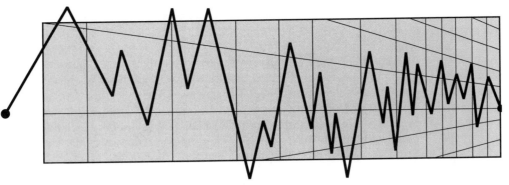

LEARNING OBJECTIVES

After reading this chapter you will understand:

- what a medium-term note is.

- the difference between the primary offering of a medium-term note and a corporate bond.

- what a structured medium-term note is and the flexibility it affords issuers.

- what a syndicated loan is.

- the basic terms of a loan.

- the two different ways a syndicated loan can be sold; either through assignments or participations.

- the difference between the various types of preferred stock; including fixed-rate, adjustable-rate, auction, and remarketed preferred stock.

- who are the major buyers of preferred stock.

- the basic provisions in the Bankruptcy Reform Act of 1978.

- the difference between a liquidation and a reorganization.

- the principle of absolute priority in a bankruptcy and the different hypotheses as to why there typically is a violation of absolute priority.

Thus far, we have discussed two senior corporate instruments: corporate bonds and commercial paper. In this chapter, we look at three other senior corporate instruments: medium-term notes, banks loans, and preferred stock. The first two are corporate debt obligations and the third is a form of equity that has a superior claim to common stock in the case of liquidation of a corporation.

MEDIUM-TERM NOTES

A medium-term note (MTN) is a corporate debt instrument, with the unique characteristic that notes are offered continuously to investors by an agent of the issuer. Investors can select from several maturity ranges: 9 months to 1 year, more than 1 year to 18 months, more than 18 months to 2 years, and so on up to 30 years. Medium-term notes are registered with the Securities and Exchange Commission under Rule 415 (the shelf registration rule) which gives a corporation the maximum flexibility for issuing securities on a continuous basis.

The term "medium-term note" to describe this corporate debt instrument is misleading. Traditionally, the term "note" or "medium-term" was used to refer to debt issues with a maturity greater than 1 year but less than 10 years. Certainly this is not a characteristic of MTNs since they have been sold with maturities from nine months to 30 years, and even longer. For example, in July 1993, Walt Disney Corporation issued a security with a 100-year maturity off its medium-term note shelf registration.

General Motors Acceptance Corporation first used medium-term notes in 1972 to fund automobile loans with maturities of five years and less. The purpose of the MTN was to fill the funding gap between commercial paper and long-term bonds. It is for this reason that they are referred to as "medium term." The medium-term notes were issued directly to investors without the use of an agent. Only a few corporations issued MTNs in the 1970s. About $800 million of MTNs were outstanding by 1981. The market was hampered from developing for two reasons. First, because the issues must be registered with the SEC, registration costs made the issuance of MTNs expensive relative to other funding sources. This cost could be avoided by privately placing MTNs. However, as we explained in Chapter 21, private placements carry a higher interest cost. Second, there was no secondary market for MTNs.

The modern-day medium-term note was pioneered by Merrill Lynch in 1981. The first medium-term note issuer was Ford Motor Credit Company. By 1983, GMAC and Chrysler Financial used Merrill Lynch as an agent to issue medium-term notes. Merrill Lynch and other investment banking firms committed funds to make a secondary market for MTNs, thereby improving liquidity. In 1982, Rule 415 was adopted making it easier for issuers to sell registered securities on a continuous basis.

Although we elected to discuss medium-term notes in our discussion of domestic corporate debt, they are also issued by foreign corporations, federal agencies, supranational institutions, and sovereign countries.

Size of Market and Issuers[1]

The public offering of MTNs by U.S. corporations increased from $5.5 billion in 1983, to $74.2 billion in 1992. By year-end 1992, $330 billion was issued over this ten-year period. In 1983 there were 12 issuers of MTNs. By 1992, 402 U.S. corporations had issued MTNs over the ten-year period, including 155 financial corporations and 247 nonfinancial corporations.

The growth of the domestic medium-term note market and its importance as a funding source can be seen by comparing it to the amount of domestic public corporate debt issued. The ratio of outstanding MTNs to the amount of outstanding public corporate debt (MTNs plus public corporate bonds) was 9% in 1989 and 16% in 1992. Because MTNs are mostly investment grade debt obligations, a more appropriate measure of the relative size of the market is the volume of investment-grade MTN issuance as a percentage of total investment-grade debt issuance. Using this measure, the share of investment-grade debt issued as MTNs increased from 18% in 1983 to 37% in 1992, reaching a peak of 42% in 1990.

Borrowers have flexibility in designing MTNs to satisfy their own needs. They can issue fixed- or floating-rate debt. The coupon payments can be denominated in U.S. dollars or in a foreign currency. In Chapter 21, we described the various security structures. MTNs have been designed with the same features. For example, there are MTNs backed by equipment trust certificates issued by railways and subordinated notes issued by bank holding companies. In Chapter 27, we discuss asset-backed securities.

When the treasurer of a corporation is contemplating an offer of either a MTN or corporate bonds, there are two factors that affect the decision. The most obvious is the cost of the funds raised after consideration of registration and distribution costs. This cost is referred to as **all-in-cost of funds**. The second is the flexibility afforded to the issuer in structuring the offering. The tremendous growth in the MTN market is evidence of the relative advantage of MTNs with respect to cost and flexibility for some offerings. However, the fact that there are corporations that raise funds by issuing both bond and MTNs is evidence that there is no absolute advantage in all instances and market environments.

---

[1] Unless otherwise indicated, the data cited in this chapter was reported in Leland E. Crabbe, "The Anatomy of the Medium-Term Note Market," *Federal Reserve Bulletin* (August 1993), pp. 752-68.

As with corporate bonds and commercial paper, MTNs are rated by the nationally recognized rating companies. More than 99% of all MTNs issued since 1983 received an investment grade rating at the time of issuance. By year-end 1992, 98% of the outstanding MTNs were rated investment grade. Of the $74 billion in MTNs offered in 1992, $51 billion were rated single A. There were six firms who offered a total of $540 million in 1992 who were rated one notch below investment grade (Ba).

The Primary Market

Medium-term notes differ from corporate bonds in the manner in which they are distributed to investors when they are initially sold. Although some investment-grade corporate bond issues are sold on a best-efforts basis, typically they are underwritten by investment bankers. MTNs have been traditionally distributed on a best-efforts basis by either an investment banking firm or other broker/dealers acting as agents. Another difference between corporate bonds and MTNs is that when MTNs are offered they are usually sold in relatively small amounts on a continuous or an intermittent basis, while corporate bonds are sold in large discrete offerings.

A corporation that wants an MTN program will file a shelf registration with the SEC for the offering of securities. While the SEC registration for MTN offerings is between $100 and $1 billion, once the total is sold, the issuer can file another shelf registration.[2] The registration will include a list of the investment banking firms, usually two to four, that the corporation has arranged to act as agents to distribute the MTNs. The large New York-based investment banking firms dominate the distribution market for MTNs.

The issuer then posts rates over a range of maturities: for example, nine months to one year, one year to eighteen months, eighteen months to two years, and annually thereafter. Table 24-1 provides an example of an offering rate schedule for a medium-term note program. Usually, an issuer will post rates as a spread over a Treasury security of comparable maturity. For example, in the 2- to 3-year maturity range, the offering rate is 35 basis points over the 2-year Treasury. Since the 2-year Treasury is shown in the table at 4%, the offering rate is 4.35%. Rates will not be posted for maturity ranges that the issuer does not desire to sell. For example, in Table 24-1 the issuer does not wish to sell MTNs with a maturity of less than 2 years.

The agents will then make the offering rate schedule available to their investor base interested in MTNs. An investor who is interested in the offering will contact the agent. In turn, the agent contacts the issuer to confirm the terms of the transaction. Since the maturity range in the offering rate schedule does not specify a maturity date, the investor can choose the final maturity, subject to approval by the issuer. The minimum size that an investor can purchase of an MTN offering typically ranges from $1 million to $25 million.

The rate offering schedule can be changed at any time by the issuer either in response to changing market conditions or because the issuer has raised the desired amount of funds at a given maturity. In the latter case, the issuer can either not post a rate for that maturity range or lower the rate.

---

[2] Crabbe, "The Anatomy of the Medium-Term Note Market."

Table 22-1

An Offering Rate Schedule for a Medium-Term Note Program

Medium-Term Notes			Treasury Securities	
Maturity Range	Yield (percent)	Yield Spread of MTN over Treasury Securities (basis points)	Maturity	Yield (percent)
9 months to 12 months	(a)	(a)	9 months	3.35
12 months to 18 months	(a)	(a)	12 months	3.50
18 months to 2 years	(a)	(a)	18 months	3.80
2 years to 5 years	4.35	35	2 years	4.00
3 years to 4 years	5.05	55	3 years	4.50
4 years to 5 years	5.60	60	4 years	5.00
5 years to 6 years	6.05	60	5 years	5.45
6 years to 7 years	6.10	40	6 years	5.70
7 years to 8 years	6.30	40	7 years	5.90
8 years to 9 years	6.45	40	8 years	6.05
9 years to 10 years	6.60	40	10 years	6.20
10 years	6.70	40	10 years	6.30

a No rate posted

Source: Leland E. Crabbe, "The Anatomy of the Medium-Term Note Market," Federal Reserve Bulletin (August 1993), p. 753.

Structured MTNs

At one time the typical MTN was a fixed-rate debenture that was noncallable. Of the $283 billion outstanding, most have this characteristic.[3] It is common today for issuers of MTNs to couple their offerings with transactions in the derivative markets (options, futures/forwards, swaps, caps, and floors) so as to create debt obligations with more interesting risk/return features than are available in the corporate bond market. Specifically, an issue can be floating-rate over all or part of the life of the security and the coupon reset formula can be based on a benchmark interest rate, equity index or individual stock price, a foreign exchange rate, or a commodity index. There are even MTNs with coupon reset formulas that vary inversely with a benchmark interest rate. That is, if the benchmark interest rate increases (decreases), the coupon rate decreases (increases). Debt instruments with this coupon characteristic are called **inverse floating rate-securities** and we will take a closer look at them in Chapter 23. MTNs can have various embedded options included.

---

[3] Crabbe, "The Anatomy of the Medium-Term Note Market."

MTNs created when the issuer simultaneously transacts in the derivative markets are called **structured notes**. It is estimated today that new issue volume of structured notes is 20% to 30% of new issuance volume.[4] The most common derivative instrument used in creating structured notes is a swap. The development of the MTN market has been fostered by commercial banks involvement in the swap market. While commercial banks offer swaps, they are restricted by the Glass-Steagall Act in their underwriting of corporate securities. However, banks may act as agents in distributing corporate debt obligations, as they do with commercial paper. The structured MTN product allows banks to participate in the distribution of corporate debt in which they realize fee income from distribution and from swaps.

By using the derivative markets in combination with an offering, borrowers are able to create investment vehicles that are more customized for institutional investors to satisfy their investment objectives, but who are forbidden from using swaps for hedging. Moreover, it allows institutional investors who are restricted to investing in investment-grade debt issues the opportunity to participate in other asset classes to make a market play. For example, an investor who buys an MTN whose coupon rate is tied to the performance of the S&P 500 is participating in the equity market without owning common stock. If the coupon rate is tied to a foreign stock index, the investor is participating in the equity market of a foreign country without owning foreign common stock. In exchange for creating a structured note product, borrowers can reduce their funding costs by as much as 10 to 15 basis points.[5]

How do borrowers or their agents find investors who are willing to buy structured notes? As explained in Chapter 5, in a typical offering of a corporate bond, the sales force of the underwriting firm will solicit interest in the offering from its customer base. That is, the sales forces will make an inquiry. In the structured note market, the process is often quite different. Because of the small size of an offering and the flexibility to customize the offering in the swap market, investors can approach an issuer through its agent about designing a security for their needs. This process of customers inquiring of issuers or their agents to design a security is called a *reverse inquiry*. Transactions that originate from reverse inquiries account for a significant share of MTN transactions.[6]

BANK LOAN MARKET

As an alternative to the issuance of securities, a corporation can raise funds by borrowing from a single bank, or from a group of banks called a syndicate of banks. The amount of commercial and industrial loans outstanding as of August 1993 was $591 billion, while at the same time commercial paper outstanding by nonfinancial corporations was $159 billion. While at one time, bank loans were held in the loan portfolio of the bank that made the loan, in

---

[4] Crabbe, "The Anatomy of the Medium-Term Note Market."

[5] James Nevler, "A Crash Course in Structured Notes," *Global Finance* (October 1993), pp. 43-7.

[6] Crabbe, "The Anatomy of the Medium-Term Note Market."

recent years a market has developed to sell off these loans to other banks and nonbank entities.

Syndicated Bank Loans

A **syndicated bank loan** is one in which a group of banks provides funds to the borrower. The need for a group of banks arises because the amount sought by a borrower may be too large for any one bank to be exposed to the credit of that borrower. Therefore, the syndicated bank loan market is used by borrowers who seek to raise a large amount of funds in the loan market rather than through the issuance of securities.

A syndicated loan is arranged by either a bank or a securities house. The arranger then lines up the syndicate. Each bank in the syndicate provides the funds for which it has committed. The banks in the syndicate have the right to subsequently sell their parts of the loan to other banks.

Characteristics of Bank Loans to Corporations

Senior bank loans have a priority position over subordinated lenders (bondholders) with respect to repayment of interest and principal. The interest rate on a syndicated bank loan is a rate that *floats*, which means that the loan rate is based on some reference rate. The loan rate is periodically reset at the reference rate plus a spread. The reference rate is typically LIBOR, although it could be the prime rate (i.e., the rate that a bank charges its most creditworthy customers) or the rate on certificates of deposits.

The term of the loan is fixed. A syndicated loan is typically structured so that it is amortized according to a predetermined schedule, and repayment of principal begins after a specified number of years (typically not longer than five or six years). However, loans in which no repayment of the principal is made until the maturity date can be arranged. Such loans are referred to as **bullet loans**.

Distribution of Loans

Senior loans are distributed by two methods—assignments and participations. Each method has its advantages and relative disadvantages, though the assignment method is the more desirable of the two.

When the holder of a loan is interested in selling his portion, he can do so by passing his interest in the loan by method of **assignment**. In this procedure, the seller transfers all his rights completely to the holder of the assignment, now called the **assignee**. The assignee is said to have **privity of contract** with the borrower. Because of the clear path between the borrower and assignee, the assignment is the more desirable choice of transfer and ownership.

A **participation** involves a holder of a loan "participating out" a portion of his holding in that particular loan. The holder of the participation does not become a party to the loan agreement. His relationship is not with the borrower but with the seller of the participation. Unlike an assignment, a participation does not confer privity of contract on the holder of the participation. However, the holder of the participation has the right to vote on certain legal matters concerning amendments to the loan agreement.

These matters include changes regarding maturity, interest rate, and issues concerning the loan collateral.

Because syndicated loans can be sold in the manner described above, they have become marketable. In response to the large amount of bank loans issued in the 1980s and their strong credit protection, some commercial banks and securities houses have shown a willingness to commit capital and resources to facilitate trading as broker-dealers. Senior bank loans have also been securitized through the same innovations (discussed in Chapters 25 and 27) used for the securitization of mortgage loans.[7]

The further development of the senior bank loan market will no doubt eventually erode the once important distinction between a security and a loan: a security has long been seen as a marketable financial asset, while a loan was not marketable. Interestingly, the trading of these loans is not limited to **performing loans**, which are loans whose borrowers are fulfilling contractual commitments. There is also a market in the trading of **nonperforming loans** (i.e., loans in which the borrower has defaulted).

PREFERRED STOCK

Preferred stock is a class of stock, not a debt instrument, but it shares characteristics of both common stock and debt. Like the holder of common stock, the preferred stockholder is entitled to dividends. Unlike those on common stock, however, dividends are a specified percentage of par or face value. The percentage is called the dividend rate; it need not be fixed, but may float over the life of the issue.

Almost all preferred stock limits the securityholder to the specified amount. Historically, there have been issues entitling the preferred stockholder to participate in earnings distribution beyond the specified amount (based on some formula). Preferred stock with this feature is referred to as **participating preferred stock**.

Failure to make preferred-stock dividend payments cannot force the issuer into bankruptcy. Should the issuer not make a preferred-stock dividend payment (usually made quarterly), one of two things can happen, depending on the terms of the issue. The dividend payment can accrue until it is fully paid—stock with this feature is called **cumulative preferred stock**. If a dividend payment is missed and the securityholder must forgo the payment, the preferred stock is said to be **noncumulative preferred stock**. Failure to make dividend payments may result in imposition of certain restrictions on management. For example, if dividend payments are in arrears, preferred stockholders might be granted voting rights.

Preferred stock has two important similarities with debt, particularly in the case of cumulative preferred stock: (1) the returns to preferred stockholders promised by the issuer are fixed, and (2) preferred stockholders have priority over common stockholders with respect to dividend payments and distribution of assets in the case of bankruptcy. (The position of noncumula-

---

[7] For a discussion of the trading and securitization of senior bank loans, see John H. Carlson and Frank J. Fabozzi (eds.), *The Trading and Securitization of Senior Bank Loans* (Chicago: Probus Publishing, 1992).

tive preferred stock is considerably weaker.) It is because of this second feature that preferred stock is called a senior security. It is senior to common stock. On a balance sheet, preferred stock is classified as equity.

Almost all preferred stock has a sinking fund provision, and some preferred stock is convertible into common stock. Preferred stock may be issued without a maturity date. This is called **perpetual preferred stock**.

As with corporate bonds, preferred stock is rated. The four nationally recognized commercial rating companies that rate corporate bonds also rate preferred stock (Duff & Phelps, Inc., Fitch Investors Service, Inc., Moody's Investors Service, Inc., and Standard & Poor's.)

As of year-end 1990, there were approximately 1,400 preferred stock issues outstanding with a par value of only $58 billion. To see how small this market is, consider that at year-end 1990 the estimated size of the domestic corporate bond market was $1.3 trillion. The amount of medium-term notes issued in 1990 alone was $41 billion, and the amount in 1991 was $71 billion.

Historically, utilities have been the major issuers of preferred stock, accounting for more than half of each year's issuance. Since 1985, major issuers have become financially oriented companies, such as finance companies, banks, thrifts, and insurance companies. Utilities issuance is now less than 30% of annual preferred stock issuance. In 1992, only 22% of the total preferred stock issued was by utilities, compared to 62% for financially oriented companies.[8]

Tax Treatment of Dividends

Unlike debt, payments made to preferred stockholders are treated as a distribution of earnings. This means that they are not tax-deductible to the corporation under the current tax code. Interest payments are tax-deductible, not dividend payments. While this raises the after-tax cost of funds if a corporation issues preferred stock rather than borrowing, there is a factor that reduces the cost differential: a provision in the tax code exempts 70% of qualified dividends from federal income taxation if the recipient is a qualified corporation. For example, if Corporation A owns the preferred stock of Corporation B, for each $100 of dividends received by A, only $30 will be taxed at A's marginal tax rate. The purpose of this provision is to mitigate the effect of double taxation on corporate earnings.

There are two implications of this tax treatment of preferred stock dividends. First, the major buyers of preferred stock are corporations seeking tax-advantaged investments. Second, the cost of preferred stock issuance is lower than it would be in the absence of the tax provision because the tax benefits are passed through to the issuer by the willingness of buyers to accept a lower dividend rate.

Types of Preferred Stock

There are four types of preferred stock: (1) fixed rate, (2) adjustable rate, and (3) auction, and (4) remarketed. We will describe each type.

With **fixed-rate preferred stock**, the dividend rate is fixed as long as the issue is outstanding. Prior to 1982, all publicly issued preferred stock was the

---

[8] Richard S. Wilson, "Nonconvertible Preferred Stock," Chapter 13 in Frank J. Fabozzi and T. Dessa Fabozzi (eds.), *The Handbook of Fixed Income Securities* (Burr Ridge, IL: Irwin Publishing, 1995).

fixed-rate type. Between 1982 and 1988, the other types of preferred stock dominated the new issue market. Since 1989, however, more than 60% of new offerings have been fixed-rate preferred stock. This has been motivated by the decline in interest rates since 1989 to historic low levels and the desire of issuers to lock in these levels.

In May of 1982, the first adjustable-rate preferred stock issue was sold in the public market.[9] The dividend rate on an **adjustable-rate preferred stock** (**ARPS**) is fixed quarterly and based on a predetermined spread from the highest of three points on the Treasury yield curve. The predetermined spread is called the dividend reset spread. The three points on the yield curve (called the benchmark rate) to which the dividend reset spread is either added or subtracted is the highest of: (1) the 3-month Treasury bill rate, (2) the 2-year constant maturity rate, or (3) a 10-year or 30-year constant maturity rate.[10] The motivation for linking the dividend rate to the highest of the three points on the Treasury yield curve is to provide the investor with protection against unfavorable shifts in the yield curve.

Most ARPS are perpetual, with a floor and ceiling imposed on the dividend rate of most issues. Because most ARPS are not putable, however, ARPS can trade below par if after issuance the spread demanded by the market to reflect the issuer's credit risk is greater than the dividend reset spread.

For the years 1983 and 1984 the volume and number of issues of ARPS exceeded that of fixed-rate preferred stock. The major issuers of ARPS have been bank holding companies. There are two reasons that bank holding companies have become major issuers of ARPS. First, floating-rate obligations provide a better liability match, given the floating-rate nature of their assets. Second, bank holding companies are seeking to strengthen their capital positions, and regulators permit bank holding companies to count perpetual preferred stock as part of their primary capital. Issuing ARPS provides not only a better asset/liability match, but also permits bank holding companies to improve primary capital without having to issue common stock.

The popularity of ARPS declined when instruments began to trade below their par value—because the dividend reset rate is determined at the time of issuance, not by market forces. In 1984, a new type of preferred stock, **auction preferred stock** (**APS**), was designed to overcome this problem, particularly for corporate treasurers who sought tax-advantaged short-term instruments to invest excess funds.[11] The dividend rate on APS is set periodically, as with ARPS, but the dividend rate is established through an auction process.[12] Participants in the auction consist of current holders and potential buyers.

---

[9] Private placement of ARPS occurred as early as 1978—once again illustrating how an innovation is first developed in this market.

[10] The Treasury constant maturity rate is reported in the Federal Reserve Report H.15(519). It is based on the closing market bid yields on actively traded Treasury securities.

[11] Each investment bank developed its own trademark name for APS. The instrument developed by Shearson Lehman/American Express was called Money Market Preferred (MMP). Salomon Brothers called their APS Dutch Auction Rate Transferable Securities (DARTS).

[12] The auction process is described in Richard S. Wilson, "Money Market Preferred Stock," Chapter 4 in Frank J. Fabozzi (ed.), *Floating Rate Instruments: Characteristics, Valuation and Portfolio Strategies* (Chicago: Probus Publishing, 1986).

The dividend rate that participants are willing to accept reflects current market conditions.

In the case of **remarketed preferred stock (RP)**, the dividend rate is determined periodically by a remarketing agent who resets the dividend rate so that any preferred stock can be tendered at par and be resold (remarketed) at the original offering price. An investor has the choice of dividend resets every 7 days or every 49 days. From 1985 to 1988, APS and RP became the dominant type of preferred stock issued.

BANKRUPTCY AND CREDITOR RIGHTS

In this chapter and the previous one, we discussed "senior" corporate securities. By senior we mean that the holder of the security has priority over the equity owners in the case of bankruptcy of a corporation. And, as we have explained, there are creditors who have priority over other creditors. In this section, we will provide an overview of the bankruptcy process and then look at what actually happens to creditors in bankruptcies.

The Bankruptcy Process

The law governing bankruptcy in the United States is the Bankruptcy Reform Act of 1978.[13] One purpose of the act is to set forth the rules for a corporation to be either liquidated or reorganized. The **liquidation** of a corporation means that all the assets will be distributed to the holders of claims on the corporation and no corporate entity will survive. In a **reorganization**, a new corporate entity will result. Some holders of the claim of the bankrupt corporation will receive cash in exchange for their claims, others may receive new securities in the corporation that results from the reorganization, and others may receive a combination of both cash and new securities in the resulting corporation.

Another purpose of the bankruptcy act is to give a corporation time to decide whether to reorganize or liquidate, and then the necessary time to formulate a plan to accomplish either decision. The time is allowed because when a corporation files for bankruptcy, the act grants the corporation protection from creditors who seek to collect their claims.[14] A company that files for protection under the bankruptcy act generally becomes a "debtor-in-possession," and continues to operate its business under the supervision of the court.

The bankruptcy act is comprised of 15 chapters, each chapter covering a particular type of bankruptcy. Of particular interest to us are Chapter 7 and Chapter 11 bankruptcies. Chapter 7 deals with the liquidation of a company; Chapter 11 deals with the reorganization of a company.

Absolute Priority: Theory and Practice

When a company is liquidated, creditors receive distributions based on the "absolute priority rule" to the extent assets are available. The absolute priority

---

[13] For a discussion of the Bankruptcy Reform Act of 1978 and a nontechnical description of its principal features, see Jane Tripp Howe, "Investing in Chapter 11 and Other Distressed Companies," Chapter 20 in Fabozzi and Fabozzi (eds.), *The Handbook of Fixed Income Securities: Fourth Edition.*

[14] The petition for bankruptcy can be filed either by the company itself, in which case it is called a *voluntary bankruptcy,* or be filed by its creditors, in which case it is called an *involuntary bankruptcy.*

rule is the principle that senior creditors are paid in full before junior creditors are paid anything. For secured creditors and unsecured creditors, the absolute priority rule guarantees their seniority to equityholders.

In liquidations, the absolute priority rule generally holds, In contrast, there is a good body of literature that argues that strict absolute priority has not been upheld by the courts or the SEC.[15] Studies of actual reorganizations under Chapter 11 have found that the violation of absolute priority is the rule rather the exception.[16]

Failure of the courts to follow strict absolute priority has implications for the capital structure decision (that is, choice between debt and equity) of a firm. The view by financial economists that the firm is effectively owned by the creditors who have sold the shareholders a call option on the firm's assets is not sustainable if the stockholders are not viewed as residual claimants.[17]

There are several hypotheses that have been suggested as to why in a reorganization the distribution made to claimholders will diverge from that required by the absolute priority principle. The **incentive hypothesis** argues that the longer the negotiation process among the parties, the greater the bankruptcy costs and the smaller the amount to be distributed to all parties. This is because in a reorganization, a committee representing the various claimholders is appointed with the purpose of formulating a plan of reorganization. To be accepted, a plan of reorganization must be approved by at least two-thirds of the amount and a majority of the number of claims voting, and at least two-thirds of the outstanding shares of each class of interests. Consequently, a lengthy bargaining process is expected. The longer the negotiation process among the parties, the more likely that the company will be operated in a manner that is not in the best interest of the creditors and, as a result, the smaller the amount to be distributed to all parties. Since all impaired classes including equityholders, generally must approve the plan of reorganization, creditors often convince equityholders to accept the plan by offering to distribute some value to them.

The **recontracting process hypothesis** argues that the violation of absolute priority reflects a recontracting process between stockholders and senior creditors that gives recognition to the ability of management to preserve value on

---

[15] See, for example, William H. Meckling, "Financial Markets, Default, and Bankruptcy," *Law and Contemporary Problems* 41, (1977), pp. 124-77; Merton H. Miller, "The Wealth Transfers of Bankruptcy: Some Illustrative Examples," *Law and Contemporary Problems* 41, (1977), pp. 39-46; Jerold B. Warner, "Bankruptcy, Absolute Priority, and the Pricing of Risky Debt Claims," *Journal of Financial Economics* 4, (1977), pp. 239-76; and, Thomas H. Jackson, "Of Liquidation, Continuation, and Delay: An Analysis of Bankruptcy Policy and Nonbankruptcy Rules," *American Bankruptcy Law Journal* 60, (1986), pp. 399-428.

[16] See: Julian R. Franks and Walter N. Torous, "An Empirical Investigation of U.S. Firms in Reorganization," *Journal of Finance*, (July 1989), pp. 747-69; Lawrence A. Weiss, "Bankruptcy Resolution: Direct Costs and Violation of Priority of Claims," *Journal of Financial Economics* (1990), pp. 285-314; and Frank J. Fabozzi, Jane Tripp Howe, Takashi Makabe, and Toshihide Sudo, "Recent Evidence on the Distribution Patterns in Chapter 11 Reorganizations," *Journal of Fixed Income* (Spring 1993), pp. 6-23.

[17] Fischer Black and Myron Scholes "The Pricing of Options and Corporate Liabilities," *Journal of Political Economy* 81 (1973), pp. 637-54. Also, in the derivation of the pricing of risky debt, Robert Merton assumes that absolute priority holds, see Robert Merton, "The Pricing of Corporate Debt: The Risk Structure of Interest Rates," *Journal of Finance* 29 (1974), pp. 449-70.

behalf of stockholders.[18] According to the **stockholders' influence on reorganization plan hypothesis** creditors are less informed about the true economic operating conditions of the firm than management is. As the distribution to creditors in the plan of reorganization is based on the valuation by the firm, creditors without perfect information suffer the loss.[19] According to Wruck, managers generally have a better understanding than creditors or stockholders about a firm's internal operations, while creditors and stockholders can have better information about industry trends. Management may therefore use its superior knowledge to present the data in a manner which reinforces its position.[20]

The essence of the **strategic bargaining process hypothesis** is that the increasing complexity of firms that declare bankruptcy will accentuate the negotiating process and result in an even higher incidence of violation of the absolute priority rule. The likely outcome is further supported by the increased number of official committees in the reorganization process as well as the increased number of financial and legal advisors.

There are some who argue that creditors will receive a higher value in reorganization than they would in liquidation, in part because of the costs associated with liquidation.[21] Finally, the lack of symmetry in the tax system (negative taxes are not permitted, although loss deductions may be carried forward) results in situations in which the only way to use all current loss deductions is to merge.[22] The tax system may encourage continuance or merger and discourage bankruptcy.

Consequently, while investors in the debt of a corporation may feel that they have priority over the equity owners and priority over other classes of debtors, the actual outcome of a bankruptcy may be far different from what the terms of the debt agreement state.

Fabozzi, Howe, Makabe, and Sudo examined the extent of violation of the absolute priority rule among three broad groups: secured creditors, unsecured creditors and equityholders, and also among various types of debt and equity securities. They also provided evidence on which asset class bears the cost of violations of absolute priority, and an initial estimate of total distributed value relative to liquidation value. Their findings suggest that unsecured creditors bear a disproportionate cost of reorganization, and that more senior unsecured creditors may bear a disproportionate cost relative to the junior unsecured creditors, while equityholders often benefit from violations of absolute priority.

---

[18] Douglas G. Baird and Thomas H. Jackson, "Bargaining After the Fall and the Contours of the Absolute Priority Rule," *University of Chicago Law Review* 55 (1988), pp. 738-89.

[19] L.A. Bebchuk, "A New Approach to Corporate Reorganizations," *Harvard Law Review* 101 (1988), pp. 775-804.

[20] Karen Hooper Wruck, "Financial Distress, Reorganization, and Organizational Efficiency," *Journal of Financial Economics* 27 (1990), pp. 419-44.

[21] Michael C. Jensen, "Eclipse of the Public Corporation," *Harvard Business Review* 89 (1989), pp. 61-2; and Wruck, "Financial Distress, Reorganization, and Organizational Efficiency."

[22] J.I. Bulow and J.B. Shoven. "The Bankruptcy Decision," *Bell Journal of Economics*, 1978. For a further discussion of the importance of net operating losses and the current tax law, see Fabozzi, et al "Recent Evidence on the Distribution Patterns in Chapter 11 Reorganizations."

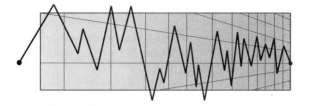

SUMMARY

Medium-term notes are corporate debt obligations offered on a continuous basis. They are registered with the SEC under the shelf registration rule and are offered through agents. The rates posted are for various maturity ranges, with maturities as short as nine months to as long as 30 years. MTNs have been issued simultaneously with transactions in the derivatives market, particularly the swap market, to create structured MTNs. These products allow issuers greater flexibility in creating MTNs that are attractive to investors who seek to hedge or undertake a market play that they might otherwise be prohibited from doing.

Bank loans represent an alternative to the issuance of securities. A syndicated bank loan is one in which a group of banks provides funds to the borrower. Senior bank loans have a priority position over subordinated lenders (bondholders) with respect to payment of interest and repayment of principal and the principal repayment is structured so that the borrowed amount is amortized according to a predetermined schedule. Senior loans are distributed by the two methods of assignments and participations. Senior bank loans have become marketable, and are now more actively traded.

Preferred stock, as a class of stock, shares characteristics of both common stock and debt. Because a special provision in the tax code allows taxation of only a portion of dividends when they are received by a corporation, the major buyers of preferred stock are corporations. There are three types of preferred stock besides the traditional fixed-rate preferred stock. Adjustable-rate preferred stock pays dividends according to a predetermined spread over the highest of three points on the Treasury yield curve. Auction preferred stock is designed to overcome the fact that ARPS can trade below par value; its dividend rate resets periodically based on the results of an auction. The dividend rate of remarketed preferred stock is reset periodically by a remarketing agent so that any preferred stock tendered can be resold (remarketed) at the original offering price.

The Bankruptcy Reform Act of 1978 governs the bankruptcy process in the United States. Chapter 7 of the bankruptcy act deals with the liquidation of a company. Chapter 11 deals with the reorganization of a company. Creditors receive distributions based on the absolute priority rule to the extent assets are available. This means that senior creditors are paid in full before junior creditors are paid anything. Generally, this rule holds in the case of liquidations. In contrast, the absolute priority rule is typically violated in a reorganization.

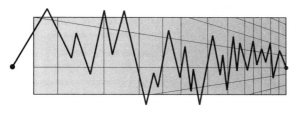

QUESTIONS

1. In what ways does a medium-term note differ from a corporate bond?

2. What derivative instrument is commonly used in creating a structured medium-term note?

3. Indicate why you agree or disagree with the following statements.

   a. "Most medium-term note issues are rated noninvestment grade at the time of offering."

   b. "Typically a corporate issuer with an MTN program will post rates for every maturity range."

   c. "An offering rate schedule for a medium-term note program is fixed for two years after the securities are registered."

4. Which is the more attractive source of financing for a corporation—corporate bonds or medium-term notes?

5. What is meant by reverse inquiry?

6. What is a syndicated bank loan?

7. What is the reference rate typically used for a syndicated bank loan?

8. What is the difference between an amortized bank loan and a bullet bank loan?

9. Explain the two ways in which a bank can sell its position in a syndicated loan and the advantages and disadvantages of each way.

10. a. Why are corporate treasurers the main buyers of preferred stock?

    b. What was the reason for the popularity of auction and remarketed preferred stock?

11. What is the difference between a liquidation and a reorganization?

12. What is the difference between a Chapter 7 and Chapter 11 bankruptcy filing?

13. What is meant by a "debtor-in-possession"?

14. What is meant by the principle of "absolute priority"?

15. Comment on the following statement: "An investor who purchases the mortgage bonds of a corporation knows that should the corporation become bankrupt, mortgage bondholders will be paid in full before the common stockholders receive any proceeds."

16. Give three reasons to explain why absolute priority might be violated in a reorganization.

Municipal Securities Market

LEARNING OBJECTIVES

After reading this chapter you will understand:

- who buys municipal securities and why the securities are attractive investments to these buyers.

- the types of municipal securities and why they are issued.

- how municipal inverse floaters are created.

- the risks unique to investors in municipal securities.

- the primary and secondary markets for municipal securities.

- yield spreads within the municipal market.

- the degree of regulation of the municipal securities market.

In this chapter we discuss municipal securities and the market in which they trade. Municipal bonds are securities issued by state and local governments and by their creations, such as "authorities" and special districts. There are both tax-exempt and taxable municipal bonds. Interest on tax-exempt municipal bonds is exempt from federal income taxation. The large majority of municipal bonds outstanding are tax-exempt. Interest may or may not be taxable at the state and local level. Municipal securities come in a variety of types, with different redemption features, credit risks, and liquidity.

Municipal securities are issued for various purposes. Short-term notes typically are sold in anticipation of the receipt of funds from taxes or proceeds from the sale of a bond issue, for example. The proceeds from the sale of short-term notes permit the issuing municipality to cover seasonal and temporary imbalances between outlays for expenditures and tax inflows. Municipalities issue long-term bonds as the principal means for financing both (1) long-term capital projects such as the construction of schools, bridges, roads, and airports, and (2) long-term budget deficits that arise from current operations.

INVESTORS IN MUNICIPAL SECURITIES

The single most important advantage of municipal securities to investors is the exemption of interest income from federal taxation. The investor groups who purchase these securities benefit the most from this exemption. The three categories of investors dominating the municipal securities market are households (retail investors), commercial banks, and property and casualty insurance companies. Although these three groups have dominated the market since the mid-1950s, their relative participation has shifted. It is the tax code that influences the relative demand for municipal securities.

Retail investor participation in the municipal securities market has fluctuated considerably since 1972. With some interruptions, retail investor market share had been trending downward, but in 1981 the trend was reversed, and individual investors are now the largest holders of municipal securities. Individual investors may purchase municipal securities directly or through mutual funds and unit trusts. The Tax Act of 1990 served to increase the attractiveness of municipal securities by raising the maximum marginal tax rate to 33%. In fact, the effective tax rate is higher than 33% because of various limitations placed on deductions that households may take. The 1992 act raised the top marginal tax rate to 39.6%, making the ownership of municipal bonds even more attractive.

While individual investors are not entitled to deduct any interest cost that they incur to purchase municipal securities, commercial banks (before the Tax Reform Act of 1986) were entitled to deduct 80% of the interest cost of funds used to purchase municipal bonds. This made the after-tax yield on the securities particularly attractive. The 1986 Tax Act repealed this special exemption for banks for securities purchased after August 7, 1986. As a result, the demand for municipal securities by banks has declined dramatically. However, commercial banks hold the obligations of state and local governments for a variety of reasons besides shielding income from federal taxation. Most state and local governments mandate that public deposits at a bank be collateralized. Although Treasury or federal agency securities can serve as collateral, in fact the use of municipal securities is favored. Obligations of state and local governments may also be used as collateral when commercial banks borrow at the discount window of the Federal Reserve. Furthermore, banks frequently serve as underwriters or market makers of municipal securities, and these functions require maintaining inventories of these securities.

Purchases of municipal securities by property and casualty companies are primarily a function of their underwriting profits and investment income. As explained in Chapter 4, profitability depends primarily upon the difference between revenues generated from insurance premiums and investment income and the cost of claims filed; and claims on property and casualty companies are difficult to anticipate. Varying court awards for liability suits, the effect of inflation upon replacement and repair costs, and the unpredictability of weather are the chief factors that affect the level of claims. Premiums for various types of insurance are also subject to competitive pressures and to approval from state insurance commissioners.

Therefore, the profitability of property and casualty companies is cyclical. Normally, intense price competition follows highly profitable years. During these high-income periods, property and casualty companies typically step up their purchases of municipal securities in order to shield income from income taxes. Lower rate increases for premiums are usually granted by state insurance commissioners during this time. Underwriting losses traditionally begin to exact a toll, as premium and investment income fails to keep pace with claims settlement costs. As underwriting losses mount, property and casualty insurance companies curtail their investment in municipal securities. The profitability cycle is completed when they win rate increases from state commissioners after sustaining continued underwriting losses. The 1986 Tax Act includes several provisions that reduced, but did not eliminate, the demand for municipal securities by property and casualty insurance companies.

FEATURES OF MUNICIPAL SECURITIES

Municipal bonds are issued with one of two debt retirement structures or a combination of both. Either a bond has a serial maturity structure or a term maturity structure. A **serial maturity** structure requires a portion of the debt obligation to be retired each year. A **term maturity** structure provides for the debt obligation to be repaid on a final date. Usually term bonds have maturities ranging from 20 to 40 years and retirement schedules (sinking fund provisions) that begin 5 to 10 years before the final term maturity. Municipal bonds may be called prior to the stated maturity date, either according to a mandatory sinking fund or at the option of the issuer.

In Chapter 21, we described zero-coupon bonds, floating-rate bonds, and putable bonds in the corporate bond market. In the municipal market there are securities with these features.

TYPES OF MUNICIPAL SECURITIES

There are basically two types of municipal bond security structures: general obligation bonds and revenue bonds. There are also securities that share characteristics of both general obligation and revenue bonds.

General Obligation Bonds

General obligation bonds are debt instruments issued by states, counties, special districts, cities, towns, and school districts. Usually, a general obligation bond is secured by the issuer's unlimited taxing power. Some general obligations bonds are backed by taxes that are limited as to revenue sources and maximum property-tax millage amounts. Such bonds are known as **limited-tax general obligation bonds**. For smaller governmental entities such as school districts and towns, the only available unlimited taxing power is on property. For larger general obligation bond issuers such as states and big cities, tax revenue sources are more diverse, and may include corporate and individual income taxes, sales taxes, and property taxes. The security pledges for these larger issuers, such as states, are sometimes referred to as **full faith and credit obligations**.

Additionally, certain general obligation bonds are secured not only by the issuer's general taxing powers to create revenues accumulated in a general fund, but also by certain identified fees, grants, and special charges, which provide additional revenues from outside the general fund. Such bonds are known as **double-barreled** in security because of the dual nature of the revenue sources.

Revenue Bonds

The second basic type of security structure is found in a **revenue bond**. Such bonds are issued for either project or enterprise financing where the bond issuers pledge to the bondholders the revenues generated by the operating projects financed. The following list provides examples of revenue bonds.[1]

- *Airport bonds*: The revenues securing these bonds come from either traffic-generated sources—such as landing fees, concession fees, and airline fueling fees—or lease revenues from one or more airlines for the use of a specific facility such as a terminal or hangar.

- *College and university bonds*: The revenues securing these bonds include dormitory room rental fees, tuition payments, and sometimes the general assets of the college or university as well.

- *Hospital bonds*: The security for these bonds depends on federal and state reimbursement programs (such as Medicaid and Medicare), third-party commercial payers (such as Blue Cross, HMOs, and private insurance), and individual patient payments.

- *Single-family mortgage bonds*: These bonds are secured by the mortgages and loan repayments on single-family homes. Security features vary but can include Federal Housing Administration (FHA), Veterans Administration (VA), or private mortgage insurance.[2]

- *Multifamily bonds*: These bonds are issued for multifamily housing projects for senior citizens and low-income families. Some housing revenue bonds are secured by mortgages that are federally insured; others receive federal government operating subsidies or interest-cost subsidies; still others receive only local property tax reductions as subsidies.

- *Industrial bonds*: Generally, these bonds are issued by state and local governments on behalf of individual corporations and businesses. The security for these bonds usually depends on the economic soundness of the particular corporation or business involved.

---

[1] These descriptions are adapted from Frank J. Fabozzi, T. Dessa Fabozzi, and Sylvan G. Feldstein, *Municipal Bond Portfolio Management* (Burr Ridge, IL: Irwin, 1994).

[2] Mortgage insurance is discussed in Chapter 24.

- *Public power bonds*: These bonds are secured by revenues to be produced from electrical operating plants. Some bonds are for a single issuer, who constructs and operates power plants and then sells the electricity. Other public power revenue bonds are issued by groups of public and private investor-owned utilities for joint financing to construct one or more power plants.

- *Resource recovery bonds*: A resource recovery facility converts refuse (solid waste) into commercially saleable energy, recoverable products, and a residue to be landfilled. The revenues securing these bonds are (1) fees paid by those who deliver the waste to the facility for disposal, (2) revenues from steam, electricity, or refuse-derived fuel sold to either an electric power company or another energy user, and (3) revenues from the sale of recoverable materials such as aluminum and steel scrap.

- *Seaport bonds*: The security for these bonds can include specific lease agreements with the benefiting companies, or pledged marine terminal and cargo tonnage fees.

- *Sports complex and convention center bonds*: These bonds usually receive revenues from sporting or convention events held at the facilities and, in some instances, from earmarked outside revenues such as local motel and hotel room taxes.

- *Student loan bonds*: Student loan repayments under student loan revenue bond programs are sometimes 100% guaranteed either directly by the federal government or by a state guaranty agency.

- *Toll road and gas tax bonds*: There are generally two types of highway revenue bonds. Bond proceeds of the first type are used to build such specific revenue-producing facilities as toll roads, bridges, and tunnels. For these pure enterprise-type revenue bonds, the pledged revenues usually are the monies collected through tolls. The second type of highway revenue bond is one where bondholders are paid by earmarked revenues outside of toll collections, such as gasoline taxes, automobile registration payments, and driver's license fees.

- *Water bonds*: Water revenue bonds are issued to finance the construction of water-treatment plants, pumping stations, collection facilities, and distribution systems. Revenues usually come from connection fees and charges paid by the users of the water systems.

Hybrid and Special Bond Securities

Some municipal bonds that have the basic characteristics of general obligation bonds and revenue bonds have more issue-specific structures as well. The examples we discuss here are insured bonds, bank-backed municipal bonds, refunded bonds, moral obligation bonds, and "troubled city" bailout bonds.

Insured bonds—Insured bonds, in addition to being secured by the issuer's revenue, are also backed by insurance policies written by commercial insurance companies. Insurance on a municipal bond is an agreement by an insurance company to pay the bondholder any bond principal and/or coupon interest that is due on a stated maturity date but that has not been paid by the bond issuer. Once issued, this municipal bond insurance usually extends for the term of the bond issue, and it cannot be canceled by the insurance company.

Because municipal bond insurance reduces credit risk for the investor, the marketability of certain municipal bonds can be greatly expanded. Municipal bonds that benefit most from the insurance would include lower-quality bonds, bonds issued by smaller governmental units not widely known in the financial community, bonds that have a sound though complex and difficult-to-understand security structure, and bonds issued by infrequent local-government borrowers who do not have a general market following among investors.

Of course, a major factor for an issuer to obtain bond insurance is that its creditworthiness without the insurance is substantially lower than what it would be with the insurance. That is, the interest cost savings are only of sufficient magnitude to offset the cost of the insurance premium when the underlying creditworthiness of the issuer is lower.

Most insured municipal bonds are insured by one of the following insurance companies that are primarily in the business of insuring municipal bonds: AMBAC Indemnity Corporation; Capital Guaranty Insurance Company; Connie Lee Insurance Company; Financial Guaranty Insurance Company; Financial Security Assurance, Inc.; and Municipal Bond Investors Insurance Corporation. In 1993, over 35% of all new municipal issues were insured.

Bank-backed municipal bonds—Since the 1980s, municipal obligations have been increasingly supported by various types of credit facilities provided by commercial banks. The support is in addition to the issuer's cash flow revenues.

There are three basic types of bank support: letter of credit, irrevocable line of credit, and revolving line of credit. A **letter-of-credit agreement** is the strongest type of support available from a commercial bank. Under this arrangement, the bank is required to advance funds to the trustee if a default occurs. An **irrevocable line of credit** is not a guarantee of the bond issue though it does provide a level of security. A **revolving line of credit** provides a source of liquidity for payment of maturing debt in the event no other funds of the issuer are currently available. Because a bank can cancel a revolving line of credit without notice if the issuer fails to meet certain covenants, bond security depends entirely on the creditworthiness of the municipal issuer.

Refunded bonds—Although originally issued as either revenue or general obligation bonds, municipals are sometimes refunded. A refunding usually occurs when the original bonds are escrowed or collateralized by direct obligations guaranteed by the government. By this it is meant that a portfolio of securities guaranteed by the government are placed in trust. The portfolio of securities is assembled such that the cash flow from all the securities matches the obligations that the issuer must pay. For example, suppose that a municipality has a 7%, $100 million issue with 12 years remaining to maturity. The municipality's obligation is to make payments of $3.5 million every six months for the next 12 years, and $100 million 12 years from now. If the issuer wants to refund this issue, a portfolio of U.S. government obligations can be purchased that has a cash flow of $3.5 million every six months for the next 12 years and $100 million 12 years from now.

Once this portfolio of securities whose cash flow matches that of the municipality's obligation is in place, the refunded bonds are no longer secured as either general obligation or revenue bonds, instead they are supported by the portfolio of securities held in an escrow fund. Such bonds, if escrowed with securities guaranteed by the U.S. government, have little if any credit risk. They are the safest municipal bond investments available.

The escrow fund for a refunded municipal bond can be structured so that the refunded bonds are to be called at the first possible call date or a subsequent call date established in the original bond indenture. Such bond's are known as **prefunded municipal bonds**. While refunded bonds are usually retired at their first or subsequent call date, some are structured to match the debt obligation to the retirement date. Such bonds are known as **escrowed-to-maturity bonds**.

There are three reasons why a municipal issuer may refund an issue by creating an escrow fund. First, many refunded issues were originally issued as revenue bonds. Included in revenue issues are restrictive-bond covenants. The municipality may wish to eliminate these restrictions. The creation of an escrow fund to pay the bondholders legally eliminates any restrictive-bond covenants. This is the motivation for the escrowed-to-maturity bonds. Second, some issues are refunded in order to alter the maturity schedule of the obligation. Finally, when interest rates have declined after a municipal security has been issued, there is a tax-arbitrage opportunity available to the issuer by paying existing bondholders a lower interest rate and using the proceeds to create a portfolio of U.S. government securities paying a higher interest rate.[3] This is the motivation for the prefunded bonds.

Moral obligation bonds—A moral obligation bond is a security structure for state-issued bonds legally authorizing but not requiring the state legislature to make an appropriation out of general state tax revenues.

Troubled city bailout bonds—These bonds are structured to appear as pure revenue bonds, but in essence they are not. Revenues come from general-purpose taxes and revenues that otherwise would have gone to the state's or the city's general fund. These bond structures were created to bail out underlying general obligation bond issuers from severe budget deficits. Examples are the New York State Municipal Assistance Corporation of the City of New York Bonds (MAC) and the State of Illinois Chicago School Finance Authority Bonds.

Money Market Products

Tax-exempt money market products include municipal notes, commercial paper, variable-rate demand obligations, and a hybrid of the last two products.

Municipal notes include tax anticipation notes (TANs), revenue anticipation notes (RANs), grant anticipation notes (GANs), and bond anticipation notes (BANs). These are temporary borrowings by states, local governments, and special jurisdictions. Usually, notes are issued for a period of 12 months,

---

[3] Since the interest rate that a municipality must pay on borrowed funds is less than the interest rate paid by the U.S. government, in the absence of any restrictions in the tax code, a municipal issuer can realize a tax arbitrage. This can be done by issuing a bond and immediately investing the proceeds in a U.S. government security. There are tax rules that prevent such arbitrage. Should a municipal issuer violate the tax-arbitrage rules, the IRS will rule the issue to be taxable. However, if subsequent to the issuance of a bond interest rates decline so that the issuer will find it advantageous to call the bond, the establishment of the escrow fund will not violate the tax-arbitrage rules.

although it is not uncommon for notes to be issued for periods as short as three months and for as long as three years. TANs and RANs (also known as TRANs) are issued in anticipation of the collection of taxes or other expected revenues. These are borrowings to even out irregular flows into the treasuries of the issuing entity. BANs are issued in anticipation of the sale of long-term bonds.

As with commercial paper issued by corporations, **tax-exempt commercial** paper is used by municipalities to raise funds on a short-term basis ranging from 1 day to 270 days. The dealer sets interest rates for various maturity dates and the investor then selects the desired date. Provisions in the 1986 Tax Act have restricted the issuance of tax-exempt commercial paper. Specifically, the act limits the new issuance of municipal obligations that are tax-exempt, and as a result, every maturity of a tax-exempt municipal issuance is considered a new debt issuance. Consequently, very limited issuance of tax-exempt commercial paper exists. Instead, issuers use one of the next two products to raise short-term funds.

Variable-rate demand obligations (VRDOs) are floating-rate obligations that have a nominal long-term maturity but have a coupon rate that is either reset daily or every seven days. The investor has an option to put the issue back to the trustee at any time with seven days notice. The put price is par plus accrued interest.

The commercial paper/VRDO hybrid is customized to meet the cash flow needs of an investor. As with tax-exempt commercial paper, there is flexibility in structuring the maturity, because the remarketing agent establishes interest rates for a range of maturities. Although the instrument may have a long nominal maturity, there is a put provision as with a VRDO. Put periods can range from 1 day to over 360 days. On the put date, the investor can put back the bonds, receiving principal and interest, or the investor can elect to extend the maturity at the new interest rate and put date posted by the remarketing agent at that time. Thus the investor has two choices when initially purchasing this instrument: the interest rate and the put date. Interest is generally paid on the put date if the date is within 180 days. If the put date is more than 180 days forward, interest is paid semiannually.

Commercial paper dealers market these products under a proprietary name. For example, the Merrill Lynch product is called Unit Priced Demand Adjustable Tax-Exempt Securities, or UPDATES. Lehman Brothers markets these simply as money market municipals. Goldman Sachs refers to these securities as flexible rate notes, and Smith Barney Shearson markets them as BITS (Bond Interest Term Series).

Municipal Derivative Securities

In recent years, a number of municipal products have been created from the basic fixed-rate municipal bond. This has been done by splitting up cash flows of newly issued bonds as well as bonds existing in the secondary market. These products have been created by dividing the coupon interest payments and principal payments into two or more bonds classes, or tranches. The resulting bond classes may have far different yield and price volatility characteristics than the underlying fixed-rate municipal bond from which they were created. By expanding the risk/return profile available in the municipal marketplace, institutional investors have more flexibility in structuring municipal bond portfolios either to satisfy a specific asset/liability objective or to make an interest rate or yield curve bet more efficiently. In exchange for such benefits, municipal issuers benefit by being able to issue securities at a lower interest cost.

The name **derivative securities** has been attributed to these bond classes because they derive their value from the underlying fixed-rate municipal bond. Much of the development in this market has paralleled that of the taxable, and specifically the mortgage-backed securities, market discussed in Chapters 25 and 26. The ability of investment bankers to create these securities has been enhanced by the development of the municipal swap market.

A common type of derivative security is one in which two classes of securities, a **floating-rate security** and an **inverse floating-rate bond**, are created from a fixed-rate bond.[4] The coupon rate on the floating-rate security is reset based on the results of an auction. The auction can take place anywhere between 7 days and 35 days. The coupon rate on the floating-rate security changes in the same direction as market rates. The inverse floating-rate bond receives the residual interest; that is, the coupon interest paid on this bond is the difference between the fixed-rate on the underlying bond and the floating-rate security. Thus the coupon rate on the inverse floating-rate bond changes in the opposite direction of interest rates.

The sum of the interest paid on the floater and inverse floater (plus fees associated with the auction) must always equal the sum of the fixed-rate bond from which they were created. A minimum interest rate is established as a floor on the inverse floater—typically the floor is zero. As a result, a cap (maximum interest rate) will be imposed on the floater such that the combined floor of zero on the inverse floater and the cap on the floater is equal to the total interest rate on the fixed-rate bond from which they were created.

Inverse floaters can be created in one of three ways. First, a municipal dealer can buy in the secondary market a fixed-rate municipal bond and place it in a trust. The trust then issues a floater and an inverse floater. The second method is similar to the first except that the municipal dealer uses a newly issued municipal bond to create a floater and an inverse floater. These two methods are illustrated in Figure 23-1. The third method is to create an inverse floater without the need to create a floater. This is done by using interest rate swaps which we described in Chapter 12. More specifically, a market for municipal swaps has developed.

The dealer determines the ratio of floaters to inverse floaters. For example, an investment banking firm may purchase $100 million of the underlying bond in the secondary market and issue $50 million of floaters and $50 million of inverse floaters. The dealer may opt for a 60/40 or any other split. The floaters/inverse floaters determines the leverage of the inverse floaters and thus affects its price volatility when interest rates change. Specifically, it can be shown that the duration of an inverse floater is a multiple of the underly-

---

4 For examples of other derivative securities, see Chapter 4 of Fabozzi, Fabozzi, and Feldstein, *Municipal Bond Portfolio Management.*

ing fixed-rate issue from which it was created. The multiple is determined by the leverage. To date, the most popular split of floaters and inverse floaters has been 50/50. In such instances, the inverse floater will have double the duration of the fixed-rate bond from which it is created. Determination of the leverage will be set based upon the desires of investors at the time of the transaction.

The investor in the inverse floater can purchase the corresponding floater at auction and combine his two positions to effectively own the underlying fixed-rate bond. This can be done if interest rates are rising and the investor wishes to close out his inverse floater position. The market for inverse floaters is not highly liquid at this time, so it represents an easy way to convert this position into a synthetic fixed-rate bond. In the future, the investor may opt to split the issue again, retaining the inverse floater. This is a valuable option for investors. As a result, the yield on this bond will generally be less than the yield on a comparable fixed-rate bond that does not have this option.

Several investment banking firms active in the municipal bond market have developed proprietary products. Merrill Lynch's institutional floaters are called *FLOATS* and its inverse floaters are called *RITES* (Residual Interest Tax Exempt Securities). Goldman Sachs' proprietary products are called *PARS* (Periodic Auction Reset Securities), which are floaters, and *INFLOS*, which are inverse floaters. Lehman Brothers' proprietary products are called *RIBS* (Residual Interest Bonds) and *SAVRS* (Select Auction Variable Rate Securities).

CREDIT RISK

While municipal bonds at one time were considered second in safety only to U.S. Treasury securities, today there are new concerns about the credit risks of municipal securities.[5] The first concern came out of the New York City billion-dollar financial crisis in 1975. On February 25, 1975, the state of New York's Urban Development Corporation defaulted on a $100 million note

Figure 23-1
Creation of a Municipal Inverse Floater

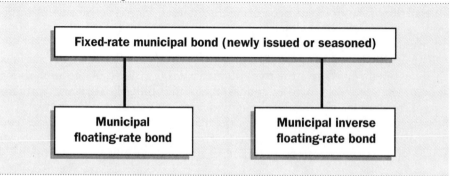

---

[5] For a history of defaults of municipal bonds, see Chapter 2 in Sylvan G. Feldstein and Frank J. Fabozzi, *The Dow Jones-Irwin Guide to Municipal Bonds* (Homewood, IL: Dow Jones-Irwin, 1987).

issue that was the obligation of New York City; many market participants had been convinced that the state of New York would not allow the issue to default. Although New York City was able later to obtain a $140 million revolving credit from banks to cure the default, lenders became concerned that the city would face difficulties in repaying its accumulated debt, which stood at $14 billion on March 31, 1975.[6] This financial crisis sent a loud and clear warning to market participants in general: Regardless of supposedly ironclad protection for the bondholder, when issuers such as large cities have severe financial difficulties, the financial stakes of public employee unions, vendors, and community groups may be dominant forces in balancing budgets. This reality was reinforced by the federal bankruptcy law that took effect in October 1979, which made it easier for the issuer of a municipal security to go into bankruptcy.

The second reason for concern about municipal securities credit risk is the proliferation in this market of innovative financing techniques to secure new bond issues. In addition to the established general obligation bonds and revenue bonds, there are now more non-voter-approved, innovative, and legally untested security mechanisms. These innovative financing mechanisms include moral obligation bonds and commercial bank-backed letters of credit bonds, to name a few. What distinguishes these newer bonds from the more traditional general obligation and revenue bonds is that there is no history of court decisions or other case law that firmly establishes the rights of the bondholders and the obligations of the issuers. It is not possible to determine in advance the probable legal outcome if the newer financing mechanisms were to be challenged in court. This is illustrated most dramatically by the bonds of the Washington Public Power Supply System (WPPSS) where bondholder rights to certain revenues were not upheld by the highest court in the state of Washington.

As with corporate bonds, many institutional investors in the municipal bond market rely on their own in-house municipal credit analysts for determining the creditworthiness of a municipal issue; other investors rely on the nationally recognized rating companies. The two leading rating companies are Moody's and Standard & Poor's, and the assigned rating system is essentially the same as that used for corporate bonds.

In evaluating general obligation bonds, the commercial rating companies assess information in four basic categories.[7] The first category includes information on the issuer's debt structure to determine the overall debt burden. The second category relates to the issuer's ability and political discipline to maintain sound budgetary policy. The focus of attention here usually is on the issuer's general operating funds and whether it has maintained at least balanced budgets over three to five years. The third category involves determining the specific local taxes and intergovernmental revenues available to the issuer, as well as obtaining historical information both on tax collection rates,

---

[6] *Securities and Exchange Commission Staff Report on Transactions in Securities of the City of New York* (Washington, D.C.: U.S. Government Printing Office, 1977), p. 2. The reasons for the New York City financial crisis are documented in Donna E. Shalala and Carol Bellamy, "A State Saves a City: The New York Case," *Duke Law Journal* (January 1976), pp. 1119-26.

[7] Although there are many similarities in how Moody's and Standard & Poor's approach the credit rating of general obligation bonds, there are differences in their approaches as well. For a discussion of these differences, see Fabozzi, Fabozzi, and Feldstein, *Municipal Bond Portfolio Management.*

which are important when looking at property tax levies, and on the dependence of local budgets on specific revenue sources. The fourth and last category of information necessary to the credit analysis is an assessment of the issuer's overall socioeconomic environment. The determinations that have to be made here include trends of local employment distribution and composition, population growth, real estate property valuation, and personal income, among other economic factors.

While there are numerous security structures for revenue bonds, the underlying principle in rating is whether the project being financed will generate sufficient cash flow to satisfy the obligations due bondholders.[8] A natural question to ask is: How good are the ratings? Of the municipal securities that were rated by a commercial rating company in 1929 and plunged into default in 1932, 78% had been rated double-A or better, and 48% had been rated triple-A. Since then the ability of rating agencies to assess the creditworthiness of municipal securities has evolved to a level of general industry acceptance and respectability. In most instances, ratings adequately describe the financial condition of the issuers and identify the credit risk factors. A small but significant number of recent instances still have caused market participants to reexamine their reliance on the opinions of the rating companies. One example is the bonds of the Washington Public Power Supply System mentioned above. The two major commercial rating companies gave their highest ratings to these bonds in the early 1980s. While these high-quality ratings were in effect, WPPSS sold over $8 billion in long-term bonds. By 1986 over $2 billion of these bonds were in default.

TAX RISK

The investor in municipal securities is exposed to the same risks affecting corporate bonds plus an additional one that may be labeled "tax risk." There are two types of tax risk to which tax-exempt municipal securities buyers are exposed. The first is the risk that the federal income tax rate will be reduced. The higher the marginal tax rate, the greater the value of the tax exemption feature. As the marginal tax rate declines, the price of a tax-exempt municipal security will decline. When in 1995 there were Congressional proposals regarding the introduction of a flat tax with a low tax rate, municipal bonds began trading at lower prices.

The second type of tax risk is that a municipal bond issued as a tax-exempt issue may be eventually declared by the Internal Revenue Service to be taxable. This may occur because many municipal revenue bonds have elaborate security structures that could be subject to future adverse congressional action and IRS interpretation. A loss of the tax-exemption feature will cause the municipal bond to decline in value in order to provide a yield comparable to similar taxable bonds. As an example, in June of 1980, the Battery Park City Authority sold $97.315 million in notes, which at the time of issuance legal counsel advised were exempt from federal income taxation. In November of 1980, however, the IRS held that interest on these notes was not exempt. The

---

[8] A comprehensive discussion of the analysis of various revenue bond structures is found in: Sylvan G. Feldstein, Frank J. Fabozzi and Irving M. Pollack (eds.), *The Municipal Bond Handbook Volume II* (Homewood, IL: Dow Jones-Irwin, 1993); and Feldstein and Fabozzi, *Dow Jones-Irwin Guide to Municipal Bonds*.

issue was not settled until September 1981, when the Authority and the IRS signed a formal agreement resolving the matter so as to make the interest on the notes tax-exempt.

THE PRIMARY MARKET

A substantial number of municipal obligations are brought to market each week. A state or local government can market its new issue by offering bonds publicly to the investing community or by placing them privately with a small group of investors. When a public offering is selected, the issue usually is underwritten by investment bankers and/or municipal bond departments of commercial banks. Public offerings may be marketed by either competitive bidding or direct negotiations with underwriters. When an issue is marketed via competitive bidding, the issue is awarded to the bidder submitting the best bid.

Usually state and local governments require a competitive sale to be announced in a recognized financial publication, such as *The Bond Buyer*, which is a trade publication for the municipal bond industry. *The Bond Buyer* also provides information on upcoming competitive sales and most negotiated sales, as well as the results of previous weeks.

Most states mandate that general obligation issues be marketed through competitive bidding, but generally this is not required for revenue bonds. Recent scandals involving financial contributions of underwriters to elected officials have made some municipalities concerned with whether they are receiving the lowest cost funding possible. Consequently, more municipalities are requiring competitive bidding for both general obligation and revenue issues.

An **official statement** describing the issue and the issuer is prepared for new offerings. Municipal bonds have legal opinions which are summarized in the official statement. The relationship of the legal opinion to the safety of the bond is twofold. First, bond counsel determines if the issue is indeed legally able to issue the bonds. Second, bond counsel verifies that the issuer has properly prepared for the bond sale by having enacted various required ordinances, resolutions, and trust indentures and without violating any other laws and regulations.

THE SECONDARY MARKET

Municipal bonds are traded in the over-the-counter market supported by municipal bond dealers across the country. Markets are maintained on smaller issuers (referred to as "local general credits") by regional brokerage firms, local banks, and by some of the larger Wall Street firms. Larger issuers (referred to as "general names") are supported by the larger brokerage firms and banks, many of whom have investment banking relationships with these issuers. There are brokers who serve as intermediaries in the sale of large blocks of municipal bonds among dealers and large institutional investors. In addition to these brokers and the daily offerings sent out over *The Bond Buyer*'s "munifacts" teletype system, many dealers advertise their municipal bond offering for the retail market in what is known as *The Blue List*. This is a 100-plus-page booklet published every weekday by the Standard & Poor's Corporation that gives municipal securities offerings and prices.

In the municipal bond markets, an odd lot of bonds is $25,000 or less in par value for retail investors. For institutions, anything below $100,000 in par value is considered an odd lot. Dealer spreads depend on several factors. For the retail investor, the spread can range from as low as one-quarter of one point ($12.50 per $5,000 par value) on large blocks of actively traded bonds to four points ($200 per $5,000 of par value) for odd lot sales of an inactive issue. For institutional investors, the dealer spread rarely exceeds one-half of one point ($25 per $5,000 of par value).

The convention for both corporate and Treasury bonds is to quote prices as a percentage of par value with 100 equal to par. Municipal bonds, however, generally are traded and quoted in terms of yield (yield to maturity or yield to call). The price of the bond in this case is called a **basis price**. The exception is certain long-maturity revenue bonds. A bond traded and quoted in dollar price (actually, as a percentage of par value) is called a **dollar bond**.

REGULATION OF THE MUNICIPAL SECURITIES MARKET[9]

Congress has specifically exempted municipal securities from both the registration requirements of the Securities Act of 1933 and the periodic reporting requirements of the Securities Exchange Act of 1934. Antifraud provisions apply nevertheless to offerings of or dealings in municipal securities.

Historically, the reasons for the exemption afforded municipal securities appear to relate to (1) a desire for governmental comity, (2) the absence of recurrent abuses in transactions involving municipal securities, (3) the greater level of sophistication of investors in this segment of the securities markets (that is, institutional investors once dominated the market), and (4) the fact that there were few defaults by municipal issuers. Consequently, between enactment of federal securities acts in the early 1930s and the early 1970s, the municipal securities market was relatively free from federal regulation.

In the early 1970s, however, circumstances changed. As incomes rose, individuals participated in the municipal securities market to a much greater extent, and public concern over selling practices occurred with greater frequency. Moreover, the financial problems of some municipal issuers, notably New York City, made market participants aware that municipal issuers have the potential to experience severe financial difficulties approaching bankruptcy levels.

Congress passed the Securities Act Amendment of 1975 to broaden federal regulation in the municipals market. This legislation brought brokers and dealers in the municipal securities market, including banks that underwrite and trade municipal securities, under the regulatory umbrella of the Securities Exchange Act of 1934. The legislation mandates also that the SEC establish a 15-member Municipal Securities Rulemaking Board (MSRB) as an independent, self-regulatory agency, whose primary responsibility is to develop rules governing the activities of banks, brokers, and dealers in municipal securities. Rules adopted by the MSRB must be approved by the SEC. The MSRB has no enforcement or inspection authority. That authority is vested

---

[9] Parts of this section are drawn from Thomas F. Mitchell, "Disclosure and the Municipal Bond Industry," Chapter 40, and Nancy H. Wotjas, "The SEC and Investor Safeguards," Chapter 42 in Frank J. Fabozzi, Sylvan G. Feldstein, Irving M. Pollack, and Frank Zarb (eds.), *The Municipal Bond Handbook: Volume I* (Homewood, IL: Dow Jones-Irwin, 1983).

with the SEC, the National Association of Securities Dealers, and certain regulatory banking agencies such as the Federal Reserve Bank.

The Securities Act Amendment of 1975 does not require municipal issuers to comply with the registration requirement of the 1933 act or the periodic reporting requirement of the 1934 act, despite several legislative proposals to mandate financial disclosure. Even in the absence of federal legislation dealing with the regulation of financial disclosure, however, underwriters began insisting upon greater disclosure as it became apparent that the SEC was exercising stricter application of the antifraud provisions. Moreover, underwriters recognized the need for improved disclosure to sell municipal securities to an investing public that has become much more concerned about the financial risk of municipal issuers.

On June 28, 1989, the SEC formally approved the first bond disclosure rule, effective January 1, 1990. While the disclosure rule has several exemptions, in general it applies to new issue municipal securities offerings of $1 million or more. In early 1994, both the SEC and other interested parties were reviewing proposals to enhance the credit disclosure for municipal bonds in both the primary and secondary markets, as well as discussing guidelines for underwriters who make financial contributions to elected public officials.

YIELDS ON MUNICIPAL BONDS

Because of the tax-exempt feature of municipal bonds, the yield on municipal bonds is less than that on Treasuries with the same maturity. As we noted in Chapter 16, the ratio of municipal yields to Treasury yields varies over time and yield spreads within the municipal bond market are attributable to differences between credit ratings (that is, quality spreads) and differences between maturities (maturity spreads).

Quality Spreads

Our statement in Chapter 16 about quality spreads between credit ratings for corporate bonds over the interest rate cycle is true for municipal bonds: quality spreads widen during recessionary periods, but narrow during periods of economic prosperity. Another factor that can cause changes in the quality spread is a temporary oversupply of issues within a market sector. For example, a substantial new-issue volume of high-grade state general obligation bonds may tend to decrease the spread between high-grade and lower-grade revenue bonds. In a weak market environment, it is easier for high-grade municipal bonds to come to market than weaker ones. Therefore, it is not uncommon for high grades to flood weak markets, while at the same time there is a relative scarcity of medium- and lower-grade municipal bond issues.

Maturity Spreads

In the municipal bond market, several benchmark curves exist. In general, a benchmark yield curve is constructed for AAA rated state general obligations. Figure 23-2 shows such a yield curve on November 18, 1994.

In the Treasury and corporate bond markets, it is not unusual to find at different times all four shapes for the yield curve described in Chapter 16. In

Figure 23-2

The AAA State General Obligation Yield Curve and U.S.
Treasury Yield Curve after 40% Tax

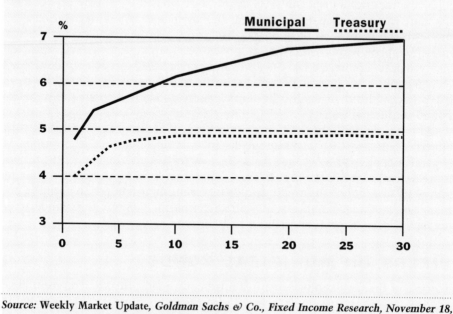

Source: **Weekly Market Update,** *Goldman Sachs & Co., Fixed Income Research, November 18,*
1994, p. A-5. Copyright 1994 by Goldman Sachs.

general, the municipal yield curve is positively sloped. There was a brief
period when the municipal yield curve became inverted. In fact, during the
period when the Treasury yield curve was inverted, the municipal yield curve
maintained its upward-sloping shape. Prior to 1986 the municipal yield curve
was consistently steeper than the Treasury yield curve as measured by the
spread between the 30-year and 1-year issue. Between 1986 and 1990, the
steepness was comparable. In 1991, the municipal yield curve became steeper
than the Treasury yield curve. Figure 23-2 compares the two yield curves
assuming a 40% tax rate on Treasury coupon interest.

Spreads between General Market and In-State Issues

There is another reason for spreads between municipal issues. Bonds of
municipal issuers located in certain states yield considerably less than issues
of identical credit quality coming from other states that trade in the "general
market." One reason is that states often exempt interest from in-state issues
from state and local personal income taxes, while interest from out-of-state
issues is generally not exempt. Consequently, in states with high income
taxes such as New York and California, strong investor demand for in-state
issues will reduce their yields relative to bonds of issuers located in states
where state and local income taxes are not important considerations.

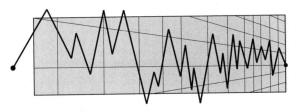

SUMMARY

Municipal securities are issued by state and local governments and their authorities, with the coupon interest on most issues being exempt from federal income taxes. The primary investors in these securities are households (including mutual funds), commercial banks, and property and casualty insurance companies. Changes in the tax law have had an effect on the relative attractiveness of municipal securities for these three groups of investors.

The two basic security structures are general obligation bonds and revenue bonds. The former are secured by the issuer's general taxing power. Revenue bonds are used to finance specific projects and are dependent on revenues from those projects to satisfy the obligations. There are also hybrid securities that have certain characteristics of both general obligation and revenue bonds, and some securities that have unique structures. Municipal money market products include notes, commercial paper, variable-rate demand notes, and a hybrid of commercial paper and variable-rate demand notes. Derivative securities have been created from the basic fixed-rate municipal bond, the most popular being inverse floaters.

Municipal bonds may be retired with a serial maturity structure, a term maturity structure, or a combination of both. As in the case of corporate bonds, there are zero-coupon bonds and floating-rate bonds. Investing in municipal securities exposes investors to the same qualitative risks as investing in corporate bonds, with the additional risk that a change in the tax law may affect the price of municipal securities adversely.

Because of the tax-exempt feature, yields on municipal securities are lower than those on comparably rated taxable securities. Within the municipal bond market, there are quality spreads and maturity spreads. Typically, the municipal yield curve is upward sloping. Moreover, there are yield spreads related to differences between in-state issues and general market issues.

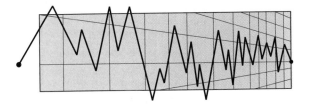

QUESTIONS

1. Explain why you agree or disagree with the following statement: "All municipal bonds are exempt from federal income taxes."

2. Explain why you agree or disagree with the following statement: "All municipal bonds are exempt from state and local taxes."

3. If Congress changes the tax law so as to increase marginal tax rates, what will happen to the price of municipal bonds?

4. Why would a property and casualty insurance company shift its allocation of funds from corporate bonds to municipal bonds?

5. What is the difference between a general obligation bond and a revenue bond?

6. Which type of bond would an investor analyze when using an approach similar to that for analyzing a corporate bond?

7. What is the tax risk associated with investing in a municipal bond?

8. "An insured municipal bond is safer than an uninsured municipal bond." Indicate whether you agree or disagree with this statement.

9. In your view, would the typical AAA or AA rated municipal bond be insured?

10. Explain the different types of refunded bonds.

11. Give two reasons why an issuing municipality would want to refund an outstanding bond issue.

12. a. What are the three basic types of bank support for a bank-backed municipal security?

b. Which is the strongest type of support available from a commercial bank?

13. Why has there been a decline in the issuance of tax-exempt commercial paper?

14. a. Explain how an inverse floating-rate municipal bond can be created.

b. Who determines the leverage of an inverse floater?

c. What is the duration of an inverse floater?

15. For years, observers and analysts of the debt market believed that municipal securities were free of any risk of default. Why do most people now believe that municipal debt can carry a substantial amount of credit or default risk?

16. a. What is typically the benchmark yield curve in the municipal bond market?

b. What can you say about the typical relationship between the yield on short-term and long-term municipal bonds?

17. a. Historically, the municipal market has not been highly regulated. Explain why.

b. Has the situation changed?

The Mortgage Market

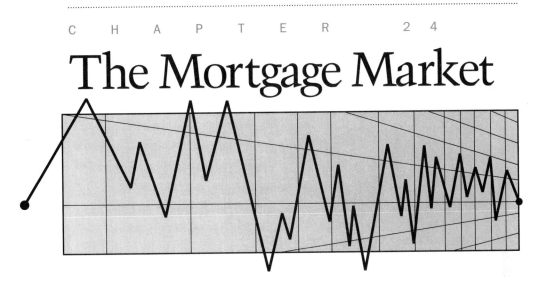

LEARNING OBJECTIVES

After reading this chapter you will understand:

- what a mortgage is.

- who the major originators of mortgages are and the mortgage origination process.

- the risks associated with the mortgage origination process and the embedded options in the transaction.

- what mortgage servicing involves.

- the risks associated with mortgage servicing.

- the different types of mortgage insurance.

- the risks faced by private mortgage insurers.

- the traditional fixed-rate, level-payment, fully amortized mortgage instrument, and its cash flow characteristics.

- what prepayments are.

- deficiencies of the traditional mortgage, including mismatch and tilt problems.

- alternative mortgage instruments, their cash flow characteristics, and how they attempt to correct for the deficiencies of the traditional mortgage instrument.

- the factors that affect defaults.

While the American dream may be to own a home, the major portion of the funds to purchase one must be borrowed. The market where these funds are borrowed is called the **mortgage market** or the housing finance market. This sector of the debt market is by far the largest in the world with an estimated size, as of the first quarter of 1993, of $4.1 trillion—far exceeding the $1.9 trillion U.S. government securities market and $1.4 trillion corporate bond market.

The mortgage market has undergone significant structural changes since the 1980s. Innovations have occurred in terms of the design of new mortgage instruments and the development of products that use pools of mortgages as collateral for the issuance of a security. Such securities are called **mortgage-backed securities**.

The mortgage market is a collection of markets which includes a primary market, or origination market, and a secondary market where mortgages trade. In this chapter we also review the various types of mortgage instruments. We discuss the development of the current secondary mortgage market in Chapter 25, where we explain the securitization of mortgage loans. The reason we postpone our discussion of the development of the secondary market is because its development is tied to the development of the market for mortgage-backed securities.

WHAT IS A MORTGAGE?

By definition, a **mortgage** is a pledge of property to secure payment of a debt. Typically, property refers to real estate, which is often in the form of a house; the debt is the loan given to the buyer of the house by a lender. Thus, a mortgage might be a pledge of a house to secure payment of a loan. If a homeowner (the **mortgagor**) fails to pay the lender (the **mortgagee**), the lender has the right to foreclose the loan and seize the property in order to ensure that it is repaid.

When the lender makes the loan based on the credit of the borrower and on the collateral for the mortgage, the mortgage is said to be a **conventional mortgage**. The lender may require the borrower to obtain mortgage insurance to insure against default by the borrower.

The types of real estate properties that can be mortgaged are divided into two broad categories: residential and nonresidential properties. The former category includes houses, condominiums, cooperatives, and apartments. Residential real estate can be subdivided into single-family (one-to-four family) residences and multifamily residences (apartment buildings in which more than four families reside). Nonresidential property includes commercial and farm properties. Table 24-1 shows the amount of debt outstanding as of the first quarter of 1993. About 75% ($3 trillion) of the mortgage debt outstanding is for one-to-four family residences.

Table 24-1

Mortgage Debt Outstanding by Type of Property as of the First Quarter of 1993

Type of property	Millions of dollars
One-to-four family residences	$2,976,287
Multifamily residences	293,382
Commercial	707,041
Farm	80,040
Total	$4,056,750

Source: **Federal Reserve Bulletin,** *December 1993, Table A38.*

INVESTORS

Table 24-2 indicates the holders of the $3 trillion mortgage debt outstanding for one-to-four family residences. There are four general categories listed in the table: major financial institutions, federal and related agencies, mortgage pools or trusts, and individuals and others. The federal and related agencies that invest in mortgages are discussed in this chapter and the next. Their purpose is to provide liquidity to the mortgage market. The category of mortgage pools and trusts will become clear in the next chapter when we discuss the securitization of mortgage loans. Basically, the mortgages held in mortgage pools and trusts are those used as collateral for the issuance of a mortgage-backed security. Note from Table 24-2 that almost half the outstanding mortgages for one-to-four family residences are held by mortgage pools and trusts as collateral for mortgage-backed securities.

As for financial institutions, the two major investors in mortgages are commercial banks and thrifts (i.e., savings institutions). At one time, thrifts were by far the major investors in mortgages. Regulatory and tax considerations encouraged them to invest in mortgages, and until quite recently they tried to keep mortgages in their portfolios. Today, however, both because they have become more conscious of the problem of matching maturities and because the tax benefits have been reduced by the 1986 Tax Act, S&Ls have tended to sell a good portion of what they originate and to become increasingly dependent on the fees generated from originating and servicing mortgages.

The participation in the mortgage market by other institutional investors such as pension funds appears to be small based on the statistics reported in Table 24-2. However, other institutions invest in mortgages through their ownership of mortgage-backed securities.

MORTGAGE ORIGINATORS

The original lender is called the **mortgage originator**. Mortgage originators include commercial banks, thrifts, mortgage bankers, life insurance companies, and pension funds. The three largest originators for all types of residential mortgages are commercial banks, thrifts, and mortgage bankers,

Table 24-2

Holders of One-to-Four Family Mortgages as of the First Quarter of 1993

Holder	Dollars (in millions)	Percent
Major financial institutions		
Commercial banks	$ 506,976	17.0%
Savings institutions[1]	480,398	16.1
Life insurance companies	11,316	0.4
Total	$ 998,690	33.5%
Federal and related agencies		
Government National Mortgage Assoc. $	37	0.0%
Farmers Home Administration	18,149	0.6
Federal Housing and Veteran's Admin.	5,631	0.2
Resolution Trust Corporation	11,375	0.4
Federal National Mortgage Assoc.	127,252	4.3
Federal Land Banks	1,679	0.1
Federal Home Loan Mortgage Corp.	32,831	1.1
Total	$ 196,954	6.7%
Mortgage pools or trusts[2]		
Government National Mortgage Assoc. $	412,798	13.9%
Federal Home Loan Mortgage Corp.	415,279	14.0
Federal National Mortgage Assoc.	448,483	15.0
Farmers Home Administration	10	0.0
Private mortgage conduits	137,000	4.6
Total	$ 1,413,570	47.5%
Individuals and others[3]	$ 367,072	12.3%
Total of all types of holders	$ 2,976,286	100.0%

[1] Includes savings banks and savings and loan associations.

[2] Outstanding principal balances of mortgage-backed securities insured or guaranteed by the agency indicated.

[3] Other holders include mortgage companies, real estate investment trusts, state and local credit agencies, state and local retirement funds, noninsured pension funds, credit unions, and finance companies.

Source: Federal Reserve Bulletin, *December 1993*, Table A38.

originating more than 95% of mortgages each year. Mortgage bankers, (or more appropriately, mortgage brokers) typically do not invest in the mortgages they originate but rather sell the mortgages to other entities that will invest in them.[1]

Prior to 1990, thrifts were the largest originators, followed by commercial banks. In 1990, thrift origination declined; with an increase in commercial bank origination, the share of thrift origination dropped below that of commercial banks. In 1990, mortgage bankers' share of origination was the largest.

Originators may generate income for themselves in several ways. They typically charge an **origination fee** which fee is expressed in terms of points, where each point represents 1% of the borrowed funds. For example, an origination fee of two points on a $100,000 mortgage represents $2,000. Originators also charge application fees and certain processing fees. Another source of revenue is the profit that might be generated from selling a mortgage at a higher price than it originally cost. This profit is called **secondary marketing profit**. Of course, if mortgage rates rise, an originator will realize a loss when the mortgages are sold in the secondary market. Finally, the mortgage originator may hold the mortgage in its investment portfolio.

The Origination Process

A potential homeowner who wants to borrow funds to purchase a home will apply for a loan from a mortgage originator. The individual who seeks funds completes an application form that provides personal financial information, and pays an application fee; then the mortgage originator performs a credit evaluation of the applicant. The two primary factors in determining whether the funds will be lent are the (1) **payment-to-income** (**PTI**) ratio, and (2) the **loan-to-value** (**LTV**) ratio. The former is the ratio of monthly payments to monthly income and is a measure of the ability of the applicant to make monthly payments (both mortgage and real estate tax payments). The lower this ratio, the greater the likelihood that the applicant will be able to meet the required payments.

The difference between the purchase price of the property and the amount borrowed is the borrower's down payment. The LTV is the ratio of the amount of the loan to the market (or appraised) value of the property. The lower this ratio, the greater the protection the lender has if the applicant defaults on the payments and the lender must repossess and sell the property. For example, if an applicant wants to borrow $150,000 on property with an appraised value of $200,000, the LTV is 75%. Suppose the applicant subsequently defaults on the mortgage. The lender can then repossess the property and sell it to recover the amount owed. But the amount that will be received by the lender depends on the market value of the property. In our example, even if conditions in the housing market are weak, the lender will still be able to recover the proceeds lent if the value of the property declines by $50,000. Suppose instead that the applicant wanted to borrow $180,000 for the same property. The LTV would then be 90%. If the lender had to sell the property because the applicant defaults, there is less protection for the lender.

---

[1] The term mortgage banking refers to the activities of originating, servicing, and securitizing of mortgages.

If the lender decides to lend the funds, it sends a commitment letter to the applicant. This letter commits the lender to provide funds to the applicant. The length of time of the commitment varies between 30 and 60 days. At the time of the commitment letter, the lender will require that the applicant pay a commitment fee. It is important to understand that the commitment letter obligates the lender—not the applicant—to perform. The commitment fee that the applicant pays is lost if the applicant decides not to purchase the property or uses an alternative source of funds to purchase the property. Thus the commitment letter states that for a fee the applicant has the right but not the obligation to require the lender to provide funds at a certain interest rate and on certain terms.

At the time the application is submitted, the mortgage originator will give the applicant a choice among various types of mortgages. Basically, the choice is between a fixed-rate mortgage or an adjustable-rate mortgage. In the case of a fixed-rate mortgage, the lender typically gives the applicant a further choice of when the interest rate on the mortgage will be determined; the three choices may be: (1) at the time the loan application is submitted, (2) at the time a commitment letter is issued to the borrower, or (3) at the closing date (the date that the property is purchased).

These choices (i.e., the right to decide whether to close on the property and the right to select when to set the interest rate) granted to the applicant by the mortgage originator, exposes the latter to certain risks. We will discuss these risks, as well as how a mortgage originator must protect itself against these risks.

Mortgage originators can: (1) hold the mortgage in their portfolio, (2) sell the mortgage to an investor that wishes to hold the mortgage in its portfolio or that will place the mortgage in a pool of mortgages to be used as collateral for the issuance of a security, or (3) use the mortgage as collateral for the issuance of a security. When a mortgage is used as collateral for the issuance of a security, the mortgage is said to be **securitized**. We discuss the process of securitizing mortgage loans in Chapter 25.

When a mortgage originator intends to sell the mortgage, it will obtain a commitment from the potential investor (buyer). Two government-sponsored enterprises and several private companies buy mortgages. As these agencies and private companies pool these mortgages and sell them to investors, they are called **conduits**.

The two agencies, the Federal Home Loan Mortgage Corporation and the Federal National Mortgage Association (discussed further below), purchase only **conforming mortgages**. A conforming mortgage is one that meets the underwriting standards established by these agencies for being in a pool of mortgages underlying a security that they guarantee. Three underwriting standards established by these agencies in order to qualify as a conforming mortgage are a maximum PTI, a maximum LTV, and a maximum loan amount. If an applicant does not satisfy the underwriting standards, the mortgage is called a **nonconforming mortgage**. Loans that exceed the maximum loan amount are called **jumbo mortgages**.

Mortgages acquired by the agency may be held as investments in their portfolio or securitized. The securities offered are discussed in Chapter 25. Two examples of private conduits are the Residential Funding Corporation (a subsidiary of General Motors Acceptance Corporation) and PruHome. Private conduits typically will securitize the mortgages purchased rather than hold them as an investment. Both conforming and nonconforming mortgages are purchased.

Nonconforming mortgages do not necessarily have greater credit risk. For example, an individual with an annual income of $500,000 may apply for a mortgage loan of $250,000 on real estate that she wants to purchase for $1 million. This would be a nonconforming mortgage because the amount of the mortgage exceeds the limit currently established for a conforming mortgage, yet the individual's income can easily accommodate the monthly mortgage payments. Moreover, the lender's risk exposure is minimal, as it has lent $250,000 backed by collateral of $1 million.

The mortgage rate that the originator will set on the loan will depend on the mortgage rate required by the investor who plans to purchase the mortgage. There are different mortgage rates for delivery at different times (30 days, 60 days, or 90 days)

The Risks Associated with Mortgage Origination

The loan applications being processed and the commitments made by a mortgage originator together are called its **pipeline**. **Pipeline risk** refers to the risks associated with originating mortgages. This risk has two components: price risk and fallout risk.

Price risk refers to the adverse effects on the value of the pipeline if mortgage rates rise. If mortgage rates rise, and the mortgage originator has made commitments at a lower mortgage rate, it will either have to sell the mortgages when they close at a value below the funds lent to homeowners, or retain the mortgages as a portfolio investment earning a below-market mortgage rate. The mortgage originator faces the same risk for mortgage applications in the pipeline where the applicant has elected to fix the rate at the time the application is submitted.

Fallout risk is the risk that applicants or those who were issued commitment letters will not close (complete the transaction by purchasing the property with funds borrowed from the mortgage originator). The chief reason that potential borrowers may cancel their commitment or withdraw their mortgage application is that mortgage rates have declined sufficiently so that it is economic to seek an alternative source of funds. Fallout risk is the result of the mortgage originator giving the potential borrower the right but not the obligation to close (that is, the right to cancel the agreement). This is why we say that the mortgage originator has effectively sold the potential borrower an option. There are reasons other than a decline in mortgage rates to cause a potential borrower to fall out of the pipeline. There may be an unfavorable property inspection report, or the purchase could have been predicated on a change in employment that does not occur.

Mortgage originators have several alternatives to protect themselves against pipeline risk. To protect against price risk, the originator could get a commitment from the agency or the private conduit to whom the mortgage originator plans to sell the mortgage.[2] This sort of commitment is effectively a forward contract: the mortgage originator agrees to deliver a mortgage at a future date, and another party (either one of the agencies or a private conduit) agrees to buy the mortgage at that time at a predetermined price (or mortgage rate).

Consider what happens, however, if mortgage rates decline and potential borrowers elect to cancel the agreement. The mortgage originator has agreed to deliver a mortgage with a specified mortgage rate. If the potential borrower does not close, and the mortgage originator has made a commitment to deliver the mortgage to an agency or private conduit, the mortgage originator cannot back out of the transaction. As a result, the mortgage originator will realize a loss—it must deliver a mortgage at a higher mortgage rate in a lower mortgage rate environment. This is fallout risk.

Mortgage originators can protect themselves against fallout risk by entering into an agreement with an agency or private conduit for optional rather than mandatory delivery of the mortgage. In such an agreement, the mortgage originator is effectively buying an option that gives it the right, but not the obligation, to deliver a mortgage. The agency or private conduit has sold that option to the mortgage originator and therefore charges a fee for allowing optional delivery. Recall that fallout risk is the result of mortgage originators selling options to potential borrowers. Therefore, it makes economic sense for a mortgage originator to protect itself against fallout risk by buying an option.

MORTGAGE SERVICERS

Every mortgage loan must be serviced. Servicing of a mortgage loan involves collecting monthly payments and forwarding proceeds to owners of the loan; sending payment notices to mortgagors; reminding mortgagors when payments are overdue; maintaining records of principal balances; administering an escrow balance for real estate taxes and insurance purposes; initiating foreclosure proceedings if necessary; and furnishing tax information to mortgagors when applicable.

Servicers include bank-related entities, thrift-related entities, and mortgage bankers. As of 1989, the *American Banker* survey found that bank-related servicers had 43% of the market share and thrift-related servicers 20%. The market share of the latter has decreased since 1987 (when it reached 29%) because thrifts have been forced to sell off servicing rights in an attempt to bolster capital to satisfy the risk-based capital guidelines imposed by FIRREA. While the market shares of bank-related and thrift-related thrifts have been affected by regulatory requirements, particularly those relating to capital requirements, there are direct capital constraints on mortgage bankers.

Profit margins from mortgage servicing have been declining. Economies of scales in the servicing of mortgages is critical. While there are hundreds of small mortgage-servicing companies, a survey conducted in the first half of

---

[2] This commitment that the mortgage originator obtains to protect itself should not be confused with the commitment that the mortgage originator gives to the potential borrower.

1990 by *Inside Mortgage Finance* found that 30 mortgage servicers accounted for more than $500 billion in servicing volume (i.e, the amount of principal serviced).[3] Yet no one firm has more than 3% of the servicing market. Recent efforts have been to consolidate operations through mergers and acquisitions, and the increased purchasing of mortgage-servicing rights.

Mortgage-Servicing-Rights Transfer Market

There is a secondary market for servicing rights (i.e., the market for the transfer of the right to service a mortgage loan). The sale of servicing rights must be approved by the investor in the loans, or in the case of a mortgage loan that has been securitized, by the conduit that has securitized it.

There are brokers and listing services specializing in the trading of servicing rights. The service transfer brokerage industry includes major investment banking firms such as Merrill Lynch, Salomon Brothers, and Bear Stearns. But the industry seems to be fragmented, as evidenced by the description of the industry in 1988 as a "cottage-industry, run mainly by middle-aged entrepreneurs from offices outside the big cities."[4]

Revenue and Costs Associated with Mortgage Servicing

There are five sources of revenue from mortgage servicing. The primary source is the servicing fee. This fee is a fixed percentage of the outstanding mortgage balance. Consequently, the revenue from servicing declines over time as the mortgage balance amortizes. The second source of servicing income arises from the interest that can be earned by the servicer from the escrow balance that the borrower often maintains with the servicer.

The third source of revenue is the float earned on the monthly mortgage payment. This opportunity arises because of the delay permitted between the time the servicer receives the payment and the time that the payment must be sent to the investor. Fourth, there are several sources of ancillary income. First, a late fee is charged by the servicer if the payment is not made on time. Second, many servicers receive commissions from cross-selling their borrowers credit life and other insurance products. Third, fees can also be generated from selling mailing lists.

Finally, there are other benefits of servicing rights for servicers who are also lenders. Their portfolio of borrowers is a potential source for other loans such as second mortgages, automobile loans, and credit cards.

The periodic costs of servicing mortgage loans are predominately the cost of labor and computer systems. Estimates of the average total annual servicing cost per loans in 1988 range from $149 to $162. The lower of the two figures is from KPMG Peat Marwick's Mortgage Servicing Performance Study; the higher figure is from a study by the Mortgage Bankers Association of America.

Risks Associated with Servicing

The major source of revenue is the usually the servicing fee in the early years of a portfolio. Since that fee is a percentage of the outstanding mortgage bal-

---

[3] As reported in Guy D. Cecala, "Mortgage Servicing Is Where the Action Is," *United States Banker* (October 1990), p. 35.

[4] "$150 Billion Industry," *United States Banker* (December 1988), p. 14.

ance, any payments made in excess of the monthly mortgage payment reduces future revenue. Such payments are called prepayments and are explained later in this chapter. A payoff of a mortgage loan by prepayment or foreclosure makes the servicing rights of that loan worthless. Consequently, the value of the servicing rights depends upon prepayments that are related to the level of interest rates and foreclosures. As interest rates decline below the rate on the mortgage loan (called the **contract rate**), the likelihood of a borrower prepaying all or a portion of his or her loan increases. A rise in the level of interest rates will reduce prepayments.

What this means is that the value of servicing rights depends in a complicated way on the level of interest rates. More specifically, there are two opposite effects on the expected cash flow when interest rates change. The expected cash flow is equal to the expected mortgage balance times the servicing fee, minus the expected servicing cost. A fall (rise) in interest rates will decrease (increase) the expected future cash flow; and a fall (rise) in interest rates will increase (decrease) the present value of that cash flow. In typical ranges for interest rates, the dollar value of the servicing fee will move in the same direction as the change in interest. Consequently, unlike typical fixed-rate coupon securities (whose price moves in the direction opposite to that of the change in interest rates), the value of the servicing rights tends to move in the same direction. This is magnified by the affects on the other revenue sources as discussed below.

Hedging the value of servicing rights against prepayments is not simple. The usual capital market instruments and derivatives used to hedge fixed income securities cannot effectively hedge the value of servicing rights. As we shall explain in Chapter 26, mortgage-backed derivatives securities that can be used for this purpose have been developed.

In addition to the servicing fee, a change in interest rates will effect the revenue earned on the escrow balances. The effect, however, will not be symmetric. When interest rates rise, higher revenue will be generated; however, when interest rates fall there are two adverse consequences. First, lower interest revenue will be earned. However, if they fall by a sufficient amount, some mortgage loans will be paid off, requiring the payout to the borrower of the escrowed balance. Therefore, no interest revenue will be earned on these loans. Similarly, interest earned on the monthly mortgage payment float will be in the same direction as the change in interest rates.

In addition to risk due to prepayments, there is inflation risk. The cost of servicing will rise over time due to inflation. Moreover, a servicer must continue to service a mortgage despite the decline in the servicing fee as the mortgage balance declines over time as a result of amortization. Higher costs due to inflation and lower servicing fees due to amortization reduce the profitability of servicing a loan over time.

MORTGAGE INSURERS

There are two types of mortgage-related insurance. The first type is originated by the lender to insure against default by the borrower and is called **mortgage insurance**. It is usually required by lenders on loans with loan-to-value (LTV) ratios greater than 80%. The amount insured will be some percentage of the loan and may decline as the LTV ratio declines. While the insurance is required by the lender, the cost of the insurance is borne by the borrower, usually through a higher contract rate.

There are two forms of mortgage insurance: insurance provided by a government agency, and private mortgage insurance. The federal agencies that provide this insurance to qualified borrowers are the Federal Housing Administration (FHA), the Veterans Administration (VA), and the Federal Farmers Administration (FmHA). Private mortgage insurance can be obtained from a mortgage insurance company such as Mortgage Guaranty Insurance Company (owned by Northwestern Mutual) and PMI Mortgage Insurance Company (owned by Sears, Roebuck).

The second type of mortgage-related insurance is acquired by the borrower, usually with a life insurance company, and is typically called **credit life**. Unlike mortgage insurance, this type is not required by the lender. The policy provides for a continuation of mortgage payments after the death of the insured person, which allows the survivors to continue living in the house. Since the insurance coverage decreases as the mortgage balance declines, this type of mortgage insurance is simply a term policy.

While both types of insurance have a beneficial effect on the creditworthiness of the borrower, the first type is more important from the lender's perspective. Mortgage insurance is sought by the lender when the borrower is viewed as being capable of meeting the monthly mortgage payments, but does not have enough funds for a large down payment. For example, suppose a borrower seeks financing of $100,000 to purchase a single-family residence for $110,000, thus making a down payment of $10,000. The LTV ratio is 90.9%, exceeding the uninsured maximum LTV of 80%. Even if the lender's credit analysis indicates that the borrower's payment-to-income ratio (PTI) is acceptable, the mortgage loan cannot be granted. However, if a private mortgage insurance company insures a portion of the loan, then the lender is afforded protection. Mortgage insurance companies will write policies to insure a maximum of 20% of loans with a LTV ranging from 80% to 90%, and a maximum of 25% of loans with an LTV ranging from 90% to 95%. The lender is still exposed to default by the borrower on the noninsured portion of the mortgage loan and, in the case of private mortgage insurers, exposed to the risk that the insurer will default.

To illustrate what will happen if a borrower covered by private mortgage insurance defaults, suppose that in our previous example mortgage insurance is obtained for $15,000, and a default occurs when the market value of the property is $94,000, and the outstanding mortgage balance is $98,000. The mortgage insurer has two choices. It can simply pay the claim by giving the lender $15,000, thereby fulfilling its insurance obligation. The lender then has $15,000 plus the mortgaged property with a value of $94,000, producing a total value of $104,000 and a profit of $6,000. A more economical alternative for the mortgage insurer would be to pay off the mortgage balance of $98,000 and take title to the property. It can then sell the property for $94,000, realizing a loss of $4,000. This loss, however, is less than the $15,000 loss that would result by paying the claim.

The Mortgage Insurance Industry

The mortgage insurance industry took off in the 1970s and continued to grow until the early 1980s. The share of private mortgage insurance, relative to the total mortgage market, grew from 15% in the 1970s to 30% in 1983-84.[5]

In the 1970s and in 1980, the mortgage insurance industry was extremely profitable. However, for the remainder of the 1980s, profitability declined and subsequently underwriting losses were realized. According to Moody's Investor's Service, in 1979 mortgage insurers' total losses were only $39 million, representing 13% of premiums earned. By 1982, total losses increased to $210 million, representing 60% of premiums earned and producing an underwriting loss of about $40 million. By 1985, the industry as a whole had losses that exceeded premiums with a loss in excess of $1 billion. As a result, between 1985 and April 1988 almost half the industry stopped writing mortgage insurance.

The underwriting losses that were realized in 1982 and 1983 were due in part to the default rate that resulted from the 1981–82 recession. Even following the recession, there were increased claims and underwriting losses due to a variety of reasons, including: (1) underpricing of mortgage insurance, (2) lax or fraudulent underwriting standards by mortgage originators, and (3) localized economic problems (in certain parts of Texas, Louisiana, and Oklahoma, for example).

Default Risks Associated with Mortgage Insurance Underwriting

The upheavals of the industry discussed above point to the various sources of default risk to which insurers are exposed. These underwriting sources can be classified into the following broad categories: (1) normal (or actuarial) risks, (2) originator underwriting risks, (3) national economic risks, and (4) local economic risks. Below we summarize these risks and discuss measures taken to manage these risks.

Normal risks—Insurers expect that a certain percentage of the borrowers will default due to unique circumstances not directly attributable to any of the other categories of default risk. A loss of employment in a period of rising national and local employment rates would be an example. Death or prolonged illness of the primary wage earner of the borrowing family would be another example.

Originator underwriting risk—At one time, mortgage originators such as banks and thrifts would retain the mortgage loan in their portfolio. As a consequence, they kept underwriting standards tight. Since local lending was common, lenders were familiar with economic and real estate market conditions in their geographical area. However, as mortgage bankers, as well as banks and thrifts, began originating mortgages with the intention of selling them in the secondary market, some either became lax in their underwriting standards or in certain instances deliberately misrepresented information to mortgage insurers and investors about the borrower and/or property.

---

[5] Bill Simpson, "Private Mortgage Insurance on the Rebound," *Secondary Mortgage Market* (Spring 1989), p. 7.

Moreover, national mortgage originators were not as familiar with local real estate markets.

To manage this type of default risk, mortgage insurers have become less reliant on the credit analysis of mortgage originators. Instead, they have established their own credit analysis departments and undertaken more extensive quality control programs. They use this information to assess and analyze performance, continually revising their underwriting standards. For example, when analysis of claims with different types of mortgage designs showed that claims on adjustable-rate mortgages were greater than on fixed-rate mortgages, mortgage insurers changed insurance rates to reflect the greater default risk.

In the case of mortgage insurance policies written for mortgage loans in which fraudulent or misleading information is suspected, mortgage insurers have been more aggressive in fighting such claims submitted by investors. Since the investor is not necessarily the mortgage originator, this exposes investors to fraudulent practice. However, investors have a claim on the mortgage originator and servicer for misrepresentations and warranties that it makes in the sale of a mortgage.

National economic risks—Default rates are positively related to national economic conditions. As national unemployment levels increase, claims increase. The extreme case of national economic risk is catastrophic risk in which an economic depression and substantial nationwide decline in property values results in a surge of claims.

Local economic risks—While the national economy may be thriving, regions within the United States may suffer high levels of unemployment and depressed property values. Some mortgage insurers have handled this problem by not writing policies in problem regions or potential problem regions. Others have responded by controlling this risk through geographical diversification of policies, coupled with differential rates, to reflect the geographical location of the property.[6]

THE TRADITIONAL MORTGAGE

Now that we understand the players in the mortgage market, we turn to the characteristics or design of the mortgage loan. Both mortgage design and the origin of the funds financing housing mortgages have, since the Great Depression, undergone revolutionary changes and been affected by spectacular innovations. Until the Great Depression, mortgages were not fully amortized as they are now. Instead they were balloon instruments where the principal is not amortized, or only partially amortized at maturity, leaving the debtor with the problem of refinancing the balance. Sometimes the bank could even ask for repayment of the outstanding balance on demand or relatively short notice, even if the mortgagor was fulfilling its obligations. This system of mortgage financing proved disastrous during the Great Depression, and contributed to its depth and personal distress, as banks that were afflicted by loan losses and depositor withdrawals found it necessary to liquidate their mortgage loans, and debtors found it impossible to refinance their debt.

---

[6] Another reason for differential rates by region—more specifically by state—is the affect of state laws on foreclosure costs.

By the middle of the 1930s this experience led to the widespread adoption of a much superior instrument called the **fixed-rate**, **level-payment**, **fully amortized mortgage** (**level-payment fixed-rate mortgage**, for short). This development was encouraged by the newly created Federal Housing Administration (FHA), whose assignments included providing for affordable insurance to protect the lender's claim against nonperformance by the borrower. This insurance is desirable not only for the lender but also for the borrower who, with insurance, would usually be able to secure better terms. The FHA specified the kind of mortgages it was prepared to insure and one of the requirements was that the instrument had to be a level-payment fixed-rate mortgage. The level-payment fixed-rate mortgage is also referred to as a **traditional mortgage**.

Characteristics of the Fixed-Rate, Level-Payment, Fully Amortized Mortgage

The basic idea behind the design of the traditional mortgage is that the borrower pays interest and repays principal in equal installments over an agreed-upon period of time, called the maturity or term of the mortgage. Thus at the end of the term, the loan has been fully amortized. The interest rate is generally above the risk-free rate because of servicing costs, default risk that is present despite the collateral, and some further risks discussed below. The frequency of payment is typically monthly, and the prevailing term of the mortgage is 20 to 30 years; in recent years an increasing number of 15-year mortgages have been originated.

Each monthly mortgage payment for a level-payment fixed-rate mortgage is due on the first of each month and consists of: (1) interest of 1/12th of the fixed annual interest rate times the amount of the outstanding mortgage balance at the beginning of the previous month; and (2) a repayment of a portion of the outstanding mortgage balance (principal).

The difference between the monthly mortgage payment and the portion of the payment that represents interest equals the amount that is applied to reduce the outstanding mortgage balance. The monthly mortgage payment is designed so that after the last scheduled monthly payment of the loan is made, the amount of the outstanding mortgage balance is zero (i.e., the mortgage is fully repaid).

To illustrate a level-payment fixed-rate mortgage, consider a 30-year (360-month), $100,000 mortgage with an 8.125% mortgage rate. The monthly mortgage payment would be $742.50.[7] Table 24-3 shows for selected months how

---

[7] Calculation of the monthly mortgage payment is just a basic application of the present value of an annuity. It can be determined as follows:

$$\text{Monthly mortgage payment} = \frac{\text{Amount of funds borrowed}}{\text{Present value of an annuity of \$1 per month}}$$

The present value of an annuity of $1 per month can be calculated as follows:

$$\text{PV of an annuity of \$1 per month} = \frac{1 - \dfrac{1}{(1+r)^n}}{r}$$

where n = number of months of the mortgage
r = simple monthly interest rate (annual interest rate/12)

each monthly mortgage payment is divided between interest and repayment of principal. At the beginning of month 1, the mortgage balance is $100,000, the amount of the original loan. The mortgage payment for month 1 includes interest on the $100,000 borrowed for the month. Since the interest rate is 8.125%, the monthly interest rate is 0.0067708 (0.08125 divided by 12). Interest for month 1 is therefore $677.08 ($100,000 times 0.0067708). The $65.41 difference between the monthly mortgage payment of $742.50 and the interest of $677.08 is the portion of the monthly mortgage payment that represents repayment of principal. This $65.41 in month 1 reduces the mortgage balance.

The mortgage balance at the end of month 1 (beginning of month 2) is then $99,934.59 ($100,000 minus $65.41). The interest for the second monthly mortgage payment is $676.64, the monthly interest rate (0.0066708) times the mortgage balance at the beginning of month 2 ($99,934.59). The difference between the $742.50 monthly mortgage payment and the $676.64 interest is $65.86, representing the amount of the mortgage balance paid off with that monthly mortgage payment. Notice that the last mortgage payment in month 360 is sufficient to pay off the remaining mortgage balance. When a loan repayment schedule is structured in this way, so that the payments made by the borrower will completely pay off the interest and principal, the loan is said to be **fully amortizing**. Table 24-3 is then referred to as an **amortization schedule**.

As Table 24-3 clearly shows, *the portion of the monthly mortgage payment applied to interest declines each month and the portion applied to reducing the mortgage balance increases.* The reason for this is that as the mortgage balance is reduced with each monthly mortgage payment, the interest on the mortgage balance declines. Since the monthly mortgage payment is fixed, an increasingly larger portion of the monthly payment is applied to reduce the principal in each subsequent month.

Prepayments and Cash Flow Uncertainty

Our illustration of the cash flow from a level-payment fixed-rate mortgage assumes that the homeowner does not pay off any portion of the mortgage balance prior to the scheduled due date. But homeowners do pay off all or part of their mortgage balance prior to the maturity date. Payments made in excess of the scheduled principal repayments are called **prepayments**.

Prepayments occur for one of several reasons. First, homeowners prepay the entire mortgage when they sell their home. The sale of a home may occur because of a change of employment that necessitates moving, the purchase of a more expensive home ("trading up"), or a divorce in which the settlement requires sale of the marital residence. Second, the borrower may be moved to

---

For example, consider the $100,000, 30-year, 8.125% mortgage. Then, the monthly mortgage payment is:

$$\frac{\$100,000}{\text{Present value of an annuity of \$1 per month}}$$

As $n = 360$ and $r = 0.0067708$ (= 0.08125/12), the present value of an annuity of $1 per month is:

$$\frac{1 - \dfrac{1}{(1.0067708)^{360}}}{.0067708} = 134.681$$

The monthly mortgage payment is then:

$$\frac{\$100,000}{134.681} = \$742.50$$

Table 24-3
Amortization Schedule for a Level-Payment Fixed-Rate Mortgage

Mortgage loan: $100,000
Mortgage rate: 8.125%
Monthly payment: $742.50
Term of loan: 30 years (360 months)

Month	Beginning mortgage balance	Monthly payment	Monthly interest	Scheduled principal repayment	Ending mortgage balance
1	100,000.00	742.50	677.08	65.41	99,934.59
2	99,934.59	742.50	676.64	65.86	99,868.73
3	99,868.73	742.50	676.19	66.30	99,802.43
4	99,802.43	742.50	675.75	66.75	99,735.68
25	98,301.53	742.50	665.58	76.91	98,224.62
26	98,224.62	742.50	665.06	77.43	98,147.19
27	98,147.19	742.50	664.54	77.96	98,069.23
74	93,849.98	742.50	635.44	107.05	93,742.93
75	93,742.93	742.50	634.72	107.78	93,635.15
76	93,635.15	742.50	633.99	108.51	93,526.64
141	84,811.77	742.50	574.25	168.25	84,643.52
142	84,643.52	742.50	573.11	169.39	84,474.13
143	84,474.13	742.50	571.96	170.54	84,303.59
184	76,446.29	742.50	517.61	224.89	76,221.40
185	76,221.40	742.50	516.08	226.41	75,994.99
186	75,994.99	742.50	514.55	227.95	75,767.04
233	63,430.19	742.50	429.48	313.02	63,117.17
234	63,117.17	742.50	427.36	315.14	62,802.03
235	62,802.03	742.50	425.22	317.28	62,484.75
289	42,200.92	742.50	285.74	456.76	41,744.15
290	41,744.15	742.50	282.64	459.85	41,284.30
291	41,284.30	742.50	279.53	462.97	40,821.33
321	25,941.42	742.50	175.65	566.85	25,374.57
322	25,374.57	742.50	171.81	570.69	24,803.88
323	24,803.88	742.50	167.94	574.55	24,229.32
358	2,197.66	742.50	14.88	727.62	1,470.05
359	1,470.05	742.50	9.95	732.54	737.50
360	737.50	742.50	4.99	737.50	0.00

pay off part of the mortgage balance as market rates fall below the mortgage rate. Third, in the case of homeowners who cannot meet their mortgage obligations, the property is repossessed and sold. The proceeds of such a sale are used to pay off the mortgage in the case of a conventional mortgage. For an insured mortgage, the insurer will pay off the mortgage balance. Finally, if property is destroyed by fire or if another insured catastrophe occurs, the insurance proceeds are used to pay off the mortgage. We will look more closely at the factors that affect prepayment behavior in Chapter 25.

The effect of prepayments is that the amount and timing of the cash flow from a mortgage is not known with certainty. For example, all that the investor in a $100,000, 8.125% 30-year FHA-insured mortgage knows is that as long as the loan is outstanding, interest will be received and the principal will be repaid at the scheduled date each month; then at the end of the 30 years, the investor would have received $100,000 in principal payments. What the investor does not know—the uncertainty—is for how long the loan will be outstanding, and therefore what the timing of the principal payments will be. This is true for all mortgage loans, not just level-payment fixed-rate mortgages.

Deficiencies of the Traditional Mortgage

There are problems with the traditional mortgage design. In the presence of high and variable inflation, this mortgage design suffers from two basic and serious shortcomings: these may be labeled the "mismatch" problem and the "tilt" problem.

Savings and loan associations have faced the mismatch problem during most of the post-World War II period, because mortgages—a very long-term asset—have been financed largely by depository institutions that obtain their funds through deposits that are primarily, if not entirely, of a short-term nature. These institutions have engaged inevitably in a highly speculative activity: borrowing short and lending very long. That is, there is a mismatch of the maturity of the assets (i.e., mortgages) and the liabilities raised to fund those assets. Speculation of this sort will prove a losing proposition if interest rates rise, as is bound to happen in the presence of significant inflation. The institution may be earning the contractual rate, but to attract the deposits needed to finance the loan, it will have to pay the current higher market rate. Considering that the intermediation margin or spread is modest—some 100 to 200 basis points—it will not take much inflation or rise in interest rates before an institution runs into a loss.

Another way to explain the mismatch problem is in terms of the balance sheet rather than the income statement. The difference between lending and borrowing rates will cause the lending institution to become technically insolvent, in the sense that the market value of their assets will be insufficient to cover their liabilities. The reason for this is that the institution's liabilities are related to the face value of its mortgage assets, but the market value of these assets will be below the face value of the mortgage loan. For these reasons both losses and technical insolvencies have occurred on a large scale since the late 1960s, especially in the 1970s and early 1980s

One obvious way to resolve this is for the institution that primarily finances fixed-rate mortgages to lengthen its liabilities through term deposits or analogous instruments. Actually, this has been done in recent years, but only to a modest extent. In fact, it is doubtful that this approach could go very far in meeting the problem, for what has made S&Ls so popular is unquestionably the highly liquid, riskless nature of their deposits. If they were allowed to finance mortgages only by long-term deposits, we might expect a substantial decline in the volume of funds available to them for mortgage financing. A second alternative is to create a different mortgage design than the traditional mortgage, the adjustable-rate mortgage, which we will discuss shortly.

The tilt problem refers to what happens to the real burden of mortgage payments over the life of the mortgage as a result of inflation. If the general price level rises, the real value of the mortgage payments will decline over time. If a homeowner's real income rises over time, this coupled with a decline in the real value of the mortgage payments will mean that the burden of the mortgage payments will decline over time. Thus, the homeowner's mortgage obligation places a greater burden in real terms in the initial years. In other words, the real burden is "tilted" to the initial years. This discourages people from purchasing a home because of the greater real burden of the mortgage payments in their early years. The tilt problem is behind the development of other types of mortgage instruments which we describe later in this chapter.

THE MISMATCH PROBLEM AND THE CREATION OF ADJUSTABLE-RATE MORTGAGES

One way to resolve the mismatch problem is redesigning the traditional mortgage so as to produce a mortgage loan whose return would match the short-term market rates, thus better matching the cost of the liabilities. One instrument satisfying these requirements, and that has won considerable popularity, is the **adjustable-rate mortgage**.

An adjustable-rate mortgage (ARM) is a loan in which the contract rate is reset periodically in accordance with some appropriately chosen reference rate. This mortgage design represents an approach applied to many other instruments, such as bank loans. By using a reference rate that is a short-term rate, depository institutions are able to improve the matching of their returns to their cost of funds. Equivalently, an instrument earning the market rate could be expected to remain close to par whether interest rates rise or fall, thus avoiding the problems of technical insolvency that have plagued the S&Ls relying on the traditional mortgage. Note also that, with high and variable rates of inflation, an adjustable-rate, in principle, reduces risk for the borrower—reduced inflation generally is accompanied by a fall in interest rates, which will benefit borrowers with an adjustable-rate mortgage.

Outstanding ARMs call for resetting the contract rate either every month, six months, year, two years, three years or five years. The contract rate at the reset date is equal to a reference rate plus a spread. The spread is typically between 200 and 300 basis points, reflecting market conditions, the features of the ARM, and the increased cost of servicing an ARM compared to a fixed-rate mortgage.

Reference Rate

Two categories of reference rates have been used in ARMs: market-determined rates and calculated rates based on the cost of funds for thrifts. Market-determined rates have been limited to Treasury-based rates. The reference rate will have an important impact on the performance of an ARM and how they are priced.

The cost of funds index for thrifts is based on the monthly weighted average interest cost for liabilities of thrifts. The two more popular indexes are the Eleventh Federal Home Loan Bank Board District Cost of Funds Index (COFI) and the National Cost of Funds Index, the former being the most popular.

The Eleventh District includes the states of California, Arizona, and Nevada. The cost of funds is calculated by first computing the monthly interest expenses for all thrifts included in the Eleventh District. The interest expenses are summed and then divided by the average of the beginning and ending monthly balance. The index value is reported with a one-month lag. For example, June's Eleventh District COFI is reported in July. The contract rate for a mortgage based on the Eleventh District COFI is usually reset based on the previous month's reported index rate. For example, if the reset date is August, the index rate reported in July will be used to set the contract rate. Consequently, there is a two-month lag by the time the average cost of funds is reflected in the contract rate. This obviously is an advantage to the borrower when interest rates are rising and a disadvantage to the investor. The opposite is true when interest rates are falling.

The National Cost of Funds Index is calculated based on all federally-insured S&Ls. A median cost of funds is calculated rather than an average. This index is reported with about a one and 1 ½ month delay. The contract rate is typically reset based on the most recently reported index value.

Features of Adjustable-Rate Mortgages

To encourage borrowers to accept ARMs rather than fixed-rate mortgages, mortgage originators generally offer an initial contract rate that is less than the prevailing market mortgage rate. This below-market initial contract rate, set by the mortgage originator based on competitive market conditions, is commonly referred to as a **teaser rate**. At the reset date, the reference rate plus the spread determines the new contract rate. For example, suppose that one-year ARMs are typically offering a 200 basis point spread over the reference rate. Suppose also that the reference rate is 5.5%, so that the initial contract rate should be 7.5%. The mortgage originator might set an initial contract rate of 6.75%, a rate 75 basis points below the current value of the reference rate plus the spread.

A pure ARM is one that resets periodically and has no other terms that affect the monthly mortgage payment. However, the monthly mortgage payment, and hence, the investor's cash flow, are affected by other terms. These are due to periodic caps and lifetime rate caps and floors.

Periodic caps limit the amount that the interest rate may increase or decrease at the reset date. The periodic rate cap is expressed in percentage points. The most common rate cap on annual reset loans is 2%. Looking at this provision from the perspective of option theory, what is a periodic cap on the interest rate? Effectively the lender or investor has given the homeowner the right to borrow money at a below-market interest rate should the reference rate plus the spread exceed the periodic cap. Thus, the lender or investor has sold the homeowner an option on an interest rate. In fact, because the cap goes into effect each year, the lender or investor has not sold one option but a package of options. Similarly, the homeowner has given the lender or investor the right to earn an above-market interest rate should the reference rate plus the spread fall below the periodic cap.

Most ARMs have an upper limit on the mortgage rate that can be charged over the life of the loan. This **lifetime loan cap** is expressed in terms of the initial rate, the most common lifetime cap being 5% to 6%. For example, if the initial mortgage rate is 7% and the lifetime cap is 5%, the maximum interest rate that the lender can charge over the life of the loan is 12%. Many ARMs also have a lower limit (floor) on the interest rate that can be charged over the life of the loan.

Once again, looking at the lifetime cap as an option, the lender or investor has effectively sold the homeowner an option on an interest rate. What about a lifetime floor? In this case, the homeowner is compensating the lender or investor should the interest rate fall below the floor. Therefore, the homeowner has sold the lender or investor an option. From the lender's or investor's perspective, an ARM with a lifetime cap and floor is equivalent to a "collar"—a maximum interest rate and a minimum interest rate. This, then, is equivalent to selling an option (the cap) at one interest rate and buying an option (the floor) at a lower interest rate.

Assessment of Adjustable-Rate Mortgages

On the whole, the adjustable-rate mortgage has the merit of providing a manageable solution to the problem of mismatch of maturities. To borrowers, these mortgages reduce the risk associated with uncertain inflation. Unfortunately, the merits of the ARM have been significantly impaired by arbitrary and misguided regulatory rules, particularly interest rate caps. These caps, meant to protect the borrower, might make sense if rates were unilaterally set by the lender, but they do not make sense when they are tied to an objective market rate, or to the cost of funds to the lending institution. Furthermore, we know that an increase in nominal rates tends to occur when there is an appreciable rise in inflation, in which case the borrower, in general, can afford to pay the higher interest rate while it lasts.

The main effect of caps is to increase the risk of inflation to intermediary lenders who have no way of putting a cap on the rate they have to pay. Nor is a floor adequate compensation, because borrowers have the right to repay. Of course, some of the expected loss will tend to be recouped by a higher spread, and thus finally unloaded on some borrowers; even so, it would be best to leave the matter of caps to private bargaining.

Unfortunately, regulators have still not grasped these simple principles. Nor have they understood that in many cases the consumer generally pays for "consumer protection" in the form of higher rates or other less favorable terms. Finally, the adjustable-rate mortgage is not a satisfactory answer to inflation-swollen interest rates because it does not address the tilt problem as the payments are still based on a nominal rather than a real interest rate.

Balloon Mortgages

A variant of the adjustable-rate mortgage is the **balloon/reset mortgage**. The primary difference between a balloon/reset mortgage design and the one described above is that the mortgage rate is reset less frequently.

While new to the U.S. mortgage market, the balloon mortgage has long been used in Canada where it is referred to as a *rollover mortgage*. In this mortgage design the borrower is given long-term financing by the lender but at specified future dates the contract rate is renegotiated. Thus, the lender is providing long-term funds for what is effectively short-term borrowing, how short depending on the frequency of the renegotiation period. Effectively it is a short-term balloon loan in which the lender agrees to provide financing for the remainder of the term of the mortgage. The balloon payment is the original amount borrowed less the amount amortized.

The Federal Home Loan Bank Board attempted to introduce this mortgage design in January 1980 when it proposed a prototype rollover mortgage design. The prototype called for the contract rate to be renegotiated every three to five years (with the specific time period being determined at the time the mortgage is originated), with a maximum contract rate change of 50 basis points for each year in the renegotiation period (i.e., 150 basis points if renegotiated every three years and 250 basis points if every five years), and the lender guaranteeing to provide new financing. There were several proposals as to how the new contract rate should be determined.

While the rollover mortgage was hailed as an important step in alleviating the mismatch problem faced by thrifts, it did not catch on until 1990, and they are now called balloon/reset mortgages, or simply balloon mortgages. Two government-sponsored enterprises, Fannie Mae and Freddie Mac, have programs for the purchase of these mortgages. Freddie Mac's 30-year balloon/resets, for example, can have either a renegotiation period of 5 years ("30-due-in-5" FRMs) or 7 years ("30-due-in-7" FRMs). If certain conditions are met, Freddie Mac guarantees the extension of the loan. The contract rate set by Freddie Mac is based on its 30-year, single-family, fixed-rate, 60-day-delivery mortgage rate. If the borrower elects to extend the mortgage, a nominal processing fee is charged.

Hybrid Mortgages

ARMs that can be converted into fixed-rate mortgages are called **convertible ARMs**. There are also fixed-rate mortgages whose mortgage rate can fall if interest rates drop by some predetermined level—these are called **reducible fixed-rate mortgages**. Unlike convertible ARMs, reducible FRMs have not been a popular financing vehicle to borrowers. Convertible ARMs and reducible FRMs are hybrid mortgages with built-in refinancing options. These hybrid mortgage instruments reduce the cost of refinancing.[8]

A convertible ARM gives the borrower the choice of converting to a fixed-rate mortgage. However, the new rate could be either a rate determined by the

---

[8] For a more detailed discussion of these instruments, see Arnold Kling, "Refinancing Express," *Secondary Mortgage Markets* (Spring 1988), pp. 2-6.

lender or a market-determined rate. As an example of the latter, the rate could be some interest rate spread over the mortgage commitment rates established by one of the agencies that purchase mortgages. The trend today is toward a market-determined rate. A borrower typically can convert at any date between the first and the fifth times that the mortgage rate is reset. The lender charges a nominal fee for conversion.

In the case of a fixed-rate mortgage that may be adjusted downward, the borrower can exercise the option to have the mortgage adjusted only if some predetermined index rate falls below a certain level (called the *trigger rate*). Usually this option is not granted for the entire life of the mortgage, but typically only for the first five or six years.

Hybrid mortgage instruments reduce the cost of refinancing substantially. At the same time, investors in convertible ARMs and reducible fixed-rate mortgages must be compensated for holding them because they have effectively sold an option to borrowers.

THE TILT PROBLEM AND THE CREATION OF OTHER MORTGAGE INSTRUMENTS

The traditional mortgage was designed so that the borrower would repay the debt in constant nominal installments. This form of repayment would seem highly desirable from the debtor's point of view, so long as inflation was zero or small, because a level nominal repayment rate in that case implies a level real rate of repayment. However, when there is significant inflation the traditional mortgage turns into a malfunctioning, very undesirable vehicle for home financing. The reason is not, as frequently supposed, that inflation increases interest rates. To be sure, with a 10% rate of inflation we would expect the nominal interest rate to rise by roughly 10 percentage points—say, from 5% to 15%. But this rise does not, per se, make the lender any better off or the borrower any worse off, as the increase is offset by inflation losses and gains, leaving the real rate largely unchanged. The higher interest rate is, by and large, compensated for by the erosion of the principal in terms of purchasing power. (In nominal terms, the higher rate is offset by the rise in the value of the property.)

Rather, the reason for the unsatisfactory performance of the traditional mortgage lies in the "tilt" effect: with 10% steady inflation, if the nominal payment is level, then the real payment will decrease at 10% per year. By the twentieth year, it will be down to some 15% of the initial installment payment. If the creditor is to receive the same real amount as in the absence of inflation, the gradual erosion of the repayments in terms of purchasing power will have to be made up by sufficiently high initial real (and hence nominal) payments. Indeed, with the interest rate rising from 5% to 15%, the first payment on a long-term mortgage will rise roughly threefold.

The nature of the distortion or tilt in the real payment path is illustrated in Figure 24-1 for different rates of inflation. Notice that for an 8% rate of inflation, the path starts at more than twice the no-inflation level, to terminate at well below half. The high initial payment caused by inflation has the effect of foreclosing home ownership to large segments of the population, or forcing buyers to scale down their demands. Indeed, not many people would be able to pay a multiple of what they were paying in the preinflation period for the same home. This is especially true in the case of young people who have little asset accumulation.

The first thing to note about this problem is that it is not addressed by the adjustable-rate mortgage. That mortgage uses throughout a nominal interest rate comparable to the fixed-rate mortgage. In particular, the critical early payment will be roughly as high as with a traditional mortgage. Actually, one can show that the adjustable rate is, in some ways, even worse for borrowers than the traditional mortgage. It starts with a rate as high as the traditional mortgage independently of inflation, and will make a substantial jump every time the interest rate is adjusted and the payment shifts from one nominal level to another—even though the rate of payment is level as long as the interest rate does not change.

Can the tilt problem be remedied? It is clear that in principle a solution must involve reducing the interest rate used in the early payments and recouping later. Three mortgage designs (with many variants) have been offered to solve the tilt problem: the graduated-payment mortgage, the price-level adjusted mortgage, and the dual-rate mortgage.

Figure 24-1
Nature of Tilt Problem: Real Value of Monthly Payments

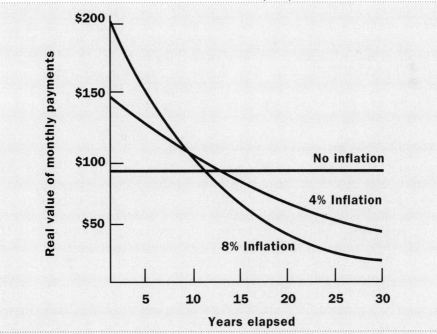

Source: D. Tucker, "The Variable-Rate Graduated Payment Mortgage," **Real Estate Review** *(Spring 1975), p. 72.*

Graduated-Payment Mortgage

A **graduated-payment mortgage** (GPM) is one in which the nominal monthly payment grows at a constant rate during a portion of the life of the contract, thereafter leveling off. The mortgage rate is fixed for the life of the loan, despite the fact that the monthly mortgage payment gradually increases. The terms of a GPM plan include (1) the mortgage rate, (2) the term of the mortgage, (3) the number of years over which the monthly mortgage payment will increase (and when the level payments will begin), and (4) the annual percent increase in the mortgage payments. The most popular 30-year GPM plan permitted by the FHA to qualify for its insurance calls for monthly payments that increase by 7.5% for five years, then at the beginning of the sixth year remain constant for the remaining 25 years. The monthly mortgage payments under this GPM program for a $100,000, 30-year, 10% mortgage would be:

$667.04 per month in the first year.
$717.06 per month in the second year.
$770.84 in the third year.
$828.66 in the fourth year.
$890.80 in the fifth year.
$957.62 for the remaining term of the mortgage, beginning with the sixth year.

Because this mortgage design involves a fixed rate over the life of the loan, while the rate of inflation may be highly variable over the same period, the GPM is not likely to succeed in assuring the debtor anything approaching a level real repayment stream. Thus, it does not solve the tilt problem. It should be apparent that it cannot solve the mismatching problem. These shortcomings have probably contributed to the decreasing popularity of GPMs in recent years. In fact, the only two basic mortgage designs that can provide a more or less foolproof solution to both problems are the price-level-adjusted mortgage and the dual-rate mortgage.

Price-Level-Adjusted Mortgage

This mortgage design is similar to the traditional mortgage except that monthly payments are designed to be level in purchasing-power terms rather than in nominal terms, and that the fixed rate is in the "real" rather than the nominal rate.[9] To compute the monthly payment under a price-level-adjusted mortgage (PLAM), the following terms of the contract must be specified: (1) the real interest rate, (2) the term of the loan, and (3) the index to be used to measure the price level, usually the Consumer Price Index (CPI). Using an ordinary mortgage table, the annual payment and the unpaid balance at the end of each year, corresponding to the stipulated real interest and maturity, can then be computed. These figures represent payments and balances in real terms. To compute the payments actually due in each year, multiply the real payment by an inflation-correction factor equal to the ratio of the stipulated

---

[9] The real rate is the interest rate that one could expect to prevail if there were no inflation in the economy.

index in the last year to the value of the index in the initial year. Similarly, to compute the actual debt, multiply the real debt by the inflation correction factor.[10]

The PLAM is not a new concept; it has been used for decades in many countries with high inflation, where the housing industries could not possibly have survived with the traditional mortgage. These include Finland right after World War II, many South American countries, and Israel. Somewhat surprisingly, it has not been used to any significant extent in the United States. This is largely explained because no innovation in home financing has been possible without some sanction of government regulators, and regulators have been unimaginative, and rather disinclined toward real indexation of any type. Critical in this respect has been HUD's lack of approval for FHA insurance. Quite recently, however, HUD seems about ready to change this attitude and to issue regulations to standardize these mortgages. PLAM may soon be making its debut in the United States.

Dual-Rate Mortgage

Also referred to as the **inflation-proof mortgage**, the dual-rate mortgage (DRM) is similar in spirit and objective to the PLAM: payments start low—at mortgage rates of around 10%, for example, payments would start around 30% to 40% below those required by the traditional mortgage or by the ARM. They then rise smoothly at the rate of inflation, if any, achieving, like the PLAM, annual payments approximately level in terms of purchasing power. Finally, by construction, the debt is fully amortized by the end of the contract.

The DRM differs from the PLAM in that the amount owed by the borrower is computed on the basis of a floating short-term rate. This has several important consequences. First, just as in the case of other instruments where a fluctuating rate is indexed to short-term market rates, the market value of the instrument is not subject to interest rate risk but should instead remain close to par, except of course for credit risk. Second, there is little danger of prepayments due to refinancing (i.e., of the borrower taking the option to repay when rates fall) for the DRM rate would automatically fall. And finally, it can be financed through the existing institution of short-term nominal deposits.

A DRM requires specification of three parameters. First, the "payment" rate is specified as a "real" rate of interest fixed for the life of the loan, much as with a PLAM. The purpose of this rate is not to establish how much the debtor will pay but rather how the amount will be paid, to make possible a desirable and affordable distribution of payments over the life of the instrument. Second, the "effective" or "debiting" rate is specified; this is a short-term rate that, as in the ARM, determines how much the borrower effectively pays (or is debited) and how much the creditor earns. This changes periodically, say, once a year, on the basis of an agreed-upon reference short-term rate such as the one-year Treasury bill rate. Third, the life of the mortgage is specified, just as for any other fully amortized mortgage contract.

So far the DRM has had rather limited application in the United States, in good measure because it has not yet received FHA approval for insurance. It

---

[10] For a discussion of the PLAM see, Susan E. Woodward and David A. Crowe, "A Power-Packed Mortgage," *Secondary Mortgage Markets* (Fall 1988), pp. 2-7.

has had some application abroad and should have a future also in the United States after the PLAM has been introduced. There are a number of variants of the DRM that improve the working of the instrument in some directions, at the cost of deterioration in other directions.[11]

DEFAULT RISK FOR MORTGAGES

Default risk is the risk that the homeowner/borrower will default. For federally insured mortgages, this risk is minimal. For privately insured mortgages, the risk can be gauged by the credit rating of the private insurance company that has insured the mortgage. For conventional mortgages (mortgages without insurance), the credit risk depends on the borrower.

Studies of Default

There are several studies of mortgage loan defaults. The measure of default used in these studies is the **conditional default rate**, which is the probability that a mortgage loan will default this year. Alternatively, the conditional default rate is the percentage of mortgage loans that start the year and default sometime during the year. It is a conditional measure because it is the probability of default given that a mortgage loan has survived to this year.[12] Measuring default in this way is better than measuring it in terms of the percentage of mortgage loans that were originated and subsequently defaulted, because the conditional default rate relates defaults to a particular point in time and to a particular set of economic conditions.

One of the first extensive statistical studies of conditional default rates was by Peters, Pinkus, and Askin.[13] Their database included 503,000 conventional fixed-rate 1 to 4 family, owner-occupied mortgage loans sold to Freddie Mac between 1973 and 1980. Of the sample mortgage loans, only about 1,000 (0.2%) defaulted during the study period. In a later study, Van Order examined 725,000 conventional fixed-rate single-family mortgage loans originated from 1973 to 1983 and purchased by Freddie Mac.[14] The default experience of these mortgage loans was investigated through the middle of 1990.

One of the key characteristics of a mortgage loan that affects defaults is the LTV ratio at origination (called **original LTV**). The higher the original LTV (or, equivalently, the less equity the borrower has in the property), the higher the probability of default. This finding was supported by Van Order's findings for the default rate by original LTV.[15] In addition, Van Order found that the origination year was significant in explaining defaults, with 1976 and 1981 being the worst years.

---

[11] For a further discussion of the DRM, its variants, and the difference between the PLAM and DRI, see Chapter 7 of Frank J. Fabozzi and Franco Modigliani, *Mortgage and Mortgage-Backed Securities Markets* (Boston: Harvard Business School Press, 1992).

[12] In other fields, conditional rates or probabilities are referred to as "hazard rates."

[13] Helen F. Peters, Scott M. Pinkus, and David J. Askin, "Default: The Last Resort," *Secondary Mortgage Markets* (August 1984), pp. 16-22.

[14] Robert Van Order, "The Hazards of Default," *Secondary Mortgage Markets* (Fall 1990), pp. 29-32.

[15] This was also found by Peters, Pinkus, and Askin, "Default: The Last Resort"; and by Scott Brown, et al. for FHA/VA loans as well as conventional loans in *Analysis of Mortgage Servicing Portfolios* (New York: Financial Strategies Group, Prudential-Bache Capital Funding, December 1990).

Unfortunately, many default models using original LTV have underestimated the level of deliquencies in recent years. Mismeasurement of the amount of equity borrowers have in their homes is the chief cause. Such mismeasurement is due to two factors: declining home prices and removal of equity via second mortgages or home equity lines of credit.

A study by Bendt, Ramsey, and Fabozzi examined not just the original LTV and its impact on default rates, but also the current LTV.[16] The **current LTV** considers the loan value to the estimated current market price. Figure 24-2 shows the effects of changing property values on the distribution of LTVs. Almost all original LTVs fall under 80% in a large pool of nonconforming mortgage loans (100,000 plus) analyzed, and none go above 90%. Adjusted for declines in property values, however, nearly 40% have current LTVs above 80% and about 15% have current LTVs above 90%.

The Bendt-Ramsey-Fabozzi study also examined defaults taking into consideration second mortgages. Figure 24-3 shows that borrowers with second mortgages behind their first mortgage become delinquent twice as often as borrowers without second mortgages. As Figure 24-4 shows, even adjusting for the higher LTVs which take into account second mortgages, borrowers with second mortgages have higher deliquency rates compared to borrowers with the same LTV without any seconds. On average, deliquency rates are about 25% higher—possibly because the combined monthly payments on a first and second mortgage would be higher than the same sized first mortgage.

Empirical studies also suggest that there is a seasoning effect for default rates. That is, default rates tend to decline as mortgage loans become seasoned. The reason for the seasoning effect on default rates is twofold. First, since a borrower typically knows shortly after moving into a home whether or not he or she can afford to make the mortgage payments, default rates are higher in the earlier years. Second, the longer a borrower remains in a home, the lower the LTV ratio (i.e., the greater the equity in the home), and therefore the incentive to default declines.

Van Order also examined several characteristics of the borrower that he hypothesized would affect default rates. For example, the payment-to-income (PTI) ratio is a measure of the burden of the mortgage payments. It is expected that the higher this ratio at origination, the greater the probability of default. Van Order found that the probability of default increased only slightly the higher this burden. As he notes, this conclusion is only tentative because his sample did not include many observations with high PTIs. None of the other borrower characteristics appeared to significantly affect default rates.

State Foreclosure Laws and Default Losses

State foreclosure laws significantly affect default losses. These state laws differ in three primary ways: foreclosure procedures, statutory right of redemption, and deficiency judgment.[17] **Foreclosure procedures** can be either judicial or nonjudicial. The former is done under court supervision, resulting in a

---

[16] Douglas L. Bendt, Chuck Ramsey, and Frank J. Fabozzi, "The Rating Agencies' Approach: New Evidence," Chapter 6 in Frank J. Fabozzi, Chuck Ramsey, and Frank Ramirez (eds.), *Whole-Loan CMOs* (Buckingham, PA: Frank J. Fabozzi Associates).

[17] Terrence M. Clauretie and Thomas N. Herzog, "How State Laws Affect Foreclosure Costs," *Secondary Mortgage Markets* (Spring 1989), pp. 26-7.

Figure 24-2

Percentage of Loans without Second Mortgages within LTV Ranges

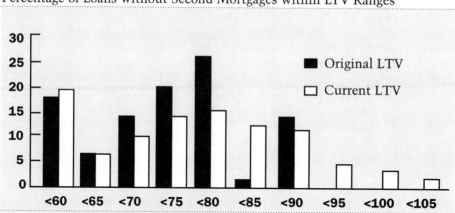

Data source: Mortgage Risk Assessment Corporation

Source: Frank J. Fabozzi, Chuck Ramsey, and Frank Ramirez, **Collateralized Mortgage Obligations: Structures and Analysis** *(Buckingham, PA: Frank J. Fabozzi Associates, 1994).*

Figure 24-3

Percentage Delinquencies

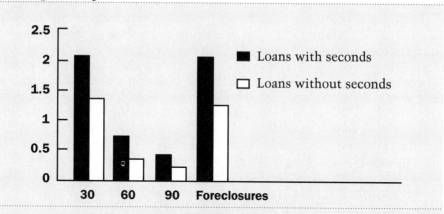

Data source: Mortgage Risk Assessment Corporation

Source: Frank J. Fabozzi, Chuck Ramsey, and Frank Ramirez, **Collateralized Mortgage Obligations: Structures and Analysis** *(Buckingham, PA: Frank J. Fabozzi Associates, 1994).*

lengthening of the time to sell the property. This delay increases the losses associated with a foreclosure because of the opportunity loss on funds that could be reinvested, additional taxes and insurance that must be paid, and legal expenses. Moreover, the property value might decline in the interim due to lack of maintenance or downturn in property values. In a nonjudicial foreclosure,[18] a sale can be made faster because there is no court proceeding;

---

[18] Such foreclosure procedures are also called power of sale procedures, foreclosures by advertisement, or a trustee's sale.

Figure 24-4

Percentage Delinquencies by LTV Range

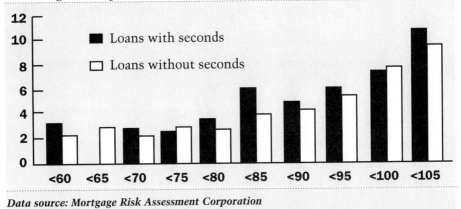

Data source: Mortgage Risk Assessment Corporation

Source: Frank J. Fabozzi, Chuck Ramsey, and Frank Ramirez, Collateralized Mortgage Obligations: Structures and Analysis (Buckingham, PA: Frank J. Fabozzi Associates, 1994).

therefore, the costs associated with foreclosure are reduced. There are 23 states that permit only judicial foreclosure.[19]

A **statutory right of redemption** is a right granted to the borrower to redeem the property by paying any deficiencies, including legal expenses, for a specified period *after* a foreclosure.[20] Twenty-nine states grant this right to borrowers.[21] If this right allows the borrower the right to occupy the property after foreclosure, there is the standard moral hazard problem which could result in deterioration of the property, as well as reluctance of potential buyers to bid on property where moral hazard exists. This will result in lower bid prices being received.

A **deficiency judgment** allows the lender to recover any deficiencies from the borrower's personal assets. While the costs of recovery and the limited personal assets of the borrower may make pursuit of this right by the lender uneconomic, its existence may discourage a default in some instances. This would occur in cases where the borrower has the capacity to pay and sufficient personal assets to satisfy any judgment, but whose property value has declined so that no equity remains in the property (i.e., the LTV is 1 or higher). Only six states do not allow deficiency judgments.[22]

An empirical study by Clauretie and Herzog, based on data from private mortgage insurance and FHA claims, investigated the effect of state laws on losses.[23] A statistical analysis of the data found that losses are significantly

---

[19] Clauretie and Herzog, "How State Laws Affect Foreclosure Costs," p. 26.

[20] An equitable right of redemption gives the borrower the right to redeem the property by paying all deficiencies and legal costs *before* a foreclosure. This right is granted to borrowers in all states.

[21] Clauretie and Herzog, "How State Laws Affect Foreclosure Costs," p. 26.

[22] Clauretie and Herzog, "How State Laws Affect Foreclosure Costs," p. 27.

[23] Clauretie and Herzog, "How State Laws Affect Foreclosure Costs," pp. 27-8.

lower in states with nonjudicial foreclosure procedures and a deficiency judgment right;[24] losses are greater where states grant a statutory right of redemption. These researchers found that on a $100,000 loan, lenders are exposed to potential additional losses of $500 to $1,000 if a property is located in a state with only a judicial foreclosure process and statutory right of redemption.

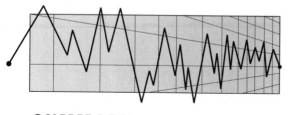

SUMMARY

A mortgage is a pledge of property to secure payment of a debt. The mortgage market is a collection of markets which includes a primary market, or origination market, and a secondary market where mortgages trade.

The original lender is called the mortgage originator; the three largest are commercial banks, thrifts, and mortgage bankers. The two primary factors in determining whether the funds will be lent are the payment-to-income ratio and the loan-to-value ratio. The risks associated with originating mortgages pipeline risk) include price risk and fallout risk.

Every mortgage loan must be serviced. Servicers include bank-related entities, thrift-related entities, and mortgage bankers. There is a secondary market for servicing rights (i.e., the market for the transfer of the right to service a mortgage loan). The value of servicing rights depends in a complicated way on the level of interest rates.

Mortgage insurance may be required by the original lender to insure against default by the borrower. The insurance is provided by private mortgage insurance companies or, if the borrower qualifies, by a federal agency. To manage default risk, mortgage insurers have become less reliant on the credit analysis of mortgage originators. Instead, they have established their own credit analysis departments and undertaken more extensive quality control programs.

There are different types of mortgage designs. The traditional type of mortgage, characterized by a fixed rate, level (nominal) payment, and full amortization, performed well in the first years of the postwar period, becoming the dominant vehicle for house financing. But this method began to falter with high and variable inflation. The traditional mortgage design suffers from two basic and serious shortcomings: the mismatch problem and the tilt problem.

Several mortgage designs are in use today to remedy these two problems. The adjustable-rate mortgage (ARM) addresses the mismatch problem, but not the tilt problem. The graduated-payment mortgage was designed to remedy the tilt problem, but not the mismatch problem. New production of the graduated-payment mortgage has ceased, a clear indication that this mortgage

---

[24] The deficiency judgment was not found to be statistically significant for the FHA data. The low default rates in California in the study period and the fact that California was one of only six states that did not have a deficiency judgment may have caused this result.

design was not an effective remedy for the tilt problem. Two other solutions, the price-level-adjusted mortgage (PLAM) and the dual-rate mortgage (DRM), address fairly effectively both problems, but neither of these instruments has yet been adopted on a large scale in the United States.

Regardless of the mortgage design, there is uncertainty with regard to the cash flow because of prepayments. Prepayments are any payments made in excess of the contractual monthly mortgage payment. Also, there is default risk associated with investing in mortgage loans. One of the key characteristics of a mortgage loan that affects defaults is the loan-to-value ratio at origination. The higher the LTV or, equivalently, the less equity the borrower has in the property, the higher the probability of default. State foreclosure laws significantly affect default losses. For mortgage loans insured by private mortgage insurance companies, an investor must be concerned with the credit risk of the insurer.

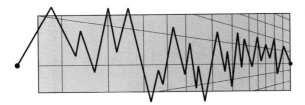

QUESTIONS

1. What are the sources of revenue arising from mortgage origination?

2. What are the risks associated with the mortgage origination process?

3. What are the two primary factors in determining whether funds will be lent to an applicant for a mortgage loan?

4. What can mortgage originators do with a loan after originating it?

5. What is meant by the servicing of a mortgage?

6. What are the risks associated with mortgage servicing?

7. a. What is the difference between mortgage insurance and credit life insurance.

   b. Which type of mortgage-related insurance may be required by a mortgage originator?

   c. What factor will determine whether a lender requires the borrower to obtain mortgage-related insurance?

8. What are the types of underwriting risks faced by mortgage insurance companies?

9. What is a conventional mortgage?

10. Explain why in a fixed-rate, level-payment mortgage the amount of the mortgage payment applied to interest declines over time while the amount applied to the repayment of principal increases.

11. Consider the following fixed-rate, level-payment mortgage: the maturity is 360 months; the amount borrowed equals $100,000; the annual mortgage rate is 10%; and the monthly mortgage payment equals $877.57.

a. Construct an amortization schedule for the first ten months.

b. What will the mortgage balance be at the end of the 360th month?

12. Why is the interest rate on a mortgage loan not necessarily the same as the interest rate that the investor receives?

13. What is meant by the "mismatch problem" associated with fixed-rate, level-payment mortgages?

14. a. Why is the cash flow of a mortgage unknown?

b. In what sense has the investor in a mortgage granted the borrower (homeowner) a call option?

15. a. What features of an adjustable-rate mortgage will affect its cash flow?

b. What are the two categories of reference rates used in adjustable-rate mortgages?

16. a. What is a balloon mortgage?

b. In what way is a balloon mortgage a type of adjustable-rate mortgage?

17. What is the motivation for the design of price-level-adjusted mortgages and dual-rate mortgages?

18. What is meant by a conforming mortgage and a nonconforming mortgage?

19. What is the problem with using the original LTV to assess the likelihood that a seasoned mortgage will default?

20. Indicate three ways in which state foreclosure laws can affect default losses.

The Market for Mortgage Pass-Through Securities

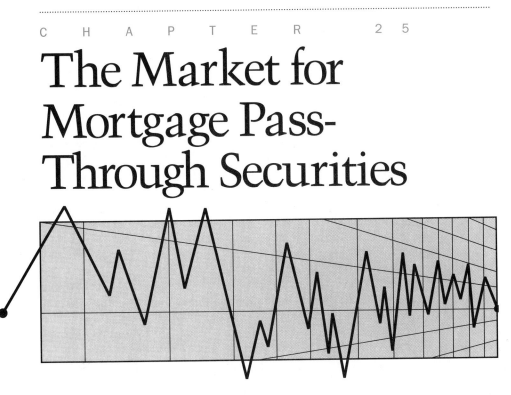

LEARNING OBJECTIVES

After reading this chapter you will understand:

- the development of the current mortgage market, and the role of public and private conduits.

- the investment characteristics of mortgage pass-through securities.

- the different types of pass-through securities.

- the importance of prepayments to the valuation of pass-through securities.

- the industry convention for determining the cash flow of a pass-through.

- the factors that affect prepayments.

- why prepayment risk can be divided into contraction risk and extension risk.

- what is meant by the average life of a pass-through security.

- the investment characteristics of stripped mortgage-backed securities.

We noted in Chapter 24 that in the 1960s and 1970s the majority of all mortgages originated in depository institutions. These institutions kept the mortgages they originated in their portfolio. Some difficulties were inevitable even then, as the depository institutions, especially the S&Ls, were encouraged by legislation and regulation to confine their deposit-seeking and lending activities to their local market. As depository institutions obtained their funds from local citizens, there tended to be a poor allocation of capital; some regions had an excess supply of funds and low rates, and others had shortages and high rates.

This problem found a partial remedy with the entrance of a new participant—the mortgage bankers. Unlike thrifts and commercial banks, mortgage bankers did not provide funds from deposit taking. Instead, they originated mortgages and sold them, not just to life insurance companies but to thrifts in other parts of the country looking for a mortgage investment. They provided a brokerage function, laying the foundation for a national mortgage market. This would seem more like an adequate market, bringing mortgage rates throughout the country closer, and reducing the shortage of mortgage money in high-demand regions of the country.

While the mortgage market operated this way through the late 1960s, it had a major shortcoming in that it was dependent on the availability of funds from thrifts and banks, whether local or national. With the inception of the period of high and variable inflation and interest rates in the late 1960s, disintermediation, induced by ceiling rates on deposits, led to wide shortfalls in the funds available to all depository institutions. To counter or at least limit this problem, what was needed was a mortgage market that was not dependent on deposit-taking institutions. This could be accomplished by developing a strong secondary mortgage market that would attract institutional investors besides deposit-taking institutions and life insurance companies.

The driving force in the development of a strong secondary market was a financial innovation that involved the packaging (or "pooling") of mortgages and the issuance of securities collateralized by these mortgages. These securities are called **mortgage-backed securities**. There are three types of mortgage-backed securities (1) mortgage pass-through securities, (2) stripped mortgage-backed securities, and (3) collateralized mortgage obligations. We will discuss the first two in this chapter and will devote Chapter 26 to the third. We begin this chapter with a discussion of the development of the secondary mortgage market.

DEVELOPMENT OF THE SECONDARY MORTGAGE MARKET

The foundations for the secondary mortgage market can be traced back to the Great Depression and the legislation that followed. Congress's response to the Depression and its effects on financial markets was to establish several public-purpose agencies. The Federal Reserve provided better liquidity for commercial banks through the Federal Reserve discount window. Liquidity for thrifts was provided by the creation of the Federal Home Loan Banks (FHLBs), which were granted the right to borrow from the Treasury.

Another creation of Congress, the Federal Housing Administration (FHA), addressed the problems with the prevailing mortgage loan design which required a balloon payment that the lender could require the homeowner to repay at any time. It was this government agency that developed and promoted the fixed-rate level-payment, fully amortized mortgage we discussed in the previous chapter. The FHA also reduced credit risk for investors by offering insurance against mortgage defaults. However, not all mortgages could be insured, because the mortgage applicant had to satisfy FHA underwriting standards, which made the FHA the first to standardize mortgage terms. While we may take this for granted today, standardization was essential for the development of a secondary mortgage market. In 1944, the Veterans Administration began insuring qualified mortgages.

Who was going to invest in these mortgages? Thrifts could do so, especially with the inducement provided by several advantages reviewed earlier. But the investment would be illiquid in the absence of a market in which mortgages trade. Congress thought of that, too. It created another agency, the Federal National Mortgage Association (FNMA). This agency, popularly known as "Fannie Mae," was charged with the responsibility to create a liquid secondary market for FHA- and VA-insured mortgages, which it tried to accomplish by buying mortgages. Fannie Mae needed a funding source in case it faced a liquidity squeeze. Congress provided this by giving Fannie Mae a credit line with the Treasury.

Despite the creation of Fannie Mae, the secondary mortgage market did not develop to any significant extent. During periods of tight money, Fannie Mae could do little to mitigate the housing crisis. In 1968, Congress divided Fannie Mae into two organizations: the current Fannie Mae, and the Government National Mortgage Association (popularly known as "Ginnie Mae"). Ginnie Mae's function is to use the "full faith and credit of the U.S. government" to support the FHA and VA mortgage market. Two years later in 1970, Congress authorized Fannie Mae to purchase conventional mortgage loans (i.e., those not insured by the FHA or VA) and created the Federal Home Loan Mortgage Corporation (popularly known as "Freddie Mac") to provide support for FHA/VA insured mortgages and conventional mortgages.

Ginnie Mae accomplished its objective by guaranteeing securities issued by private entities who pooled mortgages together, and then used these mortgages as collateral for the security sold. Freddie Mac and Fannie Mae purchased mortgages, pooled these mortgages, and issued securities using the pool of mortgages as collateral. The securities created are called **mortgage pass-through securities**. They are purchased by many types of investors (domestic and foreign) who had previously shunned investment in the mortgage market. In the 1980s, private issuers of mortgage pass-through securities who did not use the backing of the three agencies but instead used some form of private credit enhancement, began issuing pass-through securities backed by conventional family mortgages and commercial real estate mortgages. What is important to understand here is that it was the process of securitizing mortgages that resulted in the strong secondary mortgage market that exists today.

MORTGAGE PASS-THROUGH SECURITIES

As noted in Chapter 24, investing in mortgages exposes the investor to default risk and prepayment risk. A more efficient way is to invest in a mortgage pass-through security. This is a security created when one or more holders of mortgages form a collection (pool) of mortgages and sell shares or participation certificates in the pool. A pool may consist of several thousand or only a few mortgages. The first mortgage pass-through security was created in 1968.

Risk-averse investors should prefer investing in a fraction of a pool to investing in a single mortgage, just as investors prefer to hold a diversified portfolio of stocks rather than an individual stock. Individual mortgages expose the investor to unique (or unsystematic) risk and systematic risk. The risks are that the homeowner will prepay the mortgage at some unfavorable time and that the borrower may default on the loan. One reason that prepayments occur is because of changes in mortgage interest rates. The other reason is unrelated to the movement of mortgage interest rates.

Unsystematic prepayment risk is the risk of an adverse change in the speed at which prepayments are made that is not attributable to a change in mortgage interest rates. Systematic prepayment risk is an unfavorable change in prepayments attributable to a change in mortgage interest rates. Systematic risk in the case of default rates represents widespread default rates perhaps because of severe economic recession. Holding a diversified portfolio of mortgages in the form of a mortgage pass-through security reduces most unsystematic risk, leaving only systematic risk. In addition, a mortgage pass-through security is considerably more liquid than an individual mortgage.

When a mortgage is included in a pool of mortgages that is used as collateral for a mortgage pass-through security, the mortgage is said to be securitized. More than one-third of one- to four-family mortgages have been securitized. Only 22% of conventional mortgages have been securitized, but 85% of FHA/VA insured mortgages have been. Only 7% of multifamily mortgages have found their way into a pool of mortgages backing a pass-through security.

Cash Flow Characteristics

The cash flow of a mortgage pass-through security depends on the cash flow of the underlying mortgages. The cash flow consists of monthly mortgage payments representing interest, the scheduled repayment of principal, and any prepayments.

Payments are made to security holders each month. Neither the amount nor the timing, however, of the cash flow from the pool of mortgages is identical to that of the cash flow passed through to investors. The monthly cash flow for a pass-through is less than the monthly cash flow of the underlying mortgages by an amount equal to servicing and other fees. The other fees are those charged by the issuer or guarantor of the pass-through for guaranteeing the issue.[1] The coupon rate on a pass-through, called the **pass-through coupon rate**, is less than the mortgage rate on the underlying pool of mortgage loans by an amount equal to the servicing and guaranteeing fees.

---

[1] Actually, the servicer pays the guarantee fee to the issuer or guarantor.

The timing of the cash flow is also different. The monthly mortgage payment is due from each mortgagor on the first day of each month, but there is a delay in passing through the corresponding monthly cash flow to the securityholders. The length of the delay varies by the type of pass-through security.

Not all of the mortgages that are included in a securitized pool of mortgages have the same mortgage rate and the same maturity. Consequently, when describing a pass-through security, a weighted-average coupon rate and a weighted average maturity are determined. A **weighted-average coupon rate**, or WAC, is found by weighting the mortgage rate of each mortgage loan in the pool by the amount of the mortgage outstanding. A **weighted-average maturity**, or WAM, is found by weighting the remaining number of months to maturity for each mortgage loan in the pool by the amount of the mortgage outstanding.

Grantor Trust Structure

An entity issuing a mortgage pass-through security wants to make sure that it is not taxed on the interest payments when they are received from homeowners, because it is simply acting as a conduit to pass those payments through to the securityholders. Under the tax law, the issuer is not treated as a taxable entity if the pass-through security is issued through a legal structure known as a **grantor trust**.

TYPES OF MORTGAGE PASS-THROUGH SECURITIES

The three major types of pass-through securities are guaranteed by agencies created by Congress to increase the supply of capital to the residential mortgage market and to provide support for an active secondary market. While Fannie Mae and Freddie Mac are commonly referred to as "agencies" of the U.S. government, both are corporate instrumentalities of the U.S. government. The stock of these two entities trades on the New York Stock Exchange; therefore they are effectively quasi-private corporations. They do not receive a government subsidy or appropriation, and are taxed like any other corporation. Fannie Mae and Freddie Mac are more appropriately referred to as government-sponsored enterprises. Their guarantee does not carry the full faith and credit of the U.S. government. In contrast, Ginnie Mae is a federally related institution because it is part of the Department of Housing and Urban Development. As such, its guarantee carries the full faith and credit of the U.S. government.

The securities associated with these three entities are known as **agency pass-through securities**. About 98% of all pass-through securities are agency pass-through securities. The balance of mortgage pass-through securities are privately issued securities called **private-label mortgage pass-through securities**. While the major portion of pass-through issues have residential mortgages as their collateral, pass-throughs collateralized by mortgages on commercial property have also been issued.

Government National Mortgage Association (GNMA)

Ginnie Mae mortgage-backed securities represent the largest proportion of mortgage pass-through securities outstanding. They are guaranteed by the full faith and credit of the U.S. government with respect to timely payment of both interest and principal. That is, the interest and principal will be paid when due even if mortgagors fail to make their monthly mortgage payments.

While Ginnie Mae provides the guarantee, it is not the issuer. Pass-through securities are issued by lenders it approves, such as thrifts, commercial banks, and mortgage bankers. These lenders receive approval only if the underlying mortgages satisfy the underwriting standards established by Ginnie Mae. When it guarantees securities issued by approved lenders, Ginnie Mae permits these lenders to convert illiquid individual mortgages into liquid securities backed by the U.S. government. In the process Ginnie Mae accomplishes its goal to supply funds to the residential mortgage market and provide an active secondary market. For the guarantee, Ginnie Mae receives a fee called the **guaranteeing fee**.

The security guaranteed by Ginnie Mae is called a **mortgage-backed security** (MBS); it is sold in minimum denominations of $25,000 and in increments of $5,000 thereafter. The first MBS was issued in 1968. Only mortgages insured or guaranteed by either the Federal Housing Administration, the Veterans Administration, or the Farmers Home Administration can be included in a mortgage pool guaranteed by Ginnie Mae.

The Federal Home Loan Mortgage Corporation

The second largest category of agency pass-through securities are those issued by the Federal Home Loan Mortgage Corporation (FHLMC). The security issued by Freddie Mac is called a **participation certificate** (PC). The first PCs were issued in 1971. Most of the pools of mortgages underlying Freddie Mac participation certificates consist of conventional mortgages, although participation certificates with underlying pools consisting of FHA-insured and VA-guaranteed mortgages have been issued.

Freddie Mac has two programs from which it creates PCs: the Cash Program and the Guarantor/Swap Program. The underlying loans for both programs are conventional mortgages (i.e., mortgages not backed by a government agency). Conventional Regular PCs are issued under the Cash Program. In this program the mortgages that back the PC include individual conventional one- to four-family mortgage loans that Freddie Mac purchases from mortgage originators, pools, and sells. Under the Conventional Guarantor/Swap Program, Freddie Mac allows originators to swap pooled mortgages for PCs backed by those mortgages. For example, a thrift may have $50 million of mortgages. It can swap these mortgages for a Freddie Mac PC whose underlying mortgage pool is the $50 million mortgage pool the thrift swapped for the PC.

Both programs provide capital to the residential mortgage market and foster a secondary mortgage market. The Guarantor/Swap Program was designed specifically to provide liquidity to the troubled thrift industry. It allows thrifts to swap mortgages trading below par (mortgage rates lower than the current mortgage rate) without recognizing an accounting loss for financial reporting purposes. The PC that the thrift gets in exchange for the mortgage pool can then be: (1) held as an investment, (2) used as collateral for either short-term or long-term borrowing, or (3) sold.

Freddie Mac offers pass-throughs with one of two types of guarantees. All PCs issued under Freddie Mac's Gold PC program are guaranteed with respect to the timely payment of interest and principal. The **Gold PC** was first issued in the fall of 1990 and is the only type of PC that will be issued by Freddie Mac in the future. The other PCs are guaranteed with respect to the timely payment of interest but the scheduled principal is passed through as it is collected, with Freddie Mac guaranteeing only that the scheduled payment will be made no later than one year after it is due.

Federal National Mortgage Association

While it was created by Congress in 1938, the Federal National Mortgage Association (FNMA), in its current form, is the newest player in the agency pass-through securities market. Fannie Mae was charged by Congress with promoting a secondary market for conventional and FHA/VA single- and multifamily mortgages. To meet that obligation, since 1972 it has purchased these mortgages and held them as investments. It was not until 1981 that Fannie Mae pooled these mortgages and issued its first pass-throughs called mortgage-backed securities (MBS). These pass-throughs are guaranteed with respect to the timely payment of both interest and principal.

Private-Label Pass-Through Securities

Private-label pass-through securities are issued by thrifts, commercial banks, and private conduits. Private conduits may purchase nonconforming mortgages, pool them, and then sell pass-through securities whose collateral is the underlying pool of nonconforming mortgages. The underlying pool may be fixed-rate or adjustable-rate mortgages.

While the amount of private-label pass-through securities outstanding is small relative to agency pass-through securities, this market can be expected to grow significantly. The private conduits that issue these securities effectively are doing what the government created the agency conduits to do, without any guarantees (implicit or explicit) from the U.S. government. In this case, they are providing a secondary market for nonconforming mortgages.[2]

Unlike agency pass-through securities, private-label pass-through securities are rated by the commercial rating companies that we described in Chapter 21. Often they are supported by credit enhancements so that they can obtain a high rating. Most private-label pass-through securities have a rating of at least double A. The development of private credit enhancement is the

---

[2] Several legislative acts and regulatory changes helped foster the development of the private mortgage-backed securities market. The Secondary Mortgage Market Enhancement Act of 1984 included provisions to improve the marketability of mortgage-related securities earning a double-A quality rating or better from one of the nationally recognized commercial rating companies.

key to the success of this market and, indeed, the key to the development of all asset securitization. We shall describe credit enhancements in Chapter 27 when we discuss asset-backed securities. Also unlike agency pass-through securities, private-label pass-through securities must be registered with the Securities and Exchange Commission.

PREPAYMENT CONVENTIONS AND CASH FLOW[3]

In order to value a pass-through security, it is necessary to project its cash flow. The difficulty is that the cash flow is unknown because of prepayments. The only way to project a cash flow is to make some assumption about the prepayment rate over the life of the underlying mortgage pool. The prepayment rate assumed is called the "prepayment speed," or simply "speed." The yield calculated based on the projected cash flow is called a **cash flow yield**.

Estimating the cash flow from a pass-through requires making an assumption about future prepayments. Several conventions have been used as a benchmark for prepayment rates: FHA experience, the conditional prepayment rate, and the Public Securities Association (PSA) prepayment benchmark. While the first convention is no longer used, we discuss it because of its historical significance.

In the early stages of the development of the pass-through market, cash flows were calculated assuming no prepayments for the first 12 years at which time all the mortgages in the pool were assumed to prepay. This naive approach was replaced by the "FHA prepayment experience" approach, which also is no longer in use. This prepayment assumption, based on the prepayment experience for 30-year mortgages derived from an FHA table on mortgage survival factors, was once the most commonly used benchmark for prepayment rates. It calls for the projection of the cash flow for a mortgage pool on the assumption that the prepayment rate will be the same as the FHA experience with 30-year mortgage loans.

Despite the method's past popularity, prepayments based on FHA experience are not necessarily indicative of the prepayment rate for a particular pool, mainly because FHA prepayments are for mortgages originated over all sorts of interest rate periods. Prepayment rates are tied to interest rate cycles, however, so an average prepayment rate over various cycles is not very useful in estimating prepayments. Moreover, new FHA tables are published periodically, causing confusion about which FHA table prepayments should be based on. Finally, because FHA mortgages are assumable—unlike FNMA, FHLMC, and most nonconforming mortgages which have due-on-sale provisions—FHA statistics underestimate prepayments for non-FHA mortgages. Because estimated prepayments using FHA experience may be misleading, the resulting cash flow is not meaningful for valuing pass-throughs.

Conditional Prepayment Rate

Another benchmark for projecting prepayments and the cash flow of a pass-through requires assuming that some fraction of the remaining principal in

---

[3] This section and the one to follow are adapted from Chapter 3 of Frank J. Fabozzi, Charles Ramsey, and Frank R. Ramirez, *Collateralized Mortgage Obligations: Structures and Analysis* (New Hope, PA: Frank J. Fabozzi Associates, 1994).

the pool is prepaid each month for the remaining term of the mortgage. The prepayment rate assumed for a pool, called the **conditional prepayment rate** (CPR), is based on the characteristics of the pool (including its historical prepayment experience) and the current and expected future economic environment. It is referred to as a "conditional" rate because it is conditional on the remaining mortgage balance.

The CPR is an annual prepayment rate. To estimate monthly prepayments, the CPR must be converted into a monthly prepayment rate, commonly referred to as the **single-monthly mortality rate** (SMM). The following formula can be used to determine the SMM for a given CPR:

$$SMM = 1 - (1 - CPR)^{1/12} \tag{25.1}$$

Suppose that the CPR used to estimate prepayments is 6%. The corresponding SMM is:

$$SMM = 1 - (1 - 0.06)^{1/12} = 1-(0.94)^{0.08333} = 0.005143$$

An SMM of $w\%$ means that approximately $w\%$ of the remaining mortgage balance at the beginning of the month, less the scheduled principal payment, will prepay that month. That is:

$$\text{Prepayment for month} = SMM \times (\text{Beginning mortgage balance for month} \\ - \text{Scheduled principal payment for month}) \tag{25.2}$$

For example, suppose that an investor owns a pass-through in which the remaining mortgage balance at the beginning of some month is $290 million. Assuming that the SMM is 0.5143% and the scheduled principal payment is $3 million, the estimated prepayment for the month is:

$$0.005143 \times (\$290,000,000 - \$3,000,000) = \$1,476,041$$

PSA Prepayment Benchmark

The Public Securities Association (PSA) prepayment benchmark is expressed as a monthly series of annual prepayment rates.[4] The PSA benchmark assumes that prepayment rates are low for newly originated mortgages and then will speed up as the mortgages become seasoned.

The PSA benchmark assumes the following CPRs for 30-year mortgages: a CPR of 0.2% for the first month, increased by 0.2% per year per month for the next 30 months, when it reaches 6% per year; and then a 6% CPR for the remaining years. This benchmark, referred to as *100% PSA* or simply *100 PSA*, is graphically depicted in Figure 25-1. Mathematically, 100 PSA can be expressed as follows:

if $t \le 30$ then CPR = 6% $(t/30)$
if $t > 30$ then CPR = 6%

where t is the number of months since the mortgage originated.

---

[4] This benchmark is commonly referred to as a prepayment model, suggesting that it can be used to estimate prepayments. However, characterization of this benchmark as a prepayment model is inappropriate because it is simply a market convention of prepayment behavior.

Figure 25-1

Graphical Depiction of 100 PSA

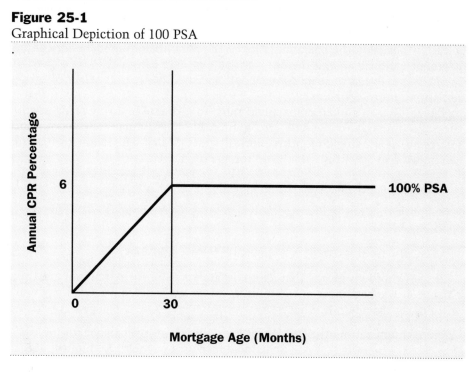

Slower or faster speeds are then referred to as some percentage of PSA. For example, 50 PSA means one-half the CPR of the PSA benchmark prepayment rate; 150 PSA means 1.5 times the CPR of the PSA benchmark prepayment rate; 300 PSA means three times the CPR of the PSA benchmark prepayment rate. This is illustrated graphically in Figure 25-2 for 50 PSA, 100 PSA, and 150 PSA. A prepayment rate of 0 PSA means that no prepayments are assumed.

The CPR is converted to an SMM using Equation (25.1). For example, the SMMs for month 5, month 20, and months 31 through 360 assuming 100 PSA are calculated as follows.

Month 5:   CPR $= 6\%\ (5/30) = 1\% = .01$
             SMM $= 1 - (1 - 0.01)^{1/12}$
             $= 1 - (0.99)^{0.083333} = 0.000837$

Month 20:   CPR $= 6\%\ (20/30) = 4\% = 0.04$
             SMM $= 1 - (1 - 0.04)^{1/12}$
             $= 1 - (0.96)^{0.083333} = 0.003396$

Months 31–360: CPR $= 6\%$
             SMM $= 1 - (1 - 0.06)^{1/12}$
             $= 1 - (0.94)^{0.083333} = 0.005143$

The SMMs for month 5, month 20, and months 31 through 360 assuming 165 PSA are computed as follows.

Figure 25-2
Graphical Depiction of 50 PSA, 100 PSA, and 150 PSA

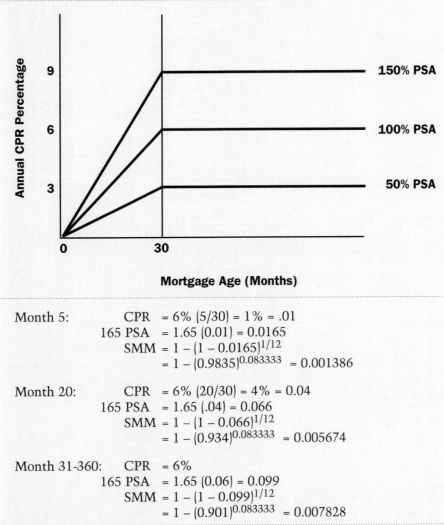

Month 5:	CPR	$= 6\% \ (5/30) = 1\% = .01$
	165 PSA	$= 1.65 \ (0.01) = 0.0165$
	SMM	$= 1 - (1 - 0.0165)^{1/12}$
		$= 1 - (0.9835)^{0.083333} = 0.001386$

Month 20:	CPR	$= 6\% \ (20/30) = 4\% = 0.04$
	165 PSA	$= 1.65 \ (.04) = 0.066$
	SMM	$= 1 - (1 - 0.066)^{1/12}$
		$= 1 - (0.934)^{0.083333} = 0.005674$

Month 31-360:	CPR	$= 6\%$
	165 PSA	$= 1.65 \ (0.06) = 0.099$
	SMM	$= 1 - (1 - 0.099)^{1/12}$
		$= 1 - (0.901)^{0.083333} = 0.007828$

Notice that the SMM assuming 165 PSA is not just 1.65 times the SMM assuming 100 PSA. It is the CPR that is a multiple of the CPR assuming 100 PSA.

Illustration of Monthly Cash Flow Construction

We now show how to construct a monthly cash flow for a hypothetical pass-through given a PSA assumption. For the purpose of this illustration, the underlying mortgages for this hypothetical pass-through are assumed to be fixed-rate, level-payment mortgages with a weighted-average coupon (WAC) rate of 8.125%. It will be assumed that the pass-through rate is 7.5% with a weighted-average maturity (WAM) of 357 months.

Table 25-1 shows the cash flow for selected months assuming 100 PSA. The cash flow is broken down into three components: interest (based on the pass-through rate), the regularly scheduled principal repayment, and prepayments based on 100 PSA. We will go through Table 25-1 column by column.

Table 25-1
Monthly Cash Flow for a $400 Million, 7.5% Pass-Through Rate with a WAC of 8.125% and a WAM of 357 Months Assuming 100 PSA

Mo.	Outstanding balance	SMM	Mortgage payment	Net interest	Scheduled principal	Prepayment	Total principal	Total cash flow
1	400,000,000	0.00067	2,975,868	2,500,000	267,535	267,470	535,005	3,035,005
2	399,464,995	0.00084	2,973,877	2,496,656	269,166	334,198	603,364	3,100,020
3	398,861,631	0.00101	2,971,387	2,492,885	270,762	400,800	671,562	3,164,447
4	398,190,069	0.00117	2,968,399	2,488,688	272,321	467,243	739,564	3,228,252
5	397,450,505	0.00134	2,964,914	2,484,066	273,843	533,493	807,335	3,291,401
6	396,643,170	0.00151	2,960,931	2,479,020	275,327	599,514	874,841	3,353,860
7	395,768,329	0.00168	2,956,453	2,473,552	276,772	665,273	942,045	3,415,597
8	394,826,284	0.00185	2,951,480	2,467,664	278,177	730,736	1,008,913	3,476,577
9	393,817,371	0.00202	2,946,013	2,461,359	279,542	795,869	1,075,410	3,536,769
10	392,741,961	0.00219	2,940,056	2,454,637	280,865	860,637	1,141,502	3,596,140
11	391,600,459	0.00236	2,933,608	2,447,503	282,147	925,008	1,207,155	3,654,658
12	390,393,304	0.00254	2,926,674	2,439,958	283,386	988,948	1,272,333	3,712,291
13	389,120,971	0.00271	2,919,254	2,432,006	284,581	1,052,423	1,337,004	3,769,010
14	387,783,966	0.00288	2,911,353	2,423,650	285,733	1,115,402	1,401,134	3,824,784
15	386,382,832	0.00305	2,902,973	2,414,893	286,839	1,177,851	1,464,690	3,879,583
16	384,918,142	0.00322	2,894,117	2,405,738	287,900	1,239,739	1,527,639	3,933,378
17	383,390,502	0.00340	2,884,789	2,396,191	288,915	1,301,033	1,589,949	3,986,139
18	381,800,553	0.00357	2,874,992	2,386,253	289,884	1,361,703	1,651,587	4,037,840
19	380,148,966	0.00374	2,864,730	2,375,931	290,805	1,421,717	1,712,522	4,088,453
20	378,436,444	0.00392	2,854,008	2,365,228	291,678	1,481,046	1,772,724	4,137,952
21	376,663,720	0.00409	2,842,830	2,354,148	292,503	1,539,658	1,832,161	4,186,309
22	374,831,559	0.00427	2,831,201	2,342,697	293,279	1,597,525	1,890,804	4,233,501
23	372,940,755	0.00444	2,819,125	2,330,880	294,005	1,654,618	1,948,623	4,279,503
24	370,992,132	0.00462	2,806,607	2,318,701	294,681	1,710,908	2,005,589	4,324,290
25	368,986,543	0.00479	2,793,654	2,306,166	295,307	1,766,368	2,061,675	4,367,841
26	366,924,868	0.00497	2,780,270	2,293,280	295,883	1,820,970	2,116,852	4,410,133

Table 25-1 *Continued from previous page*

Mo.	Outstanding balance	SMM	Mortgage payment	Net interest	Scheduled principal	Prepayment	Total principal	Total cash flow
27	364,808,016	0.00514	2,766,461	2,280,050	296,406	1,874,688	2,171,094	4,451,144
28	362,636,921	0.00514	2,752,233	2,266,481	296,879	1,863,519	2,160,398	4,426,879
29	360,476,523	0.00514	2,738,078	2,252,978	297,351	1,852,406	2,149,758	4,402,736
30	358,326,766	0.00514	2,723,996	2,239,542	297,825	1,841,347	2,139,173	4,378,715
100	231,249,776	0.00514	1,898,682	1,445,311	332,928	1,187,608	1,520,537	2,965,848
101	229,729,239	0.00514	1,888,917	1,435,808	333,459	1,179,785	1,513,244	2,949,052
102	228,215,995	0.00514	1,879,202	1,426,350	333,990	1,172,000	1,505,990	2,932,340
103	226,710,004	0.00514	1,869,538	1,416,938	334,522	1,164,252	1,498,774	2,915,712
104	225,211,230	0.00514	1,859,923	1,407,570	335,055	1,156,541	1,491,596	2,899,166
105	223,719,634	0.00514	1,850,357	1,398,248	335,589	1,148,867	1,484,456	2,882,703
200	109,791,339	0.00514	1,133,751	686,196	390,372	562,651	953,023	1,639,219
201	108,838,316	0.00514	1,127,920	680,239	390,994	557,746	948,740	1,628,980
202	107,889,576	0.00514	1,122,119	674,310	391,617	552,863	944,480	1,618,790
203	106,945,096	0.00514	1,116,348	668,407	392,241	548,003	940,243	1,608,650
204	106,004,852	0.00514	1,110,607	662,530	392,866	543,164	936,029	1,598,560
205	105,068,823	0.00514	1,104,895	656,680	393,491	538,347	931,838	1,588,518
300	32,383,611	0.00514	676,991	202,398	457,727	164,195	621,923	824,320
301	31,761,689	0.00514	673,510	198,511	458,457	160,993	619,449	817,960
302	31,142,239	0.00514	670,046	194,639	459,187	157,803	616,990	811,629
303	30,525,249	0.00514	666,600	190,783	459,918	154,626	614,545	805,328
304	29,910,704	0.00514	663,171	186,942	460,651	151,462	612,113	799,055
305	29,298,591	0.00514	659,761	183,116	461,385	148,310	609,695	792,811
350	4,060,411	0.00514	523,138	25,378	495,645	18,334	513,979	539,356
351	3,546,432	0.00514	520,447	22,165	496,435	15,686	512,121	534,286
352	3,034,311	0.00514	517,770	18,964	497,226	13,048	510,274	529,238
353	2,524,037	0.00514	515,107	15,775	498,018	10,420	508,437	524,213
354	2,015,600	0.00514	512,458	12,597	498,811	7,801	506,612	519,209
355	1,508,988	0.00514	509,823	9,431	499,606	5,191	504,797	514,228
356	1,004,191	0.00514	507,201	6,276	500,401	2,591	502,992	509,269
357	501,199	0.00514	504,592	3,132	501,199	0	501,199	504,331

- *Column 1* ref is the month.
- *Column 2* gives the outstanding mortgage balance at the beginning of the month. It is equal to the outstanding balance at the beginning of the previous month reduced by the total principal payment in the previous month.
- *Column 3* shows the SMM for 100 PSA. Two things should be noted. First, for month 1, the SMM is for a pass-through that has been seasoned three months; that is, the CPR is 0.8%. This is because the WAM is 357. Second, from month 27 on, the SMM is 0.00514, which corresponds to a CPR of 6%.
- *Column 4* shows the total monthly mortgage payment. Notice that the payment declines over time as prepayments reduce the mortgage balance outstanding. There is a formula to determine what the monthly mortgage balance will be for each month given prepayments.[5]
- *Column 5* gives the monthly interest paid to the pass-through investor. This value is determined by multiplying the outstanding mortgage balance at the beginning of the month by the pass-through rate of 7.5% and dividing by 12.
- *Column 6* gives the regularly scheduled principal repayment. This is the difference between the total monthly mortgage payment (the amount shown in column 4) and the gross coupon interest for the month. The gross coupon interest is 8.125% multiplied by the outstanding mortgage balance at the beginning of the month, then divided by 12.
- *Column 7* reports the prepayment for the month. The prepayment is found by using Equation (25.2). For example, in month 100, the beginning mortgage balance is $231,249,776, the scheduled principal payment is $332,298, and the SMM at 100 PSA is 0.00514301 (only 0.00514 is shown in the table to save space). So the prepayment is: 0.00514301 × ($231,249,776 − $332,928) = $1,187,608.
- *Column 8* shows the total principal payment, which is the sum of columns 6 and 7.
- *Column 9* gives the projected monthly cash flow for this pass-through. The monthly cash flow is the sum of the interest paid to the pass-through investor (column 5) and the total principal payments for the month (column 8).

Table 25-2 shows selected monthly cash flows for the same pass-through assuming 165 PSA.

---

[5] The formula is presented in Chapter 20 of Frank J. Fabozzi, *Fixed Income Mathematics: Analytical and Statistical Techniques* (Chicago: Probus Publishing, 1993).

Table 25-2

Monthly Cash Flow for a $400 Million, 7.5% Pass-Through Rate with a WAC of 8.125% and a WAM of 357 Months Assuming 165 PSA

Mo.	Outstanding balance	SMM	Mortgage payment	Net interest	Scheduled principal	Prepayment	Total principal	Total cash flow
1	400,000,000	0.00111	2,975,868	2,500,000	267,535	442,389	709,923	3,209,923
2	399,290,077	0.00139	2,972,575	2,495,563	269,048	552,847	821,896	3,317,459
3	398,468,181	0.00167	2,968,456	2,490,426	270,495	663,065	933,560	3,423,986
4	397,534,621	0.00195	2,963,513	2,484,591	271,873	772,949	1,044,822	3,529,413
5	396,489,799	0.00223	2,957,747	2,478,061	273,181	882,405	1,155,586	3,633,647
6	395,334,213	0.00251	2,951,160	2,470,839	274,418	991,341	1,265,759	3,736,598
7	394,068,454	0.00279	2,943,755	2,462,928	275,583	1,099,664	1,375,246	3,838,174
8	392,693,208	0.00308	2,935,534	2,454,333	276,674	1,207,280	1,483,954	3,938,287
9	391,209,254	0.00336	2,926,503	2,445,058	277,690	1,314,099	1,591,789	4,036,847
10	389,617,464	0.00365	2,916,666	2,435,109	278,631	1,420,029	1,698,659	4,133,769
11	387,918,805	0.00393	2,906,028	2,424,493	279,494	1,524,979	1,804,473	4,228,965
12	386,114,332	0.00422	2,894,595	2,413,215	280,280	1,628,859	1,909,139	4,322,353
13	384,205,194	0.00451	2,882,375	2,401,282	280,986	1,731,581	2,012,567	4,413,850
14	382,192,626	0.00480	2,869,375	2,388,704	281,613	1,833,058	2,114,670	4,503,374
15	380,077,956	0.00509	2,855,603	2,375,487	282,159	1,933,203	2,215,361	4,590,848
16	377,862,595	0.00538	2,841,068	2,361,641	282,623	2,031,931	2,314,554	4,676,195
17	375,548,041	0.00567	2,825,779	2,347,175	283,006	2,129,159	2,412,164	4,759,339
18	373,135,877	0.00597	2,809,746	2,332,099	283,305	2,224,805	2,508,110	4,840,210
19	370,627,766	0.00626	2,792,980	2,316,424	283,521	2,318,790	2,602,312	4,918,735
20	368,025,455	0.00656	2,775,493	2,300,159	283,654	2,411,036	2,694,690	4,994,849
21	365,330,765	0.00685	2,757,296	2,283,317	283,702	2,501,466	2,785,169	5,068,486
22	362,545,596	0.00715	2,738,402	2,265,910	283,666	2,590,008	2,873,674	5,139,584
23	359,671,922	0.00745	2,718,823	2,247,950	283,545	2,676,588	2,960,133	5,208,083
24	356,711,789	0.00775	2,698,575	2,229,449	283,338	2,761,139	3,044,477	5,273,926
25	353,667,312	0.00805	2,677,670	2,210,421	283,047	2,843,593	3,126,640	5,337,061

Table 25-2 *Continued from previous page*

Mo.	Outstanding balance	SMM	Mortgage payment	Net interest	Scheduled principal	Prepayment	Total principal	Total cash flow
26	350,540,672	0.00835	2,656,123	2,190,879	282,671	2,923,885	3,206,556	5,397,435
27	347,334,116	0.00865	2,633,950	2,170,838	282,209	3,001,955	3,284,164	5,455,002
28	344,049,952	0.00865	2,611,167	2,150,312	281,662	2,973,553	3,255,215	5,405,527
29	340,794,737	0.00865	2,588,581	2,129,967	281,116	2,945,400	3,226,516	5,356,483
30	337,568,221	0.00865	2,566,190	2,109,801	280,572	2,917,496	3,198,067	5,307,869
100	170,142,350	0.00865	1,396,958	1,063,390	244,953	1,469,591	1,714,544	2,777,933
101	168,427,806	0.00865	1,384,875	1,052,674	244,478	1,454,765	1,699,243	2,751,916
102	166,728,563	0.00865	1,372,896	1,042,054	244,004	1,440,071	1,684,075	2,726,128
103	165,044,489	0.00865	1,361,020	1,031,528	243,531	1,425,508	1,669,039	2,700,567
104	163,375,450	0.00865	1,349,248	1,021,097	243,060	1,411,075	1,654,134	2,675,231
105	161,721,315	0.00865	1,337,577	1,010,758	242,589	1,396,771	1,639,359	2,650,118
200	56,746,664	0.00865	585,990	354,667	201,767	489,106	690,874	1,045,540
201	56,055,790	0.00865	580,921	350,349	201,377	483,134	684,510	1,034,859
202	55,371,280	0.00865	575,896	346,070	200,986	477,216	678,202	1,024,273
203	54,693,077	0.00865	570,915	341,832	200,597	471,353	671,950	1,013,782
204	54,021,127	0.00865	565,976	337,632	200,208	465,544	665,752	1,003,384
205	53,355,375	0.00865	561,081	333,471	199,820	459,789	659,609	993,080
300	11,758,141	0.00865	245,808	73,488	166,196	100,269	266,465	339,953
301	11,491,677	0.00865	243,682	71,823	165,874	97,967	263,841	335,664
302	11,227,836	0.00865	241,574	70,174	165,552	95,687	261,240	331,414
303	10,966,596	0.00865	239,485	68,541	165,232	93,430	258,662	327,203
304	10,707,934	0.00865	237,413	66,925	164,912	91,196	256,107	323,032
305	10,451,827	0.00865	235,360	65,324	164,592	88,983	253,575	318,899
350	1,235,674	0.00865	159,202	7,723	150,836	9,384	160,220	167,943
351	1,075,454	0.00865	157,825	6,722	150,544	8,000	158,544	165,266
352	916,910	0.00865	156,460	5,731	150,252	6,631	156,883	162,614
353	760,027	0.00865	155,107	4,750	149,961	5,277	155,238	159,988
354	604,789	0.00865	153,765	3,780	149,670	3,937	153,607	157,387
355	451,182	0.00865	152,435	2,820	149,380	2,611	151,991	154,811
356	299,191	0.00865	151,117	1,870	149,091	1,298	150,389	152,259
357	148,802	0.00865	149,809	930	148,802	0	148,802	149,732

FACTORS AFFECTING PREPAYMENT BEHAVIOR

In this section we review the factors that have been observed to affect prepayments. The factors that affect prepayment behavior are: (1) the prevailing mortgage rate, (2) characteristics of the underlying mortgage pool, (3) seasonal factors, and (4) general economic activity.

Prevailing Mortgage Rate

The current mortgage rate affects prepayments in three ways. First, the spread between the prevailing mortgage rate and the contract rate paid by the homeowner affects the incentive to refinance. (By contract rate we mean the rate on the mortgage loan.) Second, the path of mortgage rates since the loan was originated affects prepayments through a phenomenon referred to as refinancing burnout. Both the spread and path of mortgage rates affect prepayments that are the product of refinancing. The third way in which the prevailing mortgage rate affects prepayments is through its effect on the affordability of housing and housing turnover. We discuss each below.

Spread between contract rate and prevailing mortgage rate—The single most important factor affecting prepayments because of refinancing is the current level of mortgage rates relative to the borrower's contract rate. The greater the difference between the two, the greater the incentive to refinance the mortgage loan. For refinancing to make economic sense, the interest savings must be greater than the costs associated with refinancing the mortgage. These costs include legal expenses, origination fees, title insurance, and the value of the time associated with obtaining another mortgage loan. Some of these costs—such as title insurance and origination points—will vary proportionately with the amount to be financed. Other costs such as the application fee and legal expenses are typically fixed.

Historically, it has been observed that when mortgage rates fall to more than 200 basis points below the contract rate, prepayment rates increase. However, the creativity of mortgage originators in designing mortgage loans such that the refinancing costs are folded into the amount borrowed has changed the view that mortgage rates must drop dramatically below the contract rate to make refinancing economic. Moreover, mortgage originators now do an effective job of advertising to make homeowners cognizant of the economic benefits of refinancing.

Path of mortgage rates—The historical pattern of prepayments and economic theory suggests that it is not only the level of mortgage rates that affects prepayment behavior but also the path that mortgage rates take to get to the current level. To illustrate why, suppose the underlying contract rate for a pool of mortgage loans is 11% and that three years after origination, the prevailing mortgage rate declines to 8%. Consider two possible paths of the mortgage rate in getting to the 8% level. In the first path, the mortgage rate declines to 8% at the end of the first year, then rises to 13% at the end of the second year, and then falls to 8% at the end of the third year. In the second path, the mortgage rate rises to 12% at the end of the first year, continues its rise to 13% at the end of the second year, and then falls to 8% at the end of the third year.

If the mortgage rate follows the first path, those who can benefit from refinancing will more than likely take advantage of this opportunity when the mortgage rate drops to 8% in the first year. When the mortgage rate drops again to 8% at the end of the third year, the likelihood is that prepayments because of refinancing will not surge; those who can benefit by taking advantage of the refinancing opportunity will have done so already when the mortgage rate declined for the first time. This is the prepayment behavior referred to as the **refinancing burnout** (or simply, burnout) **phenomenon**.

In contrast, the expected prepayment behavior when the mortgage rate follows the second path is quite different. Prepayment rates are expected to be low in the first two years. When the mortgage rate declines to 8% in the third year, refinancing activity and therefore prepayments are expected to surge. Consequently, the burnout phenomenon is related to the path of mortgage rates.

Level of mortgage rates—As we discussed earlier, prepayments occur because of housing turnover and refinancing. Our focus so far has been on the factors that affect prepayments caused by refinancing. The level of mortgage rates affects housing turnover to the extent that a lower rate increases the affordability of homes.

Characteristics of the Underlying Mortgage Loans

The following characteristics of the underlying mortgage loans affect prepayments: (1) the contract rate; (2) whether the loans are conventional or FHA/VA guaranteed; (3) the amount of seasoning; (4) the type of loan, for example, a 30-year level payment mortgage, 5-year balloon mortgage, etc.; and (4) the geographical location of the underlying properties.

Seasonal Factors

There is a well-documented seasonal pattern in prepayments. This pattern is related to activity in the primary housing market, with home buying increasing in the spring, and gradually reaching a peak in the late summer. Home buying declines in the fall and winter. Mirroring this activity are the prepayments that result from the turnover of housing as home buyers sell their existing homes and purchase new ones. Prepayments are low in the winter months and begin to rise in the spring, reaching a peak in the summer months. However, probably because of delays in passing through prepayments, the peak may not be observed until early fall.

General Economic Activity

Economic theory would suggest that general economic activity affects prepayment behavior through its effect on housing turnover. The link is as follows: a growing economy results in a rise in personal income and in opportunities for worker migration; this increases family mobility and as a result increases housing turnover. The opposite holds for a weak economy. Some researchers suggest that prepayments can be projected by identifying and forecasting the turnover rate of the single-family housing stock.[6]

---

[6] See, for example, Joseph C. Hu, "An Alternative Prepayment Projection Based on Housing Activity," in Frank J. Fabozzi (ed.), *The Handbook of Mortgage-Backed Securities* (Chicago: Probus Publishing, 1988), pp. 639-48.

Although some modelers of prepayment behavior may incorporate macro-economic measures of economic activity such as gross domestic product, industrial production, or housing starts, the trend has been to ignore them or limit their use to specific applications. There are two reasons why macroeconomic measures have been ignored by some modelers. First, empirical tests suggest that the inclusion of macroeconomic measures does not significantly improve the forecasting ability of a prepayment model.[7] Second, as explained later, prepayment models are based on a projection of a path for future mortgage rates. The inclusion of macroeconomic variables in a prepayment model would require the forecasting of the value of these variables over long time periods.

Macroeconomic variables, however, have been used by some researchers in prepayment models to capture the effect of housing turnover on prepayments by specifying a relationship between interest rates and housing turnover. This is the approach used, for example, in the Prudential Securities Model.[8]

Prepayment Models

A prepayment model is a statistical model that is used to forecast prepayments. It begins by modeling the statistical relationships among the factors that are expected to affect prepayments. One study suggests that the four factors discussed above—refinancing incentives, burnout, seasoning, and seasonality—explain about 95% of the variation in prepayment rates.[9] These factors are then combined into one model. For example, in the Goldman Sachs prepayment model, the effects interact proportionally through the following multiplicative function, which is used to project prepayments:

$$\text{monthly prepayment rate} = (\text{refinancing incentive}) \times (\text{seasoning multiplier}) \times (\text{month multiplier}) \times (\text{burnout multiplier})$$

where the various multipliers are adjustments for the effects we discussed earlier in this chapter.

The product of a prepayment forecast is not one prepayment rate but a set of prepayment rates for each month of the remaining term of a mortgage pool. The set of monthly prepayment rates, however, is not reported by Wall Street firms or vendors. Instead, a single prepayment rate is reported. One way to convert a set of monthly prepayment rates into a single prepayment rate is to calculate a simple average of the prepayment rates. The obvious drawback to this approach is that it does not take into consideration the outstanding balance each month. An alternative approach is to use some type of weighted average, selecting the weights to reflect the amount of the monthly cash flow corresponding to a monthly prepayment rate. This is done by first computing the cash-flow yield for a pass-through given its market price and the set of monthly prepayment rates. Then a single prepayment rate (CPR or PSA multiple) that gives the same cash-flow yield is found.

---

[7] Scott F. Richard and Richard Roll, "Prepayments on Fixed-Rate Mortgage-Backed Securities," *Journal of Portfolio Management*, (Spring 1989), pp. 78-9.

[8] Lakbhir S. Hayre, Kenneth Lauterbach, and Cyrus Mohebbi, "Prepayment Models and Methodologies," in Frank J. Fabozzi (ed.), *Advances and Innovations in the Bond and Mortgage Markets*, (Chicago, IL: Probus Publishing, 1989) p. 338.

[9] Scott F. Richard, "Relative Prepayment Rates on Thirty-Year FNMA, FHLMC and GNMA Fixed Rate Mortgage-Backed Securities," in Frank J. Fabozzi (ed.), *Advances and Innovations in the Bond and Mortgage Markets*, pp. 351-69.

SECONDARY MARKET

The secondary market for instruments issued as part of the more popular agency programs is highly liquid. Pass-throughs are quoted in the same manner as U.S. Treasury coupon securities. A quote of 94-05 means 94 and 5/32nd of par value, or 94.15625% of par value.

The yield corresponding to a price must be qualified by an assumption concerning prepayments. While yields are frequently quoted, remember that the yield is based on some underlying prepayment assumption. Consequently, a yield of 9% based on 150% PSA means that it is assumed that the underlying mortgages will prepay at a rate equal to 150% PSA. A yield number without qualification as to the prepayment assumption is meaningless.

In fact, even with specification of the prepayment assumption, the yield number is meaningless in terms of the relative value of a pass-through. For an investor to realize the yield based on some PSA assumption, a number of conditions must be met: (1) the investor must reinvest all the cash flows at the calculated yield, (2) the investor must hold the pass-through security until all the mortgages have been paid off, and (3) the assumed prepayment rate must actually occur over the life of the pass-through. Now, if all this is likely, then we can trust the yield numbers. Otherwise, investors must be cautious in using yield numbers to evaluate pass-through securities.

There are many seasoned issues of the same agency with the same coupon rate outstanding at any given time. Each issue is backed by a different pool of mortgages. For example, there are many seasoned pools of GNMA 8s. One issue may be backed by a pool of mortgages all for California properties, while another may be backed by a pool of mortgages for primarily New York City homes. Others may be backed by a pool of mortgages on homes in several regions of the country.

Which pools are dealers referring to when they talk about, say, GNMA 8s? They are not referring to any specific pool but they mean a "generic" security even though the prepayment characteristics of pass-throughs of underlying pools from different parts of the country are different. Thus, the projected PSA prepayment rates for pass-through securities reported by dealer firms are for generic pass-throughs. A particular pool purchased may have a materially different prepayment speed from the generic benchmark. Moreover, when an investor purchases a pass-through without specifying a pool number, the seller can deliver the worst-paying pools from the securities it holds.

PREPAYMENT RISKS ASSOCIATED WITH PASS-THROUGH SECURITIES

An investor who owns pass-through securities does not know what the cash flow will be because that depends on prepayments. The risk associated with prepayments is called **prepayment risk**.

To understand prepayment risk, suppose an investor buys a 10% coupon Ginnie Mae at a time when mortgage rates are 10%. Consider what will happen to prepayments if mortgage rates decline to, say, 6%. There will be two adverse consequences. First, we know from the basic property of fixed-income securities in Chapter 17 that the price of an option-free bond will rise. But in the case of a pass-through security, the rise in price will not be as large as that of an option-free bond because a fall in interest rates increases the borrower's incentive to prepay the loan and refinance the debt at a lower rate. This results in the same adverse consequence faced by holders of callable corporate and municipal bonds. As in the case of those instruments, the upside price potential of a pass-through security is truncated because of prepayments. This is a characteristic of all callable bonds. This should not be surprising, because a mortgage loan effectively grants the borrower the right to call the loan at par value. The second adverse consequence is that the cash flow must be reinvested at a lower rate. These two adverse consequences when mortgage rates decline is referred to as **contraction risk**.

Now look at what happens if mortgage rates rise to 15%. The price of the pass-through, like the price of any bond, will decline. But again it will decline more because the higher rates will tend to slow down the rate of prepayment, in effect increasing the amount invested at the coupon rate, which is lower than the market rate. Prepayments will slow down, because homeowners will not refinance or partially prepay their mortgages when mortgage rates are higher than the contract rate of 10%. Of course this is just the time when investors want prepayments to speed up so that they can reinvest the prepayments at the higher market interest rate. This adverse consequence of rising mortgage rates is called **extension risk**.

Therefore, prepayment risk encompasses contraction risk and extension risk. Prepayment risk makes pass-through securities unattractive for certain financial institutions to hold from an asset/liability perspective. The following are reasons why particular institutional investors may find pass-throughs unattractive.

1. Thrifts and commercial banks, as we explained in Chapter 3, want to lock in a spread over their cost of funds. Their funds are raised on a short-term basis. If they invest in fixed-rate pass-through securities, they will be mismatched because a pass-through is a longer-term security. In particular, depository institutions are exposed to extension risk when they invest in pass-through securities.

2. To satisfy certain obligations of insurance companies, pass-through securities may be unattractive. More specifically, consider a life insurance company that has issued a four-year GIC. The uncertainty about the cash flow from a pass-through security and the likelihood that slow prepayments will result in the instrument being long-term, make it an unappealing investment vehicle for such accounts. In such instances, a pass-through security exposes the insurance company to extension risk.

3. Consider a pension fund that wants to satisfy long-term liabilities by locking in prevailing interest rates. Buying a pass-through security exposes the pension fund to the risk that prepayments will speed up and the maturity of the investment will shorten considerably. Prepayments will speed up when interest rates decline, thereby forcing reinvestment of prepayments at a lower interest rate. In this case, the pension fund is exposed to contraction risk.

We can see that some institutional investors are concerned with extension risk and others with contraction risk when they purchase a pass-through security. Is it possible to alter the cash flow of a pass-through so as to reduce the contraction risk and extension risk for institutional investors? This can be done, as we explain in Chapter 26.

Yield Spread to Treasuries

While we have explained that it is not possible to calculate a yield with certainty, it has been stated that pass-through securities offer a higher yield than Treasury securities. Typically, the comparison is between Ginnie Mae pass-through securities and Treasuries, for both are free of default risk. Presumably, the difference between the two yields primarily represents prepayment risk. The question should be whether the premium the investor receives in terms of higher yield for bearing prepayment risk is adequate. This is where option-pricing models applied to pass-through securities have been used. Option-pricing models let us determine if the pass-through security is offering the proper compensation for accepting prepayment risk.

The yield spread between private-label pass-through securities and agency pass-through securities reflects both credit risk and prepayment risk. The reason for the difference in prepayment risk lies in the nature of the underlying mortgages. For example, in the case of Ginnie Mae pass-through securities, the underlying mortgages are FHA- or VA-insured mortgages. Borrowers who obtain such government guarantees have different prepayment characteristics compared to holders of nongovernment-insured mortgages. Specifically, when interest rates decline, prepayments on FHA/VA-insured mortgages do not increase as fast as those for non-FHA/VA-insured mortgages. This reflects the fact that borrowers who obtain government-guaranteed mortgages typically do not have the ability to take on refinancing costs as rates decline. There are similar differences between the prepayment patterns of Ginnie Mae pass-through securities and the two other agency pass-through securities.

When we speak of comparing the yield of a mortgage pass-through security to a comparable Treasury, what does "comparable" mean? The stated maturity of a mortgage pass-through security is an inappropriate measure because of amortization of the mortgage loan. Instead, market participants have used two measures: Macaulay duration, and average life. As we explain in Chapter 17, Macaulay duration is a weighted-average term to maturity where the weights are the present value of the cash flows. The more commonly used measure is the average life.

Average Life

The **average life** of a mortgage-backed security is the average time to receipt of principal payments (scheduled principal payments and projected prepayments), weighted by the amount of principal expected. Mathematically, the average life is expressed as follows:

$$\text{Average life} = \sum_{t=1}^{T} \frac{t \times \text{Principal received at time } t}{12 \,(\text{Total principal})}$$

where T is the number of months.

The average life of a pass-through depends on the PSA prepayment assumption. The average life is shown below for different prepayment speeds for the pass-through we used to illustrate the cash flow for 100 PSA and 165 PSA in Tables 25-1 and 25-2.

PSA speed	50	100	165	200	300	400	500	600	700
Average life	15.11	11.66	8.76	7.68	5.63	4.44	3.68	3.16	2.78

STRIPPED MORTGAGE-BACKED SECURITIES

A stripped mortgage-backed security, introduced by Fannie Mae in 1986, is one example of a **derivative mortgage security**. (The other is the collateralized mortgage obligation discussed in the next chapter.) A mortgage pass-through security divides the cash flow from the underlying pool of mortgages on a pro rata basis to the securityholders. A stripped mortgage-backed security is created by altering that distribution of principal and interest from a pro rata distribution to an unequal distribution. The result is that the securities created will have a price/yield relationship that is different from the price/yield relationship of the underlying pass-through security. Stripped mortgage-backed securities, if properly used, provide a means by which investors can hedge prepayment risk.[10]

The first generation of stripped mortgage-backed securities were "partially stripped." We can see this by looking at the stripped mortgage-backed securities issued by Fannie Mae in mid-1986. The Class B stripped mortgage-backed securities were backed by FNMA pass-through securities with a 9% coupon. The mortgage payments from the underlying mortgage pool are distributed to Class B-1 and Class B-2 so that both classes receive an equal amount of the principal, but Class B-1 receives one-third of the interest payments while Class B-2 receives two-thirds.

In a subsequent issue, Fannie Mae distributed the cash flow from the underlying mortgage pool in a far different way. Using FNMA 11% coupon pools, Fannie Mae created Class A-1 and Class A-2. Class A-1 was given 4.95% of the 11% coupon interest, while Class A-2 received the other 6.05%. Class A-1 was given 99% of the principal payments, while Class A-2 was allotted only 1% of the principal payments.

In early 1987, stripped mortgage-backed securities began to be issued where all the interest is allocated to one class called the **interest-only** (or IO) **class**, and all the principal to an other class called the **principal-only** (PO) **class**. The IO class receives no principal payments.

The PO security is purchased at a substantial discount from par value. The yield an investor realizes depends on the speed at which prepayments are made. The faster the prepayments, the higher the investor's yield. For example, suppose there is a mortgage pool consisting of only 30-year mortgages, with $400 million in principal, and that investors can purchase POs backed by this mortgage pool for $175 million. The dollar return on this investment will be $225 million. How quickly that dollar return is recovered by PO investors determines the yield that will be realized. In the extreme case, if all homeowners in the underlying mortgage pool decide to prepay their mortgage

---

[10] For a further discussion, see Lakhbir S. Hayre, Errol Mustafa, and Vincent Pica, "Stripped Mortgage-Backed Securities," Chapter 14 in Frank J. Fabozzi (ed), *The Handbook of Mortgage-Backed Securities* (Chicago, Il Probus Publishing, 1995).

loans immediately, PO investors will realize the $225 million immediately. At the other extreme, if all homeowners decide to remain in their homes for 30 years and make no prepayments, the $225 million will be spread out over 30 years, which would result in a lower yield for PO investors.

Consider how the price of the PO would be expected to change as mortgage rates in the market change. When mortgage rates decline below the coupon rate, prepayments are expected to speed up, accelerating payments to the PO holder. Thus, the cash flow of a PO improves (in the sense that principal repayments are received earlier). The cash flow will be discounted at a lower interest rate because the mortgage rate in the market has declined. The result is that the PO price will increase when mortgage rates decline. When mortgage rates rise above the coupon rate, prepayments are expected to slow down. The cash flow deteriorates (in the sense that it takes longer to recover principal repayments). Couple this with a higher discount rate, and the price of a PO will fall when mortgage rates rise.

An IO has no par value. In contrast to the PO investor, the IO investor wants prepayments to be slow. The reason is that the IO investor receives interest only on the amount of the principal outstanding. When prepayments are made, less dollar interest will be received as the outstanding principal declines. In fact, if prepayments are too fast, the IO investor may not recover the amount paid for the IO.

Let's look at the expected price response of an IO to changes in mortgage rates. If mortgage rates decline below the coupon rate, the prepayments are expected to accelerate. This would result in a deterioration of the expected cash flow for an IO. While the cash flow will be discounted at a lower rate, the net effect typically is a decline in the price of an IO. If mortgage rates rise above the coupon rate, the expected cash flow improves, but the cash flow is discounted at a higher interest rate. The net effect may be either a rise or fall for the IO. Thus, we see an interesting characteristic of an IO: its price tends to move in the same direction as the change in mortgage rates when mortgage rates fall below the coupon rate, *and* for some range of mortgage rates above the coupon rate.[11] Both POs and IOs exhibit substantial price volatility when mortgage rates change. The greater price volatility of the IO and PO compared to the pass-through is due to the fact that the combined price volatility of the IO and PO must add up to the price volatility of the pass-through.

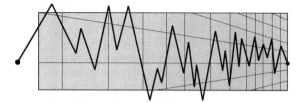

SUMMARY

The mortgage market at one time was primarily a local market: members of the community made deposits in local thrifts, which loaned the funds to local citizens who wanted to purchase a home. Because of imbalance between local

11 For a more detailed discussion of the price characteristics of IOs and POs and their valuation, see Andrew S. Carron, "Mortgage Strips," Chapter 19; Steven J. Carlson and Timothy D. Sears, "Stripped Mortgage Pass-Throughs: New Tools for Investors," Chapter 21; and R. Blaine Roberts, "The Relative Valuation of IO/PO Stripped Mortgage-Backed Securities," Chapter 20, in Fabozzi (ed.), *The Handbook of Mortgage-Backed Securities, second ed.*

supply and demand, mortgage bankers came into being to provide funds to regions of the country that needed funds from regions with surplus funds. This system, however, remained dependent on deposits at thrifts and banks, which became unstable due to interest rate ceilings that were imposed. A secondary market has developed to securitize mortgages, thereby allowing other investors to provide a steadier supply of funds to the mortgage market.

The basic mortgage-backed security is the mortgage pass-through security. The types of mortgage pass-through securities are agency and private-label pass-through securities. The nonagency pass-through securities require private credit enhancements in order to receive a high credit rating. Mortgage pass-through securities can be backed by either fixed-rate or adjustable-rate mortgage loans.

A projection of prepayments is necessary to determine the cash flow of a pass-through security. The assumed prepayment speed is based on the factors affecting prepayment behavior. There are four factors that affect prepayment behavior: (1) the prevailing mortgage rate, (2) characteristics of the underlying mortgage pool, (3) seasonal factors, and (4) general economic activity. A prepayment model begins by modeling the statistical relationships among the factors that are expected to affect prepayments. The product of a prepayment forecast is a set of prepayment rates for each month of the remaining term of a mortgage pool which are then converted into a PSA speed. The PSA prepayment benchmark is a series of conditional prepayment rates and is simply a market convention that describes in general the pattern of prepayments. A measure commonly used to estimate the life of a pass-through is its average life.

The prepayment risks associated with investing in mortgage pass-through securities can be decomposed into contraction risk and extension risk. Prepayment risk makes pass-through securities unattractive for certain financial institutions to hold from an asset/liability perspective.

A stripped mortgage-backed security is a derivative mortgage-backed security that is created by redistributing the interest and principal payments to two different classes. The most common types of stripped mortgage-backed securities are the interest-only and principal-only securities.

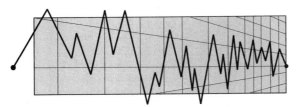

QUESTIONS

1. What is a mortgage pass-through security?

2. Describe the cash flow of a mortgage pass-through security.

3. How has securitization enhanced the liquidity of mortgages?

4. a. What are the different types of agency pass-through securities?

   b. Which type of agency pass-through carries the full faith and credit of the U.S. government?

5. What is a private-label pass-through security?

6. What is meant by the WAC and WAM of a pass-through security?

7. Explain whether all agency pass-through securities guarantee the timely payment of interest and scheduled principal.

8. What is an agency swap program?

9. Why is an assumed prepayment speed necessary to project the cash flow of a pass-through?

10. a. A cash flow for a pass-through typically is based on some prepayment benchmark. Describe the benchmark.

   b. What are the limitations of this benchmark?

11. What does a conditional prepayment rate of 8% mean?

12. What is the relationship between the conditional prepayment rate and the single monthly mortality rate?

13. If a CPR of 9% is assumed, what is the SMM?

14. a. What does 150 PSA mean?

   b. What is the SMM assuming 150 PSA for months 3, 25, and 240?

15. What is meant by prepayment risk, contraction risk, and extension risk?

16. Why would a pass-through backed by fixed-rate mortgages with a WAM of 250 months be an unattractive investment for a savings and loan association?

17. What is meant by the average life of a pass-through?

18. What are the factors that affect prepayments?

19. a. What is a principal-only security?

   b. What is an interest-only security?

20. a. How is the price of an interest-only security expected to change when interest rates change?

   b. Will the investor in an interest-only security recover the amount invested?

The Market for Collateralized Mortgage Obligations

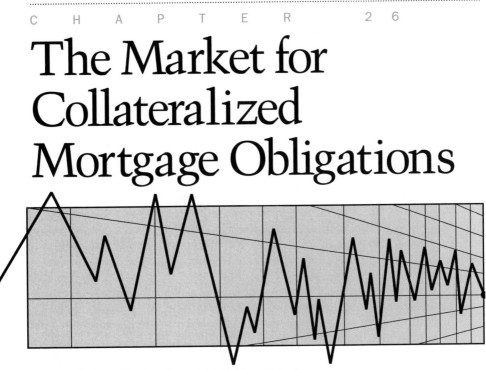

LEARNING OBJECTIVES

After reading this chapter you will understand:

- why and how a collateralized mortgage obligation is created.

- what a sequential-pay CMO is.

- how the average life of a sequential-pay CMO compares to that of the collateral from which it is created.

- what an accrual tranche is and the effect of an accrual tranche on the average life of sequential-pay tranches in the CMO structure.

- how a floater and an inverse floater are created from a CMO tranche.

- what a planned amortization class tranche is and how it is created.

- what a support or companion tranche is.

- what is meant by a REMIC.

- the difference between an agency CMO, a private-label CMO, and a whole loan CMO.

This chapter is adapted from Chapters 1 through 7 of Frank J. Fabozzi, Charles Ramsey, and Frank Ramirez, *Collateralized Mortgage Obligations: Structures and Analysis* (New Hope, PA: Frank J. Fabozzi Associates, 1994), second ed.

In the previous chapter we noted the prepayment risk associated with investing in mortgage pass-through securities. Some institutional investors are concerned with extension risk and others with contraction risk when they invest in a pass-through. This problem can be mitigated by redirecting the cash flows of mortgage-related products (pass-through securities or a pool of loans) to different bond classes, called **tranches**, so as to create securities that have different exposure to prepayment risk and therefore different risk/return patterns than the mortgage-related product from which they were created.

When the cash flows of mortgage-related products are redistributed to different bond classes, the resulting securities are called **collateralized mortgage obligations** (CMO). The creation of a CMO cannot eliminate prepayment risk; it can only distribute the various forms of this risk among different classes of bondholders. In the world of fixed-income securities, the growth of the U.S. mortgage-backed securities market holds all records, with the CMO sector now dominant. The CMO's major financial innovation, which is responsible for the rapid growth of this market, is that the securities created more closely satisfy the asset/liability needs of institutional investors, thereby broadening the appeal of mortgage-backed products to traditional fixed-income investors.

The focus in this chapter is on CMOs. The reason we devote an entire chapter to this topic is twofold. First, it is the largest and fastest growing sector of the mortgage-backed securities market. Second, the CMO provides an excellent illustration of financial engineering. While there are many different types of CMOs that have been created, we will only look at four of the key innovations in the CMO market: sequential-pay tranches, accrual tranches, floating-rate/inverse floating-rate tranches, and planned amortization class bonds. We begin with the simplest type of CMO structure.

SEQUENTIAL-PAY TRANCHES

The first CMO was created in 1983 and was structured so that each class of bond would be retired sequentially. Such structures are referred to as **sequential-pay** CMOs.

Illustration of a Sequential-Pay CMO

To illustrate a sequential-pay CMO, we discuss FRR-01,[1] a hypothetical deal made up to illustrate the basic features of the structure. The collateral for this hypothetical CMO is a hypothetical pass-through with a total par value of $400 million and the following characteristics: (1) the pass-through coupon rate is 7.5%, (2) the weighted-average coupon (WAC) is 8.125%, and (3) the weighted average maturity (WAM) is 357 months. This is the same pass-through that we used in Chapter 25 to describe the cash flow of a pass-through based on some PSA assumption.

From this $400 million of collateral, four bond classes or tranches are created. Their characteristics are summarized in Table 26-1. The total par value of the four tranches is equal to the par value of the collateral (i.e., the pass-through

---

[1] All CMO structures are given a name. In our illustration we use FRR, the initials of the last names of the authors who created the hypothetical CMOs presented in this chapter.

security). In this simple structure, the coupon rate is the same for each tranche and also the same as the coupon rate on the collateral. There is no reason why this must be so, and, in fact, typically the coupon rate varies by tranche.

Remember that a CMO is created by redistributing the cash flow—interest and principal—to the different tranches based on a set of payment rules. The payment rules at the bottom of Table 26-1 describe how the cash flow from the pass-through (i.e., collateral) is to be distributed to the four tranches. There are separate rules for the payment of the coupon interest and the payment of principal, the principal being the total of the regularly scheduled principal payment and any prepayments.

In FRR-01, each tranche receives periodic coupon interest payments based on the amount of the outstanding balance at the beginning of the month. The disbursement of the principal, however, is made in a special way. A tranche is not entitled to receive principal until the entire principal of the tranche before it has been paid off. More specifically, tranche A receives all the principal payments until the entire principal amount owed to that bond class, $194,500,000, is paid off; then tranche B begins to receive principal and continues to do so until it is paid the entire $36,000,000. Tranche C then receives principal, and when it is paid off, tranche D starts receiving principal payments.

While the priority rules for the disbursement of the principal payments are known, the precise amount of the principal in each period is not. This will depend on the cash flow—and therefore principal payments—of the collateral, which depends on the actual prepayment rate of the collateral. An assumed PSA speed allows the cash flow to be projected. Table 25-2 of Chapter 25 shows the cash flow (interest, regularly scheduled principal repayment, and

Table 26-1

FRR-01: A Hypothetical Four-Tranche Sequential-Pay Structure

Tranche	Par Amount	Coupon Rate
A	$194,500,000	7.5%
B	36,000,000	7.5
C	96,500,000	7.5
D	73,000,000	7.5
Total	$400,000,000	

Payment rules

1. *For payment of periodic coupon interest:* Disburse periodic coupon interest to each tranche on the basis of the amount of principal outstanding at the beginning of the period.

2. *For disbursement of principal payments:* Disburse principal payments to tranche A until it is completely paid off. After tranche A is completely paid off, disburse principal payments to tranche B until it is completely paid off. After tranche B is completely paid off, disburse principal payments to tranche C until it is completely paid off. After tranche C is completely paid off, disburse principal payments to tranche D until it is completely paid off.

prepayments) assuming 165 PSA. Assuming that the collateral does prepay at 165 PSA, the cash flow available to all four tranches of FRR-01 will be precisely the cash flow shown in Table 26-2.

To demonstrate how the priority rules for FRR-01 work, Table 26-2 shows the cash flow for selected months assuming the collateral prepays at 165 PSA. For each tranche, the table shows: (1) the balance at the end of the month, (2)

Table 26-2

Monthly Cash Flow for Selected Months for FRR-01 Assuming 165 PSA

Mo.	Tranche A Balance	Principal	Interest	Tranche B Balance	Principal	Interest
1	194,500,000	709,923	1,215,625	36,000,000	0	225,000
2	193,790,077	821,896	1,211,188	36,000,000	0	225,000
3	192,968,181	933,560	1,206,051	36,000,000	0	225,000
4	192,034,621	1,044,822	1,200,216	36,000,000	0	225,000
5	190,989,799	1,155,586	1,193,686	36,000,000	0	225,000
6	189,834,213	1,265,759	1,186,464	36,000,000	0	225,000
7	188,568,454	1,375,246	1,178,553	36,000,000	0	225,000
8	187,193,208	1,483,954	1,169,958	36,000,000	0	225,000
9	185,709,254	1,591,789	1,160,683	36,000,000	0	225,000
10	184,117,464	1,698,659	1,150,734	36,000,000	0	225,000
11	182,418,805	1,804,473	1,140,118	36,000,000	0	225,000
12	180,614,332	1,909,139	1,128,840	36,000,000	0	225,000
75	12,893,479	2,143,974	80,584	36,000,000	0	225,000
76	10,749,504	2,124,935	67,184	36,000,000	0	225,000
77	8,624,569	2,106,062	53,904	36,000,000	0	225,000
78	6,518,507	2,087,353	40,741	36,000,000	0	225,000
79	4,431,154	2,068,807	27,695	36,000,000	0	225,000
80	2,362,347	2,050,422	14,765	36,000,000	0	225,000
81	311,926	311,926	1,950	36,000,000	1,720,271	225,000
82	0	0	0	34,279,729	2,014,130	214,248
83	0	0	0	32,265,599	1,996,221	201,660
84	0	0	0	30,269,378	1,978,468	189,184
85	0	0	0	28,290,911	1,960,869	176,818
95	0	0	0	9,449,331	1,793,089	59,058
96	0	0	0	7,656,242	1,777,104	47,852
97	0	0	0	5,879,138	1,761,258	36,745
98	0	0	0	4,117,880	1,745,550	25,737
99	0	0	0	2,372,329	1,729,979	14,827
100	0	0	0	642,350	642,350	4,015
101	0	0	0	0	0	0
102	0	0	0	0	0	0
103	0	0	0	0	0	0
104	0	0	0	0	0	0
105	0	0	0	0	0	0

Continued on next page

Table 26-2 *Continued from previous page*

		Tranche C			Tranche D	
Mo.	Balance	Principal	Interest	Balance	Principal	Interest
1	96,500,000	0	603,125	73,000,000	0	456,250
2	96,500,000	0	603,125	73,000,000	0	456,250
3	96,500,000	0	603,125	73,000,000	0	456,250
4	96,500,000	0	603,125	73,000,000	0	456,250
5	96,500,000	0	603,125	73,000,000	0	456,250
6	96,500,000	0	603,125	73,000,000	0	456,250
7	96,500,000	0	603,125	73,000,000	0	456,250
8	96,500,000	0	603,125	73,000,000	0	456,250
9	96,500,000	0	603,125	73,000,000	0	456,250
10	96,500,000	0	603,125	73,000,000	0	456,250
11	96,500,000	0	603,125	73,000,000	0	456,250
12	96,500,000	0	603,125	73,000,000	0	456,250
95	96,500,000	0	603,125	73,000,000	0	456,250
96	96,500,000	0	603,125	73,000,000	0	456,250
97	96,500,000	0	603,125	73,000,000	0	456,250
98	96,500,000	0	603,125	73,000,000	0	456,250
99	96,500,000	0	603,125	73,000,000	0	456,250
100	96,500,000	1,072,194	603,125	73,000,000	0	456,250
101	95,427,806	1,699,243	596,424	73,000,000	0	456,250
102	93,728,563	1,684,075	585,804	73,000,000	0	456,250
103	92,044,489	1,669,039	575,278	73,000,000	0	456,250
104	90,375,450	1,654,134	564,847	73,000,000	0	456,250
105	88,721,315	1,639,359	554,508	73,000,000	0	456,250
175	3,260,287	869,602	20,377	73,000,000	0	456,250
176	2,390,685	861,673	14,942	73,000,000	0	456,250
177	1,529,013	853,813	9,556	73,000,000	0	456,250
178	675,199	675,199	4,220	73,000,000	170,824	456,250
179	0	0	0	72,829,176	838,300	455,182
180	0	0	0	71,990,876	830,646	449,943
181	0	0	0	71,160,230	823,058	444,751
182	0	0	0	70,337,173	815,536	439,607
183	0	0	0	69,521,637	808,081	434,510
184	0	0	0	68,713,556	800,690	429,460
185	0	0	0	67,912,866	793,365	424,455
350	0	0	0	1,235,674	160,220	7,723
351	0	0	0	1,075,454	158,544	6,722
352	0	0	0	916,910	156,883	5,731
353	0	0	0	760,027	155,238	4,750
354	0	0	0	604,789	153,607	3,780
355	0	0	0	451,182	151,991	2,820
356	0	0	0	299,191	150,389	1,870
357	0	0	0	148,802	148,802	930

the principal paid down (regularly scheduled principal repayment plus prepayments), and (3) interest. In month 1, the cash flow for the collateral consists of principal payment of $709,923 and interest of $2.5 million (0.075 times $400 million divided by 12). The interest payment is distributed to the four tranches based on the amount of the par value outstanding. So, for example, tranche A receives $1,215,625 (0.075 times $194,500,000 divided by 12) of the $2.5 million. The principal, however, is all distributed to tranche A. Therefore, the cash flow for tranche A in month 1 is $1,925,548. The principal balance at the end of month 1 for tranche A is $193,790,076 (the original principal balance of $194,500,000 less the principal payment of $709,923). No principal payment is distributed to the three other tranches because there is still a principal balance outstanding for tranche A. This will be true for months 2 through 80.

After month 81, the principal balance will be zero for tranche A. For the collateral, the cash flow in month 81 is $3,318,521, consisting of a principal payment of $2,032,196 and interest of $1,286,325. At the beginning of month 81 (end of month 80), the principal balance for tranche A is $311,926. Therefore, $311,926 of the $2,032,196 of the principal payment from the collateral will be disbursed to tranche A. After this payment is made, no additional principal payments are made to this tranche as the principal balance is zero. The remaining principal payment from the collateral, $1,720,271, is disbursed to tranche B. According to the assumed prepayment speed of 165 PSA, tranche B then begins receiving principal payments in month 81.

Table 26-2 shows that tranche B is fully paid off by month 100, when tranche C begins to receive principal payments. Tranche C is not fully paid off until month 178, at which time tranche D begins receiving the remaining principal payments. The maturity (i.e., the time until the principal is fully paid off) for these four tranches assuming 165 PSA would be 81 months for tranche A, 100 months for tranche B, 178 months for tranche C, and 357 months for tranche D.

Effect on Average Life

Let's look at what has been accomplished by creating the CMO. In Chapter 25 we indicated that the average life for of the pass-through is 8.76 years, assuming a prepayment speed of 165 PSA. Table 26-3 reports the average life of the collateral and the four tranches assuming different prepayment speeds. Notice that the four tranches have average lives that are both shorter and longer than the collateral, thereby attracting investors who have a preference for an average life different from that of the collateral.

There is still a major problem: there is considerable variability of the average life for the tranches. We'll see how this can be tackled later on. However, there is some protection provided for each tranche against prepayment risk. This is because prioritizing the distribution of principal (i.e., establishing the payment rules for principal) effectively protects the shorter-term tranche A in this structure against extension risk. This protection must come from somewhere; it comes from the three other tranches. Similarly, tranches C and D provide protection against extension risk for tranches A and B. At the same

Table 26-3
Average Life for the Collateral and the Four Tranches of FRR-01

Prepayment speed (PSA)	Collateral	Average life for			
		Tranche A	Tranche B	Tranche C	Tranche D
50	15.11	7.48	15.98	21.02	27.24
100	11.66	4.90	10.86	15.78	24.58
165	8.76	3.48	7.49	11.19	20.27
200	7.68	3.05	6.42	9.60	18.11
300	5.63	2.32	4.64	6.81	13.36
400	4.44	1.94	3.70	5.31	10.34
500	3.68	1.69	3.12	4.38	8.35
600	3.16	1.51	2.74	3.75	6.96
700	2.78	1.38	2.47	3.30	5.95

time, tranches C and D benefit because they are provided protection against contraction risk, the protection coming from tranches A and B.

ACCRUAL BONDS

In FRR-01, the payment rules for interest provide for all tranches to be paid interest each month. In many sequential-pay CMO structures, at least one tranche does not receive current interest. Instead, the interest for that tranche would accrue and be added to the principal balance. Such a bond class is commonly referred to as an **accrual tranche**, or a **Z bond** (because the bond is similar to a zero-coupon bond). The interest that would have been paid to the accrual bond class is then used to speed up pay down of the principal balance of earlier bond classes.

Illustration of an Accrual Tranche

To see this, consider FRR-02, a hypothetical CMO structure with the same collateral as FRR-01 and with four tranches, each with a coupon rate of 7.5%. The difference is in the last tranche, Z, which is an accrual. The structure for FRR-02 is shown in Table 26-4.

Table 26-5 shows cash flows for selected months for tranches A and B. Look at month 1 and compare it to month 1 in Table 26-2. Both cash flows are based on 165 PSA. The principal payment from the collateral is $709,923. In FRR-01, this is the principal paydown for tranche A. In FRR-02, the interest for tranche Z, $456,250, is not paid to that tranche but instead is used to pay down the principal of tranche A. So, the principal payment to tranche A in Table 26-5 is $1,166,173, the collateral's principal payment of $709,923 plus the interest of $456,250 that was diverted from tranche Z.

Table 26-4

FRR-02: A Hypothetical Four-Tranche Sequential-Pay Structure
with an Accrual Bond Class

Tranche	Par amount	Coupon Rate
A	$194,500,000	7.5%
B	36,000,000	7.5
C	96,500,000	7.5
Z (Accrual)	73,000,000	7.5
Total	$400,000,000	

Payment rules

1. *For payment of periodic coupon interest:* Disburse periodic coupon interest to tranches A, B, and C on the basis of the amount of principal outstanding at the beginning of the period. For tranche Z, accrue the interest based on the principal plus accrued interest in the previous period. The interest for tranche Z is to be paid to the earlier tranches as a principal paydown.

2. *For disbursement of principal payments:* Disburse principal payments to tranche A until it is completely paid off. After tranche A is completely paid off, disburse principal payments to tranche B until it is completely paid off. After tranche B is completely paid off, disburse principal payments to tranche C until it is completely paid off. After tranche C is completely paid off, disburse principal payments to tranche Z until the original principal balance plus accrued interest is completely paid off.

Effect on Average Life

The expected final maturity for tranches A, B, and C has shortened as a result of the inclusion of tranche Z. The final payout for tranche A is 64 months rather than 81 months; for tranche B it is 77 months rather than 100 months; and for tranche C it is 112 rather than 178 months.

The average lives for tranches A, B, and C are shorter in FRR-02 compared to FRR-01 because of the inclusion of the accrual bond. For example, at 165 PSA, the average lives are as follows:

Structure	Tranche A	Tranche B	Tranche C
FRR-02	2.90	5.86	7.87
FRR-01	3.48	7.49	11.19

The reason for the shortening of the nonaccrual tranches is that the interest that would be paid to the accrual bond is being allocated to the other tranches. Tranche Z in FRR-02 will have a longer average life than tranche D in FRR-01.

Thus, shorter-term tranches and a longer-term tranche are created by including an accrual bond. The accrual bond has appeal to investors who are concerned with reinvestment risk. Since there are no coupon payments to reinvest, reinvestment risk is eliminated until all the other tranches are paid off.

Table 26-5

Monthly Cash Flow for Selected Months for Tranches A and B
of FRR-02 Assuming 165 PSA

Mo.	Balance	Tranche A Principal	Interest	Balance	Tranche B Principal	Interest
1	194,500,000	1,166,173	1,215,265	36,000,000	0	225,000
2	193,333,827	1,280,997	1,208,336	36,000,000	0	225,000
3	192,052,829	1,395,531	1,200,330	36,000,000	0	225,000
4	190,657,298	1,509,680	1,191,608	36,000,000	0	255,000
5	189,147,619	1,623,350	1,182,173	36,000,000	0	225,000
6	187,524,269	1,736,446	1,172,027	36,000,000	0	225,000
7	185,787,823	1,848,875	1,161,174	36,000,000	0	225,000
8	183,938,947	1,960,543	1,149,618	36,000,000	0	225,000
9	181,978,404	2,071,357	1,137,365	36,000,000	0	225,000
10	179,907,047	2,181,225	1,124,419	36,000,000	0	225,000
11	177,725,822	2,290,054	1,110,786	36,000,000	0	225,000
12	175,435,768	2,397,755	1,096,474	36,000,000	0	255,000
60	15,023,406	3,109,398	93,896	36,000,000	0	225,000
61	11,914,007	3,091,812	74,463	36,000,000	0	225,000
62	8,822,195	3,074,441	55,139	36,000,000	0	225,000
63	5,747,754	3,057,282	35,923	36,000,000	0	225,000
64	2,690,472	2,690,472	16,815	36,000,000	349,863	225,000
65	0	0	0	35,650,137	3,023,598	222,813
66	0	0	0	32,626,540	3,007,069	203,916
67	0	0	0	29,619,470	2,990,748	185,122
68	0	0	0	26,628,722	2,974,633	166,430
69	0	0	0	23,654,089	2,958,722	147,838
70	0	0	0	20,695,367	2,943,014	129,346
71	0	0	0	17,752,353	2,927,508	110,952
72	0	0	0	14,824,845	2,912,203	92,655
73	0	0	0	11,912,642	2,897,096	71,454
74	0	0	0	9,015,546	2,882,187	56,347
75	0	0	0	6,133,358	2,867,475	38,333
76	0	0	0	3,265,883	2,852,958	20,412
77	0	0	0	412,925	412,925	2,581
78	0	0	0	0	0	0

Continued on next page

FLOATING-RATE TRANCHES

The CMO structures discussed above offer a fixed coupon rate on all tranches. If CMO classes could be created only with fixed-rate coupons, the market for CMOs would be limited. Many financial institutions prefer floating-rate assets, which provide a better match for their liabilities.

As explained in Chapter 21, a floating-rate municipal security can be created from fixed-rate collateral by creating a floater and an inverse floater. A floating-rate CMO tranche can be created in the same way. We will illustrate the creation of a floating-rate and inverse floating-rate bond class using the

Table 26-5 *continued from previous page*

Mo.	Balance	Tranche C Principal	Interest	Balance	Tranche Z Principal	Interest
1	96,500,000	0	603,125	73,000,000	–456,250	456,250
2	96,500,000	0	603,125	73,456,250	–459,102	459,102
3	96,500,000	0	603,125	73,915,352	–461,971	461,971
4	96,500,000	0	603,125	74,377,323	–464,858,	464,858
5	96,500,000	0	603,125	74,842,181	–467,764	467,764
6	96,500,000	0	603,125	75,309,944	–470,687	470,687
7	96,500,000	0	603,125	75,780,632	–473,629	473,629
8	96,500,000	0	603,125	76,254,261	–476,589	476,589
9	96,500,000	0	603,125	76,730,850	–479,568	479,568
10	96,500,000	0	603,125	77,210,417	–482,565	482,565
11	96,500,000	0	603,125	77,692,983	–485,581	485,581
12	96,500,000	0	603,125	78,178,564	–488,616	488,616
70	96,500,000	0	603,125	112,209,468	–701,309	701,309
71	96,500,000	0	603,125	112,910,777	–705,692	705,692
72	96,500,000	0	603,125	113,616,469	–710,103	710,103
73	96,500,000	0	603,125	114,326,572	–714,541	714,541
74	96,500,000	0	603,125	115,041,113	–719,007	719,007
75	96,500,000	0	603,125	115,760,120	–723,501	723,501
76	96,500,000	. 0	603,125	116,483,621	–728,023	728,023
77	96,500,000	2,425,710	603,125	117,211,644	–732,573	732,573
78	94,074,290	2,824,504	587,964	117,944,217	–737,151	737,151
79	91,249,786	2,810,565	570,311	118,681,368	–741,759	741,759
80	88,439,221	2,796,816	552,745	119,423,126	–746,395	746,395
110	9,701,953	2,467,192	60,637	143,967,757	–899,798	889,798
111	7,234,762	2,458,796	45,217	144,867,555	–905,422	905,422
112	4,775,966	2,450,558	29,850	145,772,978	–911,081	911,081
113	2,325,408	2,325,408	14,534	146,684,059	–799,707	799,707
114	0	0	0	147,483,765	1,512,045	921,774
115	0	0	0	145,971,721	1,498,508	912,323
116	0	0	0	144,473,213	1,485,089	902,958
117	0	0	0	142,988,123	1,471,787	893,676
118	0	0	0	141,516,336	1,458,601	884,477
119	0	0	0	140,057,735	1,445,530	875,361
120	0	0	0	138,612,205	1,432,573	866,326

hypothetical CMO structure FRR-02, which is a four-tranche sequential-pay structure with an accrual bond. We can select any of the tranches from which to create a floating-rate and inverse floating-rate tranche. In fact, we can create these two securities for more than one of the four tranches or for only a portion of one tranche.

In this case, we create a floater and an inverse floater from tranche C. The par value for this tranche is $96.5 million, and we create two tranches that have a combined par value of $96.5 million. We refer to this CMO structure with a floater and an inverse floater as FRR-03. It has five tranches, designated A, B, FL, IFL, and Z, where FL is the floating-rate tranche and IFL is the inverse floating-rate tranche. Table 26-6 describes FRR-03. Any reference rate can be used to create a floater and the corresponding inverse floater. The reference rate for setting the coupon rate for FL and IFL in FRR-03 is taken as one-month LIBOR.

The amount of the par value of the floating-rate tranche will be some portion of the $96.5 million. There are an infinite number of ways to cut up the $96.5 million between the floater and inverse floater, and final partitioning will be driven by the demands of investors. In the FRR-03 structure, we made the floater from $72,375,000, or 75% of the $96.5 million. The coupon rate on the floater is set at one-month LIBOR plus 50 basis points. So, for example, if LIBOR is 3.75% at the reset date, the coupon rate on the floater is 3.75% plus 0.5%, or 4.25%. There is a cap on the coupon rate for the floater (discussed later).

Unlike a floating-rate note in the corporate bond market, whose principal is unchanged over the life of the instrument, the floater's principal balance declines over time as principal payments are made. The principal payments to

Table 26-6
FRR-03: A Hypothetical Five-Tranche Sequential-Pay Structure with Floater, Inverse Floater, and Accrual Bond Classes

Tranche	Par amount	Coupon rate
A	$194,500,000	7.50%
B	36,000,000	7.50
FL	72,375,000	1-mo. LIBOR + 0.50
IFL	24,125,000	$28.50 - 3 \times (1\text{-mo. LIBOR})$
Z (Accrual)	73,000,000	7.50
Total	$400,000,000	

Payment rules

1. *For payment of periodic coupon interest:* Disburse periodic coupon interest to tranches A, B, FL, and IFL on the basis of the amount of principal outstanding at the beginning of the period. For tranche Z, accrue the interest based on the principal plus accrued interest in the previous period. The interest for tranche Z is to be paid to the earlier tranches as a principal paydown. The maximum coupon rate for FL is 10%; the minimum coupon rate for IFL is 0%.

2. *For disbursement of principal payments:* Disburse principal payments to tranche A until it is completely paid off. After tranche A is completely paid off, disburse principal payments to tranche B until it is completely paid off. After tranche B is completely paid off, disburse principal payments to tranches FL and IFL until they are completely paid off. The principal payments between tranches FL and IFL should be made in the following way: 75% to tranche FL and 25% to tranche IFL. After tranches FL and IFL are completely paid off, disburse principal payments to tranche Z until the original principal balance plus accrued interest is completely paid off.

the floater are determined by the principal payments from the tranche from which the floater is created. In our CMO structure, this is tranche C.

Since the floater's par value is $72,375,000 of the $96.5 million, the balance is the inverse floater. Assuming that one-month LIBOR is the reference rate, the coupon rate on the inverse floater takes the following form:

$$K - L \times (\text{1-mo. LIBOR})$$

In FRR-04, K is set at 28.50% and L at 3. Thus, if one-month LIBOR is 3.75%, the coupon rate for the month is:

$$28.50\% - 3 \times (3.75\%) = 17.25\%$$

K is the cap or maximum coupon rate for the inverse floater. In FRR-04, the cap for the inverse floater is 28.50%.

The L or multiple in the formula to determine the coupon rate for the inverse floater, is called the **coupon leverage**. The higher the coupon leverage, the more the inverse floater's coupon rate changes for a given change in one-month LIBOR. For example, a coupon leverage of 3.0 means that a 100-basis point change in one-month LIBOR will change the coupon rate on the inverse floater by 300 basis points; a coupon leverage of 0.7 means that the coupon rate will change by 70 basis points for a 100-basis point change in one-month LIBOR. Inverse floaters with a wide variety of coupon leverages are available in the market. Participants refer to low-leverage inverse floaters as those with a coupon leverage between 0.5 and 2.1; medium-leverage as those with a coupon leverage higher than 2.1 but not exceeding 4.5; and high-leverage as those with a coupon leverage higher than 4.5. At the time of issuance, the issuer determines the coupon leverage according to investor desire. In FRR-03 the coupon leverage is set at 3.

Let's see how the total interest paid on the floater and inverse floater can be supported by the tranche with a coupon rate of 7.5% from which they are created. The coupon rate for the floating-rate class is: 1-mo. LIBOR plus 0.50. For the inverse floater the coupon rate is:

$$28.50 - 3 \times (\text{1-mo. LIBOR})$$

Since the floater is 75% of the $96.5 million and the inverse floater is 25%, the weighted average coupon rate is:

$$0.75 (\text{Floater coupon rate}) + 0.25 (\text{Inverse floater coupon rate})$$

The weighted-average coupon rate is 7.5%, regardless of the level of LIBOR. For example, if one-month LIBOR is 9%, then:

Floater coupon rate = 9.0% + 0.5% = 9.5%
Inverse floater coupon rate = 28.5 − 3 × (9.0%) = 1.5%
Weighted average coupon rate = 0.75 (9.5%) + 0.25 (1.5%) = 7.5%

Consequently, the 7.5% coupon rate on the tranche from which these two tranches were created can support the aggregate interest payments that must be made to them.

As in the case of the floater, the principal paydown of an inverse floater will be a proportionate amount of the principal paydown of tranche C.

Because one-month LIBOR is always positive, the coupon rate paid to the floating-rate bond class cannot be negative. If there are no restrictions placed on the coupon rate for the inverse floater, however, it is possible for the coupon rate for that bond class to be negative. To prevent this, a floor, or minimum, can be placed on the coupon rate. In many structures, the floor is set at zero. Once a floor is set for the inverse floater, a cap or ceiling is imposed on the floater. In FRR-03, a floor of zero is set for the inverse floater. The floor results in a cap or maximum coupon rate for the floater of 10%. This is found by substituting zero for the coupon rate of the inverse floater in the formula for the weighted-average coupon rate, and then setting the formula equal to 7.5%.

The cap for the floater and the inverse floater, the floor for the inverse floater, the coupon leverage, and the margin spread are not determined independently. Given four of these variables, the fifth will be determined.

PLANNED AMORTIZATION CLASS TRANCHES

The CMO innovations discussed above attracted many institutional investors who had previously either avoided investing in mortgage-backed securities or allocated only a nominal portion of their portfolio to this sector of the fixed-income market. While some traditional corporate bond buyers shifted their allocation to CMOs, a majority of institutional investors remained on the sidelines, concerned about investing in an instrument that they continued to perceive as posing significant prepayment risk because of the substantial average life variability despite the innovations designed to reduce prepayment risk.

Potential demand for a CMO product with less uncertainty about the cash flow increased in the mid-1980s because of two trends in the corporate bond market. First was the increased event risk faced by investors, highlighted by the RJR Nabisco leveraged buyout in 1988. The second trend was a decline in the number of triple-A rated corporate issues. Traditional corporate bond buyers sought a structure with both the characteristics of a corporate bond (either a bullet maturity or a sinking-fund type schedule of principal repayment) and high credit quality. While CMOs satisfied the second condition, they did not satisfy the first.

In March 1987, the M.D.C. Mortgage Funding Corporation CMO Series 0 included a class of bonds referred to as "stabilized mortgage reduction term bonds" or "SMRT" bonds; another class in its CMO Series P was referred to as "planned amortization class bonds" or "PAC" bonds. The Oxford Acceptance Corporation III Series C CMOs included a class of bonds referred to as a "planned redemption obligation bonds" or "PRO" bonds. The characteristic common to these three bonds is that, if the prepayments are within a specified range, the cash-flow pattern is known.

The greater predictability of the cash flow for these classes of bonds, now referred to exclusively as **PAC bonds**, occurs because there is a principal repayment schedule that must be satisfied. PAC bondholders have priority over all other classes in the CMO issue in receiving principal payments from the underlying collateral. The greater certainty of the cash flow for the PAC bonds comes at the expense of the non-PAC classes, called the **support** or **companion bonds**. It is these bonds that absorb the prepayment risk. Because PAC bonds have protection against both extension risk and contraction risk, they are said to provide two-sided prepayment protection.

Illustration

To illustrate how to create a PAC bond, we will use as collateral the $400 million pass-through with a coupon rate of 7.5%, an 8.125% WAC, and a WAM of 357 months. The second column of Table 26-7 shows the principal payment (regularly scheduled principal repayment plus prepayments) for selected months assuming a prepayment speed of 90 PSA, and the third column shows the principal payments for selected months assuming that the pass-through prepays at 300 PSA.

The last column of Table 26-7 gives the *minimum* principal payment if the collateral speed is 90 PSA or 300 PSA for months 1 to 349. (After month 346, the outstanding principal balance will be paid off if the prepayment speed is between 90 PSA and 300 PSA.) For example, in the first month, the principal payment would be $508,169.52 if the collateral prepays at 90 PSA and $1,075,931.20 if the collateral prepays at 300 PSA. Thus, the minimum principal payment is $508,169.52, as reported in the last column of Table 26-7. In month 103, the minimum principal payment is also the amount if the prepayment speed is 90 PSA, $1,446,761, compared to $1,458,618.04 for 300 PSA. In month 104, however, a prepayment speed of 300 PSA would produce a principal payment of $1,433,539.23, which is less than the principal payment of $1,440,825.55 assuming 90 PSA—so $1,433,539.23 is reported in the last column of Table 26-7. In fact, from month 104 on, the minimum principal payment is the one that would result assuming a prepayment speed of 300 PSA over its life.

In fact, if the collateral prepays at *any* speed between 90 PSA and 300 PSA over its life, the minimum principal payment would be the amount reported in the last column of Table 26-7. For example, if we had included principal payment figures assuming a prepayment speed of 200 PSA, the minimum principal payment would not change: from month 11 through month 103, the minimum principal payment is that generated from 90 PSA; but from month 104 on, the minimum principal payment is that generated from 300 PSA.

This characteristic of the collateral allows for the creation of a PAC bond, assuming that the collateral prepays over its life at a speed between 90 PSA to 300 PSA. A schedule of principal repayments that the PAC bondholders are entitled to receive before any other tranche in the CMO is specified. The monthly schedule of principal repayments is as specified in the last column of Table 26-7, which shows the minimum principal payment. While there is no assurance that the collateral will prepay between these two speeds, a PAC bond can be structured to assume that it will.

Table 26-8 shows a CMO structure, FRR-04, created from the $400 million, 7.5% coupon pass-through with a WAC of 8.125% and a WAM of 357 months. There are just two tranches in this structure: a 7.5% coupon PAC bond created assuming 90 to 300 PSA with a par value of $243.8 million, and a support bond with a par value of $156.2 million.

Table 26-9 reports the average life for the PAC bond and the support bond in FRR-04 assuming various *actual* prepayment speeds. Notice that between 90 PSA and 300 PSA, the average life for the PAC bond is stable at 7.26 years. However, at slower or faster PSA speeds, the schedule is broken, and the average life changes—lengthening when the prepayment speed is less than 90 PSA, and shortening when it is greater than 300 PSA. Even so, there is much greater variability for the average life of the support bond.

Table 26-7

Monthly Principal Payment for $400 Million, 7.5% Coupon Pass-Through with a WAC of 8.125% and a WAM of 357 Month Assuming Prepayment Rates of 90 PSA and 300 PSA

Month	At 90 PSA	At 300 PSA	Minimum principal payment—PAC schedule
1	508,169.52	1,075,931.20	508,169.52
2	569,843.43	1,279,412.11	569,843.43
3	631,377.11	1,482,194.45	631,377.11
4	692,741.89	1,683,966.17	692,741.89
5	753,909.12	1,884,414.62	753,909.12
6	814,850.22	2,083,227.31	814,850.22
7	875,536.68	2,280,092.68	875,536.68
8	935,940.10	2,474,700.92	935,940.10
9	996,032.19	2,666,744.77	996,032.19
10	1,055,784.82	2,855,920.32	1,055,784.82
11	1,115,170.01	3,041,927.81	1,115,170.01
12	1,174,160.00	3,224,472.44	1,174,160.00
13	1,232,727.22	3,403,265.17	1,232,727.22
14	1,290,844.32	3,578,023.49	1,290,844.32
15	1,348,484.24	3,748,472.23	1,348,484.24
16	1,405,620.17	3,914,344.26	1,405,620.17
17	1,462,225.60	4,075,381.29	1,462,225.60
18	1,518,274.36	4,231,334.57	1,518,274.36
101	1,458,719.34	1,510,072.17	1,458,719.34
102	1,452,725.55	1,484,126.59	1,452,725.55
103	1,446,761.00	1,458,618.04	1,446,761.00
104	1,440,825.55	1,433,539.23	1,433,539.23
105	1,434,919.07	1,408,883.01	1,408,883.01
211	949,482.58	213,309.00	213,309.00
212	946,033.34	209,409.09	209,409.09
213	942,601.99	205,577.05	205,577.05
346	618,684.59	13,269.17	13,269.17
347	617,071.58	12,944.51	12,944.51
348	615,468.65	12,626.21	12,626.21
349	613,875.77	12,314.16	3,432.32
350	612,292.88	12,008.25	0
351	610,719.96	11,708.38	0
352	609,156.96	11,414.42	0
353	607,603.84	11,126.28	0
354	606,060.57	10,843.85	0
355	604,527.09	10,567.02	0
356	603,003.38	10,295.70	0
357	601,489.39	10,029.78	0

Table 26-8

FRR-04 CMO Structure with One PAC Bond and One Support Bond

Tranche	Par amount	Coupon rate
P (PAC)	$243,800,000	7.5%
S (Support)	156,200,000	7.5
Total	$400,000,000	

Payment rules

1. *For payment of periodic coupon interest:* Disburse periodic coupon interest to each tranche on the basis of the amount of principal outstanding at the beginning of the period.

2. *For disbursement of principal payments:* Disburse principal payments to tranche P based on its schedule of principal repayments. Tranche P has priority with respect to current and future principal payments to satisfy the schedule. Any excess principal payments in a month over the amount necessary to satisfy the schedule for tranche P are paid to tranche S. When tranche S is completely paid off, all principal payments are to be made to tranche P regardless of the schedule.

Table 26-9

Average Life for PAC Bond and Support Bond in FRR-04
Assuming Various Prepayment Speeds

Prepayment rate (PSA)	PAC Bond (P)	Support Bond (S)
0	15.97	27.26
50	9.44	24.00
90	7.26	18.56
100	7.26	18.56
150	7.26	12.57
165	7.26	11.16
200	7.26	8.38
250	7.26	5.37
300	7.26	3.13
350	6.56	2.51
400	5.92	2.17
450	5.38	1.94
500	4.93	1.77
700	3.70	1.37

In practice, all CMO structures typically do not have just one PAC tranche; rather, there are several PAC tranches created from the same tranche. For example, several PAC tranches that pay off in sequence can be created with a total par value equal to $243.8 million, which is the amount of the single PAC bond in FRR-04. This allows for the creation of PACs with a wide-range of average lives.

CREDIT RISK

A CMO can be viewed as a business entity. The assets of this business are the collateral; that is, the pass-through securities or pool of mortgage loans backing the deal. The collateral for a CMO is held in trust for the exclusive benefit of all the bondholders. The liabilities are the payments due to the CMO bond classes. The liability obligation consists of the par value and periodic interest payment that is owed to each tranche. The CMO—or, equivalently, the business—is structured so that, even under the worst possible consequences concerning prepayments, all the liabilities will be satisfied.

Credit-risk exposure depends on who the issuer of the CMO is. An issuer is either (1) a Freddie Mac, Fannie Mae, or Ginnie Mae, or (2) a private entity. A CMO issued by one of the first group is referred to as an **agency CMO**. Those issued by a private entity can be divided into two types. A private entity that issues a CMO but whose underlying collateral is a pool of pass-throughs guaranteed by an agency is called a **private-label CMOs**. If the collateral for a CMO is a pool of unsecuritized mortgages loans the structure is referred to as a **whole-loan CMO**.

As we noted in Chapter 25, the guarantee of a government-sponsored enterprise depends on the financial capacity of the agency. CMOs issued by private entities are rated by commercial rating companies. There are various ways that such issues can be credit-enhanced, as described in the next chapter when we discuss asset-backed securities.

TAX CONSIDERATIONS

The issuer of a CMO wants to be sure that the trust created to pass through the interest and principal payments is not treated as a taxable entity. A provision of the Tax Reform Act of 1986, called the Real Estate Mortgage Investment Conduit (REMIC), specifies the requirements that an issuer must fulfill so that the legal entity created to issue a CMO is not taxable. Most CMOs today are created as REMICs. While it is common to hear market participants refer to a CMO as a REMIC, not all CMOs are REMICs.

THE CMO MARKET TODAY

Table 26-10 shows the number of deals and the dollar volume of CMOs issued between the inception of the market in 1982 until 1993. It is not surprising today to see CMO structures with as many as 70 tranches. The last column of Table 26-10 shows the average number of tranches per deal by year. Between 1983 and 1985, the average number of tranches in a CMO deal was

Table 26-10

Issuance Volume of Collateralized Mortgage Obligations: 1982 to 1993*

Year	Number of deals	Dollar volume (in millions)	Number of tranches	Average number of tranches per deal
1982	1	$ 50	2	2.0
1983	8	4,748	53	6.6
1984	18	9,903	143	7.9
1985	59	16,515	434	7.4
1986	89	49,838	951	10.7
1987	94	58,875	1,020	10.9
1988	156	77,066	1,796	11.5
1989	236	95,209	2,608	11.1
1990	280	112,993	3,802	13.6
1991	440	200,810	7,077	16.1
1992	504	260,410	9,688	19.2
1993	441	271,180	10,597	24.0

Note: The information presented here includes agency and non-agency CMO/REMICs.

Source: Wall Street Analytics, Inc.

around seven. With the introduction in 1986 of the planned amortization class (PAC), the average number of tranches per deal increased to more than ten. The deals since 1986 when PACs were introduced typically included only one or two PAC tranches. By 1992, there was an average of 19 tranches per deal, and in 1993 there were about 24 tranches per deal.

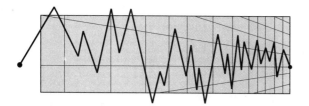

SUMMARY

Collateralized mortgage obligations are bond classes created by redirecting the cash flows of mortgage-related products (pass-throughs and whole loans). The creation of a CMO cannot eliminate prepayment risk, it can only redistribute the various forms of this risk among different classes of bonds called tranches.

In a CMO there are rules for the distribution of interest and principal from the collateral. The first CMOs were structured so that each class of bond would be retired sequentially, and hence such structures are referred to as sequential-pay CMOs. The average life of the tranches differs from that of the collateral. An accrual tranche allows the creation of shorter-term and longer-term average life tranches than is possible in a sequential-pay CMO without the inclusion of an accrual tranche. From any of the fixed-rate tranches, a floater and inverse floater can be created.

Despite the redistribution of prepayment risk with sequential-pay and accrual CMOs, there is still considerable prepayment risk. That is, there is still considerable average life variability for a given tranche. This problem has been mitigated by the creation of a planned amortization class tranche. This type of CMO tranche reduces average life variability. The bonds included in a CMO structure that provide the better protection for PAC tranches are the support or companion tranches.

The credit-risk exposure depends on whether the issuer is an agency CMO (i.e., the issuer is Ginnie Mae, Fannie Mae, or Freddie Mac) or a nonagency CMO. Agency CMOs are perceived to have no credit risk. Nonagency CMOs can be divided into private-label CMOs in which the underlying collateral is a pool of agency pass-throughs and whole-loan CMOs in which the underlying collateral is a pool of whole loans. Nonagency CMOs expose investors to credit risk.

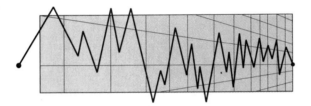

QUESTIONS

1. How does a collateralized mortgage obligation alter the cash flow from mortgages so as to shift the prepayment risk across various classes of bondholders?

2. "By creating a CMO, an issuer eliminates the prepayment risk associated with the underlying mortgages." Do you agree with this statement?

3. Explain why Wall Street often refers to a CMO as "customized securities."

4. Explain the effect of including an accrual tranche in a CMO structure on the average lives of the other tranches in a sequential-pay structure.

5. What types of investors would be attracted to an accrual bond?

6. Suppose that a tranche from which an inverse floater is created has an average life of 5 years. What will the average life of the floater be?

7. The following quotation is taken from a 1991 issue of *Bondweek:*

   First Interstate Bank of Texas will look into buying several different types of collateralized mortgage obligation tranches when it starts up its buy program sometime after the second quarter of 1991, according to Jules Pollard, V.P. Pollard said he will con-

sider replacing maturing adjustable-rate mortgage pass-throughs with short companion tranches and planned amortization classes because the ARMS have become rich....Pollard did not provide a dollar figure on the planned investments, which will be made to match fund the bank's liabilities. When he does invest he said he prefers government-guaranteed securities or those with implied guarantees.

   a. Describe the types of securities that Pollard is buying and selling.

   b. Given the preference stated in the last sentence of the quotation, what issuers is Pollard likely to prefer, and what issuers would he reject?

8. Describe how the schedule for a PAC tranche is created.

9. Explain the role of a support bond in a CMO structure.

10. What was the motivation for the creation of PAC bonds?

11. Suppose that a savings and loan association has decided to invest in mortgage-backed securities and is considering the following two securities: a Freddie Mac pass-through security with a WAM of 340 months, or a PAC tranche of a Freddie Mac CMO issue with an average life of 2 years. Which mortgage-backed security would probably be better from an asset/liability perspective?

12. Suppose that a PAC bond with an average life of four years is created assuming prepayments speeds of 80 PSA and 350 PSA. If the collateral pays at 100 PSA over its life, what will this PAC tranche's average life be?

13. Suppose that $1 billion of pass-throughs is used to create a CMO structure with a PAC bond having a par value of $700 million and a support bond having a par value of $300 million.

   a. Which of the following will have the greatest average life variability: the collateral, the PAC bond, or the support bond? Why?

   b. Which of the following will have the least average life variability: the collateral, the PAC bond, or the support bond? Why?

14. Suppose that the $1 billion of collateral in the previous question was divided into a PAC bond having a par value of $800 million and a support bond having a par value of $200 million. Will the PAC bond in this CMO structure have more or less protection than the PAC bond in the previous question?

15. It is not uncommon in a CMO structure for the issuer to carve up the support bond into several tranches. One type of support bond is created by giving a portion of the support bonds a repayment schedule. Such a tranche is called a PAC II or Level II PAC. Each PAC bond in the structure is called PAC I or Level I PAC. For example, suppose that $1 billion of pass-throughs is used to create a CMO structure with a PAC bond having a par value of $700 million (PAC I), a PAC II having a

par value of $100 million, and a support bond without a schedule that has a par value of $200 million.

a. Will the PAC I or PAC II have the smaller average life variability? Why?

b. Will the support bond without a schedule or the PAC II have the greater average life variability? Why?

16. In discussing the CMO market, the popular press sometimes refers to this sector of the mortgage-backed securities market as the riskiest sector and refers to the pass-through sector as the "safest" sector. Comment on these sorts of reference.

17. What types of CMO issues require a credit rating?

18. What is meant by a whole-loan CMO?

19. What is meant by a REMIC?

20. Indicate why you agree or disagree with the following statement: "All CMOs are REMICs."

The Market for Asset-Backed Securities

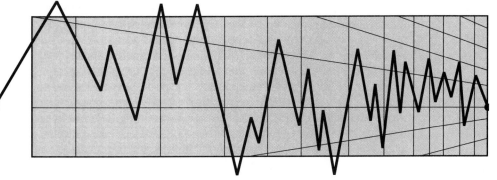

LEARNING OBJECTIVES

After reading this chapter you will understand:

• what is meant by the securitization of assets.

• the different types of asset-backed securities.

• the three most common types of asset-backed securities.

• the cash flow characteristics of asset-backed securities.

• the credit risk associated with asset-backed securities.

• the various forms of credit enhancements.

• the benefits to issuers, investors, and borrowers of securitization.

• potential implications of securitization for the financial system.

In the previous two chapters, we discussed securities backed by a pool of standard mortgage loans. Market participants refer to asset-backed securities as securities backed by one of the following types of loan obligations: (1) installment loans, (2) leases, (3) receivables, (4) home equity loans, and (5) revolving lines of credit.

In this chapter we will discuss the basic features of asset-backed securities. The process of creating securities backed by assets is referred to as **asset securitization**. At the end of this chapter, we explain the various benefits for issuers, borrowers, and investors as well as the far-ranging implications for the U.S. financial system of asset securitization.

ISSUERS OF AND COLLATERAL FOR ASSET-BACKED SECURITIES

As of December 1992, the cumulative issuance of asset-backed securities was $205 billion.[1] Table 27-1 reports the annual public issuance since the first issuance of asset-backed security in March 1985 by the type of collateral. Notice that about half of the cumulative issuance occurred in 1991 and 1992.

Table 27-2 reports the issuers by type and Table 27-3 shows the ten largest issuers of asset-backed securities through 1992. These ten entities issued 68% of asset-backed securities through 1992.

Table 27-4 shows the total principal amount issued by collateral type. As can be seen from this table, the three most common types of asset-backed securities are those backed by retail automobile loans, credit card receivables, and home equity loans. The latter includes home equity lines of credit and home equity second mortgage loans. The cumulative amount issued of these three types of asset-backed securities was $181 billion of the $205 billion issued.

Table 27-1

Public Issuance of Asset-Backed Securities through 1992 by Type of Collateral (Cumulative Issuance: $209 billion)

		Collateral type			
Year	Total issuance	Automobile loans	Credit card receivables	Home equity loans	Other
1985	$ 1.2	$ 0.9	$ 0.3	$ 0	$ 0
1986	10.0	9.7	0.3	0	0
1987	10.1	6.4	2.4	1.3	0
1988	15.6	5.5	7.4	2.7	0
1989	24.6	7.8	11.1	2.7	3.0
1990	42.7	11.6	22.7	5.6	2.8
1991	50.5	15.0	20.8	10.4	4.3
1992	51.2	19.6	15.8	6.0	9.8

Source: Tracy Hudson van Eck, "Asset-Backed Securities," Chapter 26 in Frank J. Fabozzi and T. Dessa Fabozzi (eds), The Handbook of Fixed Income Securities (Burr Ridge, IL: Irwin Professional Publishing, 1994), Exhibit 26-1, p. 585.

[1] Tracy Hudson van Eck, "Asset-Backed Securities," Chapter 26 in Frank J. Fabozzi and T. Dessa Fabozzi (eds.), *The Handbook of Fixed Income Securities* (Burr Ridge, IL: Irwin Professional Publishing, 1995). The other market statistics reported in this section are also taken from this source.

Table 27-2
Asset-Backed Securities by Type of Issuer through 1992

Type of issuer	Percent of cumulative issuance
Banks	40.3%
Vehicle finance companies	31.5
Retailers	6.5
Thrifts	3.8
Other	17.9
Total	100.0%

Source: Tracy Hudson van Eck, "Asset-Backed Securities," Chapter 26 in Frank J. Fabozzi and T. Dessa Fabozzi (eds), **The Handbook of Fixed Income Securities** *(Burr Ridge, IL: Irwin Professional Publishing, 1995), Exhibit 26-3, p. 585.*

Table 27-3
Ten Largest Asset-Backed Securities Issuers through 1992

Issuer	Principal amount issued ($ billions)	Percent of total ABS issuance (%)
Citibank	$ 27.6	13.4%
General Motors Acceptance Corp.	26.4	12.8
Chrysler Financial	22.6	11.0
Household Finance	12.2	5.9
Ford Credit	11.8	5.7
Sears	9.8	4.8
MBNA	7.9	3.9
Security Pacific	7.5	3.7
Discover	7.2	3.5
First Chicago	6.9	3.4

Source: Tracy Hudson van Eck, "Asset-Backed Securities," Chapter 26 in Frank J. Fabozzi and T. Dessa Fabozzi (eds), **The Handbook of Fixed Income Securities** *(Burr Ridge, IL: Irwin Professional Publishing, 1995), Exhibit 26-4, p. 587.*

The first asset-backed securities backed by automobile loans were issued by Marine Midland in May 1985. These issues are referred to as Certificates for Automobile Receivables or CARs. The first two public issues of credit card asset-backed securities were issued by RepublicBank Delaware (a subsidiary of RepublicBank Corporation of Texas) and Bank of America in January and February 1987, respectively. The first offering was collateralized by $200

Table 27-4

Asset-Backed Securities Chronology by Collateral Type Through 1992

Collateral type	Date of first issue	Total principal amount ($ millions)
Computer leases	March 1985	$1,847.8
Retail automobile loans	May 1985	76,363.6
Affiliate notes	July 1986	638.0
Light truck loans	July 1986	187.4
Credit card receivables	January 1987	80,238.4
Standard truck loans	June 1987	478.6
Trade receivables	September 1987	311.5
Automobile leases	October 1987	470.0
Consumer loans	November 1987	1,092.5
Boat loans	September 1988	1,202.5
Manufactured housing loans	September 1988	7,653.7
Equipment leases	October 1988	214.6
RV loans	December 1988	1,525.8
Home equity loans	January 1989	24,718.0
Harley Davidson motorcycle loans*	July 1989	86.1
Timeshare receivables	August 1989	111.5
Wholesale dealer vehicle loans	August 1990	5,900.0
Wholesale dealer truck loans	December 1990	300.0
Small business loans	January 1992	349.8
Railroad car leases	May 1992	998.4
Prefabricated home loans	June 1992	249.9
Agricultural equipment loans	September 1992	1,052.4
Total		$205,990.5

*Private placement transactions not inluded in total

Source: *Tracy Hudson van Eck, "Asset-Backed Securities," Chapter 26 in Frank J. Fabozzi and T. Dessa Fabozzi (ed.),* The Handbook of Fixed Income Securities *(Burr Ridge, IL: Irwin Professional Publishing, 1995), Exhibit 26-2, p. 586.*

million of 227,000 Visa and MasterCard accounts that were seasoned three months. The second offering was by Bank of America (California Credit Card Trust 1987-A), a $400 million issue backed by 840,000 Visa accounts. These issues were called CARDs (Certificates for Amortizing Revolving Debts). The first credit card-backed securities not collateralized by Visa and/or MasterCard accounts were issued in early 1988 by the retailers Sears, Montgomery Ward, and J.C. Penney.

Table 27-4 provides a chronology indicating when the first asset-backed security with a specific collateral type was issued.

The first public offering of an asset-backed security was in March 1985 by Sperry Lease Finance Corporation (now Unisys). The issue was collateralized by $192 million of lease-backed notes.

Because of the repayment of principal, the amount outstanding of asset-backed securities is less than the amount of cumulative issuance. As of December 1992, the amount outstanding was $125 billion.

FEATURES OF ASSET-BACKED SECURITIES

The two key features of asset-backed securities are its cash flow and its credit risk. We discuss each below.

Cash Flow

In creating an asset-backed security, issuers have drawn from the structures used in the mortgage-backed securities market described in the previous two chapters. Asset-backed securities have been structured as pass-throughs and as structures with multiple bond classes or tranches just like collateralized mortgage obligations. An example of the latter is the asset-backed security backed by automobile loans offered by Asset Backed Securities Corporation, a subsidiary of First Boston Corporation. This issue also goes down in the record books as the largest non-government debt issue in history: $4 billion. General Motors Acceptance Corporation originated the automobile loans used as collateral. There were three bond classes with average lives of 1.1, 2.2, and 3.0 years.

For asset-backed securities backed by automobile loans, borrowers pay regularly scheduled monthly loan payments (interest and scheduled principal repayments) and may make prepayments. For securities backed by automobile loans, prepayments result from: (1) sales and tradeins requiring full payoff of the loan, (2) repossession and subsequent sale of the automobile, (3) loss or destruction of the vehicle, (4) payoff of the loan with cash to save interest cost, and (5) refinancing of the loan at a lower interest cost.

While refinancings may be a major reason for prepayments of mortgage loans, they are of minor importance for automobile loans. Moreover, the interest rates for the automobile loans underlying several issues are substantially below market rates if they are offered by manufacturers as part of a sales promotion. There is good historical information on the other causes of prepayments. Therefore, the cash flow of securities backed by automobile loans do not have a great deal of uncertainty despite prepayments.

Today there are deals that include one or two PAC tranches. These tranches are targeted to investors who want virtual certainty of cash flow. The support tranches offer higher yield to investors who are willing to accept the greater cash flow uncertainty. However, the average life variability of support tranches in such deals is no where as great as for collateralized mortgage obligations.

For credit card receivable asset-backed securities, interest to holders of credit card-backed issues is paid monthly. In contrast to automobile loan asset-backed securities, the principal is not amortized. Instead, for a specified period of time, referred to as the **lockout period** or **revolving period**, the principal payments made by credit card borrowers are retained by the trustee and reinvested in additional receivables. The lockout period can vary from 18 months to 10 years. After the lockout period, the principal is no longer reinvested but paid to investors. This period is referred to as the **principal-amortization period**.

There are provisions in credit card receivable-backed securities that requires earlier amortization of the principal if certain events occur. Such provisions. which are referred to as either **early amortization** or **rapid amortization**, are included to safeguard the credit quality of the issue. The only way that the cash flow can be altered is by the triggering of the early amortization provision.

Early amortization is invoked if the trust is not able to generate sufficient income to cover the investor coupon and the servicing fee. Other events that may trigger early amortization are the default of the servicer, credit support decline below a specified amount, or the issuer violating agreements regarding pooling and servicing.

The cash flow of home-equity-backed loans are interest, regularly schedule principal repayments, and prepayments, just as with mortgage-backed securities. Thus, it is necessary to have a prepayment model and a default model to forecast cash flows. Prepayment speeds are measured in terms of conditional prepayment rates. There are differences in the prepayment behavior for home-equity loans and standard mortgage loans. Wall Street firms involved in making markets in home-equity-loan-backed securities have developed prepayment models for these loans.

Credit Risk

Asset-backed securities expose investors to credit risk. The nationally recognized rating organizations that rate corporate debt issues also rate asset-backed securities.[2] In analyzing the credit quality of the pool of loans, the rating companies look at the following factors: whether the loans were properly originated; whether the loans comply with consumer lending laws; the characteristics of the loans; and the underwriting standards used by the originator.

All asset-backed securities are credit enhanced. Credit-enhancement is used to provide greater protection to investors against losses (i.e., defaults by the borrowers of the underlying loans). The amount of credit enhancement necessary depends on two factors. One factor is the historical loss experience on similar loans made by the lender; the other factor is the rating sought by the issuer. For a given historical loss experience, more credit enhancement is needed to obtain a triple-A rating than to obtain a single-A rating.

---

[2] For a discussion of how one rating company, Fitch Investors Service, assesses the credit risk of an asset-backed security, see Mary Griffin Metz and Suzanne Mistretta, "Evaluating Credit Risk of Asset-Backed Securities," Chapter 27 in *The Handbook of Fixed Income Securities.*

Credit enhancement can take one or more of the following forms: third-party guarantees, reserve funds or cash collateral, recourse to the issuer, overcollateralization, and senior/subordinated structures. A **third-party guarantee** can be either a letter of credit from a bank or a policy from an insurance company. The rating of the third-party guarantor must be at least as high as the rating sought. Thus, if the third-party guarantor has a single-A rating, a triple-A rating for the asset-backed security can not be obtained by using only this guarantee.

A **reserve fund** or **cash collateral** is a fund established by the issuer of the asset-backed security that may be used to make principal and interest payments when there are losses. Recourse to the issuer specifies that if there are losses, securityholders can look to the investor to make up all or part of the losses.

Overcollateralization involves establishing a pool of assets with a greater principal amount than the principal amount of the asset-backed securities. For example, the principal amount of an issue may be $100 million but the principal amount of the pool of assets is $102 million.

In a **senior/subordinated structure** two classes of asset-backed securities are issued. The senior class has priority over the subordinated class with respect to the payment of principal and interest from the pool of assets. Thus, it is the subordinated piece that accepts the greater credit risk and provides protection for the senior class. The protection is greater, the larger the amount of the principal of the subordinated class relative to the senior class. Thus, for a $100 million issue, greater protection against losses is afforded the senior class if the principal for that class is $70 million and the subordinated class is $30 than if it is $80 million for the senior class and $20 million for the subordinated class.

Today, the most common type of credit enhancement is the cash collateral and the senior/subordinated structure. In automobile-loan-backed securities, credit enhancement typically consists of a combination of subordination, a partially funded reserve account, and a mechanism to build in some overcollateralization.[3] The amount of credit enhancement necessary to obtain a particular credit rating is based on a cash flow analysis of the security structure undertaken by a commercial rating company from whom a rating is sought.

BENEFITS OF ASSET SECURITIZATION AND IMPLICATIONS FOR FINANCIAL MARKETS

The traditional system for financing the acquisition of assets called for one financial intermediary (such as a commercial bank, thrift, or insurance company) to: (1) originate a loan; (2) retain the loan in its portfolio of assets, thereby accepting the credit risk associated with the loan; (3) service the loan; and (4) obtain funds from the public with which to finance its assets (except for the small amount representing the institution's equity). Asset securitization is radically different from the traditional system for financing the acquisition of assets.

With asset securitization more than one institution may be involved in lending capital. A lending scenario can look like this: (1) a bank can originate a loan; (2) the bank can sell the loans it originates to an investment banking firm that creates a security backed by the pool of loans; (3) the investment

---

[3] Metz and Mistretta, "Evaluating Credit Risks of Asset-Backed Securities," p. 602.

banker can obtain credit enhancement from a third-party guarantor; (4) the investment banker can sell the right to service the loans to a company specializing in servicing loans; and (5) the investment banking firm can sell the securities to individuals and institutional investors. Besides the original bank, an investment bank, an insurance company, a third-party guarantor, a servicing company, an individual, and other institutional investors participate. The originating bank in our example does not have to absorb the credit risk, service the loan, or provide the funding.

To facilitate the securitization of consumer installment debt and other financial assets, legislation patterned after the Real Estate Mortgage Investment Conduit provision in the tax code was introduced in 1993—the Financial Asset Securitization Investment Trust (FASIT).

What are the ideal asset characteristics for securitization? According to one investment banking firm, First Boston Corporation, the ideal characteristics are: (1) understandable credit characteristics, (2) well-defined payments pattern/predictable cash flows, (3) average maturity of a least one year, (4) low delinquency and low default rates, (5) total amortization, (6) diverse borrowers, and (7) high liquidation value.[4]

Let us look at how asset securitization can be beneficial to issuers, investors, and borrowers.

Benefits to Issuers

The most commonly cited benefits of securitization are (1) obtaining a lower cost of funds, (2) more efficient use of capital, (3) managing rapid portfolio growth, (4) better asset/liability management, (5) enhanced financial performance, and (6) diversification of funding sources.[5]

Obtaining a lower cost of funds—Segregating assets and using them as collateral for a security offering lets the issuing entity obtain lower funding costs. This is because investors look to the credit quality of the underlying pool of assets rather than the credit quality of the issuer of the asset-backed securities. The following two examples illustrate this.

The first asset-backed security was issued by Sperry Lease Financial Corporation and was backed by lease receivables. Because the issue was structured so that the cash flow from the underlying leases would be sufficient to satisfy the interest and principal payments, the security received a triple-A rating. At the time, Sperry Lease Financial Corporation had a lower credit rating. Bank of America issued asset-backed securities backed by credit card receivables. The securities received a triple-A rating, a rating higher than Bank of America's. It has been estimated that Bank of America saved at least 150 basis points over what it would have had to pay by issuing debt with a similar maturity.[6]

More efficient use of capital—For financial institutions that must meet risk-based capital guideline requirements, the sale of assets can free up capital. Recall from Chapter 3 that current risk-based capital guidelines for depository institutions require a certain percentage of capital for each asset category

---

[4] As reported in Christine A. Pavel, *Securitization* (Chicago: Probus Publishing, 1989), p.18.

[5] William Haley, "Securitizing Automobile Receivables," Chapter 3 in Philip L. Zweig (ed.), *The Asset Securitization Handbook* (Homewood, IL: Dow Jones-Irwin, 1989), p. 75.

[6] Lowell L. Bryan, "Introduction," Chapter 1 in *The Asset Securitization Handbook*, p. 18.

that a depository institution has. The percentage is supposed to reflect the credit risk associated with the asset. Often, however, the capital requirements are higher than the actual risks associated with the asset. By securitizing assets and selling these securities, the capital required will reflect the actual risks associated with the assets. This will result in a reduction of excess capital requirements.[7]

Through securitization, manufacturing corporations or their captive finance companies gain the opportunity to obtain greater leverage than the credit rating companies might judge acceptable otherwise. As an example, consider General Motors Acceptance Corporation or Chrysler Financial Corporation. These finance companies might have a ratio of automobile receivables-to-liabilities (a measure of financial leverage) of 8 or 10 to 1, acceptable for this industry according to the credit rating companies. Proper structure of an asset-backed security would allow reduction of credit-risk exposure so that the financing companies retain only a fraction of the credit risk associated with the assets.

Shifting the credit risk from the originator of the loan to another party reduces the issuer's return together with its risk. At the same time, the issuer may keep or sell the rights to service the loans. Earnings from the business come from fee income rather than interest rate spread income.

Managing rapid portfolio growth—As the business of a financial or non-financial entity grows, growth potential will be limited by capital constraints. Selling assets through securitization provides a means for quickly raising capital while keeping the asset, and hence the debt, off the balance sheet—thus, avoiding capital requirements. The risk-based capital guidelines for depository institutions encourage the practice of securitization of assets.

Better asset/liability management—Because assets expose financial institutions to prepayment risk, it can be difficult to establish a liability structure consistent with the structure of the uncertain cash flow of these assets. Securitization passes the prepayment risk to the investor. This gives the financial institution a means for funding assets whose maturity matches that of the asset.

Enhancing financial performance—When loans are sold via securitization at a yield lower than the interest rate on the loan, the originator realizes the spread. This spread partially reflects the fee for servicing the loans and partially reflects conversion of an illiquid loan into a more liquid security backed by loans and with credit enhancements. This source of spread can of course, be eroded by competition, which will tend to reallocate the abnormal spread between final borrowers and final lenders.

Diversification of sources—Investors who ordinarily could not make loans or finance receivables can invest in these securities. This provides more sources of capital for both financial and non-financial entities.

Benefits to Investors

Securitization converts illiquid loans into securities with greater liquidity and reduced credit risk. Credit risk is reduced because (1) it is backed by a

---

[7] For a discussion of the role of asset securitization for asset/liability management of depository institutions, see Anand Bhattacharya and Thomas Zimmerman, "Asset Securitization: Prospects and Issues," Chapter 4 in Frank J. Fabozzi and Atsuo Konishi (eds.), *Asset/Liability Management* (Burr Ridge, IL: Irwin Probus Publishing, 1996).

diversified pool of loans, and (2) there is credit enhancement. This permits investors to broaden their universe of investment opportunities. It also tends to improve returns through the reduction of the cost of intermediation.

Benefits to Borrowers

Because a financial or nonfinancial entity can securitize a loan it originates, or sell it to some entity that will securitize it, the lender now has a more liquid asset that it can sell if capital is needed. This should reduce the spread between lending rates and default-free assets such as Treasury securities. As the market for asset-backed securities matures, competition among originators should produce lower lending-rate spreads in loan markets.

Implications of Securitization for Financial Markets

Securitization has major implications for financial markets as well as the structure of financial institutions such as banks and thrifts. Securitization eventually may replace the traditional system of indirect financing. To understand why, let's briefly review the role of financial intermediaries, particularly banks and thrifts.

In Chapter 2, we explained that financial intermediaries act as conduits in bringing savers and borrowers together. They perform this function in several ways. First, banks and thrifts are in a better position than individual investors to assess credit risk. After evaluating credit risk, they may agree to grant a loan and hold that loan in their investment portfolio. Furthermore, being in a position to distribute their assets over many different borrowers and industries, they achieve risk reduction through diversification. The returns to investors are further made safe by government-guaranteed liabilities (e.g., their insured certificates of deposit).

Second, the maturities of loans sought by borrowers may be different from those that investors want. Banks and thrifts acquire short-term funds and grant loans with longer maturities. This satisfies the objective of investors who may want shorter-term investments and borrowers who want longer-term funds; that is, the institution provides maturity intermediation—though at their risk.

Finally, the amount of funds sought by borrowers is typically greater than any one individual investor would be willing to lend. Banks and thrifts make large-denomination loans to borrowers and offer investors investments with smaller denominations. That is, they provide denomination intermediation, transforming very large assets into quite divisible ones.

Securitization provides direct financing between borrowers and investors, short-circuiting the traditional intermediaries. Pooling of assets reinforced by private credit enhancement reduces credit risk to more acceptable levels for investors. Recasting cash flows so as to create different bond classes or tranches provides varying maturities acceptable to a wide range of investors. Thus, securitization serves a role similar to maturity intermediation while shifting its risk to the ultimate lenders. The availability of securities with smaller denominations than the underlying loans accomplishes denomination intermediation. The success of securitization indicates that it is a more efficient method for linking borrowers and investors than traditional financing through financial intermediaries. Consequently, the role of banks and thrifts may have to be reassessed.

The true innovations in this market are not really the securities themselves, rather they are (1) the reduction of risk through pooling of assets and private credit enhancement, and (2) the repackaging of the cash flows from assets in a way that relieves the intermediary of reliance on its own assets to finance the credit—i.e., they permit off-balance-sheet financing.

These practices are already spreading to other countries. For example, securitization of personal loans occurred in France in 1990. The first public asset-backed deal in Canada, issued in May 1991, was for $350 million (Canadian) dollars backed by automobile loans purchased from Chrysler Credit Canada.

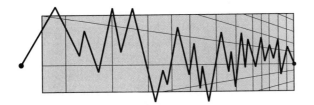

SUMMARY

Market participants refer to asset-backed securities as securities backed by consumer installment loans and receivables and loans other than standard mortgage loans. The three most common types of asset-backed securities are backed by automobile loans (CARS), credit card receivables (CARDS), and home equity loans (HELS).

In creating an asset-backed security, issuers have drawn from the structures used in the mortgage-backed securities market. Asset-backed securities have been structured as pass-throughs and as structures with multiple bond classes just like collateralized mortgage obligations.

Asset-backed securities expose investors to credit risk. All asset-backed securities are credit enhanced to provide greater protection to investors against losses. Credit enhancement can take one or more of the following forms: third-party guarantees, reserve funds or cash collateral, recourse to the issuer, overcollateralization, and senior/subordinated structures.

Securitization of assets—that is, pooling loans and selling securities backed by the pool of loans—benefits issuers, investors, and borrowers alike. Securitization may be the wave of the future, as it appears to be a more efficient mechanism for bringing borrowers and investors together than traditional financing through intermediaries.

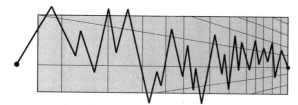

QUESTIONS

1. What is the cash flow for automobile-loan-backed securities?

2. Why are prepayments of minor importance for automobile-loan backed securities?

3. What type of tranches have been included in CARS deals to reduce the cash flow uncertainty?

4. Explain what happens to the principal repaid by borrowers in a credit-card-receivable-backed security.

5. What is the significance of a lockout period in a CARD deal?

6. What is the role of the early amortization provision in a CARD deal?

7. How can the cash flow of a credit card receivable backed security be altered prior to the principal-amortization period?

8. What is the cash flow of a home equity loan backed security and what are the difficulties of projecting the cash flow?

9. Why is credit enhancement necessary in structuring an asset-backed security?

10. What are the factors that determine the amount of credit enhancement needed in structuring an asset-backed security?

11. Explain each of the following forms of credit enhancement: a. third-party guarantees; b. reserve funds or cash collateral; c. recourse to the issuer; d. overcollateralization; e. senior/subordinated structures

12. An asset-backed security has been credit enhanced with a letter of credit from a bank with a single A credit rating. If this is the only form of credit enhancement, explain whether this issue can be assigned a triple-A credit rating.

13. An issuer is considering the following two credit enhancement-structures backed by a pool of automobile loans. Explain which structure would receive a higher credit rating:

Total principal value of asset-backed security: $300 million

Principal value for	Structure I	Structure II
Pool of automobile loans	$ 304 million	$ 301 million
Senior class	250	270
Subordinated class	50	30

14. In a 1989 study entitled "Globalization and Canada's Financial Markets," a research report prepared for the Economic Council of Canada, the following was reported:

An important feature of the increasing significance of

some aspects of financial activity is the greater use of financial markets and instruments that intermediate funds directly—a process called "market intermediation," which involves the issuance of, and trading in, securities such as bonds or stocks—as opposed to "financial intermediation," in which the financial institution raises funds by issuing a claim on itself and provides funds in the form of loans.

Why is asset securitization an example of "market intermediation"?

15. Identify two benefits which a consumer of bank services and a borrower of bank funds gets from the bank's freedom to securitize any loan they may make.

16. In classifying financial innovations, the Bank for International Settlement refers to "liquidity-generating instruments." Two characteristics of liquidity-generating instruments are that they increase the liquidity of the market and they allow borrowers to draw upon new sources of funds. Explain why asset securitization results in liquidity-generating instruments.

17. Not all assets can be easily securitized. What are the characteristics of an asset that make it attractive for securitization?

18. The quotation below appeared in an article entitled "Burlington Uses New Structure in Lease Deal," that appeared in *BondWeek*:

Burlington Northern Railroad was expected to hit the market last Friday with the first issue of pass-through securities backed by leases from railroad equipment lease

pools, according to Karl Essig, head of asset-backed securities structuring and origination at sole-manager Morgan Stanley. The pass-through structure made the deal more marketable and channeled cashflow enabled the deal to obtain a higher rating, he noted. "The structure was a very significant advance in obtaining ratings," Essig said.

Most of the leases' average lives were too long to qualify for the target Aa3/A+ rating. By channeling the different cashflows together, Burlington was able to add lease diversity and create an aggregate average life of an acceptable level for the desired rating, said Steven Schiffman, director of corporate finance at Burlington.

. . . The $117 million public offering, Burlington Northern Railroad Pass-through Trust 1990-A, was offered in two pass-through tranches, which had average lives of 8.8 and 16.7 years, respectively. . . They were backed by seven different leases for automobile racks, new covered hoppers, new gondola cars, box cars, new locomotives and two for remanufactured locomotives, according to Schiffman.

a. At the time of issuance, Burlington Northern Railroad was rated A3/BBB+. Explain how this structure enabled Burlington to issue debt at a lower cost than would be possible by issuing traditional bonds.

b. Why do you think the issue was structured to have two classes of pass-throughs?

Exchange-Traded Interest Rate Futures and Options

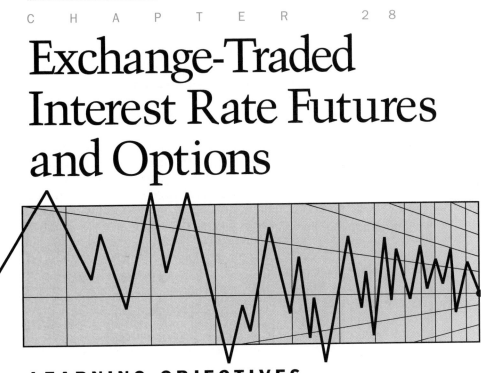

LEARNING OBJECTIVES

After reading this chapter you will understand:

- the features of interest rate futures contracts.

- the Treasury bond and note futures contract.

- the delivery options embedded in the Treasury bond and note futures contract and their impact on the futures price.

- the features of interest rate options contracts.

- what futures options are, their trading mechanics, and the reasons for their popularity.

- the empirical evidence on the pricing efficiency of futures options.

- the limitations of applying the Black-Scholes option-pricing model to options on fixed-income securities.

- an overview of more appropriate models for pricing interest rate options.

- potential applications of interest rate futures and options by institutional money managers and borrowers.

This is the first of two chapters that describe derivative contracts or instruments that investors and issuers can use to control interest rate risk. Basically, the underlying economic variable for these derivative contracts is some interest rate. The derivative contract either is based directly on an interest rate, or it is based indirectly on an interest rate by making a debt obligation the underlying instrument for the contract. In this chapter we describe three derivative contracts to control interest rate risk: interest rate futures, interest rate options, and options on futures. We cover portfolio strategies using these contracts, unique features for pricing them, and considerations of pricing efficiency.

Futures contracts are products created by exchanges. Options on futures, a new derivative product that we will introduce in this chapter, are also created by exchanges. Options, however, can be exchange-traded products or OTC options. While market participants rely almost exclusively on exchange-traded products in the case of options on common stocks and options on stock indexes, institutional investors and issuers make greater use of the over-the-counter options market to create tailor-made contracts to control interest rate risk. In the next chapter we will discuss OTC options when we focus on customized interest rate risk control instruments.

INTEREST RATE FUTURES CONTRACTS

In October 1975, the Chicago Board of Trade (CBT) pioneered trading in a futures contract based on a fixed-income instrument—Government National Mortgage Association certificates. Three months later, the International Monetary Market (IMM) of the Chicago Mercantile Exchange began trading futures contracts based on 13-week Treasury bills. Other exchanges soon followed with their own interest rate futures contracts.

Features of Actively Traded Contracts

Interest rate futures contracts can be classified by the maturity of their underlying security. Short-term interest rate futures contracts have an underlying security that matures in less than one year. The maturity of the underlying security of long-term futures contracts exceeds one year. Examples of the former are the futures contracts in which the underlying is a three-month Treasury bill, a three-month Eurodollar certificate of deposit, one-month LIBOR, and 30-day federal funds. All of these contracts are traded on the Chicago Mercantile Exchange. Examples of long-term futures are contracts in which the underlying is a Treasury bond, a Treasury note, or a municipal bond index. The more actively traded contracts traded in the United States are described below. There are also interest rate futures contracts traded in other countries.

Treasury bill futures—Treasury bill futures and Eurodollar futures contracts are futures whose underlying instrument is a short-term debt obligation. The Treasury bill futures contract, which is traded on the IMM, is based on a 13-week (three-month) Treasury bill with a face value of $1 million. More specifically, the seller of a Treasury bill futures contract agrees to deliver to the buyer at the settlement date a Treasury bill with 13 weeks remaining to maturity and a face value of $1 million. The Treasury bill delivered can be newly issued or seasoned. The futures price is the price at which the Treasury bill will be sold by the short and purchased by the buyer. For example, a nine-month Treasury bill futures contract requires that nine months from now the short deliver to the long \$1 million face value of a Treasury bill with 13 weeks remaining to maturity. The Treasury bill could be a newly issued 13-week Treasury bill or a Treasury bill that was issued one year prior to the settlement date and therefore at the settlement has only 13 weeks remaining to maturity.

As we explain in Chapter 19, Treasury bills are quoted in the cash market in terms of an annualized yield on a bank discount basis, where:

$$Y_D = \frac{D}{F} \times \frac{360}{t}$$

where

Y_D = annualized yield on a bank discount basis (expressed as a decimal)

D = dollar discount, which is equal to the difference between the face value and the price of a bill maturing in t days

F = face value

t = number of days remaining to maturity

The dollar discount (D) is found by:

$$D = Y_D \times F \times \frac{t}{360}$$

In contrast, the Treasury bill futures contract is not quoted directly in terms of yield but instead on an index basis that is related to the yield on a bank discount basis as follows:

Index price = $100 - (Y_D \times 100)$

For example, if Y_D is 8%, the index price is: $100 - (0.08 \times 100) = 92$.

It will be seen that the **index price** of an instrument differs from its actual price because it is the price of an instrument with the same annual yield but maturing in a year. The primary purpose of this convention is that all instruments with the same annual yield will have the same price, regardless of maturity. Conversely, instruments with the same price will have the same yield to maturity and bank discount basis. This clearly facilitates comparison of annual yields across maturities.

Given the price of the futures contract, the futures yield on a bank discount basis for the futures contract is determined as follows:

$$Y_D = \frac{100 - \text{Index price}}{100}$$

To see how this works, suppose that the index price for a Treasury bill futures contract is 92.52. The futures yield on a bank discount basis for this Treasury bill futures contract is:

$$Y_D = \frac{100 - 92.52}{100} = 0.0748 \text{ or } 7.48\%$$

The price that the buyer of a futures contract must pay the seller at the settlement date is called the **invoice price**. In the case of the Treasury bill futures contract, the invoice price that the buyer of $1 million face value of 13-week Treasury bills must pay at settlement is found by first computing the dollar discount, as follows:

$$D = Y_D \times \$1,000,000 \times \frac{t}{360}$$

where t is either 90 or 91 days. Typically, the number of days to maturity of a 13-week Treasury bill is 91 days.

The invoice price is then:

$$\text{Invoice price} = \$1,000,000 - D$$

For example, for the Treasury bill futures contract with an index price of 92.52 (and a yield on a bank discount basis of 7.48%), the dollar discount for the 13-week Treasury bill to be delivered with 91 days to maturity is:

$$D = 0.0748 \times \$1,000,000 \times \frac{91}{360} = \$18,907.78$$

The invoice price is: $\$1,000,000 - \$18,907.78 = \$981,092.22$.

The minimum index price fluctuation or "tick" for this futures contract is 0.01. A change of 0.01 for the minimum index price translates into a change in the yield on a bank discount basis of one basis point (0.0001). The change in the value of one basis point will change the dollar discount, and therefore the invoice price, by:

$$0.0001 \times \$1,000,000 \times \frac{t}{360}$$

For a 13-week Treasury bill with 91 days to maturity, the change in the dollar discount is:

$$0.0001 \times \$1,000,000 \times \frac{91}{360} = \$25.28$$

For a 13-week Treasury bill with 90 days to maturity, the change in the dollar discount would be $25. Despite the fact that a 13-week Treasury bill typically has 91 days to maturity, market participants commonly refer to the value of a basis point for this futures contract as $25.

Eurodollar CD futures—Eurodollar certificates of deposit (CDs) are denominated in dollars but represent the liabilities of banks outside the United States. The contracts are traded on both the International Monetary Market of the Chicago Mercantile Exchange and the London International Financial Futures Exchange. The rate paid on Eurodollar CDs is the London Interbank Offered Rate (LIBOR).

The three-month Eurodollar CD is the underlying instrument for the Eurodollar CD futures contract. As with the Treasury bill futures contract, this contract is for $1 million of face value and is traded on an index-price basis. The index-price basis in which the contract is quoted is equal to 100 minus the annualized futures LIBOR. For example, a Eurodollar CD futures price of 94.00 means a futures three-month LIBOR of 6%.

The minimum price fluctuation (tick) for this contract is 0.01 (or 0.0001 in terms of LIBOR). This means that the price value of a basis point for this contract is $25, found as follows. The simple interest on $1 million for 90 days is equal to:

$1,000,000 \times (\text{LIBOR} \times 90/360)$

If LIBOR changes by one basis point (0.0001), then:

$1,000,000 \times (0.0001 \times 90/360) = \$25$

The Eurodollar CD futures contract is a cash settlement contract. That is, the parties settle in cash for the value of a Eurodollar CD based on LIBOR at the settlement date. The Eurodollar CD futures contract is one of the most heavily traded futures contracts in the world. It is frequently used to trade the short end of the yield curve, and many hedgers have found this contract to be the best hedging vehicle for a wide range of hedging situations.

Treasury bond futures—The underlying instrument for a Treasury bond futures contract is $100,000 par value of a hypothetical 20-year, 8% coupon bond. The futures price is quoted in terms of par being 100. Quotes are in 32nds of 1%. Thus a quote for a Treasury bond futures contract of 97-16 means 97 and 16/32nds, or 97.50. So, if a buyer and seller agree on a futures price of 97-16, this means that the buyer agrees to accept delivery of the hypothetical underlying Treasury bond and pay 97.50% of par value, and the seller agrees to accept 97.50% of par value. Since the par value is $100,000, the futures price that the buyer and seller agree to pay for this hypothetical Treasury bond is $97,500.

The minimum price fluctuation for the Treasury bond futures contract is a 32nd of 1%. The dollar value of a 32nd for a $100,000 par value (the par value for the underlying Treasury bond) is $31.25. Thus, the minimum price fluctuation is $31.25 for this contract.

We have been referring to the underlying as a hypothetical Treasury bond. Does this mean that the contract is a cash settlement contract, as is the case with stock index futures described in Chapter 15? The answer is no. The seller of Treasury bond futures who decides to make delivery rather than liquidate his position by buying back the contract prior to the settlement date must deliver some Treasury bond. But what Treasury bond? The Chicago Board of Trade allows the seller to deliver one of several Treasury bonds that the CBT declares is acceptable for delivery. The specific bonds that the seller may deliver are published by the CBT prior to the initial trading of a futures contract with a specific settlement date.

Table 28-1 shows the Treasury issues that the seller could have selected from to deliver to the buyer of the September 1994 futures contract. The CBT makes its determination of the Treasury issues that are acceptable for delivery from all outstanding Treasury issues that meet the following criteria: an issue must have at least 15 years to maturity from the date of delivery, if not callable; in the case of callable bonds, the issue must not be callable for at least 15 years from the first day of the delivery month.

The delivery process for the Treasury bond futures contract makes the contract interesting. At the settlement date, the seller of a futures contract (the

Table 28-1

Acceptable Treasury Bonds and Corresponding Conversion Factors for Settlement in September 1994

Issue		
Coupon	Maturity	Conversion factor
7¼	05/15/16	0.9236
7¼	11/15/16	0.9486
8¾	05/15/17	1.0777
8⅞	08/15/17	1.0908
9⅞	11/15/15	1.1892
8⅛	08/15/19	1.0132
8⅞	02/15/19	1.0928
9⅛	05/15/18	1.1184
8½	02/15/20	1.0537
9¼	02/15/16	1.1265
8¾	05/15/20	1.0811
10⅝	08/15/15	1.2634
8½	08/15/21	1.0135
11¼	02/15/15	1.3230
8	11/15/21	1.0000
7¼	08/15/22	0.9167
7⅝	11/15/22	0.9583
11¾	11/15/14	1.3242
7¼	02/15/23	0.9024
9	11/15/18	1.1060
6¼	08/15/23	0.8040
8¾	08/15/20	1.0811
7⅞	02/15/21	0.9862
8½	05/15/21	1.0137

short) is required to deliver the buyer (the long) $100,000 par value of an 8%, 20-year Treasury bond. Since no such bond exists, the seller must choose from one of the acceptable deliverable Treasury bonds that the CBT has specified. Suppose the seller is entitled to deliver $100,000 of a 6%, 20-year Treasury bond to settle the futures contract. The value of this bond, of course, is less than the value of an 8%, 20-year bond. If the seller delivers the 6%, 20-year, this would be unfair to the buyer of the futures contract who contracted to receive $100,000 of an 8%, 20-year Treasury bond. Alternatively, suppose the seller delivers $100,000 of a 10%, 20-year Treasury bond. The value of a 10%, 20-year Treasury bond is greater than that of an 8%, 20-year bond, so this would be a disadvantage to the seller.

How can this problem be resolved? To make delivery equitable to both parties, the CBT has introduced **conversion factors** for determining the invoice price of each acceptable deliverable Treasury issue against the Treasury bond futures contract. The conversion factor is determined by the CBT before a contract with a specific settlement date begins trading. Table 28-1 shows for each of the acceptable Treasury issues the corresponding conversion factor.[1] The conversion factor is constant throughout the trading period of the futures contract. The short must notify the long of the actual bond that will be delivered one day before the delivery date.

The invoice price for the Treasury bond futures contract is the futures price plus accrued interest. However, as just noted, the seller can deliver one of several acceptable Treasury issues and to make delivery fair to both parties, the invoice price must be adjusted based on the actual Treasury issue delivered. It is the conversion factors that are used to adjust the invoice price. The invoice price is:

Invoice price = Contract size × Futures contract settlement price ×
Conversion factor + Accrued interest

Suppose the Treasury bond futures contract settles at 94-08 and that the short elects to deliver a Treasury bond issue with a conversion factor of 1.20. The futures contract settlement price of 94-08 means 94.25% of par value. As the contract size is $100,000, the invoice price the buyer pays the seller is:

$100,000 × 0.9425 × 1.20 + Accrued interest = $113,100 + Accrued interest

In selecting the issue to be delivered, the short will select from all the deliverable issues the one that is cheapest to deliver. This issue is referred to as the **cheapest-to-deliver issue** and it plays a key role in the pricing of a futures contract. The cheapest-to-deliver issue is determined by participants in the market as follows. For each of the acceptable Treasury issues from which the seller can select, the seller calculates the return that can be earned by buying that issue and delivering it at the settlement date. Note that the seller can calculate the return since he knows the price of the Treasury issue now and the futures price at which he agrees to deliver the issue. The return so calculated is called the **implied repo rate**. The cheapest-to-deliver issue is then the one issue among all acceptable Treasury issues with the highest implied repo rate since it is the issue that would give the seller of the futures contract the highest return by buying and then delivering the issue. This is depicted in Figure 28-1.

In addition to the choice of which acceptable Treasury issue to deliver—sometimes referred to as the **quality option** or **swap option**—the short position has two more options granted under CBT delivery guidelines. The short position is permitted to decide when in the delivery month the delivery will actually take place. This is called the **timing option**. The other option is the right of the short position to give notice of intent to deliver up to 8:00 P.M. Chicago time after the closing of the exchange (3:15 P.M. Chicago time) on the date when the futures settlement price has been fixed. This option is referred to as the **wild card option**. The quality option, the timing option, and the wild

---

1 The conversion factor is based on the price that a deliverable bond would sell for at the beginning of the delivery month if it were to yield 8%.

Figure 28-1

Determination of Cheapest-to-Deliver Issue Based on the Implied Repo Rate

Implied repo rate: Rate of return by buying an acceptable Treasury issue, shorting the Treasury bond futures, and delivering the issue at the settlement date.

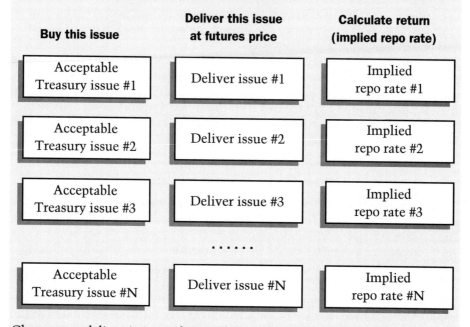

Cheapest-to-deliver is issue that produces maximum implied repo rate

card option (in sum referred to as the **delivery options**), mean that the long position can never be sure of which Treasury bond will be delivered or when it will be delivered. The delivery options are summarized in Table 28-2.

The contract specification for the Treasury bond futures has been used in other countries to design a futures contract on their government bond.

Treasury note futures—Modeled after the Treasury bond futures contract, the underlying instrument for the Treasury note futures contract is $100,000 par

Table 28-2

Delivery Options Granted to the Short (Seller) of a CBT Treasury Bond Futures Contract

Delivery option	Description
Quality or swap option	Choice of which acceptable Treasury issue to deliver
Timing option	Choice of when in delivery month to deliver
Wild card option	Choice to deliver after the closing price of the futures contract is determined

value of a hypothetical 10-year, 8% Treasury note. There are several acceptable Treasury issues that may be delivered by the short. An issue is acceptable if the maturity is not less than 6.5 years and not greater than 10 years from the first day of the delivery month. The delivery options granted to the short position and the minimum price fluctuation are the same as for the Treasury bond futures contract.

Bond Buyer's Municipal Bond Index futures—Traded on the CBT, the underlying product for this contract is a basket, or index, of 40 municipal bonds. The Bond Buyer, publisher of *The Bond Buyer* (a trade publication of the municipal bond industry), serves as the index manager for the contract and prices each bond in the index based on prices received between 1:30 and 2:00 P.M. (Central Standard Time) from five municipal bond brokers. It is necessary to obtain several independent prices from brokers because municipal bonds trade in the over-the-counter market.

Once the prices are received from the five pricing brokers for a given issue, the lowest and the highest prices are dropped. The remaining three prices are then averaged, and the resulting value is referred to as the appraisal value. The appraisal value for each issue then is divided by a conversion factor that equates the bond to an 8% issue. This gives a converted price for each issue. The converted prices then are summed and divided by 40, for an average converted price on the index. The index is revised bimonthly, when newer issues are added, and older issues or issues that no longer meet the criteria for inclusion in the index are dropped.[2] A **smoothing coefficient** is calculated on the index revision date so that the index will not change merely because of changes in the composition of the index. The average converted dollar price for the index is multiplied by this coefficient to get the index value for a particular date.

As delivery on all 40 bonds in the index is not possible, the contract is a cash settlement contract, with settlement price based on the value of the index on the delivery date. The contract is quoted in points and 32nds of a point. For example, suppose the settlement price for the contract is 93-21. This translates into a price of 93 and $21/32$, or 93.65635. The dollar value of a contract is equal to $1,000 times the Bond Buyer Municipal Bond Index. For example, the dollar value based on the settlement price is:

$1,000 \times 93.65635 = \$93,656.35$

Pricing of Interest Rate Futures Contracts

In Chapter 10, we explained how the price of a futures contract can be determined based on arbitrage arguments. We showed that the theoretical futures price depends on the cash market price, the financing cost, and the cash yield on the underlying instrument. In the case of stock index futures, the cash yield on the underlying instrument is the expected stream of cash dividends earned until the settlement date. For interest rate futures, the cash yield is the coupon interest earned until the settlement date, not the yield to maturity. Therefore, for an interest rate futures contract, the theoretical futures price is:

Futures price = Cash market price + Cash market price × (28.1)
(Financing cost – Cash yield on bond)

---

[2] The inclusion criteria, as well as the revision process and pricing of the index, are spelled out in a publication entitled *The Chicago Board of Trade's Municipal Bond Futures Contract*, 1987.

The futures price can trade at a discount or a premium to the cash price, depending on whether the cost of carry ("carry" for short) is positive (i.e., the cash yield on the bond is greater than the financing cost) or negative (i.e., the cash yield on the bond is less than the financing cost). In the case of interest rate futures, the financing cost is determined by rates at the short end of the yield curve. The cash yields for Treasury bonds and Treasury notes will be determined by yields at the long-term and intermediate-term maturity sectors of the yield curve, respectively. Therefore, the shape of the yield curve will determine carry and, in turn, whether the futures price will trade at a premium, at a discount, or equal to the cash market price. This is summarized in Table 28-3.

The shape of the yield curve also influences when the short will choose to deliver (i.e., exercise the timing option). If carry is positive, it will be beneficial for the short to delay delivery until the last permissible settlement date. If carry is negative, the short will deliver on the first permissible settlement date.

To derive the theoretical futures price in Chapter 10 using the arbitrage argument, several assumptions had to be made; we explained the implications of these assumptions for the divergence between the actual futures price and the theoretical futures price for any futures contract. In Chapter 15, we highlighted the limitations as applied to stock index futures. Here we will do the same for interest rate futures.

Interim cash flows—In Chapter 10, we explained that the model assumes no interim cash flows due to variation margin or coupon interest payments but that these can be incorporated. The unique aspect of interest rate futures is that if interest rates rise, the short will receive margin as the futures price decreases; the margin can then be reinvested at a higher interest rate. If interest rates fall, there will be variation margin that must be financed by the short, but because interest rates have declined, this can be financed at a lower cost. Thus there seems to be an advantage to the short as interest rates change. Correspondingly, there is a disadvantage to the long.

Deliverable bond is not known—The arbitrage arguments used to derive Equation (28.1) assumed that only one instrument is deliverable. But the futures contracts on Treasury bonds and Treasury notes are designed to allow the short the choice of delivering one of a number of deliverable issues (the quality or swap option). Because there may be more than one deliverable, market participants track the price of each deliverable bond and determine which bond is the cheapest to deliver. The futures price will then trade in relation to the cheapest-to-deliver issue.

There is the risk that while an issue may be the cheapest to deliver at the time a position in the futures contract is taken, it may not be the cheapest to deliver after that time. A change in the cheapest-to-deliver can dramatically alter the futures price.

Table 28-3

Effect of Shape of Yield Curve on Futures Price

Shape of Yield Curve	Carry	Futures Price
Normal	Positive	Sell at a discount to cash price
Inverted	Negative	Sell at a premium to cash price
Flat	Zero	Be equal to the cash price

What are the implications of the quality (swap) option on the futures price? Because the swap option is an option granted by the long to the short, the long will want to pay less for the futures contract than indicated by Equation (28.1). Therefore, as a result of the quality option, the theoretical futures price as given by Equation (28.1) must be adjusted as follows:

$$\text{Futures price} = \text{Cash market price} + \text{Cash market price} \times \quad (28.2)$$
$$\text{(Financing cost} - \text{Cash yield on bond)} - \text{Value of quality option}$$

Market participants have employed theoretical models in attempting to estimate the fair value of the quality option. These models are beyond the scope of this chapter.

Delivery date is not known—In the pricing model based on arbitrage arguments, a known delivery date is assumed. For Treasury bond and note futures contracts, the short has a timing and wild card option, so the long does not know when the securities will be delivered. The effect of the timing and wild card options on the theoretical futures price is the same as with the quality option. These delivery options should result in a theoretical futures price that is lower than the one suggested in Equations (28.1) and (28.2), as shown below:

$$\text{Futures price} = \text{Cash market price} + \text{Cash market price} \times \quad (28.3)$$
$$\text{(Financing cost} - \text{Cash yield on bond)} - \text{Value of quality option} - \text{Value of timing option} - \text{Value of wild card option}$$

Or alternatively:

$$\text{Futures price} = \text{Cash market price} + \text{Cash market price} \times \quad (28.4)$$
$$\text{(Financing cost} - \text{Cash yield on bond)} - \text{Delivery Options}$$

Market participants attempt to value the delivery option in order to apply Equation (28.4).

Deliverable is not a basket of securities—The municipal index futures contract is a cash settlement contract based on a basket of securities. The difficulty in arbitraging this futures contract is that it is too expensive to buy or sell every bond included in the index. Instead, as we explained in Chapter 15 in our discussion of the pricing of stock index futures, a portfolio containing a smaller number of bonds may be constructed to "track" the index. The arbitrage, however, is no longer risk-free because there is tracking-error risk.

Pricing Efficiency of Interest Rate Futures

When interest rate futures began trading, some market observers noted that futures prices for Treasury bonds were less than their theoretical price. These earlier observers concluded that this meant the market is inefficient. Yet researchers have been quick to point out that divergence between actual and theoretical futures prices was due to the delivery options granted to the short as discussed earlier.[3] The empirical question then becomes what is the value of these options.

---

[3] See Gerald D. Gay and Steven Manaster, "The Quality Option Implicit in Futures Contracts," *Journal of Financial Economics* (September 1984), pp. 353-70; and "Implicit Delivery Options and Optimal Delivery Strategies for Financial Futures Contracts," *Journal of Financial Economics* (May 1986), pp. 41-72.

In two separate studies Kane and Marcus examine the value of the quality option and the wild card option.[4] Using a simulation approach to analyze these two delivery options, they find that each has a significant influence on the price of Treasury bond futures; each option reduces the value of the futures contract by roughly $0.20 (based on a futures price of $72). Michael Hemler finds that the quality option has somewhat less of an effect for Treasury bond futures contracts.[5]

Applications of Interest Rate Futures

We will describe six ways in which market participants can employ interest rate futures. They can be used to:

- speculate on the movement of interest rates.
- control the interest rate risk of a portfolio (alter duration).
- hedge against adverse interest rate movements.
- enhance returns when futures are mispriced.
- allocate funds between stocks and bonds.
- provide portfolio insurance (dynamic hedging).

Speculating on the movement of interest rates—The price of a futures contract moves in the opposite direction from interest rates: when rates rise (fall), the futures price will fall (rise). An investor who wants to speculate that interest rates will rise (fall) can sell (buy) interest rate futures. Before interest rate futures were available, investors who wanted to speculate on interest rates did so with the long-term Treasury bond: shorting it if they expected interest rates to rise, and buying it if they expected interest rates to fall. There are three advantages of using interest rate futures instead of the cash markets (trading long-term Treasuries themselves). First, transactions costs are lower for futures compared to cash markets. Second, margin requirements are lower for futures than for Treasury securities; using futures thus permits greater leverage. Finally, it is easier to sell short in the futures market than in the Treasuries market. We repeat here what we said when we discussed the use of stock index futures to speculate on stock price movements, however: making speculation easier for investors is not the function of interest rate futures contracts.

Controlling the interest rate risk of a portfolio—Stock index futures can be used to change the market risk of a diversified stock portfolio, that is, to alter the beta of a portfolio. Likewise, interest rate futures can be used to alter the interest rate sensitivity of a portfolio. As we explained in Chapter 17, duration is a measure of the interest rate sensitivity of a bond portfolio.

Investment managers with strong expectations about the direction of the future course of interest rates will adjust the durations of their portfolios so as to capitalize on their expectations. Specifically, if a manager expects rates to increase, the duration will be shortened; if interest rates are expected to decrease, the duration will be lengthened. While investment managers can alter the durations of their portfolios with cash market instruments, a quick

---

[4] Alex Kane and Alan Marcus, "The Quality Option in the Treasury Bond Futures Market: An Empirical Assessment," *Journal of Futures Markets* (Summer 1986), pp. 231-48, and "Valuation and Optimal Exercise of the Wild Card Option in the Treasury Bond Futures Market," *Journal of Finance* (March 1986), pp. 195-207.

[5] Michael J. Hemler, "The Quality Delivery Option in Treasury Bond Futures Contracts," doctoral dissertation, Graduate School of Business, University of Chicago, March 1988.

and inexpensive means for doing so (on either a temporary or permanent basis) is to use futures contracts.

Hedging against adverse interest rate movements—Interest rate futures can be used to hedge against adverse interest rate movements by locking in either a price or an interest rate. Because in most applications the bond or the rate to be hedged is not identical to the bond or the rate underlying the futures contract, hedging with interest rate futures involves cross-hedging. The following are some examples of hedging with interest rate futures.

1. Suppose that a pension fund manager knows that bonds must be liquidated in 40 days to make a $5 million payment to the beneficiaries of the pension fund. If interest rates rise in 40 days, more bonds will have to be liquidated to realize $5 million. The pension fund manager can hedge by selling bonds in the futures market to lock in a selling price. This is an example of a sell or short hedge.[6]

2. A pension fund manager may use a long hedge when substantial cash contributions are expected and the pension fund manager is concerned that interest rates may fall. Also, a money manager who knows that bonds are maturing in the near future and who expects that interest rates will fall can employ a long hedge. In both cases, interest rate futures are used to hedge against a fall in interest rates that would cause cash flows to be invested at an interest rate lower than current rates.

3. Suppose a corporation plans to sell long-term bonds two months from now. To protect itself against a rise in interest rates, the corporation can sell interest rate futures now.

4. A thrift or commercial bank can hedge its cost of funds by locking in a rate using the Eurodollar CD futures contract.[7]

5. Suppose a corporation plans to sell commercial paper one month from now. Treasury bill futures or Eurodollar CD futures can be used to lock in a commercial paper rate.[8]

6. Investment banking firms can use interest rate futures to protect both the value of positions held by their trading desks and positions assumed by underwriting bonds. An example of the latter is a 1979 Salomon Brothers underwriting of $1 billion of IBM bonds. To protect itself against a rise in interest rates, which would reduce the value of the IBM bonds, Salomon Brothers sold (shorted) Treasury futures. In October 1979, interest rates rose following an announcement by the Federal Reserve Board that it was allowing interest rates more flexibility to move. While the value of the IBM bonds held by

---

[6] For evidence of the effectiveness of hedging corporate bonds with interest rate futures, see Joanne Hill and Thomas Schneeweis, "Risk Reduction Potential of Financial Futures for Corporate Bond Positions," in Gerald Gay and Robert W. Kolb (eds.), *Interest Rate Futures: Concepts and Issues* (Richmond, VA: Dame, 1982), pp. 307-23. For an illustration of hedging a corporate bond with Treasury futures, see Mark Pitts and Frank J. Fabozzi, *Interest Rate Futures and Options* (Chicago: Probus Publishing, 1989), Chapter 9. For evidence on the effectiveness of hedging municipal bonds with the municipal bond index futures contract, see Richard Bookstaber and Hal Heaton, "On the Hedging Performance of the New Municipal Bond Futures Contract," in Frank J. Fabozzi and T. Dessa Garlicki (editors), *Advances in Bond Analysis and Portfolio Strategies* (Chicago: Il: Probus Publishing, 1987).

[7] See Michael Smirlock, "An Analysis of Hedging Certificates of Deposit with Interest Rate Futures: Bank and Contract Specific Evidence," in *Advances in Futures and Options Research*, Vol. 2, Part B, 1986, pp. 153-70.

[8] For an illustration, see Chapter 9 in Pitts and Fabozzi, *Interest Rate Futures and Options*.

Salomon Brothers declined in value, so did the Treasury bond futures contracts; but because Salomon Brothers sold these futures it realized a gain, reducing the loss on the IBM bonds it underwrote.

Enhancing returns when futures are mispriced—In Chapter 15, we explained that institutional investors look for the mispricing of stock index futures to create arbitrage profits and thereby enhance portfolio returns. We referred to this strategy as index arbitrage because it involves a stock index. If interest rate futures are mispriced even after considering the pricing problems we discussed earlier, institutional investors can enhance returns in the same way that they do in equities.

Allocating funds between stocks and bonds—A pension sponsor may wish to alter the composition of the pension's funds between stocks and bonds, that is, change its asset allocation. Suppose that a pension sponsor wants to shift a $1 billion fund from its current allocation of $500 million in stocks and $500 million in bonds to $300 million in stocks and $700 million in bonds. This can be done directly by selling $200 million of stocks and buying a like amount of bonds. The costs associated with shifting funds in this manner are: (1) the transactions costs with respect to commissions and bid-ask spreads, (2) the market impact costs, and (3) the disruption of the activities of the money managers employed by the pension sponsor.

An alternative course of action is to use interest rate futures and stock index futures. Assume the pension sponsor wants to shift $200 million from stocks to bonds. Buying an appropriate number of interest rate futures and selling an appropriate number of stock index futures can achieve the desired exposure to stocks and bonds. Futures positions can be maintained or slowly liquidated as funds invested in the cash markets are actually shifted. The advantages of using financial futures contracts are: (1) transactions costs are lower, (2) market impact costs are avoided or reduced by allowing the sponsor time to buy and sell securities in the cash market, and (3) activities of the money managers employed by the pension sponsor are not disrupted.[9]

Portfolio insurance (dynamic hedging)—In Chapter 15, we explained that a put option on a portfolio can be created synthetically with a portfolio of Treasury bills and stock index futures. This strategy requires rebalancing, or dynamic hedging, of the portfolios. While dynamic hedging is employed more commonly in the case of stock portfolios, bond portfolio managers have shown some interest in this strategy.[10]

EXCHANGE-TRADED INTEREST RATE OPTIONS

Interest rate options can be written on cash instruments or futures. At one time, there were several exchange-traded option contracts whose underlying

---

[9] See Roger Clarke, "Asset Allocation Using Futures," Chapter 16 in Robert Arnott and Frank J. Fabozzi (eds.), *Asset Allocation* (Chicago, IL: Probus Publishing, 1988); and Mark Zurak and Ravi Dattatreya, "Asset Allocation Using Futures Contracts," Chapter 20 in Frank J. Fabozzi and Gregory Kipnis (eds.), *The Handbook of Stock Index Futures and Options* (Homewood, IL: Probus Publishing, 1988).

[10] For an explanation and illustration of portfolio insurance for fixed-income portfolios, see Colin Negrych and Dexter Senft, "Portfolio Insurance Using Synthetic Puts—The Reasons, Rewards, and Risks," Chapter 12 in Frank J. Fabozzi (ed.), *The Handbook of Fixed Income Options* (Chicago: Probus Publishing, 1989); or Erol Hakanoglu, Robert Kopprasch, and Emmanuel Roman, "Portfolio Insurance in the Fixed Income Market," Chapter 11 in Frank J. Fabozzi (ed.), *Fixed Income Portfolio Strategies* (Chicago: Probus Publishing, 1989).

instrument was a debt instrument. This type of contract is referred to as **options on physicals**. The most liquid exchange-traded option on a fixed-income security at the time of this writing is an option on Treasury bonds traded on the Chicago Board Options Exchange. For reasons explained later, options on futures have been far more popular than options on physicals.

Exchange-Traded Futures Options

An **option on futures** contract, commonly referred to as a **futures option**, gives the buyer the right to buy from or sell to the writer a designated futures contract at a designated price at any time during the life of the option. If the futures option is a call option, the buyer has the right to purchase one designated futures contract at the exercise price. That is, the buyer has the right to acquire a long futures position in the designated futures contract. If the buyer exercises the call option, the writer (seller) acquires a corresponding short position in the futures contract.

A put option on a futures contract grants the buyer the right to sell one designated futures contract to the writer at the exercise price. That is, the option buyer has the right to acquire a short position in the designated futures contract. If the put option is exercised, the writer acquires a corresponding long position in the designated futures contract. There are futures options on all the interest rate futures contracts reviewed in the previous section.

Mechanics of trading futures options—As the parties to the futures option will realize a position in a futures contract when the option is exercised, the question is: what will the futures price be? That is, at what price will the long be required to pay for the instrument underlying the futures contract, and at what price will the short be required to sell the instrument underlying the futures contract?

Upon exercise, the futures price for the futures contract will be set equal to the exercise price. The position of the two parties is then immediately marked-to-market based on the then-current futures price. Thus, the futures position of the two parties will be at the prevailing futures price. At the same time, the option buyer will receive from the option seller the economic benefit from exercising. In the case of a call futures option, the option writer must pay the difference between the current futures price and the exercise price to the buyer of the option. In the case of a put futures option, the option writer must pay the option buyer the difference between the exercise price and the current futures price.

For example, suppose an investor buys a call option on some futures contract in which the exercise price is 85. Assume also that the futures price is 95 and that the buyer exercises the call option. Upon exercise, the call buyer is given a long position in the futures contract at 85 and the call writer is assigned the corresponding short position in the futures contract at 85. The futures position of the buyer and the writer is immediately marked-to-market by the exchange. Since the prevailing futures price is 95 and the exercise price is 85, the long futures position (the position of the call buyer) realizes a gain of 10 while the short futures position (the position of the call writer) realizes a loss of 10. The call writer pays the exchange 10 and the call buyer receives from the exchange 10. The call buyer who now has a long futures position at 95 can either liquidate the futures position at 95 or maintain a long futures position. If the former course of action is taken, the call buyer sells a futures contract at the prevailing futures price of 95. There is no gain or loss from liquidating the position. Overall, the call buyer realizes a gain of 10. If the call buyer elects to hold the long futures position, then she will face the same risk and reward of holding such a position. But she still has realized a gain of 10 from the exercise of the call option.

Suppose instead that the futures option is a put rather than a call, and the current futures price is 60 rather than 95. Then if the buyer of this put option exercises it, the buyer would have a short position in the futures contract at 85; the option writer would have a long position in the futures contract at 85. The exchange then marks the position to market at the then-current futures price of 60, resulting in a gain to the put buyer of 25 and a loss to the put writer of the same amount. The put buyer who now has a short futures position at 60 can either liquidate the short futures position by buying a futures contract at the prevailing futures price of 60 or maintain the short futures position. In either case the put buyer realizes a gain of 25 from exercising the put option. Table 28-4 summarizes the position of the buyer and seller of a futures option.

There are no margin requirements for the buyer of a futures option once the option price has been paid in full. Because the option price is the maximum amount that the buyer can lose, regardless of how adverse the price movement of the underlying instrument, there is no need for margin.

Because the writer (seller) of an option has agreed to accept all of the risk (and none of the reward) of the position in the underlying instrument, the writer (seller) is required to deposit not only the margin required on the interest rate futures contract position if that is the underlying instrument, but, with certain exceptions, also the option price that is received for writing the option. In addition, as prices adversely affect the writer's position, the writer would be required to deposit variation margin as it is marked-to-market.

The price of a futures option is quoted in 64ths of 1% of par value. For example, a price of 24 means 24/64ths of 1% of par value. Since the par value of a Treasury bond futures contract is $100,000, an option price of 24 means:

$$[(24/64)/100] \times \$100,000 = \$375.$$

In general, the price of a futures option quoted at Q is equal to:

$$\text{Option price} = [(Q/64)/100] \times \$100,000.$$

Table 28-4
Futures Options

Type	Buyer has the right to and then has	If exercised, the seller then has...	and the seller pays the buyer...
Call	Purchase one futures contract @ the strike price a long futures position	a short futures position	Current futures price – Strike price
Put	Sell one futures contract @ the strike price a short futures position	a long futures position	Strike price – Current futures price

Popularity of futures options—There are three reasons why futures options on fixed-income securities have largely supplanted options on physicals as the options vehicle used by institutional investors.[11] First, unlike options on fixed-income securities, futures options on Treasury coupon futures do not require payments for accrued interest. Consequently, when a futures option is exercised, the call buyer and the put writer need not compensate the other party for accrued interest.

Second, futures options are believed to be "cleaner" instruments because of the reduced likelihood of delivery squeezes. Market participants who must deliver an instrument are concerned that at the time of delivery the instrument to be delivered will be in short supply, resulting in a higher price to acquire the instrument. As the deliverable supply of futures contracts is more than adequate for futures options currently traded, there is no concern about a delivery squeeze.

Finally, in order to price any option, it is imperative to know at all times the price of the underlying instrument. In the bond market, current prices are not as easily available as price information on the futures contract.

Applications of Interest Rate Options

There are no new strategies using interest rate options beyond what we explained in Chapters 11, 14, and 15. An institutional investor can use interest rate options to speculate on fixed-income security price movements based on expectations of interest rate movements. Because a call option increases in price if interest rates decline, an investor can buy call options if he or she expects interest rates to move in that direction. Alternatively, because the writer of a put option will benefit if the price increases, an investor who expects interest rates to fall can write put options. Purchasing put options and/or selling call options would be appropriate for an investor who expects interest rates to rise. Remember that unlike speculation in interest rate futures, interest rate options limit downside risk while reducing upside potential by the amount of the option price.

Hedging against adverse interest rate movements—Interest rate options can be used to hedge against adverse interest rate movements but still benefit from a favorable interest rate movement by setting a floor or ceiling on a rate. We will use the illustrations given earlier for interest rate futures to explain how this works and to compare the outcomes using futures and options.

1. Suppose that a pension fund manager knows that bonds must be liquidated in 40 days to make a $5 million payment to the beneficiaries of the pension fund. If interest rates rise in 40 days, more bonds will have to be liquidated to realize $5 million. The hedger will buy put options. Should interest rates rise, the value of the bonds to be sold will decline, but the put options purchased will rise in value. If the transaction is properly structured, the gain on the put options will offset the loss on the bonds. The cost of the safety bought by this strategy will then be the option price paid. If, instead, interest rates

---

[11] Laurie Goodman, "Introduction to Debt Options," Chapter 1 in Frank J. Fabozzi (ed.), *Winning the Interest Rate Game: A Guide to Debt Options* (Chicago, IL: Probus Publishing, 1985), pp. 13-4.

decline, the value of the bonds will rise. The pension fund manager will not exercise the put option. A gain equal to the rise in the bond value minus the put option price will be realized. As we explained in Chapter 14, a strategy of buying put options on securities held in a portfolio is called a protective put buying strategy.

2. Suppose a pension fund manager knows there will be substantial cash contributions flowing into the fund and is concerned that interest rates may fall. Or, suppose a money manager knows that bonds are maturing in the near future and expects interest rates to fall. In both cases, proceeds will be reinvested at a lower interest rate. Call options can be purchased in this situation. Should interest rates fall, the call options will increase in value, offsetting the loss in interest income that will result when the proceeds must be invested at a lower interest rate. The cost of this hedge strategy is the call option price. Should interest rates rise instead, the proceeds can be invested at a higher rate. The benefit of the higher rate will be reduced by the cost of the call option, which expires worthless.

3. Suppose a corporation plans to issue long-term bonds two months from now. To protect itself against a rise in interest rates, the corporation can buy put options. If interest rates rise, the interest cost of the bonds issued two months from now will be higher, but the put option will have increased in value. Buying an appropriate number of put options yields a gain on the put options sufficient to offset the higher interest cost of the bond issue. Again, the cost of this strategy is the price of the put options. Should interest rates decline instead, the corporation will benefit from a lower interest cost when the bonds are issued—a benefit reduced by the cost of the put options.

4. Suppose a thrift or commercial bank wants to make sure that the cost of its funds will not exceed a certain level. This can be done by buying put options on Eurodollar CD futures.

5. Suppose a corporation plans to sell commercial paper one month from now. Buying put options on Treasury bill futures or Eurodollar CD futures lets the corporation set a ceiling on its commercial paper interest cost.

Allocating funds between stocks and bonds—A pension sponsor may wish to alter the composition of the pension funds between stocks and bonds. Stock index options and interest rate options can be used rather than transacting in the cash market.[12]

Option-Pricing Models

In Chapters 11 and 14, we discussed two models popularly used for valuing options: the Black-Scholes model and the binomial model. There are some problems in using these models to price an option on a bond. To illustrate the problems with the Black-Scholes option-pricing model if applied to the pric-

---

[12] For an explanation and illustration, see Ravi Dattatreya, "Asset Allocation Using Futures and Options," Chapter 50 in Frank J. Fabozzi (ed.), *The Handbook of Fixed Income Securities* (Homewood, IL: BusinessOne Irwin, 1991, third ed.).

ing of interest rate options, consider a three-month European call option on a three-year zero-coupon bond.[13] The maturity value of the underlying bond is $100, and the strike price is $120. Suppose further that the current price of the bond is $75.13, the three-year risk-free rate is 10% annually, and expected price volatility is 4%. What would be the fair value for this option? Do you really need an option-pricing model to determine the value of this option?

Think about it. This zero-coupon bond will never have a price above $100 because that is the maturity value. As the strike price is $120, the option will never be exercised; its value is therefore zero. If you can get anyone to buy such an option, any price you obtain will be free money. Yet an option buyer armed with the Black-Scholes option pricing model will input the variables we assume above and come up with a value for this option of $5.60! Why is the Black-Scholes model off by so much? The answer lies in its underlying assumptions (see Table 28-5).

There are three assumptions underlying the Black-Scholes model that limit its use in pricing options on interest rate instruments. First, the probability distribution for the prices assumed by the Black-Scholes option pricing model permits some probability—no matter how small—that the price can take on any positive value. However, in the case of a zero-coupon bond, the price cannot take on a value above $100. In the case of a coupon bond, we know that the price cannot exceed the sum of the coupon payments plus the maturity value. For example, for a five-year, 10% coupon bond with a maturity value of $100, the price cannot be greater than $150 (five coupon payments of $10 plus the maturity value of $100). Thus, unlike stock prices, bond prices have a maximum value. The only way that a bond's price can exceed the maximum value is if negative interest rates are permitted. This is not likely to occur, so any probability distribution for prices assumed by an option pricing model that permits bond prices to be higher than the maximum bond value could generate nonsensical option prices. The Black-Scholes model does allow bond prices to exceed the maximum bond value (or, equivalently, allows negative interest rates). That is one of the reasons why we can get a senseless option price for the three-month European call option on the three-year zero-coupon bond.

Table 28-5

Limitations of Applying the Black-Scholes Stock Option-Pricing Model to Price Interest Rate Options

Assumptions	Fixed-income realities
The price of the underlying has some possibility of rising to any price.	There is a maximum price for a bond and any higher price assumes a negative interest rate is possible.
Short-term rates remain constant.	Changes in short-term rates cause bond prices to change.
Volatility (variance) of price is constant over the life of the option.	Bond price volatility decreases as the bond approaches maturity.

---

[13] This example is given in Lawrence J. Dyer and David P. Jacob, "Guide to Fixed Income Option Pricing Models," in Frank J. Fabozzi (ed.), *The Handbook of Fixed Income Options*, pp. 81-2.

The second assumption of the Black-Scholes option pricing model is that the short-term interest rate is constant over the life of the option. Yet the price of an interest rate option will change as interest rates change. A change in the short-term interest rate changes the rates along the yield curve. Therefore, to assume that the short-term rate will be constant is inappropriate for interest rate options. The third assumption is that the variance of prices is constant over the life of the option. Recall from Chapter 17 that as a bond moves closer to maturity its price volatility declines. Therefore, the assumption that price variance is constant over the life of the option is inappropriate.

While we have illustrated the problem of using the Black-Scholes model to price interest rate options, we can also show that the binomial option-pricing model based on the price distribution of the underlying bond suffers from the same problems. A way around the problem of negative interest rates is to use a binomial option-pricing model based on the distribution of interest rates rather than prices, and construct the binomial tree.[14] Once a binomial interest rate tree is constructed, it can be converted into a binomial price tree by using the interest rates on the tree to determine the price of the bond. Then we follow the standard procedure for calculating the option price by working backward from the value of the call option at the expiration date.

While the binomial option pricing model based on yields is superior to models based on prices, it still has a theoretical drawback. All option-pricing models to be theoretically valid must satisfy the put-call parity relationship explained in Chapter 11. The problem with the binomial model based on yields is that it does not satisfy this relationship. It violates the relationship in that it fails to take into consideration the yield curve, thereby allowing arbitrage opportunities.

The most elaborate models that take the yield curve into consideration and as a result do not permit arbitrage opportunities are called **yield curve option-pricing models** or **arbitrage-free option-pricing models**. These models can incorporate different volatility assumptions along the yield curve. The most popular model employed by dealer firms is the Black-Derman-Toy model.[15]

Pricing Efficiency of the Options Markets

In our review of the pricing efficiency of the common stock options market, we explained that there were two types of tests: (1) tests based on violations of boundary conditions and put-call parity, and (2) tests based on an option-pricing model. There have been studies of options on interest rate futures in both categories.

Jordan and Seale employ a large transactions data base (21,402 observations) for Treasury bond futures and futures options to test for both the lower bound-

---

[14] For example, in constructing the binomial tree based on interest rates, the following formula can be used:

If yield increases: If yield decreases:

$Y_{t+1} = Y_t\, e^{+s}$ $Y_{t+1} = Y_t\, e^s$

where

$\quad Y_{t+1}$ = yield to maturity in time period $t+1$
$\quad Y_t\quad$ = yield to maturity in time period t
$\quad s\quad$ = expected interest rate volatility

[15] Fischer Black, Emanuel Derman, and William Toy, "A One-Factor Model of Interest Rates and Its Application to Treasury Bond Options," *Financial Analysts Journal* (January-February 1990), pp. 24-32.

ary condition and put-call parity.[16] The time period studied is October 5, 1982 (when futures options began trading) through March 26, 1985. They find that actual prices conformed closely to the theoretical prices specified by the lower boundary and put-call parity. The deviations from put-call parity that are found were not sufficiently large to be exploitable by even the lowest-cost traders. Therefore, the findings of Jordan and Seale provide virtually no evidence for rejecting the hypothesis that the market is efficient.

Merville and Overdahl empirically examine the mispricing bias and market efficiency for call options on Treasury bond futures from December 1982 through June 1985, using several option-pricing models.[17] They find that the pricing efficiency of call options improved only marginally with the inception of futures option trading. According to their option-pricing model, they find that in-the-money options tend to be underpriced and at- and out-of-the-money options tend to be overpriced. These results, however, may be due simply to the lack of a good theoretical model to price the options.

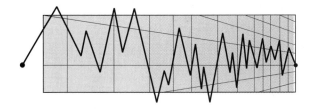

SUMMARY

In this chapter we have reviewed the markets for interest rate futures and options contracts. Currently traded interest rate futures contracts include: Treasury bill futures, Eurodollar CD futures, Treasury bond and note futures, and the Bond Buyer municipal index futures. Interest rate futures are also traded on foreign exchanges where the underlying fixed-income security is foreign debt.

The Treasury bond and note futures contracts give the short several delivery options—quality or swap option, timing option, and wild card option. All three delivery options will reduce the futures price below the theoretical futures price suggested by the standard arbitrage model.

The Bond Buyer municipal bond index futures contract is based on a basket of 40 municipal bonds priced daily by five brokers and is a cash settlement contract.

Interest rate futures can be used by institutional investors to speculate on interest rate movements, to control a bond portfolio's exposure to interest rate changes (altering duration), to enhance returns when futures are mispriced, to allocate funds between stocks and bonds (in combination with stock index

---

[16] James V. Jordan and William E. Seale, "Transactions Data Tests of Minimum Prices and Put-Call Parity for Treasury Bond Futures Options," *Advances in Futures and Options Research*, Vol. 1, Part A, 1986, pp. 63-87.

[17] Larry J. Merville and James A. Overdahl, "An Empirical Examination of the T-Bond Futures (Call) Options Markets Under Conditions of Constant and Changing Variance Rates," *Advances in Futures and Options Research*, vol. 1, Part A (1986), pp. 89-118.

futures), and to create synthetic put options (portfolio insurance or dynamic hedging). The most popular use of interest rate futures by institutional money managers and corporate financial managers is for hedging—locking in an interest rate or a price.

Interest rate options include options on fixed-income securities and options on interest rate futures contracts. The latter, more commonly called futures options, are the preferred vehicle for implementing investment strategies. Strategies using interest rate options include speculating on interest rate movements and hedging.

The assumptions underlying the Black-Scholes pricing model and the binomial model based on prices limit their application to options on fixed-income instruments. The binomial option pricing model based on yields is a better model, but it still suffers from the problem that it does not satisfy the put-call parity relationship. More sophisticated models called yield curve or arbitrage-free pricing models overcome this drawback by incorporating the yield curve into the pricing model.

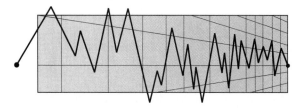

QUESTIONS

1. a. What is the underlying for the Treasury bill futures contract?

   b. If the futures price of a Treasury bills futures contract is 93.5, what is the futures yield on a bank discount basis?

   c. What is the invoice price at the settlement date for a Treasury bill futures contract if the futures price is 93.10?

2. a. What is the underlying for the Eurodollar CD futures contract?

   b. If the index price of a Eurodollar CD futures contract is 92.40, what is the annualized futures LIBOR.

3. What is the underlying for the municipal bond futures contract?

4. What does it mean if the cost of carry is positive for a Treasury bond futures contract?

5. How do you think the cost of carry will affect the decision of the short as to when in the delivery month the short will elect to deliver?

6. What is the underlying for the Treasury bond futures contract?

7. What are the delivery options granted to the seller of the Treasury bond futures contract?

8. a. What is the purpose of the conversion factors for the U.S. Treasury bond futures contract?

   b. Are the conversion factors changed once a contract with a specific settlement date begins trading?

9. How is the theoretical futures price of a Treasury bond futures contract affected by the delivery options granted to the short?

10. Suppose that the conversion factor for a particular Treasury bond that is acceptable for delivery in a Treasury bond futures contract is 0.85 and that the futures price settles at 105. Assume also that the accrued interest for this Treasury bond is 4. What is the invoice price if the seller delivers this Treasury bond at the settlement date?

11. What is the implied repo rate?

12. Explain why the implied repo rate is important in determining the cheapest-to-deliver issue?

13. As the corporate treasurer of a major corporation, you envision that the firm will have to borrow $125 million in three months' time.

   a. How could you use a Treasury bond futures contract to hedge against increased interest rates over the next quarter?

   b. Why might this not work out to be a perfect hedge?

14. What are the difficulties in pricing the municipal bond futures contract?

15. An investor owns a call option on bond X with a strike price of 100. The coupon rate on bond X is 9% and has 10 years to maturity. The call option expires today at a time when bond X is selling to yield 8%. Should the investor exercise the call option?

16. What is the difference between an option on a bond and an option on a bond futures contract?

17. If the price of a futures option is quoted at 32, what is the option price in dollars per contract?

18. Why are exchange-traded futures options more popular than exchange-traded options on physicals?

19. Suppose an investor buys a call option on some futures contract in which the exercise price is 90. Assume also that the current futures price is 95 and that the buyer exercises the option.

   a. How much must the option writer pay the option buyer?

   b. What is the resulting futures position for the option buyer and option writer?

20. Suppose an investor buys a put option on some futures contract in which the exercise price is 92. Assume also that the current futures price is 88 and that the buyer exercises the option.

   a. How much must the option writer pay the option buyer?

   b. What is the resulting futures position for the option buyer and option writer?

21. An investor wants to protect against a rise in the market yield on a Treasury bond. Should the investor purchase a put option or a call option to obtain protection?

22. Respond to the questions following each of these excerpts from an article entitled "It's Boom Time for Bond Options As Interest-Rate Hedges Bloom," published in the November 8, 1990, issue of *The Wall Street Journal.*

a. "'The threat of a large interest-rate swing in either direction is driving people to options to hedge their portfolios of long-term Treasury bonds and medium-term Treasury notes,' said Steven Northern, who manages fixed-income mutual funds for Massachusetts Financial Services Co. in Boston."

Why would a large interest rate swing in either direction encourage people to hedge?

b. "If the market moves against an option purchaser, the option expires worthless, and all the investor has lost is the relatively low purchase price, or 'premium,' of the option."

Comment on the accuracy of this statement.

c. "Futures contracts also can be used to hedge portfolios, but they cost more, and there isn't any limit on the amount of losses they could produce before an investor bails out."

Comment on the accuracy of this statement.

d. "Mr. Northern said Massachusetts Financial has been trading actively in bond and note put options. 'The concept is simple,' he said. 'If you're concerned about interest rates but don't want to alter the nature of what you own in a fixed-income portfolio, you can just buy puts'."

Why might put options be a preferable means of altering the nature of a fixed-income portfolio?

23. What arguments would be given by those who feel that the Black-Scholes model does not apply in pricing interest rate options?

24. Suppose that you are offered the following call option on a zero-coupon bond with a maturity value of 100: 2 years to expiration and strike price of 100.25.

a. Explain why the value of this option would be zero.

b. Given the assumptions that (1) the current price of the underlying zero-coupon bond is 83.96, (2) the expected price volatility is 10%, and (3) the risk-free rate is 6%, calculate the theoretical value for this call option using the Black-Scholes option-pricing model. (See Chapter 14 for the formula.) Comment on your findings.

Over-the-Counter Interest Rate Derivative Markets

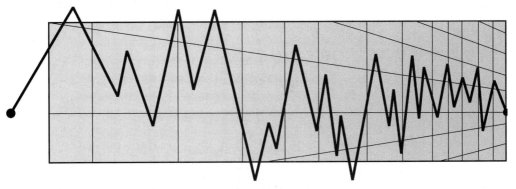

LEARNING OBJECTIVES

After reading this chapter you will understand:

- the types of over-the-counter interest rate options.

- why over-the-counter interest rate options are used by market participants.

- what a compound option is and its use.

- what a forward rate agreement is and its use.

- how an interest rate swap can be used by institutional investors and corporate borrowers.

- why the interest rate swap market has grown so rapidly.

- how the swap rate is determined.

- how to value an interest rate swap.

- the various types of interest rate swaps and reasons for their development.

- what an option on a swap is, and how it can be used.

- what an interest rate agreement (cap or floor) is, and how these agreements can be used by institutional investors and corporate borrowers.

- the relationship between an interest rate agreement and options.

- how an interest rate collar can be created.

In Chapter 28 we discussed exchange-traded interest rate futures and options and how they can be used to control interest rate risk. Commercial banks and investment banks also customize for their clients interest rate contracts useful for controlling risk or for taking positions in markets. These include interest rate options, forward rate agreements, interest rate swaps and options on swaps, interest rate agreements (caps and floors) and options on these agreements, and compound options. In this chapter we will review each of them and explain how they can be used by borrowers and institutional investors. With all of these contracts there is counterparty risk.

OVER-THE-COUNTER INTEREST RATE OPTIONS

Institutional investors who want to purchase an option on a specific Treasury security or a Ginnie Mae pass-through can do so on an over-the-counter basis. There are government and mortgage-backed securities dealers who make a market in options on specific securities.

Over-the-counter (or dealer) options typically are purchased by institutional investors who want to hedge the risk associated with a specific security. For example, a thrift may be interested in hedging its position in a specific mortgage pass-through security.[1] Typically, the maturity of the option coincides with the time period over which the buyer of the option wants to hedge, so the buyer is typically not concerned with the option's liquidity.

Besides these basic OTC options on fixed-income securities, there are the more complex options that we referred to as "exotic options" in Chapter 11. Two examples are the alternative option and the outperformance option. In our discussion of equity derivative products in Chapter 15, we explained how these two options can be used by managers of equity portfolios. They can also be used by managers of bond portfolios in betting on the better of two performing sectors of the bond market (alternative options) or the relative performance of two sectors of the bond market (outperformance options).

An option whose payoff depends on the spread between two sectors of the bond market such as between Treasuries and double-A corporates can be used by corporate treasurers to reduce risk. For example, consider a corporation that plans to sell bonds in two months. The rate that the corporate issuer will pay in two months is the Treasury rate plus the spread to Treasuries. If the corporate treasurer is satisfied with the spread but not the Treasury rate, the firm can buy an option on the spread.

A common OTC option between two sectors of the market is an option on the yield curve. Here a sector is defined as the maturity sector. The reason for the popularity of yield curve options is that there are many institutional investors whose performance is affected by a change in the shape of the yield curve. As an example of a yield curve option, consider the Goldman Sachs'

---

[1] For a detailed discussion of over-the-counter options on mortgage-backed securities, see William A. Barr, "Options on Mortgage-Backed Securities," in Frank J. Fabozzi (ed.), *The Handbook of Mortgage-Backed Securities,* third ed.(Chicago: Probus Publishing, 1992).

product called SYCURVE. This option represents the right to buy (in the case of a call option) or sell (in the case of a put option) specific segments of the yield curve. *Buying the curve* means buying the shorter maturity and selling the longer maturity; *selling the curve* means selling the shorter maturity and buying the longer maturity. The curve is defined by the spread between two specific maturities. They could be the 2-year/10-year spread, the 2-year/30-year spread, or the 10-year/30-year spread. The strike is quoted in basis points.

The yield spread is measured by the long maturity yield minus the short maturity yield. For a call option to be in the money at the expiration date, the yield spread must be positive; for a put option to be in the money at the expiration date, the yield spread must be negative. For example, a 25-basis-point call option on the 2-year/10-year spread will be in the money at the expiration date if the 10-year yield minus the 2-year yield is greater than 25 basis points. And a 35-basis-point put option on the 10-year/30-year spread will be in the money at the expiration date if the 30-year yield minus the 10-year yield is less than 35 basis points.

Yield curve options such as the SYCURVE are cash settlement contracts. In the case of the SYCURVE, if the option expires in the money, the option buyer receives $0.01 per $1 of notional amount, per in-the-money basis point at exercise. For example, suppose that $10 million notional amount of a 2-year/10-year call is purchased with a strike of 25 basis points. Suppose at the expiration date the yield spread is 33 basis points. Then the option expires 8 basis points in the money. The cash payment to the buyer of this option is: $8 \times \$0.01 \times \$10,000,000 = \$800,000$. From this amount, the option premium must be deducted.

Compound or Split-Fee Options

A **compound** or **split-fee option** is an option to purchase an option. We can explain the elements of a compound option by using a long call option on a long put option. This compound option gives the buyer of the option the right but not the obligation to require the writer of the compound option to sell the buyer a put option. The compound option would specify the following terms:

1. the day on which the buyer of the compound option has the choice of either requiring the writer of the option to sell the buyer a put option or allowing the option to expire. This date is called the **extension date**.

2. the strike price and the expiration date of the put option that the buyer acquires from the writer. The expiration date of the put option is called the **notification date**.

The payment that the buyer makes to acquire the compound option is called the **front fee**. If the buyer exercises the call option in order to acquire the put option, a second payment is made to the writer of the option. That payment is called the **back fee**.

An option that allows the option buyer to purchase a put option is called a **caput**. A **cacall** grants the option buyer the right to purchase a call option.

Compound options are most commonly used by mortgage originators to hedge pipeline risk.[2] They can also be used in any situation when the

---

[2] Pipeline risk is discussed in Chapter 24. For a discussion of how compound options can be used to hedge pipeline risk, see Anand K. Bhattacharya, "Compound Options on Mortgage-Backed Securities," Chapter 22 in *The Handbook of Fixed-Income Options* (Chicago: Probus Publishing, 1989).

asset/liability manager needs additional time to gather information about the need to purchase an option.

FORWARD RATE AGREEMENT

A **forward rate agreement** (FRA) is a customized agreement between two parties (one of whom is a dealer firm—a commercial bank or investment banking firm) where the two parties agree at a specified future date to exchange an amount of money based on a reference interest rate and a notional principal amount.

To illustrate an FRA, suppose that Industrial Products Company and an investment bank enter into the following three-month FRA whose notional principal amount is $10 million: if one-year LIBOR three months from now exceeds 9%, the investment banking firm must pay the Industrial Products Company an amount determined by the formula: (1-year LIBOR 3 months from now − 0.09) × $10,000,000.

For example, if one-year LIBOR three months from now is 12%, Industrial Products Company receives: (0.12 − 0.09) × $10,000,000 = $300,000. If one-year LIBOR three months from now is less than 9%, Industrial Products Company must pay the investment banking firm an amount based on the same formula.

Borrowers and investors can use FRAs to hedge against adverse interest rate risk by locking in a rate. To see how a borrower can use an FRA, consider the hypothetical FRA above. Suppose that the management of Industrial Products Company plans three months from now to borrow $10 million for one year. The firm can borrow funds at some spread over one-year LIBOR, which is currently 9%. The risk that the firm faces is that three months from now one-year LIBOR will be greater than 9%. Suppose further that management wishes to eliminate the risk of a rise in one-year LIBOR by locking in a rate of 9%. By entering into the hypothetical FRA, the management of Industrial Products Company has done so. Should one-year LIBOR rise above 9% three months from now, under the terms of the FRA the investment banking firm is obligated to make up the difference. If one-year LIBOR three months from now is below 9%, the Industrial Products Company does not benefit from the lower rate because it must pay the investment banking firm an amount such that the effective cost of borrowing is 9%.

INTEREST RATE SWAPS

As explained in Chapter 12, an interest rate swap is an agreement whereby two parties (called counterparties) agree to exchange periodic interest payments. The dollar amount of the interest payments exchanged is based on the notional amount. The dollar amount each counterparty pays to the other is the agreed-upon periodic interest rate multiplied by the notional amount. The only dollars that are exchanged between the parties are the interest payments, not the notional principal amount. In the most common type of swap, one party agrees to pay the other party fixed-interest payments at designated dates for the life of the contract. The other party agrees to make interest rate payments that float with some reference rate and is referred to as the floating-rate payer.

The reference rates that are commonly used for the floating rate in an interest rate swap are those on various money market instruments: Treasury bills,

London interbank offered rate (LIBOR), commercial paper, bankers acceptances, certificates of deposit, federal funds rate, and prime rate.

Interpretation of a Swap

In Chapter 12, we explained that a swap can be viewed as a package of forward contracts. There is also another important interpretation of a swap: it can be viewed as a package of cash market instruments. To understand why an interest rate swap can be interpreted as a package of cash market instruments, consider an investor who enters into a transaction to:

- buy a $50 million par of a five-year floating-rate bond that pays six-month LIBOR every six months.
- finance the purchase by borrowing $50 million for five years at a 10% annual interest rate paid every six months.

The cash flows for this transaction are set forth in Table 29-1. The second column of the table shows the cash flow from purchasing the five-year floating-rate bond. There is a $50 million cash outlay and then ten cash inflows. The amount of the cash inflows is uncertain because they depend on future LIBOR. The next column shows the cash flow from borrowing $50 million on a fixed-rate basis. The fourth column shows the net cash flow from the entire transaction. As the last column indicates, there is no initial cash flow (no cash inflow or cash outlay). In all ten six-month periods, the net position results in a cash inflow of LIBOR and a cash outlay of $2.5 million. This net position, however, is identical to the position of a fixed-rate payer/floating-rate receiver.

It can be seen from the net cash flow in Table 29-1 that a fixed-rate payer has a cash market position that is equivalent to a long position in a floating-rate bond and a short position in a fixed-rate bond—the short position being the equivalent of borrowing by issuing a fixed-rate bond.

What about the position of a floating-rate payer? It can be easily demonstrated that the position of a floating-rate payer is equivalent to purchasing a fixed-rate bond and financing that purchase at a floating rate, where the floating rate is the reference interest rate for the swap. That is, the position of a floating-rate payer is equivalent to a long position in a fixed-rate bond and a short position in a floating-rate bond.

Applications

In Chapter 12, we provided a simple illustration of how a depository institution can use an interest rate swap to alter the cash-flow character of assets or liabilities from a fixed-rate basis to a floating-rate basis or vice versa. We will provide two illustrations of application here.

Illustration 1—In the first illustration we look at how an interest rate swap can be used to alter the cash-flow characteristics of an institution's assets so as to provide a better match between assets and liabilities. The two institutions are a commercial bank and a life insurance company.

Suppose a bank has a portfolio consisting of five-year term commercial loans with a fixed interest rate. The principal value of the portfolio is $50 million, and the interest rate on all the loans in the portfolio is 10%. The loans

Table 29-1
Cash Flow for Purchase of a Five-Year Floating-Rate Bond Financed by
Borrowing on a Fixed-Rate Basis
(Cash flow in millions of dollars)

Six-month period	Floating-rate bond	Borrowing cost	Net	
0	–$ 50	+$ 50.0	$ 0	
1	+(LIBOR$_1$/2) × 50	– 2.5	+(LIBOR$_1$/2) × 50	– 2.5
2	+(LIBOR$_2$/2) × 50	– 2.5	+(LIBOR$_2$/2) × 50	– 2.5
3	+(LIBOR$_3$/2) × 50	– 2.5	+(LIBOR$_3$/2) × 50	– 2.5
4	+(LIBOR$_4$/2) × 50	– 2.5	+(LIBOR$_4$/2) × 50	– 2.5
5	+(LIBOR$_5$/2) × 50	– 2.5	+(LIBOR$_5$/2) × 50	– 2.5
6	+(LIBOR$_6$/2) × 50	– 2.5	+(LIBOR$_6$/2) × 50	– 2.5
7	+(LIBOR$_7$/2) × 50	– 2.5	+(LIBOR$_7$/2) × 50	– 2.5
8	+(LIBOR$_8$/2) × 50	– 2.5	+(LIBOR$_8$/2) × 50	– 2.5
9	+(LIBOR$_9$/2) × 50	– 2.5	+(LIBOR$_9$/2) × 50	– 2.5
10	+(LIBOR$_{10}$/2) × 50 + 50	– 52.5	+(LIBOR$_{10}$/2) × 50	– 2.5

Note: The subscript for LIBOR indicates six-month LIBOR as per the terms
    of the floating-rate bond at time t.

are interest-only loans; interest is paid semiannually, and the principal is paid
at the end of five years. That is, assuming no default on the loans, the cash
flow from the loan portfolio is $2.5 million every six months for the next five
years and $50 million at the end of five years. To fund its loan portfolio,
assume that the bank is relying on the issuance of six-month certificates of
deposit. The interest rate that the bank plans to pay on its six-month CDs is
the six-month Treasury bill rate plus 40 basis points.

The risk that the bank faces is that the six-month Treasury bill rate will be
9.6% or greater. To understand why, remember that the bank is earning 10%
annually on its commercial loan portfolio. If the six-month Treasury bill rate
is 9.6%, it will have to pay 9.6% plus 40 basis points to depositors for six-
month funds, or 10%, and there will be no spread income. Worse, if the six-
month Treasury bill rate rises above 9.6%, there will be a loss; that is, the cost
of funds will exceed the interest rate earned on the loan portfolio. The bank's
objective is to lock in a spread over the cost of its funds.

The other party in the interest rate swap illustration will be a life insurance
company that has committed itself to pay a 9% rate for the next five years on
a guaranteed investment contract (GIC) it has issued. The amount of the GIC
is $50 million. Suppose that the life insurance company has the opportunity
to invest $50 million in what it considers an attractive five-year floating-rate
instrument in a private-placement transaction. The interest rate on this
instrument is the six-month Treasury bill rate plus 160 basis points. The
coupon rate is set every six months.

The risk that the life insurance company faces is that the six-month interest rate will fall so that it will not earn enough to realize a spread over the 9% rate that it has guaranteed to the GIC holders. If the six-month Treasury bill falls to 7.4% or less, no spread income will be generated. To understand why, suppose that the six-month Treasury bill rate at the date the floating-rate instrument resets its coupon is 7.4%. Then the coupon rate for the next six months will be 9% (7.4% plus 160 basis points). Because the life insurance company has agreed to pay 9% on the GIC policy, there will be no spread income. Should the six-month Treasury bill rate fall below 7.4%, there will be a loss.

We can summarize the asset/liability problem of the bank and life insurance company as follows. The bank has lent long term and borrowed short term; if the six-month Treasury bill rate rises, spread income declines. The Life insurance company has effectively lent short term and borrowed long term; if the six-month Treasury bill rate falls, spread income declines.

Now suppose that an intermediary offers a five-year interest rate swap with a notional amount of $50 million to both the bank and the life insurance company. The terms offered to the bank are as follows:

- Every six months the bank will pay 10% (annual rate) to the intermediary.
- Every six months the intermediary will pay the six-month Treasury bill rate plus 155 basis points to the bank.

The terms offered to the insurance company are as follows:

- Every six months the life insurance company will pay the six-month Treasury bill rate plus 160 basis points per year to the intermediary.
- Every six months the intermediary will pay the bank 10% (annual rate).

What has this interest rate contract done for each entity? We will first consider the bank. For every six-month period for the life of the swap agreement, the interest rate spread for the bank will be as follows.

Annual interest rate received

From commercial loan portfolio	= 10%
From interest rate swap	= 6-month T-bill rate + 155 b.p.
Total	= 11.55% + 6-month T-bill rate

Annual interest rate paid

To CD depositors	= 6-month T-bill rate + 40 b.p.
On interest rate swap	= 10%
Total	= 10.40% + 6-month T-bill rate

Outcome

To be received	= 11.55% + 6-month T-bill rate
To be paid	= 10.40% + 6-month T-bill rate
Spread income	= 1.15%, or 115 b.p.

Thus, regardless of what happens to the six-month Treasury bill rate, the bank locks in a spread of 115 basis points.

Now we will look at the effect of the interest rate swap on the life insurance company as follows.

Annual interest rate received

From floating-rate instrument	= 6-month T-bill rate + 160 b.p.
From interest rate swap	= 10%
Total	= 11.6% + 6-month T-bill rate

Annual interest rate paid

To GIC policyholders	= 9%
On interest rate swap	= 6-month T-bill rate + 160 b.p.
Total	= 10.6% + 6-month T-bill rate

Outcome

To be received	= 11.6% + 6-month T-bill rate
To be paid	= 10.6% + 6-month T-bill rate
Spread income	= 1.0%, or 100 b.p.

Regardless of what happens to the six-month Treasury bill rate, the life insurance company locks in a spread of 100 basis points.

The interest rate swap has allowed each party to accomplish its asset/liability objective of locking in a spread.[3] It permits the two financial institutions to alter the cash-flow characteristics of its assets: from fixed to floating in the case of the bank, and from floating to fixed in the case of the life insurance company. This type of transaction is referred to as an **asset swap**. Alternatively, the bank and the life insurance company could have used the swap market to change the cash-flow nature of their liabilities. Such a swap is called a **liability swap**. While in our illustration we used a bank, an interest rate swap obviously would be appropriate for savings and loan associations that borrow short term (i.e., on a floating-rate basis) and lend long term (i.e., on fixed-rate mortgages).

Of course there are other ways that the two institutions could have chosen to accomplish the same thing. The bank might refuse to make fixed-rate commercial loans. If borrowers could find another source willing to lend on a fixed-rate basis, though, the bank has lost these customers. The life insurance company might refuse to purchase a floating-rate instrument. But suppose that the terms offered on the private-placement instrument were more attractive than what would have been offered on a comparable credit-risk floating-rate instrument, and that by using the swap market the life insurance company can earn a yield higher than if it invests directly in a five-year fixed-rate security. For example, suppose the life insurance company can invest in a comparable credit-risk five-year fixed-rate security with a yield of 9.8%. Assuming that it commits itself to a GIC with a 9% rate, this would result in spread income of 80 basis points—less than the 100-basis-point spread income it achieved by purchasing the floating-rate instrument and entering into the swap.

---

[3] Whether the size of the spread is adequate is not an issue in this illustration.

Consequently, not only can an interest rate swap be used to change the risk of a transaction by changing the cash flow characteristics of assets or liabilities, but under certain circumstances, it also can be used to enhance returns. Obviously, this depends on the existence of market imperfections.

Before we leave this illustration, look back at the floating-rate payments that the life insurance company makes to the intermediary and the floating-rate payments that the intermediary makes to the bank. The life insurance company pays the six-month Treasury bill rate plus 160 basis points, but the intermediary pays the bank the six-month Treasury bill rate plus only 155 basis points. The five-basis point difference represents the fee to the intermediary for the services of intermediation.

Illustration 2—Our second illustration considers two U.S. entities: a triple-A-rated commercial bank, and a triple-B-rated nonfinancial corporation. Each wants to raise $100 million for 10 years. The bank wants to raise floating-rate funds, while the nonfinancial corporation wants to raise fixed-rate funds. The interest rates available to the two entities in the U.S. bond market are as follows. For the bank: Floating rate = 6-month LIBOR + 30 b.p. For the nonfinancial corporation: Fixed rate = 12%.

Assume instead that both entities could issue securities in the Eurodollar bond market. The buyers in this market are typically non-U.S. investors. The criteria used by these investors to assess the default risk of bonds historically have been different from those used in the United States. Suppose that the following terms are available in the Eurodollar bond market for 10-year securities for these two entities. For the bank: Fixed rate = 10.5%. For the nonfinancial corporation: Floating rate = 6-month LIBOR + 80 b.p.

Notice that we indicate the terms that the bank could obtain on fixed-rate financing and that the nonfinancial corporation could obtain on floating-rate securities. You will see why we did this shortly. First, we will summarize the situation for the two entities in the U.S. domestic and Eurodollar bond markets, as shown below.

Floating-Rate Securities

Entity	Bond market	Rate
Bank	U.S. domestic	6-month LIBOR + 30 b.p.
Nonfinancial corp.	Eurodollar	6-month LIBOR + 80 b.p.
		Quality spread = 50 b.p.

Fixed-Rate Securities

Entity	Bond market	Rate
Bank	Eurodollar	10.5%
Nonfinancial corp.	U.S. domestic	12.0%
		Quality spread = 150 b.p.

Notice that the quality spread for floating-rate securities (50 basis points) is narrower than the quality spread for fixed-rate securities (150 basis points). This provides an opportunity for both entities to reduce the cost of raising funds. To see how, suppose each entity issued securities in the Eurodollar bond market, and then simultaneously entered into a 10-year interest rate swap with a $100 million notional principal amount offered by an intermediary. The rates available to each entity in this swap are as follows. For the bank: Pay floating rate of 6-month LIBOR + 70 b.p.; receive fixed rate of 11.3%. For the nonfinancial corp.: Pay fixed rate = 11.3%; receive floating rate = 6-month LIBOR + 45 b.p.

The cost of the issue for the bank would then be as follows.

Interest paid

On fixed-rate Eurodollar bonds issued	= 10.5%
On interest rate swap	= 6-month LIBOR + 70 b.p.
Total	= 11.2% + 6-month LIBOR

Interest received

On interest rate swap	= 11.3%

Net cost:

Interest paid	= 11.2% + 6-month LIBOR
Interest received	= 11.3%
Total	= 6-month LIBOR – 10 b.p.

The cost of the issue for the nonfinancial corporation would then be as follows.

Interest paid

On floating-rate Eurodollar bonds issued	= 6-month LIBOR + 80 b.p
On interest rate swap	= 11.3%
Total	= 12.1% + 6-month LIBOR

Interest received

On interest rate swap	= 6-month LIBOR + 45 b.p.

Net cost

Interest paid	= 12.1% + 6-month LIBOR
Interest received	= 6-month LIBOR + 45 b.p.
Total	= 11.65%

The transactions are diagrammed in Figure 29-1. By issuing securities in the Eurodollar bond market and using the interest rate swap, both entities are able to reduce their cost of issuing securities. The bank was able to issue floating-rate securities for six-month LIBOR minus 10 basis points rather than issue floating-rate securities in the U.S. domestic bond market for six-month LIBOR plus 30 basis points, thereby saving 40 basis points. The nonfinancial corporation saved 35 basis points (11.65% versus 12%) by issuing floating-rate bonds in the Eurodollar bond market and using the interest rate swap.

The point of this illustration is that if differences in quality spreads exist in different sectors of the bond markets, borrowers can use the interest rate swap to arbitrage the inconsistency. Whether they do exist is another question, which we will address below.

Figure 29-1

Diagram of Interest Rate Swap for Illustration 2

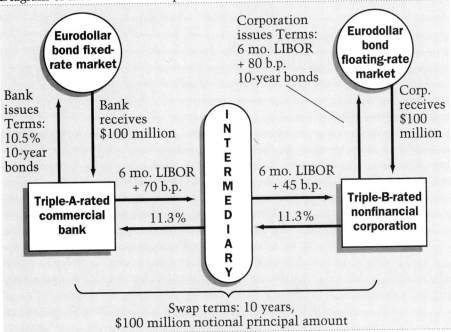

Swap terms: 10 years,
$100 million notional principal amount

Finally, we shall look once again at the intermediary in this transaction. The intermediary pays a floating rate of six-month LIBOR plus 45 basis points to the nonfinancial corporation, and receives six-month LIBOR plus 70 basis points, realizing 25 basis points for its intermediary services.

Development of the Interest Rate Swap Market

The interest rate swap was first developed in late 1981. By 1987, the market had grown to more than $500 billion (in terms of notional principal amount). What is behind this rapid growth? As our two illustrations have demonstrated, an interest rate swap is a quick way for institutional investors and corporate borrowers to change the nature of assets and liabilities or to exploit any perceived capital market imperfection.

Initial motivation for the interest rate swap market was borrower exploitation of what were perceived to be "credit arbitrage" opportunities because of differences between the quality spread between lower- and higher-rated credits in the U.S. and Eurodollar bond fixed-rate markets and the same spread in these two floating-rate markets. Note that our second illustration assumes a spread of 50 basis points in the floating-rate markets and 150 basis points in the fixed-rate markets. Publications by dealer firms[4] and academic research have suggested this credit arbitrage motivation.[5]

---

[4] See, for example, a January 1986 Salomon Brothers publication: T. Lipsky and S. Elhalaski, "Swap-Driven Primary Issuance in the International Bond Market."

[5] See, for example, James Bicksler and Andrew Chen, "An Economic Analysis of Interest Rate Swaps," *Journal of Finance* (July 1986), pp. 645-55.

Basically, the argument for swaps was based on a well-known economic principle of comparative advantage in international economics. The argument in the case of swaps is that even though a high-credit-rated issuer could borrow at a lower cost in both the fixed-rate and floating-rate markets (that is, have an absolute advantage in both), it will have a comparative advantage relative to a lower-credit-rated issuer in one of the markets (and a comparative disadvantage in the other). Under these conditions, each borrower could benefit from issuing securities in the market in which it has a comparative advantage and then swapping obligations for the desired type of financing. The swap market was the vehicle for swapping obligations.

Several observers have challenged the notion that credit arbitrage exists. It should be evident that the comparative advantage argument, while based on arbitrage, is not based on the existence of an irrational mispricing, but on assumptions of equilibrium in segmented markets. If two completely separate markets are each perfectly competitive unto themselves, but set different prices for risk, a transactor in both markets simultaneously sees an imperfectly competitive market and can make money. Those who challenge the credit-arbitrage notion argue that the differences in quality spreads in the fixed-rate and floating-rate markets represent differences in the risks that lenders face in these two markets. For example, the interest rate for a floating-rate note effectively represents a short-term interest rate. The quality spread on floating-rate notes therefore represents a spread in the short-term market. In contrast, the quality spread on fixed-rate medium- and long-term notes represents the spread in that maturity sector. There is no reason why the quality spreads have to be the same.[6]

Despite arguments that credit-arbitrage opportunities are rare in reasonably efficient international capital markets, and that, even if they did exist, they would be eliminated quickly by arbitrage, the number of interest rate swap transactions has grown substantially. Another explanation is suggested in a May 1984 contribution sponsored by Citicorp that appeared in *Euromoney*:

> *The nature of swaps is that they arbitrage market imperfections. As with any arbitrage opportunity, the more it is exploited, the smaller it becomes.*

> *But some of the causes of market imperfections are unlikely to disappear quickly. For example, insurance companies in many countries are constrained to invest mainly in instruments that are domestic in that country. That requirement will tend to favour domestic issuers artificially, and is unlikely to be changed overnight. And even in the world's most liquid markets there are arbitrage opportunities. They are small and exist only briefly. But they exist nevertheless.[7]*

As this opinion demonstrates, as early as 1984 it was argued that the difference in quality spreads in the two markets may be attributable to differences in regulations in two countries. Similarly, differences in tax treatment

---

[6] Two researchers demonstrate that differences in quality spreads between the fixed-rate and floating-rate markets are consistent with option-pricing theory. See Ian Cooper and Antonio Mello, "Default Spreads in the Fixed and in the Floating Rate Markets: A Contingent Claims Approach," *Advances in Futures and Options Research*, 3 (1988), pp. 269-90.

[7] "Swap Financing Techniques: A Citicorp Guide," Special Sponsored Section, *Euromoney* (May 1984), pp. S1-S7.

across countries also create market imperfections that can be exploited using swaps.[8] Thus, swaps can be used for regulatory or tax arbitrage.

Rather than relying exclusively on an arbitrage argument, one study suggests that the swap market grew because it allowed borrowers to raise a type of financing that was not possible prior to the introduction of interest rate swaps.[9] To explain this argument, we will look at the instruments available to borrowers prior to the introduction of interest rate swaps. They include: (1) long-term fixed-rate instruments, (2) long-term floating-rate instruments, and (3) short-term debt. The interest rate for a borrower is composed of the risk-free rate for the relevant maturity plus a credit spread. Consider borrowers with the following expectations:

- Borrower *A* believes that the risk-free rate will rise in the future, and its credit will weaken. This borrower will want to borrow long term with a fixed rate to lock in the prevailing risk-free rate and credit spread.

- Borrower *B* believes that the risk-free rate will fall in the future, but that its credit will weaken. In this case, the borrower will prefer to issue a long-term floating-rate instrument in order to lock in the credit spread, but at the same time to take advantage of an anticipated decline in the risk-free rate.

- Borrower *C* believes that the risk-free rate will fall in the future, but that its credit will strengthen in the future. The instrument of choice for this borrower is short-term floating debt. This is because its cost of funds in the future will be lower due to the expected decline in the risk-free rate and the lower credit spread that will be imposed by the market.

- Borrower *D* believes that the risk-free rate will rise in the future, and that its credit will strengthen in the future. This borrower would want to fix the risk-free rate but let the credit spread float. Which instrument will this borrower prefer to issue? None of the three instruments listed above can be used by this borrower to take advantage of its expectations.

Borrower *D* can use an interest rate swap, however, to fix the risk-free rate for the term of the swap but allow the credit spread to float.[10] In essence, this particular reason for the growth of the interest rate swap market is based on asymmetric information. That is, the borrower possesses information (or a belief) that the market does not possess—namely, that the borrower's credit will improve.

Finally, another argument suggested for the growth of the interest rate swap market is the increased volatility of interest rates that has led borrowers and lenders to hedge or manage their exposure. Even though risk/return characteristics can be replicated by a package of forward contracts, interest rate

---

[8] This applies even more so to currency swaps, which we discuss in Chapter 30. Several examples of how swaps can be used to exploit differences in taxes are given in Clifford W. Smith, Charles W. Smithson, and Lee MacDonald Wakeman, "The Evolving Market for Swaps," *Midland Corporate Finance Journal* (Winter 1986), pp. 20-32.

[9] Marcelle Arak, Arturo Estrella, Laurie Goodman, and Andrew Silver, "Interest Rate Swaps: An Alternative Explanation," *Financial Management* (Summer 1988), pp. 12-8.

[10] For an explanation of how this can be done, see Eileen Baecher and Laurie S. Goodman, *The Goldman Sachs Guide to Hedging Corporate Debt Issuance* (N.Y.: Goldman Sachs & Co., 1988).

forward contracts are not as liquid as interest rate swaps. And entering into or liquidating swap transactions has been facilitated by the standardization of documentation published by the International Swap Dealers Association in early 1987. Moreover, a swap to hedge or manage a position costs less than a package of interest rate forward contracts.

Role of the Intermediary

The role of the intermediary in an interest rate swap sheds some light on the evolution of the market. Intermediaries in these transactions have been commercial banks and investment banks, who in the early stages of the market sought out end-users of swaps. They found in their client bases those entities that needed the swap to accomplish a funding or investing objective, and they matched the two entities. In essence, the intermediary in this type of transaction performed the function of a broker.

The only time that the intermediary would take the opposite side of a swap (that is, would act as a principal) was to balance out the transaction. For example, if an intermediary had two clients that were willing to do a swap but one wanted the notional principal amount to be $100 million while the other wanted it to be $85 million, the intermediary might become the counterparty to the extent of $15 million. That is, the intermediary would warehouse or take a position as a principal to the transaction to make up the $15 million difference between client objectives. To protect itself against an adverse interest rate movement, the intermediary would hedge its position.

There is another problem in an interest rate swap that we have yet to address. The parties to the swaps we have described had to be concerned that the other party would default on its obligation. While a default would not mean any principal was lost because the notional principal amount had not been exchanged, it would mean that the objective for which the swap was entered into would be impaired. As the early transactions involved a higher and a lower credit-rated entity, the former would be concerned with the potential for default of the latter. To reduce the risk of default, many early swap transactions required that the lower credit-rated entity obtain a guarantee from a highly rated commercial bank.

As the frequency and the size of the transactions increased, many intermediaries became comfortable with the transactions and became principals instead of acting as brokers. As long as an intermediary had one entity willing to do a swap, the intermediary was willing to be the counterparty. Consequently, interest rate swaps became part of an intermediary's inventory of product positions. Advances in quantitative techniques and futures products for hedging complex positions such as swaps made the protection of large inventory positions feasible.

Yet another reason encouraged intermediaries to become principals rather than brokers in swaps. As more intermediaries entered the swap market, bid-ask spreads on swaps declined sharply. To make money in the swaps market, intermediaries had to do a sufficient volume of business, which could be done only if an intermediary had (1) an extensive client base willing to use swaps, and (2) a large inventory of swaps. This necessitated that intermediaries act as principals. For example, a survey by *Euromoney* asked 150 multinationals and supranationals to identify the characteristics that make a swap house efficient.[11] The results indicated that the speed at which a swap could be arranged for a client was the most important criterion. That speed depends on client base and inventory. The same survey also revealed clients to be less interested in brokered deals than in transactions in which the intermediary is a principal.

Consequently, we can describe the development of the swap market as one that originated to exploit real or perceived imperfections in the capital market, but that involved into a transactionally efficient market for accomplishing asset/liability objectives.

Terminology, Conventions, and Market Quotes

We have explained the basics of a swap, its applications, and development of the swap market. Here we review some of the terminology used in this market and explain how swaps are quoted.

The date that the counterparties commit to the swap is called the **trade date**. The date that the swap begins accruing interest is called the **effective date**, while the date that the swap stops accruing interest is called the **maturity date**.

While our illustrations assume that the timing of the cash flows for both the fixed-rate payer and floating-rate payer will be the same, this is rarely the case in a swap. In fact, an agreement may call for the fixed-rate payer to make payments annually but the floating-rate payer to make payments more frequently (semiannually or quarterly). Also, the way interest accrues on each leg of the transaction differs, because there are several day-count conventions in the fixed-income markets.

The terminology used to describe the position of a party in the swap markets combines cash market jargon and futures jargon, given that a swap position can be interpreted as a position in a package of cash market instruments or a package of futures/forward positions. As we have said, the counterparty to an interest rate swap is either a fixed-rate payer or floating-rate payer. There are a number of ways to describe these positions.[12]

The fixed-rate payer:

- pays fixed rate in the swap.
- receives floating in the swap.
- is short the bond market.
- has bought a swap.
- is long a swap.
- has established the price sensitivities of a longer-term liability and a floating-rate asset.

---

[11] Special Supplement on Swaps, *Euromoney* (July 1987), p. 14.

[12] Robert F. Kopprasch, John Macfarlane, Daniel R. Ross, and Janet Showers, "The Interest Rate Swap Market: Yield Mathematics, Terminology, and Conventions," Chapter 58 in Frank J. Fabozzi and Irving M. Pollack (eds.), *The Handbook of Fixed Income Securities* (Homewood, IL: Dow Jones-Irwin, 1987).

The floating-rate payer:

- pays floating rate in the swap.
- receives fixed in the swap.
- is long the bond market.
- has sold a swap.
- is short a swap.
- has established the price sensitivities of a longer-term asset and a floating-rate liability.

The first two expressions to describe the position of a fixed-rate payer and floating-rate payer are self-explanatory. To understand why the fixed-rate payer is viewed as short the bond market, and the floating-rate payer is viewed as long the bond market, consider what happens when interest rates change. Those who borrow on a fixed-rate basis will benefit if interest rates rise because they have locked in a lower interest rate. But those who have a short bond position will also benefit if interest rates rise. Thus, a fixed-rate payer can be said to be "short the bond market." A floating-rate payer benefits if interest rates fall. Because a long position in a bond benefits if interest rates fall, terminology describing a floating-rate payer as "long the bond market" has been adopted.

The convention that has evolved for quoting swaps levels is that a swap dealer sets the floating rate equal to the reference rate and then quotes the fixed rate that will apply. For example, suppose that the reference rate is three-month LIBOR and the swap is for ten years. The fixed-rate that applies is the 10-year Treasury yield plus a spread. The spread is called the **swap spread**. The fixed-rate payer/floating-rate receiver would pay the 10-year Treasury yield plus the swap spread and receive the floating rate. The fixed-rate receiver/floating rate payer would receive the 10-year Treasury yield plus the swap spread and pay the floating rate.

A dealer would quote a bid and an offer. To illustrate this convention, suppose a 10-year swap is offered by a dealer when the 10-year Treasury yield is 8.35%. The floating rate is three-month LIBOR. Suppose the dealer quotes the swap at "40–50." This means that the swap spread when the dealer is paying the fixed rate is 40 basis points, but the swap spread when the dealer is receiving the fixed rate is 50. Consequently:

1. the dealer is willing to enter into a swap in which it pays the floating-rate flat (i.e., without a spread) and receives the Treasury yield of 8.35% plus 50 basis points.

2. the dealer is willing to enter into a swap in which it pays the Treasury yield of 8.35% plus 40 basis points and receives the floating rate.

Secondary Market for Swaps

There are three general types of transactions in the secondary market for swaps. These include (1) a swap reversal, (2) a swap sale (or assignment), and (3) a swap buy-back (or close-out or cancellation).

In a **swap reversal**, the party that wants out of the transaction will arrange for a swap in which (1) the maturity on the new swap is equal to the time remaining of the original swap, (2) the reference rate is the same, and (3) the notional principal amount is the same. For example, suppose party X enters into a five-year swap with party Y with a notional principal amount of $50 million in which it pays 10% and receives LIBOR, but that two years later, X wants out of the swap. In a swap reversal, X would enter into a three-year interest rate swap, with a counterparty different from the original counterparty, let's say Z, in which the notional principal amount is $50 million, and X pays LIBOR and receives a fixed rate. The fixed rate that X receives from Z will depend on prevailing swap terms for floating-rate receivers at the initiation of the three-year swap.

While party X has effectively terminated the original swap in economic terms, there is a major drawback to this approach: party X is still liable to the original counterparty Y, as well as to the new counterparty Z. That is, party X now has two offsetting interest rate swaps on its books instead of one, and as a result it has increased its counterparty risk exposure.

The **swap sale** or **swap assignment** overcomes this drawback. In this secondary market transaction, the party that wishes to close out the original swap finds another party that is willing to accept its obligations under the swap. In our illustration, this means that X finds another party, A, that will agree to pay 10% to Y and receive LIBOR from Y for the next three years. A might have to be compensated to accept the position of X, or A might have to be willing to compensate X. Who will receive compensation depends on the swap terms at the time. For example, if interest rates have risen such that, to receive LIBOR for three years, a fixed-rate payer would have to pay 12%, then A would have to compensate X because A has to pay only 10% to receive LIBOR. The compensation would be equal to the value of the swap at the time. If, instead, interest rates have fallen so that, to receive LIBOR for three years, a fixed-rate payer would have to pay 6%, then X would have to compensate A for the value of the swap.

Once the transaction is completed, it is then A not X that is obligated to perform under the swap terms. (Of course an intermediary could act as principal and become party A to help its client X.)

In order to accomplish a swap sale, the original counterparty Y in our example, must agree to the sale. A key factor in whether Y will agree is whether it is willing to accept the credit of A. For example, if A's credit rating is triple-B while X's is double-A, Y would be unlikely to accept A as a counterparty.

A **buy-back** or **close-out sale** (or **cancellation**) involves the sale of the swap to the original counterparty. As in the case of a swap sale, one party might have to compensate the other, depending on how interest rates and credit spreads have changed since the inception of the swap.

Calculation of the Swap Rate

At the initiation of an interest rate swap, the counterparties are agreeing to exchange future interest rate payments and no upfront payments by either party are made. This means that the swap terms must be such that the present value of the cash flows for the payments to be made by the counterparties must be equal. This is equivalent to saying that the present value of the cash flows of payments to be received by the counterparties must be equal. The equivalence of the cash flows is the principle in calculating the swap rate.

For the fixed-rate side, once a swap rate is determined, the payments of the fixed-rate payer are known. However, the floating rate payments are not known because they depend on the value of the reference rate at the reset dates. For a LIBOR-based swap, the Eurodollar CD futures contract (discussed in Chapter 27) can be used to establish the forward (or future) rate for 3-month LIBOR. Given the cash flow based on the forward rate for 3-month LIBOR, the swap rate is the interest rate that will make the present value of the payments on the fixed-rate side equal to the payments on the floating-rate side.

The next question is what interest rate should be used to discount the payments. As explained in Chapter 17, the appropriate rate to discount any cash flow is the theoretical spot rate. Each cash flow should be discounted at a unique discount rate. Where do we get the theoretical spot rates? Recall from Chapter 17 that spot rates can be obtained from forward rates. It is the same 3-month LIBOR forward rates derived from the Eurodollar CD futures contract that can be used to obtain the theoretical spot rates.

We will illustrate the procedure with an example. Consider the following terms for our hypothetical swap.

Swap term: three-year swap
Notional amount: $100 million
Fixed receiver: Actual/360-day count basis and quarterly payments
Floating receiver: 3-month LIBOR, actual/360-day count basis, quarterly payments, and quarterly reset (The "actual/360-day count basis" is a market convention describing how to calculate the interest for the period.)

Our worktable for calculating the swap rate is shown in Table 29-2. The first column just lists the quarterly periods. There is a Eurodollar CD futures contract with a settlement date that corresponds to each period. The second column shows the number of days in the period for each Eurodollar CD futures contract. Column 3 shows the futures price for each contract. We know from Chapter 27 that the future 3-month LIBOR is found by subtracting the futures price from 100; this is shown in the fourth column which represents the forward (fwd) rate.

It is from the forward rates that the discount rates that will be used to discount the cash flows (payments) will be calculated. The discount factor (i.e., the present value of $1 based on the spot rate) is found as follows:[13]

$$\frac{\text{Discount factor in the previous period}}{[1 + (\text{fwd rate in previous period} \times \text{no. of days in period}/360)]}$$

The discount factors are shown in column 5 of Table 29-2.

---

[13] The formulas presented in this section are taken from Chapter 6 of Ravi E. Dattatreya, Raj E.S. Venkatesh, and Vijaya E. Venkatesh, *Interest Rate & Currency Swaps* (Chicago: Probus Publishing, 1994).

Table 29-2
Determining the Swap Rate

(1) Period	(2) Day count	(3) Futures price	(4) Fwd rate	(5) Discount factor	(6) Floating cash flow	(7) PV of floating CF	(8) Fixed cash flow	(9) PV of fixed CF
1	91		4.05	1.00000				
2	90	95.85	4.15	0.98998	1,012,500	1,002,355	1,246,888	1,234,394
3	91	95.45	4.55	0.97970	1,049,028	1,027,733	1,260,742	1,235,149
4	91	95.28	4.72	0.96856	1,150,139	1,113,979	1,260,742	1,221,104
5	91	95.10	4.90	0.95714	1,193,111	1,141,974	1,260,742	1,206,709
6	94	94.97	5.03	0.94505	1,279,444	1,209,139	1,302,305	1,230,743
7	91	94.85	5.15	0.93318	1,271,472	1,186,512	1,260,742	1,176,499
8	90	94.75	5.25	0.92132	1,287,500	1,186,200	1,246,888	1,148,783
9	91	94.60	5.40	0.90925	1,327,083	1,206,650	1,260,742	1,146,330
10	91	94.50	5.50	0.89701	1,365,000	1,224,419	1,260,742	1,130,898
11	91	94.35	5.65	0.88471	1,390,278	1,229,993	1,260,742	1,115,391
12	93	94.24	5.76	0.87198	1,459,583	1,272,727	1,288,451	1,123,504
13	91	94.21	5.79	0.85947	1,456,000	1,251,388	1,260,742	1,083,570
Total						$14,053,077		$14,053,078

The floating cash flow is found by multiplying the forward rate and the notional amount. However, the forward rate must be adjusted for the number of days in the payment period. The formula to do so is:

$$\frac{\text{Fwd rate previous period} \times \text{no. of days in period}}{360} \times \text{notional amount}$$

These values represent the payments by the floating-rate payer and the receipts of the fixed-rate receiver. The values are shown in column 6 of Table 29-2. The present value (PV) of each of these cash flows is shown in column 7 and is found by multiplying the discount factor shown in column 5 by the floating cash flow (CF) in column 6. The total present value of the floating cash flow is $14,053,077.

In order for no other payments to be exchanged between the counterparties other than the interest payments, the swap rate must be set such that the present value of the fixed cash flows is equal to the same value, $14,053,077. This can only be found by trial and error. For our hypothetical swap, when a swap rate of 4.987551% is tried, the cash flow is as shown in column 8 of the table. In determining the fixed cash flows, each cash flow must be adjusted for the day count, as follows:

$$\frac{\text{Assumed swap rate} \times \text{no. of days in period}}{360} \times \text{notional amount}$$

Multiplying the discount factors in column 5 by the fixed cash flow shown in column 8 we can obtain the present value of the fixed cash flows displayed in column 9. The total PV for the fixed cash flows is equal to $14,053,078.

---

[14] For a more detailed explanation of how this is done with more complicated swaps, see Chapter 6 of Dattatreya, Venkatesh, and Venkatesh, *Interest Rate & Currency Swaps*.

Therefore, the *swap rate* is 4.987551%, since it is this rate that equates the present value of the floating and fixed cash flows.

Given the swap rate, the swap spread can be determined. For example, since this is a three-year swap, the three-year on-the-run Treasury rate would be used as the benchmark. If the yield on that issue is 4.587551%, the swap spread is then 40 basis points.

The calculation of the swap rate for all swaps follows the same principle: equating the present value of the cash flows.[14] Later in this section the economic determinants of the swap rate are discussed.

Valuing a Swap

Once a swap transaction is completed, changes in market interest rates will change the cash flow of the floating-rate side of the swap. The value of an interest rate swap is the difference between the present value of the cash flow of the two sides of the swap. The 3-month LIBOR forward rates from the current Eurodollar CD futures contracts are used to (1) calculate the floating cash flows and (2) determine the discount factors at which to calculate the present value of the cash flows.

To illustrate this, consider the 3-year swap used to demonstrate how to calculate the swap rate. Suppose that one year later, interest rates change such that column 3 in Table 29-3 shows the prevailing futures price for the Eurodollar CD futures contract. Columns 4 and 5 show the corresponding forward rates and discount factors. Column 6 shows the floating cash flow based on the forward rates in column 4, and column 7 shows the present value of the floating cash flow using the discount factors in column 5. The total present value of the floating cash flow is $11,485,949. This means that the floating-rate payer has agreed to make payments with a value of $11,485,949 and the fixed-rate payer will receive a cash flow with this value.

Now we shall look at the fixed-rate side. The swap rate is fixed over the life of the swap. The fixed cash flow is given in column 8 of Table 29-3, and the present value based on the discount factors in column 5 is shown in column 9. The total present value of the fixed cash flows is $9,501,603. This means that the fixed-rate payer has agreed to make payments with a value

Table 29-3
Determining the Value of a Swap

(1) Period	(2) Day count	(3) Futures price	(4) Fwd rate	(5) Discount factor	(6) Floating cash flow	(7) PV of floating CF	(8) Fixed cash flow	(9) PV of fixed CF
1	91		5.25	1.000000				
2	94	94.27	5.73	0.987045	1,370,833	1,353,074	1,302,305	1,285,434
3	91	94.22	5.78	0.972953	1,448,417	1,409,241	1,260,742	1,226,642
4	90	94.00	6.00	0.958942	1,445,000	1,385,671	1,246,888	1,195,693
5	91	93.85	6.15	0.944615	1,516,667	1,432,667	1,260,742	1,190,916
6	91	93.75	6.25	0.929686	1,554,583	1,445,274	1,260,742	1,172,094
7	91	93.54	6.46	0.915227	1,579,861	1,445,931	1,260,742	1,153,865
8	93	93.25	6.75	0.900681	1,668,833	1,503,086	1,288,451	1,160,483
9	91	93.15	6.85	0.885571	1,706,250	1,511,005	1,260,742	1,116,476
Total						11,485,949		9,501,603

of $9,501,603 and the floating-rate payer will receive a cash flow with this value.

From the fixed-rate payer's perspective, a floating cash flow with a present value of $11,485,949 is going to be received, and a fixed cash flow with a present value of $9,501,603 is going to be paid out. The difference between these two present values—$1,984,346—is the *value of the swap*. It is a positive value for the fixed-rate payer because the present value of what is to be received exceeds the present value of what is to be paid out.

From the floating-rate payer's perspective, a floating cash flow with a present value of $11,485,949 is going to be paid out, and a fixed cash flow with a present value of $9,501,603 is going to be received. Once again, the difference between these two present values—$1,984,346—is the value of the swap. It is a negative value for the floating-rate payer because the present value of what is to be received is less than the present value of what is to be paid out.

Beyond the "Plain Vanilla" Swap

Thus far we have described the **plain vanilla** or **generic** interest rate swap. Nongeneric or individualized swaps have evolved as a result of the asset/liability needs of borrowers and lenders, and some are described below. Regardless of the types of interest rate swap, the valuation procedure just described can be used.

Amortizing, accreting, and roller-coaster swaps—In a generic swap, the notional principal amount does not vary over the life of the swap. Thus, it is sometimes referred to as a **bullet swap**. In contrast, for amortizing, accreting, and roller-coaster swaps, the notional principal amount varies over the life of the swap.

To explain an amortizing swap, we can use our earlier illustration of the interest rate swap between the commercial bank and the life insurance company. Recall that it was the fixed-rate commercial loans that were generating the cash flow that the bank was using to make the fixed-rate payment on the interest rate swap.

We assumed that the loans were interest-only loans and that the principal would be repaid at the end of five years. Suppose, instead, that the loan was a level-payment, fully amortized one, meaning that the principal outstanding would decline over the five years, and therefore the interest would decline over time. In such an instance, the amount received every six months from the commercial loans would be less than the fixed-rate payments to be made on the interest rate swap, if interest rates decline. This is because the principal repaid every six months would have to be reinvested at an interest rate less than 10% (the interest on the original loan balance).

An amortizing swap can be used to solve this problem. An **amortizing swap** is one in which the notional principal amount decreases in a predetermined way over the life of the swap. In situations where a liability to be funded increases over time, an **accreting swap** can be employed. An accreting swap is one in which the notional principal amount increases at a predetermined way over time. An accreting swap could be used by a lending institution that has committed to lend increasing amounts to a customer for a long-term project.

In a **roller-coaster swap**, the notional principal amount can rise or fall from period to period according to an institution's liability structure.

Zero-coupon swaps—In a **zero-coupon swap**, the fixed-rate payer does not make any payments until the maturity date of the swap but receives floating-rate payments at regular payment dates. This type of swap exposes the floating-rate payer to significant counterparty risk because this party makes regular payments but does not receive any payments until the maturity date of the swap.

Basis-rate swap—The terms of a typical interest rate swap call for the exchange of fixed- and floating-rate payments. In a **basis-rate swap**, both parties exchange floating-rate payments based on a different money market rate. As an example, assume a commercial bank has a portfolio of loans in which the lending rate is based on the prime rate, but the bank's cost of funds is based on LIBOR. The risk the bank faces is that the spread between the prime rate and LIBOR will change. This is referred to as **basis risk**. The bank can use a basis-rate swap to make floating-rate payments based on the prime rate and receive floating-rate payments based on LIBOR.

Forward-rate swaps—A **forward swap** is simply a forward contract on an interest rate swap. The terms of the swap are set today, but the parties agree that the swap will begin at a specified date in the future.

Options on Swaps

The second generation of products in the interest rate swap market is options on interest rate swaps referred to as **swaptions**. The buyer of this option has the right to enter into an interest rate swap agreement on predetermined terms by some specified date in the future. The buyer of a put or call swaption pays the writer a premium.

A **put swaption** is an option allowing the buyer to enter into an interest rate swap in which the buyer pays a fixed rate and receives a floating rate, and the writer receives a fixed rate and pays a floating rate. A **call swaption** is an option that allows the buyer to enter into an interest rate swap where the buyer pays a floating rate and receives a fixed rate, while the writer receives a floating rate and pays a fixed rate. Swaptions may be exercised at any time prior to the expiration date (i.e., American type) or only at the expiration date (i.e., European type).

A callable or a putable swap is a swap with an embedded option. A putable or callable swap effectively allows one of the parties to terminate the swap; it is therefore referred to as a **cancelable** or **terminable swap**. Putable swaps can be used in asset-based swaps when the cash flow of the fixed-rate asset enabling the fixed-rate payments is uncertain. The cash flow of the asset would be uncertain if it is (1) callable, as in the case of a callable corporate bond, a mortgage loan or pass-through security, or a loan that can be prepaid, and/or (2) exposes the investor/lender to default risk.[15]

To illustrate the use of a putable swap, suppose a savings and loan association enters into a four-year swap in which it agrees to pay 11% fixed and

---

[15] For an explanation of how putable swaps can be used to manage a portfolio of callable bonds, see Robert M. Stavis and Victor J. Haghani, "Putable Swaps: Tools for Managing Callable Assets," Chapter 21 in Frank J. Fabozzi (ed.), *The Handbook of Fixed Income Options* (Burr Ridge, IL: Irwin Publishing, 1996).

receive LIBOR. The fixed-rate payments will come from a portfolio of mortgage pass-through securities with a coupon rate of 11%. Suppose that one year after the swap begins, mortgage rates decline to 6%, resulting in large prepayments. The prepayments received will have to be reinvested at a rate less than 11%, but the S&L must still pay 11% under terms of the swap. A putable swap would give the S&L the right to pay LIBOR and receive 11%. This effectively terminates the swap.

The party in a putable or callable swap that has the right to exercise the option pays for this right. The option price can be either an upfront payment, as in the case of the options we have discussed throughout this book, or it can be an amount paid over the life of the swap by adjusting the payments exchanged.

INTEREST RATE AGREEMENTS

An interest rate agreement is an agreement between two parties whereby one party, for an upfront premium, agrees to compensate the other if a designated interest rate, called the reference rate, is different from a predetermined level. When one party agrees to pay the other when the reference rate exceeds a predetermined level, the agreement is referred to as an **interest rate cap** or **ceiling**. The agreement is referred to as an **interest rate floor** when one party agrees to pay the other when the reference rate falls below a predetermined level. The predetermined interest rate level is called the **strike rate**.

The terms of an interest rate agreement include:

1. the reference rate
2. the strike rate that sets the ceiling or floor
3. the length of the agreement
4. the frequency of settlement
5. the notional principal amount

For example, suppose that C buys an interest rate cap from D with terms as follows:.

1. The reference rate is six-month LIBOR.
2. The strike rate is 8%.
3. The agreement is for seven years.
4. Settlement is every six months.
5. The notional principal amount is $20 million.

Under this agreement, every six months for the next seven years, D will pay C whenever six-month LIBOR on the settlement date exceeds 8%. The payment will equal the dollar value of the difference between six-month LIBOR and 8% times the notional principal amount divided by two. For example, if six months from now six-month LIBOR is 11%, then D will pay C: 3% (11% minus 8%) times $20 million divided by 2, or $300,000. If six-month LIBOR is 8% or less, D does not have to pay anything to C.

As an example of an interest rate floor, assume the same terms as the interest rate cap we just illustrated. In this case, if six-month LIBOR is 11%, C receives nothing from D, but if six-month LIBOR is less than 8%, D compensates C for the difference. For example, if six-month LIBOR is 7%, D will pay C $100,000 (8% minus 7%, times $20 million divided by 2).

Interest rate caps and floors can be combined to create an **interest rate collar**. This is done by buying an interest rate cap and selling an interest rate floor. Some commercial banks and investment banking firms now write options on interest rate agreements for customers. Options on caps are called **captions**; options on floors are called **flotions**.

Risk/Return Characteristics

In an interest rate agreement, the buyer pays an upfront fee, which represents the maximum amount that the buyer can lose and the maximum amount that the writer of the agreement can gain. The only party that is required to perform is the writer of the interest rate agreement. The buyer of an interest rate cap benefits if the underlying interest rate rises above the strike rate because the seller (writer) must compensate the buyer. The buyer of an interest rate floor benefits if the interest rate falls below the strike rate, because the seller (writer) must compensate the buyer.

How can we better understand interest rate caps and interest rate floors? In essence these contracts are equivalent to a package of interest rate options. As the buyer benefits if the interest rate rises above the strike rate, an interest rate cap is similar to purchasing a package of put options on a bond or call options on an interest rate; the seller of an interest rate cap has effectively sold a package of options. The buyer of an interest rate floor benefits from a decline in the interest rate below the strike rate. Therefore, the buyer of an interest rate floor has effectively bought a package of call options on a bond or put options on an interest rate from the writer of the option.

Once again, a complex contract can be seen to be a package of basic contracts, or options in the case of interest rate agreements.

Applications

To see how interest rate agreements can be used for asset/liability management, consider the problems faced by the commercial bank and the life insurance company we used in the first illustration to demonstrate use of an interest rate swap.[16]

Recall that the bank's objective is to lock in an interest rate spread over its cost of funds. Yet because it borrows short term, its cost of funds is uncertain. The bank may be able to purchase a cap such that the cap rate plus the cost of purchasing the cap is less than the rate it is earning on its fixed-rate commercial loans. If short-term rates decline, the bank does not benefit from the cap, but its cost of funds declines. The cap therefore allows the bank to impose a ceiling on its cost of funds while retaining the opportunity to

---

[16] For additional applications in the insurance industry, see David F. Babbel, Peter Bouyoucos, and Robert Stricker, "Capping the Interest Rate Risk in Insurance Products," Chapter 21 in Frank J. Fabozzi (ed.), *Fixed Income Portfolio Strategies* (Chicago: Probus Publishing, 1989). For other applications of interest rate agreements, see Victor J. Haghani and Robert M. Stavis, "Interest Rate Caps and Floors: Tools for Asset/Liability Management," in Frank J. Fabozzi (ed.), *Advances and Innovations in Bond and Mortgage Markets* (Chicago: Probus Publishing, 1989).

benefit from a decline in rates. This is consistent with the view of an interest rate cap as simply a package of options.

The bank can reduce the cost of purchasing the cap by selling a floor. In this case, the bank agrees to pay the buyer of the floor if the underlying rate falls below the strike rate. The bank receives a fee for selling the floor, but it has sold off its opportunity to benefit from a decline in rates below the strike rate. By buying a cap and selling a floor, the bank has created a range for its cost of funds—that is, it has created a collar.

Recall the problem of the life insurance company that has guaranteed a 9% rate on a GIC for the next five years and is considering the purchase of an attractive floating-rate instrument in a private-placement transaction. The risk that the company faces is that interest rates will fall so that it will not earn enough to realize the 9% guaranteed rate plus a spread. The life insurance company may be able to purchase a floor to set a lower bound on its investment return, yet retain the opportunity to benefit should rates increase. To reduce the cost of purchasing the floor, the life insurance company can sell an interest rate cap. By doing so, however, it gives up the opportunity of benefiting from an increase in the six-month Treasury bill rate above the strike rate of the interest rate cap.

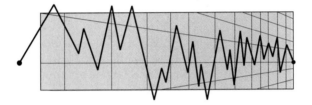

SUMMARY

In this chapter we have covered over-the-counter interest rate control contracts created by commercial banks and investment banks for their customers. Markets for these instruments have grown explosively in the 1980s.

Because of the difficulties of hedging particular bond issues or pass-through securities, many institutions find over-the-counter options more useful than exchange-traded options; these contracts can be customized to meet specific investment goals. There are also exotic options such as alternative and out-performance options. A yield curve option is an example of an exotic option. An option that allows a party the right to enter into an option is called a compound or split-fee option. These options are used primarily by mortgage originators to hedge pipeline risk.

An interest rate swap is an agreement specifying that the parties exchange interest payments at designated times. In a typical swap, one party will make fixed-rate payments, and the other will make floating-rate payments, with payments based on the notional principal amount. Participants in financial markets use interest rate swaps to alter the cash flow characteristics of their assets or liabilities, or to capitalize on perceived capital market inefficiencies.

A number of types of swaps have been developed to satisfy various needs of market participants. These include swaps in which the notional principal amount varies over the life of the swap (amortizing, accreting, and roller-coaster swaps), zero-coupon swaps, basis-rate swaps, and forward rate swaps.

The second generation of swaps is options on swaps: put and call swaptions, and putable and callable swaps.

An interest rate agreement allows one party for an upfront premium the right to receive compensation from the writer of the agreement if the reference rate is different from the strike rate. An interest rate cap calls for one party to receive a payment if the reference rate is above the strike rate. An interest rate floor lets one party receive a payment if the reference rate is below the strike rate.

An interest rate cap can be used to establish a ceiling on the cost of funding; an interest rate floor can be used to establish a floor return. Buying a cap and selling a floor creates a collar. There are also options on interest rate caps (called captions) and on floors (called flotions).

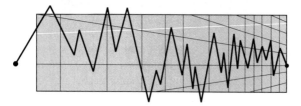

QUESTIONS

1. a. What is the motivation for the purchase of an over-the-counter option?

   b. Does it make sense for an investor who wants to speculate on interest rate movements to purchase an over-the-counter option?

2. Why does the buyer and not the seller of an over-the-counter option face counterparty risk?

3. a. What is a yield curve option?

   b. How is the payoff of a yield curve option determined?

4. a. Explain how a compound option works.

   b. We state in this chapter that compound options are most commonly used by mortgage originators to hedge pipeline risk. Why do you think compound options are used to hedge pipeline risk?

5. Suppose that three months from now the Summit Manufacturing Company plans to borrow $100 million for one year. The interest rate at which Summit Manufacturing expects to borrow is LIBOR plus 100 basis points. Currently, LIBOR is 10%.

   a. What is the funding risk that Summit Manufacturing faces?

   b. Suppose that Summit Manufacturing enters into a three-month forward rate agreement with an investment banking firm for a notional principal amount of $100 million. Terms of the FRA are as follows: If one-year LIBOR exceeds 10% three months from now, the investment banking firm must pay Summit Manufacturing; if one-year LIBOR is less than 10% three months from now, Summit Manufacturing must pay the investment banking firm. How can this FRA eliminate the risk that you identified in part a of this question?

6. The following quotation appeared in an article entitled "Recent Developments in Corporate Finance," published in the August 1990 issue of the *Federal Reserve Bulletin:*

> *Before the 1980s, it was reasonable in aggregate analysis to characterize commercial paper and bank loans as short-term debt and corporate bonds and mortgages as long-term debt. Such characterizations often were used to gauge corporate exposure to interest rate and liquidity risk, under the assumption that interest rates on short-term debt were variable whereas those on long-term debt were fixed.*
>
> *Financial developments and innovations in the past decade have made this classification of debt less useful.*

   a. What financial developments and innovations do you think this article is referring to?

   b. Why have they made the classification between short-term and long-term debt less useful?

7. Why can an interest rate swap be interpreted as a position in two cash market instruments?

8. Consider an interest rate swap with these features: maturity is five years, notional principal is $100 million, payments occur every six months, the fixed-rate payer pays a rate of 9.05% and receives LIBOR, while the floating-rate payer pays LIBOR and receives 9%. Now, suppose that at a payment date, LIBOR is at 6.5%.

What is each party's payment and receipt at that date?

9. Suppose a dealer quotes these terms on a five-year swap: fixed-rate payer to pay 9.5% for LIBOR and floating-rate payer to pay LIBOR for 9.2%.

   a. What is the dealer's bid-ask spread?

   b. How would the dealer quote the terms by reference to the yield on five-year Treasury notes?

10. a. Why would a depository institution use an interest rate swap?

   b. Why would a corporation that plans to raise funds in the debt market use an interest rate swap?

11. In determining the cash flow for the floating rate side of a LIBOR swap, explain how the cash flow is determined?

12. How is the swap rate calculated?

13. How is the value of a swap determined?

14. What types of transactions occur in the secondary market for an interest rate swap?

15. Suppose that a life insurance company has issued a three-year GIC with a fixed rate of 10%. Under what circumstances might it be feasible for the life insurance company to invest the funds in a floating-rate security and enter into a three-year interest rate swap in which it pays a floating rate and receives a fixed rate?

16. What is a swaption?

17. Give an example of why a market participant would want to use a swaption.

18. Consider the three-year swap shown in Table 29-2. Suppose that one year later the Eurodollar CD futures prices are as shown below:

Period	Day Count	Futures Price
1	91	
2	94	96.70
3	91	96.70
4	90	96.66
5	91	96.60
6	91	96.55
7	91	96.52
8	93	96.47
9	91	96.40

What is the value of the swap?

19. Suppose an S&L buy's an interest rate cap that has these terms: the reference rate is the six-month Treasury bill rate; the cap will last for five years; payment is semiannual; the strike rate is 5.5%; and the notional principal is $10 million. Suppose further that at the end of some six-month period, the six-month Treasury bill rate is 6.1%.

   a. What is the amount of the payment that the S&L will receive?

   b. What would the writer of this cap pay if the six-month Treasury rate were 5.45% instead of 6.1%?

20. How can an interest rate collar be created?

21. What is the relationship between an interest rate agreement and an interest rate option?

22. The following quotes are taken from the January 28, 1991, issue of *Bank Letter*:

   The surge in the use of derivatives, their lengthening terms and growing complexity all spell greater credit risks for the banks and securities firms that fashion these instruments, according to a recent report by Moody's Investors Service.

   The derivatives business includes creating, underwriting, trading and selling instruments including options, swaps, futures, swaptions related to debt and equity securities, commodities and foreign exchange.

   Creating "over-the-counter derivatives," with other firms as counterparties also creates new credit risks compared to the use of traded, listed instruments.

   These statements refer to two types of credit risk that banks and investment banking firms face as a result of their activities in the "derivatives business." Explain these two credit risks.

23. The following table shows information for a three-year swap. Demonstrate that the swap rate is 6.192181%.

Period	Day count	Futures price	Fwd rate	Discount factor	Floating cash flow
1	90		5.65	1.00000	
2	91	94.25	5.75	0.98592	1,428,194
3	90	94.15	5.85	0.97195	1,437,500
4	90	94.05	5.95	0.95794	1,462,500
5	91	93.88	6.12	0.94374	1,504,028
6	90	93.80	6.20	0.92952	1,530,000
7	91	93.74	6.26	0.91518	1,567,222
8	90	93.65	6.35	0.90108	1,565,000
9	91	93.50	6.50	0.88684	1,605,139
10	91	93.45	6.55	0.87251	1,643,056
11	91	93.38	6.62	0.85830	1,655,694
12	90	93.28	6.72	0.84432	1,655,000
13	91	93.20	6.80	0.83022	1,698,667

Foreign Exchange Market

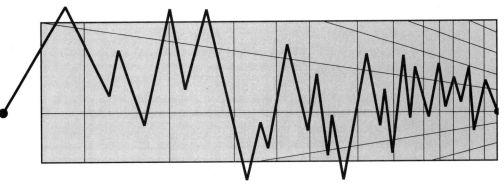

LEARNING OBJECTIVES

After reading this chapter you will understand:

- what is meant by a foreign exchange rate.

- the different ways that a foreign-exchange rate can be quoted (direct versus indirect).

- the conventions for quoting foreign exchange rates.

- what foreign-exchange risk is.

- what a cross rate is and how to calculate a theoretical cross rate.

- what triangular arbitrage is.

- the foreign exchange market structure.

- what is meant by purchasing-power parity.

- what the European Currency Unit is.

In previous chapters we have discussed how U.S. borrowers and investors need not look solely to domestic financial markets to accomplish their financial goals. Nor need foreign entities depend solely on their domestic markets. As a result, payments for liabilities made by borrowers and cash payment received by investors may be denominated in a foreign currency. In this chapter, we provide a review of the spot (or cash) foreign exchange market. In Chapter 31 we look at the markets for hedging foreign-exchange risk.

FOREIGN EXCHANGE RATES

An **exchange rate** is defined as the amount of one currency that can be exchanged per unit of another currency, or the price of one currency in terms of another currency. For example, consider the exchange rate between the U.S. dollar and the Swiss franc. The exchange rate could be quoted in one of two ways:

1. the amount of U.S. dollars necessary to acquire one Swiss franc, or the dollar price of one Swiss franc
2. the amount of Swiss francs necessary to acquire one U.S. dollar, or the Swiss franc price of one dollar.

Exchange rate quotations may be either direct or indirect. To understand the difference, it is necessary to refer to one currency as a local currency and the other as a foreign currency. For example, from the perspective of a U.S. participant, the local currency would be U.S. dollars, and any other currency, such as Swiss francs, would be the foreign currency. From the perspective of a Swiss participant, the local currency would be Swiss francs, and other currencies, such as U.S. dollars, the foreign currency.

A **direct quote** is the number of units of a local currency exchangeable for one unit of a foreign currency. An **indirect quote** is the number of units of a foreign currency that can be exchanged for one unit of a local currency. Looking at this from a U.S. participant's perspective, a quote indicating the number of dollars exchangeable for one unit of a foreign currency is a direct quote. An indirect quote from the same participant's perspective would be the number of units of the foreign currency that can be exchanged for one U.S. dollar. Obviously, from the point of view of a non-U.S. participant, the number of U.S. dollars exchangeable for one unit of a non-U.S. currency is an indirect quote; the number of units of a non-U.S. currency exchangeable for a U.S. dollar is a direct quote.

Given a direct quote, we can obtain an indirect quote (the reciprocal of the direct quote), and vice versa. For example, suppose that a U.S. participant is given a direct quote of dollars for Swiss francs of 0.7402—that is, the price of a Swiss franc is $0.7402. The reciprocal of the direct quote is 1.3508, which would be the indirect quote for the U.S. participant; that is, one U.S. dollar can be exchanged for 1.3508 Swiss francs, which is the Swiss franc price of a dollar.

In the financial press, a quote can be reported either way. Figure 30-1, taken from *The Wall Street Journal* on Friday, June 24, 1994, for quotes on June 23, 1994, shows this. All the exchange rates in the figure are between the country indicated in the first column and the U.S. dollar. Look down the first column that shows the countries until you get to "Switzerland (Franc)." Switzerland has four lines devoted to it. The first of the four lines refers to the spot or cash market exchange rate. We explain the other three lines ("30-Day Forward," "90-Day Forward," and "180-Day Forward") in Chapter 31.

Figure 30.1

Exchange Rates Reported in *The Wall Street Journal* for June 23, 1994

EXCHANGE RATES

Thursday, June 23, 1994

The New York foreign exchange selling rates below apply to trading among banks in amounts of $1 million and more, as quoted at 3 p.m. Eastern time by Bankers Trust Co., Dow Jones Telerate Inc. and other sources. Retail transactions provide fewer units of foreign currency per dollar.

Country	U.S. $ equiv. Thurs.	U.S. $ equiv. Wed.	Currency per U.S. $ Thurs.	Currency per U.S. $ Wed.
Argentina (Peso)	1.01	1.01	.99	.99
Australia (Dollar)	.7330	.7365	1.3643	1.3578
Austria (Schilling)	.08870	.08850	11.27	11.30
Bahrain (Dinar)	2.6522	2.6522	.3771	.3771
Belgium (Franc)	.03030	.03024	33.00	33.07
Brazil (Cruzeiro real) .	.0004080	.0004080	2451.04	2451.00
Britain (Pound)	1.5390	1.5305	.6498	.6534
30-Day Forward	1.5382	1.5297	.6501	.6537
90-Day Forward	1.5370	1.5282	.6506	.6544
180-Day Forward	1.5355	1.5265	.6513	.6551
Canada (Dollar)	.7202	.7222	1.3885	1.3847
30-Day Forward	.7192	.7210	1.3904	1.3869
90-Day Forward	.7166	.7178	1.3955	1.3931
180-Day Forward	.7120	.7131	1.4045	1.4023
Czech. Rep. (Koruna)				
Commercial rate	.0350557	.0350557	28.5260	28.5260
Chile (Peso)	.002438	.002438	410.24	410.24
China (Renminbi)	.115221	.115221	8.6790	8.6790
Colombia (Peso)	.001212	.001212	825.20	825.20
Denmark (Krone)	.1589	.1586	6.2949	6.3067
Ecuador (Sucre)				
Floating rate	.000463	.000463	2160.00	2160.00
Finland (Markka)	.18761	.18761	5.3302	5.3302
France (Franc)	.18240	.18213	5.4825	5.4905
30-Day Forward	.18223	.18195	5.4876	5.4960
90-Day Forward	.18197	.18164	5.4954	5.5054
180-Day Forward	.18173	.18131	5.5027	5.5155
Germany (Mark)	.6234	.6226	1.6040	1.6062
30-Day Forward	.6232	.6222	1.6047	1.6072
90-Day Forward	.6229	.6219	1.6055	1.6080
180-Day Forward	.6231	.6221	1.6050	1.6075
Greece (Drachma)	.004131	.004120	242.07	242.70
Hong Kong (Dollar)	.12937	.12938	7.7298	7.7290
Hungary (Forint)	.0097733	.0098078	102.3200	101.9600
India (Rupee)	.03212	.03212	31.13	31.13
Indonesia (Rupiah)	.0004613	.0004613	2168.00	2168.00
Ireland (Punt)	1.5110	1.5051	.6618	.6644
Israel (Shekel)	.3281	.3281	3.0480	3.0480
Italy (Lira)	.0006353	.0006346	1574.00	1575.68
Japan (Yen)	.009860	.009906	101.42	100.95

Country	U.S. $ equiv. Thu.	U.S. $ equiv. Wed.	Currency per U.S. $ Thu.	Currency per U.S. $ Wed.
30-Day Forward	.009880	.009924	101.21	100.77
90-Day Forward	.009930	.009967	100.70	100.33
180-Day Forward	.009990	.010036	100.10	99.64
Jordan (Dinar)	1.4767	1.4767	.6772	.6772
Kuwait (Dinar)	3.3695	3.3695	.2968	.2968
Lebanon (Pound)	.000595	.000595	1682.00	1682.00
Malaysia (Ringgit)	.3864	.3864	2.5880	2.5880
Malta (Lira)	2.6846	2.6846	.3725	.3725
Mexico (Peso)				
Floating rate	.2959018	.2964280	3.3795	3.3735
Netherland (Guilder) ..	.5565	.5556	1.7970	1.7998
New Zealand (Dollar) .	.5900	.5925	1.6949	1.6878
Norway (Krone)	.1434	.1432	6.9725	6.9838
Pakistan (Rupee)	.0327	.0327	30.61	30.61
Peru (New Sol)	.4705	.4705	2.13	2.13
Philippines (Peso)	.03774	.03774	26.50	26.50
Poland (Zloty)	.00004448	.00004447	22480.00	22485.00
Portugal (Escudo)	.006044	.006011	165.45	166.35
Saudi Arabia (Riyal) ..	.26667	.26667	3.7500	3.7500
Singapore (Dollar)	.6545	.6540	1.5280	1.5290
Slovak Rep. (Koruna) .	.0307220	.0307220	32.5500	32.5500
South Africa (Rand)				
Commercial rate	.2769	.2737	3.6108	3.6543
Financial rate	.2117	.2116	4.7247	4.7250
South Korea (Won)	.0012403	.0012403	806.28	806.28
Spain (Peseta)	.007530	.007480	132.80	133.68
Sweden (Krona)	.1297	.1299	7.7101	7.6961
Switzerland (Franc) ...	.7402	.7399	1.3510	1.3515
30-Day Forward	.7403	.7399	1.3508	1.3515
90-Day Forward	.7407	.7402	1.3500	1.3509
180-Day Forward	.7424	.7413	1.3470	1.3489
Taiwan (Dollar)	.036969	.036969	27.05	27.05
Thailand (Baht)	.03981	.03981	25.12	25.12
Turkey (Lira)	.0000314	.0000320	31829.14	31222.75
United Arab (Dirham) ..	.2723	.2723	3.6725	3.6725
Uruguay (New Peso)				
Financial	.201613	.201613	4.96	4.96
Venezuela (Bolivar)				
Floating rate	.00583	.00583	171.50	171.50
SDR	1.43754	1.44241	.69563	.69328
ECU	1.19500	1.19410	....	....

Special Drawing Rights (SDR) are based on exchange rates for the U.S., German, British, French and Japanese currencies. Source: International Monetary Fund.

European Currency Unit (ECU) is based on a basket of community currencies.

Reprinted by permission of The Wall Street Journal, © *June 24, 1994 Dow Jones & Co., Inc. All Rights Reserved Worldwide.*

The first two columns show the U.S. dollar equivalent (labeled in Figure 30-1 "U.S. $ equiv.") on two different days. That is, it indicates how many U.S. dollars are exchangeable for one Swiss franc. So, from a U.S. participant's perspective, it is a direct quote; from that of a Swiss participant, it is an indirect quote. For example, the Thursday number "0.7402" means that 74.02 cents can be exchanged for one Swiss franc—this is the price of one Swiss franc. The last two columns show how much of the foreign currency is necessary to exchange for one U.S. dollar—the foreign currency price of a dollar. Thus, it is an indirect quote if taken from a U.S. participant's position, but a direct quote from the perspective of a non-U.S. participant. Once again, focusing on the Thursday value, we see "1.3510", which means that 1.3510 Swiss francs can be exchanged for one U.S. dollar.

If the number of units of a foreign currency that can be obtained for one dollar—the price of a dollar or indirect quotation—rises, the dollar is said to **appreciate** relative to the foreign currency, and the foreign currency is said to **depreciate**. Thus appreciation means a decline in the direct quotation.

FOREIGN-EXCHANGE RISK

From the perspective of a U.S. investor, the cash flows of assets denominated in a foreign currency expose the investor to uncertainty as to the cash flow in U.S. dollars. The actual U.S. dollars that the investor gets depend on the exchange rate between the U.S. dollar and the foreign currency at the time the nondollar cash flow is received and exchanged for U.S. dollars. If the foreign currency depreciates (declines in value) relative to the U.S. dollar (i.e., the U.S. dollar appreciates), the dollar value of the cash flows will be proportionately less. This risk is referred to as **foreign-exchange risk.**

Any investor who purchases an asset denominated in a currency that is not the medium of exchange of the investor's country faces foreign-exchange risk. For example, a Greek investor who acquires a yen-denominated Japanese bond is exposed to the risk that the Japanese yen will decline in value relative to the Greek drachma.

Foreign-exchange risk is a consideration for issuers too. Suppose that IBM issues bonds denominated in Japanese yen. IBM's foreign-exchange risk is that at the time the coupon interest payments must be made and the principal repaid, the U.S. dollar will have depreciated relative to the Japanese yen, requiring that IBM pay more dollars to satisfy its yen obligation.

SPOT MARKET

The spot exchange rate market is the market for settlement within two business days. Since the early 1970s, exchange rates between major currencies have been free to float, with market forces determining the relative value of a currency.[1] Thus, each day a currency's price relative to that of another currency may stay the same, increase, or decrease.

For example, look at the exchange rate reported in Figure 30-1 between the U.S. dollar and the Australian dollar. The exchange rate in U.S. dollar equivalents on Wednesday was 0.7365; on Thursday it was 0.7330. Consequently, on Wednesday one Australian dollar cost 0.7365 U.S. dollars; on Thursday, it cost less U.S. dollars, 0.7330. Thus, the Australian dollar depreciated relative to the U.S. dollar; or, equivalently, the U.S. dollar appreciated relative to the Australian dollar. Figure 30-1 shows that the U.S. dollar depreciated relative to the Swiss franc between Wednesday and Thursday in the cash market. In terms of U.S. dollar equivalents, one Swiss franc cost 0.7399 U.S. dollars on Wednesday; on Thursday it cost more U.S. dollars, 0.7402.

While quotes can be either direct or indirect, the problem is defining from whose perspective the quote is given. Foreign exchange conventions in fact standardize the ways quotes are given. Because of the importance of the U.S. dollar in the international financial system, currency quotations are all relative to the U.S. dollar. When dealers quote, they either give U.S. dollars per unit of foreign currency (a direct quote from the U.S. perspective) or the number of units of the foreign currency per U.S. dollar (an indirect quote from the U.S. perspective). Quoting in terms of U.S. dollars per unit of foreign currency

---

[1] In practice, national monetary authorities can intervene in the foreign exchange market for their currency for a variety of economic reasons, so the current foreign exchange system is sometimes referred to as a "managed" floating-rate system.

is called **American terms**, while quoting in terms of the number of units of the foreign currency per U.S. dollar is called **European terms**. The dealer convention is to use European terms in quoting foreign exchange with a few exceptions. The British pound, the Irish pound, the Australian dollar, the New Zealand dollar, and the European Currency Unit (discussed later) are exceptions that are quoted in American terms.

A key factor affecting the expectation of changes in a country's exchange rate is the relative expected inflation rate. Spot exchange rates adjust to compensate for the relative inflation rate between two countries. This is the so-called **purchasing-power parity relationship**. It says that the exchange rate—the domestic price of the foreign currency—is proportional to the domestic inflation rate, and inversely proportional to foreign inflation.

CROSS RATES

Barring any government restrictions, riskless arbitrage will assure that the exchange rate between two countries will be the same in both countries. The theoretical exchange rate between two countries other than the U.S. can be inferred from their exchange rate with the U.S. dollar. Rates computed in this way are referred to as **theoretical cross rates**. They would be computed as follows for two countries, X and Y:

$$\frac{\text{Quote in American terms of currency } X}{\text{Quote in American terms of currency } Y}$$

To illustrate how this is done, let's calculate the theoretical cross rate between German marks and Japanese yen using the exchange rates shown in Figure 30-1 for Thursday, June 23, 1994. The exchange rate for the two currencies in American terms is \$0.6234 per German mark and \$0.009860 per Japanese yen. Then The number of units of Japanese yen (Y) per unit of German marks (X) is:

$$\frac{\$0.6234}{\$0.009860} = 63.23 \text{ yen/mark}$$

Taking the reciprocal gives the number of German marks exchangeable for one Japanese yen. In our example it is 0.01581.

In the real world, there are rare instances where the theoretical cross rate as computed from actual dealer dollar exchange rate quotes will differ from the actual cross rate quoted by some dealer. When the discrepancy is large enough after transactions costs, a riskless arbitrage opportunity arises. Arbitraging to take advantage of cross rate mispricing is called **triangular arbitrage**, so named because it involves positions in three currencies—the U.S. dollar and the two foreign currencies. The arbitrage keeps all rates in line.

DEALERS

Exchange rates reported in *The Wall Street Journal* are indications of the rate at which a foreign currency can be purchased in the spot market. They are the rates for which the dealer is willing to sell foreign exchange. Foreign exchange dealers, however, do not quote one price. Instead, they quote an exchange rate at which they are willing to buy a foreign currency and one at which they are willing to sell a foreign currency. That is, there is a bid-ask spread. Consequently, a U.S. investor who has received Swiss francs and wants to exchange those francs into U.S. dollars will request a quote on the bid price for Swiss francs. Another U.S. investor who wants to purchase Swiss francs in order to, say, buy a bond denominated in that foreign currency will request an offer quote.

Dealers in the foreign exchange market are large international banks and other financial institutions that specialize in making markets in foreign exchange. The former dominate the market. There is no organized exchange where foreign currency is traded, but dealers are linked by telephone and cable, and by various information transfer services. Consequently, the foreign exchange market can best be described as an interbank over-the-counter market. Most transactions between banks are done through foreign exchange brokers. Brokers are agents who do not take a position in the foreign currencies involved in the transaction. The normal size of a transaction is $1 million or more.

Dealers in the foreign exchange market realize revenue from one or more sources: (1) the bid-ask spread, (2) commissions charged on foreign exchange transactions, or (3) trading profits (appreciation of the currencies that dealers hold a long position in or depreciation of the currencies that they have a short position in) or trading losses (depreciation of the currencies that they hold a long position in or appreciation of the currencies that they have a short position in).

THE EUROPEAN CURRENCY UNIT

Since the inception of floating exchange rates in the early 1970s, there have been several attempts to develop a currency unit composed of a basket of foreign currencies that would be accepted as the unit of denomination for capital market transactions. Until early 1981, the composite currency unit that had the greatest support was the Special Drawing Right (SDR). This composite currency unit initially consisted of 16 currencies, not all of them important in global financial markets. While the SDR was subsequently redefined in 1986 to include only five major currencies, its use as an international currency unit has diminished.[2]

The most widely used composite currency unit for capital market transactions today is the European Currency Unit (ECU), created in 1979 by the European Economic Community (EEC). The currencies included in the ECU are those that are members of the European Monetary System (EMS). The weight of each country's currency is figured according to the relative importance of a country's economic trade and financial sector within the European Economic Community.

Exchange rates between the ECU and those countries not part of the EEC float freely. The exchange rate between countries in the EEC, however, may fluctuate only within a narrow range.

The increased use of ECU-denominated loans, and, more recently, the issuance of ECU-denominated government bonds by some members of the

[2] For a review of other composite currency units, see P.L. Gilbert, "The International ECU Primary Bond Market: Structure and Competition," *Cahiers BEI/EIB Papers*, European Investment Bank, Luxembourg, December 1989, pp. 23-48.

EMS, suggests the growing importance of this composite currency in international capital market transactions. The last row under the exchange rate column in Figure 30-1 indicates that on Thursday, June 23, 1994, one unit of an ECU was quoted at $1.19500.

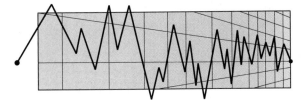

SUMMARY

We have reviewed the spot foreign exchange market and markets for hedging foreign-exchange risk. An exchange rate is defined as the amount of one currency that can be exchanged for another currency. A direct exchange rate quote is the domestic price of a foreign currency; an indirect quote is the foreign price of the domestic currency. Given a direct quote, an indirect quote can be obtained by the reciprocal of the direct quote, and vice versa. An investor or issuer whose cash flows are denominated in a foreign currency is exposed to foreign-exchange risk.

The spot exchange rate market is the market for settlement of a currency within two business days. In the developed countries, and some of the developing ones, exchange rates are free to float. According to the purchasing power parity relationship, the exchange rate between two countries—the price of the foreign currency—is proportional to the domestic price level and inversely proportional to the price level in the foreign country. Exchange rates are typically quoted in terms of the U.S. dollar.

The foreign exchange market is an over-the-counter market dominated by large international banks that act as dealers. Foreign exchange dealers quote one price at which they are willing to buy a foreign currency and one at which they are willing to sell a foreign currency.

Today, the European Currency Unit is the most widely used composite currency unit for capital market transactions. It is continuing to grow in importance as an increasing number of loans have been denominated in ECU, and some members of the Economic Monetary System have been issuing ECU-denominated government bonds.

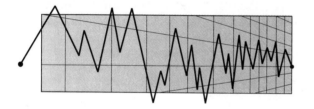

QUESTIONS

1. What risk is faced by a U.S. life insurance company that buys British government bonds?

2. Explain how direct quotes on foreign exchange are derived from indirect quotes.

3. Explain why you agree or disagree with the following statement: "Foreign exchange is traded on an organized exchange."

4. What is meant by purchasing-power parity?

5. What is triangular arbitrage?

6. The following foreign exchange rates were reported on February 8, 1991:

	German mark	Japanese yen	British pound
U.S. $	0.6874	0.00779	1.9905

The exchange rates indicate the number of U.S. dollars necessary to purchase one unit of the foreign currency.

a. From the perspective of a U.S. investor, are the foreign exchange rates direct or indirect quotes?

b. How much of each of the foreign currencies is needed to buy one U.S. dollar?

7. Given the information in the previous question, calculate the theoretical cross rates between:

a. the German mark and the Japanese yen.

b. the German mark and the British pound.

c. the Japanese yen and the British pound.

8. What is the European Currency Unit?

9. The Economic Monetary Community expects to revise the weights of the currencies comprising the ECU every five years. Why is it necessary to revise the weights?

Instruments for Controlling Foreign-Exchange Risk

LEARNING OBJECTIVES

After reading this chapter you will understand:

- what currency forward and futures contracts are.

- the limitations of forward and futures contracts for hedging long-dated foreign-exchange risk.

- what is meant by interest rate parity.

- how a forward exchange rate is determined.

- what covered interest arbitrage is.

- what a currency option is.

- the different types of exotic currency options including the lookback currency option, the average rate currency option, and the alternative currency option.

- the basic currency swap structure.

- the motivation for using currency swaps.

In Chapter 30 we explained what is meant by foreign-exchange risk. In this chapter we discuss four instruments that borrowers and investors can use to protect against adverse foreign exchange rate movements: (1) currency forward contracts, (2) currency futures contracts, (3) currency options, and (4) currency swaps.

CURRENCY FORWARD CONTRACTS

In Chapter 30 we discussed the spot rate for the Swiss franc, which appears on the first line in Figure 30-1. Now we will look at the other three lines for the Swiss franc in that figure. Each line represents the exchange rate for a forward contract.

Recall that a forward contract is one in which one party agrees to buy "something," and another party agrees to sell that same "something" at a designated price and date in the future. Each line indicates a different number of days until settlement: 30-day settlement for the first line below "Switzerland (Franc)," 90-day settlement for the second line below, and 180-day settlement for the third. Consider the quote for Thursday for the 30-day forward exchange rate. In the U.S. dollar equivalent column, the quote is "0.7403." This means that an American selling to Switzerland in Swiss francs with payment 30 days from now can, by selling forward francs, be assured of receiving 0.7403 U.S. dollars per franc. Similarly, a Swiss wanting to convert U.S. dollars into francs 30 days from now can count on paying $0.7403 for francs.

Most forward contracts have a maturity of less than two years. For longer-dated forward contracts, the bid-ask spread for a forward contract increases; that is, the size of the spread for a given currency increases with the maturity. Consequently, forward contracts become less attractive for hedging long-dated foreign currency exposure.

Also recall from Chapter 10 that forward and futures contracts can be used to lock in a foreign exchange rate. In exchange for locking in a rate, the user forgoes the opportunity to benefit from any advantageous foreign exchange rate movement but eliminates downside risk. Futures contracts that are creations of an exchange have certain advantages over forward contracts in the case of stock indexes (Chapter 15) and Treasury securities (Chapter 28). For foreign exchange, however, the forward market is the market of choice. As the foreign exchange forward market is an interbank market, data on the amount of open interest are not public.

Pricing Currency Forward Contracts

In Chapter 10, we showed the relationship between spot prices and forward prices. Arbitrage arguments can also be used to derive the relationship.[1] Consider a U.S. investor with a one-year investment horizon who has the following two choices:

- *Alternative 1*: Deposit $100,000 in a U.S. bank that pays 7% compounded annually for one year.
- *Alternative 2*: Deposit the U.S. dollar equivalent of $100,000 in German marks (DM) in a German bank that pays 9% compounded annually for one year.

---

[1] Recall that the relationship is not exact for futures prices because of the marked-to-market requirement.

The two alternatives and their outcome one year from now are depicted in Figure 31-1. Which is the best alternative? It will be the alternative that produces the largest number of U.S. dollars one year from now. Ignoring U.S. and German taxes on interest income or any other taxes, we need to know two things in order to determine the best alternative: (1) the spot exchange rate between U.S. dollars and German marks, and (2) the spot exchange rate one year from now between U.S. dollars and German marks. The former is known; the latter is not. We can determine, however, the spot rate one year from now between U.S. dollars and German marks that will make the investor indifferent between the two alternatives.

- *For Alternative 1*: The amount of U.S. dollars available one year from now would be $107,000 ($100,000 times 1.07).

- *For Alternative 2*: Assume that the spot rate is $0.6234 for one deutschemark. Then, ignoring commissions, $100,000 can be exchanged for DM 160,411 ($100,000 divided by 0.6234). The amount of German marks available at the end of one year would be DM 174,848 (DM 160,411 times 1.09).

The number of U.S. dollars that the DM 174,848 can be exchanged for depends on the exchange rate one year from now. Let F denote the exchange rate between these two currencies one year from now. Specifically, F will denote the number of U.S. dollars that can be exchanged for one German mark. Thus, the number of U.S. dollars at the end of one year from the second alternative is equal to DM 174,848 times F.

The investor will be indifferent between the two alternatives if the number of U.S. dollars is $107,000; that is, $107,000 = DM 174,848 \times F$. Solving the equation we find that F is equal to $0.6120.

Thus, if one year from now the spot exchange rate is $0.6120 for one German mark, then the two alternatives will produce the same number of U.S. dollars. If more than $0.6120 can be exchanged for one German mark, then there will be more than $107,000 at the end of one year. An exchange rate of $0.6200 for one German mark, for example, would produce $108,406 (DM 174,848 times $0.6200). The opposite is true if less than $0.6120 can be exchanged for one German mark. For example, if the future exchange rate is $0.6100, there will be $106,657 (DM 174,848 times $0.6100).

Now we will look at this from a German investor's perspective. Suppose that the German investor with a one-year investment horizon has two alternatives:

- *Alternative 1*: Deposit DM 160,411 in a German bank that pays 9% compounded annually for one year.

- *Alternative 2*: Deposit the German mark equivalent of DM 160,411 in U.S. dollars in a U.S. bank that pays 7% compounded annually for one year.

Once again, assume that the spot exchange rate is $0.6234 for one German mark. The German investor will select the alternative that generates the largest number of marks at the end of one year. The first alternative would generate DM 174,848 (DM 160,411 times 1.09). The second alternative

Figure 31-1

Outcome of Two Investment Alternatives:
Determination of Theoretical Forward Rate

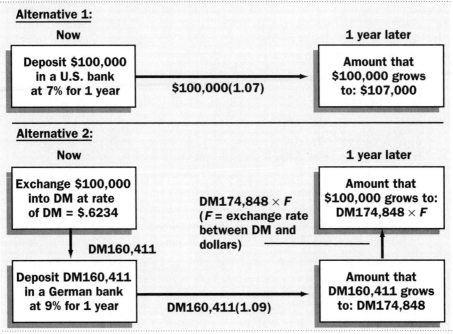

requires that deutschemarks be exchanged for U.S. dollars at the spot exchange rate. Given our assumed spot exchange rate, DM 160,411 can be exchanged for $100,000 (DM 160,411 multiplied by $0.6234). At the end of one year, the second alternative would generate $107,000 ($100,000 times 1.07). Letting F continue to denote the number of U.S. dollars needed to purchase one German mark one year from now, the German investor will realize the following amount of deutschemarks one year from now: $107,000 divided by F. The investor will be indifferent between the two alternatives if: $107,000/F$ = DM 174,848. This equation yields a value for F of $0.6120, the same exchange rate that we found when we sought the exchange rate one year from now that would make the U.S. investor indifferent between the two alternatives facing that investor.

Now suppose that a dealer quotes a one-year forward exchange rate between the two currencies. The one-year forward exchange rate fixes today the exchange rate one year from now. Thus, if the one-year forward exchange rate quoted is $0.6120 for one German mark, investing in the German bank will provide no arbitrage opportunity for the U.S. investor. If the one-year forward rate quoted is more than $0.6120 for one German mark, the U.S. investor can arbitrage the situation by selling German marks forward (and buying U.S. dollars forward for marks).

To see how this arbitrage opportunity can be exploited, suppose that the one-year forward exchange rate is $0.6200 for one German mark. Also assume that the borrowing and the lending rates within each currency are the same. Suppose that the U.S. investor borrows $100,000 for one year at 7% compounded annually and enters into a forward contract agreeing to deliver DM 174,848 one year from now at $0.6200 per German mark. That is, one year from now the investor is agreeing to deliver DM 174,848 in exchange for $108,406 (DM 174,848 multiplied by $0.6200). The $100,000 that was borrowed can be exchanged for DM 160,411 at the spot rate of $0.6234 to one German mark, which can be invested in Germany at 9%. One year from now the U.S. investor will have DM 174,848 from the investment in Germany, which can be delivered against the forward contract. The U.S. investor will receive $108,406 and repay $107,000 to satisfy the bank loan, netting $1,406. Assuming that the counterparty to the forward contract does not default, this is a riskless arbitrage situation, because a $1,406 profit is generated with no initial investment.[2] This will result in the U.S. dollar rising relative to the German mark in the forward exchange rate market, or possibly some other adjustment.[3]

On the other hand, if the one-year forward exchange rate quoted is less than $0.6120, a German investor can arbitrage the situation by buying German marks forward (and by selling U.S. dollars forward). The forward exchange rate of U.S. dollars relative to German marks will therefore fall.[4] The conclusion is that the one-year forward exchange rate must be $0.6120, because any other forward exchange rate would result in an arbitrage opportunity for either the U.S. or the German investor.

Interest Rate Parity and Covered Interest Arbitrage

We know that the spot exchange rate and the interest rates in two countries will determine the forward exchange rate. The relationship among the spot exchange rate, the interest rates in two countries, and the forward rate is called **interest rate parity**. It says that an investor, after hedging in the forward exchange rate market, will realize the same sure domestic return whether investing domestically or in a foreign country. The arbitrage process that forces interest rate parity is called **covered interest arbitrage**.

Mathematically, interest rate parity can be expressed as follows for countries A and B:

$$I\left(1 + i_A\right) = \left(I/S\right)\left(1 + i_B\right) F$$

where

  I = amount of A's currency to be invested for a time period of length t
  S = spot exchange rate which is the price of foreign currency in terms of domestic currency (units of domestic currency per unit of foreign currency)

---

[2] A German investor could also arbitrage this situation.

[3] Actually, a combination of things may occur when U.S. investors attempt to exploit this situation: (1) the spot exchange rate of U.S. dollars relative to German marks will fall as U.S. investors sell dollars and buy marks; (2) U.S. interest rates will rise in the U.S. as investors borrow in the U.S. and invest in Germany; (3) German interest rates will fall as more is invested in Germany; and (4) the one-year forward rate of U.S. dollars relative to German marks will fall. In practice, the last possibility will dominate.

[4] A combination of things may occur when German investors attempt to exploit this situation: (1) the spot exchange rate of U.S. dollars relative to German marks will rise as German investors buy dollars and sell marks; (2) German interest rates will rise as investors borrow in Germany and invest in the U.S.; (3) U.S. interest rates will fall as more is invested in the U.S.; and (4) the one-year forward rate of U.S. dollars relative to German marks will rise. In practice, the last possibility will dominate.

F = t-period forward rate or the price of foreign currency t periods from now

i_A = interest rate on an investment maturing at time t in country A

i_B = interest rate on an investment maturing at time t in country B

To illustrate, country A will represent the United States and country B will represent Germany. In our example we have:

I = \$100,000 for one year

S = \$0.6234

F = \$0.6120

i_A = 0.07

i_B = 0.09

Then according to interest rate parity this relationship holds:

$100,000 (1.07) = ($100,000/$0.6234) (1.09) ($0.6120)$

$$\$107,000 = \$107,000$$

Equivalently, interest rate parity can be expressed as:

$$(1 + i_A) = (F/S)(1 + i_B)$$

Rewriting the equation, we obtain the theoretical forward exchange rate:

$$F = S \frac{(1 + i_A)}{(1 + i_B)}$$

While we have referred so far to investors, we could use borrowers as well to illustrate interest rate parity. That is, a borrower has the choice of obtaining funds in a domestic or foreign market. Interest rate parity provides that a borrower who hedges in the forward exchange rate market will realize the same domestic borrowing rate whether borrowing domestically or in a foreign country.

To derive the theoretical forward exchange rate using the arbitrage argument, we made several assumptions. When the assumptions are violated, the actual forward exchange rate may deviate from the theoretical forward exchange rate. First, in deriving the theoretical forward exchange rate we ignored commissions and the bid-ask spread when exchanging in the spot market today and at the end of the investment horizon. Second, we assumed that the borrowing and lending rates in each currency are the same. Dropping this unrealistic assumption means that there is not a single theoretical forward exchange rate, but a band around a level reflecting borrowing and lending rates. Third, the divergence between actual and theoretical forward exchange rates can be the result of the different tax structures of the two countries. Finally, any restrictions on foreign investing or borrowing in either country that impedes arbitrage may cause a divergence between actual and theoretical forward exchange rates.

Link between Eurocurrency Market and Forward Prices

In deriving interest rate parity, we looked at the interest rate in both countries. But the interest rate in each market that participants look to in order to perform covered interest arbitrage so that interest rate parity will hold is the interest rate in the Eurocurrency market. This is the market for bank deposits and bank loans denominated in a currency other than that of the country where the bank initiating the transaction is located. Examples of transactions in the Eurocurrency market are a British bank in London that lends U.S. dollars to a French corporation, or a Japanese corporation that deposits Swiss francs in a German bank. An investor seeking covered interest arbitrage will accomplish the short-term borrowing and lending in the Eurocurrency market.

The largest sector of the Eurocurrency market is the market for bank deposits and bank loans in U.S. dollars. This sector is called the **Eurodollar market**. The seed for the Eurocurrency market was, in fact, the Eurodollar market. As international capital market transactions increased, the market for bank deposits and bank loans in other currencies developed.

CURRENCY FUTURES CONTRACTS

There are U.S.-traded foreign exchange futures contracts for the major currencies traded on the International Monetary Market (IMM), a division of the Chicago Mercantile Exchange. The futures contracts traded on the IMM are for the Japanese yen, the German mark, the Canadian dollar, the British pound, the Swiss franc, and the Australian dollar. The amount of each foreign currency that must be delivered varies by currency. For example, each British pound futures contract is for delivery of 62,500 pounds, while each Japanese yen futures contract is for delivery of 12.5 million yen.

The maturity cycle for currency futures is March, June, September, and December. The longest maturity is one year. Consequently, as in the case of a currency forward contract, currency futures are limited with respect to hedging long-dated foreign-exchange risk exposure.

Other exchanges trading currency futures in the U.S. are the Midamerica Commodity Exchange (a subsidiary of the Chicago Board of Trade) and the Financial Instrument Exchange (a subsidiary of the New York Cotton Exchange). The latter trades a futures contract in which the underlying is a U.S. dollar index. Outside the United States, currency futures are traded on the London International Financial Futures Exchange, Singapore International Monetary Exchange, Toronto Futures Exchange, Sydney Futures Exchange, and New Zealand Futures Exchange.

CURRENCY OPTION CONTRACTS

In contrast to a forward or futures contract, an option gives the option buyer the opportunity to benefit from favorable exchange rate movements but establishes a maximum loss. The option price is the cost of establishing such a risk/return profile.

Exchange-Traded Options

There are two types of foreign currency options traded on exchanges: options on the foreign currency, and futures options. The latter is an option to enter into a foreign exchange futures contract. We described the features of futures options in Chapter 23. Futures options are traded on the IMM, the trading location of the currency futures contract.

Options on foreign exchange have been traded on the Philadelphia Exchange since 1982. The foreign currencies underlying the options are the same as for the futures. There are two sorts of options traded on the Philadelphia Exchange for each currency: an American-type option and a European-type option. Recall from Chapter 11 that the former permits exercise at any time up to and including the expiration date, while the latter permits exercise only at the expiration date. The amount of foreign currency underlying each option contract traded on the Philadelphia Exchange is one-half the amount of the futures contract. For example, the Japanese yen option is for 6.25 million yen and the British pound option is for 31,250 pounds. There are also options on currencies traded on the London Stock Exchange and the London International Financial Futures Exchange.

Over-the-Counter Exotic Options

There is also an over-the-counter market for options on currencies. The markets for these products are made by commercial banks and investment banking firms. As we explained in earlier chapters, OTC options are tailor-made products to accommodate the specific needs of clients. Only options on the major currencies are traded on the exchange. An option on any other currency must be purchased in the OTC market.

There are variations on the standard call and put options in the over-the-counter market. As we explained in Chapter 11, these are called exotic options. Three common types of exotic options on currencies are the lookback currency option, average rate currency option, and alternative currency option.

A **lookback currency option** is an option where the option buyer has the right to obtain the most favorable exchange rate that prevailed over the life of the option.[5] For example, consider a two-month lookback call option to buy yen when the exchange rate between the U.S. dollar and Japanese yen is $1 for 105 yen on Day 0. Suppose that the next day, Day 1, the exchange rate changes to $1 for 110 yen—the option buyer has the right to exchange $1 for 110 yen. Suppose that on Day 2 the exchange rate changes to $1 for 108 yen. The option buyer still has the right to exchange $1 for 110 yen. Regardless of what happens to the exchange rate over the 60 days, the option buyer gets to exercise the option at the exchange rate that prevailed that gave the largest number of yen for $1 (or, equivalently, at the lowest price per yen).

An **average rate currency option**, also called an **Asian currency option**, has a payoff that is the difference between the strike exchange rate for the underlying currency and the *average* exchange rate over the life of the option for the underlying currency. In the case of a call option, if the average exchange rate for the underlying currency is greater than the strike exchange rate, then the option seller must make a payment to the option buyer. The amount of the payment is:

payoff for average rate currency call option =
(average exchange rate – strike exchange rate) × underlying units

In the case of a put option, if the strike exchange rate for the underlying currency is greater than the average exchange rate, then the option seller must make a payment to the option buyer is equal to:

---

[5] For a further discussion of these options, see Mark Garman, "Recollection in Tranquility," *Risk* (March 1989), pp. 16-9.

payoff for average rate currency put option =
(strike exchange rate – average exchange rate) × underlying units

An **alternative currency option** pays the best or worst performance of two exchange rates. For example, suppose that the two exchange rates are Japanese yen/U.S. dollar and the French franc/U.S. dollar. A strike exchange rate is established for each exchange rate. As in the case of a standard currency option, there will be a payoff if an option expires in the money. In the case of an alternative currency option, there are effectively two options—one on each foreign exchange rate. The payoff of an alternative currency option is the pay-off of the higher of the two options. In an alternative currency call option, the payoff is the best performing of the two exchange rates; in an alternative currency put option, the payoff is the worst performing of the two exchange rates.

The alternative currency option is being used by money managers who want exposure to the best, or protection against the worst, of two currencies. Alternative currency options are also called **either-or options**, **best-of-two call options**, or **worst-of-two put options**.

Pricing Currency Options

The factors that affect the price of any option were discussed in Chapter 11.[6] One of the key factors is the expected volatility of the underlying instrument or commodity over the life of the option. In the case of a standard currency option, it is the expected volatility of the exchange rate between the two currencies from the present time to the expiration of the option. The strike price also affects the option value: the higher it is, the lower the value of a call, and the higher the value of a put.

Another factor that affects the option price is the relative risk-free interest rate in the two countries. To understand why, recall the portfolio we created in Chapter 11 to replicate the payoff of a call option on an asset. A portion of the asset is purchased with borrowed funds. In the case of a currency option, this involves purchasing a portion of the foreign currency underlying the option. However, the foreign currency acquired can be invested at a risk-free interest rate in the foreign country. Consequently, the pricing of a currency option is similar to the pricing of an option on an income-earning asset such as a dividend-paying stock or an interest-paying bond.[7] At the same time the amount that must be set aside to meet the strike price depends on the domestic rate. Thus the option price, just like interest rate parity, reflects both rates.

CURRENCY SWAPS

In Chapter 12 we discussed swaps as transactions where two counterparties agree to exchange payments. In an interest rate swap, discussed in Chapter 29,

---

[6] There are other factors that affect the price of the exotic currency options.

[7] More detail on the pricing of currency options can be found in Nahum Biger and John Hull, "The Valuation of Currency Options," *Financial Management* (Spring 1983), pp. 24-8; Mark B. Garman and Steven W. Kohlhagen, "Foreign Currency Option Values," *Journal of International Money and Finance* (December 1983), pp. 231-37; and J. Orlin Grabbe, "The Pricing of Call and Put Options on Foreign Exchange," *Journal of International Money and Finance* (December 1983), pp. 239-53.

only interest payments are exchanged. In a **currency swap**, there is an exchange of both interest and principal. The best way to explain a currency swap is with an illustration.

Illustration of a Currency Swap

Assume two companies, a U.S. company and a Swiss company. Each company seeks to borrow for 10 years in its domestic currency; that is, the U.S. company seeks $100 million U.S.-dollar-denominated debt, and the Swiss company seeks SF 127 million Swiss-franc-denominated debt. For reasons that we will explore later, suppose that both companies want to issue 10-year bonds in the bond market of the other country, denominated in the other country's currency. That is, the U.S. company wants to issue the Swiss-franc equivalent of $100 million in Switzerland, and the Swiss company wants to issue the U.S.-dollar equivalent of SF 127 million in the United States.

For this illustration we will assume the following:

1. At the time that both companies want to issue their 10-year bonds, the spot exchange rate between U.S. dollars and Swiss francs is one U.S. dollar for 1.27 Swiss francs.

2. The coupon rate that the U.S. company would have to pay on the 10-year Swiss-franc-denominated bonds issued in Switzerland is 6%.

3. The coupon rate that the Swiss company would have to pay on the 10-year U.S.-dollar-denominated bonds issued in the U.S. is 11%.

By the first assumption, if the U.S. company issues the bonds in Switzerland, it can exchange the SF 127 million for $100 million. By issuing $100 million of bonds in the U.S., the Swiss company can exchange the proceeds for SF 127 million. Therefore, both get the amount of financing they seek. Assuming the coupon rates given by the last two assumptions, and assuming for purposes of this illustration that coupon payments will be made annually,[8] the cash outlays that the companies must make for the next 10 years are summarized below:

Year	U.S. Company	Swiss Company
1-10	SF 7,620,000	$ 11,000,000
10	127,000,000	100,000,000

Each issuer faces the risk that at the time the liability payment must be made its domestic currency will have depreciated relative to the other currency, requiring more of the domestic currency to satisfy the liability. That is, both are exposed to foreign-exchange risk.

In a currency swap, the two companies will issue bonds in the other's bond market. The currency swap agreement will require that:

1. the two parties exchange the proceeds received from the sale of the bonds.

---

[8] In reality U.S. coupon payments are made semiannually. The practice for bonds issued in Europe is to pay coupon interest once per year.

2. the two parties make the coupon payments to service the debt of the other party.

3. at the termination date of the currency swap (which coincides with the maturity of the bonds), both parties agree to exchange the par value of the bonds.

In our illustration, these requirements mean the following.

1. The U.S. company issues 10-year, 6% coupon bonds with a par value of SF 127 million in Switzerland and gives the proceeds to the Swiss company. At the same time, the Swiss company issues 10-year, 11% bonds with a par value of $100 million in the U.S. and gives the proceeds to the U.S. company.

2. The U.S. company agrees to service the coupon payments of the Swiss company by paying $11,000,000 per year for the next 10 years to the Swiss company; the Swiss company agrees to service the coupon payments of the U.S. company by paying SF 7,620,000 for the next 10 years to the U.S. company.

3. At the end of 10 years (this would be the termination date of this currency swap because it coincides with the maturity of the two bond issues), the U.S. company agrees to pay $100 million to the Swiss company, and the Swiss company agrees to pay SF 127 million to the U.S. company.

This currency swap is illustrated in Figure 31-2.

Now let's assess what this transaction has done. Both parties received the amount of financing they sought. The U.S. company's coupon payments are in dollars, not Swiss francs; the Swiss company's coupon payments are in Swiss francs, not U.S. dollars. At the termination date, both parties will receive an amount sufficient in their local currency to pay off the holders of their bonds. With the coupon payments and the principal repayment in their local currency, neither party faces foreign-exchange risk.

In practice, the two companies would not deal directly with each other. Instead, either a commercial bank or investment banking firm would be involved as an intermediary in the transaction either as a broker or a dealer. As a broker, the intermediary simply brings the two parties together, receiving a fee for the service. If instead the intermediary serves as a dealer, it not only brings the two parties together, but also guarantees payment to both parties. Thus, if one party defaults, the counterparty will continue to receive its payments from the dealer. Of course, in this arrangement, both parties are concerned with the credit risk of the dealer. When the currency swap market started, transactions were typically brokered. The more prevalent arrangement today is that the intermediary acts as a dealer.

As we explained in Chapter 29, an interest rate swap is nothing more than a package of forward contracts. The same is true for a currency swap; it is simply a package of currency forward contracts.

Figure 31-2
Illustration of a Currency Swap

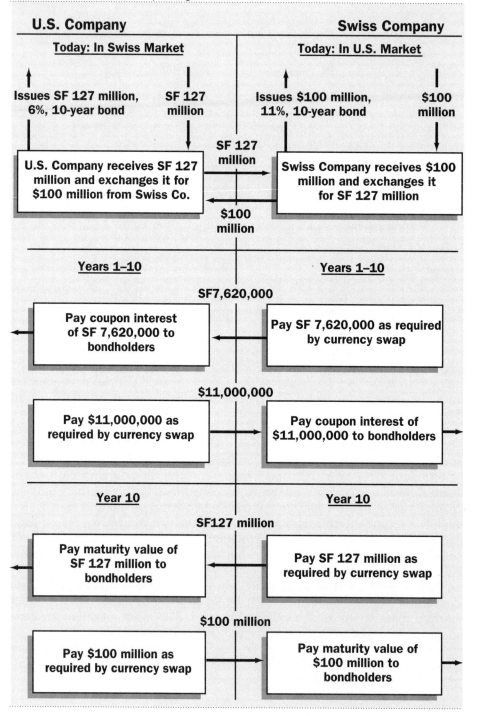

Motivation for Currency Swaps

We turn to the question of why both companies may find a currency swap beneficial. In a global financial market where there are no market imperfections because of regulations, taxes, and transactions costs, the cost of borrowing should be the same whether the issuer raises funds domestically or in any foreign capital market. In a world with market imperfections, it may be possible for an issuer to reduce its borrowing cost by borrowing funds denominated in a foreign currency and hedging the associated exchange rate risk. This is what is meant by an arbitrage opportunity. The currency swap allows borrowers to capitalize on any such arbitrage opportunities.

Prior to the establishment of the currency swap market, capitalizing on such arbitrage opportunities required use of the currency forward market. The market for long-dated forward exchange rate contracts is thin, however, which increases the cost of eliminating foreign-exchange risk. Eliminating foreign-exchange risk in our U.S.-Switzerland illustration would have required each issuer to enter 10 currency forward contracts (one for each cash payment that the issuer was committed to make in the foreign currency). The currency swap provides a more transactionally efficient means for protecting against foreign-exchange risk when an issuer (or its investment banker) has identified an arbitrage opportunity and seeks to benefit from it.

As the currency swap market has developed, arbitrage opportunities for reduced funding costs available in the early days of the swap market have become less common. In fact, it was the development of the swap market that reduced arbitrage opportunities. When these opportunities do arise, they last for only a short period of time, usually less than a day.

There is another motivation for currency swaps. Some companies seek to raise funds in foreign countries as a means of increasing their recognition by foreign investors, despite the fact that the cost of funding is the same as in the United States. The U.S. company in our illustration might have been seeking to expand its potential sources of future funding by issuing bonds today in Switzerland.

Currency Coupon Swap

In our illustration, we assumed that both parties made fixed cash-flow payments. Suppose instead that one of the parties sought floating-rate rather than fixed-rate financing. Returning to the same illustration, assume that instead of fixed-rate financing, the Swiss company wanted LIBOR-based financing. In this case, the U.S. company would issue floating-rate bonds in Switzerland. Suppose that it could do so at a rate of LIBOR plus 50 basis points. Because the currency swap calls for the Swiss company to service the coupon payments of the U.S. company, the Swiss company will make annual payments of LIBOR plus 50 basis points. The U.S. company will still make fixed-rate payments in U.S. dollars to service the debt obligation of the Swiss company in the United States Now, however, the Swiss company will make floating-rate payments (LIBOR plus 50 basis points) in Swiss francs to service the debt obligation of the U.S. company in Switzerland.

Currency swaps in which one of the parties pays a fixed rate and the counterparty a floating rate are called **currency coupon swaps**.

Swaptions

In our discussion of the interest rate swap in Chapter 29, we explained the motivation for the development of the option on an interest rate swap, called swaptions. It is not difficult to see why swaptions would be attractive in the case of currency swaps. Suppose that the 10-year bonds of either issuer are callable and that interest rates decline sufficiently in the United States so that the Swiss company will find it economic to call the bonds. The Swiss company will still be responsible for making the payments as specified in the currency swap. An option to exit the currency swap would be needed to offset these obligations.

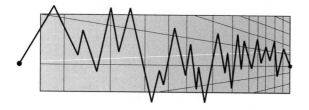

SUMMARY

Currency forward contracts, currency futures contracts, currency options, and currency swaps are four instruments that borrowers and investors can use to protect against adverse foreign exchange rate movements.

Interest rate parity gives the relationship among the spot exchange rate, the interest rates in two countries, and the forward rate. The relationship is assured by a covered interest arbitrage. Interest rate parity implies that investors and borrowers who hedge in the forward exchange rate market will realize the same domestic return or face the same domestic borrowing rate whether investing or borrowing domestically or in a foreign country.

In implementing covered interest arbitrage, the relevant interest rates are those in the Eurocurrency market—the market for bank deposits and bank loans denominated in a currency other than that of the country where the bank initiating the transaction is located. The Eurodollar market is the largest sector of this market.

There are exchange-traded options on major foreign currencies and futures options on the same currencies traded in the United States An option on any other currency must be purchased in the over-the-counter market. There are exotic currency options created by dealer firms. These include lookback currency options, average rate currency options, and alternative currency options.

A currency swap is effectively a package of currency forward contracts, with the advantage that it allows hedging of long-dated foreign-exchange risk and it is more transactionally efficient. Currency swaps are used to arbitrage opportunities in the global financial market for raising funds at less cost than in the domestic market. Arbitrage opportunities have become rare.

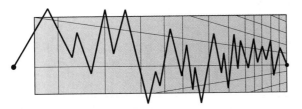

QUESTIONS

1. On February 8, 1991, the U.S. dollar/British pound spot rate was U.S. $1.9905 per pound; and the U.S. dollar/Japanese yen spot rate was U.S. $0.00779 per yen. The forward rates following were also quoted on that date:

	British pound	**Japanese yen**
30 days	1.9908	0.007774
60 days	1.9597	0.007754
90 days	1.9337	0.007736

   a. Explain what someone who enters into a 30-day forward contract to deliver British pounds is agreeing to do.

   b. Explain what someone who enters into a 90-day forward contract to buy Japanese yen is agreeing to do.

   c. What can you infer about the relationship between U.S. and British short-term interest rates and U.S. and Japanese short-term interest rates?

2. What is the drawback of using currency forward contracts for hedging long-dated positions?

3. What is meant by interest rate parity?

4. What is covered interest arbitrage?

5. Why are the interest rates in the Eurocurrency market important in covered interest arbitrage?

6. Consider this excerpt from *Euromoney* of September 1989:

Enterprise Oil itself recently purchased what it claims to be the biggest currency option obtained by a corporate client. In March it spent over $15 million as the premium on a 90-day currency option.

The Chemical [Bank]-arranged option was used to lock in exchange rate protection on $1.03 billion of a $1.45 billion liability incurred in the acquisition of US-based gas transmission company, Texas Eastern.

The need for the option arose since Enterprise Oil was paying for a dollar liability by raising sterling-denominated equity. The option is a dollar-call option which gives the company the right to buy dollars at a dollar/sterling exchange rate of $1.70 for a 90-day period.

Enterprise bought the option out-of-the-money on March 1 with dollar/sterling exchange rates at $1.73. It reduced its premium on currency options by taking the option a long way out-of-the-money.

Discuss Enterprise Oil's financing strategy and rationale for the purchase of the currency options.

7. The following excerpt is from a 1991 issue of *Corporate Financing Week:*

To purchase additional aircraft, a major international carrier needed to borrow $105 million and then convert its dollar liability to a currency matching its passenger revenues.

SBCM [Sumitomo Bank Capital Markets] executed an amortizing cross-currency swap in which the carrier pays a monthly yen amount in return for a semi-annual U.S. dollar Libor-based payment. The fixed-yen payments on the swap represent interest plus amortization of principal on the yen equivalent of the U.S. dollar borrowing, and the floating Libor payments represent semi-annual interest plus amortization of the U.S. dollar principal amount.

a. Discuss the rationale for this currency swap transaction.

b. What alternative hedging techniques might have been used to achieve the same end?

8. The following excerpt appeared in the January 14, 1991, issue of *Wall Street Letter:*

The Philadelphia Stock Exchange plans to list the first non-dollar denominated options to trade in the United States, according to sources at the exchange. The Phlx will list cross-currency options based on the relationships between the Deutsche mark and the Japanese yen, as well as British pound/yen and

pound/mark options, a spokesman confirmed.

The exchange currently lists currency options that are based on the relationship between that currency and the dollar, one Phlx member explained. "If you're not American," he added, "then the dollar doesn't do it for you." The three new cross-currency options should be attractive to the same banks and broker-dealers that currently trade dollar-based currency options, as well as non-U.S. entities that have interests in other currencies.

Cross-currency options are "a very big part of international trade and international capital markets," and are big over-the-counter products, but none currently trade on an exchange. The advantage of exchange-traded options, the Phlx member said, is that "99% of the customers don't have the credit" to trade such a product over-the-counter with a big bank.

a. What does the spokesman for the Philadelphia Exchange mean when he says: "If you're not American then the dollar doesn't do it for you."?

b. Why is the credit of customers critical in the over-the-counter market but not for an exchange-traded contract?

c. When the Philadelphia Stock Exchange filed with the SEC to list cross-currency options, the exchange indicated that the demand for this product has been "spawned by recent large fluctuations and dramatic increases in volatility levels for cross-rate options." Why would this increase the demand for cross-currency options?

9. Explain how the payoff of an average rate currency option is determined.

10. Explain whether you agree or disagree with the following statement: "As with an interest rate swap, there is no exchange of principal with a currency swap."

11. Explain whether you agree or disagree with the following statement: "A currency swap is a redundant financial instrument since a borrower can accomplish the same hedging objective with a package of foreign currency forward contracts."

12. What is the motivation for the use of a currency swap by a corporation?

Index